Virtual Environments and Advanced Interface Design

Virtual Environments and Advanced Interface Design

Edited by

WOODROW BARFIELD

THOMAS A. FURNESS III

New York   Oxford
OXFORD UNIVERSITY PRESS
1995

Oxford University Press

Oxford   New York
Athens   Auckland   Bangkok   Bombay
Calcutta   Cape Town   Dar es Salaam   Delhi
Florence   Hong Kong   Istanbul   Karachi
Kuala Lumpur   Madras   Madrid   Melbourne
Mexico City   Nairobi   Paris   Singapore
Taipei   Tokyo   Toronto

and associated companies in
Berlin   Ibadan

Published by Oxford University Press, Inc.,
200 Madison Avenue, New York, New York 10016

Oxford is a registered trademark of Oxford University Press

Library of Congress Cataloging-in-Publication Data
Virtual environments and advanced interface design / edited by
Woodrow Barfield and Thomas A. Furness, III.
p. cm.   Includes bibliographical references and index.
ISBN 0-19-507555-2
1. Human-computer interaction.   2. Virtual reality.   3. User
interfaces (Computer systems)   I. Barfield, Woodrow.   II. Furness,
Thomas A.
QA76.9.H85V54 1995
006—dc20   94-31635

9 8 7 6 5 4 3 2 1

Printed in the United States of America
on acid-free paper

This book is dedicated to the memory of
ANNIE CHENG-BARFIELD

Preface

It is an interesting time for those involved in computer and engineering science, biological and physical science, medicine, and art. This is because the tremendous advances in computer and display technology which have occurred since the late 1950s have given participants in these fields an entire new set of tools with which to work. One of these tools is the hardware that allows the user to view and manipulate images. This equipment includes display devices such as CRT and flat panel displays, and input devices such as keyboards, trackballs, and mice. Another important tool is the software which allows the user to model and render images, and to spatialize sound. It is interesting to note that the "interface" has much to do with both (hardware and software) of these tools. For example, the computing equipment that we use to perform tasks presents an interface between us and that which we are trying to accomplish. The hardware interface can either assist us in the performance of our tasks or, if not well designed, serve as a hindrance. In addition, much of the code for software applications is written as part of what we term the user interface. Such software allows the user to recover from errors, to use icons to initiate actions, and to access help. As with the hardware, if the software interface is not well designed, it will serve as a hindrance to the performance of tasks.

However, even with the tremendous advances in computing technology, users of computing systems are still, in many cases, relegated to the role of passive observer of data and processes. Furthermore, the input devices that we use to interact with computing systems are limited, providing us with very unnatural ways in which to interact with objects and to initiate actions. And, even though we see, feel, smell, and hear in three dimensions, we spend large amounts of our work and recreation time interacting with an image or text projected onto a two-dimensional display surface. Sadly, in most cases, with the computers of today, we humans are on the outside looking in. However, with the development of "Sketchpad" by Ivan Sutherland, then a graduate student at MIT, an important paradigm shift occurred in computing in the early 1960s (Sutherland, I. E., The ultimate display, *Proceedings of the IFIPS Congress*, **2**, 506–8, 1965). Sutherland came up with the idea of surrounding the user with an immersive three-dimensional view of the computer-generated world. Along with this idea came the possibility of allowing the user to look at, and experience, data and processes from the inside, that is, to become part of the computer-generated virtual world. This idea has tremendous ramifications for society including the way we work and play. The elucidation of this idea is a major theme of this book.

Given that the human is a component of the virtual environment system, we need to consider how the capabilities of the human's sensory and cognitive abilities should be utilized in the design of virtual environment equipment and in the performance of tasks within virtual environments. The consideration of the human in the design of virtual environments is a major theme of this book. Along these lines, the two main goals of this book are: (1) to acquaint the reader with knowledge concerning the technical capabilities of virtual environment equipment, and (2) to acquaint the reader with knowledge concerning the capabilities of the human senses. It is the symbiosis between these two sources of information that represents the theme to this book, that is, considering human cognitive and sensory capabilities in the design and use of virtual environments.

It should be noted that technical specifications for virtual environment equipment will change rapidly with new advances in the field; but what will not change is human sensory capabilities. Thus, to ensure that the material in the book is not quickly outdated, the authors of the chapters in this book have made a great effort to emphasize fundamental knowledge concerning the human senses and to indicate how this knowledge can be used in the design of virtual environments. In fact, by integrating knowledge of human factors and psychological principles concerning the human senses into the design of virtual environments and virtual environment technology, it is now becoming possible to take the next giant step in interface design: to create virtual worlds which not only allow us to see, hear, and feel three-dimensional computer-generated data, but also to extend our sensory capabilities in ways which we are just now beginning to explore.

This book is a collection of chapters from experts in academia, industry, and government research laboratories, who have pioneered the ideas and technologies associated with virtual environments. The book discusses the hardware, human factors, and psychological principles associated with designing virtual worlds and what we term "advanced interfaces." As is discussed in the first chapter, perhaps the best definition of interface is that "interface" means exactly what the word roots connote: inter (between) and face, or that stuff that goes between the faces (i.e., senses) of the human and the machine. Interfaces are termed *advanced* in the sense that the hardware, software, and human factors technologies associated with these interfaces go beyond that which is in widespread use today and which overcome the shortfalls of many current interfaces.

The book is divided into three main sections comprising 14 chapters overall. Because both the technological and human interfaces issues in virtual environments are covered, the book can be used as a textbook for students in the following fields: computer science, engineering, psychology, and human factors. For computer science and engineering students, the standard text in computer graphics can be used to emphasize the graphics programming side of creating virtual environments (Foley, J. D., Van Dam, A., Feiner, S. K., and Hughes, J. F., *Computer Graphics: Principles and Practice*, Addison-Wesley,

1990). In addition, the book will also be of interest to those in other scientific fields such as medicine and chemistry, as it contains a fairly comprehensive review of the concepts associated with virtual environments. Furthermore, students in the arts and sciences who wish to integrate state-of-the-art computing and display technology in their creative endeavors will find the book a good reference source for stimulating their imagination as to what can be done.

The first section of the book contains two chapters written to provide a broad introduction to virtual environments and advanced interfaces. The chapters provide basic definitions and background material which thus sets the stage for future chapters. Specifically, Chapter 1 written by the two co-editors, Barfield and Furness, attempts to coalesce the concepts and ideas associated with virtual environments and advanced interfaces, discusses the advantages of virtual environments for the visualization of data and the performance of tasks, and provides a brief list of important research issues for the field. Chapter 2, by Ellis, provides an excellent overview of virtual environments including a history of the developments in the field, and provides a basic scheme on how virtual environments can be conceptualized.

The second section of the book provides information on the software and hardware technologies associated with virtual environments. Chapter 3, by Green and Sun, focuses on issues relating to modeling of virtual environments. This is an important topic given the complexity of the images which must be represented in virtual worlds. In Chapter 4, Bricken and Coco discuss their experiences associated with developing an operating system to assist developers in designing virtual worlds. Chapter 5, by Davis and Hodges, discusses the psychological aspects of human stereo vision and presents applied data on the use of stereoscopic displays. The importance of this chapter is clear when one considers that stereoscopic views of virtual environments is one of the most compelling experiences one encounters within a virtual world. In Chapter 6, Kocian and Task provide a comprehensive discussion of the technologies associated with head-mounted displays (HMDs) including a review of the technical capabilities of available commercial HMDs. In Chapter 7, Jacob discusses principles associated with eye tracking, a technology which holds great promise for interface design especially for disabled users. In Chapter 8, Cohen and Wenzel discuss the hardware and psychological issues which relate to the design of auditory virtual environments. In addition, they present some of the basic psychophysical data related to the auditory modality. The next set of chapters focus on issues relating to haptics. These chapters are important given the trend to include more touch and force feedback in virtual environments. Chapter 9 by Kaczmarek and Bach-y-Rita provides a very comprehensive overview of tactile interfaces, including psychophysical data and equipment parameters. In Chapter 10, an important extension of the concepts in the previous chapter are presented. Hannaford and Venema discuss issues in force feedback and principles of kinesthetic displays for remote and virtual environments. Finally, in Chapter 11, MacKenzie discusses the design and use of input devices. The importance of input devices is clear when one considers how often we use our hands to perform basic gripping tasks, to gain information about the surface and shape of an object, or to determine the material properties or temperature of an object. It is obvious that significant improvements are needed in the input technology we use to manipulate virtual images.

The third section of the book contains three chapters which focus on applications and cognitive issues in virtual environments. Chapter 12, written by Barfield, Zeltzer, Sheridan, and Slater, discusses the concept of presence, the sense of actually being there, for example at a remote site as in teleoperation, or of something virtual being here, for example a virtual image viewed using an HMD. In Chapter 13, Wickens and Baker discuss the cognitive issues which should be considered when designing virtual environments. It should be noted that cognitive issues associated with human participation in virtual environments have not been given the consideration they should by the virtual environment community. In fact, issues in cognitive science show great promise in terms of providing a theoretical framework for the work being done in the virtual environment field. Finally, Chapter 14, by Barfield, Rosenberg, and Lotens, discusses the design and use of augmented reality displays, essentially the integration of the virtual with the real world.

We hope the material provided in the book stimulates additional thinking on how best to integrate humans into virtual environments and on the need for more fundamental research on issues related to virtual environments and advanced interface design.

Seattle   W.B.
January 1995   T.F. III

Contents

Part III Integration of Technology

Contributors

Paul Bach-y-Rita, MD
Department of Rehabilitation Medicine
1300 University Ave. Room 2756
University of Wisconsin
Madison, WI 53706

Polly Baker, Ph.D.
National Center for Supercomputing
  Applications
University of Illinois
405 North Mathews Ave.
Urbana, IL 61801

Woodrow Barfield, Ph.D.
Sensory Engineering Laboratory
Department of Industrial Engineering,
  Fu-20
University of Washington
Seattle, WA 98195

William Bricken, Ph.D.
Oz . . . International, Ltd
3832 140th Ave., NE
Bellevue, WA 98005

Geoffrey Coco
Lone Wolf Company
2030 First Avenue, 3rd Floor
Seattle, WA 98121

Michael Cohen, Ph.D.
Human Interface Laboratory
University of Aizu
Aizu-Wakanatsu 965-80
Japan

Elizabeth Thorpe Davis, Ph.D.
School of Psychology
Georgia Institute of Technology
Atlanta, GA 30332-0280

Stephen R. Ellis, Ph.D.
Spatial Perception and Advanced Display
  Laboratory
NASA, Ames Research Center, MS 262-2
Moffett Field, CA 94035

Thomas A. Furness III, Ph.D.
Human Interface Technology Laboratory
Department of Industrial Engineering
University of Washington
Seattle, WA 98195

Mark Green, Ph.D.
Department of Computer Science
University of Alberta
Edmonton, Alberta
Canada T6G 2H1

Blake Hannaford, Ph.D.
Department of Electrical Engineering
University of Washington
Seattle, WA 98195

Larry F. Hodges, Ph.D.
Graphics, Visualization & Usability
  Center and College of Computing
Georgia Institute of Technology
Atlanta, GA 30332-0280

Robert J. K. Jacob, Ph.D.
Department of Electrical Engineering and
  Computer Science
Tufts University
Halligan Hall
161 College Avenue
Medford, MA 02155

Kurt A. Kaczmarek, Ph.D.
Department of Rehabilitation Medicine
University of Wisconsin
1300 University Ave., Rm 2756
Madison, WI 53706

Dean F. Kocian
Armstrong Laboratories
AL/CFHV, Bldg. 248
2255 H. Street
Wright Patterson Air Force Base
OH 45433-7022

Wouter A. Lotens, Ph.D.
TNO Human Factors Research Institute
PO Box 23
3769 ZG Soesterberg
The Netherlands

I. Scott MacKenzie, Ph.D.
Department of Computing and
   Information Science
University of Guelph
Guelph, Ontario
Canada N1G 2W1

Craig Rosenberg, Ph.D.
Sensory Engineering Laboratory
Department of Industrial Engineering,
   Fu-20
University of Washington
Seattle, WA 98195

Thomas Sheridan, Ph.D.
Engineering and Applied Psychology
Massachusetts Institute of Technology
77 Massachusetts Ave #3-346
Cambridge, MA 02139

Mel Slater, Ph.D.
Department of Computer Science
Queen Mary and Westfield College
Mile End Road
University of London
London E1 4NS
United Kingdom

Hanqiu Sun, Ph.D.
Business Computing Program
University of Winnipeg
Winnipeg, Manitoba
Canada R3B 2E9

H. Lee Task, Ph.D.
Armstrong Laboratories
AL/CFHV, Bldg. 248
2255 H. Street
Wright-Patterson Air Force Base
OH 45433-7022

Steven Venema
Department of Electrical Engineering
University of Washington
Seattle, WA 98195

Elizabeth M. Wenzel, Ph.D.
Spatial Auditory Displays Laboratory
NASA-Ames Research Center
Mail Stop 262-2
Moffett Field, CA 94035-1000

Christopher D. Wickens, Ph.D.
University of Illinois
Aviation Research Laboratory
1 Airport Road
Savoy, IL 61874

David Zeltzer, Ph.D.
Principal Research Scientist
Sensory Communication Group
Research Laboratory of Electronics
Massachusetts Institute of Technology
Cambridge, MA 02139

I

INTRODUCTION TO VIRTUAL ENVIRONMENTS

Introduction to Virtual Environments and Advanced Interface Design

THOMAS A. FURNESS III AND WOODROW BARFIELD

We understand from the anthropologists that almost from the beginning of our species we have been tool builders. Most of these tools have been associated with the manipulation of matter. With these tools we have learned to organize or reorganize and arrange the elements for our comfort, safety, and entertainment.

More recently, the advent of the computer has given us a new kind of tool. Instead of manipulating matter, the computer allows us to manipulate symbols. Typically, these symbols represent language or other abstractions such as mathematics, physics, or graphical images. These symbols allow us to operate at a different conscious level, providing a mechanism to communicate ideas as well as to organize and plan the manipulation of matter that will be accomplished by other tools. However, a problem with the current technology that we use to manipulate symbols is the interface between the human and computer. That is, the means by which we interact with the computer and receive feedback that our actions, thoughts, and desires are recognized and acted upon. Another problem with current computing systems is the format with which they display information. Typically, the computer, via a display monitor, only allows a limited two-dimensional view of the three-dimensional world we live in. For example, when using a computer to design a three-dimensional building, what we see and interact with is often only a two-dimensional representation of the building, or at most a so-called $2\frac{1}{2}$ D perspective view. Furthermore, unlike the sounds in the real world which stimulate us from all directions and distances, the sounds emanating from a computer originate from a stationary speaker, and when it comes to touch, with the exception of a touch screen or the tactile feedback provided by pressing a key or mouse button (limited haptic feedback to be sure), the tools we use to manipulate symbols are primitive at best.

This book is about a new and better way to interact with and manipulate symbols. These are the technologies associated with virtual environments and what we term *advanced interfaces*. In fact, the development of virtual environment technologies for interacting with and manipulating symbols may represent the next step in the evolution of tools. The technologies associated with virtual environments will allow us to see, hear, and feel three-dimensional virtual objects and also to explore virtual worlds. Using virtual environment technology, no longer will we have to look passively at the symbols from the outside but will be able to enter into and directly interact with the world of symbols. Virtual environment technologies are just now beginning to be applied with great success to the medical and engineering sciences, and entertainment; and even though the technology is still in its infancy, the intuitiveness and power associated with viewing data and processes from within has captured the imagination of scientists and the general public alike.

However, for any tool to be useful it must help us perform a task, even if that task is gaining greater knowledge, understanding, or just plain enjoyment. Truly effective tools become an extension of our intelligence, enabling us to accomplish tasks, or at least to do something more efficiently and effectively than without the tool. But since computers are symbol manipulators, it is necessary to build ways to couple the capabilities of the machine to the capabilities of the human. This book concentrates on the nature and design of the coupling or the boundary between the human and the computer that we call the *interface* and it does this specifically in the context of the technologies associated with virtual environments.

BASIC DEFINITIONS

The introduction of a few definitions will be useful to orient the reader. We define a *virtual environment* as the representation of a computer model or database which can be interactively experienced and manipulated by the virtual environment participant(s). We define a *virtual image* as the visual, auditory, and tactile and kinesthetic stimuli which are conveyed to the sensory endorgans such that they appear to originate from within the three-dimensional space surrounding the virtual environment participant. Figure 1-1 shows a virtual environment participant stimulated by several sources of computer-generated sensory input which, if done with sufficient fidelity, creates the "virtual reality" illusion. Finally, we define a *virtual interface* as a system of transducers, signal processors, computer hardware and software that create an interactive medium through which; (1) information is conveyed to the senses in the form of three-dimensional virtual images, tactile and kinesthetic feedback, and spatialized sound and, (2) the psychomotor and physiological behavior of the user is monitored and used to manipulate the virtual environment.

The term *interface* is defined as the technology that goes between the human and the functional elements of a machine. For example, using the existing parlance of computing machinery, interfaces include those *peripherals* which provide the input/output ports to the human such as visual display terminals, keyboard, mice, etc. However, interface technology must encompass more than the hardware elements and include also the software modules and human factors considerations. These modules provide not only functionality but also the more aesthetic "look and feel" attributes of the machine. In

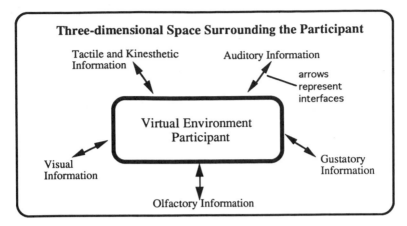

Figure 1-1 Information from several sources (typically emanating from computing technology) stimulates the virtual environment participant's sensory endorgans to create the "virtual reality" illusion. Note that currently gustatory input is not available, and olfactory input is in the early development stage.

addition, human cognitive processes should be considered part of the interface as they process and make sense of the sensory information.

Perhaps the best definition of interface, which also frees the term from that limited by the concepts of today, is that "interface" means exactly what the word roots connote: inter (between) and face, or that stuff that goes between the faces (i.e., senses) of the human and the machine. Interfaces are termed *advanced* in the sense that the hardware, software and human factors technologies associated with these interfaces go beyond that which is in widespread use and which overcome the shortfalls of many current interfaces. In the context of virtual environments the interface technologies are generally a head-mounted display for viewing stereoscopic images, a spatial tracker for locating the position of the head and hand, equipment to spatialize sound, and equipment to provide tactile and force feedback to the virtual environment participant.

A WAY OF THINKING ABOUT INTERFACES

The interface between the human and the machine can be thought to exist in "direct" and "indirect" paths. The direct paths are those which are physical or involve the transfer of signals in the form of light, sound or mechanical energy between the human and the machine. We usually think of the direct pathways as the information *medium*. The indirect pathways deal with the organization of signals according to internal models which are shared by the human and the machine. These models cause the data elements conveyed on the display to have meaning or "semantic content." Such is the nature of language. We can think of the indirect pathway as the *message* that is transmitted through the medium. Our ability to input control actions into the machine makes the medium *interactive*, in that messages can be sent in two directions.

The quality of the direct pathway or medium is governed principally by the physical aspects of the control and display components within the interface (e.g., luminance, contrast, resolution, acoustic frequency response, etc.). The quality of the indirect pathways is governed by the programming of the controls and displays (e.g., the nature of the world construct, interactive tools and heuristics, etc.). The semantic fidelity of the interface is greatly affected by training, *a priori* knowledge of the task, individual differences, and our general experience in living in a three-dimensional world.

ATTRIBUTES OF AN IDEAL MEDIUM

Ideally, the medium should be configured to match the sensory and perceptual capabilities of the human while the message programming organizes and structures the information elements (i.e., creates a message "context") to achieve an optimum coupling or match between the internal mental model of the human and the machine's interpretation and representation of the environment. Together, the message and medium create an *information environment* wherein tasks are performed. The direct and indirect paths are highly entwined and both must be considered in designing an ideal interface which promotes an accurate spatial/cognitive map of the virtual environment.

Humans have remarkable capacities for handling complex spatial and state information as long as this information is portrayed through a medium that uses our three-dimensional perceptual organization and incorporates the natural semantics of our mental models of the world (i.e., a common language). Spatial information is concerned with three-dimensional geometry of the virtual environment while state information is concerned with the state of events within the virtual environment. An ideal information environment should provide a signal transfer path to our senses which conveys information in the above context. Table 1-1 lists some of the attributes of an ideal medium intended to communicate an accurate spatial/cognitive map of the virtual environment to the user.

SHORTFALLS IN CURRENT INTERFACES

As discussed above, in order to be efficient, the ideal interface needs to match the perceptual and psychomotor capabilities of the human. This requirement exposes some of the fundamental limitations of current interfaces. For example, most current visual displays are capable of presenting only mono-scopic depth cues (e.g., linear perspective, size constancy) to display three-dimensional information, it is not possible to present stereoscopic depth cues to the user with these systems. The instantaneous field-of-view of 19-inch displays provides little stimulation to the peripheral retina which is essential to engage our senses and give us a feeling of immersion. Furthermore, our methods of

Table 1-1 Attributes of an ideal medium	
• Matches the sensory capabilities of human	• Unambiguous
• Easy to learn	• Does not consume reserve capacity
• High bandwidth bridge to the brain	• Easy prediction
• Dynamically adapts to the needs of the task	• Reliable
• Can be tailored to individual approaches	• Operates when busy
• Natural semantic language	• High semantic content (simple presentation)
• Organization of spatial/state/temporal factors	• Localization of objects
• Macroscopic vs. microscopic view	movement
• High bandwidth input	state
• Information clustering	immediacy
• Information filtering	• Sense of presence

manipulation, using keyboards and other manipulation devices, require the user to become highly skilled in order to operate these devices efficiently. Three-dimensional acoustic and tactile displays are rarely used. In a sense, the medium gets in the way of the message. These and other limitations limit the bandwidth of the channel through which information and command flow between the human and the machine. New technologies involving direct input of spatial information and use of speech show great promise, but still do not solve some of the fundamental issues of how to build a symbiotic relationship between the human and the machine such that it truly becomes a tool to extend our intellectual reach.

VIRTUAL ENVIRONMENTS

Virtual interfaces and the information environments they produce provide new alternatives for communicating information to users (Furness, 1988; Kocian, 1988; Ellis, 1991). A virtual display leads to a different "visual experience" than viewing an image using a standard computer monitor (see Figure 1-2). Instead of viewing directly one physical display screen, the virtual display creates only a small physical image (e.g., nominally one square inch) and projects this image into the eyes by optical lenses and mirrors so that the original image appears to be a large picture or full scale three-dimensional scene suspended in the world. A personal virtual display system, termed a head-mounted display, usually consists of two small image sources (e.g., a miniature cathode-ray tube or liquid crystal array) which is mounted on some headgear, and small optical elements which magnify, collimate and project this image via a mirror combiner into the eyes such that the original image appears at optical infinity. The size of the image is now a function of the magnification of the optics and not the physical size of the original image source. With two image sources and projection optics, one for each eye, a binocular virtual display is achieved, providing a 3D or stereoscopic scene. It is possible, therefore, to create a personal 3D "cinerama theater" within headgear worn by the user.

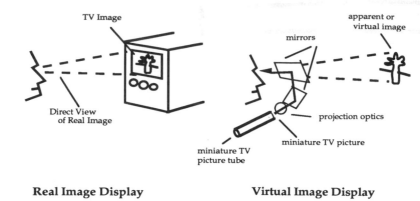

Real Image Display   Virtual Image Display

Figure 1-2   Comparison of real image and virtual image display.

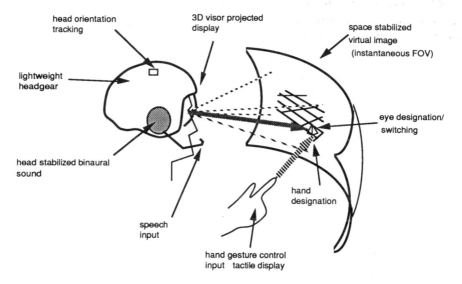

Figure 1-3   Virtual environment display system.

With a partially reflective combiner (a mirror that reflects light from the image source into the eyes), the display scene can be superimposed onto the normal physical world. In this way the virtual image can "augment" or add information to the physical world. The user can also position the image anywhere (i.e., it moves with the head). When combined with a head position sensing system, the information on the display can be stabilized relative to the physical world, thereby creating the effect of viewing a circumambience or "virtual world" which surrounds the user (Figure 1-3).

An acoustic virtual display, i.e., a system which spatializes sound, can also be created by processing a sound image in the same way that the pinnae of the ear manipulate a sound wavefront (Foster and Wenzel, 1992). A sound object

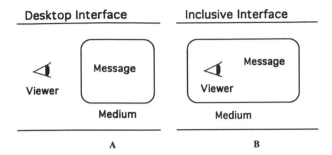

Figure 1-4 In (A) the viewer is separate from the message; in (B) the viewer and message occupy the same virtual space.

is first digitized and then convolved with head related transfer function (HRTF) coefficients which describe the finite impulse response of the ears of a "generic head" to sounds at particular angles and distances from the listener. Monaural digitized sound can thus be transformed to spatially localized binaural sound presented through stereo headphones to the subject. By using the instantaneously measured head position to select from a library of HRTF coefficients, a localized sound which is stable in space can be generated (Wenzel and Foster, 1990). These sound objects can be used either separately or as an "overlay" onto stereoscopic visual objects.

Similarly, a tactile image can be displayed by providing a two-dimensional array of vibration or pressure transducers in contact with the skin of the hand or body. Tactors, devices that stimulate tactile receptors, may be actuated as a function of the shape and surface features of a virtual object and the instantaneous position of the head and fingers.

ADVANTAGES OF VIRTUAL ENVIRONMENTS

Since virtual displays can surround the user with three-dimensional stimuli, under ideal conditions the user may feel a sense of "presence," that they are "inhabiting" a new place instead of looking at a picture. This aspect is illustrated by Figure 1-4. Normally, when we look at a video display terminal, we see an object embedded in our three-dimensional world through which a separate message is being conveyed. In order to interact effectively with this world, we have to use three cognitive models: (1) a model of our immediate environment, (2) a model of the functionality of the medium (the terminal, in this case), and (3) a model of the message and its heuristics as conveyed through this medium.

When we are "immersed" in an inclusive virtual environment, we in effect become a part of the message. The original environment and presentation medium disappear and we are required to draw upon only a single model of the new environment which represents only the message. Ultimately then we can interact within this virtual environment using the natural semantics that we use when interacting with the physical world. These factors empower the virtual interface as a medium with an unprecedented efficiency in communicating computer-generated graphical information, making it ideal for visual/spatial displays.

Other advantages of the virtual environment include the flexibility in conveying three-dimensional information simultaneously into several modalities, such as using visual and acoustic representations of an object's location and state in three-dimensional space. Multiple modality displays have a greater promise of reducing ambiguity in complex situations and perhaps a more effective way of attracting attention to critical conditions during high workload tasks. Generally, virtual interfaces also facilitate natural input behavior to the machine. In this regard, the psychomotor movement of the eyes, head, hands and body can be used as input to a virtual space and for control of three-dimensional objects.

Perhaps one of the more salient advantages of virtual interfaces is the ability to superimpose images over the physical world, thereby augmenting the normal information that could be derived from direct observation. It should also be noted that virtual environments can serve as a good means of simulating other systems, both physical and virtual (e.g., using a virtual display to simulate another virtual display).

In terms of applied applications the use of virtual environment technology offers great promise over conventional technology for product design, development, and testing. Consider for example, the manufacturing arena, a critical area for global competitiveness. According to Adam (1993); the following benefits may result from the use of virtual environment technology for manufacturing design.

1. Virtual prototyping will reduce the need for costly and time consuming physical mock-ups.
2. Engineering analysis will become more efficient as the results of simulations are integrated with virtual prototypes.
3. Operational simulations will permit the direct involvement of humans in performance and ergonomic studies.

In addition, in other domains the use of virtual environment technology will also result in significant improvements in the way data and dynamic processes are visualized. For example, scientific visualization is one application where virtual environment technology will enable scientists to enter into the world of data, to perform virtual simulations and experiments, and to circumvent the time consuming model building associated with physical mock-ups.

RESEARCH ISSUES IN VIRTUAL ENVIRONMENTS AND ADVANCED INTERFACES

Despite the great potential of virtual environment technology for solving many of the interface problems thus far discussed, several significant problems must be resolved before virtual interfaces and the environments they can create will become practical and useful (Furness, 1988). Here we list a few of the important issues that need to be resolved.

1. There is a need to develop a theoretical basis for the work done in virtual environments, and a need to develop conceptual models to assist designers of virtual worlds.
2. There is a need to develop a solid understanding of the human factors design implications of virtual interfaces.
3. There is a need to develop ways to measure the goodness of virtual environments.
4. There is a need to develop physiological and behavior tracking of virtual world participants.
5. There is a need for affordable, lightweight, high-resolution display devices
6. There is a need for inexpensive hardware architecture to support the rapid image generation and manipulation needed to generate a seamless virtual world presentation.
7. There is a need for software infrastructure and tools for constructing, managing and interacting within virtual environments.
8. There is a need to develop languages, spatial and state representations, and interactive heuristics for constructing virtual worlds.

INTRODUCTION TO THE CHAPTERS

The emerging field of virtual environments and advanced interface design is very broad, covering topics from psychology, engineering, and computer science. This book represents an attempt to integrate these topics into one source with the interface between the human and virtual environment equipment as the main underlying theme. Where appropriate, the chapter authors present both the theoretical and applied data relating to virtual environments because both are equally important. The theoretical data are important because the design of virtual environments and advanced interfaces must be based on theoretical models of human behavior. Support for this argument comes from the field of human–computer interaction where models of human behavior have proved useful in interface design. The applied information is important because much data on interface design has been generated from the fields of psychology and human factors engineering and much of this data is directly applicable to virtual environments.

To cover the broad topic of virtual environments and "advanced" interfaces, the chapters in the book are organized around three general areas. The first general topic is an introduction to virtual environments and advanced interfaces. Furness and Barfield start Part I of the book by discussing the basic components of virtual environment systems and by proposing definitions of basic terms related to virtual environments and advanced interfaces. The introductory material is concluded by Steve Ellis who provides an excellent review of the origins and elements of virtual environments which further sets the stage for subsequent chapters.

Part II of the book focuses on the current technologies used to present visual, auditory, and tactile and kinesthetic information to participants of virtual environments. The first chapter in this section describes the computer graphics and software principles associated with virtual environments, currently one of the most time consuming aspects of building virtual environments. Specifically, Green and Sun discuss modeling techniques for virtual environments and Bricken and Coco discuss the development efforts associated with VEOS, a software system for virtual environments in use at the University of Washington. The next display technology covered in this section relates to the visual display of 3D information. Davis and Hodges present the basic concepts associated with human stereo vision and stereoscopic viewing systems while Kocian and Task focus specifically on head-mounted displays. Finally, Jacob reviews eye tracking technology and the psychology of eye movements for interface input/output. The next area covered on the topic of current virtual environment technologies focuses on the design of auditory interfaces to virtual environments. Specifically, Cohen and Wenzel discuss human auditory capabilities, auditory interface design concepts, and principles of spatialized sound. The last three chapters comprising Part II focus on haptic interface technology. That is, issues which relate to the participant's interaction with virtual objects and the quality and type of· feedback received when virtual objects are manipulated. For example, Kaczmarek and Bach-y-Rita review the tactile sense and the technology used to stimulate tactile receptors. Much of this work is gleaned from their experience in designing interfaces for the disabled. In the kinesthetic domain, Hannaford and Venema discuss force feedback and kinesthetic displays for the manipulation of remote and virtual environments. Finally, MacKenzie categorizes and discusses the design and use of input devices for virtual environments and advanced interfaces.

The last part of the book focuses on the integration of virtual environment technology with the human component in the system. Barfield, Zeltzer, Sheridan, and Slater discuss the important concept of presence within a virtual environment, i.e., the feeling of actually being there at a remote site, as in the case of a teleoperator, or of a virtual object being here. They propose several potential measures for presence. In addition, Wickens discusses cognitive issues related to "virtual reality," focusing on learning, navigation, and depth cues, along with other topics. Finally, Barfield, Rosenberg, and Lotens discuss augmented reality, the concept of combining the virtual world with the real, using a system designed at the University of Washington as an example system.

SUMMARY

In summary, virtual environment technology holds great promise as a tool to extend human intelligence. However, in order to effectively couple virtual environment equipment with human cognitive, motor, and perceptual sensory capabilities, significant improvements in virtual environment technology and interface design are needed. Along these lines, much of the research and many of the ideas presented in this book are motivated by the need to design more natural and intuitive interfaces to virtual environments and to improve the technology used to present auditory, visual, tactile, and kinesthetic information to participants of virtual worlds. Finally, the book attempts to give the reader an idea as to where we are now in terms of the design and use of virtual environments, and most importantly, where we can go in the future.

REFERENCES

Adam, J. A. (1993) Virtual reality is for real, *IEEE Spectrum*, October

Ellis, S. R. (1991) Nature and origins of virtual environments a bibliographical essay, *Comput. Systems Engineering*, **2**, 321–47

Foster, S. and Wenzel, E. (1992) Three-dimensional auditory displays, *Informatique '92, Int. Conf. Interface to Real and Virtual Worlds*, Montpellier, France, 23–27 March

Furness, T. (1988) Harnessing virtual space, *SID Int. Symp., Digest of Technical Papers*, Anaheim, CA, pp. 4–7

Kocian, D. F. (1988) Design considerations for virtual panoramic display (VPD) helmet systems, *Man-Machine Interface in Tactical Aircraft Design and Combat Automation* (AGARD-CP-425), pp. 1–32

Wenzel, E. M. and Foster, S. H. (1990) Realtime digital synthesis of virtual acoustic environments, *Proc. 1990 Symp. in Interactive 3D Graphics*, March 25–28, Snowbird, VT, pp. 139–40

2

Origins and Elements of Virtual Environments

STEPHEN R. ELLIS

COMMUNICATION AND ENVIRONMENTS

Virtual environments are media

Virtual environments created through computer graphics are communications media (Licklider *et al.*, 1978). Like other media, they have both physical and abstract components. Paper, for example, is a medium for communication. The paper is itself one possible physical embodiment of the abstraction of a two-dimensional surface onto which marks may be made.[1] The corresponding abstraction for head-coupled, virtual image, stereoscopic displays that synthesize a coordinated sensory experience is an environment. These so-called "virtual reality" media have only recently caught the international public imagination (Pollack, 1989; D'Arcy, 1990; Stewart, 1991; Brehde, 1991), but they have arisen from continuous development in several technical and non-technical areas during the past 25 years (Brooks Jr., 1988; Ellis, 1990; Ellis, *et al.*, 1991, 1993; Kalawsky, 1993).

Optimal design

A well designed computer interface affords the user an efficient and effortless flow of information to and from the device with which he interacts. When users are given sufficient control over the pattern of this interaction, they themselves can evolve efficient interaction strategies that match the coding of their communications to the characteristics of their communication channel (Zipf, 1949; Mandelbrot, 1982; Ellis and Hitchcock, 1986; Grudin and Norman, 1991). But successful interface design should strive to reduce this adaptation period by analysis of the user's task and performance limitations. This analysis requires understanding of the operative design metaphor for the interface in question.

The dominant interaction metaphor for the computer interface changed in the 1980's. Modern graphical interfaces, like those first developed at Xerox PARC (Smith *et al.*, 1982) and used for the Apple Macintosh, have transformed the "conversational" interaction from one in which users "talked" to their computers to one in which they "acted out" their commands in a "desk-top" display. This so called desk-top metaphor provides the users with an illusion of an environment in which they enact wishes by manipulating symbols on a computer screen.

Extensions of the desk-top metaphor

Virtual environment displays represent a three-dimensional generalization of the two-dimensional "desk-top" metaphor.[2] These synthetic environments may be experienced either from egocentric or exocentric viewpoints. That is to say, the users may appear to actually be in the environment or see themselves represented as a "You are here" symbol (Levine, 1984) which they can control.

The objects in this synthetic universe, as well as the space itself within which they exist, may be programmed to have arbitrary properties. However, the successful extension of the desk-top metaphor to a full "environment" requires an understanding of the necessary limits to programmer creativity in order to insure that the environment is comprehensible and usable. These limits derive from human experience in real environments and illustrate a major connection between work in telerobotics and virtual environments. For reasons of simulation fidelity, previous telerobotic and aircraft simulations, which have many of the aspects of virtual environments, have had to explicitly take into account real-world kinematic and dynamic constraints in ways now usefully studied by the designers of totally synthetic environments (Hashimoto et al., 1986; Bussolari et al., 1988; Kim et al., 1988; Bejczy et al., 1990; Sheridan, 1992; Cardullo, 1993).

Environments

Successful synthesis of an environment requires some analysis of the parts that make up the environment. The theater of human activity may be used as a reference for defining an *environment* and may be thought of as having three parts: a *content*, a *geometry*, and a *dynamics* (Ellis, 1991).

Content

The *objects* and *actors* in the environment are its content. These objects may be described by *characteristic vectors* which identify their position, orientation, velocity, and acceleration in the environmental space, as well as other distinguishing characteristics such as their color, texture, and energy. The characteristic vector is thus a description of the *properties* of the objects. The subset of all the terms of the characteristic vector which is common to every actor and object of the content may be called the *position vector*. Though the actors in an environment may for some interactions be considered objects, they are distinct from objects in that in addition to characteristics they have *capacities* to initiate interactions with other objects. The basis of these initiated interactions is the storage of energy or information within the actors, and their ability to control the release of this stored information or energy after a period of time. The *self* is a distinct actor in the environment which provides a *point of view* from which the environment may be constructed. All parts of the environment that are exterior to the self may be considered the field of action. As an example, the balls on a billiard table may be considered the content of the billiard table environment and the cue ball controlled by the pool player may be considered the "self."

Geometry

The geometry is a description of the environmental field of action. It has *dimensionality*, *metrics*, and *extent*. The dimensionality refers to the number of *independent* descriptive terms needed to specify the position vector for every element of the environment. The metrics are systems of rules that may be applied to the position vector to establish an ordering of the contents and to establish the concept of geodesic or the loci of minimal distance paths between points in the environmental space. The extent of the environment refers to the range of possible values for the elements of the position vector. The environmental space or field of action may be defined as the Cartesian product of all the elements of the position vector over their possible ranges. An environmental trajectory is a time-history of an object through the environmental space. Since kinematic constraints may preclude an object from traversing the space along some paths, these constraints are also part of the environment's geometric description.

Dynamics

The dynamics of an environment are the *rules of interaction* among its contents describing their behavior as they exchange energy or information. Typical examples of specific dynamical rules may be found in the differential equations of Newtonian dynamics describing the responses of billiard balls to impacts of the cue ball. For other environments, these rules also may take the form of grammatical rules or even of look-up tables for pattern-match-triggered action rules. For example, a syntactically correct command typed at a computer terminal can cause execution of a program with specific parameters. In this case the information in the command plays the role of the energy, and the resulting rate of change in the logical state of the affected device, plays the role of acceleration.[3]

Sense of physical reality

Our sense of physical reality is a construction from the symbolic, geometric, and dynamic information directly presented to our senses. It is noteworthy that many of the aspects of physical reality are only presented in incomplete, noisy form. We, for example, generally see only part of whole objects, yet through *a priori* "knowledge" that we bring to perceptual analysis, we know them to exist in their entirety[4] (Gregory, 1968, 1980, 1981). Similarly, our goal-seeking behavior appears to filter noise by benefiting from internal dynamical models of the objects we may track or control (Kalman, 1960; Kleinman *et al.*, 1970).

Accurate perception consequently involves considerable *a priori* knowledge about the possible structure of the world. This knowledge is under constant recalibration based on error feedback. The role of error feedback has been classically mathematically modeled during tracking behavior (Jex *et al.*, 1966; McRuer and Weir, 1969; Hess, 1987) and notably demonstrated in the behavioral plasticity of visual-motor coordination (Held *et al.*, 1966; Welch, 1978; Held and Durlach, 1991) and in vestibular reflexes (Jones *et al.*, 1984; Zangemeister and Hansen, 1985; Zangemeister, 1991).

Thus, a large part of our sense of physical reality is a consequence of internal processing rather than being something that is developed only from the immediate sensory information we receive. Our sensory and cognitive interpretive systems are predisposed to process incoming information in ways that normally result in a correct interpretation of the external environment, and in some cases they may be said to actually "resonate" with specific patterns of input that are uniquely informative about our environment (Gibson, 1950; Koenderink and van Doorn, 1977; Regan and Beverley, 1979; Heeger, 1989).

These same constructive processes are triggered by the displays used to present virtual environments. However, in these cases the information is mediated through the display technology. The illusion of an enveloping environment depends on the extent to which all of these constructive processes are triggered. Accordingly, virtual environments can come in different stages of completeness, which may be usefully distinguished.

VIRTUALIZATION

Definition of virtualization

Virtualization may be defined as *the process by which a human viewer interprets a patterned sensory impression to represent an extended object in an environment other than that in which it physically exists.* A classical example would be that of a virtual image as defined in geometrical optics. A viewer of such an image sees the rays emanating from it as if they originated from a point that could be computed by the basic lens law rather than from their actual location (Figure 2-1).

Virtualization, however, extends beyond the objects to the spaces in which they themselves may move. Consequently, a more detailed discussion of what it means to *virtualize* an environment is required.

Levels of virtualization

Three levels of virtualization may be distinguished: virtual space, virtual image, and virtual environments. These levels represent identifiable points on a continuum of virtualization as synthesized sensory stimuli more and more closely realize the sensory and motor consequences of a real environment.

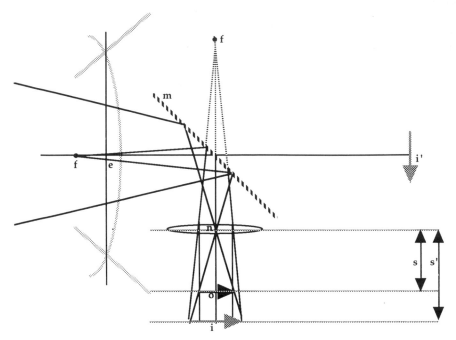

Figure 2-1 Virtual image created by a simple lens with focal length f placed at n and viewed from e through a half-silvered mirror at m appears to be straight ahead of the viewer at i'. The visual direction and accommodation required to see the virtual image clearly are quite different than what would be needed to see the real object at o. An optical arrangement similar to this would be needed to superimpose synthetic computer imagery on a view of a real scene as in a head-up display.

Virtual space

The first form, construction of a virtual space, refers to the process by which a viewer perceives a three-dimensional layout of objects in space when viewing a flat surface presenting the pictorial cues to space, that is, perspective, shading, occlusion, and texture gradients. This process, which is akin to map interpretation, is the most abstract of the three. Viewers must literally learn to interpret pictorial images (Gregory and Wallace, 1974; Senden, 1932; Jones and Hagen, 1980). It is also not an automatic interpretive process because many of the physiological reflexes associated with the experience of a real three-dimensional environment are either missing or inappropriate for the patterns seen on a flat picture. The basis of the reconstruction of virtual space must be the optic array, the patterned collection of relative lines of sight to significant features in the image, that is, contours, vertices, lines, and textured regions. Since scaling does not affect the relative position of the features of the optic array, perceived size or scale is not intrinsically defined in a virtual space.

Virtual image

The second form of virtualization is the perception of a virtual image. In conformance with the use of this term in geometric optics, it is the perception

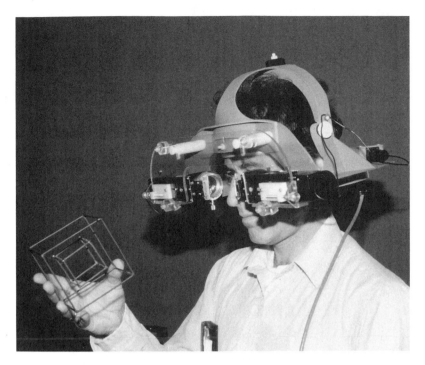

Figure 2-2   A see-through, head-mounted, virtual image, stereoscopic display that will allow the users to interact with virtual objects synthesized by computer graphics which are superimposed in their field of vision (Ellis and Bucher, 1994). (Photograph courtesy of NASA.)

of an object in depth in which accommodative,[5] vergence,[6] and (optionally) stereoscopic disparity[7] cues are present, though not necessarily consistent (Bishop, 1987). Since, virtual images can incorporate stereoscopic and vergence cues, the actual perceptual scaling of the constructed space is not arbitrary but, somewhat surprisingly, not simply related to viewing geometry (Foley, 1980, 1985; Collewijn and Erkelens, 1990; Erkelens and Collewijn, 1985a, 1985b) (Figure 2-2).

Virtual environment

The final form is the virtualization of an environment. In this case the key added sources of information are observer-slaved motion parallax, depth-of-focus variation, and wide field-of-view without visible restriction of the field of view. If properly implemented, these additional features can be consistently synthesized to provide stimulation of major space-related psychological responses and physiological reflexes such as vergence, accommodative vergence,[8] vergence accommodation[9] of the "near response" (Hung *et al.*, 1984), the optokinetic reflex[10] the vestibular-ocular reflex[11] (Feldon and Burda, 1987), and postural reflexes (White *et al.*, 1980). These features when embellished by synthesized sound sources (Wenzel *et al.*, 1988; Wightman and Kistler, 1989a,

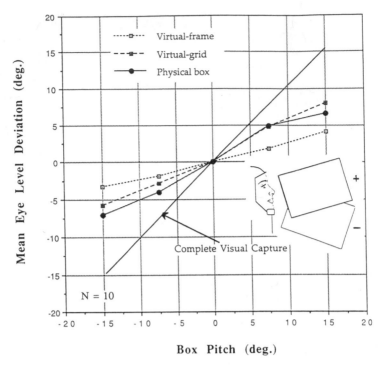

Figure 2-3 Observers who view into a visual frame of reference such as a large room or box that is pitched with respect to gravity, will have their sense of the horizon, biased towards the direction of the pitch of the visual frame. A mean effect of this type is shown for a group of 10 subjects by the trace labeled "physical box." When a comparable group of subjects experienced the same pitch in a matched virtual environment simulation of the pitch using a stereo head-mounted display, the biasing effect as measured by the slope of this displayed function was about half that of the physical environment. Adding additional grid texture to the surfaces in the virtual environment, increased the amount of visual-frame-induced bias, i.e., the so-called "visual capture" (Nemire and Ellis, 1991).

1989b; Wenzel, 1991) can substantially contribute to an illusion of telepresence (Bejczy, 1980), that is, actually being present in the synthetic environment. Measurements of the degree to which a virtual environment display convinces its users that they are present in the synthetic world can be made by measuring the degree to which these responses can be triggered in it (Figure 2-3) (Nemire and Ellis, 1991).

The fact that actors in virtual environments interact with objects and the environment by hand, head, and eye movements, tightly restricts the subjective scaling of the space so that all system gains must be carefully set. Mismatch in the gains or position measurement offsets will degrade performance by introducing unnatural visual–motor and visual–vestibular correlations. In the absence of significant time lags, humans can adapt to these unnatural correlations. However, time lags do interfere with complete visual–motor adaptation (Held and Durlach, 1991; Jones *et al.*, 1984) and when present in the imaging system can cause motion sickness (Crampton, 1990).

Environmental viewpoints and controlled elements

Virtual spaces, images or environments may be experienced from two kinds of viewpoint: egocentric viewpoints, in which the sensory environment is constructed from the viewpoint actually assumed by users, and exocentric viewpoints in which the environment is viewed from a position other than that where users are represented to be. In the latter case, they can literally see a representation of themselves. This distinction in frames of reference results in a fundamental difference in movements users must make to track a visually referenced target. Egocentric viewpoints require compensatory tracking, and exocentric viewpoints require pursuit tracking. This distinction also corresponds to the difference between inside-out and outside-in frames of reference in the aircraft simulation literature. The substantial literature on human tracking performance in these alternative reference frames, and the general literature on human manual performance, may be useful in the design of synthetic environments (Poulton, 1974; Wickens, 1986).

ORIGINS OF VIRTUAL ENVIRONMENTS

Early visionaries

The obvious, intuitive appeal that virtual environment technology has is probably rooted in the human fascination with vicarious experiences in imagined environments. In this respect, virtual environments may be thought of as originating with the earliest human cave art (Fagan, 1985), though Lewis Carroll's *Through the Looking-Glass* certainly is a more modern example of this fascination.

Fascination with alternative, synthetic realities has been continued in more contemporary literature. Aldous Huxley's "feelies" in *Brave New World* were certainly a kind of virtual environment, a cinema with sensory experience extended beyond sight and sound. A similar fascination must account for the popularity of microcomputer role-playing adventure games such as *Wizzardry*. Motion pictures, and especially stereoscopic movies, of course, also provide examples of noninteractive spaces (Lipton, 1982). Theater provides an example of a corresponding performance environment which is more interactive and has been claimed to be a source of useful metaphors for human interface design (Laural, 1991).

The contemporary interest in imagined environments has been particularly stimulated by the advent of sophisticated, relatively inexpensive, interactive techniques allowing the inhabitants of these environments to move about and manually interact with computer graphics objects in three-dimensional space. This kind of environment was envisioned in the science fiction plots of the movie TRON and in William Gibson's 1984 *Neuromancer*, yet the first actual

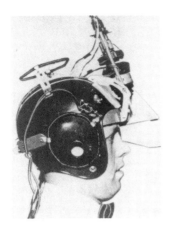
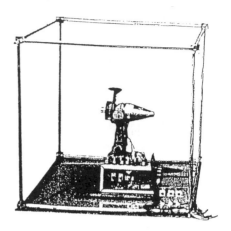
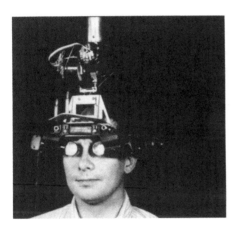
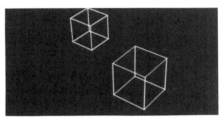

Figure 2-4 Visual virtual environment display systems have three basic parts: a head-referenced visual display, head and/or body position sensors, a technique for controlling the visual display based on head and/or body movement. One of the earliest systems of this sort developed by Philco engineers (Comeau and Bryan, 1961) used a head-mounted, binocular, virtual image viewing system, a Helmholtz coil electromagnetic head orientation sensor, and a remote TV camera slaved to head orientation to provide the visual image. Today this would be called a telepresence viewing system (upper panels). The first system to replace the video signal with a totally synthetic image produced through computer graphics, was demonstrated by Ivan Sutherland for very simple geometric forms (Sutherland, 1965, 1970 lower panels).

synthesis of such a system using a head-mounted stereo display was made possible much earlier in the middle 1960's by Ivan Sutherland (Figure 2-4) who developed special-purpose fast graphics hardware specifically for the purpose of experiencing computer-synthesized environments through head-mounted graphics displays (Sutherland, 1965, 1970).

Another early synthesis of a synthetic, interactive environment was implemented by Myron Krueger (Krueger, 1977, 1983, 1985) in the 1970's. Unlike the device developed for Sutherland, Krueger's environment was projected onto a wall-sized screen. In Krueger's VIDEOPLACE, the users' images appear in a two-dimensional graphic video world created by a computer. The VIDEOPLACE computer analyzed video images to determine when an object was touched by an inhabitant, and it could then generate a graphic or auditory response. One advantage of this kind of environment is that the remote video-based position measurement does not necessarily encumber the user with position sensors. A more recent and sophisticated version of this mode of experience of virtual environments is the implementation from the University of Illinois called, with apologies to Plato, the "Cave" (Cruz-Neira et al., 1992).

Vehicle simulation and three-dimensional cartography

Probably the most important source of virtual environment technology comes from previous work in fields associated with the development of realistic vehicle simulators, primarily for aircraft (Rolfe and Staples, 1986; CAE Electronics, 1991; McKinnon and Kruk, 1991; Cardullo, 1993) but also automobiles (Stritzke, 1991) and ships (Veldhuyzen and Stassen, 1977; Schuffel, 1987). The inherent difficulties in controlling the actual vehicles often require that operators be highly trained. Since acquiring this training on the vehicles themselves could be dangerous or expensive, simulation systems synthesize the content, geometry, and dynamics of the control environment for training and for testing of new technology and procedures.

These systems have usually cost millions of dollars and have recently involved helmet-mounted displays to re-create part of the environment (Lypaczewski et al., 1986; Barrette et al., 1990; Furness, 1986, 1987). Declining costs have now brought the cost of a virtual environment display down to that of an expensive workstation and made possible "personal simulators" for everyday use (Foley, 1987; Fisher et al., 1986; Kramer, 1992; Bassett, 1992) (Figures 2-5 and 2-6).

The simulator's interactive visual displays are made by computer graphics hardware and algorithms. Development of special-purpose hardware, such as matrix multiplication devices, was an essential step that enabled generation of real-time, that is, greater than 20 Hz, interactive three-dimensional graphics (Sutherland, 1965, 1970; Myers and Sutherland, 1968). More recent examples are the "geometry engine"(Clark, 1980, 1982) and the "reality engine" in Silicon Graphics IRIS workstations. These "graphics engines" now can project very large numbers of shaded or textured polygons or other graphics primitives per second (Silicon Graphics, 1991). Though the improved numbers may seem large, rendering of naturalistic objects and surfaces can require from 10 000 to 500 000 polygons. Efficient software techniques are also important for improved three-dimensional graphics performance. "Oct-tree" data structures, for example, have been shown to dramatically improve processing speed for inherently volumetric structures (Jenkins and Tanimoto, 1980; Meagher, 1984).

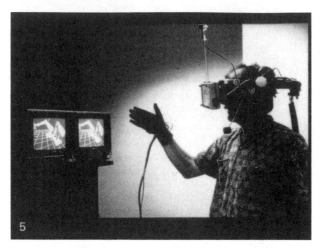

Figure 2-5 This head-mounted, stereo, virtual environment display system at the Ames Research Center Advanced Displays and Spatial Perception Laboratory is being used to control a remote PUMA robot in the Intelligent Mechanisms Laboratory. The simulation update rate varies from 12 to 30 Hz depending on the complexity of the graphics. A local kinematic simulation of the remote work site aids the operator in planning complex movements and visualizing kinematic and operational constraints on the motion of the end-effector. (Photograph courtesy of NASA.)

Figure 2-6 As in all current relatively inexpensive, head-mounted virtual environment viewing systems using LCD arrays, the view that the operator actually sees through the wide field of the LEEP® view finder (lower inset shows a part of the user's actual field of view) is significantly lower resolution than that typically seen on the graphics monitors (background matched in magnification). The horizontal pixel resolution through view finder is about 22 arcmin/pixel, vertical resolution is 24 arcmin/line. Approximately 2 arcmin/pixel are required to present resolution at the center of the visual field comparable to that seen on a standard Macintosh monochrome display viewed at 57 cm. (Photograph courtesy of NASA.)

24

Figure 2-7 Moving-base simulator of the Aerospace Human Factors Division of Ames Research Center pitched so as to simulate an acceleration. (Photograph courtesy of NASA.)

Since vehicle simulation may involve moving-base simulators, programming the appropriate correlation between visual and vestibular simulation is crucial for a complete simulation of an environment (Figure 2-7). Moreover, failure to match these two stimuli correctly can lead to motion sickness (AGARD, 1988). Paradoxically, however, since the effective travel of most moving-base simulators is limited, designers must learn how to use subthreshold visual–vestibular mismatches to produce illusions of greater freedom of movement. These allowable mismatches are built into so-called "washout" models (Bussolari *et al.*, 1988; Curry *et al.*, 1976) and are key elements for creating illusions of extended movement. For example, a slowly implemented pitch-up of a simulator can be used to help create an illusion of forward acceleration. Understanding the tolerable dynamic limits of visual–vestibular miscorrelation will be an important design consideration for wide field-of-view head-mounted displays.

The use of informative distortion is also well established in cartography (Monmonier, 1991) and is used to help create a convincing three-dimensional environment for simulated vehicles. Cartographic distortion is also obvious in global maps which must warp a spherical surface into a plane (Cotter, 1966; Robinson *et al.*, 1984) and three-dimensional maps, which often use significant vertical scale exaggeration (6–20×) to present topographic features clearly. Explicit informative geometric distortion is sometimes incorporated into maps and cartograms presenting geographically indexed statistical data (Tobler, 1963, 1976; Tufte, 1983, 1990; Bertin, 1967/1983), but the extent to which such informative distortion may be incorporated into simulated environments is constrained by the user's movement-related physiological reflexes. If the viewer is constrained to actually be *in* the environment, deviations from a natural environmental space can cause disorientation and motion sickness (Crampton, 1990; Oman, 1991). For this reason, virtual space or virtual image formats are more suitable when successful communication of the spatial information may be achieved through spatial distortions (Figure 2-8). However, even in these formats the content of the environment may have to be enhanced by aids such as graticules to help the user discount unwanted aspects of the geometric distortion (McGreevy and Ellis, 1986; Ellis *et al.*, 1987; Ellis and Hacisalihzade, 1990).

In some environmental simulations the environment itself is the object of interest. Truly remarkable animations have been synthesized from image sequences taken by NASA spacecraft which mapped various planetary surfaces. When electronically combined with surface altitude data, the surface photography can be used to synthesize flights over the surface through positions never reached by the spacecraft's camera (Hussey, 1990). Recent developments have made possible the use of these synthetic visualizations of planetary and Earth surfaces for interactive exploration and they promise to provide planetary scientists with the new capability of "virtual planetary exploration" (NASA, 1990; Hitchner, 1992; McGreevy, 1994) (Figure 2-9).

Physical and logical simulation

Visualization of planetary surfaces suggests the possibility that not only the substance of the surface may be modeled but also its dynamic characteristics. Dynamic simulations for virtual environments may be developed from ordinary high-level programming languages like Pascal or C, but this usually requires considerable time for development. Interesting alternatives for this kind of simulation have been provided by simulation and modeling languages such as SLAM II, with a graphical display interface, TESS (Pritsker, 1986). These very high languages provide tools for defining and implementing continuous or discrete dynamic models. They can facilitate construction of precise systems models (Cellier, 1991).

Another alternative made possible by graphical interfaces to computers is a simulation development environment in which the simulation is created through manipulation of icons representing its separate elements, such as integrators, delays, or filters, so as to connect them into a functioning *virtual*

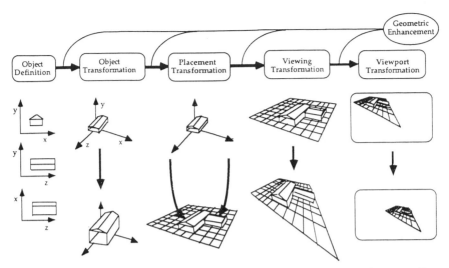

Figure 2-8 The process of representing a graphic object in virtual space allows a number of different opportunities to introduce informative geometric distortions or enhancements. These may either be a modification of the transforming matrix during the process of object definition or they may be modifications of an element of a model. These modifications may take place (1) in an object relative coordinate system used to define the object's shape, or (2) in an affine or even curvilinear object shape transformation, or (3) during the placement transformation that positions the transformed object in world coordinates, or (4) in the viewing transformation or (5) in the final viewport transformation. The perceptual consequences of informative distortions are different depending on where they are introduced. For example, object transformations will not impair perceived positional stability of objects displayed in a head-mounted format, whereas changes of the viewing transformation such as magnification will.

machine. A microcomputer program called Pinball Construction Set published in 1982 by Bill Budge is a widely distributed early example of this kind of simulation system. It allowed the user to create custom-simulated pinball machines on the computer screen simply by moving icons from a tool kit into an "active region" of the display where they would become animated. A more educational, and detailed, example of this kind of simulator was written as educational software by Warren Robinett. This program, called Rocky's Boots (Robinett, 1982), allowed users to connect icons representing logic circuit elements, that is, AND gates and OR gates, into functioning logic circuits that were animated at a slow enough rate to reveal their detailed functioning. More complete versions of this type of simulation have now been incorporated into graphical interfaces to simulation and modeling languages and are available through widely distributed systems such as the interface builder distributed with NeXt® computers.

The dynamical properties of virtual spaces and environments may also be linked to physical simulations. Prominent, noninteractive examples of this technique are James Blinn's physical animations in the video physics courses,

Figure 2-9 When high-performance computer display technology can be matched to equally high resolution helmet display technology, planetary scientists will be able to use these systems to visualize remote environments such as the surface of Mars to plan exploration and to analyze planetary surface data. (Photograph courtesy of NASA.)

The Mechanical Universe and *Beyond the Mechanical Universe* (Blinn, 1987, 1991). These physically correct animations are particularly useful in providing students with subjective insights into dynamic three-dimensional phenomena such as magnetic fields. Similar educational animated visualizations have been used for courses on visual perception (Kaiser *et al.*, 1990) and computer-aided design (Open University and BBC, 1991). Physical simulation is more instructive, however, if it is interactive and interactive virtual spaces have been constructed which allow users to interact with nontrivial physical simulations by manipulating synthetic objects whose behavior is governed by realistic dynamics (Witkin *et al.*, 1987, 1990) (Figures 2-10 and 2-11). Particularly interesting are interactive simulations of anthropomorphic figures, moving according to realistic limb kinematics and following higher level behavioral laws (Zeltzer and Johnson, 1991).

Some unusual natural environments are difficult to work in because their inherent dynamics are unfamiliar and may be nonlinear. The immediate environment around an orbiting spacecraft is an example. When expressed in a spacecraft-relative frame of reference known as local-vertical–local-horizontal, the consequences of maneuvering thrusts become markedly counter-intuitive and nonlinear (NASA, 1985). Consequently, a visualization tool designed to allow manual planning of maneuvers in this environment has taken account of these difficulties (Grunwald and Ellis, 1988, 1991, 1993; Ellis and Grunwald, 1989). This display system most directly assists planning by providing visual feedback of the consequences of the proposed plans. Its significant features enabling interactive optimization of orbital maneuvers include an "inverse dynamics" algorithm that removes control nonlinearities. Through a "geometric spread-sheet," the display creates a synthetic environment that provides the

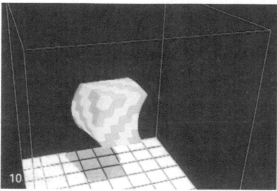

Figure 2-10 Nonrigid cube is dynamically simulated to deform when a force is applied. Though computationally expensive, this kind of dynamic simulation will markedly increase the apparent realism of virtual environments. (Photograph Courtesy of Andrew Witkin.)

user control of thruster burns which allows *independent* solutions to otherwise coupled problems of orbital maneuvering (Figures 2-12 and 2-13). Although this display is designed for a particular space application, it illustrates a technique that can be applied generally to interactive optimization of constrained nonlinear functions.

Scientific and medical visualization

Visualizing physical phenomena may be accomplished not only by constructing simulations of the phenomena but also by animating graphs and plots of the physical parameters themselves (Blinn, 1987, 1991). For example, multiple time functions of force and torque at the joints of a manipulator or limb while it is being used for a test movement may be displayed (see, for example, Pedotti *et al.* (1978)).

One application for which a virtual space display has already been demonstrated in a commercial product is in the visualization of volumetric

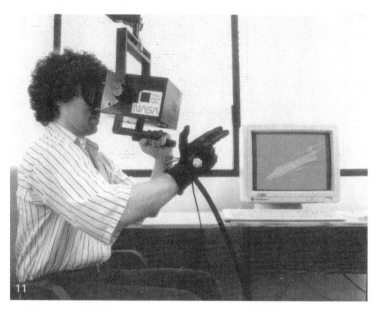

Figure 2-11 Virtual environment technology may assist visualization of the results of aerodynamic simulations. Here a DataGlove is used to control the position of a "virtual" source of smoke in a wind-tunnel simulation so the operator can visualize the local pattern of air flow. In this application the operator uses a viewing device incorporating TV monitors (McDowall, *et al.*, 1990) to present a stereo view of the smoke trail around the test model also shown in the desk-top display on the table (Levit and Bryson, 1991). (Photograph courtesy of NASA.)

medical data (Meagher, 1984). These images are typically constructed from a series of two-dimensional slices of CAT, PET, or MRI images in order to allow doctors to visualize normal or abnormal anatomical structures in three dimensions. Because the different tissue types may be identified digitally, the doctors may perform an "electronic dissection" and selectively remove particular tissues. In this way truly remarkable skeletal images may be created which currently aid orthopedic and cranio-facial surgeons to plan operations (Figures 2-14 and 2-15). These volumetric data bases are also useful for shaping custom-machined prosthetic bone implants and for directing precision robotic boring devices for precise fit between implants and surrounding bone (Taylor *et al.*, 1990). Though these static data bases have not yet been presented to doctors as full virtual environments, existing technology is adequate to develop improved virtual space techniques for interacting with them and may be able to enhance the usability of the existing displays for teleoperated surgery (Green *et al.*, 1992). Related scene-generation technology can already render detailed images of this sort based on architectural drawings and can allow prospective clients to visualize walk-throughs of buildings or furnished rooms that have not yet been constructed (Greenberg, 1991; Airey *et al.*, 1990; Nomura *et al.*, 1992).

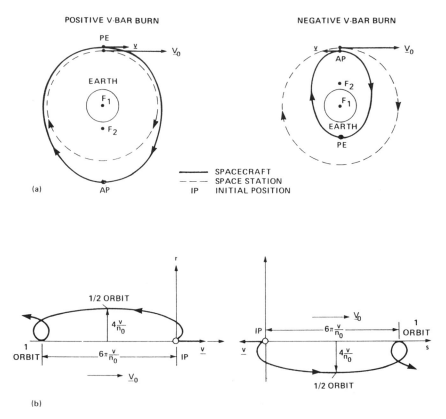

Figure 2-12 Unusual environments sometimes have unusual dynamics. The orbital motion of a satellite in a low earth orbit (upper panels) changes when thrust **v** is made either in the direction of orbital motion, **V**₀ (left) or opposed to orbital motion (right) and indicated by the change of the original orbit (dashed lines) to the new orbit (solid line). When the new trajectory is viewed in a frame of reference relative to the initial thrust point on the original orbit (Earth is down, orbital velocity is to the right, see lower panels), the consequences of the burn appear unusual. Forward thrusts (left) cause nonuniform, backward, trochoidal movement. Backward thrusts (right) cause the reverse.

Teleoperation and telerobotics and manipulative simulation

The second major technical influence on the development of virtual environment technology is research on teleoperation and telerobotic simulation (Goertz, 1964; Vertut and Coiffet, 1986; Sheridan, 1992). Indeed, virtual environments have existed before the name itself as telerobotic and teleoperations simulations. The display technology, however, in these cases was usually panel-mounted rather than head-mounted. Two notable exceptions were the head-controlled/head-referenced display developed for control of remote viewing systems by Raymond Goertz at Argonne National Laboratory (Goertz *et al.*, 1965) and a head-mounted system developed by Charles Comeau and

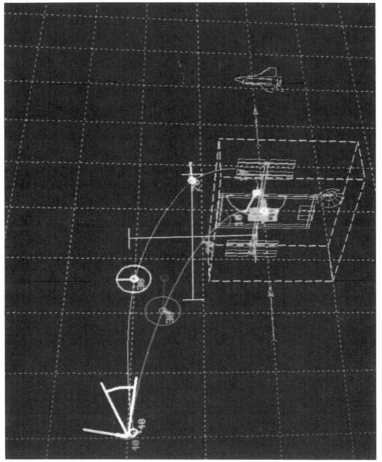

Figure 2-13 Proximity operations planning display presents a virtual space that enables operators to plan orbital maneuvers despite counter-intuitive, nonlinear dynamics and operational constraints, such as plume impingement restrictions. The operator may use the display to visualize his proposed trajectories. Violations of the constraints appear as graphics objects, i.e. circles and arcs, which inform him of the nature and extent of each violation. This display provides a working example of how informed design of a planning environment's symbols, geometry, and dynamics can extend human planning capacity into new realms. (Photograph courtesy of NASA.)

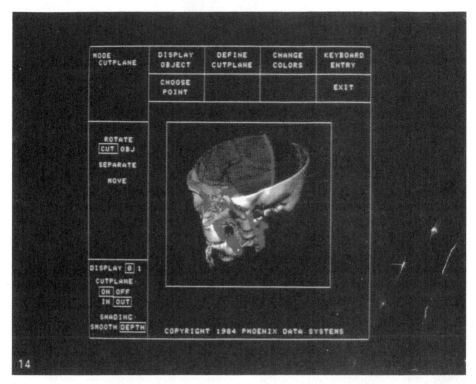

Figure 2-14 Successive CAT scan x-ray images may be digitized and used to synthesize a volumetric data set which then may be electronically processed to identify specific tissue. Here bone is isolated from the rest of the data set and presents a striking image that even nonradiologists may be tempted to interpret. Forthcoming hardware will give physicians access to this type of volumetric imagery for the cost of an expensive car. (Photograph courtesy of Octree Corporation, Cupertino, CA.)

James Bryan of Philco (Figure 2-4) (Comeau and Bryan, 1961). The development of these systems anticipated many of the applications and design issues that confront the engineering of effective virtual environment systems. Their discussions of the field-of-view/image resolution trade-off is strikingly contemporary. A key difficulty, then and now, was lack of a convenient and cheap head tracker. The current popular, electromagnetic, six-degrees-of-freedom position tracker developed by Polhemus Navigation (Raab *et al.*, 1979; see also, Ascension Technology Corp., 1990; Polhemus Navigation Systems, 1990; Barnes, 1992), consequently, was an important technological advance but interestingly was anticipated by similar work at Philco limited to electromagnetic sensing of orientation. In other techniques for tracking the head position, accelerometers optical tracking hardware (CAE Electronics, 1991; Wang *et al.*, 1990), or acoustic systems (Barnes, 1992) may be used. These more modern sensors are much more convenient than those used by the pioneering work of Goertz and Sutherland, who used mechanical position sensors, but the

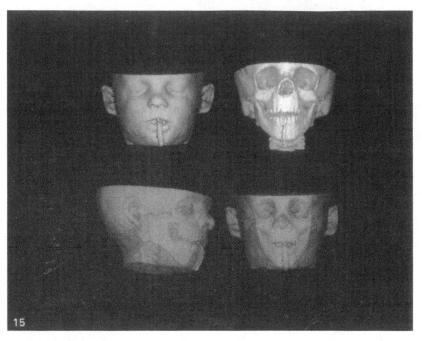

Figure 2-15 Different tissues in volumetric data sets from CAT scan X-ray slices may be given arbitrary visual properties by digital processing in order to aid visualization. Here tissue surrounding the bone is made partially transparent so as to make the skin surface as well as the underlying bone of the skull clearly visible. This processing is an example of enhancement of the content of a synthetic environment. (Photograph courtesy of Octree Corporation, Cupertino, CA.)

important, dynamic characteristics of these sensors have only recently begun to be fully described (Adelstein *et al.*, 1992).

A second key component of a teleoperation work station, or of a virtual environment, is a sensor for coupling hand position to the position of the end-effector at a remote work site. The earlier mechanical linkages used for this coupling have been replaced by joysticks or by more complex sensors that can determine hand shape, as well as position. Modern joysticks are capable of measuring simultaneously all three rotational and three translational components of motion. Some of the joysticks are isotonic (BASYS, 1990; CAE Electronics, 1991; McKinnon and Kruk, 1991) and allow significant travel or rotation along the sensed axes, whereas others are isometric and sense the applied forces and torques without displacement (Spatial Systems, 1990). Though the isometric sticks with no moving parts benefit from simpler construction, the user's kinematic coupling in his hand makes it difficult for him to use them to apply signals in one axis without cross-coupled signals in other axes. Consequently, these joysticks use switches for shutting down unwanted axes during use. Careful design of the breakout forces and detentes for the different axes on the isotonic sticks allow a user to minimize cross-coupling in control signals while separately controlling the different axes (CAE Electronics, 1991; McKinnon and Kruk, 1991).

Figure 2-16 Researcher at the University of North Carolina uses a multidegree-of-freedom manipulator to maneuver a computer graphics model of a drug molecule to find binding sites on a larger molecule. A dynamic simulation of the binding forces is computed in real time so the user can feel these forces through the force-reflecting manipulator and use this feel to identify the position and orientation of a binding site. (Photograph courtesy of University of North Carolina, Department of Computer Science.)

Although the mechanical bandwidth might have been only of the order of 2–5 Hz, the early mechanical linkages used for telemanipulation provided force-feedback conveniently and passively. In modern electronically coupled systems force-feedback or "feel" must be actively provided, usually by electric motors. Although systems providing six degrees of freedom with force-feedback on all axes are mechanically complicated, they have been constructed and used for a variety of manipulative tasks (Bejczy and Salisbury, 1980; Hannaford, 1989; Jacobson *et al.*, 1986; Jacobus *et al.*, 1992; Jacobus, 1992). Interestingly, force-feedback appears to be helpful in the molecular docking work at the University of North Carolina (Figure 2-16) in which chemists

Figure 2-17 A high-fidelity, force-reflecting two-axis joystick designed to study human tremor. (Photograph courtesy of B. Dov Adelstein.)

manipulate molecular models of drugs in a computer graphics physical simulation in order to find optimal orientations for binding sites on other molecules (Ouh-young *et al.*, 1989).

High-fidelity force-feedback requires electromechanical bandwidths over 30 Hz (see Figure 2-17 for an example of a high bandwidth system.) Most manipulators do not have this high a mechanical response. A force-reflecting joystick with these characteristics, however, has been designed and built (Figure 2-17) (Adelstein and Rosen, 1991, 1992). Because of the required dynamic characteristics for high fidelity, it is not compact and is carefully designed to protect its operators from the strong, high-frequency forces it is capable of producing (see Fisher *et al.* (1990) for some descriptions of typical manual interface specifications; also Brooks and Bejczy (1986) for a review of control sticks).

Manipulative interfaces may provide varying degrees of manual dexterity. Relatively crude interfaces for rate-controlled manipulators may allow experienced operators to accomplish fine manipulation tasks. Access to this level of proficiency, however, can be aided by use of position control, by more intuitive control of the interface, and by more anthropomorphic linkages on the manipulator (Figure 2-18).

An early example of a dextrous, anthropomorphic robotic end-effector is the hand by Tomovic and Boni (Tomovic and Boni, 1962). A more recent example is the Utah/MIT hand (Jacobson *et al.*, 1984). Such hand-like end-effectors with large numbers of degrees of freedom may be manually controlled directly by hand-shape sensors; for example, the Exos, exoskeletal hand (Exos, 1990) (Figure 2-19).

Significantly, the users of the Exos hand often turn off a number of the joints raising the possibility that there may be a limit to the number of degrees of freedom usefully incorporated into a dextrous master controller (Marcus, 1991). Less bulky hand-shape measurement devices have also been developed using fiber optic or other sensors (Zimmerman *et al.*, 1987; W Industries, 1991) (Figures 2-20, 2-22); however, use of these alternatives involves significant trade-offs of resolution, accuracy, force-reflection and calibration stability as compared with the more bulky sensors (Figure 2-21). A more recent hand-shape measurement device had been developed that combines high static and dynamic positional fidelity with intuitive operation and convenient donning and doffing (Kramer, 1992).

Photography, cinematography, video technology

Since photography, cinema, and television are formats for presenting synthetic environments, it is not surprising that technology associated with special effects for these media has been applied to virtual environments. The LEEP optics, which are commonly used in many "virtual reality" stereo-viewers, were originally developed for a stereoscopic camera system using matched camera and viewing optics to cancel the aberrations of the wide-angle lens. The LEEP system field of view is approximately $110° \times 55°$, but it depends on how the measurement is taken (Howlett, 1991). Though this viewer does not allow adjustment for interpupilary distance, its large entrance pupil (30 mm radius) removes the need for such adjustment. The stereoscopic image pairs used with these optics, however, are presented 62 mm apart, closer together than the average interpupilary distance. This choice is a useful design feature which reduces some of the likelihood that average users need to diverge their eyes to achieve binocular fusion (Figure 2-23).

An early development of a more complete environmental illusion through cinematic virtual space was Morton Heilig's "Sensorama." It provided a stereo, wide field-of-view, egocentric display with coordinated binaural sound, wind, and odor effects (Heilig, 1955). A more recent, interactive virtual space display was implemented by the MIT Architecture Machine Group in the form of a video-disk-based, interactive, map of Aspen, Colorado (Lippman, 1980). The interactive map provided a video display of what the user would have seen were he actually there moving through the town. Similar interactive uses of video-disk technology have been explored at the MIT Media Lab (Brand, 1987). One feature that probably distinguishes the multimedia work mentioned

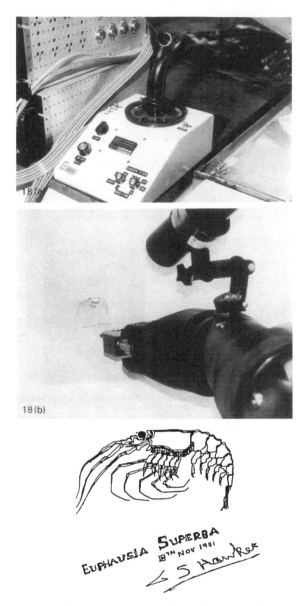

Figure 2-18 Experienced operators of industrial manipulator arms (center) can develop great dexterity (see drawing on bottom) even with ordinary two-degree-of-freedom, joystick interfaces (top) for the control of robot arms with adequate mechanical bandwidth. Switches on the control box shift control to the various joints on the arm. (Photographs courtesy of Deep Ocean Engineering, San Leandro, CA.)

Figure 2-19 An exoskeletal hand-shape measurement system in a dextrous hand master using accurate Hall effect flexion sensors, which is suitable to drive a dextrous end-effector. (Photograph courtesy of Exos, Inc, Burlington, MA.)

here from the more scientific and engineering studies reported previously, is that the media artists, as users of the enabling technologies, have more interest in synthesizing highly integrated environments including sight, sound, touch, and smell. A significant part of their goal is the integrated experience of a "synthetic place." On the other hand, the simulator designer is only interested in capturing the total experience insofar as this experience helps specific training and testing.

Role of engineering models

Since the integration of the equipment necessary to synthesize a virtual environment represents such a technical challenge in itself, there is a tendency for groups working in this area to focus their attention only on collecting and integrating the individual technologies for conceptual demonstrations in highly controlled settings. The video-taped character of many of these demonstrations often suggests system performance far beyond actually available technology. The visual resolution of the cheaper, wide-field displays using LCD technology

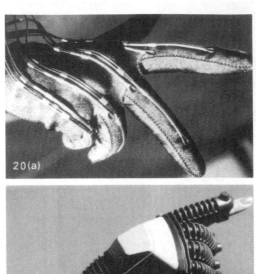

Figure 2-20 Less bulky hand-shape measuring instruments using flexible sensors (upper panel: courtesy of VPL, Redwood City, CA.; lower panel: courtesy of WA. Industries, Leicester, UK.)

Figure 2-21 A six-degree-of-freedom force reflecting joystick (Bejczy and Salisbury, 1980). (Photograph courtesy of JPL, Pasadena, CA.)

Figure 2-22 Fiber-optic flexion sensors used by VPL in the DataGlove have been incorporated into a body-hugging suit. Measurements of body shape can be used to dynamically control a computer-graphics image of the body which may be seen through the head-mounted viewing device. (Lasko-Harvill *et al.*, 1988). (Photograph courtesy of VPL, Redwood City, CA.)

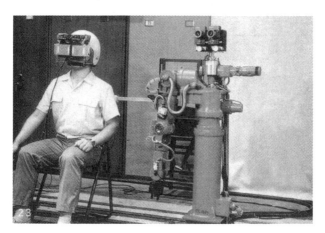

Figure 2-23 Head and hand position sensors allow the user to control the head and arm position of a teleoperations robot which provides a stereo video signal that may be seen in the viewing helmet (Tachi *et al.*, 1984, 1989). (Photograph courtesy of Susumu Tachi.)

has often been, for example, implicitly exaggerated by presentation techniques using overlays of users wearing displays and images taken directly from large format graphics monitors. In fact, the users of many of these displays are for practical purposes legally blind.

Accomplishment of specific tasks in real environments, however, places distinct real performance requirements on the simulation of which visual resolution is just an example. These requirements may be determined empirically for each task, but a more general approach is to use human performance models to help specify them. There are good general collections that can provide this background design data (e.g. Borah *et al.*, 1978; Boff *et al.*, 1986; Elkind *et al.*, 1989) and there are specific examples of how scientific and engineering knowledge and computer-graphics-based visualization can be used to help designers conform to human performance constraints (Monheit and Badler, 1990; Phillips *et al.*, 1990; Larimer *et al.*, 1991). Useful sources on human sensory and motor capacities relevant to virtual environments are also available (Howard, 1982; Blauert, 1983; Brooks and Bejczy, 1986; Goodale, 1990; Durlach *et al.*, 1991; Ellis *et al.*, 1991) (Figure 2-24).

Because widely available current technology limits the graphics and simulation update rate in virtual environments to less than 20 Hz, understanding the control characteristics of human movement, visual tracking, and vestibular responses is important for determining the practical limits to useful work in these environments. Theories of grasp, manual tracking (Jex *et al.*, 1966), spatial hearing (Blauert, 1983; Wenzel, 1991), vestibular response, and visual–vestibular correlation (Oman *et al.*, 1986; Oman, 1991) all can help to determine performance guidelines.

Predictive knowledge of system performance is not only useful for matching interfaces to human capabilities, but it is also useful in developing effective displays for situations in which human operators must cope with significant time lags, for example those >250 ms, or other control difficulties. In these circumstances, accurate dynamic or kinematic models of the controlled element allow the designer to give the user control over a predictor which he may move to a desired location and which will be followed by the actual element (Hashimoto *et al.*, 1986; Bejczy *et al.*, 1990) (Figure 2-25).

Another source of guidelines is the performance and design of existing high-fidelity systems themselves (Figures 2-26 and 2-27). Of the virtual environment display systems, probably the one with the best visual display is the CAE Fiber Optic Helmet Mounted Display, FOHMD (Lypaczewski *et al.*, 1986; Barrette *et al.*, 1990) which is used in military simulators. It presents two 83.5° monocular fields of view with adjustable binocular overlap, typically in early versions of about 38°, giving a full horizontal field of view up to 162°. Similarly, the Wright-Patterson Air Force Base Visually Coupled Airborne Systems Simulator, or VCASS display, also presents a very wide field of view, and has been used to study the consequences of field-of-view restriction on several visual tasks (Wells and Venturino, 1990). Their results support other reports that indicate that visual performance is influenced by increased field of view, but that this influence wanes as fields of view greater than 60° are used (Hatada *et al.*, 1980).

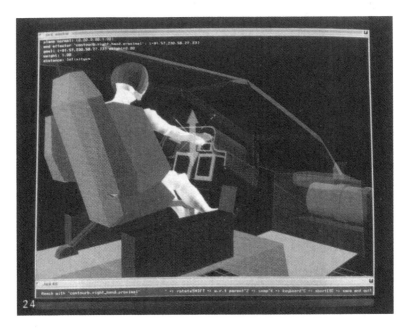

Figure 2-24 "Jack" screen (Phillips *et al.*, 1990; Larimer *et al.*, 1991) example of a graphics display system that is being developed to assist cockpit designers to determine whether potential cockpit configurations would be consistent with human performance limitations such as reach envelopes or visual field characteristics. (Photograph courtesy of NASA.)

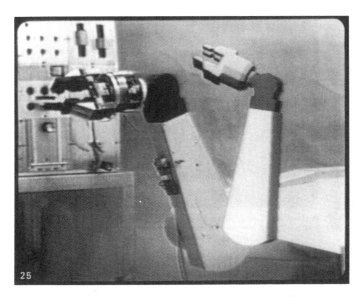

Figure 2-25 Graphic model of a manipulator arm electronically superimposed on a video signal from a remote work-site to assist users who must contend with time delay in their control actions. (Photograph courtesy of JPL, Pasadena, CA.)

Figure 2-26   Visually Coupled Airborne Systems Simulator of the Armstrong Aerospace Medical Research Laboratory of Wright-Patterson Air Force Base can present a wide field-of-view stereo display (120° × 60°) which is updated at up to 20 Hz. Head position is measured electromagnetically and may be recorded at a slower rate Visual pixel resolution 3.75 arcmin/pixel. (Photograph courtesy of AAMRL, WPAFB.)

A significant feature of the FOHMD is that the 60-Hz sampling of head position had to be augmented by signals from helmet-mounted accelerometers to perceptually stabilize the graphics imagery during head movement. Without the accelerometer signals, perceptual stability of the enveloping environment requires head-position sampling over 100 Hz, as illustrated by well-calibrated teleoperations viewing systems developed in Japan (Tachi *et al.*, 1984, 1989). In general, it is difficult to calibrate the head-mounted, virtual image displays used in these integrated systems. One solution is to use a see-through system, as illustrated by Hirose, and to compare the positions of real objects and superimposed computer-generated objects (Hirose *et al.*, 1990, 1992; Ellis and Bucher, 1994).

Technical descriptions with performance data for fully integrated systems have not been generally available or particularly detailed and accurate (Fisher *et al.*, 1986; Stone, 1991a, 1991b), but this situation should change as reports are published in the journal *Computer Systems in Engineering* and in two other new journals: *Presence: the Journal of Teleoperations and Virtual Environments* (Cambridge, MA: MIT Press) and *Pixel, the Magazine of Scientific Visualization*, (Watsonville, CA: Pixel Communications). A new book has collected much of the manufactures' material ostensibly describing performance of the component technology (Kalawsky, 1993), but due to the absence of standards

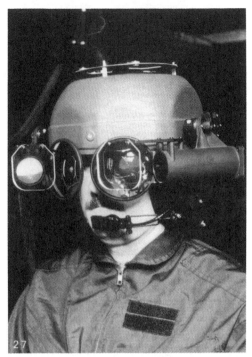

Figure 2-27 Though very expensive, the CAE Fiber Optic Helmet Mounted display, FOHUD, is probably the best, head-mounted, virtual environment system. It can present an overall visual field 162° × 83.5° with 5-arcmin resolution with a high-resolution inset of 24° × 18° of 1.5 arcmin resolution. It has a bright display, 30 Foot-Lambert, and a fast, optical head-tracker, 60-Hz sampling, with accelerometer augmentation. (Photograph courtesy of CAE Electronics, Montreal, Canada.)

and the novelty of the equipment, developers are likely to find these descriptions still incomplete.

VIRTUAL ENVIRONMENTS: PERFORMANCE AND TRADE-OFFS

Performance advances

With the state of off-the-shelf technology, it is unlikely that a fully implemented virtual environment display will today uniquely enable useful work at a price accessible to the average researcher. Those systems that have solved some of the major technological problems, that is, adequate head-tracking bandwidth, and viewing resolution comparable to existing CRT technology, do so through special-purpose hardware that is very expensive. The inherent cost of some enabling technologies, however, is not high and development continues, promising improved performance and flexibility (e.g. optical head tracking (Wang, *et al.*, 1990) and high-quality detailed volumetric display hardware for medium-cost workstations stations (OCTREE Corporation,

1991)). Medium-cost complete systems costing on the order of $200,000 have currently proved commercially useful for visualizing and selling architectural products such as custom kitchens (Nomura *et al.*, 1992). However, no matter how sophisticated or cheap the display technology becomes, there will always be some costs associated with its use. With respect to practical applications, the key question is to identify those tasks that are so enabled by use of a virtual environment display, that users will choose this display format over alternatives.

Stereoscopic visual strain

Designers of helmet-mounted displays for military applications have known that field use of stereoscopic displays is difficult because careful alignment is required to avoid problems with visual fatigue (Edwards, 1991; Melzer, 1991). Accordingly, stereo eye strain is a likely difficulty for long-term use of stereo virtual environments. However, new devices for measuring acuity, accommodation, and eye position (Takeda *et al.*, 1986) may help improve designs. Development of a self-compensating display that adjusts to the refractive state and position of the user's eyes is one possibility. As with eye strain, the neck strain caused by the helmet's mass is likely to be relieved by technical advances such as miniaturization. But there will always be a cost associated with required use of head gear and the simple solution to this problem may be to avoid protracted use as is possible with boom-mounted displays.

Resolution/field-of-view tradeoff

Another cost associated with head-mounted displays, is that though they may generally have larger fields of view than the panel-mounted alternative, they will typically have correspondingly lower spatial resolution. Eye movement recording technology has been used to avoid this trade-off by tracking the viewer's current area of fixation so that a high-resolution graphics insert can be displayed there. This technique can relieve the graphics processor of the need to display high-resolution images in the regions of the peripheral visual field that cannot resolve it (Cowdry, 1986). Reliable and robust eye tracking technology is still, however, costly, but fortunately may be unnecessary if a high-resolution insert of approximately 30° diameter may be inserted. Since in the course of daily life most eye movements may be less than 15° (Bahill *et al.*, 1975), a head-mounted display system which controls the viewing direction of the simulation need not employ eye tracking if the performance environment does not typically require large amplitude eye movements.

Unique capabilities

In view of these and certainly other costs of virtual environment displays, what unique capabilities do they enable? Since these systems amount to a communications medium, they are intrinsically applicable to practically anything, for example education, procedure training, teleoperation, high-level programming, remote planetary surface exploration, exploratory data analysis, and scientific visualization (Brooks Jr., 1988). One unique feature of the medium, however, is that it enables multiple, simultaneous, coordinated, real-time foci of control in an environment. Tasks that involve manipulation of objects in complex visual environments and also require frequent, concurrent changes in viewing position, for example, laparoscopic surgery (SAGES, 1991) are tasks that are naturally suited for virtual environment displays. Other tasks that may be mapped into this format are also uniquely suitable.

In selecting a task for which virtual environment displays may provide useful interfaces it is important to remember that effective communication is the goal, and that consequently one need not aspire to create a fully implemented virtual environment; a virtual space or a virtual image might even be superior. For non-entertainment applications, the illusion of an alternative reality is not necessarily the goal of the interface design. The case of the Matel PowerGlove,® which is no longer manufactured, is instructive. This interface device, which was derived from the Data Glove,® was marketed for video games as an intuitive control device to replace the joysticks and fire buttons. But it proved fatiguing since it required the users to keep their hands held in the air for extended periods, and yet, since no special-purpose software was ever written to exploit its unique control capacities, provided no particular advantage to its user. It was thus marketed for a pure novelty value which soon wore off. A successful virtual environment product will have to find a real communications need to fill for it to be successful in the long term.

Future mass markets

It is difficult to foretell the future practical mass-market applications for virtual environments. Like three-dimensional movies, the technology could only be a transient infatuation of visionary technophiles, but the situation is more likely analogous to the introduction of the first personal computer, the Altair. At its introduction, the practical uses for which small computers like it have become essential, word-processing, databases and spreadsheets, seemed well beyond its reach. In fact, spreadsheet programs like VISICALC had not even been conceived! Accordingly, some of the ultimate mass-market applications of virtual environments are likely unknown today. Possibly, once the world is densely criss-crossed with high bandwidth, public access, fiber-optic "information highways," mass demand will materialize for convenient, virtual environment displays of high-resolution imagery (Gore, 1990).

ACKNOWLEDGMENT

An earlier version of this article originally appeared as "Nature and origin of virtual environments: a bibliographical essay," in (1991) *Computer Systems in Engineering*, **2**, 321–46.

NOTES

1. Some new computer interfaces such as that proposed for the Apple Newton series of intelligent information appliances may resemble handwriting-recognizing magic slates on which users write commands with a stylus. See Apple Computer Co. (1992).

2. Higher dimensional displays have also been described. See Inselberg (1985) or Feiner and Beshers (1990) for alternative approaches.

3. This analogy suggests the possibility of developing an *informational mechanics* in which some measure of motion through the state space of an information-processing device may be related to the information content of the incoming messages. In such a mechanics, the proportionality constant relating the change in motion to the message content might be considered the *informational mass* of the program.

4. This "knowledge" should not be thought of as the conscious, abstract knowledge that is acquired in school. It rather takes the form of tacit acceptance of specific constraints on the possibilities of change such as those reflected in Gestalt Laws, e.g., common fate or good continuation.

5. Focusing required of the eye to make a sharp image on the retina.

6. Convergence or divergence of the eyes to produce an apparently single image.

7. The binocular disparity to a point in space is the difference of the binocular parallax of that point measured from both eyes.

8. Reflexive changes in the convergence of the eyes triggered by changes in the required focus.

9. Reflexive changes in the focusing of the eye triggered by change in convergence.

10. Reflexive tracking eye movements triggered by movement of objects subtending large visual angles.

11. Tracking eye movements triggered by vestibular stimulation normally associated with head or body movement.

REFERENCES

Adelstein, B. D., Johnston, E. R., and Ellis, S. R. (1992) A test-bed for characterizing the response of virtual environment spatial sensors *The 5th Annual ACM Symp. on User Interface Software and Technology*, Monterey, CA, ACM, pp. 15–20

Adelstein, B. D. and Rosen, M. J. (1991) A high performance two degree of freedom kinesthetic interface. Human machine interfaces for teleoperators and virtual environments, Santa Barbara, CA: NASA (CP 91035, NASA Ames Research Center, Moffett Field, CA), pp. 108–13

Adelstein, B. D. and Rosen, M. J. (1992) *Design and Implementation of a Force Reflecting Manipulandum for Manual Control Research*, Anaheim, CA: American Society of Mechanical Engineers, pp. 1–12

AGARD (1988) *Conf. Proc. N. 433: Motion Cues in Flight Simulation and Simulator Induced Sickness (AGARD CP 433)*, Springfield, VA: NTIS

Airey, J. M., Rohlf, J. H., and Brooks Jr. (1990) Towards image realism with interactive update rates in complex virtual building environments, *Computer Graphics*, **24**, 41–50

Apple Computer Co. (1992) *Newton Technology: an Overview of a New Technology from Apple*, Apple Computer Co, 20525 Mariani Ave, Cupertino CA 95014

Ascension Technology Corp. (1990) *Product Description*, Ascension Technology Corporation, Burlington VT 05402

Bahill, A. T., Adler, D., and Stark, L. (1975). Most naturally occurring human saccades have magnitudes of 15 degrees or less, *Investigative Ophthalmology*, **14**, 468–9

Barnes, J. (1992) *Acoustic 6 dof sensor*, Logitech, 6505 Kaiser Dr., Fremont CA 94555 Logitech, 6505 Kaiser Dr., Fremont CA 94555

Barrette, R., Dunkley, R., Kruk, R., Kurtz, D., Marshall, S., Williams, T., Weissman, P., and Antos, S. (1990) *Flight Simulation Advanced Wide FOV Helmet Mounted Infinity Display (AFHRL-TR-89-36)*, Air Force Human Resources Laboratory

Bassett, B. (1992) *Virtual Reality Head-mounted Displays*, Virtual Research, 1313 Socorro Ave, Sunnyvale CA, 94089 Virtual Research, 1313 Socorro Ave, Sunnyvale CA, 94089

BASYS (1990) *Product Description*, Basys Gesellschaft für Anwender und Systemsoftware mbH, Nuremberg, Germany

Bejczy, A. K. (1980) Sensor controls and man-machine interface for teleoperation, *Science*, **208**, 1327–35

Bejczy, A. K., Kim, W. S., and Venema, S. C. (1990) The phantom robot: predictive displays for teleoperation with time delay. *Proc. of the IEEE Int. Conf. on Robotics and Automation*, 13–18 May 1990, New York: IEEE, pp. 546–51

Bejczy, A. K. and Salisbury Jr, K. S. (1980) Kinesthetic coupling between operator and remote manipulator. Advances in computer technology, *Proc. ASME Int. Computer Technology Conf.*, San Francisco, CA, pp. 197–211

Bertin, J. (1967/1983) *Semiology of Graphics: Diagrams, Networks, Maps*, Madison, WI: University of Wisconsin Press

Bishop, P. O. (1987) Binocular vision, in R. A. Moses and W. M. Hart, Jr (Eds), *Adlers Physiology of the Eye*, Washington, DC: Mosby, pp. 619–89

Blauert, J. (1983) *Spatial Hearing*, Cambridge, MA: MIT Press

Blinn, J. F. (1987) The mechanical universe: an integrated view of a large animation project (Course Notes: Course #6), *Proc. of the 14th Ann. Conf. on Computer Graphics and Interactive Techniques*, Anaheim, CA: ACM SIGGRAPH and IEEE Technical Committee on Computer Graphics

Blinn, J. F. (1991) The making of the mechanical universe, in S. R. Ellis, M. K. Kaiser, and Grunwald (Eds), *Pictorial Communication in Virtual and Real Environments*, London: Taylor and Francis, pp. 138–55

Boff, K. R., Kaufman, L., and Thomas, J. P. (1986) *Handbook of Perception and Human Performance*, New York: Wiley

Borah, J., Young, L. R., and Curry, R. E. (1978) *Sensory Mechanism Modelling* (USAF ASD Report AFHRL TR 78-83), Air Force Human Resources Laboratory

Brand, S. (1987) *The Media Lab: Inventing the Future at MIT*, New York: Viking

Brehde, D. (1991) CeBIT: Cyberspace-Vorstoss in eine andere Welt (Breakthrough into another world), *Stern*, **44**, 130–42

Brooks Jr., F. (1988) Grasping reality through illusion–interactive graphics serving science, *Proc. Chi '88*, 15–19 May 1988, Washington, DC, pp. 1–12

Brooks, T. L. and Bejczy, A. K. (1986) *Hand Controllers for Teleoperation* (NASA CR 175890, JPL Publication 85-11), JPL

Bussolari, S. R., Young, L. R., and Lee, A. T. (1988) The use of vestibular models for design and evaluation of flight simulation motion, *AGARD Conf. Proc. N. 433: Motion Cues in Flight Simulation and Simulator Induced Sickness*, Springfield, VA: NTIS (AGARD CP 433)

CAE Electronics (1991) *Product Literature*, CAE Electronics, Montreal, Canada CAE Electronics, Montreal, Canada

Cardullo, F. (1993) *Flight Simulation Update 1993*, Binghamton, New York: Watson School of Continuing Education, SUNY Binghamton

Cellier, F. (1991) *Modeling Continuous Systems*, New York: Springer-Verlag

Clark, J. H. (1980) A VLSI geometry processor for graphics, *IEEE Computer*, **12**, 7

Clark, J. H. (1982) The geometry engine: a VLSI geometry system for graphics, *Computer Graphics*, **16**(3), 127–33

Collewijn, H. and Erkelens, C. J. (1990) Binocular eye movements and the perception of depth, in E. Kowler (Ed.), *Eye Movements and their Role in Visual and Cognitive Processes*, Amsterdam: Elsevier Science Publishers, pp. 213–62

Comeau, C. P. and Bryan, J. S. (1961) Headsight television system provides remote surveillance, *Electronics*, November, 86–90

Cotter, C. H. (1966) *The Astronomical and Mathematical Foundations of Geography*, New York: Elsevier

Cowdry, D. A. (1986) *Advanced Visuals in Mission Simulators in Flight Simulation*, Springfield, VA: NTIS (AGARD), pp. 3.1–3.10

Crampton, G. H. (1990) *Motion and Space Sickness*, Boca Raton, FL: CRC Press

Cruz-Neira, C., Sandin, D. J., DeFanti, T. A., Kenyon, R. V., and Hart, J. C. (1992) The cave: audio visual experience automatic virtual environment, *Communications of the ACM*, **35**, 65–72

Curry, R. E., Hoffman, W. C., and Young, L. R. (1976) *Pilot Modeling for Manned Simulation* (AFFDL-TR-76-124), Air Force Flight Dynamics Laboratory Publication

D'Arcy, J. (1990) Re-creating reality, *MacCleans*, **103**, 36–41

Durlach, N. I., Sheridan, T. B., and Ellis, S. R. (1991) *Human Machine Interfaces for Teleoperators and Virtual Environments* (NASA CP91035), NASA Ames Research Center

Edwards, O. J. (1991) *Personal Communication*, S-TRON, Mountain View, CA 94043

Elkind, J. I., Card, S. K., Hochberg, J., and Huey, B. M. (1989) *Human Performance Models for Computer-Aided Engineering*, Washington, DC: National Academy Press

Ellis, S. R. (1990) Pictorial communication, *Leonardo*, **23**, 81–6

Ellis, S. R. (1991) Prologue, in S. R. Ellis, M. K. Kaiser, and A. J. Grunwald (Eds), *Pictorial Communication in Virtual and Real Environments*, London: Taylor and Francis, pp. 3–11

Ellis, S. R. and Bucher, U. J. (1994) Distance perception of stereoscopically presented virtual objects superimposed on physical objects by a head-mounted display. *Proc. of the 38th Annual Meeting of the Human Factors and Ergonomics Society*, Nashville, TN

Ellis, S. R. and Grunwald, A. J. (1989) *The Dynamics of Orbital Maneuvering: Design and Evaluation of a Visual Display Aid for Human Controllers*, Springfield, VA: NTIS, (AGARD FMP symposium CP 489), pp. 29-1–29-13

Ellis, S. R. and Hacisalihzade, S. S. (1990) Symbolic enhancement of perspective displays, *Proc. of the 34th Ann. Meeting of the Human Factors Society*, Santa Monica, CA, 1465–9

Ellis, S. R. and Hitchcock, R. J. (1986) Emergence of Zipf's law: spontaneous encoding optimization by users of a command language, *IEEE Trans. Systems Man Cybern.*, **SMC-16**, 423–7

Ellis, S. R., Kaiser, M. K., and Grunwald, A. J. (1991; 1993 2nd edn) *Pictorial Communication in Virtual and Real Environments*, London: Taylor and Francis

Ellis, S. R., McGreevy, M. W., and Hitchcock, R. (1987) Perspective traffic display format and airline pilot traffic avoidance, *Human Factors*, **29**, 371–82

Erkelens, C. J. and Collewijn, H. (1985a) Eye movements and stereopsis during dichoptic viewing of moving random dot stereograms, *Vision Research*, **25**, 1689–1700

Erkelens, C. J. and Collewijn, H. (1985b). Motion perception during dichoptic viewing of moving random dot stereograms, *Vision Research*, **25**, 583–8

Exos (1990) *Product literature*, Exos, 8 Blanchard Rd., Burlington, MA

Fagan, B. M. (1985) *The Adventures of Archaeology*, Washington, DC: National Geographic Society

Feiner, S. and Beshers, C. (1990) Worlds within worlds: metaphors for exploring *n*-dimensional virtual worlds, *Proc. of 3rd Ann. Symp. on User Interface Technology*, Snowbird, UT, 3–5 October 1990, ACM 429902

Feldon, S. E. and Burda, R. A. (1987) The extraocular muscles: Section 2, the oculomotor system, in R. A. Moses and W. M. Hart Jr (Eds), *Adlers physiology of the eye*, Washington, DC: Mosby, pp. 122–68

Fisher, P., Daniel, R., and Siva, K. V. (1990) Specification of input devices for teleoperation, *IEEE Int. Conf. on Robotics and Automation*, Cincinnati, OH: IEEE, pp. 540–5

Fisher, S. S., McGreevy, M., Humphries, J., and Robinett, W. (1986) Virtual environment display system, *ACM 1986 Workshop on 3D Interactive Graphics*, Chapel Hill, NC, 23–24 October 1986, ACM

Foley, J. D. (1987) Interfaces for Advanced Computing, *Sci. American*, **257**, 126–35

Foley, J. M. (1980) Binocular distance perception, *Psychological Rev.*, **87**, 411–34

Foley, J. M. (1985) Binocular distance perception: egocentric distance tasks, *J. Exp. Psychology: Human Perception Perform.*, **11**, 133–49

Furness, T. A. (1986) The supercockpit and its human factors challenges, *Proc. of the 30th Ann. Meeting of the Human Factors Society*, Dayton, OH, pp. 48–52

Furness, T. A. (1987) Designing in virtual space, in W. B. Rouse and K. R. Boff (Eds), *System Design*, Amsterdam: North-Holland

Gibson, J. J. (1950) *The Perception of the Visual World*, Boston: Houghton Mifflin

Goertz, R. C. (1964) Manipulator system development at ANL, *Proc. of the 12th RSTD Conf.* Argonne National Laboratory, pp. 117–36

Goertz, R. C., Mingesz, S., Potts, C., and Lindberg, J. (1965) An experimental head-controlled television to provide viewing for a manipulator operator, *Proc. of the 13th Remote Systems Technology Conf.*, pp. 57–60

Goodale, M. A. (1990) *Vision and Action: The Control of Grasping*, Norwood, NJ: Ablex Publishing Corporation

Gore, A. (1990) Networking the future, *Washington Post*, July 15, B3

Green, P., Satava, R., Hill, J., and Simon, I. (1992) Telepresence: advanced teleoperator technology for minimally invasive surgery, *Surgical Endoscopy*, **6**, 62–7

Greenberg, D. P. (1991) Computers and architecture, *Sci. American*, **264**, 104–9

Gregory, R. L. (1968) Perceptual illusions and brain models, *Proc. R. Soc.*, B, **171**, 278–96

Gregory, R. L. (1980) Perceptions as hypotheses, *Phil. Trans. R. Soc.*, B, **290**, 181–97

Gregory, R. L. (1981) *Mind in Science*, London: Weidenfeld and Nicolson

Gregory, R. L. and Wallace, J. G. (1974) Recovery from early blindness: a case study, in R. L. Gregory (Ed.), *Concepts and Mechanisms of Perception*, London: Methuen, pp. 65–129

Grudin, J. and Norman, D. (1991) Language evolution and human-computer interaction (submitted for publication)

Grunwald, A. J. and Ellis, S. R. (1988) *Interactive Orbital Proximity Operations Planning System* (NASA TP 2839), NASA Ames Research Center

Grunwald, A. J. and Ellis, S. R. (1991) Design and evaluation of a visual display aid for orbital maneuvering, in S. R. Ellis, M. K. Kaiser, and A. J. Grunwald (Ed.), *Pictorial Communication in Virtual and Real Environments*, London: Taylor and Francis, 207–31

Grunwald, A. J. and Ellis, S. R. (1993) A visual display aid for orbital maneuvering: experimental evaluation, *AIAA J. Guid. Control*, **16**, 145–50

Hannaford, B. (1989) A design framework for teleoperators with kinesthetic feedback, *IEEE Trans. Robot. Automation*, **5**, 426–34

Hashimoto, T., Sheridan, T. B., and Noyes, M. V. (1986) Effects of predictive information in teleoperation with time delay, *Japanese J. Ergonomics*, **22**, 2

Hatada, T., Sakata, H., and Kusaka, H. (1980) Psychophysical analysis of the sensation of reality induced by a visual wide-field display, *SMPTE J.*, **89**, 560–9

Heeger, D. J. (1989) Visual perception of three-dimensional motion, *Neural Comput.*, **2**, 127–35

Heilig, M. L. (1955) El cine del futuro (The cinema of the future), *Espacios, Apartado Postal Num 20449, Espacios S. A., Mexico* (No. 23–24, January–June)

Held, R. and Durlach, N. (1991) Telepresence, time delay and adaptation, in S. R. Ellis, M. K. Kaiser, and A. J. Grunwald (Eds), *Pictorial Communication in Virtual and Real Environments*, London: Taylor and Francis, 232–46

Held, R., Efstathiou, A., and Greene, M. (1966) Adaptation to displaced and delayed visual feedback from the hand, *J. Exp. Psychology*, **72**, 887–91

Hess, R. A. (1987) Feedback control models, in G. Salvendy (Ed.), *Handbook of Human Factors*, New York: Wiley

Hirose, M., Hirota, K., and Kijma, R. (1992) Human behavior in virtual environments, *Symp. on Electronic Imaging Science and Technology*, San José, CA: SPIE

Hirose, M., Kijima, R., Sato, Y., and Ishii, T. (1990) A study for modification of actual environment by see-through HMD, *Proc. of the Human Interface Symp.*, Tokyo, October 1990

Hitchner, L. E. (1992) Virtual planetary exploration: a very large virtual environment (course notes), *SIGGRAPH '92*, Chicago, IL: ACM, pp. 6.1–6.16

Howard, I. (1982) *Human Visual Orientation*, New York: Wiley

Howlett, E. M. (1991) *Product Literature*, Leep Systems, 241 Crescent Street, Waltham, MA

Hung, G., Semlow, J. L., and Cuiffreda, K. J. (1984) The near response: modeling, instrumentation, and clinical applications, *IEEE Trans. Biomed. Eng.* **31**, 910–19

Hussey, K. J. (1990) *Mars the Movie (video)*, Pasadena, CA: JPL Audiovisual Services

Inselberg, A. (1985) The plane with parallel coordinates, *The Visual Computer*, **1**, 69–91

Jacobson, S. C., Iversen, E. K., Knutti, D. F., Johnson, R. T., and Biggers, K. B. (1986) Design of the Utah/MIT dextrous hand, *IEEE Int. Conf. on Robotics and Automation*, San Francisco, CA: IEEE, 1520–32

Jacobson, S. C., Knutti, D. F., Biggers, K. B., Iversen, E. K., and Woods, J. E. (1984) The Utah/MIT dextrous hand: work in progress, *Int. J. Robot. Res.*, **3**, 21–50

Jacobus, H. N. (1992) *Force Reflecting Joysticks*, CYBERNET Systems Corporation Imaging and Robotics, 1919 Green Road, Suite B-101, Ann Arbor, MI 48105

Jacobus, H. N., Riggs, A. J., Jacobus, C. J., and Weinstein, Y. (1992). Implementation issues for telerobotic handcontrollers: human–robot ergonomics, in M. Rahmini, and W. Karwowski (Eds), *Human–Robot Interaction*, London: Taylor and Francis, pp. 284–314

Jenkins, C. L. and Tanimoto, S. I. (1980) Oct-trees and their use in representing three-dimensional objects, *Computer Graphics and Image Processing*, **14**, 249–70

Jex, H. R., McDonnell, J. D., and Phatak, A. V. (1966) *A Critical Tracking Task for Man–Machine Research Related to the Operator's Effective Delay Time* (NASA CR 616) NASA

Jones, G. M., Berthoz, A., and Segal, B. (1984) Adaptive modification of the vestibulo-ocular reflex by mental effort in darkness, *Brain Res.*, **56**, 149–53

Jones, R. K. and Hagen, M. A. (1980) A perspective on cross cultural picture perception, in M. A. Hagen (Ed.), *The Perception of Pictures*, New York: Academic Press, pp. 193–226

Kaiser, M. K., MacFee, E., and Proffitt, D. R. (1990) *Seeing Beyond the Obvious: Understanding Perception in Everyday and Novel Environments*, Moffett Field, CA: NASA Ames Research Center

Kalawksy, R. S. (1993) *The Science of Virtual Reality and Virtual Environments*, Reading, MA: Addison-Wesley

Kalman, R. E. (1960) Contributions to the theory of optimal control, *Bolatin de la Sociedad Matematico Mexicana*, **5**, 102–19

Kim, W. S., Takeda, M., and Stark, L. (1988) On-the-screen visual enhancements for a telerobotic vision system, *Proc. of the 1988 Int. Conf. on Systems Man and Cybernetics*, Beijing, 8–12 August 1988, pp. 126–30

Kleinman, D. L., Baron, S., and Levison, W. H. (1970) An optimal control model of human response, part I: theory and validation, part II: prediction of human performance in a complex task, *Automatica*, **6**, 357–69

Koenderink, J. J. and van Doorn, A. J. (1977) How an ambulant observer can construct a model of the environment from the geometrical structure of the visual inflow, in G. Hauske and E. Butenandt (Eds), *Kybernetik*, Munich: Oldenberg

Kramer, J. (1992) *Company Literature on Head Mounted Displays*, Virtex/Virtual Technologies, P.O. Box 5984, Stanford, CA 94309

Krueger, M. W. (1977) *Responsive Environments, NCC Proc.*, pp. 375–85

Krueger, M. W. (1983) *Artificial Reality*, Reading, MA: Addison-Wesley

Krueger, M. W. (1985) VIDEOPLACE—an artificial reality, *SIGCHI 85 Proc.*, April, 1985, ACM, pp. 35–40

Larimer, J., Prevost, M., Arditi, A., Bergen, J., Azueta, S., and Lubin, J. (1991) Human visual performance model for crew-station design, *Proc. of the 1991 SPIE*, San José, CA, February 1991, pp. 196–210

Lasko-Harvill, A., Blanchard, C., Smithers, W., Harvill, Y., and Coffman, A. (1988) From DataGlove to DataSuit, *Proc. of IEEE CompConn88*, San Francisco, CA, 29 February–4 March 1988, pp. 536–8

Laural, B. (1991) *Computers as Theatre*, Reading, MA: Addison-Wesley

Levine, M. (1984) The placement and misplacement of you-are-here maps, *Environment and Behavior*, **16**, 139–57

Levit, C. and Bryson, S. (1991) A virtual environment for the exploration of three-dimensional steady flows, *SPIE*, February, **1457**

Licklider, J. C. R., Taylor, R., and Herbert, E. (1978) The computer as a communication device, *Int. Sci. Technol.*, April, 21–31

Lippman, A. (1980) Movie maps: an application of optical video disks to computer graphics, *Computer Graphics*, **14**, 32–42

Lipton, L. (1982) *Foundations Of Stereoscopic Cinema*, New York: Van Nostrand

Lypaczewski, P. A., Jones, A. D., and Vorhees, M. J. W. (1986) Simulation of an advanced scout attack helicopter for crew station studies, *Proc. of the 8th Interservice/Industry Training Systems Conf.*, Salt Lake City, UT, pp. 18–23

Mandelbrot, B. (1982) *The Fractal Geometry of Nature*, San Francisco: Freeman

Marcus, O. B. (1991) *Personal communication*, Exos, 8 Blanchard Rd., Burlington, MA

McDowall, I. E., Bolas, M., Pieper, S., Fisher, S. S., and Humphries, J. (1990) Implementation and integration of a counterbalanced CRT-base stereoscopic display for interactive viewpoint control in virtual environment applications, *Stereoscopic Displays and Applications II*. San José, CA: SPIE

McGreevy, M. W. (1994) Virtual reality and planetary exploration, in A. Wexelblat (Ed.), *Virtual Reality Applications: Software*, New York: Academic Press, 163–97

McGreevy, M. W. and Ellis, S. R. (1986) The effect of perspective geometry on judged direction in spatial information instruments, *Human Factors*, **28**, 439–56

McKinnon, G. M. and Kruk, R. (1991) Multiaxis control of telemanipulators, in S. R. Ellis, M. K. Kaiser, and A. J. Grunwald (Ed.), *Pictorial Communication in Virtual and Real Environments*, London: Taylor and Francis, pp. 247–64

McRuer, D. T. and Weir, D. H. (1969) Theory of manual vehicular control, *Ergonomics*, **12**, 599–633

Meagher, D. (1984) A new mathematics for solids processing, *Computer Graphics World*, November, 75–88

Melzer, J. (1991) *Personal communication*, Kaiser Electronics, San José, CA 95134

Monheit, G. and Badler, N. I. (1990) *A Kinematic Model of the Human Spine and Torso* (Technical Report MS-CIS-90-77), University of Pennsylvania, Philadelphia, PA, 29 August 1990

Monmonier, M. (1991) *How to Lie with Maps*, Chicago: University of Chicago Press

Myers, T. H. and Sutherland, I. E. (1968) On the design of display processors, **11**, 410–14

NASA (1985) *Rendezvous/Proximity Operations Workbook, RNDZ 2102*, Lyndon B. Johnson Space Center, Mission Operations Directorate Training Division

NASA (1990) Computerized reality comes of age, *NASA Tech. Briefs*, **14**, 10–12

Nemire, K. and Ellis, S. R. (1991) Optic bias of perceived eye level depends on structure of the pitched optic array, *32nd Ann. Meeting of the Psychonomic Society*, San Francisco, CA, November 1991

Nomura, J., Ohata, H., Imamura, K., and Schultz, R. J. (1992) Virtual space decision support system and its application to consumer showrooms, *CG Int. '92*, Tokyo, Japan

OCTREE Corporation (1991) *Product Literature*, OCTREE Corporation, Cupertino, CA 95014

Oman, C. M. (1991) Sensory conflict in motion sickness: an observer theory approach, in S. R. Ellis, M. K. Kaiser, and A. J. Grunwald (Eds), *Pictorial Communication in Virtual and Real Environments*, London: Taylor and Francis, pp. 362–76

Oman, C. M., Lichtenberg, B. K., Money, K. E., and McCoy, R. K. (1986) MIT/Canada Vestibular Experiment on the SpaceLab 1- Mission: 4 Space motion sickness: systems, stimuli, and predictability, *Exp. Brain Res.*, **64**, 316–34

Open University and BBC (1991) *Components of Reality Video #5. 2 for Course T363: Computer Aided Design*, Walton Hall, Milton Keynes, MK7 6AA, UK

Ouh-young, M., Beard, D., and Brooks Jr, F. (1989). Force display performs better than visual display in a simple 6D docking task, *Proc. IEEE Robotics and Automation Conf.*, May 1989, 1462–6

Pedotti, A., Krishnan, V. V., and Stark, L. (1978) Optimization of muscle force sequencing in human locomotion, *Math. Biosci.*, **38**, 57–76

Phillips, C., Zhao, J., and Badler, N. I. (1990) Interactive real-time articulated figure manipulation using multiple kinematic constraints, *Computer Graphics*, **24**, 245–50

Polhemus Navigation Systems (1990) *Product Description*, Polhemus Navigation Systems, Colchester, VT, 05446

Pollack, A. (1989) What is artificial reality? Wear a computer and see, *New York Times*, 10 April 1989, A1L

Poulton, E. C. (1974) *Tracking Skill and Manual Control*, New York: Academic Press

Pritsker, A. A. B. (1986) *Introduction to Simulation and SLAM II (3rd edn)*, New York: Wiley

Raab, F. H., Blood, E. B., Steiner, T. O., and Jones, H. R. (1979) Magnetic position and orientation tracking system, *IEEE Trans. Aerospace Electronic Syst.*, **AES-15**, 709–18

Regan, D. and Beverley, K. I. (1979) Visually guided locomotion: psychophysical evidence for a neural mechanism sensitive to flow patterns, *Science*, **205**, 311–13

Robinett, W. (1982) *Rocky's Boots*, Fremont, CA: The Learning Company

Robinson, A. H., Sale, R. D., Morrison, J. L., and Muehrcke, P. C. (1984) *Elements of Cartography (5th edn)*, New York: Wiley

Rolfe, J. M., and Staples, K. J. (1986) *Flight Simulation*, London: Cambridge University Press

SAGES (1991) Panel on Future Trends in Clinical Surgery, *American Surgeon*, March

Schuffel, H. (1987) Simulation: an interface between theory and practice elucidated with a ship's controllability study, in R. Bernotat, K.-P. Gärtner, and H. Widdel (Eds), *Spektrum der Anthropotechnik*, Wachtberg-Werthoven, Germany: Forschungsinstitut für Anthropotechnik, 117–28

Senden, M. V. (1932) *Raum und Gestaltauffassung bei operierten Blindgeborenen vor und nach Operation*, Leibzig: Barth

Sheridan, T. B. (1992) *Telerobotics, Automation and Human Supervisory Control*, Cambridge, MA: MIT Press

Silicon Graphics (1991) *Product Literature*, Silicon Graphics Inc., Mountain View, CA

Smith, D. C., Irby, C., Kimball, R., and Harslem, E. (1982) The star user interface: an overview, *Office Systems Technology*, El Segundo, CA: Xerox Corporation, pp. 1–14

Spatial Systems (1990) *Spaceball Product Description*, Spatial Systems Inc., Concord, MA 01742

Stewart, D. (1991) Through the looking glass into an artificial world-via computer, *Smithsonian Mag.*, January, 36–45

Stone, R. J. (1991a) Advanced human-system interfaces for telerobotics using virtual reality and telepresence technologies, *Fifth Int. Conf. on Advanced Robotics*, Pisa, Italy, IEEE, pp. 168–73

Stone, R. J. (1991b) *Personal communication*, The National Advanced Robotics Research Centre, Salford, UK

Stritzke, J. (1991) *Automobile Simulator*, Daimler-Benz AG, Abt FGF/FS, Daimlerstr. 123, 1000, Berlin 48, Germany

Sutherland, I. E. (1965) The ultimate display, *International Federation of Information Processing*, **2**, 506–8

Sutherland, I. E. (1970) Computer Displays, *Sci. American*, **222**, 56–81

Tachi, S., Hirohiko, A., and Maeda, T. (1989) Development of anthropomorphic tele-existence slave robot, *Proc. of the Int. Conf. on Advanced Mechatronics*, Tokyo, 21–24 May 1989, pp. 385–90

Tachi, S., Tanie, K., Komoriya, K., and Kaneko, M. (1984) Tele-existence (I) Design and evaluation of a visual display with sensation of presence, *Proc. of the 5th Int.*

Symp. on Theory and Practice of Robots and Manipulators, Udine, Italy, 26–29 June 1984 (CISM-IFToMM-Ro Man Sy '84), pp. 245–53

Takeda, T., Fukui, Y., and Lida, T. (1986) Three dimensional optometer, *Appl. Optics*, **27**, 2595–602

Taylor, R. H., Paul, H. A., Mittelstadt, B. D., Hanson, W., Kazanzides, P., Zuhars, J., Glassman, E., Musits, B. L., Williamson, B., and Bargar, W. L. (1990) An image-directed robotic system for hip replacement surgery, *Japanese R. S. J.*, **8**, 111–16

Tobler, W. R. (1963) Geographic area and map projections, *Geog. Rev.*, **53**, 59–78

Tobler, W. R. (1976) The geometry of mental maps, in R. G. Golledge and G. Rushton (Eds), *Spatial Choice and Spatial Behavior*, Columbus, OH: The Ohio State University Press

Tomovic, R. and Boni, G. (1962) An Adaptive Artificial Hand, *IRE Trans. Automatic Control*, **AC-7**, April, 3–10

Tufte, E. R. (1983) *The Visual Display of Quantitative Information*, Cheshire, CO: Graphics Press

Tufte, E. R. (1990) *Envisioning Information*, Cheshire, CO: Graphics Press

Veldhuyzen, W. and Stassen, H. G. (1977) The internal model concept: an application to modeling human control of large ships, *Human Factors*, **19**, 367–80

Vertut, J. and Coiffet, P. (1986) *Robot Technology: Teleoperations and Robotics: Evolution and Development Vol. 3A and Applications and Technology Vol. 3B* (English Translation), Englewood Cliffs, NJ: Prentice Hall

Wang, J.-F., Chi, V., and Fuchs, H. (1990) A real-time optical 3D tracker for head-mounted display systems, *Computer Graphics*, **24**, 205–15

Welch, R. B. (1978) *Perceptual Modification: Adapting to Altered Sensory Environments*, New York: Academic Press

Wells, M. J. and Venturino, M. (1990) Performance and head movements using a helmet-mounted display with different sized fields-of-view, *Optical Eng.*, **29**, 810–77

Wenzel, E. M. (1991) Localization in virtual acoustic displays, *Presence*, **1**, 80–107

Wenzel, E. M., Wightman, F. L., and Foster, S. H. (1988) A virtual display system for conveying three-dimensional acoustic information, *Proc. of the 32nd Meeting of the Human Factors Society*, Anaheim, CA, 22–24 October 1988, pp. 86–90

White, K. D., Post, R. B., and Leibowitz, H. W. (1980) Saccadic eye movements and body sway, *Science*, **208**, 621–3

Wickens, C. D. (1986) The effects of control dynamics on performance, in K. R. Boff, L. Kaufman, and J. P. Thomas (Eds), *Handbook of Perception and Human Performance*, New York: Wiley

Wightman, F. L. and Kistler, D. J. (1989a) Headphone simulation of free-field listening I: stimulus synthesis, *J. Acoustical Soc. America*, **85**, 858–67

Wightman, F. L. and Kistler, D. J. (1989b) Headphone simulation of free-field listening II: psycho-physical validation, *J. Acoustical Soc. America*, **85**, 868–78

W Industries (1991) *Product Literature*, ITEC House, 26–28 Chancery St., Leicester LE1 5WD, UK

Witkin, A., Fleisher, K., and Barr, A. (1987) Energy constraints on parameterised models, *Computer Graphics*, **21**, 225–32

Witkin, A., Gleicher, M., and Welch, W. (1990) Interactive dynamics, *Computer Graphics*, **24**, 11–22

Zangemeister, W. H. (1991) Voluntary presetting of the vestibular ocular reflex permits gaze stabilization despite perturbation of fast head movement, in S. R. Ellis, M.

K. Kaiser, and A. J. Grunwald (Eds), *Pictorial Communication in Virtual and Real Environments*, London: Taylor and Francis, pp. 404–16

Zangemeister, W. H. and Hansen, H. C. (1985) Fixation suppression of the vestibular ocular reflex and head movement correlated EEG potentials, in J. K. O'Reagan and A. Levy-Schoen (Eds), *Eye Movements: From Physiology to Cognition*, Amsterdam: Elsevier, pp. 247–56

Zeltzer, D. and Johnson, M. B. (1991) Motor planning: specifying the behavior and control of autonomous animated agents, *J. Visualization Computer Animation*, **2**, 74–80

Zimmerman, T., Lanier, J., Blanchard, C., Bryson, S., and Harvil, Y. (1987) A hand gesture interface device, *Proc. of the CHI and GI*, Toronto, Canada, 5–7 April 1987, ACM, pp. 189–92

Zipf, G. K. (1949) *Human Behavior and the Principle of Least Effort*, Cambridge, MA: Addison-Wesley

II
VIRTUAL ENVIRONMENT TECHNOLOGIES

VIRTUAL ENVIRONMENT MODELING

3

Computer Graphics Modeling for Virtual Environments

MARK GREEN AND HANQIU SUN

Modeling is currently one of the most important areas in virtual environments research (Bishop *et al.*, 1992). Of all the software areas, this is the area that we know the least about. Modeling has been an active research area in computer graphics for many decades, and is still a major research area. Many of the modeling issues addressed in computer graphics and virtual environments are also of concern to researchers in robotics, mechanical engineering and biomechanics, so progress in modeling can have an impact on many fields. Modeling is difficult since most of the objects that we would like to model, such as people, animals, and airplanes, are quite complex. They have a large amount of geometrical detail and move in complex ways. This difficulty is compounded by the different fields that use modeling techniques, since each field has its own requirements and priorities. For example, it is highly unlikely that the same model of a human figure would be optimal for applications in both virtual environments and biomechanics.

The following criteria can be used as a basis for evaluating different modeling techniques.

Accuracy. The model should be an accurate representation of the real-world object. Ideally, we would like all of our models to be precise representations of the real-world objects, and not simply approximations to them. But, in reality accuracy comes with a price, usually increased display time or memory usage. The amount of accuracy required often depends upon the application. For example, in some applications it is acceptable to approximate a sphere with a large number of polygons, but for a large number of computer-aided design (CAD) applications the precise mathematical representation of the sphere is required. Since the polygonal representation can be drawn faster, it is often used in applications where display speed is more important than accuracy.

Display speed. Many applications place restrictions on the time available to display individual objects. In the case of interactive applications, short display times increase the level of interaction between the user and the model. In large

CAD applications there may be many objects, therefore, the time required to display individual objects becomes an important consideration in the usability of the application even if a high level of interactivity is not required.

Manipulation efficiency. While display is the most frequent operation performed on a model, there are several other common operations that must also be performed efficiently. If the model represents an object that moves, such as a human figure, it must be possible to modify the model in real-time to reflect its motion. In the case of the human model, in order to get the figure to walk, it must be possible to modify the joint angles efficiently at both the knees and hips. In an environment with several moving objects it must be possible to detect collisions between objects. Collision detection is an operation that is performed frequently, so it must be efficient.

Ease of use. Creating good models is a complex task. The modeler must produce an accurate representation of both the object's geometry and behavior. This task should not be complicated by the modeling technique, it should make it as easy as possible to develop good models. We would like to have modeling techniques that make it possible to quickly specify the geometry of complex objects, but at the same time be able to control every detail of its geometry. Controlling detail often requires access to the individual points that define the geometry, but for any nontrivial object, working at this level is very time consuming and tedious. There is a need for modeling techniques that allow the user to control the level of detail that they work at and provide an efficient way of defining geometry.

Breadth. The breadth of a modeling technique is the range of objects that it can represent. A good modeling technique allows us to efficiently produce accurate models of many different kinds of object. It is much easier to produce modeling software if only a few modeling techniques need to be supported, which is only possible if these modeling techniques are quite broad.

In addition to these general criteria, virtual environment applications have the additional criterion of real-time display. That is, it must be possible to display the model at a fixed frame rate that is dictated by the application. This can be done by having fast enough display algorithms or simplifying the model so it can be displayed within the allocated time.

In general there has not been a good transfer of modeling knowledge from the computer graphics field to virtual environments. Virtual environment researchers who started in computer graphics are well aware of the available modeling techniques, and this chapter will have very little of interest to them. However, a large number of virtual environment researchers and developers have limited knowledge of computer graphics and the modeling techniques that have been developed there. This chapter addresses this audience and attempts to outline the basic issues behind modeling. The modeling literature is quite extensive, and for someone unfamiliar with the area it can be quite difficult to find relevant information. A large number of modeling techniques are not applicable to virtual environments for a variety of reasons. The most common reason is that they produce models that cannot be displayed in real-time. Other reasons include concentration on aspects of the model that are not of much interest to virtual environments, or poor support for motion and other manipulations that are required in virtual environment applications. This chapter should provide the basic background required to find the relevant modeling literature for particular virtual environment applications.

This chapter reviews the computer graphics modeling techniques that are useful in the construction of virtual environments. The emphasis in this review is on the techniques that are directly applicable to the design of virtual worlds, little emphasis is placed on techniques that cannot be used interactively. Modeling techniques can be divided into two groups, geometrical and behavioral. *Geometrical modeling* deals with representing the geometry or shape of objects. Essentially it is the study of graphical data structures. *Behavior modeling* deals with how the motion or behavior of these objects can be described. In computer graphics these are often viewed as two different topics, though some researchers have investigated modeling techniques that incorporate both geometry and behavior. In computer graphics geometrical modeling is usually called modeling and behavioral modeling is usually called animation. This is because a considerable amount of modeling is done without concern for the motion of the object (for example, computer-aided design). In virtual environments both of these areas are combined and called modeling, since it makes very little sense to have objects in a virtual environment that have no means of behaving or reacting to the user.

This chapter is divided into three main sections. The next section reviews the main geometrical modeling techniques that are used in the development of virtual environments. The second section reviews behavioral modeling techniques and their use in virtual environments. The last section describes a simple virtual environment that we have constructed. This example illustrates the application of different geometrical and behavioral modeling techniques.

GEOMETRICAL MODELING

Geometrical modeling deals with the representation and processing of geometrical or shape information. It covers the data structures that are used to represent geometrical information and the algorithms that are used to construct and manipulate these data structures. The following three criteria can be used to evaluate a modeling technique for use in virtual environments:

1. Interactive display
2. Interactive manipulation
3. Ease of construction.

The model is used to generate the images that are seen by the user. These images must be updated at least ten times per second, therefore, it must be possible to display the model quickly or easily convert it into a representation that can be quickly displayed. This is by far the most important criterion. Behavioral modeling quite often changes the geometry of an object, therefore it must be possible to modify the model quickly to reflect its behavior. Constructing good models is currently a very time-consuming task. Modeling techniques that make it possible to construct models quickly, or build tools for their construction are obviously desirable.

Basic principles

A modeling technique can be divided into two main parts, which are called *primitives* and *structure*. The primitives are the atomic units that are used to build the geometrical description of the object. They are the basic building-blocks that are used in the production of object geometry. The choice of primitives determines the range of objects that can be constructed with the modeling system. The structure part of the modeling technique determines how the primitives are combined to produce new objects. This subsection covers the basic ideas behind the most popular modeling structure, hierarchical modeling, and the remaining subsections cover some to the more popular modeling primitives. More details on the modeling techniques discussed in this section can be found in standard computer graphics and geometrical modeling textbooks (Foley *et al.*, 1990; Mantyla, 1988).

There are two key concepts that have been developed in computer graphics for structuring geometrical models, which are hierarchical modeling and masters and instances. Both of these concepts are reviewed in this subsection. *Hierarchical modeling* is based on the use of a tree structure to represent the parts of an object. To illustrate this point consider a simple model of a human body. We can view the body as a tree structure of limbs. The root of this structure can be placed between the neck and the upper back. From this root, there are subtrees for the neck and upper back. The neck branch leads to the head, and the upper back branch leads to the left upper arm, right upper arm, and lower back. Similarly the left upper arm is the root of a subtree that also contains the left lower arm and the palm and fingers of the left hand. This tree structure is shown in Figure 3-1. The tree structure provides a convenient and natural way of dividing complex objects into their subparts.

Hierarchical modeling also provides us with a convenient way of modifying the model. A transformation can be attached to each node of the tree. This transformation specifies how the current node is positioned and oriented with respect to its parent. In the case of our human-body model, a transformation at the upper left arm node can be used to move the left arm. If a rotation is added to this transformation the arm can be rotated either forwards or backwards (a different rotation can be used to move the arm left or right). Since the tree is based on the structure of the object, these transformations make sense in terms of the object's properties. For example, adding a rotation to the upper left arm node not only rotates the upper left arm, but also all the nodes in its subtree, including all of the left arm.

In computer graphics 4×4 matrices are used to represent transformations.

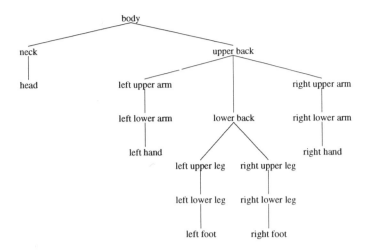

Figure 3-1 Hierarchical model of the human body.

The matrices for the standard transformations, such as translation, scale, rotate, and shear, can be found in any of the standard computer graphics textbooks (Foley *et al.*, 1990). Two transformations can be combined by multiplying their transformation matrices. An object can be both scaled and rotated by multiplying together the matrices for the scale and the rotate transformations. This is the real key to the power of hierarchical models. Each node has its own coordinate system that is defined in terms of its parent's coordinate system and the transformation matrix at that node. This coordinate system is called the local coordinate system for the node. For example, the geometry of the lower left arm can be defined in its own coordinate system, that can then be converted to its parent's coordinate system by a transformation matrix attached to its node. This means that each of the object's subparts can be developed independently and then combined by the transformation matrices at the nodes.

A hierarchical model is easy to display, the display operation is based on a depth first traversal of the tree. In order to display the model, all the primitives in the tree must be converted to the same coordinate system. This global coordinate system is called the world coordinate system. This conversion is based on a current transformation matrix called the CTM. At the root of the tree the CTM is set to the identity matrix. All the primitives at the root node are transformed by the CTM and drawn. Next, the first child of the root node is processed. This is done by first pushing the CTM on to a stack, multiplying the current CTM by the transformation matrix for the child node, giving a new CTM, then all the primitives at the child node are transformed by the new CTM and drawn. This whole process is repeated with this node's children. When we go down the tree the CTM is pushed onto the stack, and when we go back up the tree the CTM is popped off of the stack. This ensures that the second and subsequent children of a node have the correct CTM. The process of traversing and drawing a hierarchical model is quite efficient and most graphics workstations have special-purpose hardware to assist with this operation.

Another powerful technique from computer graphics modeling is *masters* and *instances*. To see how this technique works consider a simple model of a car. In this model there are four wheels that all have the same geometry. In a naive approach to modeling, the user would produce four identical copies of the wheel geometry. This is not a good approach for the following three reasons. First, there is a very good chance that the user will make mistakes while entering the geometry for the four wheels, resulting in four wheels with slightly different geometry. Second, when the user wants to change the wheel geometry (change it from a black wall to a white wall tire), all four copies of the wheel must be changed. This is both a time-consuming and error-prone task, since the user must remember where all the copies of the wheel are located. Third, it is a waste of the user's time. The user has already entered the wheel geometry once, he or she should not be forced to repeat the process three more times. The use of masters and instances solves all of these problems. First, the geometry for the object, in this case the wheel, is entered once and stored in a master. Second, each time that the object is required, an instance of the master is created. An instance is essentially a pointer to the master. Therefore, each wheel will have identical geometry, and when the master is changed all of the instances are automatically updated.

One possible concern at this point is that each wheel is located at a different position and orientation in space, and since each instance is just a pointer to its master, how can this be handled? Hierarchical modeling handles this automatically. Each instance is a separate node in the modeling hierarchy, therefore, it will have its own transformation matrix that positions and orients the instance in space. Each wheel will have a different transformation matrix that places it on the car.

Most 3D graphics packages, such as Silicon Graphics' GL and PHIGS, support both hierarchical models and masters and instances. In most of these packages the masters are called either segments or objects, and the instances are created by calling the master in essentially the same way that a procedure is called in a programming language. Thus, there is no reason why these techniques cannot be used in virtual environment construction.

Polygons

Polygons are the most common modeling primitive. A *polygon* is a region of a 3D plane, where the boundary of this region is specified by a connected list of line segments. In most graphics packages a polygon is specified by a list of vertices. These vertices are used to determine the plane that the polygon lies in, and form the end points of the line segments that define the polygon's region. The vertices must be specified in a particular order, in most cases this is the counterclockwise direction when looking down on the polygon. A typical polygon with its vertices is shown in Figure 3-2.

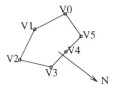

Figure 3-2 A typical polygon with its surface normal.

The internal representation of a polygon used in most modeling packages consists of two parts, the plane equation for the polygon and its vertices. The plane equation has the form:

$$Ax + By + Cz + D = 0$$

The points (x,y,z), that lie on the plane of the polygon satisfy this equation. The vector (A,B,C) is the normal vector for the polygon, and it is used in lighting calculations and to determine the front and back sides of the polygon. For an arbitrary point (x,y,z), the plane equation can be used to divide 3D space into three regions. If a point satisfies the plane equation, then it lies on the plane of the polygon (but, not necessarily in the polygon). If the value of the equation is positive, the point lies in front of the polygon, and if it is negative it lies behind the polygon. As will be shown later, this information can be used to classify the space occupied by the model.

Internally, the storage of the vertices is often separated from the storage of the polygons themselves. There is typically one table for the vertices and one for the polygons. An entry in the polygon table has a list of pointers to the entries in the vertex table for its vertices. Similarly each entry in the vertex table has a list of the polygons it belongs to. A vertex often appears in more than one polygon, so this technique saves storage space and facilitates editing the model.

Most of the display algorithms for polygons are based on the use of scan conversion and a z-buffer. The display algorithms consist of a sequence of steps or transformations, so this process is usually called a display pipeline. The first step in the display pipeline is to convert the polygons to eye coordinates. The eye coordinate system is centered on the viewer's eyes with the z axis pointing along the line of sight. Thus, the eye coordinate system represents the user's view of the scene. The next step of the pipeline is to project the polygons from the 3D eye coordinate space to 2D screen space. This is normally performed by a perspective projection. Both the transformation to eye coordinates and the perspective projection can be represented by 4×4 matrices so they can be combined with the standard modeling transformations.

The last step in the display pipeline is to convert the polygons into the pixels that represent it on the screen. When we do this we want to display only the parts of the polygon that are visible to the viewer. In other words, the parts of the polygon that are covered by other polygons in the model should not be displayed. This is called hidden surface removal. The standard polygon display algorithm is based on scan conversion. The display screen can be viewed as a matrix of pixels, and the scan conversion process considers one row of this matrix at a time. All the pixels in the polygon that intersect this row are computed and drawn on the screen. The following is the basic outline of the scan conversion process. First, the polygon is decomposed into its non-horizontal edges. These edges are then sorted on their maximum y values to produce an edge table (ET) that contains the edges in descending order. The individual rows or scan lines of the polygon are considered one at a time starting with the largest y value in the polygon. A second table, called the active edge table (AET), contains all the edges that intersect the current scan line. First, all the edges in the ET whose maximum y value equals the current scan line are moved to the AET. Second, the AET is sorted on the x value of the edge for the current scan line. Third, the edges in the AET are considered in pairs, and all the pixels between their x values are filled. Fourth, all the edges whose minimum y value is equal to the current scan line are removed from the AET.

The above process fills in all of the pixels that are covered by the polygon, but it does not solve the hidden surface problem. One way of doing this is to use a z-buffer. A z-buffer is an array that is the same size as the display screen. This array stores the current z value for each of the pixels displayed on the screen. When the screen is cleared the z-buffer is set to an infinite distance from the eye. In the scan conversion process the z-buffer is checked before each pixel is drawn. If the value in the z-buffer is larger than the z value of the current point on the polygon (the polygon is closer to the viewer) then the pixel is drawn and the z-buffer is updated. Otherwise, the object for the current pixel is closer to the viewer than the polygon, so the pixel is not drawn. Note that this approach to hidden surface removal can be used for any type of object that can be drawn, it is not restricted to polygons.

A number of real-time algorithms for displaying and manipulating polygon-based models are based on the use of binary space partitioning or BSP trees (Fuchs *et al.*, 1980; Naylor, 1990). A *BSP tree* is a binary tree that has a polygon at each node. Each node has two subtrees called front and back. The front subtree contains polygons that are in front of the polygon at the node, and the back subtree contains polygons that are behind the polygon at the node. The polygon surface normal is used to determine the polygons that are in front and behind the polygon at the node.

A BSP tree solves the hidden surface problem independently of the position of the viewer. The polygons can be displayed with hidden surfaces removed by traversing the BSP tree in a particular way. At each node the position of the viewer with respect to the polygon at the node is determined. If the viewer is in front of the polygon, we first display the back subtree, then the polygon at the node, and then the front subtree. Since the viewer is in front of the polygon at the node, the polygons in the back subtree cannot hide any of the other polygons, so they are drawn first. If the viewer is behind the polygon at the node, the polygons are displayed in the reverse order. The BSP tree display algorithm is shown in Figure 3-3. We can determine whether the viewer is in front of the polygon by substituting the position of the viewer into the polygon's equation. If the result is positive, the viewer is in front of the

```
display_tree(n : node) {

    if(viewer in front of n.polygon) {
            display_tree(n.back);
            display_polygon(n.polygon);
            display_tree(n.front);
    } else {
            display_tree(n.front);
            display_polygon(n.polygon);
            display_tree(n.back);
    }

}
```

Figure 3-3 The BSP tree display algorithm.

polygon, and if the result is negative the viewer is behind the polygon. In practice a stack-based algorithm is used to avoid the procedure-call overhead required for recursion.

Constructing a good BSP tree is harder than displaying one (Fuchs *et al.*, 1983). The basic algorithm is to select one of the polygons in the model as the root of the tree, divide the rest of the polygons into front and back sets, and recursively apply the algorithm until the front and back sets are empty. The basic outline of the algorithm is shown in Figure 3-4.

The split_polygon procedure splits a polygon into two lists, one containing the parts of the polygon that are in front of the root polygon and the other containing the parts that are behind the root polygon. The select_polygon function selects one of the polygons in the list as the root of the tree. The

```
build_tree(polygon_list p) {
        polygon k, j;
        polygon_list positive_list, negative_list;
        polygon_list positive_parts, negative_part;

        k = select_polygon(p);
        positive_list = NULL;
        negative_list = NULL;
        forall polygons j in p, such that j <> k {
                        split_polygon(k,j,positive_part,negative_parts)
                        add_list(positive_list,positive_pasts);
                        add_list(negative_list,negative_parts);
        }

        return(make_tree(build_tree(positive_list), k, build_tree(negative_list)));

}
```

Figure 3-4 The BSP tree construction algorithm.

efficiency of the resulting tree depends upon this function. One way of constructing a good BSP tree is to select the polygon that cuts the fewest other polygons in the model. Unfortunately, this is a very expensive computation, since every polygon on the list must be compared to all the other polygons on the list, at each step of the algorithm. A more efficient technique is to randomly select a small number of polygons from this list and determine the number of polygons that they cut. The one that cuts the fewest polygons is selected.

Algorithms have been developed for real-time manipulation of BSP trees, including CSG operations (Naylor, 1990). BSP trees can also be used to partition space into regions. Each leaf node in a BSP tree defines a region of 3D space that is bounded by the polygons on the path taken to reach that node. This can be used to efficiently determine the subvolume of 3D space that the user is currently in, and determine the closest objects to the user for the purposes of collision detection and grab processing.

Polygons have a number of important advantages. First, they are very easy to display and their display algorithms are very efficient. This is very important in virtual environments where display speed is the important criterion. Second, polygons are very easy to specify. The user only needs to provide a list of vertices to completely determine the polygon, and it is fairly easy to determine this set. This is not the case for most of the other modeling primitives. A large number of man-made objects have flat faces, so polygons can be used to accurately model them. Fourth, polygons have been used extensively in computer graphics for close to 30 years, so their properties and algorithms are very well understood.

There are also disadvantages to using polygons. First, polygons do a very poor job of modeling objects that have curved surfaces. A large number of polygons are required to model a curved surface, and when the viewer gets close enough to the surface it will look like a collection of flat surfaces and not a smooth curve. Second, a large number of polygons are often required to model interesting objects. This makes it difficult to construct the model, and display will be time consuming.

Curves and surfaces

Curves and surfaces give us a way of modeling objects that have curved surfaces. The mathematics behind these primitives is more complicated than polygons, and many different types of curves and surfaces have been developed. In this subsection the basic ideas behind curves and surfaces are outlined along with their advantages and disadvantages. More information on these primitives can be found in the standard computer graphics and geometrical modeling text books (Barsky, 1988; Bartels *et al.*, 1987).

The common curve primitives are based on *parametric polynomials*. A parameter, t, is defined along the length of the curve, such that $t = 0$ at one end of the curve and $t = 1$ at the other end of the curve. Intermediate values of t generate points along the curve. Three polynomials are used to represent the

x, y and z coordinates of the points along the curve. These polynomials are functions of t and have the following form:

$$x(t) = \sum_{i=0}^{n} a_i t^i$$

$$y(t) = \sum_{i=0}^{n} b_i t^i$$

$$z(t) = \sum_{i=0}^{n} c_i t^i$$

In most computer graphics applications third-degree polynomials are used. The curve is drawn by evaluating the polynomial at particular values of t and then connecting the resulting points by lines. Efficient algorithms for doing this can be found in the graphics literature and some graphics workstations have implemented these algorithms in hardware.

The big question is where do the polynomial coefficients come from? There is no way to easily guess the coefficients for a particular curve. Over the years many techniques have been developed for determining the coefficients, and the main difference between the different types of curves is the way the polynomial coefficients are computed. Most techniques use a set of *control points* to determine the shape of the curve. A control point is a point in 3D space that is used to control the shape of a curve. A control point can represent a point that the curve must either pass through or lie close to. Alternatively, a control point can be used to specify the slope or tangent of the curve at a particular point. One example of the use of control points is the specification of a Bezier curve. For this type of curve four control points are used to specify the shape of a cubic curve. The first and the last control points specify the two end points of the curve. The second control point controls the slope of the curve at the first end point, and the third control point controls the slope of the curve at the second end point. This is illustrated in Figure 3-5. By moving these control points the user can easily change the position and shape of the curve.

A surface can be represented in essentially the same way as a curve, except that a bivariate polynomial is used. A surface is basically a two-dimensional structure embedded in a 3D space. A two-dimensional coordinate system can be constructed on the surface. These coordinates are usually represented by

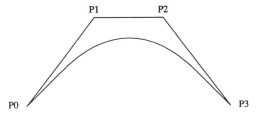

Figure 3-5   A Bezier curve with its control points.

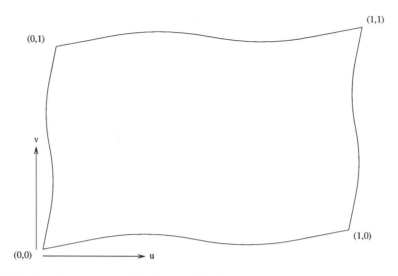

Figure 3-6 A surface patch with its coordinate system.

the variables u and v, and both of these variables are normally restricted to the range 0 to 1. For each value of (u,v) there is a corresponding point on the surface. The four corners of the surface have the (u,v) coordinates $(0,0)$, $(1,0)$, $(0,1)$ and $(1,1)$. This coordinate system is illustrated in Figure 3-6.

As in the case of curves, a surface is represented by three bivariate polynomials, one each for the x, y, and z coordinates of the points on the surface. These polynomials can be expressed in the following way:

$$x(u,v) = \sum_{i=0}^{n} \sum_{j=0}^{m} a_{ij} u^i v^j$$

$$y(u,v) = \sum_{i=0}^{n} \sum_{j=0}^{m} b_{ij} u^i v^j$$

$$z(u,v) = \sum_{i=0}^{n} \sum_{j=0}^{m} c_{ij} u^i v^j$$

In most cases bicubic polynomials are used giving 16 coefficients for each polynomial.

The coefficients for the surface polynomials are determined in essentially the same way as they are for curves. For curves four control points were used, and in the case of surfaces 16 control points are used. The control points either specify points on or near the surface, or the slope or shape of the surface.

Quite often more than one curve of surface segment is required to represent an object. In the case of surfaces these segments are called *patches*, and a representation using a collection of patches is called a *piecewise representation*. In a piecewise representation the patches are placed side by side and joined at their edges. Two patches are joined by having them share control points along (and sometime near) their common edge. This construction is similar to the construction of a patchwork quilt. For example, a sphere can be approximated by eight patches; four patches for the northern hemisphere and four patches for the southern hemisphere. In each hemisphere, each of the four patches is triangular in shape and covers 90 degrees of the radius at the equator.

There are several advantages to using curve and surface primitives. The obvious advantage is that they can accurately represent objects that have curved surfaces, producing a much more accurate model. Second, they can reduce the number of primitives that are required to model a complex object. This has the dual advantage of decreasing the amount of space required to store the model and decreasing the amount of time required to process it. Third, a number of sophisticated commercial modeling tools use this representation, therefore, it is possible to import models produced using these tools into a virtual environment modeling system.

There are also several disadvantages to using this type of modeling primitive. First, display algorithms for curves and surfaces are not as efficient as the algorithms for polygons, therefore, a model using them may be restricted to fewer objects. Second, the algorithms for manipulating curves and surface are more complicated than those for other modeling primitives, making them more difficult to program and debug. Third, curves and surfaces are not as widely supported in graphics packages as polygons are.

Procedural modeling

A *procedural model* is any modeling technique that uses a procedure to generate the primitives in the model. A large number of procedural models are based on physics or biology and tend to combine geometry and behavior into one model. An example of this approach that we have used is a model of the swimming behavior of fish. Fish change their shape when they are swimming. For example, a fish increases the size of its tail in order to swim faster, therefore, the geometry of the fish depends upon the speed at which it is swimming. Our procedural model takes into account the swimming motion at each step of the simulation to generate the polygons that are displayed in the current frame.

A simple physical model can be used to model objects that deform. For example a deformable cube can be modeled by eight point masses located at the corners of the cube. Springs connect each point mass to the other seven point masses in the cube. The rest lengths of these springs maintain the cube shape when no additional forces are applied to the cube. If the viewer picks up the cube by one of its corners, the cube will deform in such a way that it becomes longer and thinner. Similarly, if the cube is dropped it will deform when it strikes the ground.

Using a procedural model has the following main advantages. First, if an accurate physical or biological model is used the resulting object is quite realistic and convinces the viewer that he or she is interacting with the real object. Second, since the model combines geometry and behavior, the behavior modeling part becomes much simpler and the geometry of the object can reflect its current behavior. Third, if a good physical or biological model of the object can be found, then the modeling task is greatly simplified, since all the modeler needs to do is implement the model. Fourth, special procedural modeling tools have been developed that significantly simplify the implementation of procedural models (Green and Sun, 1988).

Procedural models also have a number of disadvantages. First, in some cases good physical or biological models of the object do not exist. In this case the modeler not only needs to develop the model, but also the underlying physics. Second, in the case of physical models there is the problem of solving the equations in the model. These are quite often differential equations that may be hard to solve and consume a considerable amount of computing time. Techniques for solving these equations are reviewed and compared in the article by Green (1989).

The following two subsections describe two of the more popular procedural models, fractals and particle systems.

Fractals

Fractals are a technique for modeling objects that have an irregular outline. This technique was first used to model geographical features such as rivers and mountains. Fractals are a *stochastic* modeling primitive in the sense that they are based on a random process. A fractal primitive consists of a standard modeling primitive, such as a polygon or a surface patch, plus a stochastic process that is used to modify the underlying primitive. The stochastic process that is used in fractals is called *fractional Brownian motion*. This process is self-similar, which is a desirable property for a stochastic process used in modeling applications. A process is *self-similar* if it retains its basic properties when it is scaled. This implies that when the model is scaled it will have the same basic shape. To see why this is important consider a fractal model of a mountain. When the viewer is far away from the mountain, only the basic outline of the mountain can be seen. When the viewer flies towards the mountain, more details of the mountain appear as the viewer gets closer to it. As the user gets closer, the mountain should have the same basic shape, it should not change shape as it is approached. The self-similar nature of the stochastic process guarantees this.

Fractals are a good example of database amplification (Smith, 1984). In this modeling technique a procedure is used to generate the information in the model. The modeler specifies the base primitive and the parameters of the stochastic process, then the fractal process generates a collection of primitives that represents the object. In the case of a mountain, the modeler specifies a set of polygons that give the general outline of the mountain and then the fractal process generates a large number of polygons that represent the details of the mountain. The modeler only needs to specify a small amount of information, and the fractal process amplifies it to produce a large number of geometrical primitives.

One algorithm for approximating a fractal process is called stochastic subdivision (Fournier *et al.*, 1982). In this algorithm the base primitive is divided into smaller parts. In the case of a triangle or quadrilateral base primitive, the primitive is divided into four smaller triangles or quadrilaterals. When this subdivision occurs a random displacement is added to the subdivision points. This adds additional structure and detail to the model. Some care must be taken in the generation of the random displacements, the techniques for doing this are outlined in the article by Fournier *et al.* (1982).

In the case of virtual environments fractals are used to generate static objects that are mainly used for background. For these objects the fractal process can be used once to generate the object and then the resulting set of polygons can be displayed in the environment. In general the fractal process is not used to generate a new set of primitives on each screen update, since it requires a considerable amount of time to generate it. The fractal process could also be used to change the level of detail of the object as the user moves closer to it.

The main advantages of fractals is that they can be used to generate very complex objects with a minimal amount of work, and these objects can have a very irregular structure. The main disadvantage of this technique is that it generates a large number of primitives, that consume a large amount of display time. Also, it can only be used for static objects, and not the objects that exhibit behavior in the environment.

Particle systems

Particle systems are another form of procedural model based on using a large number of very simple primitives to model a complex object. Particle systems were originally used to model fire (Reeves, 1983; Reeves and Blau, 1985). Since then they have been used to model water, grass, trees and snow. Particle systems also make use of stochastic processes and often combine geometry and behavior into the same modeling structure.

A particle system consists of a collection of very simple primitives called *particles*. Each particle has a collection of properties, such as position, velocity, color, size, and lifetime. The set of properties associated with a particle depends upon the particular modeling application. The initial values of the particle's properties are generated using a random process. Usually a uniform random process is used, and the modeler specifies the mean value and the range of values for the property. The particles are usually generated by a source that has a location in 3D space.

A particle system evolves over time. At each time step of its lifetime the following computations are performed:

1. Generate new particles at the source
2. Update the particle properties
3. Remove dead particles from the system
4. Draw the particles.

In the first step a random number of new particles are generated at the source. The initial properties of these particles are set using the random process outlined above. Each particle is also assigned a lifetime that is used to determine how long it will remain in the system. A lifetime of infinity can be used if the particle should not be removed from the system.

In the second step the properties of all the existing particles are updated. For example, if a particle has a position and velocity, the acceleration of gravity is added to the velocity and then the new velocity is added to its position, as shown in the following equations:

$$v = v + a \, dt$$

$$p = p + v \, dt$$

where a is the acceleration of the particle (including the acceleration of gravity), v is the particle's velocity, p is the particle's position and dt is the size of the time step (the time between updates in the virtual environment). This will generate a simple dynamic behavior. In this step the lifetime of the particle is decremented.

In the third step all the particles with a lifetime of zero are removed from the system. In the final step all the particles are drawn. The geometry of a particle is quite simple, usually either a single pixel or a small polygon. The section on Slink world contains an example of the use of particle systems in a virtual environment.

Particle systems have the following advantages. First, they provide a way of combining simple geometry and behavior into an object that is visually interesting. For example, it is easy to model fire and water fountains using particle systems. Second, since a procedural model is used, it is easy to specify a particle system, the modeler only needs to specify the parameters for the random processes that generate the particle properties. Third, since each particle has a simple geometry they are easy to display and the display process is quite efficient.

Particle systems have the following disadvantages. First, since the dynamics of the particle system must be computed in each time step, there is an added time requirement for the use of particle systems. Second, since the geometry of each particle is quite simple, there is a limited range of objects that can be modeled using this approach.

Special virtual environment issues

Virtual environments differ in three main ways from other types of computer graphics modeling. First, virtual environments have a much wider range of objects. In most computer graphics applications there is one main object or a small collection of objects. A virtual environment must provide a significant number of interesting objects in order to be successful. Second, some of the objects in a virtual environment must have their own behavior. In most computer graphics applications the objects are either static or only perform simple motions, such as translation or rotation. Third, the objects in a virtual environment must be able to respond to the viewer. When the viewer interacts with an object, the object must respond in a reasonable way, it cannot ignore the viewer's actions. This is not the case in most computer graphics applications. These differences place additional requirements on the modeling techniques and software used in virtual environments. These requirements are briefly outlined in this section.

Reusability is one of the main additional requirements. Each virtual environment requires a wide range of objects. A considerable effort is required to develop the geometry and behavior of each of these objects. This investment can be better justified if they can be used in more than one environment. If there is a library of standard objects, the effort required to develop a new virtual environment is significantly reduced. Model reusability is also important in other graphics applications, but in virtual environments it is likely to be an important factor in the successful development of commercial applications.

There are two things that must be done in order to meet this requirement. First, provide tools that support the independent development and manipulation of objects. The model of each object should not be tied into the model of the entire environment in such a way that it cannot be separated from it. This strongly suggests the use of hierarchical modeling techniques, where the objects can be placed at the leaves of the modeling hierarchy. Second, there must be standard ways of recording and transmitting the models of individual objects. This format should include a hierarchical or structured description of the object's geometry along with its behavior. This will allow for the widespread sharing of objects.

At run-time the model should provide some assistance with interaction processing. For example, when the viewer makes a grab gesture the user interface must determine the object that the viewer is attempting to grab. Similarly, if the viewer makes a pointing gesture, the user interface must determine the object that is being selected. Both of these operations nominally require an examination of all the objects in the model. If the model is quite large this requires a considerable amount of time, and this processing must be performed in every update cycle. There are several ways that the modeling software can facilitate these computations. First, it can provide simplified geometry that can be used in grab and pointing tests. For example, a complex object can be replaced by a bounding box that significantly reduces the number of comparisons that must be made. Also the structure of the model can be used to divide up the space occupied by the environment. Only the objects that are currently seen by the viewer are candidates for grab and pointing operations. In the case of grab operations, only the objects within the viewer's reach need to be considered. If the modeling software can provide these tools the user interface part of the environment is much easier to produce and much more efficient.

Finally the geometry must be structured in such a way that it is easy to specify the object's behavior. The object's behavior will require changing certain aspects of its geometry. For example, consider the case of a human figure that walks. If the model consists of a non-hierarchical collection of polygons, changing the model to reflect its leg motion will be quite difficult. Instead, if a hierarchical model is used, such as the one shown in Figure 3-1 that has a branch for each leg, the leg motion can be produced by changing a transformation matrix. When building the geometrical model the modeler must be aware of the types of behaviors that will be required, and structure the model in such a way that these behaviors are easy to produce.

BEHAVIOR MODELING

Most modeling research in computer graphics and virtual environments has concentrated on geometrical modeling, but this is only the start of the story. In an interesting virtual world, the objects must interact with the user and each other. This implies that the objects must be able to move and change their physical properties (such as color or facial expression). The problem of making objects move has been studied in computer animation for a considerable length of time. Some of the techniques that have been developed in computer animation are of use in virtual worlds, but there is one major difference between these two fields that limits the techniques that can be transferred between them. In computer animation the animator has complete control over the environment, while in virtual worlds this is not the case, since the user is free to interact with the environment in arbitrary ways. An animator can completely plan the motion that will occur in an animation. The virtual world designer does not have this ability, since he or she does not have complete control over the environment, the best they can do is specify how the objects will react to particular situations.

In the following subsections, traditional animation techniques for modeling object behavior and their potential use in virtual environments are reviewed. Then the ideas behind behavioral animation are introduced followed by a discussion of the relation model that provides a convenient and efficient way of specifying behavior for virtual environments.

Traditional animation techniques

Before the use of computer technology, animation was done by hand. An animation is produced by a sequence of still images whose continuous display shows a smooth movement. Each of the images in an animation is called a *frame*. Before computers these frames were generated by hand drawing, where every detail of a motion in each frame was drawn by hand. The idea of *keyframing* is used to separate the important actions from the details of how the motion is performed. By using keyframing, the main parts of a motion are drawn by an animator with a high degree of skill, and the rest of the frames are filled in by animators with less skill. Here the key drawings (keyframes) do not capture the entire motion, but define the key poses or events in the motion. These key frames are sufficient to guide the in-betweener from one pose to another of the object or character being animated.

Today traditional hand-drawn animation has been replaced by computer animation, but the essential idea of keyframing for generating motion sequences has not changed. Rather than keyframing a sequence by hand, computers are used for this traditional role. Various control techniques have been introduced to achieve this goal. Kinematics and dynamics are the two major techniques for defining and interpolating key poses in a motion.

Animation languages and interactive systems are the two major environments for using either kinematic or dynamic control techniques. A brief discussion of these important control components for computer-generated animation, in terms of their basic ideas and current research, is given below.

Kinematics and dynamics

Kinematics and dynamics are the two major control techniques used in computer animation, where *kinematics* is based on geometrical transformations, and *dynamics* (also called physically derived control) is based on the use of forces, torques, and other physical properties to produce motion.

Kinematics. Kinematics describes a motion by geometrical transformations, such as rotation, scaling, translation, and shear. No knowledge of the physical properties of the object are used in motion control. In keyframe animation, the extremes of a motion or critical junctures in a motion sequence are explicitly specified using geometrical transformations. In-between frames are generated by various interpolation methods such as linear interpolation, parabolic interpolation, or cubic-spline interpolation.

Either forward or inverse kinematics can be used in motion control. In forward kinematics the transformation matrices in the modeling hierarchy are manipulated and used to compute the positions of the object's subparts. Inverse kinematics operates in the opposite direction, the positions of the object's subparts at the leaves of the tree are specified, and the transformation matrices are computed from these positions. Since the motion produced by kinematics is based on geometrical transformations, in a complex environment it can be difficult to produce the desired motion using this technique.

In the early 1960s, the temporal behavior of interpolated points on a path was first noticed by animation researchers. The *P-curve* technique was introduced by Baecker (1969) in his GENESYS system, where a P-curve is used to define both the trajectory of the point and the dynamics of its motion. This technique was later extended to three dimensions by Csuri (1975). The technique of using *moving point constraints* between keyframes was developed by Reeves (1981). This technique allows the specification of multiple paths and the speed of interpolation by connecting matching points in two adjacent keyframes and using a P-curve to show how they transform over time. The sets of keyframes and moving points form a constraint or patch network for controlling the desired dynamics.

The use of kinematic positioning coupled with constraint specifications has been used by Badler (Badler *et al.*, 1986) as a promising solution to complex animation tasks. A constraint includes spatial regions, orientation zones, and time expressions. Multiple constraints on body position or orientation can be specified and the motion is controlled by a constraint satisfaction system. Three-dimensional input devices have been used for manipulating and positioning objects. These devices are also used for visually establishing multiple constraints and motion goals.

Keyed parameters, which control the positioning of the objects in the keyframes, have been used for animating 3D objects. A keyed parameter could be part of a transformation matrix, or a vertex or control point that defines part of the geometry of the object. Once an appropriately parameterized model is created, the parameters can be keyed and interpolated to produce an animation. One well-known example of a parameterized model is the facial animation system created by Parke (1982). Using the keyed parameters of the model, a sequence of facial expressions can be created by modifying the parameters, as needed, for each movement.

Motion goals have been used with kinematic control. With a predefined motion goal, much of the burden of generating explicit motion descriptions is shifted to the animation software. One system using this technique is the skeleton control model of Zeltzer (1982). A motion goal such as walking or running is parsed into a sequence of motion skills, where each skill is further divided into a set of local motor programs predefined in terms of kinematic transformations.

Dynamics. Dynamics applies physical laws to produce the object's movement, instead of positioning the object by geometrical transformations. In this approach, motion is calculated in terms of the object's mass and inertia, applied force and torque, and other physical effects of the environment. As a result, the motion produced is physically more accurate, and appears more attractive and natural. One goal in computer animation is to establish control techniques for dynamics and use dynamics to provide a minimal user interface to highly complex motion. In addition, dynamics is generally considered a useful tool in the fields of robotics and biomechanics.

Dynamics, also called physically derived control, takes into account a body's mass and inertia as well as the various forces acting on the body. The equations of motion are used to relate the acceleration of the mass (object) to the forces and/or torques acting upon it. The well-known Newtonian equation of motion, $F = ma$, is used to produce the motion of a particle. In this equation, F is the force vector acting on the point mass, m, and a is the acceleration the mass experiences. Given the acceleration, the velocity and position along the path of motion can be computed. A torque is produced when a force acts at a point on the body other than its center of mass. The basic equation for computing torque has the form: $T = p \times f$, where $p = (x,y,z)$ is the point being acted on and $f = (fx,fy,fz)$ is the force applied to it. Similar to a force, a torque can be represented as a 3D vector in space. Other types of forces, such as gravity, and spring and damper, can also be modeled and integrated into the dynamic environment when they are necessary.

A wide variety of dynamic formulas have been discovered since 1500. One example is Newton's three laws of motion. These laws explain why objects move and the relationships that exist between force and motion. The methods used for integrating individual forces in 3D vector space are well defined in physics. In computer animation, various forces and torques acting on and in the object's body can be divided into a few types. For instance, the gravitational force can be calculated automatically. Interactions with the ground, other collisions, and joint limits can be modeled by springs and dampers. Internally produced motions such as muscles in animals or motors in robots can be specified using an interactive interface.

Developing good formulations of the dynamic equations for articulated bodies, including humans and animals, has been a research challenge for computer animation. A good dynamics formulation produces a set of equations that can be efficiently solved and provide the animator with an intuitive and flexible control mechanism. An articulated body is modeled with rigid segments connected together at joints capable of less than 6 degrees of freedom. Because of the interactions between connected segments, the dynamics equations are coupled and must be solved as a system of equations, one equation for each degree of freedom. Numerous formulations of the dynamics equations for rigid bodies have been defined. Although derived from different methodologies, all the equations produce the same results. The most significant equations include the Euler equations (Wells, 1969), the Gibbs–Appell formulation (Horowitz, 1983; Pars, 1979; Wilhelms, 1985), the Armstrong recursive formulation (Armstrong, 1979; Armstrong and Green, 1985), and the Featherstone recursive formulation (Featherstone, 1983).

The Euler equations are defined by three translational equations and three rotational equations. It is simple to solve these equations, if the accelerations are given and the forces and torques are desired. But, the equations do not properly deal with constraints at the joints. The Gibbs–Appell equations are a nonrecursive form that has $O(n^4)$ time complexity for n degrees of freedom. These equations express the generalized force at each degree of freedom as a function of the mass distribution, acceleration, and velocity of all segments distal to this degree of freedom. Thus, this method allows considerable flexibility in designing joints. The Armstrong recursive formulation can be thought of as an extension of the Euler equations with multiple segments. The method is built on tree structures and is suitable for certain types of joints. The complexity of the method is linear in the number of joints. The Featherstone method is a recursive linear dynamics formulation, and is flexible in the types of joints.

The use of dynamic control for the problem of collision response between rigid objects is discussed by Moore and Wilhelms (Moore and Wilhelms, 1988). In this technique, a collision is treated as a kinematic problem in terms of the relative positions of objects in the environment. The response of arbitrary bodies after collision in the environment is modeled using springs, and an analytical response algorithm for articulated rigid bodies is also applied to conserve the linear and angular momentum of linked structures.

A general control model for the dynamics of arbitrary three-dimensional rigid objects has been proposed by Hahn (Hahn, 1988). This model takes into account various physical qualities such as elasticity, friction, mass, and moment of inertia to produce the dynamic interactions of rolling and sliding contacts. Another technique used for the dynamic control of collisions between rigid bodies (Baraff, 1989) starts from the problem of resting contact. The forces between systems of rigid bodies, either in motion or stationary, with no-colliding contact are analytically formulated, and the formulation can then be modified to simulate the motion of colliding bodies.

Spacetime constraints (Witkin and Kass, 1988) is a technique that combines both the what and how requirements of a motion into a system of dynamic control equations. A motion can be described not only by the task to be performed, such as "jump from here to there," but by how the task should be performed, "jump hard or little." These requirements are specified by coupling the constraint functions representing forces and positions over time to the equations of the object's motion. The solution to this problem is the motion that satisfies the "what" constraints with the "how" criteria optimized.

Another major research direction in dynamic control is the modeling and animation of elastically deformable materials, such as rubber, cloth, paper, and flexible metals. This technique employs elasticity theory to construct differential equations that represent the shape and motion of deformable materials when they are subjected to applied forces, constraints and interactions with other objects. The models are active since they are physically based; the descriptions of shape and motion are unified to yield realistic dynamics as well as realistic statics in a natural way.

Summary. Both kinematics and dynamics can be used to compute the motion of an object. These techniques differ in their computational cost, the level of detail at which the motion must be specified, and the ease with which it can be specified. These three factors influence the choice between these two techniques.

Kinematics is computationally cheaper than dynamics. In kinematics the modeler establishes the key positions in the object's motion, usually by adjusting transformation matrices or key parameters in the model. When the motion is performed, the individual frames in the animation are produced by interpolating the matrices or key parameters. This process is not computationally demanding. On the other hand, with dynamics a system of differential equations must be solved. A new solution value must be produced for each frame of the animation. Depending upon the formulation of the dynamics equations, and the solution technique used, this can be a very demanding computational process, and techniques for solving these equations in real-time are a major research problem.

In kinematics every detail of the object's motion must be specified by the modeler. The modeling software is simply interpolating the modeler's specification, it cannot add to the motion of the object. With dynamics some aspects of the object's motion can be left to the modeling software. For example, if an object is not supported it will fall under the influence of gravity until it reaches some object that can support it. In a kinematic system this motion must be specified by the modeler, otherwise the object will remain suspended in space with no visible means of support. In dynamics this type of motion can be produced automatically. Similarly, collisions between objects can be automatically handled by dynamics software. The automatic production of these aspects of the object's motion can greatly simplify the modeler's task, since he or she can concentrate on the high-level details of the motion. Since kinematics is based on interpolating transformation matrices, it is not suitable for virtual environment applications where the object must respond to its environment.

The ease of specification issue is not as easy to deal with, since it depends upon the nature of the motion and the modeler's skill. With kinematics the modeler has detailed control over the motion of the object, and specifying its motion in the key frames in a straightforward activity. Once the keyframes have been correctly specified, the interpolation will produce close to the correct motion, and fine tuning the motion only involves changing adjacent keyframes. The problem with this is that specifying the keyframes is a long and tedious process, and the resulting motion will not respond to other actions within the environment. Also, when there are multiple moving objects, synchronizing the motion of the objects can be quite difficult. With dynamics, the main problem is specifying the forces and torques that are acting on the object. In some cases it can be quite easy to compute these values, and in other cases it may be close to impossible. The main advantage that dynamics has is that the modeler can work at a higher level than is possible with kinematics, and if a well-known physical process is being simulated force and torque values may be readily available. Dynamics also concentrates more on the object's reactions, therefore, it is more suitable for environments where there is a considerable amount of interaction between objects.

Programming and interactive tools

Programming and interactive tools are two major approaches to the specification of motion. *Programming* uses a textual description to describe the motion, while *interactive tools* use a visual description. Textual descriptions rely on the power of a computer language to convey natural and versatile motion expressions. Visual descriptions rely on the user's ability to directly interact with and manipulate the objects displayed on the computer screen, in either a two- or three-dimensional space.

The programming approach. Animation languages provide a programming means for specifying and controlling motion. The object geometry, temporal relationship of parts, and variations in the motion are explicitly described using a textual description in a programming language. Using an animation language gives the animator complete control over the process. The motion concepts and processes are expressed in terms of abstract data types and procedures. Once a program is created, the rest of the process of producing the animation is completely automatic. The programming approach is suitable for algorithmic control, or when the movement simulates a physical process. Certain sophisticated motions and some special motion effects can easily be animated with the programming approach. One major disadvantage with using programming, however, is the time lag between specifying the motion and viewing the result. The animator does not see any of the resulting motion until the program is complete and the full animation is rendered.

Three approaches have emerged in the development of animation languages. These are subroutine libraries, preprocessors, and complete languages. Subroutine libraries are used to supply graphical functions that are added to a pre-existing high-level language. The library can be linked with programs in a regular programming language at execution time. Examples of subroutine libraries include the ACM Core system and PHIGS. These graphics packages support two- and three-dimensional transformations, perspective projection, drawing primitives, and control structures. A subroutine package can be both language and device independent. The cost of using a subroutine package is fairly low, but subroutine calls are not the most natural way of specifying the motion. That is, there is a large semantic gap between the motion and its specification.

A graphics preprocessor is an extension to a compiler that augments the syntax of an existing language with new (graphics) commands and data types. New graphical features are recognized and incorporated into the language. The preprocessor program works prior to the interpreter or compiler, and its output is passed to the language compiler and processed as usual. From the user's viewpoint, a new graphics language that fully incorporates an existing high-level language as well as graphics commands is created. This technique has been widely used in the design of graphics languages. It reduces the semantic gap by providing better syntax for the graphics functionality, but the language designer is constrained by the syntax and semantics of the existing language.

A complete programming language with original graphics syntax and semantics is the third approach to developing, manipulating, and displaying visual images. In this approach the expense of a preprocessor is avoided, but considerable effort is required to produce a complete programming language. Also, a new compiler is required for the language. In practice, few graphics languages have been implemented using this technique.

ASAS (Reynolds, 1978, 1982), designed at the Architecture Machine Group, is an extension of the Lisp programming environment. This language includes geometric objects, operators, parallel control structures and other features to make it useful for computer graphics applications. The operators are applied to the objects under the control of modular programming structures. These structures, called actors, allow parallelism, independence, and optionally, synchronization. Also, the extensibility of ASAS allows it to grow with each new application.

CINEMIRA (Thalman and Magnenat-Thalmann, 1984) is a high-level, three-dimensional animation language based on data abstraction. The language is an extension of the high-level Pascal language. It allows the animator to write structured scripts by defining animated basic types, actor types and camera types.

The interactive approach. Interactive techniques have generated considerable interest in the animation community due to their flexibility. Basically, interactive control refers to graphical techniques that allow the animator to design motions in real-time while watching the animation develop on the graphics screen. For example, the "keyed" parameters of a model can be continuously modified by connecting their values to numeric input devices. The model is displayed while this interaction occurs, so the animator gets instant feedback on his or her actions. The parameter values specified using this approach can be stored in a hierarchically structured database. The values in this database can be interpolated to produce the animation sequence, and the animator can quickly return to certain keyframes to fine tune the animation. The two important features of this approach are that the animator directly interacts with the model being animated, and quickly receives feedback on his or her actions.

There are three interaction tasks that are typically supported by interactive animation systems. The first task is selecting the part of the model that the animator wants to modify. In the case of hierarchical models this involves navigating through the model until the transformation or parameter to be modified is reached. In other modeling structures some way of naming components of the model or navigating through its structure must be provided.

The second task is modifying the values stored in the model. These values include transformations and the keyed parameters in the model. These modifications could also include changing the positions of the subparts at the leaves of the modeling hierarchy. If inverse kinematics is supported by the animation system, these modifications could also be reflected in higher levels of the modeling structure.

The third task is specifying the procedures that act on the model and the times at which they are active. These procedures could be dynamics models, in which case the animator must specify the forces and torques that act on the model as a function of time. In the case of procedural animation the animator must specify the procedures to execute, the parameters to these procedures, and the times at which they are active.

Two well-known interactive animation systems are BBOP and EM (Hanrahan and Sturman, 1985; Sturman, 1984). Both of these systems were developed at the New York Institute of Technology for the animation of human forms and other models that have a hierarchical structure. The BBOP system was based on a traditional hierarchical modeling scheme with transformation matrices on each arc of the modeling structure. The animator used a joystick to navigate through the modeling structure and adjust the transformation matrices along the arcs. The EM system was more general and was based on the use of keyed parameters. A special animation language was used to describe the structure of the model and the parameters that the animator could manipulate. As in BBOP a joystick was used to navigate through the structure of the model and various input devices could be used to interactively modify the model's parameters.

Researchers at the University of Pennsylvania (Badler *et al.*, 1986) have used a 3SPACE digitizer for manipulating and positioning three-dimensional objects. With this device, the positioning of an articulated figure is handled by visually establishing multiple goals, and then letting a straightforward tree-traversal algorithm simultaneously satisfy all the constraints.

The MML system (Green and Sun, 1988) uses a combination of programming and interactive techniques to construct models and specify their behavior. MML is based on the use of procedural modeling to define the geometry of the objects and motion verbs to specify their behavior. The procedures used to describe the object's geometry consist of a collection of parameterized production rules. The parameters give the animator some control over the object's geometry when it is generated. The motion of the object is specified in terms of motion verbs, which are elementary units of motion for the object. Both the production rules and the motion verbs are specified using a programming language. This programming language is an extension of the C programming language.

The result of compiling the program is an interactive interface to the object's geometry and behavior. The animator can interactively select values for the production parameters, and then view the resulting geometry on a graphics display. The animator can then modify the parameters to fine tune the geometry of the object. This is a highly interactive process, since the generation of the object geometry is essentially instantaneous. Once the object geometry has been generated, the animator can specify its motion by selecting motion verbs from a menu. After a motion verb is selected the animator enters values for its parameters and specifies the times when the motion verb is active. The MML system then computes the object's motion, which the animator can interactively preview from within the MML system. After viewing the animation, the animator can return to the motion verbs and edit their parameters and the times when they are active.

Summary. Programming languages support the widest range of motion specification, essentially any motion that can be described in an algorithmic way can be specified using the programming language approach. The main problem with this approach is its ease of use, the animator must be a programmer and must understand the details of the desired motion. The interactive approach does not cover as wide a range of motions, but provides a more convenient and easier to use interface to motion specification. The animator does not need to have programming skills to use this approach, and quite often the motion specification can be developed significantly faster using this approach. Thus, the main trade-off is between the range of motions that can be specified and the ease with which these motions can be specified.

This trade-off has led to the development of mixed systems, such as MML, that use both programming and interactive techniques. By combining these two approaches, the resulting system can handle a wider range of motions and at the same time still have the ease of use properties of the interactive systems.

Virtual environment issues

A virtual environment places the user in virtual three-dimensional space, in which he or she can view, touch, and manipulate the objects as people do in the real world. Working in this environment requires a large amount of information, direct manipulation, fast update rate, and active user control over the objects. How can the techniques used for computer animation be used for this purpose? To answer this question, we take a quick look at the use of each of these techniques in the development of virtual environments.

The use of kinematics provides the user with a simple and predictable control means over an object's behavior. A real-time response is possible if kinematics is used for controlling the behavior, especially when the hardware supports the matrix manipulations used in kinematics. These features make kinematics a good choice for controlling the behavior in a virtual environment from a computational point of view. But, kinematics requires the modeler to specify the motion at a very detailed level, and once the motion starts there is no possibility for interaction with the user, since the motion is based on the interpolation of predefined keyframes or keyvalues. Dynamics produces physically realistic motion, but its use requires considerable computing power for solving the dynamic equations. In some cases, physically realistic motion may not be necessary, but a reasonable response time is crucial. While dynamics is more costly it allows the modeler to work at a higher level and allows for the possibility of user interaction. For example, if collision processes are accurately modeled, the user can interact with the object by hitting it or walking into it. All the interactions are purely mechanical, no aspects of behavior or personality are shown. Programming, as a general tool, is best used to generate the primitive behaviors that can be interactively combined to produce more complex behaviors. It should not be used as the direct interface with the virtual environment, because of its textual debugging cycle. Interactive techniques seem to be well suited to virtual environments that have a rich graphical structure. But, it is not clear whether they are flexible enough to cover the wide range of behaviors required in virtual environments.

There is one major difference between computer animation and virtual environments that makes it difficult to transfer the techniques developed in computer animation to virtual environments. Computer animation is based on the assumption that the animator is in complete control of all the objects in the animation. The animator specifies in detail the motion of every single object in the animation, and is aware of every single action that will occur in the animation. In a virtual environment the modeler cannot make that assumption. The major participant in the virtual environment is the user, who is free to move anywhere in the environment and interact with any of its objects. Thus, the modeler does not have complete control over the environment, he or she must provide an environment that responds to the user. The modeler cannot predict ahead of time all the actions that will occur in the environment, and he or she does not have complete control over its objects.

Due to this difference some animation techniques, such as keyframing and kinematics, may not be useful in some virtual environments. When an animator keyframes a motion sequence he or she knows exactly where all the objects in the animation are. In a virtual environment this is not the case, objects can be moved while the environment is running. As a result, a keyframed motion could result in objects moving through each other or an object coming to rest at a location where it has no visible support. Both kinematics and keyframing are only based on information provided by the animator and have no way of determining the current state of the environment. Thus, they have no way of reacting to changes that occur in the environment.

Some animation techniques, such as dynamics, are better since they can respond to the state of the environment. In the case of dynamics, objects can respond to collisions with other objects and will not stay suspended in space without support.

The behavior modeling techniques that are used in virtual environments must be able to sense the current state of the environment and must be able to respond to the events that occur there. The modeler must be able to state how the object responds to the events that occur in the environment and the user's actions. This response must take into account the current state of the environment and the other actions that are occurring around the object. Thus, we need modeling techniques that are oriented towards the behavior of objects, instead of specifying their detailed motion in particular circumstances.

Behavioral animation

Behavioral animation is a more recent animation technique based on describing an object's general behavior, instead of describing its motion at each point in time. As objects become more complicated the effort required to specify their motion increases rapidly. Using traditional animation techniques the details of each motion must be individually specified, and each time the situation or environment changes the motion must be respecified. In behavioral animation the object's responses to certain situations are specified, instead of its motion in a particular environment at a particular time. Thus, the environment can be changed without respecifying the motion. In a virtual environment the modeler does not have complete control over the environment, since the user is free to interact with it in an arbitrary way. Since behavioral animation deals with how objects react to certain situations, this approach is ideal for virtual environments.

In this section the basic issues in behavioral animation are outlined, and some of the techniques that have been used are reviewed. This section concludes with a discussion of a new behavioral animation technique.

Behavior control issues

Traditional animation techniques deal with the motion of a single object in a controlled environment. However, in virtual environments there are multiple moving objects and the modeler does not have complete control over the environment. There are many special control issues that are not involved in the motion of a single object, but are important for motion in a virtual environment. The three key issues are: degrees of freedom, implicit behavior structure, and indirect environment control.

Animating a single object can be difficult if its model has a large number of degrees of freedom. Examples of such models are trees with many branches and human figures with a large number of body segments. An object with a large number of degrees of freedom (object parts that can move) implies a large control problem. The task of animating these objects is more complex than animating one with a simple model, such as a ball or a box. In complex models there is also the problem of coordinating the object's subparts. For example, in a human model the arms should swing while the figure walks. In addition, the swinging of the arms must match the pace of the walk.

In a virtual environment motion control is not simply a matter of scaling up the techniques used for single objects. In this domain, an object's motion is not isolated to the object itself, but dynamically influenced by the environment in a very complex way. A virtual environment includes the environment boundaries, obstacles, static and dynamic objects, and unpredictable events. These additional factors introduce additional degrees of freedom in the modeling and control of object motion. The additional complexity introduced by the environment can be seen from an example of two objects in a simple environment. When two objects are moving together, their motions are influenced by each other. One natural influence is the avoidance behavior between the two objects. While avoiding each other, one object might change course, use a different speed, or perform other evasive actions. One moving object can show interest in the other, or dislike the other object, while it follows, copies, and disturbs the first object's motion. If one of them stretches his/her arms, the other may need to avoid the stretched arms or perform a similar reaction.

When the simple two-object environment is extended to a more general environment with boundaries, obstacles, other static and dynamic objects, and events, the motion of the objects is further constrained by the environment. In this case, the motion is not just affected by the other object, but by the entire contents of the environment. Each of them contributes to the modeling of an object's motion. Avoiding possible collisions with other objects in the environment is the first consideration. This consideration may vary an object's motion whenever the possibility of a collision arises. Besides collision avoidance, many other environmental influences can be modeled, which could cover every pair of moving objects in the environment. All of these influences contribute to the large number of degrees of freedom that must be considered when specifying an object's motion. Techniques for controlling the explosive growth of the control space are required.

An explicit structure is used to model the physical connections between the subparts of a single object's body. Realistic motion can easily be produced if such a structure is found. Examples of this structure are the tree-like structure of articulated human figures, and the muscle groups used in facial expression animation. With an explicit structure, a single object's motion, even if it has a large number of degrees of freedom, can be easily controlled. Structuring an object's motion is one way of limiting the growth of the control problem.

When an object is placed in an environment, the object's motion is not only affected by its own model, but also by the surrounding environment. However, structures for modeling environmental influences on the dynamic behavior of an object have not been used in computer animation or virtual environments. Instead, a predefined sequence of motions is used for animating the object. The sequence exactly specifies the behavior of an object at every time step and every location along a predefined path. The animation is produced from one action to the next, and from one object to the next, with each motion produced in its own control space. Essentially, the same control mechanism used for a single object's motion is used for producing the motion of a collection of objects.

Behavioral animation tries to avoid these problems by concentrating on the behavior or response of the object, instead of its detailed motion in a particular situation. Dividing the motion into behaviors provides a way of modularizing the motion specification, which is one way of controlling its complexity. Also interactions between behaviors can handle the cases of complex motions and interactions between objects.

Previous approaches

Several approaches have been proposed for behavioral animation. These approaches are: the sensor-effector approach, the rule-based approach, and the predefined environment approach.

The *sensor-effector* approach (Braitenberg, 1984; Travers, 1988; Wilhelms and Skinner, 1989) is one of the first approaches to behavior specification. This approach uses three control components: sensors, effectors, and a neural network between the sensors and effectors. An object's motion in an environment is based on how the environment is sensed and how the sensed information is processed through the neural network. The output signals from the network are used to trigger various effectors, which produce the object's motion. This approach essentially simulates the way humans and animals normally perform in the real world.

The *rule-based* approach (Coderre, 1988; Reynolds, 1987) is another solution to the problem of behavior specification. As with the sensor-effector approach, this approach uses input and output components, taking the sensed information as its inputs and motor controls as its outputs. Between the inputs and outputs, a set of behavioral rules is used to map from the sensors to the motors, instead of the neural network used in the sensor-effector approach. Behavioral rules are used to determine the proper motion, such as when and what actions should be produced. Rule selection can be represented by a decision tree, where each branch contributes one control alternative. The alternative branches rank the order of importance for selecting a particular motion, depending on the weights and thresholds that are used by the behavior rules.

Another approach to solving the problem of behavior animation is based on the use of a predefined environment (Ridsdale, 1988). Since the environment is known, the motion behavior in the environment can be carefully planned. One typical application of this approach is to select one optimal path in the environment, either the shortest path or the path using minimal energy for the moving object. This minimal path is derived from all the alternatives, which are precomputed in a visibility graph, starting from an initial position in the environment. This approach is mainly used in applications with static environments.

The use of the sensor-effector approach depends on an understanding of real neural networks. Our understanding of these connections has progressed over the years, but it is still an open research problem. Behavior rules appear to be an easier way to specify the motion. However, the use of rules is less efficient due to the rule-interpreting process, which travels through the decision tree. For dynamic environments, this inefficiency becomes worse since a large decision tree must be built to cover all the possibilities in the environment. The motion produced by the predefined environment approach depends on a static environment. If the environment is changed in any way the entire motion computation process must be repeated.

A new behavior specification technique

To effectively address the problem of behavior animation, a new behavior control scheme has been developed. This scheme is based on constructing a set of primitive behaviors for each object, and a set of structuring mechanisms for organizing the primitives into motion hierarchies that produce complex behaviors.

Each primitive behavior describes one environmental influence on the motion(s) of an object. There are many environmental influences that could be imposed on an object's motion. These influences include the environment's boundaries, obstacles, static and dynamic objects, and events.

An object's primitive behaviors are based on object-to-object influences. Each of them models one interaction between two objects, one representing the source and the other responding to the source. A *source* object can be eithera static or dynamic object in the environment, while a *responder* object is a dynamic object that responds to the stimulus presented by the source object. The source and responder objects in a behavior primitive could be the same object. In this case the object is influenced by itself. Consider a room environment with chairs and a dancer. Here, the dancer is the only responder object and the room boundaries, chairs as well as the dancer can be source objects that influence the dancer's motion in the room.

The influence from a source object to a responder object is described by an enabling condition and a responsive behavior. An *enabling condition* is one or more properties sensed from the source by the responder. Examples of enabling conditions are an object's color, an object's size, the distance to another object, whether an object is in sight, and an object's motivation. A *responsive behavior* is the motion that occurs when the enabling condition becomes true. It is a primitive response produced by the responder object. Examples of responsive behaviors for a human model are a walking step, a dance step, a body turn, a head turn, an arm raise, a side step, and a pause.

The behavior primitives are called *relations*. A relation is in one of the four states: $S_{potential}$, S_{active}, $S_{suspended}$, $S_{terminated}$. These four states indicate the ready, active, blocked, or terminated state of a relation. For the formal definition of relation and its theoretical foundation see Sun (1992).

A relation is specified using a frame-like syntax consisting of both local control properties for the relation and the control body that produces the response. The local control properties of a relation include the source and responder names, relation name, enabling condition, initial state, response duration, and parameters for controlling the response strength. The control body of a relation describes the response that the responder performs. This part of the frame is modeled using a procedural language.

The responses of several relations can be combined to produce more complex behaviors. A relation only performs its response while it is in the active state. During a motion, a relation's state can be dynamically changed from one state to another based on its enabling condition, interactions with other relations, or other structuring mechanisms imposed on the relation.

While a relation is in the potential state, it can be automatically triggered to the active state when its enabling condition becomes true. An active relation continues performing its behavior until its enabling condition becomes false or its response duration is over. At that time, the relation's state is automatically changed to potential. This automatic triggering mechanism determines the independent dynamic behavior of the relations. One example of this is the "avoid_chair" relation, whose source is a chair and the responder is a dancer. A distance threshold between the two objects forms the enabling condition that triggers an avoiding behavior in the dancer, such as a body turn. This avoiding behavior is used whenever the dancer is too close to the chair.

A relation only describes a simple behavior in an environment. To model global, dynamic, and complex environmental behaviors, additional structuring mechanisms are used to organize the activities of the relations. Four mechanisms are used, which are: selective control, interactive control, pattern control, and sequential control. Most of these control mechanisms are implemented by changing the states of relations.

The *selective control* mechanism is used to select the relations used in the current environment and behavior. There are two selective controls: environment and behavior. In the first case, if the environment contains both the source and responder objects the relation is included in the current motion. This process can be automated by the animation system. In the second case, the user selects the relations used in the animation. A relation is selected if it is applicable in the current behavior, which can be done by the user through an interactive interface. Once a relation is selected, it can be placed in either the potential or the suspended state.

After selection, an interactive control mechanism is used to specify the possible interactions among the relations. Any active relation can issue a state control to another relation causing it to change its state. There are four types of state controls that can be issued by an active relation. These are: activating, potentializing, suspending, and terminating. An *activating* control is issued when the behavior of the called relation assists in the current behavior. A *potentializing* control is issued to allow the called relation to actively participating in the motion when its enabling condition becomes true. A *suspending* control is issued to temporarily prohibit the active use of the called relation. This control explicitly produces a priority order amongst the relations. A *terminating* control is issued when the called relation is no longer usable in the current application. These four types of state control can be either textually specified in the relation's definition or interactively specified through the animation system.

The pattern control mechanism is used to group relations into pattern structures. Two patterning structures are used, which are: time reference and relation reference. *Time reference* structures a group of relations to take part in the motion at a particular point in time. When this time is reached all the relations in the group are switched to the potential state. Similarly, *relation reference* structures a group of relations with respect to another relation. When this relation becomes active all the relations in the group are switched to the potential state. Both structures simulate potential grouping behavior relative to some context. Whether these relations will actively perform their actions depends on their enabling conditions. If these relations are modeled with the default true enabling condition, they will be directly changed to the active state when the pattern becomes active.

The sequential control mechanism is the fourth structuring mechanism, and it is used for modeling sequential behaviors. This control level is based on the behavior patterns produced in the previous level. These patterns are composite units that can be individually selected, ordered, and scheduled in a sequential time space. The ordering control determines the order of the selected patterns in a sequential behavior. The scheduling control adjusts the duration of each pattern in the order. A looping control facility can be used to repeat several patterns, or a list of ordered patterns can call another list to form a branched control structure.

An interactive control environment for specifying the sequential and other relation control structures has been produced. Details of this approach are presented in Sun and Green (1991, 1993) and this model is used as the basis for the OML language that is now part of the MR toolkit.

EXAMPLE—SLINK WORLD

A simple example is presented in this section to illustrate how the above techniques are used in practice. Slink world is a simple environment that is inhabited by one or more creatures that are called slinks (simple linked creatures). A slink has a large yellow face, a cylindrical segment for its body, and cylindrical segments for its arms and legs. Each slink has its own personality, which is reflected in the shape of its mouth. An upturned mouth indicates a happy personality, a downturned mouth indicates a grumpy personality and a horizontal mouth indicates a "don't care" personality. Slink world has a gently rolling terrain with several pine trees. Slink world also has a simple weather system consisting of a prevailing wind that blows in one direction over the environment at ground level. When it reaches the end of the environment it moves upwards and travels in the opposite direction at the top of the environment. Again when the wind reaches the end of the environment it blows down to ground level. A collection of flakes (triangle-shaped objects) continuously travel in the wind system. Most of the features of this environment can be specified by the user through the use of an environment description file. This file specifies the properties of all the slinks in the environment, the nature of the terrain, the positions of the pine trees, and other parameters of the environment. Figure 3-7 shows a static image of the environment.

In this environment the positive z axis is the up direction. The ground level is represented by a height map, a two-dimensional array that gives the z value

Figure 3-7 Slink world.

for certain values of the x and y coordinates. The user specifies the size of the environment in meters and the size of the height map. The distance between adjacent entries in the map can be computed from this information. Linear interpolation is used to compute the z values between entries in the array. Increasing this size of the height map improves the visual quality of the environment (and the number of polygons to be displayed), but also increases the amount of memory and display time required. The gently rolling terrain is generated by a function with two sine terms. The first term is a function of the x coordinate and the second term is a function of the y coordinate. The amplitude and frequency of the sine functions are user-specified parameters. This function is used to generate the values stored in the height map. Whenever the user or one of the slinks moves they follow the terrain, that is their feet are at the z value specified by the height map.

A procedural model is used to generate the pine trees. The environment description file contains the (x,y) position of each tree and its height. The procedural model first computes the z value at the (x,y) position, and this value becomes the base of the tree. A cylindrical segment is used as the tree trunk. The height of the tree is used to compute the number of branching levels. Each branching level consists of a number of branches evenly spaced around the circumference of the trunk. The number and length of each branch depend upon the relative height of the branching level. Each branch is a green cylindrical segment that slopes downward.

A volume representation is used for the wind. This representation is based on dividing the 3D space for the environment into a large number of cubical subvolumes. Each subvolume has its own wind velocity that is represented by a 3D vector. A 3D array is used to represent the entire value, with each array entry storing the velocity vector for one of the cubical subvolumes. The (x,y,z) coordinates of a point are used to index into this array to determine the wind velocity at that point. The contents of this array are pre-computed at the start of each program run. The size of this array determines the quality of the simulation. A large array will produce good flake motion, but will require extra memory and a longer time to generate.

The wind field is used to generate the flake's motion. Each flake uses a simple physical model based on its current position, velocity and acceleration. The current position of the flake is used to determine the wind velocity operating on it. The wind velocity, multiplied by a constant, is added to the flake's acceleration. A drag force, based on the flake's velocity, is also computed and added to its acceleration. The acceleration multiplied by the current time step is added to the flake's current velocity to give its new velocity. Similarly, the velocity multiplied by the current time step is added to the flake's position to give its new position. If a flake is blown out of the environment's volume it is placed at a random position in the environment. The number of flakes determines the visual complexity and interest of this effect. A minimum of 50 to 100 flakes is required to produce an interesting effect. Even though the motion of each flake is quite simple, computing the motion of a large number of flakes can consume a significant amount of time.

A hierarchical model is used to represent each of the slinks. This model is shown in Figure 3-7. The hierarchical model is generated procedurally given the height and mood of the slink. Since a hierarchical model is used, the position of the slink's arms and legs can easily be changed without affecting the rest of the model. This is used for the slink's walking behavior.

The main part of the slink model is its behavior. The slink's behavior can be divided into three parts, its autonomous motion, its reaction to other objects in the environment and its reaction to the user. The autonomous behavior forms the basis for the other behaviors. The basic autonomous behavior is the slink's walking motion. This is done by modifying the rotation matrices at the top of the left and right legs. A simple periodic function is used to generate the joint angles, such that the left and right legs are always 180 degrees out of phase. The autonomous motion also follows the terrain so the slink's feet are always on the ground. Finally, this part of the slink's behavior keeps the slink within the environment. When a slink approaches the edge of the environment, its direction of motion is changed so it will remain in the environment.

The main reaction that the slink has to other objects in the environment is avoiding collisions. There are two types of objects in the environment, static objects and dynamic objects. The main static objects are the trees, while the main dynamic objects are the other slinks. Collision avoidance with static objects is quite simple, since their position is a known constant. When the slink approaches a static object, it simply changes its direction of motion to avoid a collision with that object. In the case of dynamic objects the situation is not quite as simple, since the other object is also in motion. There are two approaches that could be used, one is to attempt to predict the motion of the other object and determine if there will be a collision in the next time step. If this is the case, the slink will change its direction of motion. This strategy does not always work, since both slinks could change their directions of motion in such a way that they collide with each other in the current time step. Another approach is to use a larger radius in collision detection. A slink will avoid any dynamic object that is closer than two time steps (for example). This is a more conservative strategy, but it will avoid collisions most of the time. Problems occur when there are more than two slinks in a small area. In this case avoiding a collision between two of the slinks may cause a collision with a third slink. These situations are difficult to detect, and for real-time simulations the detection computations are usually too expensive.

The most complicated part of the slink's behavior is its reaction to the user. This reaction is determined by the user's actions and the slink's mood. Without any user action the slink will be naturally curious about the user. The slink will periodically determine the position of the user and move in that direction for a short period of time. The frequency of these actions depends upon the slink's mood. If the slink is in a good mood it will frequently check the user's position and thus has a tendency to follow the user. On the other hand, if the slink has a bad mood the checks will be infrequent and the slink will tend to stay away from the user. All the behaviors at this level are overridden by the lower-level behaviors. For example, if a slink is following the user, it will interrupt this motion if there is a potential collision with another object.

The slink can respond to the user's actions in several ways. If the user makes a friendly gesture to the slink, such as a waving motion, the slink will tend to come closer to the user. On the other hand, if the user makes an aggressive gesture, such as a fist, the slink will move away from the user out of fear. The slink's behavior is also determined by the user's walking motion. If the user walks slowly towards the slink, it will stay in its current position and wait for the user to approach it. If the user walks quickly, the slink will be afraid of the user and will try to move away from the user as quickly as possible. A combination of user behaviors will cause a more dramatic response on the part of the slink.

The slink behavior is produced by a collection of relations. Each slink has a small amount of state information that includes the current time step within the walking motion, its current position, current orientation and mood. The slink relations both access and change this information to produce the slink behavior.

The autonomous behavior is produced by two relations, which are called step and boundary. The step relation increments the time step in the walking motion, computes the new leg angles, and updates the position of the slink taking into account the current terrain. The boundary relation determines if the slink is close to the environment boundary and if it is, changes the slink orientation so it moves away from the boundary.

The reaction to the objects in the environment is handled by two relations. The avoid_tree relation avoids collisions with the trees in the environment. A collision is detected by comparing the position of the slink with all the trees in the environment. If this distance is less than a step distance the orientation of the slink is changed to avoid the collision. The avoid_slink relation is used to avoid collisions with other slinks. It compares the position of the slink with the positions of the other slinks in the environment. If this distance is less than a threshold, the orientation of the slink is changed.

The slink's reaction to the user is produced by four relations. The curious relation periodically examines the position of the user and if the slink has a happy mood, points it towards the user. The call relation is activated when the user makes a calling gesture. When this occurs the call relation triggers the curious relation to the active state with a greater than normal strength. As long as the user makes the call gesture this relation will be active and point the slink towards the user. The mad relation becomes active when the user makes a threatening gesture. This relation changes the orientation of the slink so that it is pointing away from the user. The chase relation is active when the user is moving and its response is determined by the user's speed. If the user is moving slowly, the slink turns towards the user and thus starts walking towards the user. If the speed of the user is greater than a certain threshold the slink will become afraid of the user. This is done by changing the orientation of the slink to point away from the user and doubling its walking speed. All the user response relations can be blocked by the other relations. This ensures that the slink does not run into another object while it is responding to the user.

CONCLUSIONS

Some of the common geometrical and behavioral modeling techniques have been presented here. A large number of the geometrical modeling techniques that have been developed in computer graphics can also be used in virtual environments. In adapting these techniques to virtual environments, the modeler must be careful to use those techniques that do not require a large amount of computation time and be careful to structure the geometry so that its behavior can easily be specified.

The behavioral modeling techniques that have been developed in computer graphics do not transfer quite so easily to virtual environments. Most of these techniques have been developed in the context of computer animation, where the animator is in complete control over the environment. In virtual environments this is definitely not the case, since the user is free to move anywhere and can interact with any of the objects in the environment. Behavioral modeling techniques seem to be well suited to virtual environments since they concentrate on how the object behaves and not the details of its motion in a particular animation. This allows the modeler to define the object's behavior in terms of how it reacts to the user and other objects in the environment. More research is needed in the area of behavioral animation and its application to virtual environments.

REFERENCES

Armstrong, W. W. (1979) Recursive solution to the equations of motion of an N-link manipulator, *Proc. Fifth World Congress on the Theory of Machines and Mechanisms*, pp. 1343–6

Armstrong, W. W. and Green, M. W. (1985) The dynamics of articulated rigid bodies for purposes of animation, *Proc. Graphics Interface*, **85**, 407–15

Badler, N. I., Manoochehri, K. H., and Baraff, D. (1986) Multi-dimensional input techniques and articulated figure positioning by multiple constraints, *Proc. of Workshop on Interactive 3D Graphics*, pp. 151–69

Baecker, R. M. (1969) Picture-driven Animation, *Proc. Spring Joint Computer Conf. 34*, AFIPS Press, pp. 273–88

Baraff, D. (1989) Analytical methods for dynamic simulation of non-penetrating rigid bodies, *Computer Graphics*, **23**, 223–32

Barsky, B. (1988) *Computer Graphics and Geometric Modeling Using Beta-splines*, New York: Springer-Verlag

Bartels, R., Beatty, J., and Barsky, B. (1987) *An Introduction to Splines for Use in Computer Graphics and Geometric Modeling*, Los Altos, CA: Morgan Kaugman

Bishop, G. *et al.* (1992) Research directions in virtual environments: report of an NSF invitational workshop, *Computer Graphics*, **26**, 153–77

Braitenberg, V. (1984) *Vehicles: Experiments in Synthetic Psychology*, Cambridge, MA: MIT Press

Coderre, B. (1988) Modeling behavior in petworld, in *Artificial Life*, New York: Addison-Wesley

Csuri, C. (1975) Computer Animation, *Computer Graphics*, **9**, 92–101

Featherstone, R. (1983) The calculation of robot dynamics using articulated-body inertias, *Int. J. Robot. Res.*, **2**, 13–30

Foley, J., van Dam, A., Feiner, S., and Hughes, J. (1990) *Computer Graphics, Principles and Practice*, New York: Addison-Wesley

Fournier, A., Fussell, D., and Carpenter, L. (1982) Computer rendering of stochastic models, *Commun. ACM*, **25**, 371–84

Fuchs, H., Abram, G., and Grant, E. (1983) Near real-time shaded display of rigid objects, *SIGGRAPH 83*, 65–72

Fuchs, H., Kedem, Z., and Naylor, B. (1980) On visible surface generation by *a priori* tree structures, *SIGGRAPH 80*, 124–33

Green, M. (1989) Using dynamics in computer animation: control and solution issues, in *Mechanics, Control, and Animation of Articulated Figures*, N. Badler, B. Barsky and D. Zeltzer (Eds), Cambridge, MA: Morgan-Kaufman

Green, M. and Sun, H. (1988) A language and system for procedural modeling and motion, *IEEE Computer Graphics and Applications*, **8**, 52–64

Hahn, J. (1988) Realistic animation of rigid bodies, *Computer Graphics*, **22**, 299–308

Hanrahan, P. and Sturman, D. (1985) Interaction animation of parameteric models, *Visual Computer*, 260–6

Horowitz, R. (1983) Model reference adaptive control of mechanical manipulators, *Ph.D. Thesis*

Mantyla, M. (1988) *An Introduction to Solid Modeling*, Computer Science Press

Moore, M. and Wilhelms, J. (1988) Collision detection and response for computer-animation, *SIGGRAPH 88*, 289–98

Naylor, B. (1990) Binary space partitioning trees: an alternative representation of polytopes, *CAD*, **22**, 250–2

Parke, F. I. (1982) Parameterized models for facial animation, *Computer Graphics and Applications*, **2**, 61–8

Pars, L. A. (1979) *A Treatise on Analytical Dynamics*, Woodbridge, CT: Ox Bow Press

Reeves, W. (1981) Inbetweening for computer animation utilizing moving point constraints, *SIGGRAPH 81*, 263–9

Reeves, W. (1983) Particle systems—a technique for modeling a class of fuzzy objects, *SIGGRAPH 83*, 359–76

Reeves, W. and Blau, R. (1985) Approximate and probabilistic algorithms for shading and rendering particle systems, *SIGGRAPH 85*, 313–22

Reynolds, C. W. (1978) Computer animation in the world of actors and scripts, *SM Thesis*, Architecture Machine Group, MIT

Reynolds, C. W. (1982) Computer animation with scripts and actors, *Computer Graphics*, **16**, 289–96

Reynolds, C. (1987) Flocks, herds and schools: a distributed behavioral model, *Computer Graphics*, **21**, 25–34

Ridsdale, G. (1988) The director's apprentice: animating figures in a constrained environment, *Ph.D. Thesis*

Smith, A. R. (1984) Plants, fractals, and formal languages, *Computer Graphics*, **18**, 1–10

Sturman, D. (1984) Interactive keyframe animation of 3-D articulated models, *Graphics Interface '84 Proc.*, pp. 35–40

Sun, H. (1992) A relation model for animating adaptive behavior in dynamic environments, *Ph.D. Thesis*, University of Alberta

Sun, H. and Green, M. (1991) A technique for animating natural behavior in complex scenes, *Proc. 1991 Int. Conf. Systems, Man, and Cybernetics*, pp. 1271–7

Sun, H. and Green, M. (1993) The use of relations for motion control in an environment with multiple moving objects, *Graphics Interface '93 Proc.*, 209–18

Thalmann, D. and Magnenat-Thalmann, N. (1984) CINEMIRA: a 3-D computer animation language based on actor and camera data types, *Technical Report, University of Montreal*

Travers, M. (1988) Animal construction kits, in *Artificial Life*, New York: Addison-Wesley

Wells, D. A. (1969) *Lagrangian Dynamics (Shaum's Outline Series)*, New York

Wilhelms, J. (1985) Graphical simulation of the motion of articulated bodies such as humans and robots, with particular emphasis on the use of dynamic analysis, *Doctoral Disertation*, Computer Science Div., University of California

Wilhelms, J. and Skinner, R. (1989) An interactive approach to behavioral control, *Proc. of Graphics Interface '89*, pp. 1–8

Witkin, A. and Kass, M. (1988) Spacetime constraints, *Computer Graphics*, **22**, 159–68

Zeltzer, D. (1982) Motor control techniques for figure animation, *IEEE Computer Graphics and Applications*, **2**, 53–9

4

VEOS: The Virtual Environment Operating Shell

WILLIAM BRICKEN AND GEOFFREY COCO

Computer technology has only recently become advanced enough to solve the problems it creates with its own interface. One solution, virtual reality (VR), immediately raises fundamental issues in both semantics and epistemology.

Broadly, virtual reality is that aspect of reality which people construct from information, a reality which is potentially orthogonal to the reality of mass. Within computer science, VR refers to interaction with computer-generated spatial environments, environments constructed to include and immerse those who enter them.

VR affords non-symbolic experience within a symbolic environment

Since people evolve in a spatial environment, our knowledge skills are anchored to interactions within spatial environments. VR design techniques, such as scientific visualization, map digital information onto spatial concepts. When our senses are immersed in stimuli from the virtual world, our minds construct a closure to create the experience of inclusion. *Participant inclusion is* the defining characteristic of VR. (Participation within information is often called *immersion.*) Inclusion is measured by the degree of *presence* a participant experiences in a virtual environment.

We currently use computers as symbol processors, interacting with them through a layer of symbolic mediation. The computer user, just like the reader of books, must provide cognitive effort to convert the screen's representations into the user's meanings. VR systems, in contrast, provide interface tools which support natural behavior as input and direct perceptual recognition of output. The idea is to access digital data in the form most easy for our comprehension; this generally implies using representations that look and feel like the thing they represent. A physical pendulum, for example, might be represented by an accurate three-dimensional digital model of a pendulum which supports direct spatial interaction and dynamically behaves as would an actual pendulum.

Immersive environments redefine the relationship between experience and representation, in effect eliminating the syntax-semantics barrier. Reading, writing, and arithmetic are cast out of the computer interface, replaced by direct, non-symbolic environmental experience.

Before we can explore the deeper issues of experience in virtual environments, we must develop an infrastructure of hardware and software to support "tricking the senses"[1] into believing that representation is reality. The VEOS project was designed to provide a rapid prototyping infrastructure for exploring virtual environments. In contrast to basic research in computer science, this project attempted to synthesize known techniques into a unique functionality, to redefine the concept of interface by providing interaction with environments rather than with symbolic codes.

This chapter presents some of the operating systems techniques and software tools which guided the early development of virtual reality systems at the University of Washington Human Interface Technology Lab. We first describe the structure of a VR system. This structure is actually the design basis of the Virtual Environment Operating Shell (VEOS) developed at HITL. Next, the goals of the VEOS project are presented and the two central components of VEOS, the Kernel and FERN, are described. The chapter concludes with a description of entity-based programming and of the applications developed at HITL which use VEOS. As is characteristic of VR projects, this chapter contains multiple perspectives, approaching description of VEOS as a computational architecture, as a biological/environmental modeling theory, as an integrated software prototype, as a systems-oriented programming language, as an exploration of innovative techniques, and as a practical tool.

COMPONENT TECHNOLOGIES

Computer-based VR consists of a suite of four interrelated technologies:

Behavior transducers: hardware interface devices
Inclusive computation: software infrastructure
Intentional psychology: interaction techniques and biological constraints
Experiential design: functionally aesthetic environments.

Behavior transducers map physically natural behavior onto digital streams. *Natural behavior* in its simplest form is what two-year-olds do: point, grab, issue single-word commands, look around, toddle around. Transducers work in both directions, from physical behavior to digital information (sensors such as position trackers and voice recognition) and from digital drivers to subjective experience (displays such as stereographic monitors and motion platforms).

Inclusive computation provides tools for construction of, management of, and interaction with inclusive digital environments. Inclusive software techniques include pattern-matching, coordination languages, spatial parallelism, distributed resource management, autonomous processes, inconsistency maintenance, behavioral entities and active environments.

Intentional psychology seeks to integrate information, cognition and behavior. It explores structured environments that respond to expectation as well as action, that reflect imagination as well as formal specifications. It defines the interface between the digital world and ourselves: our sensations, our perceptions, our cognition, and our intentions. Intentional psychology incorporates physiological models, performance metrics, situated learning, multiple intelligences, sensory cross-mapping, transfer effects, participant uniqueness, satisficing solutions, and choice-centered computation.

Experiential design seeks to unify inclusion and intention, to make the virtual world feel good. The central design issue is to create particular inclusive environments out of the infinite potentia, environments which are fun and functional for a participant. From the perspective of a participant, there is no interface, rather there is a world to create (M. Bricken, 1991). The conceptual tools for experiential design may include wands, embedded narrative, adaptive refinement, individual customization, interactive construction, multiple concurrent interpretations, artificial life, and personal, mezzo and public spaces.

Taxonomies of the component technologies and functionalities of VR systems have only recently begun to develop (Naimark, 1991; Zeltzer, 1992; Robinett, 1992), maturing interest in virtual environments from a pretaxonomic phenomenon to an incipient science. Ellis (1991) identifies the central importance of the environment itself, deconstructing it into content, geometry, and dynamics.

VR unifies a diversity of current computer research topics, providing a uniform metaphor and an integrating agenda. The physical interface devices of VR are similar to those of the teleoperation and telepresence communities. VR software incorporates real-time operating systems, sensor integration, artificial intelligence, and adaptive control. VR worlds provide extended senses, traversal of scale (size-travel), synesthesia, fluid definition of self, super powers, hyper-sensitivities, and metaphysics. VR requires innovative mathematical approaches, including visual programming languages, spatial representations of mathematical abstractions, imaginary logics, void-based axiomatics, and experiential computation. The entirely new interface techniques and software methodologies cross many disciplines, creating new alignments between knowledge and activity.

VR provides the cornerstone of a new discipline: *computer humanities*.

THE STRUCTURE OF A VR SYSTEM

As a technology matures, the demands on the performance of key components increase. In the case of computer technology, we have passed through massive mainframes to personal computers to powerful personal workstations. A growth in complexity of software tasks has accompanied the growth of hardware capabilities. At the interface, we have gone from punch cards to command lines to windows to life-like simulation. Virtual reality applications present the most difficult software performance expectations to date. VR challenges us to synthesize and integrate our knowledge of sensors, databases, modeling, communications, interface, interactivity, autonomy, human physiology, and cognition — and to do it in real-time.

VR software attempts to restructure programming tools from the bottom up, in terms of *spatial, organic models*. The primary task of a virtual environment operating system is to make computation transparent, to empower the participant with *natural interaction*. The technical challenge is to create mediation languages which enforce rigorous mathematical computation while supporting intuitive behavior. VR uses spatial interaction as a mediation tool. The prevalent textual interface of command lines and pull-down menus is replaced by physical behavior within an environment. Language is not excluded, since speech is a natural behavior. Tools are not excluded, since we handle physical tools with natural dexterity. The design goal for natural interaction is simply *direct access to meaning*, interaction not filtered by a layer of textual representation. This implies both eliminating the keyboard as an input device, and minimizing the use of text as output.

Functional architecture

Figure 4-1 presents a functional architecture for a generic VR system; Figure 4-1 is also the architecture of VEOS. The architecture contains three subsystems: transducers, software tools, and computing system. Arrows indicate the direction and type of dataflow. In actual implementations, the operating system is involved with all transactions. Figure 4-1 illustrates direct dataflow paths, hiding the fact that all paths are mediated by the underlying hardware. Participants and computer hardware are shaded with multiple boxes to indicate that the architecture supports any number of active participants and any number of hardware resources.[2] Naturally, transducers and tools are also duplicated for multiple participants.

This functional model, in addition to specifying a practical implementation architecture, provides definition for the essential concepts of VR.

The *behavior and sensory transducing subsystem* (labeled participant, sensors and display) converts natural behavior into digital information and digital information into physical consequence. Sensors convert our actions into binary-encoded data, extending the physical body into the virtual environment with position tracking, voice recognition, gesture interfaces, keyboards and joysticks, midi instruments and bioactivity measurement devices. Displays provide sensory stimuli generated from digital models and tightly coupled to personal expectations, extending the virtual environment into the realm of experience with wide-angle stereo screens, surround projection shells, head-mounted displays, spatial sound generators, motion platforms, olfactory displays, and tactile feedback devices.

The behavior transducing subsystem consists of these three components:

The participant. VR systems are designed to integrate the human participant into the computational process. The participant interprets the virtual world perceptually and generates actions physically, providing human transduction of imagination into behavior.

Sensors (input devices). Sensors convert both the natural behavior of the participant and measurements of events occurring in the physical world into

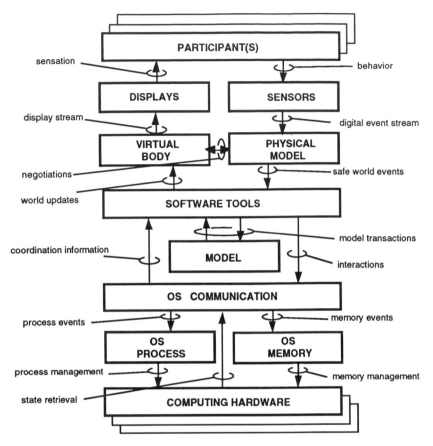

Figure 4-1   VEOS system architecture.

digital streams. They transduce physical measurement into patterned representation.

Displays (output devices). Displays convert the digital model expressed as display stream instructions into subjective sensory information perceived as sensation by the participant. They physically manifest representation.

The *virtual toolkit subsystem* (the physical model, virtual body, software tools and model) coordinates display and computational hardware, software functions and resources, and world models. It provides a wide range of software tools for construction of and interaction with digital environments, including movement and viewpoint control; object inhabitation; boundary integrity; editors of objects, spaces and abstractions; display, resource and time management; coordination of multiple concurrent participants; and history and statistics accumulation.

The virtual toolkit subsystem consists of four software components:

The *physical model* maps digital input onto a realistic model of the participant and of the physical environment the participant is in. This model is responsible for screening erroneous input data and for assuring that the semantic intent of the input is appropriately mapped into the world database.

The *virtual body* customizes effects in the virtual environment (expressed as digital world events) to the subjective display perspective of the participant.[3] The virtual body is tightly coupled to the physical model of the participant in order to enhance the sensation of presence. Differences between physical input and virtual output, such as lag, contradiction, and error, can be negotiated between these two components of the body model without interacting with the world model. The physical model and the virtual body comprise a *participant system* (Minkoff, 1993).

Virtual world *software tools* program and control the virtual world, and provide techniques for navigation, manipulation, construction, editing, and other forms of participatory interaction. All transactions between the model and the system resources are managed by the tool layer.

The virtual world *model* is a database which stores world state and the static and dynamic attributes of objects within the virtual environment. Software tools access and assert database information through model transactions. During runtime, the database undergoes constant change due to parallel transactions, self-simplification, canonicalization, search-by-sort processes, process demons, and function evaluations. The database is better viewed as a turbulent fluid than as a stable crystal.

The *computational subsystem* (the operating system and hardware) customizes the VR software to a particular machine architecture. Since machine-level architectures often dictate computational efficiency, this subsystem is particularly important for ensuring real-time performance, including update rates, complexity and size of worlds, and responsiveness to participant behavior.

The computational subsystem consists of these components:

The operating system *communications* management (messages and networking) coordinates resources with computation. The intense interactivity of virtual worlds, the plethora of external devices, and the distributed resources of multiple participants combine to place unusual demands on communication models.

The operating system *memory* management (paging and allocation) coordinates data storage and retrieval. Virtual worlds require massive databases, concurrent transactions, multimedia datatypes, and partitioned dataspaces.

The operating system *process* management (threads and tasks) coordinates computational demands. Parallelism and distributed processing are prerequisite to VR systems.

The computational *hardware* provides digital processing specified by the operating system. Machine architectures can provide coarse and fine grain parallelism, homogeneous and heterogeneous distributed networks, and specialized circuitry for real-time performance.

Operating systems also manage input and output transactions from physical sensors and displays. Some data transactions (such as head position sensing used for viewpoint control) benefit from having minimal interaction with the virtual world. Real-time performance can be enhanced by specialized software which directly links the input signal to the output response.[4]

Presence

Presence is the impression of being within the virtual environment. It is the suspension of disbelief which permits us to share the digital manifestation of fantasy. It is a reunion with our physical body while visiting our imagination.

The traditional *user interface* is defined by the boundary between the physical participant and the system behavior transducers. In a conventional computer system, the behavior transducers are the monitor and the keyboard. They are conceptualized as specific tools. The user is an interrupt. In contrast, *participant inclusion* is defined by the boundary between the software model of the participant and the virtual environment. Ideally the transducers are invisible, the participant feels like a local, autonomous agent with a rendered form within an information environment. The degree of presence achieved by the virtual world can be measured by the ease of the subjective shift on the part of the participant from attention to interface to attention to inclusion.

An *interface* is a boundary which both separates and connects. A traditional interface separates us from direct experience while connecting us to a representation of information (the semantics-syntax barrier). The keyboard connects us to a computational environment by separating concept from action, by sifting our intention through a symbolic filter.

Interface provides access to computation by objectifying it. Displays, whether command line, window or desk-top, present tokens which we must interpret through reading. Current multimedia video, sound and animation provide images we can watch and interact with within the two-dimensional space of the monitor. VR provides three-dimensional interaction we can experience.

Conventionally we speak of the "software interface" as if the locale of human–computer interaction were somehow within the software domain. The human interface, the boundary which both separates and connects us, is our skin. *Our bodies are our interface.* VR inclusion accepts the entirety of our bodily interface, internalizing interactivity within an environmental context.

The architectural diagram in Figure 4-2 is composed of three nested inclusions (physical, digital, virtual). The most external is physical reality, the participant's physical body on one edge, the computational physical hardware on the other. All the other components of a VR system (software, language, virtual world) are contained within the physical. Physical reality *pervades* virtual reality.[5] For example, we continue to experience physical gravity while flying around a virtual environment.

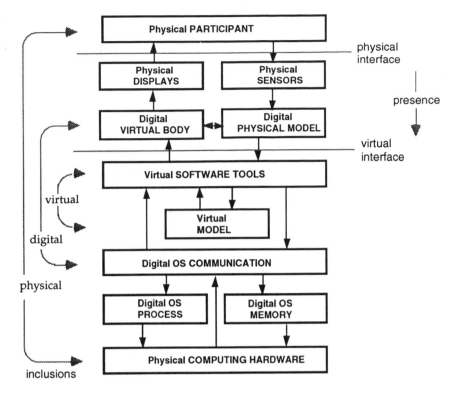

Figure 4-2   Presence and inclusion.

One layer in from the physical edges of the architecture are the software computational systems. A participant interfaces with behavior transducers which generate digital streams. The hardware interfaces with systems software which implements digital computations. Software, the *digital reality*, is contained within physical reality and, in turn, pervades virtual reality.

The innermost components of the architecture, the virtual world tools and model, form the virtual reality itself.[6] Virtual software tools differ from programming software tools in that the virtual tools provide a non-symbolic look-and-feel. Virtual reality seamlessly mixes a computational model of the participant with an anthropomorphized model of information. In order to achieve this mixing, both physical and digital must pervade the virtual.

Humans have the ability to focus attention on physicality, using our bodies, and on virtuality, using our minds. In the VR architecture, the participant can focus on the physical/digital interface (watching the physical display) and on the digital/virtual interface (watching the virtual world). Although the digital is necessary for both focal points, VR systems make digital mediation transparent by placing the physical in direct correspondence with the virtual.

As an analogy, consider a visit to an orbiting space station. We leave the physically familiar Earth, transit through a domain which is not conducive to human inhabitation (empty space), to arrive at an artificial domain (the space station) which is similar enough to Earth to permit inhabitation. Although the

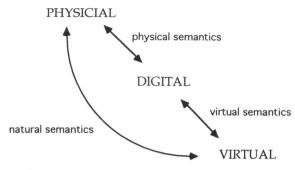

Figure 4-3 Types of semantics.

space station exists in empty space, it still supports a limited subset of natural behavior. In this analogy the Earth is, of course, physical reality. Empty space is digital reality, the space station is virtual reality. A virtual environment operating system functions to provide an inhabitable zone in the depths of symbolic space. Like the space station, virtual reality is pervaded by essentially alien territory, by binary encodings transacted as voltage potentials through microscopic gates. Early space stations on the digital frontier were spartan, the natural behavior of early infonauts (i.e., programmers) was limited to interpretation of punch cards and hex dumps. Tomorrow's digital space stations will provide human comfort by shielding us completely from the emptiness of syntactic forms.

Another way to view the architecture of a VR system is in terms of meaning, of semantics (Figure 4-3). A VR system combines two mappings, from physical to digital and from digital to virtual. When a participant points a physical finger, for example, the digital database registers an encoding of pointing. *Physical semantics* is defined by the map between behavior and digital representation. Next, the "pointing" digit stream can be defined to fly the participant's perspective in the virtual environment. *Virtual semantics* is defined by the map between digital representation and perceived effect in the virtual environment. Finally, *natural semantics* is achieved by eliminating our interaction with the intermediate digital syntax. In the example, physical pointing is felt to "cause" virtual flying.

By creating a closed loop between physical behavior and virtual effect, the concepts of digital input and output are essentially eliminated from perception. When natural physical behavior results in natural virtual consequences, without apparent digital mediation, we achieve presence in a new kind of reality, virtual reality. When I knock over my glass, its contents spill. The linkage is direct, natural, and non-symbolic. When I type on my keyboard, I must translate thoughts and feelings through the narrow channel of letters and words. The innovative aspect of VR is to provide, for the first time, natural semantics within a symbolic environment. I can literally spill the image of water from the representation of a glass, and I can do so by the same sweep of my hand.

Natural semantics affords a surprising transformation. By passing through digital syntax twice, we can finesse the constraints of physical reality.[7] Through presence, we can map physical sensations onto imaginary capacities. We can point to fly. Double-crossing the semantics-syntax barrier allows us to *experience imagination*.

Natural semantics can be very different from physical semantics because the virtual body can be any digital form and can enact any codable functionality. The virtual world is a *physical simulation* only when it is severely constrained. We add collision detection constraints to simulate solidity; we add inertial constraints to simulate Newtonian motion. The virtual world itself, without constraint, is one of potential. Indeed, this is the motivation for visiting VR: although pervaded by both the physical and the digital, the virtual is *larger in possibility* than both.[8]

The idea of a natural semantics that can render representation irrelevant (at least to the interface) deeply impacts the intellectual basis of our culture by questioning the nature of knowledge and representation and by providing a route to unify the humanities and the sciences. The formal theory of VR requires a reconciliation of digital representation with human experience, a reconstruction of the idea of meaning.

THE VIRTUAL ENVIRONMENT OPERATING SHELL (VEOS)

The Virtual Environment Operating Shell (VEOS) is a software suite operating within a distributed UNIX environment that provides a tightly integrated computing model for data, processes, and communication. VEOS was designed from scratch to provide a comprehensive and unified management facility for generation of, interaction with, and maintenance of virtual environments. It provides an infrastructure for implementation and an extensible environment for prototyping distributed VR applications.

VEOS is platform independent, and has been extensively tested on the DEC 5000, Sun 4, and Silicon Graphics VGX and Indigo platforms. The programmer's interface to VEOS is XLISP 2.1, written for public domain by David Betz. XLISP provides programmable control of all aspects of the operating shell. The underlying C implementation is also completely accessible.

Within VEOS, the *Kernel* manages processes, memory, and communication on a single hardware processor. *FERN* manages task decomposition on each node and distributed computing across nodes. FERN also provides basic functions for entity-based modeling. *SensorLib* provides a library of device drivers. The *Imager* provides graphic output. Only the VEOS Kernel and FERN are discussed in this chapter.

Other systems built at HITL enhance the performance and functionality of the VEOS core. *Mercury* is a participant system which optimizes interactive performance. *UM* is the generalized mapper which provides a simple graph-based interface for constructing arbitrary relations between input signals, state information, and output. The *Wand* is a hand-held interactivity device which allows the participant to identify, move, and change the attributes of virtual objects.

We first provide an overview of related work and the design philosophy for the VEOS architecture. Then we present the central components of VEOS: the Kernel, FERN, and entities. The chapter closes with a description of some applications built using VEOS. For a deeper discussion of the programming and operating system issues associated with VEOS, see Coco (1993). In contrast to previous sections which discussed interface and architectural theory, this section addresses issues of software design and implementation.

VR software systems

Virtual reality software rests upon a firm foundation built by the computer industry over the last several decades. However, the actual demands of a VR system (real-time distributed, multimedia, multiparticipant, multisensory environments) provide such unique performance requirements that little research exists to date that is directly relevant to whole VR systems. Instead, the first generation of VR systems have been *assembled* from many relevant component technologies available in published academic research and in newer commercial products.[9]

The challenge, then, for the design and implementation of VR software is to select and integrate appropriate technologies across several areas of computational research (dynamic databases, real-time operating systems, three-dimensional modeling, real-time graphics, multisensory input and display devices, fly-through simulators, video games, etc.). We describe several related software technologies that have contributed to the decisions made within the VEOS project.

As yet, relatively few turnkey VR systems exist, and of those most are entertainment applications. Notable examples are the multiparticipant interactive games such as LucasArt's Habitat™, W Industries arcade game system, Battletech video arcades, and Network Spector™ for home computers. Virtus Walkthrough™ is one of the first VR design systems.

Architectures for virtual reality systems have been studied recently by several commercial (Blanchard et al., 1990; VPL, 1991; Grimsdale, 1991; Appino et al., 1992) and university groups (Zeltzer et al., 1989; Bricken, 1990; Green et al., 1991; Pezely et al., 1992; Zyda et al., 1992; West et al., 1992; Grossweiler et al., 1993).

Other than at the University of Washington, significant research programs that have developed entire VR systems exist at the University of North Carolina at Chapel Hill (Holloway et al., 1992), MIT (Zeltzer et al., 1989), University of Illinois at Chicago (Cruz-Neira et al., 1992), University of Central Florida (Blau et al., 1992), Columbia University (Feiner et al., 1992), NASA Ames (Wenzel et al., 1990; Fisher et al., 1991; Bryson et al., 1992), and within many large corporations such as Boeing, Lockheed, IBM, Sun, Ford, and AT&T.[10]

More comprehensive overviews have been published for VR research directions (Bishop et al., 1992), for VR software (Zyda et al., 1993), for system architectures (Appino et al., 1992), for operating systems (Coco, 1993), and for participant systems (Minkoff, 1993). HITL has collected an extensive bibliography on virtual interface technology (Emerson, 1993).

VR development systems can be grouped into *tool kits* for programmers and *integrated software* for novice to expert computer users. Of course some kits, such as 3D modeling software packages, have aspects of integrated systems. Similarly, some integrated systems require forms of scripting (i.e. programming) at one point or another.

Toolkits

The MR Toolkit was developed by academic researchers at the University of Alberta for building virtual environments and other 3D user interfaces (Green *et al.*, 1991). The toolkit takes the form of subroutine libraries which provide common VR services such as tracking, geometry management, process and data distribution, performance analysis, and interaction. The MR Toolkit meets several of the design goals of VEOS, such as modularity, portability and support for distributed computing. MR, however, does not strongly emphasize rapid prototyping; MR programmers use the compiled languages C, C++, and FORTRAN.

Researchers at the University of North Carolina at Chapel Hill have created a similar toolkit called VLib. VLib is a suite of libraries that handle tracking, rigid geometry transformations and 3D rendering. Like MR, VLib is a programmer's library of C or C++ routines which address the low-level functionality required to support high-level interfaces (Robinett and Holloway, 1992).

Sense8, a small company based in Northern California, produces an extensive C language software library called WorldToolKit^{TM} which can be purchased with 3D rendering and texture acceleration hardware. This library supplies functions for sensor input, world interaction and navigation, editing object attributes, dynamics, and rendering. The single loop simulation model used in WorldToolKit is a standard approach which sequentially reads sensors, updates the world, and generates output graphics. This accumulates latencies linearly, in effect forcing the performance of the virtual body into a co-dependency with a potentially complex surrounding environment.

Silicon Graphics, an industry leader in high-end 3D graphics hardware, has recently released the *Performer* software library which augments the graphics language GL. Performer was designed specifically for interactive graphics and VR applications on SGI platforms. Autodesk, a leading CAD company which began VR product research in 1988, has recently released the Cyberspace Developer's Kit, a C++ object library which provides complete VR software functionality and links tightly to AutoCAD.

Integrated systems

When the VEOS project began in 1990, VPL Research, Inc. manufactured RB2^{TM}, the first commercially available integrated VR system (Blanchard *et al.*, 1990; VPL, 1991). At the time, RB2 supported a composite software suite which coordinated 3D modeling on a Macintosh, real-time stereo image generation on two Silicon Graphics workstations, head and hand tracking using proprietary devices, dynamics and interaction on the Macintosh, and runtime communication over Ethernet. The graphics processing speed of the Macintosh created a severe bottleneck for this system. VEOS architects had considerable design experience with the VPL system; its pioneering presence in the marketplace helped define many design issues which later systems would improve.

Division, a British company, manufactures VR stations and software. Division's ProVision™ VR station is based on a transputer ring and through the aid of a remote PC controller runs dVS, a director/actors process model (Grimsdale, 1991). Each participant resides on one station; stations are networked for multiparticipant environments. Although the dVS model of process and data distribution is a strong design for transputers, it is not evident that the same approaches apply to workstation LANs, the target for the VEOS project.

Perhaps the most significant distributed immersive simulation systems today are the military multiparticipant tank combat simulator, SIMNET (Blau *et al.*, 1992) and the advanced military VR simulation system, NPSNET (Zyda *et al.*, 1992), developed at the Naval Postgraduate School.

VEOS design philosophy

The negotiation between theory and implementation is often delicate. Theory pays little attention to the practical limitations imposed by specific machine architectures and by cost-effective computation. Implementation often must abandon rigor and formality in favor of making it work. In sailing the digital ocean, theory provides the steerage, implementation provides the wind.

The characteristics of the virtual world impose several design considerations and performance requirements on a VR system. The design of VEOS reflects multiple objectives, many practical constraints, and some compromises (Bricken, 1992a).

The dominant design decision for VEOS was to provide broad and flexible capabilities. The mathematical ideals include simplicity (a small number of independent primitives), integration (all primitives are composable), and expressability (primitives and compositions represent all programming domains) (Coco, 1993).

As a research vehicle, VEOS emphasizes functionality at the expense of performance. Premature optimization is a common source of difficulty in software research. So our efforts were directed first towards demonstrating that a thing can be done at all, then towards demonstrating how well we could do it. Since a research prototype must prepare for the future, VEOS is designed to be as generic as possible; it places very little mechanism in the way of exploring diverse and unexpected design options. It is possible to easily replicate procedural, declarative, functional, and object-oriented programming styles within the VEOS pattern-matching computing framework.

Naturally, the VEOS project has passed through several phases over its three years of development. VEOS 2.2 has the desired conceptual structure, but quickly becomes inefficient (relative to a 30 frame-per-second update rate) when the number of active nodes grows beyond a dozen (Coco and Lion, 1992). VEOS 3.0 emphasizes performance.

Table 4-1 VEOS practical design decisions.

Research prototype, 5–10 years ahead of the marketplace
Functional rather than efficient
Rapidly reconfigurable
Synthesis of known software technologies
Incorporates commercially available software when possible

VR is characterized by a rapid generation of applications ideas; it is the potential of VR that people find exciting. However, complex VR systems take too much time to reconfigure. VEOS was designed for rapid prototyping. The VEOS interface is interactive, so that a programmer can enter a new command or world state at the terminal, and on the next frame update the virtual world displays that change. VR systems must avoid hardwired configurations, because a participant in the virtual world is free to engage in almost any behavior. For this reason, VEOS is reactive, it permits the world to respond immediately to the participant (and to the programmer).

The broad-bandwidth display and the multisensory interaction of VR systems create severe demands on sensor integration. Visual, audio, tactile, and kinesthetic displays require the VR database to handle multiple data formats and massive data transactions. Position sensors, voice recognition, and high-dimensional input devices overload traditional serial input ports. An integrated hardware architecture for VR should incorporate asynchronous communication between dedicated device processors in a distributed computational environment.

When more than one person inhabits a virtual world, the perspective of each participant is different. This can be reflected by different views on the same graphical database. But in the virtual world, multiple participants can have divergent models embodied in divergent databases as well. Each participant can occupy a unique, personalized world, sharing the public database partition and not sharing private database partitions.

With the concept of entities, VEOS extends programming metaphors to include first-class environments, biological models, and systems-oriented programming. A programming metaphor is a way to think about and organize symbolic computation. The biological/environmental metaphor introduced in VEOS originates from the artificial life community (Langton, 1988; Meyer and Wilson, 1991; Varela and Bourgine, 1992); it is a preliminary step toward

Table 4-2 VEOS functionality.

General computing model
Interactive rapid prototyping
Coordination between distributed, heterogeneous resources
Parallel decomposition of worlds (modularity)
Multiple participants
Biological/environmental modeling

providing a programming language for modeling autonomous systems within an inclusive environment (Varela, 1979; Maturana and Varela, 1987).

The VEOS kernel

The VEOS Kernel is a significant effort to provide transparent low-level database, process, and communications management for arbitrary sensor suites, software resources, and virtual world designs. The Kernel facilitates the VR paradigm shift by taking care of operating system details without restricting the functionality of the virtual world. The Kernel is implemented as three tightly integrated components:

SHELL manages node initialization, linkages, and the LISP interface.
TALK manages internode communications.
NANCY manages the distributed pattern-driven database.

The fundamental unit of organization in the Kernel is the *node*. Each node corresponds to exactly one UNIX process. Nodes map to UNIX processors which ideally map directly to workstation processors.

Nodes running the VEOS Kernel provide a substrate for distributed computing. Collections of nodes form a distributed system which is managed by a fourth component of the VEOS system, FERN. FERN manages sets of uniprocessors (for example, local area networks of workstations) as pools of nodes.

The VEOS programming model is based on entities. An *entity* is a coupled collection of data, functionality, and resources, which is programmed using a biological/environmental metaphor. Each entity within the virtual world is modular and self-contained, each entity can function independently and autonomously.

In VEOS, everything is an entity (the environment, the participant, hardware devices, software programs, and all objects within the virtual world). Entities provide database modularity, localization of scoping, and task decomposition. All entities are organizationally identical. Only their structure, their internal detail, differs. This means that a designer needs only one metaphor, the entity, for developing all aspects of the world. Changing the graphical image, or the behavioral rules, or even the attached sensors, is a modular activity. We based the entity concept on distributed object models (Jul *et al.*, 1988).

Entities are multiplexed processes on a single node. As well as managing nodes, FERN also manages sets of entities, providing a model of lightweight processing and data partitioning. From the perspective of entity-based programming, the VEOS Kernel is a transparent set of management utilities.

The SHELL is the administrator of the VEOS Kernel. It dispatches initializations, handles interrupts, manages memory, and performs general housekeeping. There is one SHELL program for each node in the distributed computing system. The programmer interface to the SHELL is the LISP programming language, augmented with specialized Kernel functions for database and communications management. LISP permits user configurability of the VEOS environment and all associated functions. LISP can also be seen as a rapid prototyping extension to the native VEOS services.

TALK provides internode communication, relying on common UNIX operating system calls for message passing. It connects UNIX processes which are distributed over networks of workstations into a virtual multiprocessor. TALK is the sole mechanism for internode communication. Message passing is the only kind of entity communication supported by TALK, but, depending on context, this mechanism can be configured to behave like shared memory, direct linkage, function evaluation and other communication regimes.

TALK uses two simple point-to-point message-passing primitives, *send* and *receive*. It uses the LISP functions *throw* and *catch* for process sharing on a single node. Messages are transmitted asynchronously and reliably, whether or not the receiving node is waiting. The sending node can transmit a message and then continue processing. The programmer, however, can elect to block the sending node until a reply, or handshake, is received from the message destination. Similarly, the receiving node can be programmed to accept messages at its own discretion, asynchronously and nonblocking, or it can be programmed to react in a coupled, synchronous mode.

An important aspect of VEOS is consistency of data format and programming metaphor. The structure of messages handled by TALK is the same as the structure of the data handled by the database. The VEOS database uses a communication model which partitions communication between processes from the computational threads within a process (Gelertner and Carriero, 1992). Database transactions are expressed in a pattern-directed language.

Pattern-directed data transactions

NANCY, the database transaction manager, provides a content addressable database accessible through pattern-matching. The database supports local, asynchronous parallel processes, a desirable quality for complex, concurrent, interactive systems. NANCY is a variant of the Linda *parallel database model* to manage the coordination of interprocess communication (Arango *et al.*, 1990). In Linda-like languages, communication and processing are independent, relieving the programmer from having to choreograph interaction between multiple processes. Linda implementations can be used in conjunction with many other sequential programming languages as a mechanism for interprocess communication and generic task decomposition (Gelertner and Philbin, 1990; Cogent Research, 1990; Torque Systems, 1992).

The Linda approach separates programming into two essentially orthogonal components, *computation* and *coordination*. Computation is a singular activity, consisting of one process executing a sequence of instructions one step at a time. Coordination creates an ensemble of these singular processes by establishing a communication model between them. Programming the virtual world is then conceptualized as defining "a collection of asynchronous activities that communicate" (Gelertner and Carriero, 1992).

NANCY adopts a uniform data structure, as do all Linda-like approaches. In Linda, the data structure is a *tuple*, a finite ordered collection of atomic elements of any type. Tuples are a very simple and general mathematical structure. VEOS extends the concept of a tuple by allowing nested tuples, which we call *grouples*.

A *tuple database* consists of a set of tuples. Since VEOS permits nested tuples, the database itself is a single grouple. The additional level of expressibility provided by nested tuples is constrained to have a particular meaning in VEOS. Basically, the nesting structure is mapped onto logical and functional rules, so that the control structure of a program can be expressed simply by the depth of nesting of particular grouples. Nesting implements the concept of containment, so that the contents of a grouple can be interpreted as a set of items, a *grouplespace*.

Grouples provide a consistent and general format for program specification, inter-entity communication and database management. As the VEOS database manager, NANCY performs all grouple manipulations, including creation, destruction, insertion, and copying of grouples. NANCY provides the access functions *put*, *get* and *copy* for interaction with grouplespace. These access functions take patterns as arguments, so that sets of similar grouples can be retrieved with a single call.

Structurally, the database consists of a collection of fragments of information, labeled with unique syntactic identifiers. Collections of related data (such as all of the current properties of Cube-3, for example) can be rapidly assembled by invoking a parallel pattern match on the syntactic label which identifies the sought-after relation. In the example, matching all fragments containing the label "Cube-3" creates the complete entity known as Cube-3. The approach of fragmented data structures permits dynamic, interactive construction of arbitrary entity collections through real-time pattern-matching. Requesting "all-blue-things" creates a transient complex entity consisting of all the things in the current environment that are blue. The blue-things entity is implemented by a dynamic database thread of things with the attribute "color = blue."

Performance of the access functions is improved in VEOS by *association matching*. When a process performs a *get* operation, it can block, waiting for a particular kind of grouple to arrive in its perceptual space (the local grouplespace environment). When a matching grouple is *put* into the grouplespace, usually by a different entity, the waiting process gets the grouple and continues.

Putting and getting data by pattern-matching implements a Match-and-Substitute capability which can be interpreted as the substitution of equals for equals within an algebraic mathematical model. These techniques are borrowed from work in artificial intelligence, and are called *rewrite systems* (Dershowitz and Jouannaud, 1990).

Languages

Rewrite systems include expert systems, declarative languages, and blackboard systems. Although this grouping ignores differences in implementation and programming semantics, there is an important similarity. These systems are variations on the theme of inference or computation over rule-based or equational representations. Declarative languages such as FP, Prolog, lambda calculus, Mathematica, and constraint-based languages all traverse a space of possible outcomes by successively matching variables with values and substituting the constrained value. These languages each display the same trademark attribute: their control structure is *implicit* in the structure of a program's logical dependencies.

The VEOS architects elected to implement a rewrite approach, permitting declarative experimentation with inference and meta-inference control structures. Program control structure is expressed in LISP. As well, this model was also strongly influenced by the language Mathematica (Wolfram, 1988).

LISP encourages prototyping partly because it is an interpreted language, making it quite easy to modify a working program without repeated takedowns and laborious recompilation. Using only a small handful of primitives, LISP is fully expressive, and its syntax is relatively trivial to comprehend. But perhaps the most compelling aspect of LISP for the VEOS project is its program–data equivalence. In other words, program fragments can be manipulated as data and data can be interpreted as executable programs. Program–data equivalence provides an excellent substrate for the active message model (von Eicken *et al.*, 1992). LISP expressions can be encapsulated and passed as messages to other entities (data partitions) and then evaluated in the context of the receiving entity by the awaiting LISP interpreter.

In terms of availability, LISP has been implemented in many contexts: as a production-grade development system (FranzLisp, Inc.), as a proprietary internal data format (AutoLisp from AutoDesk, Inc.), as a native hardware architecture (Symbolics, Inc.), and most relevantly as XLISP, a public domain interpreter (Betz and Almy, 1992). Upon close inspection, the XLISP implementation is finely-tuned, fully extendible, and extremely portable.

FERN: distributed entity management

The initial two years of the VEOS project focused on database management and Kernel processing services. The third year (1992) saw the development of FERN, the management module for distributed nodes and for lightweight processes on each node. With its features of systems orientation, biological modeling and active environments, FERN extends the VEOS Kernel infrastructure to form the entity-based programming model. We first discuss related work which influenced the development of FERN, then we describe entities in detail.

Distributed computation

Multiprocessor computing is a growing trend (Spector, 1982; Li and Hudak, 1989; Kung *et al.*, 1991). VR systems are inherently multicomputer systems, due primarily to the large number of concurrent input devices which do not integrate well in real-time over serial ports. The VEOS architects chose to de-emphasize short-term performance issues of distributed computing, trusting that network-based systems would continue to improve. We chose instead to focus on conceptual issues of semantics and protocols.

The operating systems community has devoted great effort towards providing seamless extensions for distributed virtual memory and multi-processor shared memory. Distributed shared memory implementations are inherently platform specific since they require support from the operating systems kernel and hardware primitives. Although this approach is too low level for the needs of VEOS, many of the same issues resurface at the application level, particularly protocols for coherence.

IVY (Li and Hudak, 1989) was the first successful implementation of distributed virtual memory in the spirit of classical virtual memory. IVY showed that through careful implementation, the same paging mechanisms used in a uniprocessor virtual memory system can be extended across a local area network.

The significance of IVY was twofold. First, it is well known that virtual memory implementations are afforded by the tendency for programs to demonstrate locality of reference. Locality of reference compensates for lost performance due to disk latency. In IVY, locality of reference compensates for network latency as well. In an IVY program, the increase in total physical memory created by adding more nodes sometimes permits a superlinear speed-up over sequential execution. Second, IVY demonstrates the performance and semantic implications of various memory coherence schemes. These coherence protocols, which assure that distributed processes do not develop inconsistent memory structures, are particularly applicable to distributed grouplespace implementations.

MUNIN and MIDWAY (Carter *et al.*, 1992; Bershad *et al.*, 1992) represent deeper explorations into distributed shared memory coherence protocols. Both systems extended their interface languages to support programmer control over the coherence protocols. In MUNIN, programmers always use release consistency but can fine-tune the implementation strategy depending on additional knowledge about the program's memory access behavior. In MIDWAY, on the other hand, the programmer could choose from a set of well-defined coherence protocols of varying strength. The protocols ranged from the strongest, *sequential consistency*, which is equivalent to the degenerate distributed case of one uniprocessor, to the weakest, *entry consistency*, which makes the most assumptions about usage patterns in order to achieve efficiency. Each of these protocols, when used strictly, yields correct deterministic behavior.

Lighweight processes

The VEOS implementation also needed to incorporate some concept of *threads*, cooperating tasks each specified by a sequential program. Threads can be implemented at the user level and often share single address spaces for clearer data-sharing semantics and better context-switch performance. Threads can run in parallel on multiple processors or they can be multiplexed preemptively on one processor, thus allowing n threads to execute on m processors, an essential facility for arbitrary configurations of VEOS entities and available hardware CPUs.

This generic process capability is widely used and has been thoroughly studied and optimized. However, thread implementations normally have system dependencies such as the assembly language of the host CPU, and the operating system kernel interface. Inherent platform specificity combined with the observation that generic threads may be too strong a mechanism for VEOS requirements suggest other lightweight process strategies.

The driving performance issue for VR systems is frame update rate. In many application domains, including all forms of signal processing, this problem is represented in general by a discrete operation (or computation) which should occur repeatedly with a certain frequency. Sometimes, multiple operations are required simultaneously but at different frequencies. The problem of scheduling these discrete operations with the proper interleaving and frequency can be solved with a *cyclic executive* algorithm. The cyclic executive model is the *de facto* process model for many small real-time systems.

The cyclic executive control structure was incorporated into VEOS for two reasons. It provided a process model that can be implemented in a single process, making it highly general and portable. It also directly addressed the cyclic and repetitive nature of the majority of VR computation. This cyclic concept in VEOS is called *frames*.

The design of VEOS was strongly influenced by object-oriented programming. In Smalltalk (Goldberg, 1984), all data and process is discretized into objects. All parameter passing and transfer of control is achieved through messages and methods. VEOS incorporates the Smalltalk ideals of modular processes and hierarchical code derivation (classes), but does not enforce the object-oriented metaphor throughout all aspects of the programming environment. More influential was EMERALD (Jul *et al.*, 1988). The EMERALD system demonstrates that a distributed object system is practical and can achieve good performance through the mechanisms of object mobility and compiler support for tight integration of the runtime model with the programming language. EMERALD implements intelligent system features like location-transparent object communication and automatic object movement for communication or load optimization. As well, EMERALD permits programmer knowledge of object location for fine-tuning applications. EMERALD was especially influential during the later stages of the VEOS project, when it became more apparent how to decompose the computational tasks of VR into entities. In keeping with the ideal of platform independence, however, VEOS steered away from some EMERALD features such as a compiler and tight integration with the network technology.

Entities

An *entity* is a collection of resources which exhibits behavior within an environment. The entity-based model of programming has a long history, growing from formal modeling of complex systems, object-oriented programming, concurrent autonomous processing and artificial life. Agents, actors, and guides all have similarities to entities (Agha, 1988; Oren *et al.*, 1990).

An entity is a stand-alone executable program that is equipped with the VEOS functionalities of data management, process management, and inter-entity communication. Entities act as autonomous systems, providing a natural metaphor for responsive, situational computation. In a virtual environment composed of entities, any single entity can cease to function (if, for example, the node supporting that entity crashes) without effecting the rest of the environment.

Entities provide a uniform, singular metaphor and design philosophy for the organization of both physical (hardware) and virtual (software) resources in VEOS. Uniformity means that we can use the same editing, debugging, and interaction tools for modifying each entity.

The biological/environmental metaphor for programming entities provides functions that define perception, action and motivation within a dynamic environment. *Perceive* functions determine which environmental transactions an entity has access to. *React* functions determine how an entity responds to environmental changes. *Persist* functions determine an entity's repetitive or goal-directed behavior.

The organization of each entity is based on a mathematical model of inclusion, permitting entities to serve as both objects and environments. Entities which *contain* other entities serve as their environment; the environmental component of each entity contains the global laws and knowledge of its contents. From a programming context, entities provide an integrated approach to variable scoping and to evaluation contexts. From a modeling point of view, entities provide modularity and uniformity within a convenient biological metaphor, but most importantly, from a VR perspective, entities provide first-class environments, *inclusions*, which permit modeling object/ environment interactions in a principled manner.

Synchronization of entity processes (particularly for display) is achieved through frames. A frame is a cycle of computation for an entity. Updates to the environment are propagated by an entity as discrete actions. Each behavioral output takes a local tick in local time. Since different entities will have different workloads, each usually has a different frame rate. As well, the frame rate of processes internal to an entity is decoupled from the rate of activity an entity exhibits within an environment. Thus, entities can respond to environmental perturbances (reacting) while carrying out more complex internal calculations (persisting).

To the programmer, each entity can be conceptualized to be a virtual processor. Actual entity processing is transparently multiplexed over available physical processors. The entity virtual processor is non-preemptive; it is intended to perform only short discrete tasks, yielding quickly and voluntarily to other entities sharing the same processor.

Entities can function independently, as worlds in themselves, or they can be combined into complex worlds with other interacting entities. Because entities can access computational resources, an entity can use other software modules available within the containing operating system. An entity could, for instance, initiate and call a statistical analysis package to analyze the content of its memory for recurrent patterns. The capability of entities to link to other systems software makes VEOS particularly appealing as a software testing and integration environment.

Systems-oriented programming

In object-oriented programming, an object consists of static data and responsive functions, called methods or behaviors. Objects encapsulate functionality and can be organized hierarchically, so that programming and bookkeeping effort is minimized. In contrast, entities are objects which include interface and computational resources, extending the object metaphor to a systems metaphor. The basic prototype entity includes VEOS itself, so that every entity is running VEOS and can be treated as if it were an independent operating environment. VEOS could thus be considered to be an implementation of *systems-oriented programming*.

Entities differ from objects in these ways:

- *Environment.*   Each entity functions concurrently as both object and environment. The environmental component of an entity coordinates process sharing, control and communication between entities contained in the environment. The root or global entity is the virtual universe, since it contains all other entities.
- *System.*   Each entity can be autonomous, managing its own resources and supporting its own operation without dependence on other entities or systems. Entities can be mutually independent and organizationally closed.
- *Participation.*   Entities can serve as virtual bodies. The attributes and behaviors of an inhabited entity can be determined dynamically by the physical activity of the human participant at runtime.

In object-oriented systems, object attributes and inheritance hierarchies commonly must be constructed by the programmer in advance. Efficiency in object-oriented systems usually requires compiling objects. This means that the programmer must know in advance all the objects in the environment and all their potential interactions. In effect, the programmer must be omniscient. Virtual worlds are simply too complex for such monolithic programming. Although object-oriented approaches provide modularity and conceptual organization, in large-scale applications they can result in complex property and method variants, generating hundreds of object classes and forming a complex inheritance web. For many applications, a principled inheritance hierarchy is not available, forcing the programmer to limit the conceptualization of the world. In other cases, the computational interaction between objects is context dependent, requiring attribute structures which have not been preprogrammed.

Since entities are interactive, their attributes, attribute values, relationships, inheritances and functionality can all be generated dynamically at runtime. Structures across entities can be identified in real-time based on arbitrary patterns, such as partial matches, unbound attribute values (i.e., abstract objects), ranges of attribute values, similarities, and analogies. Computational parallelism is provided by a fragmented database which provides opportunistic partial evaluation of transactions, regardless of transaction ownership. For coordination, time itself is abstracted out of computation, and is maintained symbolically in data structures.

Although world models composed of collections of objects provide conceptual parallelism (each object is independent of other objects), programming with objects paradoxically enforces sequential modeling, since messages from one object are invariably expected to trigger methods in other objects. Objects are independent only to the extent that they do not interact, but interaction is the primary activity in a virtual world. The essential issue is *determinism*: current object-oriented methodologies expect the programmer to conceptualize interaction in its entirety, between all objects across all possibilities. In contrast, entities support strong parallelism. Entities can enter and leave a virtual environment independently, simply by sending the change to the environment entity which contains them. An autonomous entity is only *perturbed* by interactions; the programmer is responsible for defining subjective behavior locally rather than objective interaction globally. For predictability, entities rely on *equifinality*: although the final result is predictable, the paths to these results are indeterminant.

Dynamic programming of entity behavior can be used by programmers for debugging, by participants for construction and interaction, and by entities for autonomous self-modification. Since the representation of data, function, and message is uniform, entities can pass functional code into the processes of other entities, providing the possibility of genetic and self-adaptive programming styles.

Entity organization

Each entity has the following components:

- A *unique name.* Entities use unique names to communicate with each other. Naming is location transparent, so that names act as paths to an entity's database partition.
- A *private partition* of the global database. The entity database consists of three subpartitions (external, boundary, and internal), and contains an entity's attributes, recorded transactions, environmental observations, observable form, and internal structure.
- Any number of *processes.* Conceptually, these processes operate in parallel within the context of the entity, as the entity's internal activities. Collectively, they define the entity's behavior.
- Any number of *interactions.* Entities call upon each other's relational data structures to perform communication and joint tasks. Interactions are expressed as perceptions accompanied potentially by both external reactions and internal model building.

The functional architecture of each entity is illustrated in Figure 4-4 (Minkoff, 1992). FERN manages the distributed database and the distributed processes within VEOS, providing location transparency and automated coordination between entities. FERN performs three internal functions for each entity:

Communication. FERN manages transactions between an entity and its

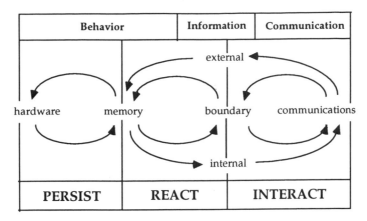

Figure 4-4   Functionality, resources, and processes in an entity.

containing environment (which is another entity) by channeling and filtering accessible global information. TALK, the communication module, facilitates inter-node communication.

Information.   Each entity maintains a database of personal attributes, attributes and behaviors of other perceived entities, and attributes of contained entities. The database partitions use the pattern language of NANCY, another basic module, for access.

Behavior.   Each entity has two functional loops that process data from the environment and from the entity's own internal states. These processes are LISP programs.

Internal resources.   The data used by an entity's processes is stored in five resource areas (Figure 4-4): hardware (device streams which provide or accept digital information), memory (local storage and workspace) and the three database partitions (external, boundary and internal). These internal resources are both the sources and the sinks for the data created and processed by the entity.

The three database partitions store the entity's information about self and world.[11] Figure 4-5 illustrates the dual object/environment structure of entities.

The *boundary* partition contains data about the self that is meant to be communicated within the containing environment and thus shared with as many other entities in that environment as are interested. The boundary is an entity's self-presentation to the world. The boundary partition is both readable and writable. An entity reads a boundary (of self or others) to get current state information. An entity writes to its own boundary to change its perceivable state.

The *external* partition contains information about other entities that the self-entity perceives. The external is an entity's perception of the world. An entity can set its own perceptual filters to include or exclude information about the world that is transacted in its external. The external is readable only, since

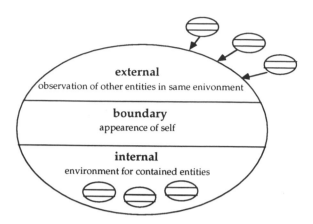

Figure 4-5 Entities as both object and environment.

it represents externally generated and thus independent information about the world.

The *internal* partition consists of data in the boundary partitions of contained entities. This partition permits an entity to serve as an environment for other entities. The internal is readable only, since it serves as a filter and a communication channel between contained entities.

The other two resources contain data about the entity that is never passed to the rest of the world. These connect the entity to the physical world of computational hardware.

The *memory* contains internal data that is not directly communicated to other entities. Memory provides permanent storage of entity experiences and temporary storage of entity computational processes. Internal storage can be managed by NANCY, by LISP, or by the programmer using C.

The *hardware* resource contains data which is generated or provided by external devices. A position tracker, for example, generates both location and orientation information which would be written into this resource. A disk drive may store data such as a behavioral history, written by the entity for later analysis. An inhabited entity would write data to a hardware renderer to create viewable images.

Internal processes. Internal processes are those operations which define an entity's behavior. Behavior can be private (local to the entity) or public (observable by other entities sharing the same environment). There are three types of behavioral processes: each entity has two separate processing regimes (*React* and *Persist*), while communications is controlled by a third process (*Interact*). By decoupling local computation from environmental reactivity, entities can react to stimuli in a time-critical manner while processing complex responses as computational resources permit.

The *Interact* process handles all communication with the other entities and with the environment. The environmental component of each entity keeps track of all contained entities. It accepts updated boundaries from each entity and stores them in the internal data-space partition. The environmental process also updates each contained entity's external partition with the current state of the world, in accordance with that entity's perceptual filters. Interaction is usually achieved by sending messages which trigger behavioral methods.[12]

The *React* process addresses pressing environmental inputs, such as collisions with other entities. It reads sensed data and immediately responds by posting actions to the environment. This cycle handles all real-time interactions and all reactions which do not require additional computation or local storage. React processes only occur as new updates to the boundary and external partitions are made.

The *Persist* process is independent of any activity external to the entity. The Persist loop is controlled by resources local to the specific entity, and is not responsive in real-time. Persist computations typically require local memory, function evaluation, and inference over local data. Persist functions can copy data from the shared database and perform local computations in order to generate information, but there are no time constraints asserted on returning the results.

The Persist mechanism implements a form of cooperative multitasking. To date, the responsibility of keeping the computational load of Persist processes balanced with available computational resources is left to the programmer. To ensure that multitasking simulates parallelism, the programmer is encouraged to limit the number of active Persist processes, and to construct them so that each is relatively fast, is atomic, and never blocks.

Coherence

FERN provides a simple coherence mechanism for shared grouplespaces that is based on the same message flow control facility as streamed methods. At the end of each frame, FERN takes an inventory of the boundary partitions of each entity on the node, and attempts to propagate the changes to the sibling entities of each of the entities in that environment. Some of these siblings may be maintained by the local node, in which case the propagation is relatively trivial. For local propagation, FERN simply copies the boundary attributes of one entity into the externals of other entities. For remote sibling entities, the grouplespace changes are sent to the nodes on which those entities reside where they are incorporated into the siblings' externals.

Because of mismatched frame rates between nodes, change propagation utilizes a flow-control mechanism. If the logical stream to the remote node is not full, some changes can be sent to that node. If the stream is full, the changes are cached until the stream is not full again. If an entity makes further changes to its boundary while there is still a cached change waiting from that entity, the intermediate value is lost. The new change replaces the previous one and continues to wait for the stream to clear. As the remote nodes digest previous change messages, the stream clears and changes are propagated.

This coherence protocol guarantees the two things. First, if an entity makes a single change to its boundary, the change will reach all subscribing sibling entities. Second, the last change an entity makes to its boundary will reach its siblings. This protocol does not guarantee the intermediate changes because

FERN cannot control how many changes an entity makes to its boundary each frame, while it must limit the stack of work that it creates for interacting nodes.

To tie all the FERN features together, Figure 4-6 provides a graphical overview of the FERN programming model (Coco, 1993).

Programming entities

Since VEOS supports many programming styles, and since it incorporates techniques from operating systems, database and communication theory, object-oriented programming, theorem proving, artificial intelligence, and interactive interface, it is not possible to present here a complete programming guide. Rather, we will discuss the unique function calls available for entities that support the biological/environmental programming metaphor. FERN functions in this section are indicated by typewriter font. Since these are LISP functions, they include the standard LISP parentheses. Angle brackets enclose argument names. An ellipsis within the parentheses indicates arguments which are unspecified. Function names in the text are written in complete words; during actual programming, these function names are abbreviated.

An entity is defined by the LISP function (fern-entity...). This function bundles a collection of other LISP functions which specify all of the entity's initial constructs, forming the entity's capabilities and behavioral disposition. These initializing commands establish the memory allocation, process initialization, and potential activities of an entity.

(fern-entity...) actually defines a *class* of entities; each time the function is called, an instance of the entity class is created. Instances are initialized by (fern-new-entity ⟨fern-entity-definitions⟩). The entity definition itself is a first-class citizen that can be loaded unevaluated, bound to a symbol, stored in the grouplespace, or sent as a message. Within an entity definition, the code can include other entity definitions, providing an inheritance mechanism.

The functions normally included within (fern-entity...) define the following characteristics.

- *Attributes* (fern-put-boundary-attribute...) Properties which are associated with state values are constructed within the entity's boundary resource. Examples of common attributes are listed in Table 4-3.
- *Workspace* (fern-put-local...) Local memory and private workspace resources are reserved within a local partition of the database.
- *Behavior* (fern-define-method...) Methods which define an entity's response to the messages it receives are defined as functions which are evaluated within the local context.
- *Processes* (fern-persist...) Persistent processes within an entity are defined and initialized. An entity can engage in many processes which timeshare an entity's computational process resources.
- *Perceptions* (fern-perceive...) When specific changes occur in an entity's environment, the entity is immediately notified, modeling a perceptual capability. An entity can only access data which it can perceive.

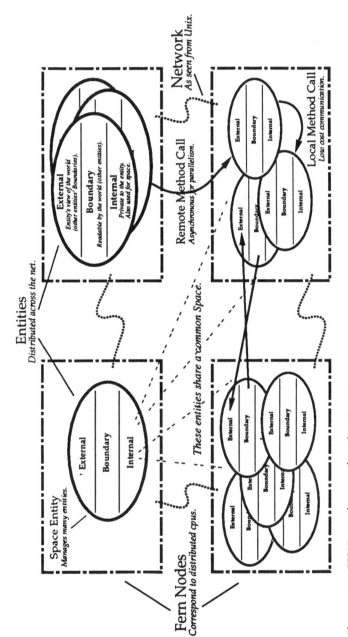

Figure 4-6 FERN topology and entity structure.

129

- *Peripherals* (sensor-init...) Connections to any physical sensors or input devices used by the entity are established and initialized.
- *Functionality* (define ⟨function-name⟩...) Any particular functions required to achieve the above characteristics are defined within the entity's local context.

As well as defining entities, FERN includes functions for initializing the computational environment (fern-init...), changing the platforms which form the processor pool (fern-merge-pool...), running the FERN process on each node (fern-run...), and providing debugging, timing, and connectivity information. FERN also provides management facilities for all functions (fern-close) (fern-detach-pool...) (fern-dispose-entity...) (fern-undefine-method...) (fern-unperceive).

Object/environment relationships are created by (fern-enter ⟨space-id⟩). The contained entity sends this registration message to the containing entity. Entities within a space can access only the perceivable aspects of other entities *in the same space.* That entities can both act as spaces and enter other spaces suggests a hierarchical nature to spaces. However, any hierarchy significance must be implemented by the application. Spaces as such are primarily a dataspace partitioning mechanism.

Entities can select and filter what they perceive in a space with (fern-perceive ⟨attribute-of-interest⟩). These filters constrain and optimize search over the shared dataspace. For example, should an entity wish to perceive changes in the color of other entities in its environment, the following code would be included in the entity's definition: (fern-perceive "color"). This code will automatically optimize the shared dataspace for access to color changes by the interested entity, posting those changes directly in the external partition of the entity.

Processes. All FERN application tasks are implemented as one of three types of entity processes:

- react (fern-perceive ⟨attribute⟩ :react ⟨react-function⟩)
- persist (fern-persist ⟨persist-function⟩)
- interact (fern-define-method ⟨message-name⟩...)
  (fern-send ⟨entity⟩ ⟨message-name⟩).

React processes are triggered when entities make changes to the shared grouplespace. Since reactions occur only as a function of perception, they are included with the perceive function. For example, an entity may want to take a specific action whenever another entity changes color:

(fern-perceive "color" :react (take-specific-action))

Persist processes can be used to perform discrete computations during a frame of time (for example, applying recurrent transformations to some object or viewpoint each frame). Persist processes can also be used in polling for data from devices and other sources external to VEOS. The following simple

Table 4-3 Common attributes of entities.

Name
    concise (human readable)
    verbose (human readable)
    system-wide
Spatial
    location in three dimensions
    orientation in three dimensions
    scale
Visual
    picture-description
    color
    visibility
    opacity
    wireframe
    texture-description
    texture-map
    texture-scale
Aural
    sound-description
    loudness
    audibility
    sound-source
    Doppler
    roll-off
    midi-description
    midi-note (pitch, velocity, sustain)
Dynamic
    mass
    velocity
    acceleration

example reads data from a dataglove and sends it to the relocate-hand method of a renderer entity, updating that data once every rendering frame:

```
(fern-persist '(poll-hand))
```

```
(define poll-hand ( )
  (let ((data (read-position-of-hand)))
    (if data (fern-send renderer "relocate-hand" data) )))
```

When persist processes involve polling, they often call application specific primitives written in C. The (read-position-of-hand) primitive would most likely be written in C since it accesses devices and requires C level constructs for efficient data management.

During a single frame, FERN's cyclic executive evaluates every persist process installed on that node exactly once. For smoother node performance, FERN interleaves the evaluation of persist processes with evaluation of queued asynchronous messages. When a persist process executes, it runs to completion like a procedure call on the node's only program stack. In comparison, preemptive threads each have their own stack where they can leave state information between context switches.

Interact processes are implemented by object-oriented messages and methods.[13] Like Smalltalk, FERN methods are used to pass data and program control between entities. An entity can invoke the methods of other entities by sending messages. The destination entity can be local or remote to the sending entity and is specified by the destination entity's unique id. A method is simply a block of code that an entity provides with a well-defined interface. The following method belongs to a renderer entity, and calls the hand update function.[14]

> (fern-define-method "relocate-hand" new-position
>   (lambda (new-position) (render-hand new-position)))

Messages. Messages can be sent between entities by three different techniques, asynchronous (fern-send...), synchronous (fern-sequential-send...) and stream (fern-stream-send...).

Asynchronous messages are most common and ensure the smoothest overall performance. An entity gets program control back immediately upon sending the message regardless of when the message is handled by the receiving entity. The following message might be sent to a renderer entity by the hand entity to update its display position:

> (fern-send renderer "relocate-hand" current-position)

When the receiving entity is remote, a message is passed to the Kernel inter-node communication module and sent to the node where the receiving entity resides. When the remote node receives the message, it posts it on the asynchronous message queue. When the receiving entity is local, a message is posted to the local message queue and handled by FERN in the same way as remote messages.

Although asynchronous message delivery is guaranteed, there is no guarantee when the receiving entity will actually execute the associated method code. As such, an asynchronous message is used when timing is not critical for correctness. In cases where timing is critical, there are common idioms for using asynchronous semantics to do synchronization. Or, if desired, FERN also provides synchronous messages.

Synchronous messages assure control of timing by passing process control from the sending to the receiving entity, in effect simulating serial processing in a distributed environment. When an entity sends a synchronous message, it blocks, restarting processing again only when the receiving entity completes its processing of the associated method and returns an exit value to the sending entity.

Although the VEOS communication model is inherently asynchronous, there are two occasions when synchronous messages may be desirable: when the sending entity needs a return value from the receiving entity, or when the sending entity needs to know exactly when the receiving entity completes processing of the associated method. Although both of these occasions can be handled by asynchronous means, the asynchronous approach may be more complicated to implement and may not achieve the lowest latency. The most important factor in choosing whether to use synchronous or asynchronous messages is whether the destination entity is local or remote. In the remote case, synchronous messages will sacrifice local processor utilization because the entire node blocks waiting for the reply, but in doing so the sending entity is assured the soonest possible notification of completion. In the local case, a synchronous method call reduces to a function call and achieves the lowest overall overhead.

A third message-passing semantic is needed to implement a communications pacing mechanism between entities. Because interacting entities may reside on different nodes with different frame rates, they may each have different response times in transacting methods and messages.

Stream messages implement a flow-control mechanism between entities. In cases where one entity may generate a stream of messages faster than a receiving entity can process them, stream messages provide a pacing mechanism, sending messages only if the stream between the two nodes is not full. Streams ensure that sending entities only send messages as fast as receiving entities can process them. The user can set the size of the stream, indicating how many buffered messages to allow. A larger stream gives better throughput because of the pipelining effect, but also results in "bursty" performance due to message convoying.

Streams are usually used for transmission of *delta* information, information indicating changes in a particular state value. Polling a position tracker, for example, provides a stream of changes in position. Streams are useful when data items can be dropped without loss of correctness.

Examples of FERN usage

Entering a world.   To enter a new environment, an entity notifies the entity which manages that environment (as an internal partition). Subsequent updates to other entities within that environment will automatically include information about the incoming entity.

Follow.   By associating an entity's position with the location of another entity (for example, Position-of-A = Position-of-B + offset), an entity will follow another entity. Following is dependent on another entity's behavior, but is completely within the control of the following entity.

Move with joystick.   The joystick posts its current values to its boundary. A virtual body using the joystick to move would react to the joystick boundary, creating an information linkage between the two activities.

Inhabitation.   The inhabiting entity uses the inhabited entity's relevant boundary information as its own, thus creating the same view and movements as the inhabited entity.

Portals.   An entity sensitive to portals can move through the portal to another location or environment. Upon entering the portal, the entity changes its boundary attributes to the position, orientation, and other spatial values defined by the portal.

A simple programming example. Finally, we present a complete FERN program to illustrate basic biological/environmental concepts within a functional programming style. When called within a LISP environment, this program creates a *space* entity, which in turn creates two other entities, *tic* and *toc*. All three entities in this simple example exist on one node; the default node is the platform on which FERN is initialized.[15]

Tic and *toc* each enter the space which created them, and each establishes a single attribute which stores a numerical value. Jointly subscribing to *space* permits each entity to perceive the attributes of the other. *Tic* persists in incrementing its attribute value, prints that current value to the console, and stores the new value. *Toc* persists in decrementing its attribute value. The perceive function of each looks at the current value of the other entity's attribute and prints what it sees to the console of the default platform. The console output of the program follows.[16]

```
(define simple-communications-test ()
  (let (
    (space '(entity-specification
      (new-entity tic)
      (new-entity toc)))
    (tic '(entity-specification
      (enter (copy.source))
      (put.attribute '("tics" 0))
      (perceive "tocs"
        :react '(lambda (ent value) (print "Tic sees: " value)))
      (persist
        '(let ((new-value (1+ (copy.attribute "tics"))))
          (print "Tic says: " new-value)
          (put.attribute '("tics" ,new-value)))) ))
    (toc '(entity-specification
      (enter (copy.source))
      (put.attribute '("tocs" 1000))
      (perceive "tics"
        :react '(lambda (ent value) (print "Toc sees: " value)))
      (persist
        '(let ((new-value (1- (copy.attribute "tocs"))))
          (print "Toc says: " new-value)
          (put.attribute '("tocs" ,new-value)))) )) )
    (run space) ))
```

Simple-communications-test generates asynchronous varieties of the following output:

```
Tic says 1
Toc says 999
Tic says 2
Toc says 998
Toc sees 2
```

```
Tic sees 998
Toc says 997
Tic says 3
Toc says 996
Toc sees ...
```

The sequence of persisting to change tics and tocs remains constant for each entity, but what each entity sees depends upon communication delays in database transactions. What each entity tells you that it sees depends upon how the underlying operating system differentially manages processing resources for print statements with persist and perceive operations.

APPLICATIONS

VEOS was developed iteratively over three years, in the context of prototype development of demonstrations, theses and experiments. It was constantly under refinement, extension and performance improvement. It has also satisfied the diverse needs of all application projects, fulfilling the primary objective of its creation. Although not strictly academic research, the VEOS project does provide a stable prototype architecture and implementation that works well for many VR applications. We briefly describe several.

Tours. The easiest type of application to build with VEOS is the virtual tour. These applications provide little interactivity, but allow the participant to navigate through an interesting environment. All that need be built is the interesting terrain or environment. These virtual environments often feature autonomous virtual objects that do not significantly interact with the participant.
Examples of tours built in VEOS are:

- an aircraft walkthrough built in conjunction with Boeing Corporation,
- the TopoSeattle application where the participant could spatially navigate and teleport to familiar sites in the topographically accurate replica of the Seattle area, and
- the Metro application where the participant could ride the ever-chugging train around a terrain of rolling hills and tunnels.

Physical simulation. Because physical simulations require very precise control of the computation, they have been a challenging application domain. Coco and Lion (1992) implemented a billiard-ball simulation to measure VEOS's performance, in particular to measure the trade-offs between parallelism and message passing overhead. Most of the entity code for this application was written in LISP, except for ball-collision detection and resolution, which was written in C to reduce the overhead of the calculations.
The simulation coupled eighteen entities. Three entities provided an

interface to screen-based rendering facilities, access to a spaceball six-degree-of-freedom input device, and a command console. The rendering and spaceball entities worked together much like a virtual body. The spaceball entity acted as a virtual hand, using a persist procedure to sample the physical spaceball device and make changes to the 3D model. The imager entity acted as a virtual eye, updating the screen-based view after each model change made by the spaceball entity. The console entity managed the keyboard and windowing system.

Asynchronous to the participant interaction, fifteen separate ball entities continually recomputed their positions. Within each frame, each ball, upon receiving updates from other balls, checked for collisions. When each ball had received an update from every other ball at the end of each frame, it would compute movement updates for the next frame. The ball entities sent their new positions via messages to the imager entity which incorporated the changes into the next display update. The ball entities used asynchronous methods to maximize parallelism within each frame. Balls did not wait for all messages to begin acting upon them. They determined their new position iteratively, driven by incoming messages. Once a ball had processed all messages for one frame, it sent out its updated position to the other balls thus beginning a new frame.

Multiparticipant interactivity. In the early stages of VEOS development, Coco and Lion designed an application to demonstrate the capabilities of multiparticipant interaction and independent views of the virtual environment. Block World allowed four participants to independently navigate and manipulate moveable objects in a shared virtual space. Each participant viewed a monitor-based display, concurrently appearing as different colored blocks on each other's monitor. Block World allowed for interactions such as "tug-of-war" when two participants attempted to move the same object at the same time. This application provided experience for the conceptual development of FERN.

One recent large-scale application, designed by Colin Bricken, provided multiparticipant interaction by playing catch with a virtual ball while supporting inter-participant spatial voice communication. The Catch application incorporated almost every interaction technique currently supported at HITL including head tracking, spatial sound, 3D binocular display, wand navigation, object manipulation, and scripted movement paths.

Of particular note in the Catch application was the emphasis on independent participant perceptions. Participants customized their personal view of a shared virtual environment in terms of color, shape, scale, and texture. Although the game of catch was experienced in a shared space, the structures in that space were substantively different for each participant. Before beginning the game, each player selected the form of their virtual body and the appearance of the surrounding mountains and flora. One participant may see a forest of evergreens, for example, while concurrently the other saw a field of flowers. Participants experienced the Catch environment two at a time, and could compare their experiences at runtime through spatialized voice communication. The spatial filtering of the voice interaction provided each participant with additional cues about the location of the other participant in the divergent world.

Manufacturing. For her graduate thesis, Karen Jones worked with engineer Marc Cygnus to develop a factory simulation application (Jones, 1992). The program incorporated an external interface to the AutoMod simulation package. The resulting virtual environment simulated the production facility of the Derby Cycle bicycle company in Kent, Washington, and provided interactive control over production resources allocation. The Derby Cycle application was implemented using a FERN entity for each dynamic object and one executive entity that ensured synchronized simulation time steps. The application also incorporated the Body module for navigation through the simulation.

Spatial perception. Coming from an architectural background, Daniel Henry wrote a thesis on comparative human perception in virtual and actual spaces (Henry, 1992). He constructed a virtual model of the Henry Art Gallery on the University of Washington campus. The study involved comparison of subjective perception of size, form, and distance in both the real and virtual gallery. This application used the Body module for navigation through the virtual environment. The results indicated that the perceived size of the virtual space was smaller than the perceived size of the actual space.

Scientific visualization. Many applications have been built in VEOS for visualizing large or complex data sets. Our first data visualization application was of satellite collected data of the Mars planet surface. This application allowed the participant to navigate on or above the surface of Mars and change the depth ratio to emphasize the contour of the terrain. Another application designed by Marc Cygnus revealed changes in semiconductor junctions over varying voltages. To accomplish this, the application displayed the patterns generated from reflecting varying electromagnetic wave frequencies off the semiconductor.

Education. Meredith Bricken and Chris Byrne led a program to give local youth the chance to build and experience virtual worlds. The program emphasized the cooperative design process of building virtual environments. These VEOS worlds employed the standard navigation techniques of the wand and many provided interesting interactive features. The implementations include an AIDS awareness game, a Chemistry World and a world which modeled events within an atomic nucleus.

Creative design. Using the Universal Motivator graph configuration system, Colin Bricken designed several applications for purely creative ends. These environments are characterized by many dynamic virtual objects which display complex behavior based on autonomous behavior and reactivity to participant movements.

CONCLUSION

Operating architectures and systems for real-time virtual environments have been explored in commercial and academic groups over the last five years. One such exploration was the VEOS project, which spread over three and a half years, and is now no longer active.

We have learned that the goals of the VEOS project are ambitious; it is difficult for one cohesive system to satisfy demands of conceptual elegance, usability, and performance even for limited domains. VEOS attempted to address these opposing top-level demands through its hybrid design. In this respect, perhaps the strongest attribute of VEOS is that it promotes modular programming. Modularity has allowed incremental performance revisions as well as incremental and cooperative tool design. Most importantly, the emphasis on modularity facilitates the process of rapid prototyping that was sought by the initial design.

Now that the infrastructure of virtual worlds (behavior transducers and coordination software) is better understood, the more significant questions of the design and construction of psychologically appropriate virtual/synthetic experiences will receive more attention. Biological/environmental programming of entities can provide one route to aid in the humanization of the computer interface.

ACKNOWLEDGEMENTS

The HITL software development program was a group effort to create a satisfying software infrastructure for the entire lab. The discussion in this chapter is based upon a conceptual VR system architecture developed by Bricken over the last decade and grounded in an implementation by Coco over the last three years (Bricken, 1991a). VEOS supported parallel development of lab applications, technology demonstrations, thesis projects, and software interaction tools (Coco, 1993). Dav Lion, Colin Bricken, Andy MacDonald, Marc Cygnus, Dan Pirone, Max Minkoff, Brian Karr, Daniel Henry, Fran Taylor and several others have made significant contributions to the VEOS project.

Portions of this chapter have appeared in the *Proceedings of the 13th World Computer Congress (1994)*, **3**, 163–70, and in *Presence*, **3**(2) (Spring 1994), 111–29.

NOTES

1. The description of VR as techniques which *trick* the senses embodies a cultural value: somehow belief in digital simulation is not as legitimate as belief in physical reality. The VR paradigm shift directly challenges this view. The human mind's ability to attribute equal credibility to Nature, television, words, dreams and computer-generated environments is a *feature*, not a bug.

2. Existing serial computers are not designed for multiple concurrent participants or

for efficient distributed processing. One of the widest gaps between design and implementation of VR systems is efficient integration of multiple subsystems. VEOS is not a solution to the integration problem, nor does the project focus on basic research toward a solution. Real-time performance in VEOS degrades with more than about ten distributed platforms. We have experimented with only up to six interactive participants.

3. A graphics rendering pipeline, for example, transforms the world coordinate system into the viewpoint coordinate system of the participant. Since renderers act as the virtual eye of the participant, they are part of the participant system rather than part of the operating system.

4. The Mercury Project at HITL, for example, implements a participant system which decouples the performance of the behavior transducing subsystem from that of the virtual world through distributed processing. Even when complexity slows the internal updates to the world database, the participant is still delivered a consistently high frame rate.

5. The apparent dominance of physical reality is dependent on how we situate our senses. That is to say, physical reality is dominant only until we close our eyes. Situated perception is strongly enhanced by media such as radio, cinema and television, which invite a refocusing into a virtual world. The objective view of reality was reinforced last century by print media which presents information in an objectified, external form. Immersive media undermine the dominance of the physical simply by providing a different *place* to situate perception.

6. To be manifest, VR also requires a participant.

7. Crossing *twice* is a mathematical necessity (Spencer-Brown, 1969).

8. A thing that is larger than its container is the essence of an imaginary configuration, exactly the properties one might expect from the virtual.

9. Aside from one or two pioneering systems built in the sixties (Sutherland, 1965), complete VR systems did not become accessible to the general public until 6 June, 1989, when both VPL and Autodesk displayed their systems at two concurrent trade shows. Research at NASA Ames (Fisher *et al.*, 1986) seeded both of these commercial prototypes. At the time, the University of North Carolina was the only academic site of VR research (Brooks, 1986).

10. Of course the details of most corporate VR efforts are trade secrets.

11. This tripartite model of data organization is based on spatial rather than textual syntax. The shift is from *labels* which point to objects to *containers* which distinguish spaces. Containers differentiate an outside, an inside, and a boundary between them. Higher dimensional representation is essential for a mathematical treatment of virtual environments (Bricken and Gullichsen, 1989; Bricken, 1991b, 1992b). Text, written in one-dimensional lines, is too weak a representational structure to express environmental concepts; words simply lack an inside.

12. Technically, in a biological/environmental paradigm, behavior is under autonomous control of the entity and is *not necessarily* triggered by external messages from other entities.

13. It is appropriate to model interaction *between* entities using the objective, external perspective of object-oriented programming.

14. Lambda is LISP for "this code fragment is a function."

15. The names of actual functions have been changed in the example, to simplify reading of intent. Also, the normal mode of storing entities is the file, not the name.

16. This example is written in LISP and suffers from necessary LISP syntax. A non-programmer's interface for configuring entities could be based on filling forms, on menu selections, or even on direct interaction within the virtual environment.

REFERENCES

Agha, G. (1988) *Actors: a Model of Concurrent Computation in Distributed Systems*. MIT Press

Appino, P. A., Lewis, J. B., Koved, L., Ling, D. T., Rabenhorst, D., and Codella, C. (1992) An architecture for virtual worlds, *Presence*, **1**, 1–17

Arango, M., Berndt, D., Carriero, N., Gelertner, D. and Gilmore, D. (1990) Adventures with network linda, *Supercomputing Review*, 42–6

Bershad, B., Zekauskas, M. J., and Swadon, W. A. (1992) *The Midway Distributed Shared Memory System*, School of Computer Science, Carnegie Mellon University

Betz, D. and Almy, T. (1992) *XLISP 2.1 User's Manual*

Bishop, G. *et al.* (1992) Research directions in virtual environments: report of an NSF invitational workshop, *Computer Graphics* **26**, 153–77

Blanchard, C., Burgess, S., Harvill, Y., Lanier, J., Lasko, A., Oberman, M., and Teitel, M. (1990) Reality built for two: a virtual reality tool. *Proc. 1990 Symp. on Interactive Graphics*, Snowbird, UT, pp. 35–6

Blau, B., Hughes, C. E., Moshell, J. M., and Lisle, C. (1992) Networked virtual environments, *Computer Graphics 1992 Symp. on Interactive 3D Graphics*, p. 157

Bricken, M. (1991) Virtual worlds: no interface to design, in M. Benedikt (Ed.), *Cyberspace First Steps*, Cambridge, MA, MIT Press, pp. 363–82

Bricken, W. (1990) Software architecture for virtual reality, *Human Interface Technology Lab Technical Report P-90-4*, University of Washington

Bricken, W. (1991a) VEOS: preliminary functional architecture, *ACM Siggraph'91 Course Notes, Virtual Interface Technology*, pp. 46–53. Also *Human Interface Technology Lab Technical Report M-90-2*, University of Washington

Bricken, W. (1991b) A formal foundation for cyberspace, *Proc. of Virtual Reality '91, The Second Annual Conf. on Virtual Reality, Artificial Reality, and Cyberspace*, San Francisco: Meckler

Bricken, W. (1992a) VEOS design goals, *Human Interface Technology Lab Technical Report M-92-1*, University of Washington

Bricken, W. (1992b) Spatial representation of elementary algebra, *1992 IEEE Workshop on Visual Languages*, Seattle: IEEE Computer Society Press, pp. 56–62

Bricken, W. and Gullichsen, E. (1989) An introduction to boundary logic with the LOSP deductive engine, *Future Computing Systems* **2**

Brooks, F. (1986) Walkthrough—a dynamic graphics system for simulation of virtual buildings, *Proc. of the 1986 Workshop on Interactive 3D Graphics*, ACM 271–81

Bryson, S. and Gerald-Yamasaki, M. (1992) The distributed virtual wind tunnel, *Proc. of Supercomputing '92*, Minneapolis, MN

Carter, J. B., Bennet, J. K., and Zwaenepoel, W. (1992) *Implementation and Performance of Munin*, Computer Systems Laboratory, Rice University

Coco, G. (1993) The virtual environment operating system: derivation, function and form, *Masters Thesis*, School of Engineering, University of Washington

Coco, G. and Lion, D. (1992) Experiences with asychronous communication models in VEOS, a distributed programming facility for uniprocessor LANs, *Human Interface Technology Lab Technical Report R-93-2*, University of Washington

Cogent Research, Inc. (1990) *Kernel Linda Specification: Version 4.0. Technical Note*, Beaverton, OR

Cruz-Neira, C., Sandin, D. J., DeFanti, T., Kenyon, R., and Hart, J. (1992) The cave:

audio visual experience automatic virtual environment, *Commun. ACM* **35**, 65–72

Dershowitz, N. and Jouannaud, J.P. (1990) Chapter 6: rewrite systems, *Handbook of Theoretical Computer Science*, Amsterdam: Elsevier Science Publishers, 245–320

Ellis, S. R. (1991) The nature and origin of virtual environments: a bibliographical essay, *Computer Systems in Engineering*, **2**, 321–47

Emerson, T. (1993) Selected bibliography on virtual interface technology, *Human Interface Technology Lab Technical Report B-93-2*, University of Washington

Feiner, S., MacIntyre, B., and Seligmann, D. (1992) Annotating the real world with knowledge-based graphics on a "see-through" head-mounted display, *Proc. Graphics Interface '92*, Vancouver, Canada, pp. 78–85

Fisher, S., Jacoby, R., Bryson, S., Stone, P., McDowell, I., Bolas, M., Dasaro, D., Wenzel, E., and Coler, C. (1991) The Ames virtual environment workstation: implementation issues and requirements, *Human–Machine Interfaces for Tele-operators and Virtual Environments*, NASA, pp. 20–24

Fisher, S., McGreevy, M., Humphries, J., and Robinett, W. (1986) Virtual environment display system, *ACM Workshop on Interactive 3D Graphics*, Chapel Hill, NC

Gelertner, D. and Carriero, N. (1992) Coordination languages and their significance, *Communications of the ACM*, **35**, 97–107

Gelertner, D. and Philbin, J. (1990) Spending your free time, *Byte*, May

Goldberg, A. (1984) *Smalltalk-80* (Xerox Corporation), New York: Addison-Wesley

Green, M., Shaw, C., Liang, J., and Sun, Y. (1991) MR: a toolkit for virtual reality applications, Department of Computer Science, University of Alberta, Edmonton, Canada

Grimsdale, C. (1991) dVS: distributed virtual environment system, *Product Documentation*, Division Ltd. Bristol, UK

Grossweiler, R., Long, C., Koga, S., and Pausch, R. (1993) *DIVER: a Distributed Virtual Environment Research Platform*, Computer Science Department, University of Virginia

Henry, D. (1992) Spatial perception in virtual environments: evaluating an architectural application, *Masters Thesis*, School of Engineering, University of Washington

Holloway, R., Fuchs, H., and Robinett, W. (1992) Virtual-worlds research at the University of North Carolina at Chapel Hill, *Course #9 Notes: Implementation of Immersive Virtual Environments, SIGGRAPH '92*, Chicago, IL

Jones, K. (1992) Manufacturing simulation using virtual reality, *Masters Thesis*, School of Engineering, University of Washington

Jul, E., Levy, H., Hutchinson, N., and Black, A. (1988) Fine-grained mobility in the emerald system, *ACM Trans. Computer Systems*, **6**, 109–33

Kung, H. T., Sansom, R., Schlick, S., Steenkiste, P., Arnould, M., Bitz, F. J., Christianson, F., Cooper, E. C., Menzilcioglu, O., Ombres, D., and Zill, B. (1991) Network-based multicomputers: an emerging parallel architecture, *ACM Computer Sci.*, 664–73

Langton, C. (1988) *Artificial Life: Proc. of an Interdisciplinary Workshop on the Synthesis and Simulation of Living Systems*, New York: Addison-Wesley

Li, K. and Hudak, P. (1989) Memory coherence in shared virtual memory systems, *ACM Trans. Computer Systems*, **7**, 321–59

Maturana, H. and Varela, F. (1987) *The Tree of Knowledge*, New Science Library

Meyer, J. and Wilson, S. (1991) *From Animals to Animats: Proc. of the First Int. Conf. on Simulation of Adaptive Behavior*, Cambridge, MA: MIT Press

Minkoff, M. (1992) The FERN model: an explanation with examples, *Human Interface*

Technology Lab Technical Report R-92-3, University of Washington

Minkoff, M. (1993) The participant system: providing the interface in virtual reality, *Masters Thesis*, School of Engineering, University of Washington

Naimark, M. (1991) Elements of realspace imaging: a proposed taxonomy, *Proc. of the SPIE 1457, Stereoscopic Displays and Applications II*, Bellingham, WA: SPIE, pp. 169–79

Oren, T., Salomon, G., Kreitman, K., and Don, A. (1990) Guides: characterizing the interface, in Laurel, B. (Ed.), *The Art of Human–Computer Interface Design*, New York: Addison-Wesley

Pezely, D. J., Almquist, M. D., and Bricken, W. (1992) Design and implementation of the meta operating system and entity shell, *Human Interface Technology Lab Technical Report R-91-5*, University of Washington

Robinett, W. (1992) Synthetic experience: a proposed taxonomy, *Presence* **1**, 229–47

Robinett, W. and Holloway, R. (1992) Implementation of flying, scaling and grabbing in virtual worlds, *Computer Graphics 1992 Symp. on Interactive 3D Graphics*, p. 189

Spector, A. Z. (1982) Performing remote operations efficiently on a local computer network, *Commun. ACM*, **25**, 246–60

Spencer-Brown, G. (1969) *Laws of Form*, Bantam

Sutherland, I. (1965) The ultimate display, *Proc. of the IFIP Congress*, pp. 502–8

Torque Systems, Inc. (1992) *Tuplex 2.0 Software Specification*, Palo Alto, CA

Varela, F. (1979) *Principles of Biological Autonomy*, Amsterdam: Elsevier, North-Holland

Varela, F. and Bourgine, P. (1992) *Toward a Practice of Autonomous Systems: Proc. of the First European Conf. on Artificial Life*, MIT Press

von Eicken, T., Culler, D. E., Goldstein, S. C., and Schauser, K. E. (1992) Active messages: a mechanism for integrated communication and computation, *Commun. ACM*, 256–66

VPL (1991) *Virtual Reality Data-flow Language and Runtime System, Body Electric Manual 3.0*, VPL Research, Redwood City, CA

Wenzel, E., Stone, P., Fisher, S., and Foster, S. (1990) A system for three-dimensional acoustic 'visualization' in a virtual environment workstation, *Proc. of the First IEEE Conf. on Visualization, Visualization '90*, IEEE, pp. 329–37

West, A. J., Howard, T. L. J., Hubbold, R. J., Murta, A. D., Snowdon, D. N., and Butler, D. A. (1992) *AVIARY—a Generic Virtual Reality Interface for Real Applications*, Department of Computer Science, University of Manchester, UK

Wolfram, S. (1988) *Mathematica: a System for Doing Mathematics by Computer*, New York: Addison-Wesley

Zeltzer, D. (1992) Autonomy, interaction, and presence, *Presence*, **1**, 127–32

Zeltzer, D., Pieper, S., and Sturman, D. (1989) An integrated graphical simulation platform, *Graphics Interface '89*, Canadian Information Processing Society, pp. 266–74

Zyda, M. J., Akeley, K., Badler, N., Bricken, W., Bryson, S., vanDam, A., Thomas, J., Winget, J., Witkin, A., Wong, E., and Zeltzer, D. (1993) *Report on the State-of-the-art in Computer Technology for the Generation of Virtual Environments*, Computer Generation Technology Group, National Academy of Sciences, National Research Council Committee on Virtual Reality and Development

Zyda, M. J., Pratt, D. R., Monahan, J. G., and Wilson, K. P. (1992) NPSNET: constructing a 3D virtual world, *Computer Graphics*, **3**, 147

VISUAL DISPLAYS

5

Human Stereopsis, Fusion, and Stereoscopic Virtual Environments

ELIZABETH THORPE DAVIS AND LARRY F. HODGES

Two fundamental purposes of human spatial perception, in either a real or virtual 3D environment, are to determine where objects are located in the environment and to distinguish one object from another. Although various sensory inputs, such as haptic and auditory inputs, can provide this spatial information, vision usually provides the most accurate, salient, and useful information (Welch and Warren, 1986). Moreover, of the visual cues available to humans, stereopsis provides an enhanced perception of depth and of three-dimensionality for a visual scene (Yeh and Silverstein, 1992). (Stereopsis or stereoscopic vision results from the fusion of the two slightly different views of the external world that our laterally displaced eyes receive (Schor, 1987; Tyler, 1983).) In fact, users often prefer using 3D stereoscopic displays (Spain and Holzhausen, 1991) and find that such displays provide more fun and excitement than do simpler monoscopic displays (Wichanski, 1991). Thus, in creating 3D virtual environments or 3D simulated displays, much attention recently has been devoted to visual 3D stereoscopic displays. Yet, given the costs and technical requirements of such displays, we should consider several issues. First, we should consider in what conditions and situations these stereoscopic displays enhance perception and performance. Second, we should consider how binocular geometry and various spatial factors can affect human stereoscopic vision and, thus, constrain the design and use of stereoscopic displays. Finally, we should consider the modeling geometry of the software, the display geometry of the hardware, and some technological limitations that constrain the design and use of stereoscopic displays by humans.

In the following section we consider when 3D stereoscopic displays are useful and why they are useful in some conditions but not others. In the section after that we review some basic concepts about human stereopsis and fusion that are of interest to those who design or use 3D stereoscopic displays. Also in that section we point out some spatial factors that limit stereopsis and fusion in human vision as well as some potential problems that should be considered in designing and using 3D stereoscopic displays. Following that we discuss some software and hardware issues, such as modeling geometry and display geometry as well as geometric distortions and other artifacts that can affect human perception. Finally we summarize our tutorial and conclude with some suggestions and challenges for the future development and use of computer-generated 3D stereoscopic displays.

WHEN ARE 3D STEREOSCOPIC DISPLAYS USEFUL?

Stereoscopic displays are useful when information is presented in a perspective view rather than in a plan or bird's eye view (Barfield and Rosenberg, 1992; Yeh and Silverstein, 1992), when monocular cues provide ambiguous or less effective information than stereoscopic cues (Way, 1988; Reising and Mazur, 1990; Yeh and Silverstein, 1992), when static displays are used rather than dynamic displays (Wickens, 1990; Yeh and Silverstein, 1992), when complex scenes and ambiguous objects are presented (Cole *et al.*, 1990; Drascic, 1991; Spain and Holzhausen, 1991), when complex 3D manipulation tasks require ballistic movements or very accurate placement and positioning of tools or manipulators (Drascic, 1991; Spain and Holzhausen, 1991), and when relatively inexperienced users must perform remote 3D manipulation tasks (Drascic, 1991). In these various situations, stereopsis helps by providing information about the spatial layout of objects (e.g., their elevation or distance from the observer) or about fine depth or relative distances between objects.

Perspective views of visual scenes

In a perspective view, azimuth is represented by the x axis, elevation by the y axis, and distance from the observer by the z axis. A perspective view may improve the user's perception of the overall 3D spatial layout and performance in spatial judgment tasks, as compared to perception and performance with a plan view (Yeh and Silverstein, 1992). For example, in situational awareness tasks during flight simulation, the user may be more accurate in detecting threats, locking onto sequential targets, and intercepting those targets when provided with a perspective view rather than a plan view (Barfield *et al.*, 1992; Yeh and Silverstein, 1992). However, a perspective view does introduces certain ambiguities into the interpretation of the spatial layout. In a perspective view, absolute distance of an object cannot be determined as accurately as its azimuth position (i.e., position parallel to the image plane). The reason is that in a perspective view distance information is integrated with elevation information so that it is difficult to disentangle the two sources of information. Changing the angle from which an observer views the perspective visual scene also changes the relative compression and expansion of the y and z axes. Thus, in a perspective view there is an inherent ambiguity between position along the y axis and along the z axis. The use of stereopsis helps to resolve this ambiguity by providing another source of information about relative distances of objects from the observer.

Ambiguous or less effective monocular cues

Three-dimensional stereoscopic displays are most useful when the visual display lacks effective monocular cues (Way, 1988; Reising and Mazur, 1990; Yeh and Silverstein, 1992). For example, Wickens and his colleagues (Wickens, 1990; Wickens and Todd, 1990) reported that stereopsis, motion parallax, and interposition (occlusion) are effective cues, but linear perspective, accommodation, and relative size are not. According to Wickens, spatial perception will not be enhanced if stereopsis is added to a visual display that already contains motion parallax, but would be enhanced if stereopsis is added to a visual display with only linear perspective. There is some disagreement in the literature, however, about which cues are effective. Reising and Mazur (1990) reported that linear perspective, motion parallax, and interposition are effective cues. Perhaps if objects always are depicted on the ground, rather than above it, then perspective may be a more effective cue. Providing a ground intercept (i.e., a symbol enhancer) for objects floating above the ground also can make perspective a better depth cue (Kim *et al.*, 1987), but these symbol enhancers add clutter to the visual scene (Yeh and Silverstein, 1992). Visual clutter can make a scene more complex and, thus, may adversely affect spatial perception.

Static displays

Several investigators have shown that stereopsis is more useful in static displays or in slowly changing displays (Wickens and Todd, 1990; Yeh and Silverstein, 1992) than in more dynamic displays. For example, Wickens and Todd reported that stereoscopic displays provide greater performance gains for the static displays of air traffic control than for dynamic displays of flight-path guidance, where relative motion is a very salient cue. Note, however, others have reported that stereopsis and motion parallax provide similar information (Rogers and Graham, 1982). For example, addition of motion parallax to a visual display may reduce the ambiguity of a perspective format, just as a stereoscopic view reduces the ambiguity. Moreover, in some cases stereopsis can enhance motion cues, such as those provided by rotation or the kinetic depth effect (Sollenberger and Milgram, 1991).

Complex visual scenes and ambiguous objects

The 3D stereoscopic displays are more useful than monoscopic displays with complex or unfamiliar visual scenes (Pepper *et al.*, 1981; Cole *et al.*, 1990; Drascic, 1991; Spain and Holzhausen, 1991). For example, stereopsis may be a useful cue in a very cluttered visual scene, such as one that uses too many symbol enhancers. Moreover, stereopsis can enhance the discrimination between figure and ground in configurations that have camouflage or minimal actual depth differences and, thus, break camouflage (Yeh and Silverstein, 1990).

Complex 3D manipulation tasks

Three-dimensional stereoscopic displays are more useful than monoscopic displays for demanding, complex, 3D manipulation tasks. Tasks that require ballistic movement and/or accurate placement of manipulators and tools within the environment benefit from the use of stereoscopic displays. For example, remote performance of a complex and difficult line-threading task benefited more from the use of stereoscopic displays than from the use of monoscopic displays (Spain and Holzhausen, 1991). In this task, completion times were faster (29%) and error rates were lower (44%) for performance with a stereoscopic display than with a monoscopic display.

Inexperienced users

An initial performance advantage has been reported for inexperienced users who use stereoscopic displays rather than monoscopic displays (Drascic, 1991). For low-difficulty tasks that do not require stereopsis (viz., stereoscopic-vision independent tasks) this performance advantage may decrease with experience. For the more difficult stereoscopic-vision dependent tasks, however, experience results in little change of the performance advantage offered by stereoscopic displays.

Some useful applications of 3D stereoscopic displays

Some useful applications of 3D stereoscopic displays in virtual environments and avionics include the operation of remotely manipulated vehicles or teleoperators (Cole et al., 1990, 1991; Wickens and Todd, 1990; Drascic, 1991; Spain and Holzhausen, 1991), scientific visualization of complex data sets (Wickens and Todd, 1990), the display of aircraft locations in airspace for air traffic control (Wickens and Todd, 1990), and situational awareness in flying aircraft (Way, 1988; Reising and Mazur, 1990; Barfield et al., 1992). In all of these situations the user must infer relationships among objects located in a 3D space.

Stereoscopic versus monoscopic visual displays

Although stereoscopic visual systems can be very helpful in the above situations, monoscopic visual systems are more common for some of these applications, such as the use of teleoperated robots or remotely manipulated vehicles (Drascic, 1991). Yet, 3D stereoscopic visual displays can reduce response latencies or task execution time, reduce error rates, and reduce the amount of time needed for training (Drascic, 1991). One often experiences faster and more accurate perception of spatial layout of a remote scene as well as finer discrimination of depth between objects with stereopsis than without it. Moreover, if a remote manipulator requires steadiness of hand (e.g., in teleoperated surgery) then stereopsis is more useful than motion parallax. For example, Cole and his colleagues (Pepper et al., 1981; Cole et al., 1990) tested operators who guided a remote manipulator through a wire maze to a target. When the operators used a stereoscopic visual display they were able to perform the task with speed and accuracy. When the operators used a monoscopic display, however, they were forced to explore the wire maze in a slow trial-and-error fashion, learning from feedback provided by collisions and entanglements of the remote manipulator.

When 3D stereoscopic displays may not be useful

In considering when 3D stereoscopic displays are useful, we also have indicated some situations where they may be less useful. For instance, they may be less useful for tasks involving a plan view rather than a perspective view or for displays that represent a very dynamically changing visual scene rather than a relatively static visual scene. There are additional limitations placed on the usefulness of 3D stereoscopic displays. These limitations result from processing by the human visual system and from technological limitations and artifacts in the 3D stereoscopic displays. As an extreme example, humans with strabismus (*cross-eyed*) or anomalous stereopsis (Richards, 1971) would not benefit from stereoscopic displays as much as humans with normal stereopsis. Also, geometric distortions in the stereoscopic display may hinder stereopsis and make the 3D stereoscopic displays less useful than they could be. Below we will consider both the processing of stereopsis and fusion in the human visual system and the technical capabilities and artifacts of stereoscopic displays in light of the limitations they impose on the design and use of 3D stereoscopic displays.

STEREOPSIS AND FUSION IN HUMAN VISION

Stereopsis results from the two slightly different views of the external world that our laterally displaced eyes receive (Tyler, 1983; Schor, 1987). The binocular parallax that results from these two different views can provide information about the relative distances of objects from the observer or about the depth between objects. Stereoacuity can be characterized as the smallest depth that can be detected based on binocular parallax. Under optimal conditions, stereoacuities of less than 5″ of arc can be obtained (McKee, 1983; Westheimer and McKee, 1980), although somewhat larger stereoacuities are more common (Schor and Wood, 1983; Yeh and Silverstein, 1990; Davis *et al.*, 1992a; Patterson and Martin, 1992). (Because such stereoacuities are significantly smaller than the smallest photoreceptors in the human retina, which are approximately 30″ of arc in diameter, stereoacuity is classified as a hyperacuity.) We provide below a brief description of the binocular geometry underlying stereopsis and fusion as well as some terminology and facts about human stereopsis. We then consider some spatial factors which can affect human stereoscopic vision. More detailed descriptions can be found elsewhere (Luneburg, 1947; Ogle, 1950; Julesz, 1971; Gulick and Lawson, 1976; Tyler, 1983; Poggio and Poggio, 1984; Bishop, 1985; Arditi, 1986).

Binocular visual direction

Visual direction is the perceived spatial location of an object relative to the observer. Usually, it is measured in terms of azimuth (left and right of the point of fixation) and of elevation (above and below the point of fixation). Sometimes the binocular visual direction of an object is not the same as the monocular visual direction of either eye. (You can verify this yourself by looking at a very close object first with one eye, then with the other eye, and finally with both eyes.) Hering proposed that binocular visual direction will lie midway between the directions of the two monocular images; others have reported that the binocular visual direction will lie somewhere between the left and right monocular visual directions, but not necessarily midway (Tyler, 1983). These potential individual differences in perceived binocular visual direction imply that the perceived visual direction of objects viewed in a 3D stereoscopic display may vary somewhat from one user to the next, unless compensations are made for these individual differences.

Convergence angles and retinal disparities

For symmetric convergence of the two eyes on a fixated point in space, f_1, the angle of convergence is defined as

$$\alpha = 2 \arctan(i/2D_1) \tag{1}$$

where α is the angle of convergence, D_1 is the distance from the interocular axis to the fixated point, f_1, and i is the interocular distance (Graham, 1965; Arditi, 1986).[1] (See Figure 5-1.) For another point in space, f_2, located at a distance D_2, the angle of convergence is β (see Figure 5-1). Notice that the angle of convergence, α or β, is inversely related to the distance from the observer, D_1 or D_2 respectively, of the fixated point, f_1 or f_2; this inverse relation is a nonlinear one.

The difference in vergence angles (α-β) is equivalent to the retinal disparity between the two points in space, measured in units of visual angle. Notice that when the eyes are fixated on point f_1, the retinal image of f_1 is focused on the center of the fovea in each eye. However, the retinal image of f_2 in the right eye lies at a different position and distance from the center of the fovea than does the retinal image of f_2 in the left eye. This difference in retinal distances is the retinal disparity, δ. Usually we measure this retinal disparity as the sum of the angles, δ_L and δ_R, as shown in Figure 5-1. Angles measured from the

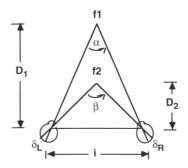

Figure 5-1   See text for an explanatiion of this figure.

center of the fovea towards the outside of each eye are negative and, conversely, those measured from the center of the fovea towards the inside of each eye are positive. So, for the example shown in Figure 5-1, both δ_L and δ_R have negative values and, thus, the resultant retinal disparity, δ, also is negative as shown in the following equation:

$$\delta = \delta_L + \delta_R \qquad (2)$$

Retinal disparity is monotonically related to the depth or exocentric distance between two objects in space. That is, at a constant distance, D_1, a larger depth corresponds to a larger retinal disparity. Moreover, this monotonic relationship between retinal disparity and depth is a nonlinear one.

In terms of vergence angles, the depth, d, between two points in space (f_1 and f_2) is given by the following equation:

$$d = (i/2)[1/\tan(\beta/2) - 1/\tan(\alpha/2)] \qquad (3)$$

where i is the interocular distance and α and β are the angles of convergence for the points in space, f_1 and f_2, respectively. However, information about the changes in the convergence angle of the eyes probably is not very useful for distances greater than one meter (Arditi, 1986) although stereopsis can be useful for much greater distances (Tyler, 1983; Boff and Lincoln, 1988; Wickens, 1990). In fact, if an observer has a retinal disparity limit of 2″ of arc, this is sufficient to discriminate between infinity and an object two miles away from the observer (Tyler, 1983).

Conversely, if we know the physical depth, d, between two points in space, f_1 and f_2, and the distance, D_1, from the observer to the fixated point, f_1, then we can approximate the value of the horizontal retinal disparity, δ, in terms of radians. This approximation is given by the following equation:

$$\delta = (id)/(D_1^2 + dD_1) \qquad (4)$$

If an object is closer than the fixation point, the retinal disparity, δ, will be a negative value. This is known as a *crossed* disparity because the two eyes must cross to fixate the closer object. Conversely, if an object is further than the fixation point, the retinal disparity will be a positive value. This is known as *uncrossed* disparity because the two eyes must uncross to fixate the further object. An object located at the fixation point or whose image falls on corresponding points in the two retinae (as defined below) has a *zero* disparity. Retinal disparity will be discussed again later, in the section on "Stereoscopic Displays afor Virtual Environments," in terms of the screen parallax of a stereoscopic 3D display.

Corresponding retinal points, theoretical and empirical horopters

Corresponding points on the two retinae are defined as being the same vertical and horizontal distance from the center of the fovea in each eye (Tyler, 1983; Arditi, 1986). (When an object is fixated by an observer's two eyes, an image of that object usually falls onto the fovea of each eye. The fovea is the part of the human retina that possesses the best spatial resolution or visual acuity.) When the two eyes binocularly fixate on a given point in space, there is a locus of points in space that falls on corresponding points in the two retinae. This locus of points is the horopter, a term originally used by Aguilonius in 1613. The horopter can be defined either theoretically or empirically.

The *Vieth–Mueller Circle* is a theoretical horopter, defined only in terms of geometrical considerations. This horopter is a circle in the horizontal plane that intersects each eye at the fovea. This circle defines a locus of points with zero disparity. However, in devising this theoretical horopter it is assumed that the mapping of the visual angle is homogeneous for the two eyes (C. W. Tyler, personal communication, 1993). For example, a position 10° from the fovea in the right eye is assumed to correspond to one at 10° from the fovea in the same direction in the left eye. Because of failures in the homogeneity and affine mapping properties, however, distortions occur. Thus, when one compares the Vieth–Mueller Circle to any of the empirically determined horopters defined below, there is a discrepancy between the theoretical and empirical horopters. The difference between the empirically determined horopter and the Vieth-Mueller Circle is known as the Hering–Hillebrand deviation. This discrepancy between the theoretical and empirical horopters suggests that relying only on theoretical calculations for the design and use of 3D stereoscopic displays may result in perceptual errors for human stereoscopic vision. Instead, one might empirically determine an observer's horopter in the 3D simulated display or virtual environment, just as one does for an observer in the real environment, then incorporate this information into the design and use of the 3D visual display.

There are several methods available to determine an *empirical horopter*. The five most common empirical horopters are the *nonius horopter* (i.e., the longitudinal horopter), the *equidistance horopter*, the *apparent fronto-parallel plane horopter*, the *singleness of vision horopter* (i.e., the fusion horopter) and the *stereoacuity horopter*. We will briefly consider the strengths and weaknesses of each of these empirical horopters. All of these horopters have been determined with eyes that are symmetrically converged; they also can be determined for eyes that are asymmetrically converged.

To determine the *nonius horopter* the subject binocularly fixates a target. Off to one side of the fixation target a vertical rod is presented so that one eye views the top half and the other eye views the bottom half. The subject's task is to align the top and bottom halves of the vertical rod so that they are collinear. This method is only useful for the central 24° of the visual field, because further into the peripheral visual field acuity is too poor to make accurate and reliable judgments. Also, because binocularly viewed visual direction may differ from monocularly viewed visual direction (see below), there may be a fixation disparity that will distort the empirically measured nonius horopter.

To determine the *equidistance horopter*, the subject binocularly fixates a target, then adjusts eccentrically located stimuli so that they appear to be the same distance from the subject as is the fixation target. To determine the *apparent frontoparallel plane horopter* the subject instead adjusts the eccentrically located stimuli so that they appear to lie in the same frontoparallel plane as the fixation target. For both of these horopters one is measuring properties of spatial perception that are unrelated to the binocular geometry. Consequently, there is an inherent ambiguity between the equidistance and apparent frontoparallel plane horopters; this ambiguity increases at more eccentric locations of the visual field. Moreover, neither of these horopters necessarily describes a locus of points that result in zero disparity. Both of these horopters, however, are relatively quick and easy to measure.

To determine the *singleness of vision horopter*, the subject binocularly fixates a target, then the distance of an eccentrically located stimulus is varied until that stimulus no longer appears single. The mean value at each eccentricity is used to describe the horopter. This method is long and tedious, requiring many judgments. Also, the region of single vision becomes larger and more difficult to judge as retinal eccentricity is increased.

To determine the *stereoacuity horopter*, the subject binocularly fixates a target, then determines the smallest detectable depth between two objects located at the same retinal eccentricity. The method is also very long and tedious. Yet, this is probably the best empirically determined horopter from a theoretical point of view.

The horopters described above have only dealt with the horizontal plane. However, Nakayama and his colleagues (Nakayama *et al.*, 1977; Nakayama, 1978) have determined a vertical horopter: a locus of points along the vertical meridian that fall on corresponding points of the two retinae. The empirical vertical horopter is a tilted straight line that passes from a point near the ground level, which lies directly below the subject's eyes, through the binocular fixation point, as originally conjectured by Helmholtz (Helmholtz, 1925).

Most of the above horopters describe a locus of points that should fall on corresponding points in the two retinae. Stereopsis, however, occurs when there is a nonzero disparity that gives rise to the percept of depth. That is, an object or visual stimulus appears closer or further than the horopter for crossed and uncrossed disparity, respectively. Stereopsis can sometimes occur even if the images are diplopic (the percept of double images). Thus, stereopsis does not necessarily depend upon fusion (the merging of the two eyes' different views into a single, coherent percept). Furthermore, there are several different types of stereopsis, as described below.

Quantitative and qualitative stereopsis

Quantitative or patent stereopsis is obtained for small disparities. In this case, there is a percept both of the direction (nearer versus further) and magnitude of the stereoscopic depth that increases monotonically with retinal disparity (see Figure 5-2). The left and right monocular images need not be fused in order for quantitative stereopsis to occur.

Qualitative or latent stereopsis is obtained for larger disparities, those that always yield a percept of diplopia (viz., doubled images). In this case, there is a percept of the direction (nearer versus further), but the magnitude of the stereoscopic depth does not increase monotonically with retinal disparity. Beyond the range of qualitative stereopsis there is no percept of stereoscopic depth and the perceived double images may appear either to collapse to the fixation plane or to have no definite location in depth. Although one can still perceive some depth with qualitative stereopsis, the presence of diplopic

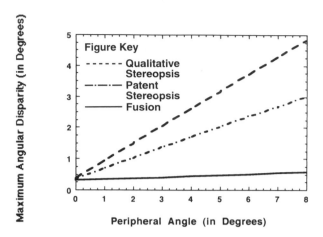

Figure 5-2a Disparity limits for fusion and for patent and qualitative stereopsis are plotted as a function of retinal eccentricity. The data shown here are redrawn from data shown in Bishop (1985) on page 637.

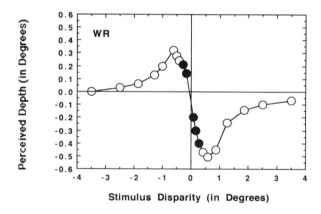

Figure 5-2b The perceived depth elicited by a bar flashed at different crossed and uncrossed disparities, relative to the fixation point. The filled circles represent fused depth percepts and the open circles represent diplopic percepts. The data shown here were redrawn from data reported in Richards (1971) on page 410.

images in a stereoscopic display may result in visual discomfort and detract from the subjective enjoyment in using stereoscopic displays. Moreover, in tasks that require fine depth perception, such as line threading or guiding a remote manipulator through a wire maze (Cole *et al.*, 1990; Spain and Holzhausen, 1991), depth information provided by qualitative stereopsis may not be accurate enough. In tasks where occlusion or interposition of objects provides adequate depth information, however, qualitative stereopsis probably also would provide adequate depth information.

Sensory fusion and diplopia

If the images in the two eyes are similar and there is only a small binocular retinal disparity, then the binocular stimuli will appear fused into the percept of a single object or stimulus (see Figure 5-2). Fine stereopsis corresponds to the range of retinal disparities over which the percept of the image remains fused; this is known as Panum's fusion area. In general, Panum's fusion area is ellipsoidal in shape. That is, a larger amount of horizontal disparity can be fused (e.g., 10' to 20' of arc at the fovea) but only a smaller amount of vertical disparity can be fused (e.g., 2.5' to 3.5'). This means that geometric distortions in the 3D stereoscopic display which introduce vertical disparities also could cause the perceived images to appear diplopic, rather than fused, whereas the same amount of horizontal disparity would not cause diplopia.

If the binocular retinal disparity is larger than Panum's fusion area, the percept is of doubled images and, thus, is diplopic rather than fused. Coarse stereopsis corresponds to the range of retinal disparities for which the percept of the image is diplopic, but depth differences are still perceived. Coarse stereopsis is a less specific process than is fine stereopsis in that coarse stereopsis can operate on dichoptic visual images which are very dissimilar in contrast, luminance, and form (Bishop, 1985).

Local and global stereopsis

Local stereopsis involves disparity processing at one location in the visual field without reference to the disparities present at other locations in the visual field or to other disparities at the same location (Tyler, 1983). Retinal stimulus features, such as size and orientation, may affect local stereoscopic processing. Moreover, local stereoscopic processing is not limited to small retinal disparities.

In contrast to local stereopsis, global stereopsis does involve interactions in disparity processing at many different locations in the visual field (Julesz, 1971). Whenever there is ambiguity as to which element in one retinal image corresponds to a given element in the other retinal image, a global process is needed to resolve the ambiguity.

Julesz (Julesz, 1971, 1978) used the term *cyclopean* for any stimulus features (e.g., depth) that are not discernible monocularly, but are revealed by disparity-processing mechanisms in the human visual system. For instance, a dynamic random dot stereogram (dRDS) may have depth cues that are not discernible monocularly, but that are revealed by stereoscopic processing. This type of pattern would be a cyclopean pattern and probably would involve global stereoscopic processing to reveal the various depths contained in the pattern. Another cyclopean pattern might be a leaf pattern or a similar pattern that is used for camouflage purposes; stereoscopic vision can provide the fine depth perception necessary to segment figure from ground and reveal camouflaged objects.

With global stereopsis, Panum's area is subject to a hysteresis effect (Fender and Julesz, 1967). That is, for a fused RDS, the two random dot images can be pulled apart by up to 2° of visual angle before fusion breaks down and diplopia results. However, diplopic random dot images must be laterally displaced by much less than 2° in order for fusion to occur. That is, the disparity limit for the breakdown of fusion is much larger than the disparity limit for the recovery of fusion from diplopic images. With local stereopsis, however, Panum's area is subject to a smaller hysteresis effect of only 6' of arc.

Spatial factors that affect human stereopsis and fusion

Stereopsis and fusion each can be affected by certain spatial characteristics of the visual patterns, such as the spatial frequency, orientation, and spatial location. Some of the important spatial characteristics of visual stimuli and how they can affect human stereopsis and fusion are described below.

Size or spatial frequency

Both stereoacuity and fusion thresholds vary as a function of size or spatial frequency content of the visual stimulus (Schor, 1987).[2] (High spatial frequencies occur when visual stimuli or objects have sharp edges or are of small size.)

Stereoacuity is finest and remains constant for visual patterns that contain spatial frequencies above 2.5 cycles per degree; stereoacuity becomes progressively worse with stimuli of lower spatial frequency content (Schor and Wood, 1983). Thus, a blurred visual pattern will result in poorer stereoacuity because the higher spatial frequencies have been eliminated by the blur. Also, the low spatial resolution available in many commercial virtual environments can result in worse stereoacuity performance than human stereoscopic vision is capable of. Three-dimensional stereoscopic displays with low spatial resolution would not be optimal for tasks which require fine depth perception, such as teleoperated surgery or remote line-threading tasks, but may be adequate for other tasks which require the perception of spatial layout, as discussed below.

The size of Panum's fusion area also is smaller for visual stimuli or objects of higher spatial frequencies than for those of lower spatial frequencies. That is, the binocular fusion limit or diplopia threshold is smallest for visual patterns that contain spatial frequencies above 2.5 cycles per degree; the fusion limit increases inversely with spatial frequency below 2.5 cycles per degree. Thus, for patterns with only high spatial frequencies viewed foveally at fixation, Panum's fusion limit is about 15' of arc; but, for patterns with only low spatial frequencies (e.g., below 0.1 cycles per degree) the fusion range can be over 6° of visual angle (Tyler, 1973; Schor, 1987). Moreover, Panum's fusion area is larger for stationary objects or those with slow temporal modulation than it is for objects that are moving or temporally modulating at faster rates (Tyler, 1983). This suggests an advantage for a 3D virtual environment system or stereoscopic display that has only limited spatial resolution: Because of the low spatial-frequency content of such displays, much larger retinal disparities can be tolerated and still result in the perception of fused images. These sorts of visual displays may be especially useful where the spatial layout of objects is important, as in a relatively static 3D stereoscopic visual display for air traffic control tasks.

Because both stereopsis and diplopia depend on the spatial frequency content of a visual pattern, a complex stimulus containing a broad range of spatial frequencies can result in the simultaneous percepts of stereopsis, fusion and diplopia. Thus, it may be beneficial to band-pass filter such visual displays to optimize performance in specific tasks.

Relative spacing of visual stimuli

For stereoacuity, as for other forms of spatial hyperacuity, the observer's sensitivity to depth is affected by the length of the compared features or stimuli as well as the distance separating them. The finest stereoacuity has been found with isolated vertical lines of 10′ to 15′ of arc in length or pairs of dots, with each dot pair vertically separated by 10′ to 15′ of arc. Increasing the length of a line or the distance between a pair of dots beyond 20′ of arc yields no improvement in stereoacuity (McKee, 1983). Moreover, stereoacuity is optimal if there is a gap of 10′ to 30′ of arc between stimuli (McKee, 1983); it is noticeably worse for stimuli that either spatially abut or are separated by much larger distances (Westheimer and McKee, 1977). These results suggest that the spatial enhancers sometimes used to improve distance and elevation judgments in perspective-view display formats could interfere with stereoscopic vision. (Remember that in a perspective view, stereopsis can help disambiguate the distance of an object from its elevation above the ground.)

Disparity scaling and disparity gradient limit

Tyler (Tyler, 1973, 1974) showed that the upper limits of both fusion and depth perception depend upon a disparity scaling effect. That is, the maximum retinal disparity that can be fused, δ_{max}, can be determined as follows:

$$\delta_{max} = cA \qquad (5)$$

where c is a disparity scaling factor and A is the visual angle subtended by the disparity gradient. (Tyler used the example of a corrugated random dot pattern, a pattern that is sinusoidally modulated in depth with a fixed spatial period. In the above equation, A would correspond to half of the spatial period of the corrugated random dot pattern.)

Burt and Julesz (1980) later showed that the maximum disparity which can be fused, δ_{max}, is proportional to the distance, R, between neighboring objects in a visual image. They stated that fusion fails, for the average observer, when the disparity gradient, δ/R, exceeds a value of 1. Thus, for densely positioned objects, the maximum disparity for fused images is *less* than it is for objects positioned further apart. In the former case, the δ_{max} may be less than the classic Panum's fusion limits.

Stereoscopic 3D display formats should be designed so that the spacing of objects within the visual scene and the rate of change of disparity across space remains within the gradient limits specified above. Otherwise, diplopia and loss of depth perception may result.

Orientation

Stereoacuity is worse for oblique or horizontal visual patterns than for vertical patterns (Ogle, 1955; Ebenholtz and Walchli, 1965; Blake *et al.*, 1976; Arditi,

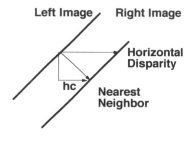

Figure 5-3 In measuring retinal disparity between the corresponding left- and right-eye's images, usually the horizontal disparity is measured. The horizontal disparity is shown in this diagram for a 45° oblique line. However, for this 45° oblique line, the nearest-neighbor disparity is indicated by the arrow pointing down and to the right. For the oblique line, the nearest-neighbor disparity is shorter than is the horizontal disparity. In this example, hc, the horizontal component of the nearest-neighbor disparity, is even shorter.

1982; Davis *et al.*, 1992a, 1992b). In fact, stereoacuity thresholds seem to be proportional to the $\cos(\theta)$, where θ is the angle of rotation in the frontoparallel plane.

In most of these cases, horizontal retinal disparity was measured. The classic interpretation is that human stereopsis only uses horizontal retinal disparity to derive depth information (Bishop, 1985). Davis *et al.* (1992a) instead proposed that human stereopsis may compute the nearest-neighbor matches of corresponding elements in the left and right images for patterns which have an orientation between vertical and 45° oblique; this proposal agrees with Ebenholtz and Walchli's (1965) interpretation of their data. So, for a 45° oblique pattern, the nearest-neighbor components would be perpendicular to the 45° oblique pattern, as shown in Figure 5-3. According to the nearest-neighbor algorithm, when only horizontal retinal disparity is measured by the experimenter, the stereoacuity of a 45° oblique pattern should be larger than that of a vertical pattern by a factor of 1.414.[3] Results consistent with the nearest-neighbor matching algorithm have been obtained using standard psychophysical methods (Davis *et al.*, 1992b; Ebenholtz and Walchli, 1965). Thus, at least for visual patterns rotated between vertical and 45° oblique orientations, stereoacuity may involve both vertical and horizontal retinal disparity components and, thus, perhaps a nearest-neighbor algorithm should be used to compute disparities for the left and right images in a 3D stereoscopic display.

Visual field location

Stereoacuity is finest for stimuli that fall on or near the fixation point (Westheimer and McKee, 1980; McKee, 1983). At a visual field eccentricity of 30' of arc, stereoacuity has fallen to half of its best value (Millodot, 1972). Moreover, stereoacuity is finest at the plane of fixation and increases when presented on either crossed or uncrossed disparity pedestals (Blakemore, 1970; Westheimer, 1979; Schumer and Julesz, 1984).

Similarly, Panum's fusion area has the smallest size (e.g., 10' to 20' of arc for horizontal disparity) for images that fall on the fovea of the retinae. The size of Panum's area is larger for images that fall in the periphery of the retinae; in fact, the size of Panum's area increases in proportion to the distance from the fovea.

Figure 5-4 This figure illustrates the stereo aperture problem. The problem can result if visual patterns are one dimensional and are of longer extent than the stereo aperture (shown by the oval shape). In this case, only nearest-neighbor disparities are encoded. That is, the only disparities which matter are those that are perpendicular to the orientation of the one-dimensional visual pattern.

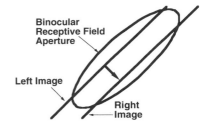

The results for stereoacuity and fusion suggest that more optimal 3D stereoscopic displays would provide finer spatial resolution near the center of gaze than in more peripheral areas of the visual field.

Potential problems in human stereopsis and fusion

Before human stereopsis and fusion can function properly in either a real or a virtual environment, there are a number of inherent problems that the human visual system must first resolve. Below we briefly describe some of those problems.

The correspondence problem and false targets

The correspondence problem is one major problem in fusing the right and left retinal images. That is, which point in one monocular image corresponds to a given point in the other monocular image? Prior to Julesz' (1960) work with random dot stereograms (RDSs), it was thought that the correspondence problem was avoided by first recognizing objects and their components in one image, then performing errorless matches with the corresponding objects and their components in the other image. Julesz showed that with RDSs, the perception of depth could precede the recognition of objects rather than follow it. Thus, for random dot patterns, as well as for many other patterns, a given element in one image does not unambiguously match an element in the other image. Marr and Poggio (1979) have rigorously considered the correspondence problem and algorithmic solutions for reducing the probability of false target matches.

The stereo aperture problem

A stereo aperture problem can result if visual patterns are one dimensional (e.g., lines and sinewave gratings) and are of longer extent than the stereo aperture. Figure 5-4 graphically shows the stereo aperture problem. According to the stereo aperture problem, only retinal disparities perpendicular to the orientation of the visual pattern are encoded (Davis *et al.*, 1992b). That is, only nearest-neighbor matching correspondence points in the right and left images are encoded. The size and orientation of this aperture result from the receptive field properties of low-level binocular mechanisms in the human visual system. We assume that for stereoacuity, the most sensitive binocular mechanism detects the depth. We also assume that these binocular mechanisms are selectively sensitive to the spatial frequency and spatial phase content of the visual pattern. The binocular mechanism need not be selectively sensitive to orientation, however, for the stereo aperture problem to occur.

Although the stereo aperture problem may exist for one-dimensional visual patterns that are vertically or obliquely oriented, it does not exist for two-dimensional patterns or for horizontally oriented one-dimensional patterns (Davis et al., 1992b).

Calibration of depth and distance from retinal disparity

A fixed retinal disparity, δ, is ambiguous. It could correspond either to a small depth between two points viewed at a relatively close distance or to a large depth between two points viewed at a relatively far distance. In theory, if we know the angle of convergence of the two eyes (e.g., the value of α in Figure 5-1) and the retinal disparity, δ, we could disambiguate whether a given retinal disparity corresponds to a small depth at a close viewing distance or a large depth at a far viewing distance. In fact, we could precisely determine the depth or absolute distance.

Extraretinal signals from the oculomotor system could provide the necessary information about convergence angle, if the interocular distance (i) is known. Although knowing the angle of convergence may be useful, its effective availability and precision are poor for the human visual system, especially for distances beyond one meter (Foley, 1977, 1980; Erkenlens and Colliwijn, 1985; Arditi, 1986; Schor, 1987).

Retinal signals based on vertical disparities as well as horizontal disparities could help disambiguate the depth or distance for a given retinal disparity; these retinal signals also could help to interpret the spatial layout of objects (Longuet-Higgins, 1982; Gillam and Lawergren, 1983; Gillam et al., 1988). These vertical disparities arise because of perspective deformations that occur in stereo geometry as a function of the distance (and spatial location) of objects. Questions exist, however, as to whether the human visual system does measure vertical disparities that could be used in calibrating distance from retinal disparities and also whether the measurements of vertical disparities are accurate enough to perform this task (Poggio and Poggio, 1984).

Visual signals based on monocular cues to depth may help humans to judge absolute distance and, thus, disambiguate depth derived from retinal disparity (Schor, 1987; Maloney and Landy, 1990; Landy et al., 1991). Precisely how these monocular cues may provide absolute distance information to stereopsis is not well understood.

Binocular visual direction

Fixation disparity (vergence disparity) may arise because sometimes the binocular visual direction is different from monocular visual direction. For example, in the binocular condition two vertical, abutting lines are seen by each eye and can be adjusted so that they are collinear. Next, in the monocular condition the upper line is viewed only by one eye, the lower line only by the other eye. In the monocular condition, if the two lines no longer appear aligned, then a fixation disparity exists. Often fixation disparities are in the range of $-5'$ to $+3'$ of arc.

Binocular rivalry, binocular suppression, and binocular luster

If the left and right monocular images fall on corresponding points of the two retinae but are very different in spatial characteristics (e.g., one is a bright bar and the other is a dark bar), binocular rivalry may result. That is, instead of perceiving both monocular images simultaneously, the monocular images may be perceived in alternation so that while the left monocular image is perceived, the right monocular image is suppressed, and vice versa. Hebbar and McAllister (1991) have shown how color quantization of stereoscopic images may inadvertently result in binocular rivalry. Increased stimulus strength (or contrast) of a monocular input will increase the prevalence of that eye over the fellow eye (Levelt, 1968; Blake, 1977). Transient, alternating suppression can become continuous suppression of one monocular image by the other. This can happen if one retinal input dominates over the input from the corresponding points of the other retina.

Suppression often occurs when the spatial stimulus presented to one eye is sufficiently different in orientation, length, or thickness from that presented to the other eye (Levelt, 1968). Temporally modulating or moving contours are particularly effective in producing rivalry and suppression (Tyler, 1983). Whereas lines and edges are rivalrous, areas of uniform brightnesses may tend to average. Often, in areas of uniform illumination, binocular luster occurs when the luminance for one eye is different from that for the fellow eye. In this case, the percept of a lustrous or shimmering surface of indeterminate depth occurs. Binocular luster can also be observed in RDSs in which all of the elements for one eye have the opposite polarity or contrast of those for the other eye.

We now have considered the binocular geometry of the human visual system as it affects 3D spatial perception as well as some spatial factors that also can influence human stereopsis and fusion. We next will examine the modeling geometry, display geometry, and geometric distortions in 3D stereoscopic displays as well as some technological limitations and artifacts in various stereoscopic displays that can affect human spatial perception of a 3D environment.

STEREOSCOPIC DISPLAYS FOR VIRTUAL ENVIRONMENTS

Stereoscopic virtual environments are different from real visual environments in two basic ways. First, virtual environments lack or are inconsistent in providing some of the visual cues that are present in real visual environments. Second, virtual environments also can contain artifacts or visual cues that do not exist in real environments. For example, in stereoscopic virtual environments, accommodation cues often can be inconsistent with convergence information when both eyes are focused on a screen that is a fixed distance from the observer. Moreover, in time-multiplexed displays, interocular cross-talk occurs between the left- and right-eye images of a scene. Presentation of visually convincing 3D virtual environments requires an understanding of both human stereopsis and of the technology used to create the 3D environment.

There are three primary approaches to incorporating stereoscopic images into virtual environment displays. First, head-mounted displays consist of separate display screens for each eye that are attached to the head along with some type of display optics and a head-tracking device (Teitel, 1990).[4] Second, time-multiplexed CRT displays present a stereoscopic image by alternating right- and left-eye views of a scene on a CRT. The image is viewed through a shutter system that occludes the left eye when the right-eye image is on the screen and vice versa (Hodges, 1992). Third, time-multiplexed projection displays operate similarly to time-multiplexed CRTs, but the images are projected onto one or more large screens (Cruz-Neira *et al.*, 1992). Projection and CRT stereoscopic displays may or may not also incorporate head-tracking. None of the existing commercial systems incorporates monitoring of eye movements or positions.

Screen parallax and retinal disparity

For any type of stereoscopic display, we are modeling what would be seen by each eye if the image were projected onto a screen or window being viewed by an observer. The simplest case is when the observer's eyes are horizontally aligned and lie in a plane parallel to a single planar projection screen on which both the left- and right-eye projected view of an image are displayed (Figure 5-5). If we choose a point, P, on the object and follow its projection vectors to each eye position, then the distance between the projected location of P on the screen, P_{left}, seen by the left eye and the projected location, P_{right}, seen by the right eye is called the *screen parallax*. Screen parallax is consistent with, but is not the same as, retinal disparity. Retinal disparity is measured on the two retinae and its value is relative to the current binocular fixation point. Screen parallax is measured on the surface of a display device and its value is dependent on the computational model of the observer (i.e., the distance from each eye position to the projection plane and the orientation of the plane relative to the plane containing the two eye positions) and the display geometry (how values are mapped onto a display screen). Points with constant screen parallax describe a straight line that is parallel to a line drawn through the two eye positions (centers of projection). Zero or no parallax results in a spatial position at the plane of the screen. Crossed or negative parallax (i.e., the left-eye view of P', is to the right of the right-eye view of P') results in an image that appears spatially in front of the display screen. Conversely, uncrossed or positive parallax results in an image that appears behind the screen.

The amount of screen parallax, in cases of crossed and uncrossed parallax, may be computed with respect to the geometric model of the scene as shown in Figure 5-6 and by the following equation:

$$p = i(D - d)/D \tag{6}$$

where p is the amount of screen parallax for a point, f_1, when projected onto a

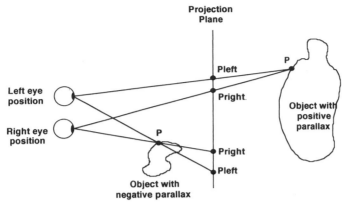

Figure 5-5 Screen parallax for cases of crossed (negative) and uncrossed (positive) parallax.

plane a distance d from the plane containing two eyepoints. The interocular distance between eyepoints is denoted by i and D is the distance from f_1 to the nearest point on the plane containing the two eyepoints.

Points with constant screen parallax describe a straight line that is parallel to a line drawn through the two eye points. This assumes that the eyepoints do not change positions when the eyes converge and accommodate on a different point. In reality the location of the first nodal point of the eye's lens system will vary slightly with convergence and possibly with accommodation (Deering, 1992). Assuming a model in which perfectly spherical eyes rotate about the eyepoint so that the eyepoint is stationary with respect to the head position and in which affine mapping properties hold, the resulting screen parallax that is computed for each point in the scene will produce proper retinal parallax for any fixation point and resultant convergence angles. This is illustrated in Figure 5-7. Points f_2 and f_3 both have the same screen disparity as point f_1. These equal screen parallaxes induce convergence angles (α, β and γ) for all three points and resultant retinal disparities ($\alpha - \beta$) and ($\alpha - \gamma$).

Screen parallax is an absolute measure of a point's distance from the plane of an observer's eyepoints. To calculate retinal disparity from screen parallax, we must look at values that are proportional to differences in screen parallax. For symmetric convergence, this calculation is straightforward for points that lie on a line along the binocular visual direction. If an observer's eyes are

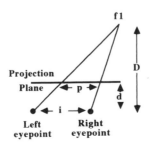

Figure 5-6 Screen parallax, p, is equal to $i(D - d)/D$.

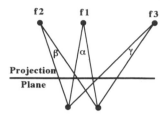

Figure 5-7   Screen parallax and convergence angles.

fixated on a point, f_1, in a stereoscopic virtual environment, then there is a screen parallax p_α associated with that point and an angle of convergence, α. Another point, f_2, with convergence angle, β, would also have an associated screen parallax, p_β. (Remember that retinal disparity is the difference in vergence angles $(\alpha - \beta)$ between two points in space, measured in units of visual angle.) For points that lie on a line along the binocular visual direction, the retinal disparity may be computed directly from the screen parallax by the following formula:

$$2[\tan^{-1}(p_\alpha/2(D - d)) - \tan^{-1}(p_\beta/2(D - d))]. \qquad (7)$$

Modeling geometry

One of the most important issues in producing good stereoscopic imagery is to guarantee that the modeling geometry implicit in the mathematical model matches the display geometry of the hardware. The display geometry must be modeled accurately by the perspective projections used to produce the left- and right-eye views of a scene.

For time-multiplexed images in which both the left- and right-eye views are shown overlaid on a single screen and for head-mounted displays in which both display screens are aligned in the same plane, an off-axis projection should be used. For an off-axis projection we assume two different centers of projection. The right-eye view will be produced by projection to a right center of projection. The left-eye view will be produced by projection to a left center of projection. (For implementation details see Hodges, 1992.) The field of view (FOV) for the stereoscopic image computed with the off-axis projection consists of three regions: a stereoscopic region that is seen by both eyes, plus two monoscopic regions, each of which is seen only by one eye. Together these three regions present a wider FOV than is achieved from a single perspective image computed with the same parameters (Williams and Parrish, 1992). In addition to this increased FOV due to the nonoverlapping regions, we also encode more information about a scene because the left- and right-eye views of the overlapping region show different perspectives of the scene.

For some head-mounted displays, the display screen for the left eye may not be coplanar with the display screen for the right eye. In this case the left- and right-eye views may be computed by rotations about a vertical axis through the scene followed by a standard perspective projection. The left-eye view is rotated from left to right. Conversely, the right-eye view is rotated from right to left. Total rotation should reflect the relative angular orientation of the left-eye display screen with respect to the right-eye display screen.

Accurate head-tracking is crucial to the presentation of spatially consistent stereoscopic images. Screen parallax information is computed based on implied eye-point positions relative to head position and head orientation. If the observer's head is not exactly in the position reported by the head-tracker, then scaling and distortion effects in the image occur. If the observer's head is further away from the center of the display than reported by the head-tracker the image is elongated in depth. If his head is closer, then the image is compacted in depth. If the observer's head is incorrectly tracked for side-to-side or up-down motion, the image is distorted by a shear transformation.

Display geometry

A stereoscopic display system provides a partitioning of three-dimensional space into volumetric spatial units known as *stereoscopic voxels* (Hodges and Davis, 1993). Each stereoscopic voxel is defined by the intersection of the lines of sight from each eye through two distinct pixels. The size and shape of stereoscopic voxels are determined by the position of each eye as well as the pixel pitch and shape. If we assume an idealized rectangular pixel shape,[5] then stereoscopic voxels can be modeled as six-sided polyhedrons with a diamond-shaped horizontal cross-section. A horizontal slice (created by one row of pixels) is shown in Figure 5-8. The distance, measured in number of pixels between the eye points, specifies the total number of discrete depth positions at which a point may be placed. In Figure 5-8, the number in each diamond cell indicates the number of pixels of parallax which defines that row of stereoscopic voxels. All stereoscopic voxels in a particular row have the same volume. They differ in shape in that each is a shear of the stereoscopic voxel which is centered between the two eyes of the observer.

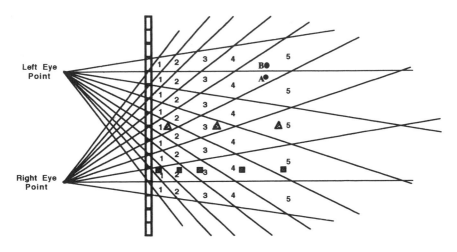

Figure 5-8 Cross-section of stereoscopic voxels.

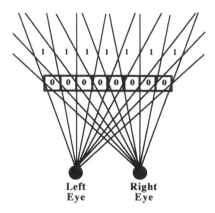

Figure 5-9 Jittering depth locations to achieve more horizontal resolution.

A point's apparent position may be defined as the center of the cross-sectional area of the stereoscopic voxel in which it resides.[6] The diamond cross-sectional shape of the stereoscopic voxels means that a point's horizontal placement can affect its apparent depth location. In Figure 5-8, point A would appear to be closer to an observer than would point B. Similarly, the distinct steps in depth at which a point may appear is affected by the point's horizontal placement. For example, the position of the triangular points in Figure 5-8 puts them in only three different depth positions (1, 3, and 5). Yet, the square points, which exist in the same range of depth, are positioned in five depth positions (1, 2, 3, 4, and 5).

Conversely, if we allow some jitter in a pixel's depth location, then we can provide an effective doubling of horizontal spatial resolution for point positioning in stereoscopic display as compared to monoscopic display. For example, if we allow points to be positioned in either rows 0 and 1 of Figure 5-9, then we have fifteen horizontal positions represented across the front of the eight-pixel screen in Figure 5-9.

We can analytically characterize a stereoscopic voxel in row j by the values, $d_{j\text{near}}$, $d_{j\text{far}}$, $d_{j\text{mid}}$, and $d_{j\text{width}}$ (Figure 5-10). The distance of nearest approach of a voxel j to the plane of the display screen is $d_{j\text{near}}$, the distance from the plane to the most-distance point of the voxel is $d_{j\text{far}}$, the distance to the largest width of the voxel is $d_{j\text{mid}}$, and the maximum width of the voxel is $d_{j\text{width}}$.

From similar triangles we can derive the following equations:

$$d_{j\text{near}} = d_{(j-2)\text{far}} \tag{8a}$$

$$d_{j\text{far}} = (j+1)pD/(i-(j+1)p) \tag{8b}$$

$$d_{j\text{mid}} = d_{(j-1)\text{far}} \tag{8c}$$

$$d_{j\text{width}} = (j+1)p(d_{j\text{far}} - d_{j\text{mid}})/(d_{j\text{far}}) \tag{8d}$$

where p is the pixel pitch, i is the interocular distance, and D is the distance from the eyeplane to projection plane.

Figure 5-10   Characterization of stereoscopic voxel.

Interocular cross-talk and ghosting

In a perfect time-multiplexed system, when the right-eye image is on the screen the left-eye image should be completely extinguished, and vice versa. In a real system, however, interocular cross-talk between the images occurs. Factors that affect the amount of interocular cross-talk include the dynamic range of the shutter, phosphor persistence, and vertical screen position of the image. The subjective impression of ghosting or image doubling is an artifact of cross-talk. Ghosting in the stereoscopic image can cause a correspondence problem for the user, as discussed previously. Factors affecting the perceived ghosting between the left- and right-eye images as a result of cross-talk are image brightness, contrast, textural complexity, and horizontal parallax. These are discussed below.

Cross-talk is caused by a combination of the effects of the leakage of the shutter in its closed state and the phosphorescence from the opposite eye's image when the shutter is in its open state. The amount of leakage in the shutter's closed state is quantified in terms of its dynamic range. The dynamic range of the shutter is defined as the ratio of the transmission of the shutter in its open state to the transmission of the shutter in its closed state. The amount of phosphorescence from the opposite eye's image is defined by phosphor persistence, or the length of time it takes for the phosphorescence to decay to 10% of its initial light output. Persistence is related to color of the object in that the P22 red, green, and blue phosphors used in most CRTs do not decay at the same rate. The red and blue phosphors have substantially faster decay rates than does the green phosphor. The phosphorescence contribution also increases in relation to distance to the bottom of the CRT screen. This increase is an artifact of the top-to-bottom scanning of an image on a raster graphics display screen. Scan lines near the top of the screen have had longer to decay when the shutter switches than do scan lines at the bottom. Yeh and Silverstein (1990) have quantified this effect as a function of image color and screen position based on P22 phosphors and a Tektronix 808-012 Four Segment Liquid Crystal (LC) Stereo Goggles in terms of extinction ratio (the luminance of the correct eye's image divided by the luminance of the opposite eye's ghost image).

Lipton (1987) has pointed out that the ghosting effect produced by cross-talk between the left- and right-eye images is mitigated by a number of factors such as image brightness, contrast, texture complexity, and horizontal parallax. The effect of these factors on perceived ghosting between the images is not as easy to quantify in terms of exact measurements but does provide useful *rules of thumb* for improving quality of images. In general, perception of ghosting in images is directly proportional to brightness, amount of horizontal parallax, and high contrast. Perception of ghosting is inversely proportional to the textural complexity or amount of detail in the image.

Collimated stereo display

Head-mounted and time-multiplexed CRT stereoscopic displays usually either physically or optically place the display screen between 40 and 80 centimeters from the observer. The resulting effective viewing volume has a depth of approximately one meter. Moving the display screen further from the observer and using primarily cross-parallax can extend the usable depth of viewing volume but at the expense of field of view. Experiments at NASA-Langley Research Center indicate that collimating the display source so that the accommodation distance is effectively at optical infinity will allow an increase in depth of viewing volume while maintaining a field of view of approximately 40° (Busquets *et al.*, 1990).

CRT refresh rate

The CRT refresh rate contributes to the perceived flicker in an image. Currently 60 and 120 Hz refresh rates are used for time-multiplexed stereoscopic display. Shutters and monitors that may be driven at approximately 60 Hz provide the observer with a 30 Hz refresh rate to each eye. Switching is usually done by a hardware double buffer with each perspective view shown at full resolution. Interactive displays are difficult to achieve because all image updates must be done in less than $\frac{1}{60}$ of a second to maintain correspondence between perspective views and the observer's eyes. The 120 Hz systems provide a 60 Hz refresh rate to each eye but at reduced vertical resolution because each frame buffer is divided into a logical left- and right-eye buffer. Interactive displays for hardware double-buffered systems are more practical because the programmer is working with the logical equivalent of four buffers: two to display the current image and two in which to draw the next stereo image (Baker, 1987). We are aware of no studies that compare the actual performance of 60 Hz full-resolution systems to 120 Hz reduced-resolution systems. It is generally assumed that a faster refresh rate is more advantageous than is full spatial resolution. It has been our experience, however, that visual interpretation of very complex images with fine detail is sometimes easier on a 60 Hz system with full resolution than on the 120 Hz system at half resolution (Ribarsky *et al.*, 1992). Also, suppose vertical disparities can convey information to the observer about absolute distance or a scaling factor to disambiguate the depth that corresponds to a given retinal disparity, as some have suggested, then in this case, the reduced vertical resolution of the faster 120 Hz stereographics display may be harmful.

Image distortion

Image distortion caused by display technology is a problem for both time-multiplexed and head-mounted displays. Two possible sources of distortion for time-multiplexed CRT displays have been analyzed by Deering (1992). The first source of distortion is that standard projection geometry assumes that the display surface of a CRT is planar. Modern CRT screens, however, are shaped as a section of a sphere or a cylinder with a radius of curvature of about two meters. The second source of distortion is that the phosphor screen on a CRT is viewed through a thick glass faceplate with an index of refraction significantly higher than that of air. For a viewing angle of 60° relative to a normal vector to the plane of the CRT, the curvature of the CRT screen can cause positional errors on the order of 1.8 centimeters. For the same viewing angle, the thickness of the glass faceplate can cause positional errors of up to 2.0 cm. These errors are both viewpoint dependent and nonlinear. Equations to compensate for these distortions are described by Deering (1992).

For head-mounted displays image distortions are introduced by the optics of the system, by improper alignment of the user's eye position with respect to the mathematical model of eye position, and by mismatches between the display's field of view and the mathematical model for field of view implicit in the software. Of particular interest are the distortions caused by the optical system in the head-mounted display. The purpose of the optical system is to provide an image to the user that is located at a comfortable distance for accommodation and magnified to provide a reasonable field of view. The optics also cause nonlinear distortions in the image so that straight lines in the model appear curved in the visual image. Robinett and Rolland (1992) have developed a computational model for the geometry of head-mounted displays to correct for these distortions. An algorithm for real-time implementation of their model has not been developed.

SUMMARY AND CONCLUSIONS

Virtual environments are becoming increasingly important for training, targeting, teleoperation, and entertainment. They offer a new human–computer interaction paradigm in which users are immersed in and actively participate within a computer-generated 3D virtual world. The use of 3D stereoscopic displays can enhance the sense of presence and add to the fun and excitement of virtual environments, but, to optimize the effectiveness of the design and use of 3D stereoscopic displays, we need to consider several related issues. We first reviewed situations where 3D stereoscopic displays can enhance human spatial perception and performance (as well as where they may not). We then considered the human component of this new human–computer interface. Specifically, we discussed the binocular geometry of human stereoscopic vision and how various spatial factors can affect human stereopsis and fusion. Finally, we considered the machine component of this new human–computer interface. Specifically, we discussed the modeling geometry of software designed to present stereoscopic images and the display geometry of the hardware on which those images are displayed. We also considered some technical limitations and artifacts that arise due to human stereoscopic vision and to the 3D stereoscopic display software and hardware. All of these issues must be considered in the design and use of 3D stereoscopic virtual environments.

ACKNOWLEDGMENTS

We thank Aries Arditi, Woody Barfield, Allison Hochstein, Bob King, Art Kirkland, Christopher Tyler, and an anonymous reviewer for helpful comments on an earlier version of this chapter.

NOTES

1. For asymmetric convergence of the two eyes, the formula for the angle of convergence is basically the same as that shown for symmetric convergence. The difference is that D now represents the perpendicular distance from the interocular axis to the frontoparallel plane which intersects the asymmetrically converged point of fixation. This interpretation of the convergence angle formula for asymmetric convergence is not exact, but it is a good approximation.

2. Spatial frequency is measured in cycles per degree (cy/deg) of visual angle, where $1°$ corresponds to approximate $\frac{1}{3}$ mm on the retina. So, a sinewave grating of 1 cy/deg would have one bright–dark pair of blurry bars falling on a width of $\frac{1}{3}$ mm of the retina. Spatial frequency is always specified in terms of the retinal image (proximal stimulus). The spatial frequency content of a visual pattern may matter for a few reasons. First, by Fourier Analysis any complex visual scene can be decomposed into a set of sinewave gratings of the appropriate spatial frequencies, orientations, etc. Second, the human visual system may perform a crude Fourier analysis of visual inputs at an early level of visual processing (i.e., the visual cortex). See Graham (1989) for more details about Fourier analysis and its relation to the early stages of human vision.

3. However, in explaining the induced effect, Arditi (1982) proposed that human stereopsis computes the *horizontal component* of the nearest-neighbor matches, as shown by h_c in Figure 5-4. This would yield somewhat different predictions from those discussed in the text.

4. Although counterbalanced CRT-based displays such as NASA's CCSV (McDowall *et al.*, 1990) or the BOOM (Cruz-Neira *et al.*, 1992) differ from head-mounted displays in terms of tracking technique and the use of CRTs instead of liquid crystal displays, their stereoscopic characteristics are similar and will not be addressed separately.

5. When displayed on a CRT, pixels actually have a Gaussian shape and adjacent pixels may blend together. LCD pixels have well-defined edges, but most head-mounted displays incorporate an optical low-pass filter to reduce the perception of this effect. Head-mounted displays (HMDs) also incorporate optics that distort size and location of pixels.

6. Alternately, we could think of the volume of a stereoscopic pixel as a measure of the *uncertainty* in the position of a point or as a type of spatial aliasing.

REFERENCES

Arditi, A. (1982) The dependence of the induced effect on orientation and a hypothesis concerning disparity computations in general, *Vision Res.*, **22**, 247–56

Arditi, A. (1986) Binocular vision, in K. R. Boff *et al.* (Eds), *Handbook of Perception and Human Performance*, New York: Wiley

Baker, J. (1987) Generating images for a time-multiplexed stereoscopic computer graphics system, in *SPIE*, vol. 761, Bellingham, WA: SPIE, pp. 44–52

Barfield, W. and Rosenberg, C. (1992) Comparison of stereoscopic and perspective display formats for exocentric judgment tasks, *Paper presented at the Annual Meeting of the Human Factors Society*, Atlanta, GA

Barfield, W., Rosenberg, C., Han, S.-H., and Furness, T. (1992) A god's eye (exocentric) versus a pilot's eye (egocentric) frame-of-reference for enhanced situational awareness, in *Proc. of the Annual Meeting of the Human Factors Society*, Atlanta, GA: Working Paper: Department of Industrial Engineering, University of Washington

Bishop, P. O. (1985) Binocular vision, in *Adler's Physiology of the Eye*, Saint Louis, MO: Mosby

Blake, R. (1977) Threshold conditions for binocular rivalry, *J. Exp. Psychol.: Human Perception Perform.*, **3**, 251–7

Blake, R., Camisa, J., and Antoinetti, D. N. (1976) Binocular depth discrimination depends on orientation, *Percept. Psychophys.*, **20**, 113–18

Blakemore, C. (1970) The range and scope of binocular depth discrimination in man, *J. Physiol. (London)*, **211**, 599–622

Boff, K. R. and Lincoln, J. E. (Eds) (1988) *Engineering data compendium: Human Perception and Performance*, Ohio: Wright-Patterson Air Force Base

Burt, P. and Julesz, B. (1980) A disparity gradient limit for binocular fusion, *Science*, **208**, 615–17

Busquets, A. M., Williams, S. P., and Parrish, R. V. (1990) Depth-viewing volume increase by collimation of stereo 3-D displays, in *IEEE Southeastern Conf., IEEE 90-260*, New Orleans

Cole, R. E., Merritt, J. O., Coleman, R., and Ikehara, C. (1991) Teleoperator performance with virtual window display, in J. O. Merritt and S. S. Fisher (Eds), *Stereoscopic Displays and Applications II, SPIE*, vol. 1457, San José, CA: pp. 111–19

Cole, R. E., Merritt, J. O., and Lester, P. (1990) Remote manipulator tasks impossible without stereo TV, in J. O. Merritt and S. S. Fisher (Eds), *Stereoscopic Displays and Applications I, SPIE*, vol. 1256, San José, CA: pp. 255–65

Cruz-Neira, Sandin, D. J., DeFanti, T. A., Kenyon, R. V., and Hart, J. C. (1992) The CAVE: Audio visual experience automatic virtual environment, *Commun. ACM*, **35**, 64–72

Davis, E. T., King, R. A., and Anoskey, A. (1992a) Oblique effect in stereopsis? in B. Rogowitz (Ed.), *Human Vision, Visual Processing, and Digital Display III, SPIE*, vol. 1666, San José, CA: pp. 465–74

Davis, E. T., King, R. A., Guenter, B., and Anoskey, A. (1992b) Anisotropies in stereo depth thresholds of luminance-modulated spatial patterns? *Perception*, **21** (suppl. 2), 83

Deering, M. (1992) High resolution virtual reality, *Computer Graphics*, **26**, 195–202

Drascic, D. (1991) Skill acquisition and task performance in teleoperation using monoscopic and stereoscopic video remote viewing, in *Proc. of the Human Factors Society 35th Annual Meeting*, pp. 1–5

Ebenholtz, S. and Walchli, R. (1965) Stereoscopic thresholds as a function of head- and object-orientation, *Vision Res.*, **5**, 455–61

Erkenlens, C. J. and Colliwijn, H. (1985) Eye movements and stereopsis during dichoptic viewing of moving random-dot stereograms, *Vision Res.*, **25**, 1689–700

Fender, D. and Julesz, B. (1967) Extension of Panum's fusional area in binocularly stabilized vision, *J. Opt. Soc. Am.*, **57**, 819–30

Foley, J. M. (1977) Effect of distance information and range on two indices of visually perceived distance, *Perception*, **6**, 449–60

Foley, J. M. (1980) Binocular distance perception, *Psychol. Rev.*, **87**, 411–34

Gillam, B., Chambers, D., and Lawergren, B. (1988) The role of vertical disparity in the scaling of stereoscopic depth perception: an empirical and theoretical study, *Percept. Psychophys.*, **44**, 473–83

Gillam, B. and Lawergren, B. (1983) The induced effect, vertical disparity and stereoscopic theory, *Percept. Psychophys.*, **34**, 121–30

Graham, C. H. (1965) Visual space perception, in C. H. Graham (Ed.), *Vision and Visual Perception*, New York: Wiley

Graham, N. V. S. (1989) *Visual Pattern Analyzers*, New York: Oxford University Press

Gulick, W. L. and Lawson, R. B. (1976) *Human Stereopsis*, New York: Oxford University Press

Hebbar, P. D. and McAllister, D. F. (1991) Color quantization aspects in stereopsis, in J. O. Merritt and S. S. Fisher (Eds), *Stereoscopic Displays and Applications II*, *SPIE*, vol. 1457, San José, CA, pp. 233–41

Helmholtz, H. von (1925) *Treatise on Physiological Optics* (Translated by J. P. C. Southall, from 3rd German edn), Optical Society of America

Hodges, L. F. (1992) Time-multiplexed stereoscopic display, *IEEE Computer Graphics and Applications*, **12**, 20–30

Hodges, L. F. and Davis, E. T. (1993) Geometric considerations for stereoscopic virtual environments, *PRESENCE: Teleoperators and Virtual Environments*, **2**(1), 34–43

Julesz, B. (1960) Binocular depth perception of computer-generated patterns, *Bell System Tech. J.*, **39**, 1125–62

Julesz, B. (1971) *Foundations of Cyclopean Perception*, Chicago: University of Chicago Press

Julesz, B. (1978) Global stereopsis: Cooperative phenomena in stereoscopic depth perception, in R. Held, *et al.* (Eds), *Handbook of Sensory Physiology: Perception*, Berlin: Springer

Kim, W. S., Ellis, S. R., Tyler, M. E., Hannaford, B., and Stark, L. W. (1987) Quantitative evaluation of perspective and stereoscopic displays in a three-axis manual tracking task, *IEEE Trans. Systems, Man Cybernet.*, **17**, 61–71

Landy, M. S., Maloney, L. T., and Young, M. J. (1991) Psychophysical estimation of the human depth combination rule, in P. S. Schenker (Ed.), *Sensory Fusion III: 3-D Perception and Recognition, SPIE*, vol. 1383, Bellingham, WA: SPIE, pp. 247–54

Levelt, W. J. M. (1968) *On Binocular Rivalry*, Hague: Mouton

Lipton, L. (1987) Factors affecting ghosting in time-multiplexed plano-stereoscopic CRT display systems, in *SPIE*, vol. 761, Bellingham, WA: SPIE, pp. 75–8

Longuet-Higgins, H. C. (1982) The role of the vertical dimension in stereoscopic vision, *Perception*, **11**, 377–86

Luneburg, R. K. (1947) *Mathematical analysis of binocular vision*, Princeton, NJ

Maloney, L. T. and Landy, M. S. (1990) Psychophysical estimation of the human depth combination rule, in W. A. Pearlman (Ed.), *Visual Communication and Image Processing IV, SPIE*, vol. 1199, Bellingham, WA; SPIE, pp. 1154–63

Marr, D. and Poggio, T. A. (1979) A computational theory of human stereo vision, *Proc. R. Soc. London*, **204**, 301–28

McDowall, I. E., Bolas, M., Pieper, S., Fisher, S. S., and Humphries, J. (1990) Implementation and integration of a counterbalanced CRT-based stereoscopic display for interactive viewpoint control in virtual environment applications, in J.

O. Merritt and S. S. Fisher (Eds), *Stereoscopic Displays and Applications, SPIE*, vol. 1256, San José, CA, pp. 136–46

McKee, S. P. (1983) The spatial requirements for fine stereoacuity, *Vision Res.*, **23**, 191–8

Millodot, M. (1972) Variations of visual acuity in the central region of the retina, *Br. J. Physiolog. Opt.*, **27**, 24–8

Nakayama, K. (1978) Geometrical and physiological aspects of depth perception, in S. Benton (Ed.), *Three Dimensional Imaging, SPIE*, vol. 120, Bellingham, WA: SPIE, pp. 2–9

Nakayama, W., Tyler, C. W., and Appelman, J. (1977) A new angle on the vertical horopter, *Investigative Ophthal. Suppl.*, **16**, 82

Ogle, K. N. (1955) Stereopsis and vertical disparity, *Arch. Ophthalmol.*, **53**, 495–504

Ogle, K. N. (1950) *Researches in Binocular Vision*, Philadelphia: Saunders

Patterson, R. and Martin, W. L. (1992) Human stereopsis, *Human Factors*, **34**, 669–92

Pepper, R. L., Smith, D. C., and Cole, R. E. (1981) Stereo TV improves operator performance under degraded visibility conditions, *Opt. Eng.*, **20**, 579–85

Poggio, G. F. and Poggio, T. (1984) The analysis of stereopsis, *Ann. Rev. Neurosci.*, **7**, 379–412

Reising, J. M. and Mazur, K. M. (1990) 3D displays for cockpits: where they payoff, in J. O. Merritt, and S. S. Fisher (Eds), *Stereoscopic Displays and Applications I, SPIE*, vol. 1256, San José, CA, pp. 35–43

Ribarsky, W., Hodges, L. F., Minsk, R., and Bruschez, M. (1992) *Visual representations of discrete multivariate data, Graphics, Visualization and Usuability Center Technical Report No. GIT-GVU-92-04*, Georgia Institute of Technology

Richards, W. (1971) Anomalous stereoscopic depth perception, *J. Opt. Soc. Am.*, **61**, 410–14

Robinett, W. and Rolland, J. (1992) A computational model for stereoscopic optics of a head-mounted display, *Presence*, **1**, 45–62

Rogers, B. and Graham, M. (1982) Similarities between motion parallax and stereopsis in human depth perception, *Vision Res.*, **22**, 261–70

Schor, C. M. (1987) Spatial factors limiting stereopsis and fusion, *Optic News*, **13**, 14–17

Schor, C. M. and Wood, I. (1983) Disparity range for local stereopsis as a function of luminance spatial frequency, *Vision Res.*, **23**, 1649–54

Schumer, R. and Julesz, B. (1984) Binocular disparity modulation sensitivity to disparities offset from the plane of fixation, *Vision Res.*, **24**, 533–42

Sollenberger, R. L. and Milgram, P. (1991) A comparative study of rotational and stereoscopic computer graphic depth cues, in *Proc. of the Human Factors Society 35th Annual Meeting*, Santa Monica, CA: Human Factors Society, pp. 1452–6

Spain, E. H. and Holzhausen, K. P. (1991) Stereoscopic versus orthogonal view displays for performance of a remote manipulation task, in J. O. Merritt and S. S. Fisher (Eds) *Stereoscopic Displays and Applications II, SPIE*, vol. 1457, San José, CA, pp. 103–10

Teitel, M. A. (1990) The eyephone: a head-mounted stereo display, in J. O. Merritt and S. S. Fisher (Eds), *Stereoscopic Displays and Applications I, SPIE*, vol. 1256, San José, CA

Tyler, C. W. (1973) *Science*, **181**, 276–8

Tyler, C. W. (1974) Depth perception in disparity gratings, *Nature*, **251**, 140–2

Tyler, C. W. (1983) Sensory processing of binocular disparity, in C. M. Schor and K. J. Ciuffreda (Eds), *Vergence Eye Movements: Basic and Clinical Aspects*, Boston: Butterworth

Way, T. C. (1988) Stereopsis in cockpit display—a part-task test, in *Proc. of the 32nd Ann. Meeting of the Human Factors Society*, pp. 58–62

Welch, R. B. and Warren, D. H. (1986) Intersensory interactions, in K. R. Boff *et al.* (Eds), *Handbook of Perception and Human Performance*, New York: Wiley

Westheimer, G. (1979) Cooperative neural processes involved in stereoscopic acuity, *Exp. Brain Res.*, **36**, 585–97

Westheimer, G. and McKee, S. P. (1977) Spatial configurations for visual hyperacuity, *Vision Res.*, **17**, 941–7

Westheimer, G., and McKee, S. P. (1980) Stereoscopic acuity with defocused and spatially filtered retinal images, *J. Opt. Soc. Am.*, **70**, 772–8

Wichanski, A. M. (1991) User benefits of visualization with 3D stereoscopic displays, in *Proc. of 1991 SPIE/SPSE Electronic Imaging Science and Technology Conf.*

Wickens, C. D. (1990) Three-dimensional stereoscopic display implemention: Guidelines derived from human visual capabilities, in J. O. Merritt and S. S. Fisher (Eds), *Stereoscopic Displays and Applications I, SPIE*, vol. 1256, San José, CA, pp. 2–11

Wickens, C. D. and Todd, S. (1990) Three-dimensional display technology for aerospace and visualization, in *Proc. of the Human Factors Society 34th Annual Meeting*, pp. 1479–83

Williams, S. P. and Parrish, R. V. (1992) *Computational algorithms for increased control of the depth-viewing volume for stereo 3-D graphic displays* (TM No. 4379), NASA

Yeh, Y.-Y. and Silverstein, L. D. (1990) Limits of fusion and depth judgment in stereoscopic color displays, *Human Factors*, **32**, 45–60

Yeh, Y. Y. and Silverstein, L. D. (1992) Spatial judgments with monoscopic and stereoscopic presentation of perspective displays, *Human Factors*, **34**, 538–600

6

Visually Coupled Systems Hardware and the Human Interface

DEAN F. KOCIAN AND H. LEE TASK

A visually coupled system (VCS) has been defined as "... a special 'subsystem' which integrates the natural visual and motor skills of an operator into the system he is controlling" (Birt and Task, 1973). A basic VCS consists of three major components: (1) a head- or helmet-mounted (or head-directed) visual display, (2) a means of tracking head and/or eye pointing direction, and (3) a source of visual information which is dependent on eye/head viewing direction. The concept of a VCS is relatively simple: an operator looks in a particular direction, the head or eye tracker determines what that direction is, and the visual information source produces appropriate imagery to be viewed on the display by the operator. In this manner the operator is visually coupled to the system represented by the visual information source. The visual information source could be a physical imaging sensor such as a television camera or it could be a synthetic source such as computer-generated imagery (the basis for a virtual reality (VR) or virtual environment system). Thus, a VR system is really a subset of a VCS which can present both real-world and virtual information to an operator, often on a see-through display. The display is usually a helmet/head-mounted display (HMD) but it could also be the interior of a dome capable of displaying a projected image or it could be a mechanically mounted display that is not supported by the head but is attached to the head which in recent times has been referred to as a binocular omni-oriented monitor (BOOM) display. Both eye-tracking and head-tracking devices have been developed but by far the least expensive and most widely used is head tracking (this is based on the reasonable assumption that the eyes will be looking in the general direction that the head is pointing). Figures 6-1 through 6-4 are photographs of some early helmet-mounted and BOOM displays. In this chapter we will concentrate primarily on helmet/head-mounted displays and helmet/head trackers.

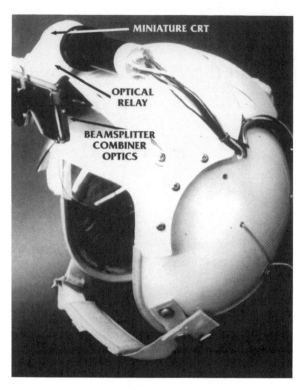

Figure 6-1 Photograph of early Autonetics helmet-mounted display circa 1968. Photograph courtesy of Armstrong Laboratory, USAF.

VISUALLY COUPLED SYSTEMS COMPONENTS

This section describes each of the three main components of a visually coupled system and defines characteristics that are used in the specification of these components. Figure 6-5 is a schematic block diagram of a visually coupled system with arrows indicating the closed-loop nature of the system. The head/helmet-mounted display is further subdivided into two main parts: the optical system and the display image source. Although these two main parts are almost always considered as a single entity (the head/helmet-mounted display), it is important to understand the characteristics and limitations of each part and how these affect the quality and utility of the HMD. For this reason these two subcomponents are treated separately. Latter sections of this chapter will deal in greater detail with the interaction of these components (and subcomponents) as they combine to make a full visually coupled system.

HMD optical systems

There are two basic types of optical systems that have been used for head/helmet-mounted virtual displays. These are: (1) the simple magnifier and

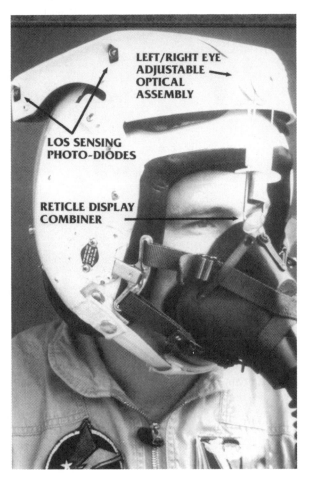

Figure 6-2 Photograph of early Honeywell infra-red helmet tracker and helmet-mounted reticle (aiming marker) display circa late 1960s. Photograph courtesy of Armstrong Laboratory, USAF.

(2) the compound microscope. This section will discuss each of these optical approaches to helmet-mounted displays.

Simple magnifier HMD optical system

As its name implies, the simple magnifier is a single lens system that produces a magnified, virtual image of the display image source. It is essentially the same as the magnifying glass that Sherlock Holmes uses to search for clues! Figure 6-6 is a simplified ray trace diagram for a simple magnifier optical system. If the display), it is important to understand the characteristics and limitations of each part and how these affect the quality and utility of the HMD. For this reason these two subcomponents are treated separately. Latter sections of this chapter will deal in greater detail with the interaction of these components (and subcomponents) as they combine to make a full visually coupled system.

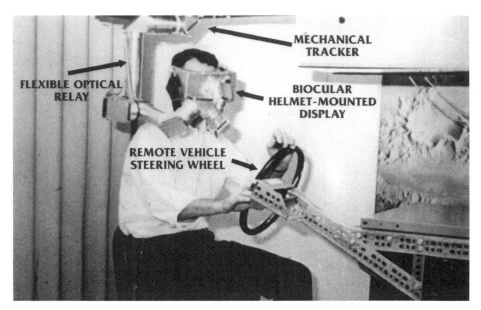

Figure 6-3 Photograph of early BOOM-type display used for remote driving of a motor vehicle circa late 1960s. Photograph courtesy of Armstrong Laboratory, USAF.

of light rays that emit from the bottom of the field of view and the solid lines are the light rays from the topmost part of the field of view. Point "P" is the furthest back from the optical system that an observer's eye can be and still see the entire field of view with no more than 50% vignetting (see section on *system characteristics*) anywhere in the field. Unlike the compound microscope optical system described next, and in Figure 6-7, the simple magnifier system does not produce a real exit pupil. Many virtual reality displays use the simple magnifier approach because it is simple and inexpensive.

The field of view of this system can be calculated using:

$$\text{FOV} = 2\arctan(S/(2F)) \tag{1}$$

where S is the linear size of the display image source, F the focal length of the lens, and FOV the field of view. It should be noted that equation (1) is only valid for the case shown in Figure 6-6 where the virtual image is located at infinity. If the display image source is not located at the focal plane of the lens, then the field of view is slightly different than that calculated using equation (1) but close enough for most applications.

The important characteristics of the simple magnifier optical system are the lens focal length (which determines magnification), the diameter of the lens (which affects eye relief distance) and the format size for which the lens was designed (which should be about the same as the size of the display image source). In addition to these basic first-order characteristics, it is also of interest to know about the imaging quality of the lens. Lenses are limited in their image quality capability by aberrations and by diffraction. Aberrations

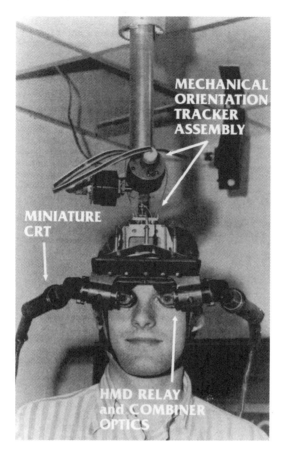

Figure 6-4 Photograph of early binocular HMD with see-through capability and mechanical head tracker (Vickers, 1973). Photograph courtesy of Armstrong Laboratory, USAF.

can be reduced by using lenses composed of multiple elements. Highest-quality lenses have sufficient optical elements to produce an image that is limited only by diffraction effects and are therefore referred to as "diffraction limited" lenses. Further discussion of this topic is well beyond the scope of this chapter, but one should be aware that lenses having the same first-order characteristics may well vary considerably in their image quality due to aberrations.

Compound microscope HMD optical system

The second basic optical system used in HMDs is based primarily on the compound microscope. Figure 6-7 is a ray-trace diagram for this type of system.

In this optical system the objective lens (also sometimes referred to as a relay lens in HMDs) produces a real image of the display image source at some intermediate location in the optical train. The eyepiece lens is then used to produce an observable virtual image of this intermediate image. As depicted in Figure 6-7, the eyepiece lens is located such that the intermediate image is at

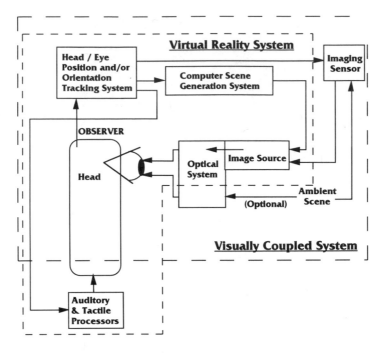

Figure 6-5 Major components of virtual reality and visually coupled system.

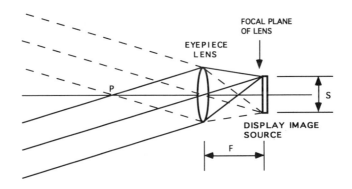

Figure 6-6 Simple magnifier optical system.

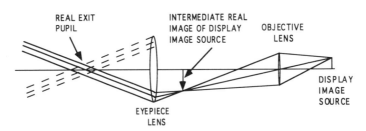

Figure 6-7 Compound microscope optical system approach for HMDs.

its focal plane, which means the exiting ray bundles are parallel and the virtual image is located at infinity. If the eyepiece lens is moved towards or away from this position, it will permit focusing to occur as in the simple magnifier case. This approach to the HMD optical system is used when it is desirable or necessary to have a long distance between the actual display image source and the eye position. Due to center of gravity and bulk considerations the display image source is often mounted at a location on the helmet, which is relatively far from the eyes thus requiring a relay lens (or objective lens) and perhaps several folding mirrors or prisms to relay the virtual image to a location that can be viewed by the eyes. Most helmet-mounted displays for airborne use have employed this basic optical design approach to improve the center of gravity of the helmet system.

In Figure 6-7 only a few rays have been traced from the display image source through the optical system. The solid lines are rays from the top part of the display. There are a similar set of rays that could be traced from the bottom of the display through the optical system, but this would result in a cluttered drawing. However, the last portion of these rays are depicted as dashed lines exiting the eyepiece lens to show how this type of optical system creates a real exit pupil which is a key characteristic of this type of optical system. For best viewing the observer's eye pupil should be in the center of the exit pupil of the system. The effect of this exit pupil in comparison with the simple magnifier optical system (and its lack of an exit pupil) is discussed further in the *system integration* section of this chapter.

Two other features of this type of optical system are worth noting: (1) the observed image is inverted compared with the image on the display (unlike the simple magnifier approach), and (2) the existence of a real intermediate image can be a problem if there is a physical surface in this same area (or close to it) since defects and debris on this surface will be imaged through the rest of the system and be visible to the observer.

The important characteristics of this optical system approach are the exit pupil size, exit pupil location (eye relief), input format size (which should be the same as the size of the display image source) and the field of view. The field of view for this type of system is not as easy to calculate, since it depends on several factors that are beyond the scope of this chapter.

It should be noted that the two optical design approaches described herein are shown in their simplest configuration using conventional, single-element lenses. Actual systems may use (and have used) multiple element lenses, flat and curved mirrors, holographic optics, gradient index optics, surface relief optics, Fresnel lenses, fiber optics and other optical components. However, even with these more elaborate optical components they can still be divided into the two classes of optical design approach presented in this section. Further information on these optical systems can be found in *Applied Optics and Optical Engineering* (Kingslake, 1965).

The two optical design approaches presented provide a convenient and useful means of categorizing HMD optics, since the two approaches have significantly different advantages and disadvantages (see section on *system integration*). However, there are other independent categorization schemes

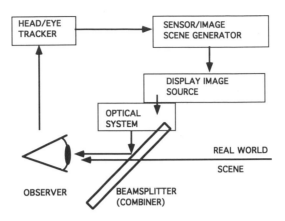

Figure 6-8 Schematic block diagram of "see-through" HMD.

that may be equally important in differentiating between systems. In particular, HMDs can be divided into "see-through" and "non-see-through" systems. A "see-through" HMD is one in which the virtual image is presented using a beamsplitter or optical combiner to permit the simultaneous viewing of the real-world scene with the virtual image superimposed. Figure 6-8 is a schematic block diagram of this type of HMD. As its name implies a "non-see-through" HMD is one in which there is no optical combiner or beamsplitter and the real-world scene is not visible behind the HMD virtual image.

The previous schematic block diagram shown in Figure 6-5, excluding the optional ambient scene pathway, is an example of the "non-see-through" HMD. Night vision goggles (NVGs) have been designed both with and without beamsplitters. The NVG community has adopted a standard terminology to refer to these two categories: *Type I* are "non-see-through" and *Type II* are "see-through" displays. Since the NVG is really a specific subset of visually coupled systems it makes sense to adopt the same categorization terminology for HMDs. Henceforth, we will use the same terminology in this chapter using *Type I* to refer to "non-see-through" (no combiner) HMDs and *Type II* to refer to "see-through" (with combiner) HMDs. (A mnemonic to aid in remembering which is which is: "Type two has see-through, type one has none.") In general, Type I systems are better suited to virtual reality applications and Type II are better suited for symbology-only, reality supplement (overlay) applications.

The coating on the optical combiner determines the relative luminance of the real-world scene and the virtual image on the HMD. Since real-world scenes can range from a few thousandths of a foot-Lambert up to several thousand foot-Lamberts (RCA Electro-Optics Handbook, 1974) it becomes a real challenge to design a system that will work for the full gamut of real-world luminance. One technique to improve the relative luminance of the HMD image with respect to the real-world scene is to use a wavelength selective coating on the combiner. The concept is to use a monochromatic or narrow spectral band display image source, and then use a combiner coating that is

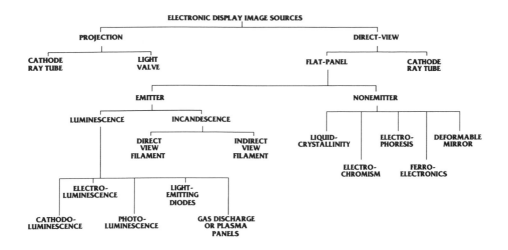

Figure 6-9 Display image source technologies.

highly reflective in the same wavelengths as the image source but is highly transmissive in the other visible wavelengths. This provides for a higher apparent luminance for the virtual image but without the reduction in real-world luminance that would occur with a wavelength neutral coating. For high, real world light levels a variable transmission filter (such as adjustable, crossed polarizers) may still be necessary to reduce the outside luminance to an acceptable level. Type II displays are probably best suited for daytime, symbology-only applications or night-time symbology and imagery applications (Task *et. al.*, 1980). Type I HMDs are best suited to virtual reality and other applications that do not require visual interaction (overlay) with the real world.

Miniature image sources for head-mounted displays

The image source is the key component technology for any visually coupled or virtual reality system. Most past and present head-mounted systems have treated the image source as an off-the-shelf component and the primary developmental thrust has been the display optics and its head-support subsystem. Programs that are enjoying the most *technical* success today are acknowledging the key role of the display image source in system performance. Using an image-source-centered developmental model, one attempts to optimize its performance for a given application first, keeping a keen eye on how its design can improve or aid the design of the remainder of the VCS or VR system.

As may be seen from Figure 6-9, there are a large number of candidate image source technologies that might be used in displays. The possible candidate technologies applicable for use in miniature displays where head-mounting of the image source dictates specialized requirements, quickly limits the number of viable candidates. Each of the remaining candidates is useful in one or more respects, but consideration of size, weight, cost, resolution, brightness, power consumption and optical system requirements for a particular miniature display application often results in radical differences in criteria for selecting a viable image source. Here, we shall cover just the mainstream candidates, concentrating primarily on those that have experienced the most widespread use to date or are currently supported by the Advanced Research Projects Agency (ARPA) High Definition Television subpanel for helmet-mounted displays or other US Department of Defense programs.

As shown in Figure 6-9, image sources can be divided into two main categories of projection and direct view. A more important distinction is whether the image source is an emitter of light (emissive) or a non-emitter (non-emissive) device. Emissive display image sources generally combine the light generation and image generation process. This fact generally implies some compromise between luminance output (and power dissipation) that can be sustained for a given level of resolution and image contrast performance. Non-emissive displays separate the light generation and image generation process. For some applications, this separation provides a distinct advantage of allowing greater luminance output for a given comparable resolution and contrast.

Both emissive and non-emissive image sources now provide a wide range of monochrome and full-color options from which to choose. Except for laser light devices, "narrow bandwidth" image source is a more accurate description for the spectral emission characteristics of most "monochrome" image sources. For HMDs utilizing see-through combiners (see Figure 6-8) that permit simultaneous viewing of the display scene overlaid on the ambient scene, monochrome image sources have been the overwhelming favorite. This is because reflective notch filters that provide efficient reflection of the HMD image to the eye can be built that also allow ambient light to be transmitted to the eye with only slight visible changes to the color of objects in the ambient scene. For HMDs, the monochrome or narrow-bandwidth image sources of choice have generally produced light in the green, yellow-green, or red portions of the spectrum. The primary reasons favoring these spectral bands are correlation with the eye's photopic response, higher luminous efficiency of the light-emitting material, better thermal saturation characteristics, better color contrast, or a combination of these factors.

The use of a wide-bandwidth color source with a see-through display greatly complicates the spectral characteristics of the display combiner's reflective/transmissive coatings and makes the colors of the HMD-generated scene dependent upon the color(s) of the ambient scene that it overlays. Thus most current HMDs, whose transmitted scene utilizes a medium to large color gamut, employ a non-see-through (type I) design.

As shown in Table 6-1, color images can be formed in four primary ways. The color-image formation process can be very important for HMDs. Among the differences that HMDs exhibit from their panel- or desk-mounted cousins is their often significant magnification of the display image source format. For HMDs with large monocular instantaneous FOVs (e.g., 70°) and relatively small image source input format size (e.g., approximately 1 inch), the

Table 6-1   Color Generation Schemes

Technique	Description	Characteristics
Spatial integration	Separate RGB pixels addressed in triads or quads	Simple and cheap but resolution equals $\frac{1}{3}$–$\frac{1}{2}$ of other techniques
Temporal integration	Separate RGB images presented in rapid succession	Compact but luminance equals $\frac{1}{3}$ of others, bandwidth must be 3×, and color break-up problem
Spatial addition	Separate RGB images superimposed on a combining surface	Good luminance and resolution, but too bulky (i.e., 3 displays needed)
Spatial subtraction	White light filtered through a transmissive CMY stack	Luminance almost unlimited, resolution limited only by diffraction, good color gamut

magnification will be quite large. Large magnification tends to make certain display defects very distracting that go unnoticed in other displays. It also can make displays with discrete pixel areas surrounded by dead areas distinct to the viewer. Thus, color generation techniques that utilize spatial integration are not an ideal choice. Color displays that utilize temporal integration (such as field-sequential color from a "white" light source) require high bandwidth and have associated human factors issues such as color break-up. Spatial addition may work well for home video projection systems but is bulky and difficult to implement for HMD applications. Spatial subtraction with its superior resolution, luminance and good color gamut holds probably the most promise for HMDs.

Empirical performance considerations for miniature image sources

Before proceeding to cover our brief overview of miniature image sources, it is necessary to establish an understanding of the performance measures to be cited as each type of miniature image source is discussed. There are many figures of merit (FOMs) used to describe various aspects of display performance. In this section we shall mainly be interested in the major FOMs of luminance, contrast, resolution, and a short discussion of interface considerations unique to miniature displays and image sources.

When discussing image source brightness (see section on *system characteristics*), we shall use the term "luminance" (L). The official international unit for luminance is candelas per meter squared (cd m^{-2}). However, in the text we shall use the unit foot-Lambert (ft-L). To convert ft-L to cd m^{-2} it is necessary to multiply the ratio of m^2/ft^2 by $1/\pi$ to obtain the multiplier of 3.426 as shown

$$1 \text{ ft-L} = 1/\pi(\text{cd ft}^{-2}) = 3.426 \text{ cd m}^{-2} \qquad (2)$$

If the luminance of a display is the same for all viewing angles then the display is said to be a diffuse (or Lambertian) emitter. Most emissive image sources (such as a cathode-ray tube (CRT)) qualify as a Lambertian emitter which means they look equally bright when viewed perpendicular to the surface or when viewed at an angle to the surface. However, most non-emissive displays do not act as Lambertian surfaces. This can be a particular problem when the display is mated with an optical system that produces a wide field of view since the edges of the field are viewed at relatively steep angles and are therefore dimmer than the center of the display. With non-emissive displays it is often necessary to add some additional optical element that acts as a diffuser to improve the luminance uniformity with respect to viewing angle.

When discussing contrast, we shall mean contrast defined as the maximum luminance minus the minimum luminance divided by the sum of the two as shown in equation (3). When using the term contrast ratio we shall mean the ratio of the maximum luminance to the minimum luminance as shown in equation (4). Equation (5) shows the relationship between these two different definitions of contrast.

$$M = (L_{max} - L_{min})/(L_{max} + L_{min}) \tag{3}$$

$$C_r = L_{max}/L_{min} \tag{4}$$

$$C_r = (1 + M)/(1 - M) \tag{5}$$

where M is the modulation contrast, and C_r the contrast ratio.

When discussing the resolution of a display (see section on *system characteristics*), it will normally be expressed in terms of elements per picture width or picture height. The reader should understand that this is a rather rough definition or expression of image quality performance and not nearly as precise as other more complicated measures of image quality. However, it allows one to form a general impression regarding the image quality of the display.

Emissive display image sources

Emissive displays provide a more varied selection of image source candidates than non-emissive displays, although non-emissive image sources may soon surpass emissive displays in total number of units produced on a yearly basis.

Lasers. Already used in dome simulators, lasers have only recently been considered for head/helmet-mounted display applications. When used for dome projection, the lower power output of the laser is wasted by the massive inefficiency of diffuse reflection from the dome surface. For HMDs, specular conservation of the laser's light should result in useful displays using milliwatt continuous-wave lasers. That the laser is quite bright is apparent from the fact that staring into a laser of this power can result in burning the retina; obviously, a primary concern is safety, for the laser should not be focused and allowed to dwell on the retina. Developing the associated optics and scanning systems needed for an HMD is under development and some years away from practical application. Optics designed to image large FOVs to the observer have yet to be demonstrated and no particular advantage is gained through the use of a laser image source with respect to the size of the optics needed to project the display image over a given instantaneous FOV. Finally, the scanning system and laser activation scheme must be extremely reliable and safe to completely eliminate the chance for short-term or long-term retinal damage.

There has also been some discussion that, because a laser emits coherent light, less power might be needed for a display. This is a misconception: it takes just as much power with a laser to produce a subjective impression of brightness as it does with any other source of light. The difference is that the laser can be strictly controlled, while an incandescent light squanders its power by radiating in all directions, only a small percentage of which can be collected with the lenses used in display optics. Also, much of the incandescent light's radiation is in the infrared portion of the electromagnetic spectrum. For raster information display to the human, the CRT has the advantage of persistence (if it is not too long) that the laser does not. Therefore, either high power levels, which may be undesirable, or high scan and refresh rates are needed to suppress flicker problems. Higher scan rates may exceed the practical bandwidth limits that can be achieved with a laser-scanned display system.

Electroluminescent (EL) displays. EL displays offer a good low-power candidate for head-mounted displays. In particular, the ARPA-funded program in active matrix EL displays appears to be showing favorable results. Current devices have a resolution of 640 pixels by 512 pixels for a display size of approximately 1.3 inches by 1.0 inch. Peak measured luminances are at about 2000 ft-L for monochrome devices but full-color devices with the filters needed to generate color are at about 1/10 the monochrome figure and improvements are expected to come in small increments. One positive note is that EL image sources may benefit from the recent initiation of the Phosphor Technology Center of Excellence (PTCE) Consortium headed by Georgia Institute of Technology and sponsored by ARPA.

Field-emission displays (FEDs). Somewhat further behind but gaining momentum, FEDs are being pursued with the hope that their promise of high energy efficiency, good brightness, high video speed, high contrast, wide viewing angle, low weight and thin package profile can be realized for a commercially viable flat color CRT. In particular, the USAF Armstrong Laboratory (AL) development program with FED Corporation located in New York is showing good promise with the new gated-point field-emitter-array (FEA) technology. In this device the three scanned electron guns of a conventional color CRT are replaced with many millions of individual electron emitter guns, groups of which are responsible for a single pixel or point of emitted light. The FEA 'micro-electron guns' are sandwiched in a thin panel separated by a vacuum from a phosphor screen. The FED Corporation proprietary version of the microguns offers low-voltage control, low current leakage, and high yield while still permitting low-cost high-voltage electron acceleration with tight electron trajectory control. Prototype 512 by 512 pixel flat-panel color displays operating at 5000 volts with a 1.8 inch by 1.8 inch active area are currently being developed. Final fabrication and test will be required before FOMs such as luminance will be known. This technology holds the promise of producing

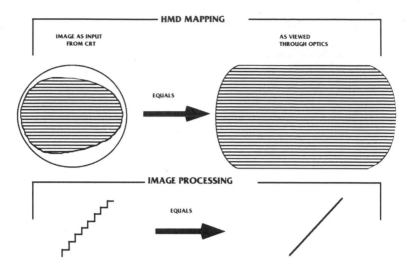

Figure 6-10   Examples of monochrome CRTs advantages for the HMD interface.

useful high-current, long-life cathodes of an ungated variety for use in conventional miniature monochrome CRTs.

Miniature CRT. The great strides being made with solid-state image sources have application to many commercial and some military display systems, and although color image sources using miniature CRTs have not fared well, significant advancements are being made in miniature monochrome CRT technology, which still makes them the current best choice for many HMDs, especially those employing a see-through combiner. The terminology "monochrome" is applied loosely here, as it is understood that we are not talking about a single wavelength in the visible spectrum, but a dominant narrow band of wavelengths that may have several lesser spectral peaks at other wavelengths. The best distinction is that monochrome visual images are formed through variations in luminance levels (gray levels) only and not by differences in color.

The vast majority of HMT/D systems built to date for high-quality VCS and VR applications have used the miniature monochrome CRT as their image source of choice. Advances in flat-panel displays are having a significant impact on miniature image source variety for virtual reality applications but miniature CRTs are also experiencing significant performance improvements.

The CRT has some significant disadvantages. These include: (1) its long front-to-back distance that makes it difficult to package into any type of military or commercial helmet assembly, (2) its requirement for special high-voltage power supplies, (3) its weight (due in part to a lack of investment in new packaging technologies), and (4) its requirement for production methods that lead to some hand assembly (making it difficult to achieve repeatability in product and low production costs).

The CRT's main advantages include its basic light conversion efficiency and superior resolution performance in small format sizes. Many of the most important reasons for using miniature CRTs stem from system requirements that other types of available image sources cannot support. Among them is that the CRT does not impose a strict allocation of display elements across the display format whose relative size and activation characteristics are fixed. Therefore, horizontal/vertical smoothing (anti-aliasing) techniques may be applied to smooth the appearance of straight edges (particularly from man-made objects) that cross the scanning format diagonally, producing stair-casing effects and visual artifacts as shown in Figure 6-10. Generally, a solid-state display requires several times the inherent resolution of a CRT to match the apparent smoothness of the CRT's imagery, especially under the image format magnification inherent in most helmet displays. Since current advanced miniature CRTs can provide in excess of one million resolution elements in a 20 millimeter format, solid-state displays for HMDs have significant performance barriers to overcome. In small sizes they currently have much lower resolution than CRTs. In addition, a CRT image source may present randomly written vector graphic information, providing only smooth line segments at any orientation on the display. This symbology may be updated at refresh rates much higher than normal video field rates to achieve much brighter peak line luminance levels for daylight viewing on helmet displays employing see-through combiners. The higher refresh rates take advantage of the higher brightness and better thermal saturation characteristics that some of the new rare earth phosphors permit. Finally, some helmet-display optical systems, particularly binocular systems with large monocular FOVs and partial overlap of the monocular fields, have significant residual distortion. The CRT's ability to employ geometry correction to its electron scan deflection circuitry, effectively allows this distortion to be removed by introducing a counterbalancing distortion to its input. Figure 6-10 illustrates this effect.

As shown in Table 6-2, several different sizes now exist for miniature CRTs. This represents a significant change from the early 1980s, when essentially one size of miniature CRT existed for use with HMDs. The smallest are generally used for the display of symbology and, as one progresses to larger CRTs, one finds they are used for the display of either symbology or imagery. The maximum anode potential also increases with size, as one would expect. It

Table 6-2 CRT performance characterization by usable phosphor area.

CRT Parameter	Format size (usable phosphor diameter in mm)				
	11.5	15.5	17.5	19	23
~Outer dia. (mm)	18.5	23	22	27	30
Length (mm)	65–80	110–120	88–94	100–120	135–145
Weight* (g)	35–45	85–100	55–70	85–135	120–140
Accel. voltage (kV)	~8	~11	~13	13.5	13.5
Deflection method	magnetic	magnetic	magnetic	magnetic	magnetic

*Assumes 6 inches of leads.

is also generally true that to produce a larger HMD FOV, the format size, and therefore the outside diameter of the CRT, must be increased to permit reasonable optical system f-numbers. Display resolution and contrast performance are almost always improved with an increased CRT format size.

CRTs are normally delivered in a single cylinder shape with one contiguous mumetal shield with its leads soldered and potted at the back of the tube. They may also come in a dual cylinder package with a larger diameter mumetal shield over the deflection yoke area and a smaller diameter shield over the back of the CRT. Again, the leads are normally soldered to the tube pins and then potted in place for about two inches of length to provide some strain relief and insulation. As of 1992, however, it is possible to obtain the 19 mm format CRT in a dual cylinder package with removable aviation connectors (AVCON) that eliminate the need for potting compounds and provide better performance while also resulting in less total weight for the complete CRT package. By mid-1995 it should also be possible to obtain the 17.5 mm format size CRT with the AVCON connectors and other package sizes will undoubtedly appear with removable connectors as someone steps in to fund the development costs for the required custom molds, etc.

The internal structures that comprise the CRT have undergone, and continue to undergo, changes, resulting in more diversity to meet special requirements for particular HMD systems. The most important subcomponents are the phosphor/faceplate system, the electron-gun design, the cathode, and the deflection yoke. More will be said about each of these areas later in the chapter, but it is worth summarizing some of the features most apparent to the user as a point of reference for further discussion.

Besides size and shape, the most noticeable difference between miniature CRTs is their faceplate system. Miniature CRTs generally employ either a fiber-optic or glass faceplate. Generally, the design requirements of the HMD optics play the biggest role in determining the type of faceplate used. However, phosphor type can also influence faceplate selection. Three general classes of phosphors are used, or have been developed, for use in miniature CRTs. These are particulate phosphors, sputtered phosphors, and single-crystal phosphors. Particulate phosphors, which came first in developmental history, have the most widespread use and color range. Each manufacturer of phosphors, and, indeed, many CRT manufacturers, have their special processing methods for particulate phosphors to optimize resolution, luminous efficiency, contrast and life characteristics. Particulate phosphors may be used with little difficulty with either glass or fiber-optic faceplates. Sputtered and single-crystal phosphors offer improvements over particulate phosphor systems for certain characteristics, such as resolution. However, because of either available processing techniques or their requirements for higher processing temperatures, they can at this time only be used with standard glass or, in some cases, hard glass (e.g., sapphire) faceplates.

Miniature CRT deflection yokes come in a variety of configurations to meet e-beam scan performance requirements and CRT size. The type used can have a significant impact on performance. Deflection is usually accomplished using magnetic deflection yokes because of their better beam forming/movement

Table 6-3 A comparison of miniature CRT deflection yoke types.

Yoke type	Sensitivity (LI^2)	Resolution	Inductance balance	Resistance (Ω)	Cross-talk	Resonant frequency	Producibility
Interleaved hanks	typical	typical	best	worst	typical	typical	typical
Stator	best	typical	typical	typical	typical	worst	best
Constant volume	typical	worst	typical	typical	worst	best	worst

properties and electrostatic deflection is employed only infrequently in miniature CRT applications. Presently, miniature CRT deflection yokes come with inductances in discrete ranges. The bulk of current miniature CRTs have deflection yoke inductances located at 15 to 20 microhenries (μH), and then jump up to a range of 100 to 150 μH. Some newer deflection yokes now exist with inductances located in the 80 to 100 μH range. Capacitance and lead resistance usually increase, with inductance. For high-speed calligraphic and raster scan systems, where large voltages may appear across the deflection yokes and fast settling times are required, lower inductance/capacitance yokes are usually employed. Table 6-3 lists the most common types of magnetic deflection yokes used with miniature CRTs and gives a general comparison of their relative advantages.

As mentioned earlier, the performance requirements placed upon the CRT normally have their primary origin in the application-specific requirements imposed by the HMD. The most common type of miniature CRT is the electromagnetic deflection (EMD)/electrostatic focus lens (ESFL) system, which has been found to be most suitable for miniature CRT applications. A representative CRT, showing the major relationships between internal components, is diagrammed in Figure 6-11. Although new and promising alternatives are being investigated, nearly all EMD/ESFL designs for CRTs use either (1) bipotential lenses or, (2) unipotential or einzel lenses. In general, better center resolution is achievable with bipotential lens CRTs than unipotential lens CRTs, because of the more favorable beam diameter magnification value of bipotential lens designs. Using Figure 6-11 to establish relationships, the potential miniature CRT buyer may form a rough estimate of resolution or beam spot size performance (ignoring the effects of the phosphor faceplate system) by asking the CRT vendor for data on the virtual crossover diameter of a given CRT and using equations (6) through (8).

$$\text{Geometric magnification} = M_1 = Q/P \qquad (6)$$

where Q is the distance from CRT deflection center to the screen, and P the distance from G_1/G_2 crossover to the deflection center.

$$\text{Electronic magnification} = M_2 = (V_3/V_4) \qquad (7)$$

where V_3 is the CRT focus voltage, and V_4 the CRT final acceleration or anode voltage.

$$\text{Overall magnification} = M_3 = M_1 \cdot M_2 \qquad (8)$$

For the CRT shown in Figure 6-11, which might operate at an acceleration potential of 13 kV, and nominal focus potential of 2.5 kV, a value for M_3 of 0.266 is obtained. This value may be multiplied by the virtual crossover diameter, supplied by the CRT manufacturer, to determine a first-order approximation to spot size, ignoring phosphor/faceplate system contributions. Unipotential lenses give better center-to-edge uniformity than bipotential lenses. This disadvantage can be overcome by using shaped fiber-optic faceplates, which minimize deflection defocusing, and using dynamic focus voltage correction, which minimizes focus lens aberrations while maintaining the significant spot minification advantage demonstrated by equation (7).

One new alternative CRT that has given rise to optimism had its origins in a joint development effort between the USAF Armstrong Laboratory and Hughes Display Products. Named for its distinguishing Decelerator Pre-focus Lens (DPFL) gun, the DPFL CRT has shown much promise. The fundamental difference between this gun design and the standard bipotential-lens CRT is that it has an additional control grid between the G_2 and G_3 grids (see Figure 6-11). The preliminary data taken from the few DPFL tubes that exist suggest that this type of CRT–electron gun combination offers a number of very desirable characteristics. Among them are: (1) nearly constant line width over

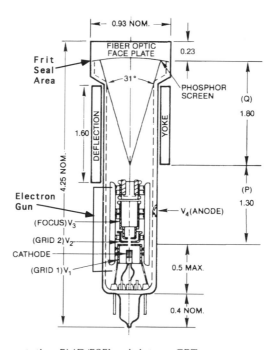

Figure 6-11 Representative EMD/ESFL miniature CRT.

Table 6-4   Recent results with new DPFL gun CRTs.*

Refresh (cycles s^{-1})	Luminance level (ft-L)	CRT serial number	Drive voltages (V)	50 per cent line width (mils)	Peak cathode loading (A cm^{-2})
	~8300	90-35122	63.5	~1.0	4.32
60	7000	90-35123	69.0	~1.15	4.90
		90-35122	63.5	1.01/1.04	4.32
120	~17 000	90-35123	69.0	1.05/1.07	4.90
		90-35122	41.2	0.98/1.00	2.26
240	~17 000	90-35123	44.8	1.01/1.04	2.56

*CRT type: Hughes Display Products 1475→ 13 kV, 30 k inches s^{-1}, 17 × 12.75 mm format.
Data taken at Hughes Display Products, Lexington, Kentucky.

a wide range of modulation voltages, (2) low modulation defocusing, (3) minimization of focus lens spherical aberration, and (4) selectable gun efficiency. Preliminary results with some recently built DPFL CRTs operated at several display refresh rates and final anode potentials of 13 000 V are shown in Table 6-4. It is interesting to note that as refresh rates go up, video modulation voltages needed to obtain the luminance levels shown go down. This decrease improves maximum obtainable video bandwidth for the amplifier which, unlike panel-mounted CRTs that must drive just a few inches of unterminated cable to the CRT, must drive several feet of unterminated cable going to the head-mounted components. The peak cathode loading also decreases significantly. This, in turn, will improve cathode life characteristics, and therefore useful CRT life. These results have a distinct advantage for CRTs that are used primarily to image calligraphic symbology overlaid on an ambient scene using Type II HMDs.

In the future, these results will be combined with improved faceplates and it is hoped improved phosphors derived from the already mentioned Phosphor Technology Center of Excellence development program. New cathodes, such as FEA cathodes, may be incorporated to provide both brighter displays and longer product lifetimes. During the next four to five years, it seems likely that nearly optimum electron-gun designs will appear for specific applications. It also seems likely that gun designs will become available providing good performance for day/night systems that require night raster presentations at the lower line rates and high-brightness daylight symbology. With the commercial incentive and investment that appears to be occurring in high-performance cathodes, it also seems reasonable to expect that cathodes exhibiting high current loading densities (4–8 A cm^{-2}) and improved operating lifetimes (>1000 hours) will become available for use in miniature CRTs. What is not so clear is whether phosphors with improved resolution and Coulombic degradation numbers (such as sputtered phosphors) will be available to match the performance gains of the CRT gun and cathode. This is because these types of phosphors will probably be expensive for large area displays and, thus, appear to have no similar commercial incentives for their development. Improvements in CRT deflection yokes will probably be incremental, at best. However, significant changes may begin to appear in CRT packaging, involving molded parts and metalized coatings for shielding that may affect yoke design and could result in improved form factors and reduced weight.

Non-emissive display image sources

Liquid crystal image sources are important and becoming more so because they operate with low voltage (a strong safety feature) and draw very low amounts of current. They adapt to both transmitted and reflected illumination (sunlight where available) and maintain a uniform contrast against rising luminance levels. For the most part, the thermal sensitivity of liquid crystals has limited their military utilization.

The major thrust in non-emissive transmissive displays for HMDs is for full color. A number of attempts at building miniature color CRTs have been made. Among them are field-sequential systems, beam penetration systems, and post-deflection acceleration systems. Most have not been found to be really useful due primarily to size and weight. Though someone may yet design and build a truly outstanding miniature color CRT, it is probably true that the demands placed on this device, where the information and light-generation functions are combined, will not permit it to be competitive with alternative approaches. The use of color in non-see-through HMDs seems to have more potential than for see-through HMDs, but, at night or in low ambient illumination conditions, even see-through HMDs may benefit significantly.

Among the most promising alternatives is one using subtractive color liquid crystal displays (LCDs) that was developed as a result of a joint program between Honeywell, Inc. and the USAF Armstrong Laboratory. Figure 6-12 shows an example of a subtractive color LCD now under development.

The (off-helmet) illuminator for the LCD pumps light into a thin, non-coherent fiber-optic cable. The illuminator consists of a xenon lamp, reflector, cold mirror (to remove IR), UV filter, RGB filter, and a lens which

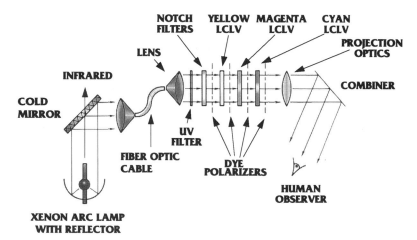

Figure 6-12 Example of helmet-mountable subtractive color image source.

focuses the light onto the cable end. The RGB filter spectrally tunes the light to match the light-valve's spectral selection characteristics.

At the other end of the cable, the light enters a premodulation section consisting of a collimating lens and field-stop. The field-stop limits the collimated light beam diameter to the light-valve's physical dimensions.

Next, the light enters the light-valve, which contains two major sections: (1) a luminance-modulation section, consisting of a chromatically neutral LCD with polarizer; and (2) a chromatic-modulation section consisting of three guest-host LCDs with polarizers. The three guest-host LCDs contain yellow (minus-blue), magenta (minus-green), and cyan (minus-red) dichroic dyes, respectively. These LCDs use liquid crystal to control the orientation of the dye molecules and thereby vary from transparent to fully colored (i.e., the liquid crystal (LC) does not modulate light directly—it only rotates the dye molecules). In principle, the three guest-host LCDs can also perform the luminance-modulation function; however, the use of a separate LCD for this purpose will give the demonstrator better luminance contrast and color purity. Future development can presumably eliminate the fourth LCD.

Finally, the light passes through a diffuser, which softens the edges of the pixels' sharp luminance profile, and enters the HMD optics. A separate non-coherent fiber-optic cable and wires with power for the thin-film electronics bring the image data to the LCD stack on the helmet.

Figure 6-13 shows the color gamut of the subtractive color LCD display as compared to that obtained from conventional color shadow mask CRTs. The color gamuts of both are mapped with respect to the Commission Internationale de l'Eclairage (CIE) 1976 uniform chromaticity-scale (UCS) diagram.

The Advanced Research Projects Agency (ARPA) is providing sustaining funds to develop versions of the LCD that contain the miniaturized thin-film transistor electronics (e.g., to provide an active-matrix LCD (AMLCD)

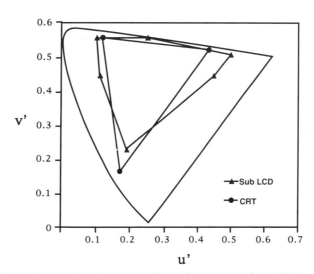

Figure 6-13   Comparison of color gamut for subtractive color LCD and CRT.

Table 6-5 Proposed performance characteristics for several subtractive color LCD displays.

Parameter	Display type		
	Monocular HMD	Binocular HMD	HDTV
Pixels (horz. × vert.)	640 × 480	1280 × 1024	1920 × 1080
Aspect ratio	4:3	5:4	~16:9
Pixel size (μm)	20	24	24
Active area (mm)	13 × 10	31 × 25	46 × 26
Diagonal (mm)	16	40	53
Transmittance	20%	10%	10%
Luminance (ft-L)	15 000	7500	7500
Primaries	RG	RGB	RGB
Colors	4096	262 144	262 144
Frame rate	72	60	60
Outer dimensions (mm) depth × width × length	20 × 21 × 50	35 × 40 × 75	50 × 40 × 75

	Performance common to all displays		
	Parameter		
Aperture ratio	70 per cent		
Lamp	84 W metal-halide		
Gray scale	6 bits/primary		
Drivers	integrated x:SI		
Data cable	optical fiber; diameter and length TDB		
Light conduit	0.25-inch optical fiber; Y-config.;* length TBD		
Light box	size, weight, and power supply TBD		

*To illuminate binocular designs with a single light box.

configuration), better cholesteric polarizers and a high-efficiency tailored spectra halide light source. An improved version that is miniaturized should be ready in late 1995.

Table 6-5 lists the relative performance characteristics for several types of subtractive color LCD image sources that may be built, at least in prototype form, within the next few years.

Figure 6-14 depicts the angular distribution of light output as measured on one of the prototype subtractive-color LCD image sources delivered to the USAF Armstrong Laboratory by Honeywell, Inc. during 1993. As can be seen, the light output is far different from that of the Lambertian distribution that a CRT provides. Recalling the earlier discussion regarding luminance uniformity, this difference has some significant implications for the design of the HMD optics that would incorporate such an image source. Used without modification, the subtractive-color LCD will only be able to work with HMDs having small exit pupils and relatively small instantaneous FOVs, and provide roughly uniform illumination across the instantaneous FOV. If some sort of diffuser can be added to permit larger angles with more uniform intensity distributions,

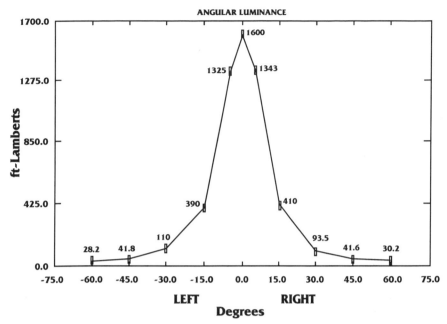

Figure 6-14   Angular distribution for light exiting the subtractive-color LCD.

then the HMD design performance specifications for exit-pupil and instantaneous FOV can be significantly increased.

Hybrid transmissive/emissive display image sources

A number of field sequential color image sources employing emissive CRT and transmissive light-valve technology are now being used successfully for HMD applications in the commercial market. It has been 24 years since the USAF Armstrong Laboratory initiated the first field sequential color system for HMDs in a joint program with Hughes Aircraft Company. In principle, that system operated using the same techniques as those employed for the CBS Laboratories Minicam Mark XII field sequential color camera system. Instead of today's light-valve technology, the system employed a servo-driven spinning color filter wheel in front of a CRT with a white phosphor. The system had a field rate of 180 Hz (60 each for red, green, and blue (RGB)) and a horizontal frequency of 39.69 kHz producing an effective vertical resolution of ~300 TV lines and a horizontal resolution of ~350 lines. The color filter wheel that rotated in front of the CRT image surface had to be driven at a precise rate of speed to insure that the correct color filter segment passed the CRT face immediately prior to readout of that color's information. Maintaining proper speed across a wide variety of ambient environments and the fact that it had poor color saturation and was bulky for head-mounting limited its usefulness. Also, with this implementation, rapid eye movement resulted in an undesirable viewing phenomen known as color break-up.

Table 6-6 Basic performance characteristics for FLC light valve.*

Parameter	Typical performance
Optical delay time	<100 μs
Optical rise (10–90%)/fall time (90–10%)	<100 μs
Allowable CRT spectral range	400–700 nm
Resolution	Limited by CRT
Clear aperture	0.50 or 1.00 in.
Operating temperature	0 to 50 °C
Electrical drive	±5 V DC
Required switching energy	<5 mJ (180 Hz operation)
Capacitance	<400 nF
Series resistance	~200 Ω
Shunt resistance	>20 mΩ

*Data taken from preliminary DI data sheet for FLC.

Today's systems, even though most still use the same 180 Hz field rate, are much improved. Using light-valve technology that provides color uniformity, reduced head-mounted weight and bulk, no moving parts, simple drive electronics, and improved CRTs/phosphors, better performance is being obtained. Of particular note are new light valves using ferroelectric liquid crystal (FLC) technology, such as those produced by DISPLAYTECH, Inc (DI). The FLC has the fastest transition time of any currently available switchable color filter and it eliminates the need for a segmented color filter aperture, as is typically required with π-cell LC technology. The DI RGB filter consists of two FLC cells, dichroic color polarizers, and a dichroic linear polarizer. The Kaiser Electro-Optics SIM-EYE™ HMD (see Figures A7 and A8 in the Appendix) is one system currently using this type of light-valve with a CRT employing a PT696 white phosphor. The basic performance characteristics of the DI FLC are shown in Table 6-6 and its color gamut using P45 as compared to that obtained from conventional color shadow mask CRTs is shown in Figure 6-15. The color gamuts of both are mapped with respect to the CIE 1976 UCS diagram.

Helmet/head tracking systems

This section discusses the functionality and system alternatives that might be considered for the selection and use of a head/helmet-mounted tracker (HMT) as part of a complete VCS or VR system. Another frequently used term for the HMT is position and orientation tracker (P&OT). In the discussion that follows, we shall use the acronyms HMT and P&OT interchangeably to refer to head/helmet tracker systems.

Most frequently, visually coupled systems (VCS) and virtual reality systems (VRS) have their visual interface to the human driven by head orientation and position (HOP) information. A few of the more elaborate systems make use of eye line-of-sight (LOS) information, as well. The quality of the HOP

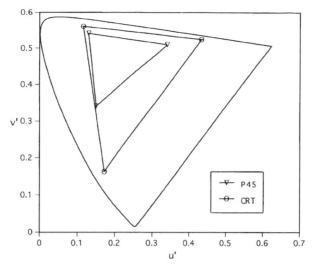

Figure 6-15   Comparison of color gamut for FLC light valve with P45 and CRT.

information must be available to a known and repeatable baseline level of accuracy to guarantee success in a particular system application. Beyond the basic requirement for HOP measurement, other HMT system parameters can also become important.

Most current HMT systems utilize some form of remote sensing system transducer pairing consisting of one or more transmitters and one or more receivers. The number of transmitter and receiver transducers required depends upon the HMT technology employed, the angular and positional coverage desired, and the specific application. Usually the receiver is mounted to the head because it provides a more desirable combination of power dissipation and weight but this is not always the case. The allocation of transducers can be further complicated, especially for VRS, if one desires to measure the position and orientation (P&O) of the operator's extremities and sometimes even the torso. This has been accomplished in a few instances by attaching additional transducers to the extremities and torso, having a fixed place to put them for initial boresight and calibration, and adding the additional amplifiers and processing power needed to compute the angular and positional locations of these extra transducers. One example of such a system was the USAF Armstrong Laboratory's Virtual Panoramic Display (VPD) magnetic helmet-mounted tracker (MHMT) developed in the late 1980s. This system could measure in a multiplexed manner the location of the heads and both hands of two observers.

Most HMT systems employ either ultrasonic, magnetic, or light energy to communicate HOP information between the transmitter/receiver pair(s). Today, the most commonly used systems utilize either optical light-sensing concepts or alternating (AC) or static (DC) magnetic fields. Each of these systems incorporates features that make it the best choice for some specific use or range of applications. In this section we will examine some of the most important features to be considered in choosing an HMT and then briefly compare performance while bypassing the lengthy process of providing a complete technical description of how each type of system operates to determine head orientation and position.

Basic concepts

To employ the HMT as a useful command and control input device, some type of sensory input must be provided to the observer to permit meaningful steering by the human operator of the HMT P&O outputs. A useful analogy is a telescopic sight on a rifle that is used to direct the LOS of its muzzle. Most current HMT systems employ either a head-mounted visual display that includes an LOS aiming reticle or an auditory signal whose audible characteristics are changed to indicate directed changes in the HMT's P&O outputs.

The most basic form of HMT visual display is a simple sighting reticle. The sighting reticle normally consists of an incandescent or light-emitting diode (LED) image source that can project a fixed image of a crosshair or similar symbology to the eye using a simple optical lens and combiner combination. The combiner transmits the reticle image to the eye and also transmits the ambient scene so that the reticle appears to be overlaid on the real-world scene. The reticle's LOS is aligned parallel to the LOS of the head-mounted transducer. Achieving parallelism is most often accomplished by sighting the display reticle on some known reference located at optical infinity and then having the HMT electronics compute the electronic calibration needed to bring the head-mounted source's signals into the desired coincidence. The LOS pointing concept and its application to slaving some remote gimbaled platform or computer output is shown graphically in Figure 6-16. The operator places the reticle over the desired aiming point bringing the LOS of the HMT into coincidence with the operator's. If the reticle is displayed as a collimated image then parallax errors, especially for aiming points close to the operator, are small. The computed LOS or HOP information is then transmitted as an analog or digital signal from the HMT electronics to the system requiring the HMT control input. In the example shown in Figure 6-16, a simple reticle display provides no direct image from the seeker head and significant open loop offset errors can occur. If an imaging helmet display is provided and boresighted (usually through some automatic calibration process), then the seeker image and HMT LOS aiming symbol can be combined visually on the helmet display for closed-loop aiming and feedback of the imaging seeker's actual LOS. Thus, significant open-loop offset errors between the operator's LOS and the slaved system's LOS can be reduced to almost negligible amounts through this powerful concept of closing the system control loop through the human operator.

The combination of an HMT and sighting reticle is commonly referred to as a helmet-mounted sight (HMS) system. As just explained, such a system provides open-loop control or cueing. Additional simple symbology whose representation is fixed in form and angular space on the display, such as dashes or dots (discretes), sometimes accompanies the sighting reticle. These addition-

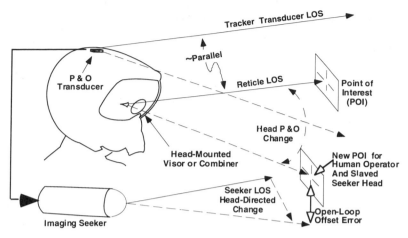

Figure 6-16   Line-of-sight (LOS) cueing relationships.

al discretes may be switched on and off based upon the P&O outputs of the HMT and system state of the system being controlled. Such an implementation can provide a coarse closed-loop feedback function to improve operator LOS cueing performance.

When the sighting reticle is replaced with a helmet-mounted display (HMD) as described earlier in this chapter, then the HMT and HMD together form a VCS or HMT/D and permit a low error closed-loop feedback system that helps the operator remain spatially coupled with the remote systems he is cueing or being cued by (see Figure 6-16). Such a system may provide one or many cueing symbols on the display that dynamically change to indicate both LOS performance and any system state changes that the current HOP outputs can affect. An aircraft-related example of multiple LOS cueing symbols would be one aiming symbol in the upper portion of the HMD FOV for designating aiming points outside the aircraft and another aiming symbol in the lower portion of the display for activating controls in an electronics or virtual cockpit. A simplified representation of this concept is shown in Figure 6-17 for an aircraft cockpit similar to current modern fighter aircraft. The lower reticle is used to designate space-stabilized electronic-cockpit switches and functions, when these are made active by the operator, that are imaged onto the HMD. The position of the electronic-cockpit switches stays fixed with respect to the cockpit while the reticle moves with the changing head LOS. When the lower reticle is placed over the electronic-cockpit switch, its visual form changes to indicate it is active and you are designating it by your current LOS. The operator must then activate the switch's function by pushing some dedicated selection button located on some control input such as the joystick. Meanwhile, the upper aiming reticle can remain active for designating outside-world targets through other electronic control loops. This concept is most useful for VCS or VR systems that employ HMDs with large instantaneous FOVs.

Finally, it is important to mention, that for the HMT relative position and orientation outputs to be meaningful in a "system sense," they must be accurately referenced to some coordinate system common to all system parts.

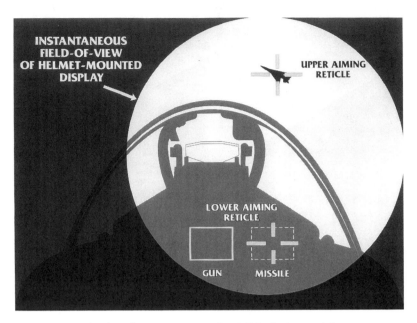

Figure 6-17   HMD display showing two active LOS aiming reticles.

Important functions and performance criteria

Today, HMT P&OT systems are often the odd man out when the design of VCS systems is being considered because these systems and technologies are considered to be mature. Following such logic, one merely has to pick something off-the-shelf that comes close to meeting specifications that are often loosely stated for static accuracy, update rate, etc. However, performing a good system integration job for a complete VCS requires a more in-depth look. Where do you start? Well, there is really no set order to a general discussion of these criteria. As shown in Table 6-7, one set of criteria has been picked for discussion here, but others would probably be just as good.

Line-of-sight (LOS), orientation, position, or all of the above

Many early systems and some systems still in use today provide only helmet (or head) azimuth (AZ) and elevation (EL) LOS information. This is often sufficient for a given application. However, many of today's more sophisticated applications display information driven by HMT-produced head P&O on the HMD with respect to several coordinate frames as shown in Figure 6-18. For this type of application helmet roll and position information are usually needed. Roll information permits symbology or imagery on the HMD, whose frame of reference is some dynamic vehicle such as an aircraft, to be derotated on the HMD. This permits structures on the HMD to be imaged with the proper perspective to the background structures in the vehicle's coordinate frame. The addition of X,Y,Z position information allows computer-generated information

Table 6-7   Helmet P&OT system criteria.

Parameter	Performance
Line-of-sight, orientation, position or all of these	AZ, EL, Roll, X, Y, Z . . . ?
Head coverage or motion box	Limited or full coverage?
Static accuracy (how much and where)	1 milliradian, several or ?
Resolution and repeatability	Arc minutes, bits or ?
Sample rate, update rate, and throughput rate	800, 240, or ?
System interfaces	IEEE 488, RS-422, or ?
Other system issues	LOS filtering, etc.

(CGI) on the HMD to properly show the parallax with respect to nearby structures that are either real as viewed with a Type II HMD or computer-generated as they would be on a Type I HMD. The general terms used to indicate display information frame of reference are "head-stabilized" for display information fixed to the head's coordinate frame and "space-stabilized" for information referenced to other non-head coordinate frames. The use of multiple reference frames is more common with Type II displays but has also been employed frequently with Type I displays.

A system offering six-degree-of-freedom (6DOF—AZ, EL, Roll, X, Y, Z) information, also offers other system advantages. For example, portions of an oculometer (eye LOS) function can be implemented using just the HMT/D. This feature is generally referred to as coordinate intersection cueing (CIC)

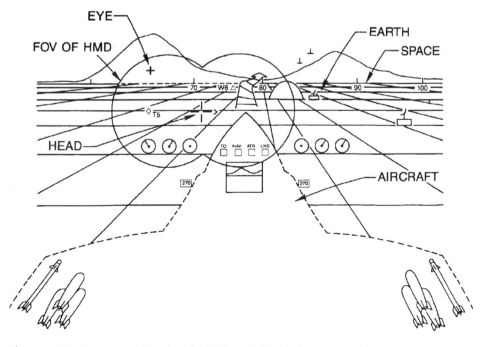

Figure 6-18   Some possible head-stabilized display imagery reference frames.

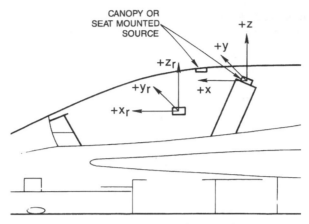

Figure 6-19   Coordinate intersection cueing reference frame geometry.

and is used primarily with Type II HMDs. As shown in Figure 6-19, CIC requires some measurement system with a separate coordinate frame that can be referenced to the coordinate of the HMT's cockpit-mounted transducer. The measurement system can then be used to measure the LOS angles to cockpit locations or switches in its reference frame (shown as X_r, Y_r, Z_r in Figure 6-19) that can be stored in the HMT's electronics nonvolatile memory. During actual operation of the HMT, these stored reference points are converted to the coordinate frame of the cockpit transducer (shown as X, Y, Z in Figure 6-19). Then using the 6DOF information from the observer's LOS as derived from the HMT, the additional coordinate transformation information is available for eye/display aiming-reticle-directed pointing to cockpit surfaces or switches, as implemented by overlaying the HMT LOS reticle on that cockpit location regardless of head location. Some sort of visual or auditory feedback is given to the operator to inform him of his instantaneous interaction with the cockpit-based or system-based controls. If the system incorporates large area active displays in front of the operator, then CIC may be circumvented by displaying an HMT-driven cursor on the panel-mounted display that he can drive with direct visual feedback. The cursor may then interact with switches imaged in the same reference frame on the panel-mounted display.

System head coverage and motion box

Closely associated with P&OT options are the HMT's physical limits of coverage for each parameter (AZ, EL, Roll, X, Y, Z) and the absolute range over which the helmet can be moved and have P&OT information accurately and reliably resolved.

Most of today's serious applications require that angular coverage follows the head to the normal limits of its angular movements. This means at least ±180 degrees in azimuth, ±90 degrees in elevation, and ±45 degrees in roll. Total 4π steradian coverage is even more desirable. At this juncture, it is worth noting that the preferred gimbal order for HMT systems is azimuth, elevation, and roll. This corresponds to most rotation platform gimbal orders that the HMT might be driving for either military or commercial applications. The implication for HMT applications is that using a particular oder for AZ, Roll, EL rotations does not get one to the same LOS as if these rotations were done in some other order (e.g., EL, AZ, Roll).

Position coverage is usually specified with respect to some design eye point over a range that is suitable for the range of operator movement allowed. Representative specifications for a military aircraft cockpit might be +20 and −6 inches in X, ±12 inches in Y, and ±6 inches in Z. In reality, especially for situations where the HMT information is driving the information displayed on the HMD, the system ought to provide coverage wherever the pilot or observer has to put his head and permit the operator to know he is able to extract reliable information from the HMD. This type of performance prevents the "out-of-motion-box" problems that cause data to "freeze" on the HMD until the head returns to a position where a good LOS solution can be obtained.

Static accuracy

Following close on the heels of any discussion of the above parameters is static accuracy. The true meaning of static accuracy and its importance is very often influenced by the demands of a given system application, the pilot's or operator's state (whether external disturbances such as vibration are a factor), the true signal-to-noise performance of the system, the angular limits for operation, and the particular function for which the system is being used. Static accuracy usually means the performance provided when the system is internally programmed to provide information over its full angular and positional limits. It is most often specified as a set of accuracies that degrade as one moves towards the system's positional limits. The limits most often stated in system-specific technical literature are those that represent performance within a few inches of the "design eye" (designated center for normal head location) and ±30 to ±70 degrees in AZ and EL.

An example would be static LOS pointing accuracy for a sensor. Generally, the static accuracy must be less than one-half the instantaneous FOV of the sensor. Thus an HMT/D-driven sensor may only require 9 milliradian accuracy if the FOV of the sensor is 20 milliradians. However, driving the operator's visual aiming point or LOS, through the use of HMT-driven HMD information, to an earth-referenced navigation way-point may require 1 to 2 milliradian accuracy, approaching that claimed for the aircraft's head-up display (HUD). HUD alignment, when accurately checked, is often more like 3 to 5 milliradians rather than the 0.5 to 1 milliradian that is claimed. Today's best HMS systems using suitable P&OT algorithms and alignment procedures can achieve static accuracies of 1 to 2 milliradians, at least throughout the angular range normally subtended by the HUD's instantaneous FOV (e.g. 30°). However, when the HMS is used "open-loop" to direct systems observed through such media as cockpit transparencies, offset errors arising from prismatic deviation through the transparency, can cause error ($>\frac{1}{2}°$) that overwhelm the basic static accuracy performance of the HMS.

Table 6-8 HMT static accuracy performance (relationship between CEP and RMS errors).

CEP	Static accuracy requirement	R from (9)	σ (RMS) degrees	σ (RMS) radians
0.50	0.2°	$1.18\sigma = 0.2°$	0.169	0.00295
0.99	0.4°	$3.03\sigma = 0.2°$	0.132	0.00230

When one is given a system pointing accuracy specification (e.g. ±3 milliradians) its meaning must be known: Does it mean that the manufacturer is guaranteeing that all points over a given angular and positional range will be determined to the stated system accuracy? Or is the manufacturer saying that the system accuracy represents some given root-mean square (RMS) error for an assumed Gaussian distribution because the estimation errors of the sampled physical signal are assumed to be Gaussian and uncorrelated. Usually the second condition is the case and the errors are stated in terms of circular error probability (CEP). Table 6-8 and equation (9) give an example of these relationships for two assumed CEP and static accuracy requirement conditions

$$R^2 = -2\sigma^2 \ln[1 - P(r \leq R)] \tag{9}$$

where $P(r \leq R) = 1 - \exp(-R/2\sigma^2)$ is the probability of a radial error not exceeding a radius of R.

Resolution and repeatability

For HMT systems, resolution and repeatability are closely related. They also have a bearing on static accuracy performance. The resolution capability of a system generally influences its maximum static accuracy. However, the signal-to-noise (S/N) performance of the transducing scheme and system electronics used, also plays a part. Most systems available today provide 12 bits of resolution (1 part in 4096) for each P&O parameter they measure. For an azimuth specification of ±180°, this means it has a basic angular resolving capability of 0.088° (~0.75 milliradian). However, if its S/N performance is better than indicated by its gross resolution performance, it might be able to operate over small angular ranges and still provide 12-bit resolution. An example would be ±90° azimuth determined to 12 bits of resolution, thus providing an angular resolving capability of 0.044°. However, because these are sampled systems, and usually update rate is also important, noise performance and settling times for the analog-to-digital electronics will determine the resolved level of the signal. The cost of the HMT electronics is also a factor. Thus, the angular resolution at the HMT system's angular limits normally reflects the system's performance limits.

Resolution performance can be a significant parameter for head-driven display presentations where small head movements can be detected on the HMD presentation under conditions of high apparent magnification. 12-bit P&O tracking systems have been observed to cause undesirable and detectable discrete jumps in the location of the display imagery on the HMD during small head movements. Newer systems that resolve orientation to 14 bits or more seem to provide enough additional resolution to make this artifact virtually undetectable. For full angular coverage, such a system can provide an angular resolution of almost 0.02°. HMT systems providing higher resolution are preferred for binocular HMD applications involving high raster line rates and partial overlap of the monocular fields, since they offer the potential of more accurate symbology placement for objects viewed by both eyes in the HMD's overlap region.

There are trade-offs associated with the improved performance. Achieving the S/N needed to attain an honest 14-bit system often impacts the transducer and electronics design. For example, the AC MHMT requires a larger source. The larger sources measure 1.25 inches to 1.5 inches square as compared to the normal 1-inch-square source and weigh between 7.5 and 9 ounces, an increase of several ounces. The ideal mounting location in military fighter aircraft is on the cockpit canopy behind the pilot. The larger and heavier MHMT source may be too heavy for mounting in some cockpit canopies (e.g. the USAF F-16) because bird-strike-induced canopy waves are more prone to cause canopy failure with the heavier MHMT source mounted in them.

The other troublesome area involving system resolution or accuracy performance occurs when the separation distance between the transmitting and receiving transducers for full-resolution performance is reached. Does the system just quit operating or does its performance degrade gracefully? For example, a 14-bit system might perform at full resolution out to a distance of 40 inches between the transmitting and receiving transducers. Beyond 40 inches it might degrade gracefully to 13 bits between 40 and 46 inches, to 12 bits between 46 and 50 inches, etc., for those conditions where the maximum full-resolution source–sensor range is exceeded.

Repeatability is closely related to resolution and to how well the complete system approaches the performance of an idealized linear system. It is important because it indicates the variation in measurement one might expect by making repeated measurements at the same position and orientation sample point. As a performance measure, it can indicate the relative stability of the location of HMT-driven information on the HMD. Generally, repeatability is specified at twice or three times the system resolution limit for any value determined within its normal operating limits, regardless of the absolute accuracy of that value. Repeatability worse than three times the resolution limit can be an indication of flaws in the design of the system.

Update rate, throughput rate, and display refresh rate

These performance measures for HMT systems have been a point of contention and misunderstanding on an almost continuing basis. Today's applications involving HMTs, especially if they involve HMT-driven computer-generated information (CGI) on the HMD, demand as high an update rate as most systems can provide. Indeed, even if the computer graphics update rate is relatively slow, several P&O samples from an HMT running at a high update rate can be used for predicting the next update point for the display of CGI on

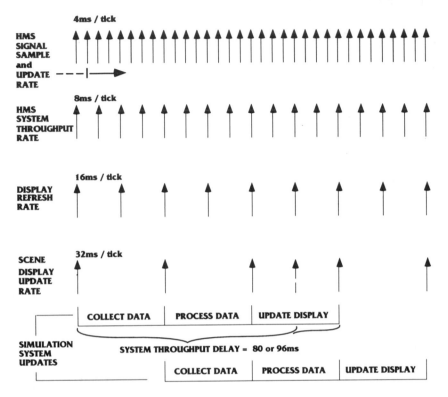

Figure 6-20 Relationships between update, throughput, and refresh rate.

the HMD, thus improving the apparent data throughput rate for the entire system. At this juncture, it is appropriate to discuss these relationships in the context of the entire visually coupled or virtual reality system and explain how the visual data on the display whose P&O is driven by the helmet or head tracker is impacted by these relationships. Figure 6-20 shows a set of hypothetical timing diagrams for the P&OT, helmet display, and computer systems that generate the virtual reality scene. As shown in Figure 6-20, there are really a number of update and throughput rate relationships for the tracker and scene generation system that should be considered.

To be meaningful, HMT update rate must be explained in terms of the sampling process and P&OT algorithm used. For instance, is one update used solely for sampling the sensed signal to remove unwanted disturbances from the signal by means of various digital filtering schemes? Or is the P&OT algorithm recursive in nature, requiring two or more updates to approach some nominal steady-state error, or both?

As sometimes defined, update rate is the rate at which the signal is sampled and at which P&OT data appear at the output. Throughput rate is the time or number of samples required for an input to be reflected as an output from the HMT system. Throughput rate is a better reflection of the "real" bandwidth of the HMT and its dynamic error. Throughput rate should be considered in terms of how many updates are required for a step input change in head P&O to show up on the system's output to an accuracy level that represents its claimed static accuracy or steady-state error.

For the HMT performance depicted by Figure 6-20, we have assumed that the HMT is sampling the head P&O many times over a 4 millisecond (ms) interval and processing or filtering these samples to reduce certain types of environmental noise. During the next 4 ms interval it computes the new P&O at the system's specified static accuracy and outputs its update at the end of the cycle to the scene-generation system. Once the HMT data pipeline is full it could produce updates to an external system at 4 ms intervals for an update rate of 250 updates per second (UPS) with an 8 ms throughput delay.

For the hypothetical system shown in Figure 6-20, a multiprocessor virtual reality system is assumed. Once the HMT data output is ready it must be collected along with other control input data on a fixed interval basis. Here we have assumed 32 ms is required. Then the next 32 ms interval is assumed to be needed to process the data and output it to the computer-generated graphics systems that will update the display scene refresh memory, and finally the display is refreshed with the updated changes to the scene. For the example based upon Figure 6-20, the "system" throughput delay is either 80 ms if the display refresh rate is for a non-interlaced scanning format or 96 ms for a 2:1 interlace scanning format. An infinite number of scenarios are possible but this example indicates how system processing requirements can build up to very long scene update delays. It should be noted that we have assumed that the HMT cycles can be "clocked" from an external system clock, normally the display refresh controller. This permits each display scene update to be the same integer multiple of P&OT updates, so that moving objects on the display appear to move smoothly (i.e. at equal distances in time), eliminating movement jitter that is often observed when unequal numbers of P&OT updates occur between consecutive scene updates.

What, then, besides improving the performance of superior forms of P&OT algorithms, are some good reasons for requiring an improved update for the HMT? One already mentioned is that it also aids the throughput delay problems for computer-generated imagery systems which must place their imagery on the HMD according to the HMT P&O updates. Using multiple HMT updates provided at high rates for a system update rate that may be much lower can permit elegant prediction algorithms to be utilized, thereby improving the effective throughput of scene placement information and its offset with respect to head movement.

Another is that a higher update rate aids one area of HMT performance that is particularly hard to quantify: system dynamic accuracy. The problem with this requirement is its measurement. Past development efforts that have investigated the measurement of HMT dynamic accuracy performance, particularly for the magnetic HMT, have resulted in budgetary estimates of three to four hundred thousand dollars to produce an adequate test fixture. This is an amount that meager development budgets have not been able to support with competing commitments of greater overall import. Perhaps a good alternative for the HMT is the achievement of higher update rates that reduce the latency

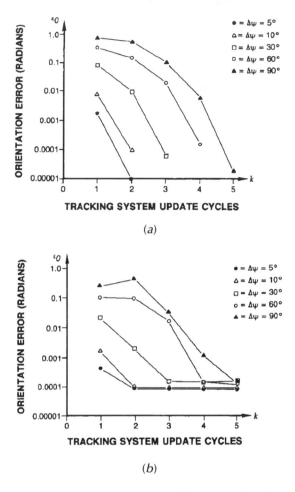

Figure 6-21 Representative MVLE P&OT performance for free-space and fixed scattering environments.

between the measured and real head position and orientation and, thus, inherently improve system dynamic accuracy.

Some of the currently more popular HMT technologies, like the AC magnetic helmet tracker, employ system P&O algorithms requiring at least two update cycles to obtain good convergence to the actual dynamic head P&O inputs. Figure 6-21 indicates the error performance obtained for a new type of minimum variance linear estimation algorithm. This algorithm provides a system error that is minimum in a least-squared-error sense. It is also designed to track field conditions at the helmet sensor, and in laboratory tests, at least, has demonstrated the capability to track the sensor down to conductive surfaces. The system hardware that was designed to run this algorithm operates at a 240 sample per second rate. Once the data pipeline is full, the system provides data at 240 UPS or every 4.17 ms. For this type of algorithm, the

Table 6-9   Update and throughput times for several HMTs.

Tracker type	Update rate (milliseconds (UPS))	Throughput rate (ms)
AC magnetic	4.167 (240)	12.5
DC magnetic	6.944 (144)	10.944*
Electro-optical (LED arrays)	4.167 (240)	4.167
Electro-optical (rotating IR planes of light)	33.33 (33)	33.33

*Supplies data at a maximum throughput rate sufficient to support an integer number of updates for a display refresh rate of 72 UPS or every 13.89 milliseconds.

higher update rate reduces the algorithm convergence problem down to manageable levels for human operator head movement rates of roughly 0–250 degrees per second that are most often encountered in normal use.

The evolution of VCS interfaces in the military aircraft cockpit and VCS and VR interfaces elsewhere is leading towards an overall integration of human sensory interfaces to maximize the use of the human's cognitive functions. Foremost among the new integrated capabilities coming on line for the man–machine interface is auditory localization. The human visual system has relatively high resolution but its processing time is relatively slow. The human auditory system is relatively coarse but its processing of input signals is much faster. Researchers working on the auditory localization problem indicate that people can move their heads between 200 and 500 degrees per second without blurring the auditory cues and that at the most sensitive locations human auditory localization error is about one degree. Maximum head rates over small arcs fall in the range of 800 to 1000 degrees per second. Some HMT algorithms being used to obtain improved static accuracy require at least one update for wave-form sampling and then another to produce an output to better than one degree error. These same algorithms may have convergence problems if sensor orientation changes by more than 1 or 2 degrees per update. Such operating characteristics beg the question of the effect on latency for the auditory localization system, which may be as important as rate. Since no system providing these very high update rates has been built, the effect on 3D audio displays is not well defined. Current estimates from technical personnel familiar with auditory localization research indicate that sampling rates between 500 and perhaps as high as 1600 updates per second may be needed, depending upon the system type, its algorithm and the throughput rates it can provide.

Table 6-9 lists some current maximum update and throughput rates for several commonly available HMT systems. As integrated-circuit technology continues to improve, the improvements may be reflected in improved update and throughput times for HMT systems.

System interfaces

Today's HMT, when used as part of a modern VCS, needs to accommodate a number of system interfaces. Systems geared for military cockpit use normally provide a 1553B interface. The update rate of 50 updates per second on some aircraft's 1553B bus is sufficient for slaving sensors, etc., but too slow for others such as image derotation on the HMD. This function may have to operate at rates of 60 to 120 UPS or higher to maintain synchronization with the helmet display raster or calligraphic imagery. A special interface, often a dedicated RS-422 channel, is required. For commercial applications other interfaces such as ethernet, a computer bus standard, or a shared memory interface may be required, especially for simulator applications. The system must also be capable of being synchronized to an external clock that is controlling the CGI or the refresh control of the HMD imagery. As already mentioned, this requirement is often critical for CGI moving objects, whose placement on the HMD is driven by the HMT outputs. It is often the case with today's HMT systems that they are not "plug-and-play" for most applications.

Other system issues

There are a number of other systems issues that ought to be considered in selecting an HMT system. Often these are not directly related to performance but may ultimately affect system performance because of limitations imposed by the operating environment.

One important issue is the number of transducers that must be installed and aligned to achieve full system head P&OT coverage. A system requiring just one transducer to achieve full coverage is a decided advantage. It takes up less space, especially in cramped fighter cockpits. The use of just one transducer external to the head simplifies its alignment to the vehicle or system datum line. It also eliminates problems that systems using multiple transducers often experience regarding maintaining relative alignment to its other transducers. Systems employing multiple transducers must have developed a successful strategy for preventing crossover from one transducer's coverage limits to another's from inducing offset errors in the HMT's P&O outputs that can cause very noticeable "jumps" in the location of imagery on the HMD.

Another issue, from which a whole series of questions regarding cost arises, relates to the type of transducer alignment hardware provided. Is it expensive and labor intensive? Or relatively cheap and automated in its use? Must multiple transducers be aligned and how is relative alignment checked? Does the alignment fixture allow one to test system P&OT static accuracy at the same time or must a different fixture be procured for this function? Can the customer become proficient enough to align the system himself or must he continually return to the manufacturer of the system for such help?

Depending upon the type of application, important issues relating to system integration and long-term performance may arise. One very important issue is system susceptibility to performance degradation due to external disturbances and materials that will be encountered in its operating environment. Can these factors be compensated for and how easily? Systems that transduce magnetic energy are bothered by conductive and ferromagnetic materials and stray fields from the helmet-mounted CRTs. Systems that transduce light energy may be bothered by sunlight or other types of light sources. Is the helmet-mounted transducer hardware compact, leaving more room for other system attachments and relatively immune to helmet flexure or obscuration by human motion? Or does the system require a significant area of real estate on the helmet or head surface making it susceptible to helmet flexure or obscuration of its transduced energy by human motion. Is it rugged and relatively immune to the abuse that personal equipment receives during normal use?

Performance specifications for several HMS system types

The discussion just concluded has attempted to cover some of the most important issues surrounding the selection and use of HMT equipment as part of a VCS. It is not possible within the constraints of this chapter to be totally inclusive, especially with the application-dependence of particular requirements and technology that is constantly evolving. Tables 6-10(a) and (b), which are an update to one included in a 1991 SPIE paper by Ferrin (Ferrin, 1991), provide a summary of basic performance characteristics for some of the newer systems. These tables primarily chart the basic performance issues and status of different technologies and cannot be used alone to make a system acquisition decision. This requires a thorough understanding of one's application and close coordination with each system vendor.

SYSTEM INTEGRATION

The preceding section presented and described the main characteristics of the major components and subcomponents of visually coupled systems. The purpose of this section is to discuss the issues associated with the integration of these components with each other and with the human operator. This should provide the reader with a sufficient understanding to be better able to specify and evaluate visually coupled systems and components.

System characteristics

There are a number of parameters that are used to characterize a visually coupled system; Table 6-11 provides a summary list of some of the more important ones. Each of these are briefly discussed in this section.

Ocularity

One of the first decisions to be made is whether a VCS will be monocular (HMD image to one eye only), biocular (same HMD image to both eyes), or binocular (independent, matched HMD images to each eye). The monocular approach is well suited for symbology-only, Type II HMDs and has the advantage of being relatively light weight (only one optical system and display image source). The binocular approach is required if stereoscopic imagery is desired but requires two independent optical systems and two sensors or image generation channels. This results in a larger and more expensive system (but more capable) than the monocular approach. The biocular approach provides

Table 6-10 Comparison of helmet tracking technologies.

(*a*)

Tracker technology category	Range of angular inputs (RMS)	Accuracy range (milliradians) (RMS)	Strengths
Electro-optical using rotating IR beams or planes of light	AZ: ±180° EL: ±70° Roll: ±35	3 to 10	Availability Simple installation
Electro-optical using LED arrays	AZ: ±180° EL: ~±60° Roll: ~±45°	1 to 10	Minimum added helmet weight High accuracy
Electro-optical using videometric techniques	AZ: ±180° EL: ~±60° Roll: ~±45°	2 to 15	No added helmet weight
Ultrasonic concepts	AZ: ±180° EL: ~±90° Roll: ~±45°	5 to 10	Minimum added helmet weight
Magnetic concepts AC or DC	AZ: ±180° EL: ~±90° Roll: ~±180°	1 to 8	Very low added helmet weight Simple mechanization Good noise immunity High accuracy Very large motion box

(*b*)

Tracker technology category	Weaknesses	Possible interference sources	Development status
Electro-optical using rotating IR beams or planes of light	Helmet weight (12 ounces) Reliability of moving parts No head position information	Helicopter rotor chop Sun modulation	Production (F4 Phantom, AH-64 Apache, and A-129 Mangusta)
Electro-optical using LED arrays	Coverage Limited motion box Covertness	Reflections IR energy sources	Prototype
Electro-optical using videometric techniques	Limited motion box Helmet surface integrity	Reflections IR energy sources	Prototype
Ultrasonic concepts	Partial blockage Stray cockpit signal returns Accuracy No head position information	Air flow and turbulence Ultrasonic noise sources Multi-path signals	Prototype
Magnetic concepts AC or DC	Ferromagnetic and/or metal conductive surfaces cause field distortion (cockpit metal, moving seat, helmet CRTs)	Changing locations for metal objects Rarely—magnetic fields	AC system in low-rate production for AH-66 Comanche Several commercial variations of AC and DC designs in production

Table 6-11 Parameters used to characterize or specify the HMD of a visually coupled system.

Ocularity (binocular, biocular, monocular
Color (monochrome, polychrome)
Type I or Type II (combiner or no combiner)
Monocular field of view
Total field of view
Binocular field of view (if applicable)
Field of regard
Resolution
Focus (image distance)
Luminance
Combiner ratio
Exit-pupil size (or eye motion box)
Eye relief
Vignetting
Interpupillary distance (IPD)
Distortion
Update rate
Refresh rate

---

for two-eye viewing but since the images are the same, stereo viewing is not possible.

Color

HMDs can be either monochrome or polychrome with the term "polychrome referring to the fact that the HMD can produce more than one color but may not be capable of full color. The vast majority of airborne HMDs developed since the early 1970s have been monochrome (usually green due to the high efficiency green phosphor cathode-ray tubes available) although some experimental (and bulky) early color systems were built (e.g., Winner, 1973). In recent years color liquid-crystal displays and liquid-crystal shutters in conjunction with white phosphor CRTs have resulted in numerous commercially available color HMDs (see section on *Applications of VCS and VCS components*).

Type I or Type II

To split or not to split, that is the question! The key to answering this question is in the application of the VCS. If the system is to be interactive with the real world then a Type II display is probably most appropriate. If the system is to be used totally independent of the real world (visually) then a Type I system is the best choice.

Monocular field of view

The monocular FOV is the angular subtense of the displayed image as measured from the pupil of one eye. The total FOV (see below) may be the same as the monocular FOV for a two-eye (binocular) HMD if the two FOVs have 100% overlap.

Total field of view

This is the total angular size of the virtual image visible to both eyes expressed in degrees. Due to the concept of partial overlap in binocular displays, it is necessary to specify both the total FOV and the binocular FOV. This may be expressed as a single number (usually in degrees) implying a circular FOV (or it may mean the diagonal of a rectangular FOV) or it may be expressed as two numbers representing the horizontal and the vertical angular size of the image. Systems have been built with FOVs as small as 5° and as large as 160° (horizontal).

Binocular field of view

This parameter refers to the size of the display field which is visible to both eyes. If an HMD has full overlap between the two eyes, then the binocular FOV and the total FOV will be the same. As in the total field of view, this is usually expressed in degrees for both the horizontal and vertical angles.

Field of regard

The term "field of regard" was created for helmet-mounted displays connected to a gimbaled (slewable) sensor (e.g., a television camera) to describe the total visual field that was potentially available for viewing. Thus, the field of regard is the angular size of the visual scene that is within the range of viewing angles possible with the particular HMD/tracker/sensor system.

Resolution

Resolution is a highly over-simplified method of providing a very limited amount of information regarding the image quality aspects of a display. The intent of this parameter is to provide an indication of the level of detail available in an image or display system. A proper discussion of this topic would take a chapter by itself (Task, 1979) so the coverage here will be limited. For solid-state display image sources the smallest available picture element (pixel) is fairly well defined, since these displays are composed of discretely addressed cells. For monochrome devices the resolution might be expressed as the distance (in linear units such as millimeters) from center to center of the individual pixels. This is referred to as the "pitch" of the display. The resolution may also only be expressed in computer terms as a number of elements across by some number of elements vertically (note that this is really a computer addressable measure and does not ensure that the display can "show" all of these elements). For HMDs it is most appropriate to convert these linear measures of resolution to angular units to better relate to visual perception. Many angular resolution units have been used to express resolution including: cycles per degree, cycles per milliradian, radians, milliradians, and arcminutes. The first two units correspond to resolution measurement methods that involve the use of a periodic or semi-periodic resolution chart (such as the 1951 Air Force Tri-Bar chart; see Kingslake, 1965). The latter three units simply refer to the angular subtense of an individual pixel which is also the angular "pitch" of the display. In order to achieve an image that has

Table 6-12   Human visual limiting resolution (acuity) expressed in various units.

1	arcminutes
0.86	cycles per milliradian
30	cycles per degree
0.29	milliradians
0.00029	radians

reasonable quality, it is desirable to have a resolution that is close to the resolving capability of the human eye. This is quite often not possible but by comparing the resolution of the display to the resolution of the eye one can get an idea of how good the image will appear. Table 6-12 is a listing of the human visual resolution (acuity) for a normal individual expressed in each of these units. All the values in Table 6-12 roughly correspond to a normal human visual capability of 20/20 (Snellen acuity).

If the HMD resolution is equal to or better than the human visual resolving capability (visual acuity) then one is assured that the HMD will provide excellent image quality. If the HMD resolution is much worse than the human visual capability (e.g., by a factor of 10) then the image will appear significantly degraded (grainy). Somewhere between these extremes is probably the best trade-off between HMD resolution and HMD field of view. Note that better HMD resolution corresponds to high numbers for the cycles per milliradian and cycles per degree units (the larger the number the better the quality) but it corresponds to low numbers for the angular units (arcminutes, milliradians, and radians) of Table 6-12 (the lower the number the better the quality). If the HMD resolution is only given in computer terms (addressable elements) it is possible to convert this to visual terms if the field of view is known. The easiest calculation is to determine the cycles per degree. This is done by dividing the number of elements by twice the field of view (in degrees). For example, if a display produces an 80° field of view and has 1280 elements then the visual resolution is $(1280/(2 \times 80))$ or 8 cycles per degree. This is only about $\frac{1}{4}$ of the human visual resolution limit of 30 cycles per degree listed in Table 6-12.

Focus (image distance)

An HMD may or may not have a focus adjustment. The primary purpose of a focus adjustment is to allow the HMD user to view the HMD image without using corrective lenses (eyeglasses). The focus adjustment range is normally given in either diopters or as a distance. A diopter is a unit of optical power equal to the reciprocal of the image distance in meters. (For a lens the diopter power is one over the focal length in meters.) For near-sighted individuals (myopes) the HMD image must be brought in closer by moving the eyepiece lens closer to the display image source (inside the focal length). For far-sighted individuals the image is actually moved "beyond infinity" in order to permit the individual to form a clear image on his retina. For near-sighted settings the diopter units are negative and for far-sighted individuals the diopter units are positive. A typical adjustment range might be from −6 diopters to +2 diopters (as in the US Army ANVIS-6 night-vision goggles).

Luminance

In strictest terms luminance is the photometeric quantity that is measured with a photometer or luminance meter that most closely corresponds to the human visual sensation of brightness. There are a number of illusions which demonstrate that luminance (what is measured) and brightness (what is visually perceived) are not the same thing. However, they quite often are erroneously used interchangeably. Luminance is typically measured in foot-Lamberts (English units) or candela per square-meter (also called a nit; international system units). The luminance specification may refer to the peak luminance or it may refer to the average luminance across the display field.

Combiner ratio

If the HMD uses a combiner or beamsplitter to superimpose the HMD image on the real world the reflection and transmission coefficient of the combiner might be expressed as a ratio or, more typically, both the transmission and reflection percentages are stated (e.g. 40 per cent transmission, 35 per cent reflection). Theoretically, the transmission and reflection percentages could add up to 100 per cent but typically there is also some absorption of the light resulting in the two values adding up to less than 100 per cent. For HMDs that use a narrow-band display image source (such as a miniature CRT with a P-43 phosphor) the combiner can be made to have different reflection and transmission values for different wavelengths by using either holographic techniques or multi-layer coatings. This wavelength selective technique can produce higher HMD image luminances without losing as much real-world scene luminance (on average, across wavelengths) although some color shift of real-world objects may occur.

Vignetting

As light travels from the display through the optical system to the eye it is quite common for some of the light rays to be blocked or to be directed in such a way that they do not make it entirely through the system to the eye. These effects can cause a reduction in the field of view (such as the case found in the simple magnifier example if the eye is located too far away from the lens) or it may cause a reduction in the amount of light the eye receives from some parts of the display (which reduces the apparent brightness of that part of the display). A full discussion of vignetting is beyond the scope of this text but the interested reader can find out more about it in any basic optics textbook (e.g., *Optics*, Klein, 1970).

Exit-pupil size (or eye-motion box)

If the HMD optical system produces a real exit pupil then the size of the exit pupil is typically measured in millimeters and is relatively easy to measure. For non-exit-pupil forming optical systems there exists a certain volume in space

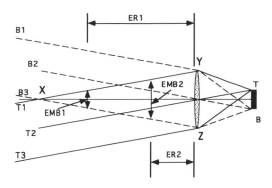

Figure 6-22 Simple magnifier optics (non-pupil-forming optical system).

within which the eye can be where the full field of view is visible and no vignetting is taking place. This volume is usually cone shaped (if the lens is circular) but there is no accepted name for this volume (see triangle XYZ in Figure 6-22). If the eye-relief distance is stated, then it is possible to determine how much the eye can move laterally before the field of view starts to be cut off. This area of possible lateral movement has, on occasion, been erroneously referred to as the exit pupil. A more appropriate name may be the "eye-motion box." Figure 6-22 is a ray-trace drawing for a simple magnifier optical system with two eye-motion box and eye-relief distance combinations marked.

Figure 6-22 shows the trade-off relationship between eye-motion box and eye relief. If the eye-relief distance is set at ER1 then the eye-motion box size is shown by EMB1. However, if the eye is only set back a distance of ER2 then the eye motion box grows to the size shown by EMB2. The triangle defined by XYZ corresponds to the area within which the eye must be in order to see the full field of view. This triangle is bounded by the lens, the top-most ray (T1) of the bundle of rays (T1, T2, T3) coming from the top of the display image source and by the bottom-most ray (B3) of the bundle of rays (B1, B2, B3) coming from the bottom of the display image source. The XYZ triangle can be made larger only by increasing the size of the lens or by decreasing the field of view (the angle between rays T1 and B3). This demonstrates the interrelationship between the field of view, lens size, eye-relief distance and eye-motion box size.

Eye-relief distance

This is the distance from the last optical surface in the HMD optical system to the front surface of the eye. This is an important parameter in that it provides some information as to whether or not the HMD is compatible with eyeglass wear. For exit-pupil forming systems the eye relief is simply the distance from the last optical surface to the plane of the exit pupil. For non-pupil forming systems the eye-relief distance and the eye-motion box can be traded off. Figure 6-22 depicts this eye-relief distance and eye-motion box size trade-off.

Interpupillary distance (IPD)

The IPD is the distance between the two optical axes in a binocular view system. This also refers to the distance between the observer's eyes. It is imperative that the binocular HMDs have either an adjustable IPD to match the observers' IPDs or have a sufficiently large exit pupil (or eye-motion box) that can accommodate the expected user population. IPDs for US Air Force personnel have been found to range from 51 mm to 76 mm (Hertzberg *et al.*, 1954).

Distortion

As its name implies, distortion is a result of nonlinear mapping from object space to image space making the image appear to be shaped somewhat differently than the object. For circularly symmetric lens systems, distortion typically increases with increasing distance (or angle) from the optical axis. This produces either a "barrel" distortion or a "pin-cushion" distortion (Kingslake, 1965; Smith, 1966). The magnitude of the distortion is typically expressed as a percentage.

Update rate

The update rate for a display system is the frequency with which the image information is recalculated (in the case of computer-generated imagery) or rescanned (in the case of a sensor such as a video camera). This is usually stated in Hertz, times per second, or updates per second.

Refresh rate

Many display types (such as a CRT) produce an image that would disappear in a fraction of a second if it were not "repainted" or refreshed. In a television monitor a scanning electron beam activates the phosphor of the screen which produces light for a short time. As the beam moves on to another part of the screen the light quickly fades or decays. For this reason it is necessary to refresh the image often enough that the flicker caused by the process will not be objectionable (and preferably not even detectable). The refresh rate is stated in Hertz, times per second just like the update rate or sometimes as refreshes per second.

Eye/optics integration

There are several trade-off issues associated with the interface between the optical system of an HMD and the human visual system. Some of the more important issues and trade-offs are presented in this section. For simplicity only the simple magnifier optical system is used for the examples presented herein.

Eye relief versus field of view

As stated earlier, a simple magnifier lens system does not have a real exit pupil. However, there is a restriction on where the eye can be in order to see

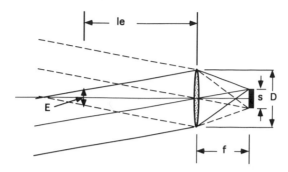

Figure 6-23 Ray trace for a simple magnifier optical system showing the relationship between eye relief (*le*), eye box size (*E*), display size (*s*), lens diameter (*D*) and lens focal length (*f*).

the entire FOV without vignetting. Figure 6-23 is a drawing of the relationship between the lens diameter, lens focal length, display size, eye relief and the eye-motion box (which has, on many occasions, been referred to as an "exit pupil").

Using Figure 6-23 and simple geometry, it is possible to derive equation (10) which mathematically describes the relationship between eye relief, eye box size ("exit pupil"), display size, lens diameter, and lens focal length.

$$E = D - \frac{(le)(s)}{f} \tag{10}$$

where E is the eye-motion box ("exit pupil") which is equivalent to the "exit pupil" diameter, D the lens diameter, s the display size, le the eye-relief distance, and f the focal length of lens. Figure 6-24 presents a graphical representation of equation (10).

At some optical eye-relief distance, the eye-motion box size is the same as the entrance pupil to the eye. This is the maximum optical eye relief possible without causing vignetting at the edge of the FOV. It should also be noted that the actual physical eye clearance will be somewhat less than this value since the entrance pupil of the eye is located about 3 mm behind the corneal surface, and since the rear principle plane of the eyepiece lens is typically not at the last optical surface of the lens system.

The previously discussed equations assumed that the eye-relief and lens diameter were such that they did not limit the FOV of the system. This, obviously, is not always the case. For a simple magnifier optical system, the FOV will be vignetted (clipped) if the observer's eye is too far from the lens. The relationship between this distance (eye to lens) can be related to the FOV remaining. When the eye is far enough from the lens that the entire FOV is not visible, then there is an ambiguity in determining the instantaneous FOV. For points that are near the edge of the field, it is possible to define the edge of the FOV as that angle at which there is no vignetting of the light from the edge, 50 per cent vignetting, or just at 100 per cent vignetting. Figure 6-25 is a drawing of the rays coming from a lens that represent the angles corresponding to 0 per

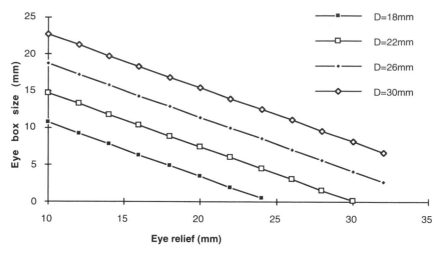

Figure 6-24 Graph of equation (10) with eye box size (*E*) versus eye relief (*le*) for several values of lens diameter (*D*) using a focal length of 25 mm and a display size of 18 mm. Note that this is for the case where the display is located at the rear focal plane of the lens (image produced at infinity; i.e., collimated).

cent, 50 per cent, and 100 per cent vignetting. Visually, what one sees is that the edge of the FOV is "fuzzy"; where this fuzziness begins is the field angle that corresponds to 0 per cent vignetting, approximately in the middle of it is the 50 per cent vignetting angle and at the very edge of the visible field is the 100 per cent point.

There are, therefore, six equations that can be used to determine the FOV based on the eye-to-lens distance and the level of vignetting that one wishes to use to define the FOV. These are listed as equations (11) through (16). Figure 6-26 is a graph of the apparent FOV as a function of eye distance for the three vignetting cases (0 per cent, 50 per cent, and 100 per cent). The graphs were produced using a focal length of 25 mm, a display size of 18 mm and a lens diameter of 18 mm.

Case 1—0% vignetting:

For $le < (f(D - e)/s)$ $\qquad$ $\text{FOV} = 2\arctan(s/(2f))$ $\qquad$ (11)

For $le > (f(D - e)/s)$ $\qquad$ $\text{FOV} = 2\arctan((D - e)/(2\,le))$ $\qquad$ (12)

Case 2—50% vignetting:

For $le < (f \times D)/s$ $\qquad$ $\text{FOV} = 2\arctan(s/(2f))$ $\qquad$ (13)

For $le > (f \times D)/s$ $\qquad$ $\text{FOV} = 2\arctan(D/(2\,le))$ $\qquad$ (14)

Case 3—100% vignetting:

For $le < (f(D + e)/s)$ $\qquad$ $\text{FOV} = 2\arctan(s/(2f))$ $\qquad$ (15)

For $le > (f(D + e)/s)$ $\qquad$ $\text{FOV} = 2\arctan((D + e)/(2\,le))$ $\qquad$ (16)

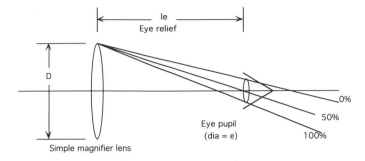

Figure 6-25 Drawing showing the rim rays that correspond to 0%, 50% and 100% vignetting for determining apparent FOV.

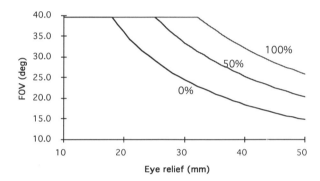

Figure 6-26 Apparent FOV versus eye distance from the lens for a system with $f = 25$ mm, $D = 18$ mm and $e = 5$ mm. Graphics generated using equations (11) through (16).

where le is the eye relief, D the lens diameter, e the eye-pupil diameter, s the display size, and f is the lens focal length.

Resolution versus field of view (FOV)

For a given display size, one can obtain a larger HMD FOV by using a shorter focal length lens. As explained in the preceding material, this results in a shorter eye-relief distance. It also will result in reduced visual resolution. The display limiting resolution can be expressed in cycles mm^{-1}, which corresponds to the highest spatial frequency pattern that can be seen (resolved) on the display. When viewed through the simple magnifier optical system, this can be converted to cycles per degree by using equation (17). Since the display size is fixed and its linear resolution (cycles mm^{-1}) is fixed, then the total number of picture elements (pixels) is also fixed. If one produces a larger FOV by reducing the focal length of the lens then the same fixed number of pixels must be spread over a larger angular area which reduces the apparent visual resolution. By combining equations (1) and (17), it is possible to generate an

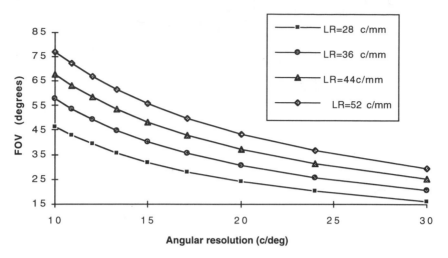

Figure 6-27 FOV versus resolution for several display linear resolutions. These curves were generated using equation (18) with a lens focal length of 25 mm, display size of 18 mm and the display located at the focal point of the lens. These curves assume that the eye is close enough to the lens that the lens diameter does not become a limiting factor.

equation which describes this trade-off between FOV and visual acuity (angular resolution). Equation (18) is the result. Note that equation (18) was derived for the limited case where the display is at the focal plane of the lens.

$$V_{\text{res}} = \frac{1}{\arctan(1/(fL_{\text{res}}))} \tag{17}$$

$$\text{FOV} = 2\arctan\{((sL_{\text{res}})/2)\tan(1/V_{\text{res}})\} \tag{18}$$

where V_{res} is the visual angular resolution (cycles per degree), L_{res} the linear display resolution (cycles mm^{-1}), f the focal length of lens (mm), s the size of display (mm), and FOV is the field of view in degrees. Figure 6-27 is a graphic representation of equation (18) showing the trade-off between HMD FOV and visual angular resolution for several display linear resolutions.

In order to get a better feel for the trade-off between FOV and visual resolution, it is possible to convert the visual angular resolution values into Snellen acuity (which may be more familiar to most people). Equation (19) converts visual angular resolution in cycles per degree to Snellen acuity by using the assumption that 20/20 visual acuity is equivalent to 30 cycles per degree visual angular resolution.

$$V_{\text{res}} = \frac{600}{xx} \tag{19}$$

where xx is the Snellen acuity (as in 20/xx), and V_{res} the visual angular

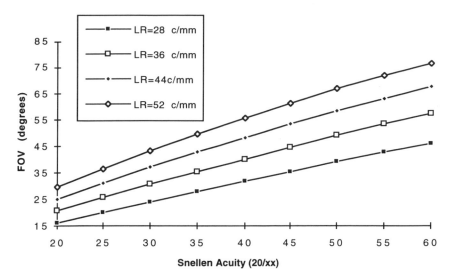

Figure 6-28   FOV versus Snellen acuity for several display linear resolutions. These were generated using equation (14) with a focal length of 25 mm, display size of 18 mm and the display at the lens focal length. It is assumed that the eye is close enough to the lens that the lens diameter does not limit the FOV.

resolution (cycles per degree). If this is substituted into equation (18), one obtains:

$$FOV = 2\arctan[((sL_{res})/2)\tan(xx/600)] \tag{20}$$

where the symbols have the same meaning as previously.

Figure 6-28 was produced using equation (20) and the same data as were used to generate Figure 6-27. The larger visual acuity numbers correspond to poorer vision/resolution.

Resolution values for HMDs and night-vision goggles (NVGs) may be expressed in cycles per milliradian, cycles per degree, or Snellen acuity. Table 6-13 is a summary of conversions between these different units. It is divided into three sets of three columns each. The first column in each set was used to generate the values shown in the other two columns of the set. The purpose of this table is to permit easy conversion from one type of unit to another. To convert from one unit to another, go to the set of columns that has the unit you want to convert *from* in the first column in the set. Then move down the column until you see the value that you are interested in and read across the row within that set to find the value converted to the other units. For example, if you knew a system had a visual resolution of 0.76 cycles per milliradian you would go to the first set of three columns, since its first column is in units of cycles per mradian. If you wished to convert this to Snellen acuity, you would look down the first column until you saw the 0.76 cycles per milliradian then look across to the last column in the set and see that this corresponds to a Snellen acuity of 20/45.

Table 6-13 Conversion table to change between Snellen acuity and visual angular resolution stated in either cycles per milliradian (c mrad^{-1}) or cycles per degree (c deg^{-1}).

V_{res} (c mrad^{-1})	V_{res} (c deg^{-1})	Snellen 20/xx	Snellen 20/xx	V_{res} (c mrad^{-1})	V_{res} (c deg^{-1})	V_{res} (c deg^{-1})	Snellen 20/xx	V_{res} (c mrad^{-1})
0.50	8.7	69	60	0.57	10.0	10.0	60	0.57
0.52	9.1	66	59	0.58	10.2	10.5	57	0.60
0.54	9.4	64	58	0.59	10.3	11.0	55	0.63
0.56	9.8	61	57	0.60	10.5	11.5	52	0.66
0.58	10.1	59	56	0.61	10.7	12.0	50	0.69
0.60	10.5	57	55	0.63	10.9	12.5	48	0.72
0.62	10.8	55	54	0.64	11.1	13.0	46	0.74
0.64	11.2	54	53	0.65	11.3	13.5	44	0.77
0.66	11.5	52	52	0.66	11.5	14.0	43	0.80
0.68	11.9	51	51	0.67	11.8	14.5	41	0.83
0.70	12.2	49	50	0.69	12.0	15.0	40	0.86
0.72	12.6	48	49	0.70	12.2	15.5	39	0.89
0.74	12.9	46	48	0.72	12.5	16.0	38	0.92
0.76	13.3	45	47	0.73	12.8	16.5	36	0.95
0.78	13.6	44	46	0.75	13.0	17.0	35	0.97
0.80	14.0	43	45	0.76	13.3	17.5	34	1.00
0.82	14.3	42	44	0.78	13.6	18.0	33	1.03
0.84	14.7	41	43	0.80	14.0	18.5	32	1.06
0.86	15.0	40	42	0.82	14.3	19.0	32	1.09
0.88	15.4	39	41	0.84	14.6	19.5	31	1.12
0.90	15.7	38	40	0.86	15.0	20.0	30	1.15
0.92	16.1	37	39	0.88	15.4	20.5	29	1.17
0.94	16.4	37	38	0.90	15.8	21.0	29	1.20
0.96	16.8	36	37	0.93	16.2	21.5	28	1.23
0.98	17.1	35	36	0.95	16.7	22.0	27	1.26
1.00	17.5	34	35	0.98	17.1	22.5	27	1.29
1.02	17.8	34	34	1.01	17.6	23.0	26	1.32
1.04	18.2	33	33	1.04	18.2	23.5	26	1.35
1.06	18.5	32	32	1.07	18.8	24.0	25	1.38
1.08	18.8	32	31	1.11	19.4	24.5	24	1.40
1.10	19.2	31	30	1.15	20.0	25.0	24	1.43
1.12	19.5	31	29	1.19	20.7	25.5	24	1.46
1.14	19.9	30	28	1.23	21.4	26.0	23	1.49
1.16	20.2	30	27	1.27	22.2	26.5	23	1.52
1.18	20.6	29	26	1.32	23.1	27.0	22	1.55
1.20	20.9	29	25	1.38	24.0	27.5	22	1.58
1.22	21.3	28	24	1.43	25.0	28.0	21	1.60
1.24	21.6	28	23	1.49	26.1	28.5	21	1.63
1.26	22.0	27	22	1.56	27.3	29.0	21	1.66
1.28	22.3	27	21	1.64	28.6	29.5	20	1.69
1.30	22.7	26	20	1.72	30.0	30.0	20	1.72

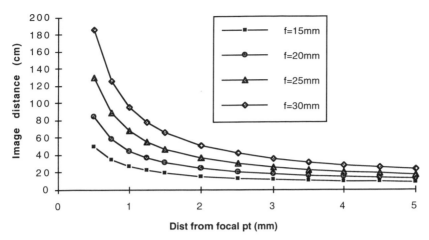

Figure 6-29 Effect of focal length and image source (display) position on virtual image distance from the eye. The horizontal axis is the distance from the focal point of the lens to the display surface (i.e., $(f - d)$ from equation (21)). The eye relief *le* used to produce these graphs was 25 mm.

Focus/accommodation

Equation (1) was derived assuming that the display was located at the focal point of the lens to produce the virtual image at infinity. However, it is not always desirable to set the virtual image distance for infinity. Specifically, it is often desirable to make the eyepiece adjustable to change the distance from the display to the rear principal plane of the eyepiece, so that people who are near-sighted or far-sighted can focus the display to compensate for their eyesight. Equation (21) describes the effect of display distance (distance from display image source to the lens) on the location of the virtual image

$$I = \frac{(d)(f)}{(f - d)} + le \tag{21}$$

where I is the virtual image distance from the eye, d the distance from lens to display, f the focal length of lens, and le the eye-relief distance (eye to lens).

Note that, if $d = f$, then the denominator is zero and the image distance I goes to infinity. If d is less than f, then the system will produce a virtual image located a finite distance from the observer. This condition will accommodate observers who are near-sighted. If d is larger than f, then the image distance I is actually negative and, strictly speaking, does not produce a virtual image in front of the eye. However, this condition is what permits the system to compensate for far-sighted observers. Figure 6-29 is a set of graphs generated using this equation for several focal length lenses using an eye-relief distance of 25 mm.

This section has investigated a few of the trade-offs that must be considered for a simple magnifier type of virtual display. In general, these same types of trade-offs hold for more complex virtual displays involving relay lenses and real

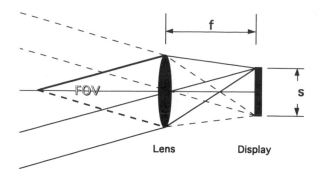

Figure 6-30 Simple magnifier HMD geometry to produce virtual image at infinity.

exit pupils. When using any of the equations listed in this section you are cautioned to make sure that the assumptions under which the particular equation was derived are met.

Optics/display image source interface

The most fundamental optics/display interface relationship for the simple magnifier HMD optical approach is described in equation (1) earlier in this chapter and repeated as equation (22) for convenience. This equation relates the HMD field of view, the lens focal length, and the size of the display image source. Figure 6-30 is a drawing of this basic system and Figure 6-31 is a graph of equation (22) showing the trade-offs of these parameters.

$$\text{FOV} = 2\arctan(S/(2f)) \tag{22}$$

where as before FOV is the angular field-of-view, S the size of display, and f the focal length of the lens.

From Figure 6-29 and equation (22) it is apparent that one can obtain a larger field of view by increasing the size of the display or by decreasing the focal length of the lens. Increasing the physical size of the display means the physical size and weight of the HMD will be greater (which is not desirable). Decreasing the focal length affects the amount of eye relief available (as discussed in the *Eye/optics integration* section). In addition, when a lens system is designed it is made for a specific format size (input size). For example, camera lenses for 35 mm cameras are designed to give good image quality over the size of the 35 mm film. If one uses this lens for a larger format the image quality may suffer considerably outside of the design range. For this reason it is not always possible to take any lens and use it with a particular size display and expect to get good image quality across the entire field of view.

Previous discussions regarding resolution of the HMD (see section on *Resolution versus field of view*) provided a simple geometric equation that did not take into account image quality aspects of the optical system. An in-depth discussion of this area is beyond the scope of this chapter but the reader should be aware that there will be at least some contrast loss due to the optics. This

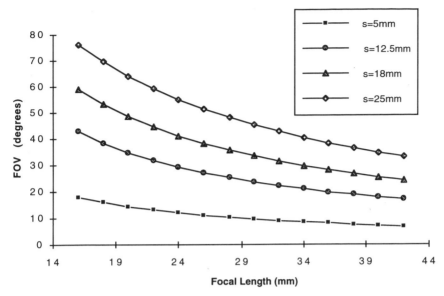

Figure 6-31 Graphical representation of equation (1) showing the trade-offs between display size, lens focal length and FOV.

means the image viewed by the observer will, in general, have less contrast than the contrast that is available on the surface of the display. The amount of contrast loss tends to be greater for finer detail objects.

Display image source/electronics interface

There are many design and interface issues surrounding the interface of the HMT/D to the remote electronics that form the bulk of the hardware for either a visually coupled or virtual reality system. It is beyond the scope of this chapter to provide a comprehensive presentation of interface design that goes beyond covering a few of the more important issues. One of the primary issues, if not the key issue, is how the system design is implemented for sending and receiving signals to and from the head-mounted components. It is particularly important for signals that create the visual scene imagery. There are two major interface issues that significantly affect the performance of the head-mounted image source that must drive the display optics. One is the remoteness of the image source from its drive electronics. This remoteness contributes to image-source bandwidth limitations and noise characteristics, especially for CRT-based systems. Secondly, the head-mounted image source is viewed under significant magnification by the head-mounted optics. Thus, any display artifacts are much more obvious than they would be for panel-mounted displays. These factors make the interconnect between the head-mounted components and their supporting electronics a key integration issue.

The proliferation of HMT/D applications relative to virtual reality and direct information display has led to increased resolution requirements for the visual scene. For a CRT-based display, a non-interlaced video display format of 1280×1024 presented at a refresh rate of 72 Hz, requires a video bandwidth slightly greater than 100 mHz for proper reproduction of the source video signal. Another requirement stems from environments which are subject to high ambient light conditions. In such environments, especially for Type II HMDs, the flat-panel or CRT image source may be required to produce a peak luminance above ten thousand foot-Lamberts to produce adequate display brightness and gray-level rendition. For a CRT-based HMT/D, the impact on the video amplification electronics is a dual requirement of wide bandwidth at large voltage swing.

Finally, the helmet display image source must image visual information from a variety of scene-generation sources, and often they all use different standards for generating the signals that ultimately must be imaged on the helmet display for the human to view. A set of carefully prepared and thoughtful standards for interfacing the head-mounted components to the remainder of the system can do much to maximize system performance while easing periodic performance upgrades and lowering system life-cycle costs.

In the remainder of this section we shall take a quick look at one approach the military is using to overcome the problems mentioned above. It is hoped that some of the system interface concepts described will stimulate similar thinking for virtual reality applications.

Military aircraft applications of HMT/D technology and the interconnect between the head and airframe electronics have the special constraints of ejection, ground egress in explosive vapor environments, and possibly more severe ambient environments. Nevertheless, the requirement for the best possible signal transmission fidelity is even more imposing for the commercial applications than the military because the visual information requirements for military systems are usually at least one generation behind due to the severe operating requirements for military vehicles. Figures 6-32 and 6-33 depict the "standardized" helmet–vehicle interface (HVI) concept developed jointly by the Armstrong Laboratory with Reynolds Industries (RI), University of Dayton Research Institute (UDRI), and Dunbar Associates for interfacing miniature CRT-based HMT/Ds between man and machine. The HVI is intentionally separated into three modules to support the quick-disconnect connector (QDC) function and facilitate system interconnect flexibility.

The key element in the system is the panel-mounted connector. Maximum system flexibility can be achieved by wiring this connector and its associated cable run to the electronics for full binocular operation. The electronics is designed to support the tracker function and drive either one or two miniature CRTs. Monocular HMD operation becomes a subset of binocular operation that can be easily supported through simple changes in the system software. Module II's end of the panel-mounted connector is then wired for either one CRT or two CRT operation depending upon the HMD it is supporting. Table 6-14 lists the key elements, performance and functions that are part of the "standardized" HVI except for the specific types of wire, shield, and cable coverings in the wiring harness.

Starting at the helmet image source, the first HVI component is the new miniature CRTs that incorporate the aviation connector (AVCON) recepta-

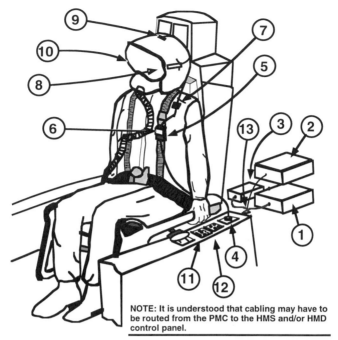

NOTE: It is understood that cabling may have to be routed from the PMC to the HMS and/or HMD control panel.

1. Display Head Electronics for CRT 1
2. Display Head Electronics for CRT 2
3. Head Position Sensor Electronics
4. Panel-Mounted Connector (PMC)
5. Video Driver Hybrids
6. Quick-Disconnect Connector (QDC)
7. Velcro Attachment to Flight Suit
8. Helmet-Mounted Display (HMD) CRT 2 Connector
9. Helmet-Mounted Sight (HMS) Position/Orientation Sensor Connect
10. Helmet-Mounted Display (HMD) CRT 1 Connector
11. Hypothetical HMS Control Panel
12. Hypothetical HMD Control Panel
13. Optional Pressure Bulkhead Feedthru Connector

Figure 6-32 Artist's concept of a "standardized" HVI interconnect.

cles. The AVCON provides a standardized pinout that all vendors can design around and be sure that their product can be operated with systems using this connector. The receptacle housing the deflection yoke leads and anode lead also holds the CRT characterization EPROM. Electronics designed to drive miniature CRTs with the AVCON connector are also able to read the EPROM data and automatically adjust their internal anode and control grid voltages, deflection drive, and video drive for maximum performance with a particular CRT. Using AVCON, a failed CRT can be replaced in about four minutes using just a simple screwdriver and when power is reapplied the electronics automatically adjusts for driving the new CRT. Most major vendors of miniature CRTs in the United States and United Kingdom are adopting the AVCON connector interface as an off-the-shelf option.

The Module III portion of the wiring harness also accommodates serial EPROMs for the tracker and optics characterization. In the case of at least the magnetic trackers, the module III ribbon cable inside the helmet provides interconnects for a hybrid preamplifier circuit that boosts signal level for better

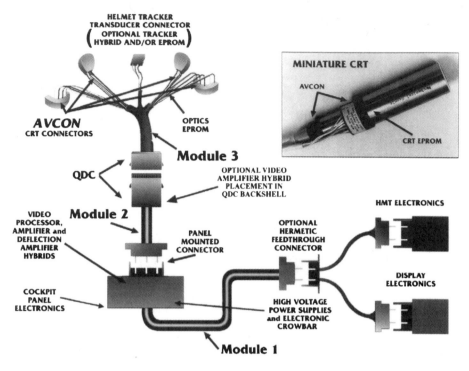

Figure 6-33 Detailed depiction of HVI wiring harness.

transmission characteristics before it travels down the cable to the system electronics. The QDC that interfaces Module III to Module II is a requirement perhaps unique to military applications but could have use in certain more demanding commercial applications, as well.

In the past, many HMT/D applications have purported to drive the display with high line rates and pixel rates. Such performance was never realized at the display optics because the CRT was driven through a long unterminated cable with significant distributed capacitance. Effectively, the cable operated as a low-pass filter of the video information. Video and deflection hybrid integrated circuits were developed as part of the HVI to improve signal transmission performance and eliminate the weight and power dissipation at the head imposed by past head-mounted solutions to this problem. The video processor, video amplifier, and video deflection hybrids include dies from Motorola, Comlinear, Harris Semiconductor, Supertex, National Semiconductor, Siliconix, and International Rectifier. The dies are incorporated into complete hybrid circuits using militarized packages by MS Kennedy. The hybrids give the HVI concept a set of standardized electronic building blocks that are low risk and high performance. Used in conjunction with improved cabling, the hybrids can support video bandwidths of greater than 100 MHz that are observable at the display optics. Maximum video bandwidths are achieved by placing the video amplifier hybrid in the back shell of the QDC. It is cooled using a new technique developed by UDRI called jet impingement cooling (JPC). JPC allows a chip whose internal heat-dissipating components are specifically laid out with this technique in mind, to be cooled efficiently at low air pressures and flow rates.

The CRT electronics crowbar and compatible high-voltage supply provide additional safety margins required for military systems. However, they also represent a stand-alone electronic solution for quick disconnects with arc suppression, where safety requirements are less stringent. The high-voltage power supply performance shown in Table 6-14 provides a level of ripple, noise, and regulation performance needed for miniature CRTs viewed under the unforgiving format magnification imposed by most HMDs.

The point here is to demonstrate by example one significant effort now underway within the military, to provide safety, interconnect flexibility, and performance benefits through the development of a standard interface. The recent availability of an interface standard is accelerating the interest in using HMT/D technology because it lowers risk, improves system life cycle costs, and provides predictable system growth options. Commercial systems may standardize on the flat panel display or other type of image source with different requirements. The expanding use of thin-film transistor technology may allow the addition of huge amounts of computational power right next to the flat panel display. Digital high-definition TV is just getting started and is likely to have a big impact on VR systems. These and other related developments will come together sooner if interface standards can be agreed upon and implemented in conjunction with technology advancements.

APPLICATIONS OF VCS AND VCS COMPONENTS

Military systems and applications

Today's drastic reductions in defense budgets are causing a redirection of technical efforts with the focus being on near-term threats. Current HMT/D systems for military aircraft have as their primary application the cueing of weapons and sensors. Thus, see-through monocular systems with a narrow-band miniature CRT image source providing symbology overlay with some intermittent display of imagery are receiving primary emphasis. Binocular displays used for the long-duration presentation of imagery for pilotage tasks using navigation and targeting sensors are coming into existence for special forces and rotary wing aircraft. However, most of these systems still utilize a narrow-band miniature CRT. The first use of color in fielded military HMDs may come through the use of low-power electroluminescent or liquid-crystal color image sources for the infantry soldier to expedite integrated command and control. Laser threats, enclosed cockpits, and renewed interest in unmanned aerial vehicles could accelerate the use of HMDs throughout the military. Also, the DOD Joint Advanced Strike Technology Program and related ARPA programs may accelerate high-resolution color image source technology availability for both military and commercial applications. Yet, it is

Table 6-14 Characteristics of government-initiated "standardized" helmet–vehicle interface (HVI).

Component	Primary features and performance	Other features
CRT connector (AVCON)	Uses screwdriver and twist-lock connector to change head-mounted CRTs when they fail or age *Operates to 70 000 foot altitude from −55 to 125 °C in high humidity and explosive vapor environments	Standardized pinout Improved CRT yield Eliminates need to scrap cable harness when CRT fails Lighter than comparable hard-wired CRT connections Provides standard mount for CRT characterization EPROM Helps standardize wire types
CRT characterization EPROM	Mounted inside CRT AVCON receptacle Provides standard format for optimizing each CRT's grid voltages and drive Same as*	Standard format allows electronics to optimally drive different vendor's CRTs Resolution, luminance, and contrast maximized for helmet display viewing conditions
Optics characterization EPROM	Mounted on Module III ribbon cable inside helmet Provides standard data packet format for optimizing each CRT's display format input Same as*	Allows any residual optical distortion to be reduced by pre-distorting CRT input Allows different vendor's optical designs to be used with common electronics
Tracker characterization EPROM (optional)	**Comes mounted on Module III connector interface to helmet tracker transducer Same as*	Allows easy exchange of different tracker transducers with automatic calibration Optimizes tracker transducer's characteristics as needed
Tracker hybrid (optional)	Same as* Same as**	If tracker transducer's output are low-level signals they can be boosted for better cable transmission characteristics
High-voltage QDC	Operates to 15 000 V and up to 15 000 foot altitude in high humidity and explosive environment	Provides safe and standardized mating and demating interface for the HMT/D
CRT video hybrid	Provides equivalent bandwidth of >100 MHz at 50 V peak to peak of video modulation when driving two feet or less of Cheminax #9530H1014 coaxial cable Same as*	Provides standard video interface Reduces discrete component count of electronics Mounts in either QDC back shell or cockpit panel depending upon required video bandwidth
CRT deflection hybrid	Provides equivalent full power bandwidth of >80 kHz with less than 3 μs settling time to 0.1% when driving 90 μH yoke Same as* except −10°C	Provides standard high-performance deflection interface Reduces discrete component count of electronics
CRT electronic crowbar	Uses spark gaps and custom electronics to crowbar CRT high-voltage power in less than 30 μs without premature "turn-off"	Provides safe and standardized backup for QDC should it fail

Table 6-14—*contd.*

Component	Primary features and performance	Other features
Electronic crowbar compatible high-voltage power supply	Same as* Anode supply ripple and noise ≤0.05% and regulation ≤0.5% All other grid voltage supplies have ripple and noise ≤0.05% and regulation ≤0.1% Same as*	Provides programmable supplies whose values can be controlled automatically by CRT characterization EPROMs Helps maximize CRT resolution, luminance, and contrast performance Reliably interfaced to electronic crowbar

likely that the first military production color HMD system will not be underway until the turn of the century, if then.

The Figures A1 through A6 and Tables A1 through A6 in the Appendix provide a brief summary of some key parameters for several current military-targeted HMT/D systems. The information in the tables associated with each figure was supplied either by the manufacturer directly or was obtained from the manufacturer's literature unless otherwise noted.

Civilian systems and applications

With the recent significant improvements in color liquid-crystal displays and liquid-crystal shutters, the number and types of HMDs available for civilian applications have grown tremendously. Probably the largest market for HMDs is the relatively low-cost entertainment field for use in interactive video games or personal viewing of television or computer output screens. In the medical field HMDs have been proposed for minimally invasive surgery and for preoperative training and preparation. For sports, racing-car drivers and skiers may be able to see their speed on miniature HMDs. HMDs as part of a visually coupled system have long been considered for remote "teleoperations" such as exploration of hazardous environments (e.g., deep-sea exploration, bomb disposal, fire-fighting, police surveillance, etc.). As the cost of these systems drops as their quality improves, the number of applications should grow accordingly, limited only by our imagination!

Figures A7 through A20 and Tables A7 through A20 in the appendix provide a brief summary of some key parameters for several currently commercially available HMDs. The information in the following tables was supplied either by the manufacturer directly or was obtained from the manufacturer's literature unless otherwise noted.

BIBLIOGRAPHY

Birt, J. A. and Task, H. L. (Eds) (1973) *A Symposium on Visually Coupled Systems: Development and Application (Aerospace Medical Division technical report AMD-TR-73-1)*, Brooks Air Force Base, Texas, November 8–10, 1972

Carollo, J. T. (Ed.) (1989) *Helmet-Mounted Displays, Proc. SPIE*, vol. 1116, Bellingham, WA: SPIE

Farrell, R. J. and Booth, J. M. (1984) *Design Handbook for Imagery Interpretation Equipment* (publication D180-19063-1), Boeing Aerospace Company, Seattle, Washington 98124, February 1984

Ferrin, F. J. (1973) F-4 visual target acquisition system, in *A Symp. on Visually Coupled Systems: Development and Application*, AMD TR-73-1, September

Ferrin, F. J. (1991) Survey of helmet tracking technologies, *SPIE, Conf. Proc., vol. 1456: Large Screen Projection, Avionic and Helmet Mounted Displays*, Orlando, FL, pp. 86–94

Gaertner Research (1991) *GRD-1000 Headtracker Specifications*, Norwalk, CN: GEC Ferranti Defense Systems, Inc.

Hertzberg, H. T. E., Daniels, G. S., and Churchill, E. (1954) Anthropometry of flying personnel-1950, *WADC Technical Report 52-321*, Wright Air Development Center, Wright-Patterson Air Force Base, OH, p. 61

Kingslake, R. (Ed.) (1965) *Applied Optics and Optical Engineering*, New York: Academic, Vol. I, pp. 232–6

Klein, M. V. (1970) *Optics*, New York: Wiley

Kocian, D. F. (1987) Design considerations for virtual panoramic display (VPD) helmet systems, *AGARD Conf. Proc. 425: The Man-Machine Interface in Tactical Aircraft Design and Combat Automation* (NTIS No. AGARD-CP-425), Neuilly Sur Seine, France: NATO Advisory Group for Aerospace Research & Development, pp. 22-1–22-32

Kocian, D. F. (1990) Visually coupled systems (VCS): Preparing the engineering research framework, *Eleventh Annual IEEE/AESS Dayton Chapter Symposium: The Cockpit of the 21st Century—Will High Tech Payoff?* pp. 28–38

Kocian, D. F. (1991) Visually coupled systems (VCS): The virtual panoramic display (VPD) "system," in K. Krishen (Ed.), *Fifth Annual Workshop on Space Operations, Applications, and Research (SOAR '91)* (NASA Conference Publication 3127, vol. 2, 548–561), Johnson Space Center, TX: NASA

Landau, F. (1990) The effect on visual recognition performance of misregistration and overlap for a biocular helmet mounted display, in *Helmet-mounted displays II, Proc. SPIE*, vol. 1290, Bellingham, WA: SPIE

Lewandowski, R. J. (Ed.) (1990) *Helmet-Mounted Displays II, Proc. SPIE*, vol. 1290, Bellingham, WA: SPIE

Moss, H. (1968) *Narrow Angle Electron Guns and Cathode Ray Tubes*, New York: Academic, pp. 145–66

Raab, F. H. (1982) *Algorithms for Position and Orientation Determination in Magnetic Helmet Mounted Sight System*, AAMRL-TR-82-045, US Air Force Armstrong Aerospace Medical Research Laboratory, Wright-Patterson AFB, OH

RCA Corporation (1974) *Electro-Optics Handbook*, RCA Technical Series EOH-11, Commercial Engineering, Harrison, NJ 07029

Ross, J. A. and Kocian, D. F. (1993) Hybrid video amplifier chip set for helmet-mounted visually coupled systems, *1993 Soc. Information Display Int. Symp. Dig. Tech. Papers*, **24**, 437–40

Self, H. C. (1972) The construction and optics problems of helmet-mounted displays, in J. A. Birt and H. L. Task (Eds), *A Symposium on Visually Coupled Systems: Development and Application (Aerospace Medical Division Technical Report AMD-TR-73-1)*, Brooks Air Force Base, TX, November 8–10

Self, H. C. (1986) *Optical Tolerances for Alignment and Image Differences for Binocular Helmet-Mounted Displays*, AAMRL-TR-86-019, May

Sherr, S. (1979) *Electronic Displays*, New York: Wiley

Shmulovich, J. and Kocian, D. F. (1989) Thin-film phosphors for miniature CRTs used in helmet-mounted displays, *Proc. Soc. Information Display*, **30**, 297–302

Smith, W. J. (1966) *Modern Optical Engineering*, New York: McGraw-Hill

Task, H. L. (1979) *An Evaluation and Comparison of Several Measures of Image Quality of Television Displays*, AAMRL-TR-79-7

Task, H. L. and Kocian, D. F. (1992) *Design and Integration Issues of Visually Coupled Systems (SPIE vol. SC54)* (Short course presented at SPIE's OE/Aerospace Sensing 1992 International Symposium, Orlando, FL)

Task, H. L., Kocian, D. F. and Brindle, J. H. (1980) Helmet mounted displays: design considerations, in W. M. Hollister (Ed.) *Advancement on Visualization Techniques*, AGARDograph No. 255, Harford House, London, October

Vickers, D. L. (1973) Sorcerer's apprentice: Head-mounted display wand, in J. A. Birt and H. L. Task (Eds), *A Symposium on Visually Coupled Systems: Development and Application (Aerospace Medical Division Technical Report AMD-TR-73-1)*, Brooks Air Force Base, TX, November 8–10, 1972, pp. 522–41

Wells, M. J., Venturino, M. and Osgood, R. K. (1989) Effect of field of view size on performance at a simple simulated air-to-air mission, in *Helmet-Mounted Displays, Proc. SPIE, vol. 1116*, March

Widdel, H. and Post, D. L. (Eds) (1992) *Color in Electronic Displays*, New York: Pelnum

Winner, R. N. (1973) A color helmet mounted display system, in J. A. Birt and H. L. Task (Eds), *Proc. A Symp. Visually-Coupled Systems*, Aerospace Medical Division Technical Report AMD-TR-73-1, Brooks Air Force Base, TX, November 8–10, 1972, pp. 334–62

APPENDIX

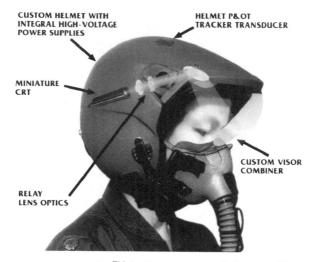

Figure A1   Kaiser Agile Eye Plus™ helmet-mounted display. Photograph courtesy of Armstrong Laboratory, USAF.

Table A1   Kaiser Agile Eye Plus™ helmet-mounted display specifications.

Parameter	Performance
Field of view	20 degrees circular
Resolution	1.87 arcminutes
Ocularity	monocular with image on custom helmet visor
Focus	infinity (adjustable: 1 meter to ∞)
Exit pupil	15 mm horz. × 12 mm vert. (unvignetted)
Eye relief	~53 mm
Luminance	~1500 ft-L at eye (symbology)
	~800 ft-L peak luminance at eye (imagery using pixel size used to estimate resolution)
See-through	yes (8% or 65% for either 13% or clear visor)
Display type	CRT with monochrome or narrow-band phosphor
Typical image source	Hughes Display Products 1425
Display/helmet type	Integrated within custom helmet shell
Weight	5.29 lb (HMT/D integrated helmet + oxygen mask)

Figure A2   Kaiser Agile Eye™ Mark III helmet-mounted display.

Table A2   Kaiser Agile Eye™ Mark III helmet-mounted display specifications.

Parameter	Performance
Field of view	20 degrees circular
Resolution	1.87 arcminutes
Ocularity	monocular with image on standard Air Force toric visor
Focus	Infinity
Exit pupil	17 mm on-axis and 15 mm off-axis (unvignetted)
Eye relief	~65 mm
Luminance	~1500 ft-L at eye (symbology)
	~800 ft-L peak luminance at eye (imagery using pixel size used to estimate resolution)
See-through	yes (8%, 19%, 70%—varies with optical density of the visor used)
Display type	CRT with monochrome or narrow band phosphor
Typical image source	Hughes Display Products 1425
Display/helmet type	attaches to standard helmet shell
Weight	4.1 lb (HMT/D + HGU-55/P helmet + oxygen mask)

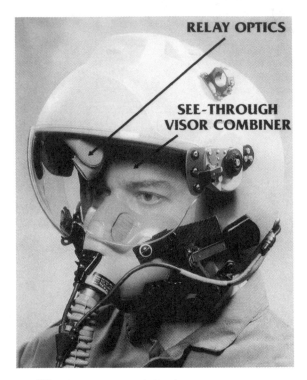

Figure A3   GEC VIPER™ helmet-mounted display.

Table A3   GEC VIPER™ helmet-mounted display specifications.

Parameter	Performance
Field of view	Slightly more than 20° circular
Resolution	1.87 arcminutes
Ocularity	monocular
Focus	infinity (adjustable: 3.3 m to ∞)
Exit pupil	15 mm horz. × 12 mm vert. (unvignetted)
Eye relief	>40 mm
Luminance	~1500 ft-L at eye (symbology)
	~800 ft-L peak luminance at eye (imagery using pixel size used to estimate resolution)
See-through	yes (~70%) and no outside-world coloration
Display type	CRT with monochrome or narrow-band phosphor
Typical image source	rank
Display/helmet type	integrated within custom helmet shell
Weight	4.3 lb (HGU-55 or 53/P helmet HMT/D + CRT + oxygen mask)

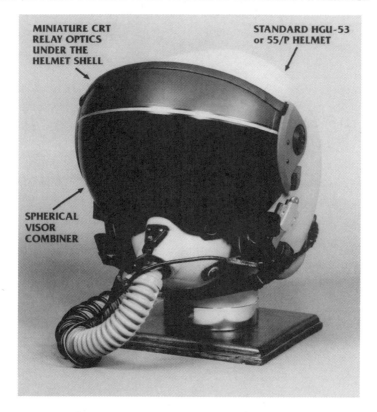

Figure A4 Honeywell Advanced Visor Display and Sight System.

Table A4 Honeywell Advanced Visor Display and Sight System specifications.

Parameter	Performance
Field of view	20° circular
Resolution	~2.0 arcminutes (CRT dependent)
Ocularity	monocular
Focus	infinity (adjustable: 1 m to ∞)
Exit pupil	15 mm circular (unvignetted)
Eye relief	69 mm
Luminance	~1300 ft-L at eye (symbology)
	~700 ft-L peak luminance at eye (pixel size for imagery used to estimate resolution)
See-through	yes (9% or 70% for either 13% tinted visor or clear visor)
Display type	CRT with monochrome or narrow-band phosphor
Typical image source	miniature CRT
Display/helmet type	module added to HGU-53/P
Weight	3.4 lb (HMT/D + HGU-53/P + helmet + auto brightness sensor) (3.55 lb w/miniature CCD video camera)

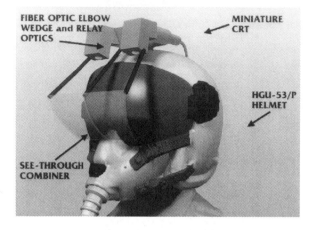

Figure A5 USAF AL Tophat helmet-mounted display. Photograph courtesy of Armstrong Laboratory, USAF.

Table A5 USAF AL Tophat helmet-mounted display specifications.

Parameter	Performance
Field of view	30° horz. × 22.5° vert. with full overlap
Resolution	1.76 arcminutes
Ocularity	monocular
Focus	infinity
Exit pupil	21 mm horz. × 15 mm vert.
Inter-pupillary adjustment	none
Eye relief	~100 mm
Luminance	~8500 ft-L at eye (symbology)
	~2000 ft-L peak luminance at eye (imagery using pixel size used to estimate resolution)
See-through	yes (~75%)
Display type	CRT with monochrome or narrow-band phosphor
Typical image source	Hughes Display Products
Display/helmet type	add-on to USAF HGU-55/P flight helmet
Weight	4.3 lb (HGU-53/P Helmet + optics/CRTs + oxygen mask)

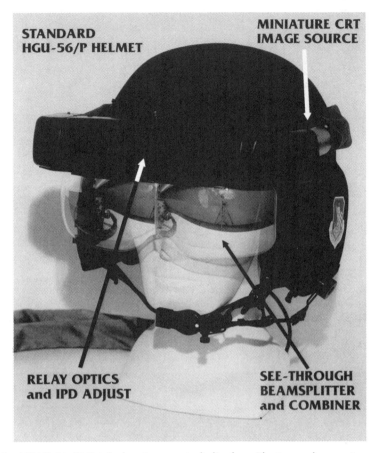

Figure A6 USAF AL BiCat helmet-mounted display. Photograph courtesy of Armstrong Laboratory, USAF.

Table A6 USAF AL BiCat helmet-mounted display specifications.

Parameter	Performance
Field of view	50° circular with full overlap
Resolution	1.87 arcminutes
Ocularity	binocular
Focus	infinity
Exit pupil	20 mm circular (unvignetted)
Inter-pupillary adjustment	62–74 mm
Eye relief	40 mm
Luminance	~1500 ft-L at eye (symbology)
	~800 ft-L peak luminance at eye (imagery using pixel size used to estimate resolution)
See-through	yes——~50%
Display type	CRT narrow-band phosphor
Typical image source	Hughes Display Products
Display/helmet type	add-on to Army HGU-56/P flight helmet
Weight	5.5 lb (HGU-56/P Helmet + optics/CRTs)

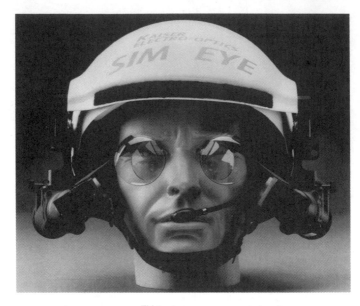

Figure A7   Kaiser Color Sim-Eye 40™ helmet-mounted display.

Table A7   Kaiser Color Sim-Eye 40™ helmet-mounted display system.

Field of view	40° diameter or 40 × 60 with partial overlap
Resolution	2.7 arcminutes
Ocularity	binocular
Focus	infinity to 3.5 feet adjustable
Exit pupil	15 mm
Luminance	6 ft-L min at eye
See-through	yes (24% min)
Display type	CRTs with field sequential liquid crystal shutters to achieve color
Weight	4.5 lb (helmet with optics and CRTs)
Approximate cost	$145 000 (Dec. 1993)

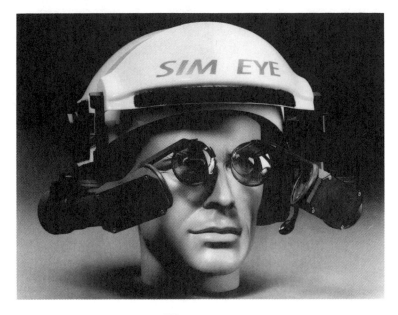

Figure A8   Kaiser Color Sim-Eye 60™ helmet-mounted display.

Table A8   Kaiser Color Sim-Eye 60™ helmet-mounted display system.

Field of view	60° diameter or 100 × 60 with 20° overlap or 80 × 60 with 40° overlap
Resolution	4.0 arcminutes
Ocularity	binocular
Focus	infinity to 3.5 feet adjustable
Exit pupil	15 mm
Luminance	6 ft-L min at eye
See-through	yes (24% min)
Display type	CRTs with field sequential liquid-crystal shutters to achieve color
Weight	5.2 lb (helmet with optics and CRTs)
Approximate cost	$165 000 (Dec. 1993)

Figure A9 Kaiser VIM™ Model 1000 pv personal viewer™.

Table A9 Kaiser VIM™ Model 1000 pv personal viewer™.

Field of view	30° vert. 100° horz.
Resolution	10.2 arcminutes
Ocularity	binocular in center region (partial overlap)
Focus	infinity (fixed)
Exit pupil	non-pupil-forming ("eyeglass compatible")
Luminance	2 to 3 ft-L
See-through	no
Display type	multiple color liquid-crystal displays ("Tiled Vision Immersion Modules")
Weight	0.94 lb (15 ounces; basic unit)
Approximate cost	$12 000 (Dec. 1993)

Figure A10   n-Vision™ Datavisor™ 9c.

Table A10   n-Vision™ Datavisor™ 9c.

Field of view	50° circular
Resolution	2 arcminutes
Ocularity	binocular
Focus	infinity (fixed)
Exit pupil	14 mm
Luminance	25 ft-L
See-through	no
Display type	CRTs with liquid-crystal shutters to achieve field sequential color
Weight	3.9 lb
Approximate cost	$70 000 (Feb. 1994)

Figure A11　Liquid Image MRG2™.

Table A11　Liquid Image MRG2™.

Field of view	85° nominally
Resolution	21 arcminutes (approx. from calculation)
Ocularity	binocular (same image to both eyes)
Focus	infinity (fixed)
Exit pupil	non-pupil-forming
Luminance	35 ft-L (estimated)
See-through	no
Display type	single color liquid-crystal display
Weight	4.0 lb
Approximate cost	$6500 (basic unit; Feb. 1994)

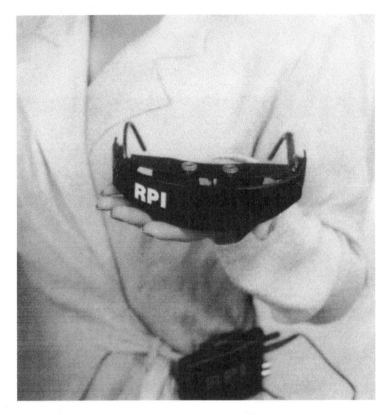

Figure A12   RPI Advanced Technology Group HMSI™ Model 1000.

Table A12   RPI Advanced Technology Group HMSI™ Model 1000.

Field of view	65° horz. × 46° vert. for entertainment or 45° horz. × 32° vert. for CAD visualization
Resolution	8.7 arcminutes (calculated)
Ocularity	binocular
Focus	Fixed (adjustable is option)
Exit pupil	
Luminance	
See-through	optional
Display type	color liquid-crystal displays
Weight	0.28 lb (4.5 ounces on head)
Approximate cost	$5000 (Feb. 1994)

Figure A13   Virtual Reality, Inc. Personal Immersive Display 131.

Table A13   Virtual Reality, Inc. Personal Immersive Display 131.

Field of view	50° diagonal
Resolution	2 arcminutes
Ocularity	binocular
Focus	fixed
Exit pupil	12 mm
Luminance	50 ft-L
See-through	optional
Display type	monochrome CRTs
Weight	"less than 3 lb"
Approximate cost	$56 000 (Feb. 94)

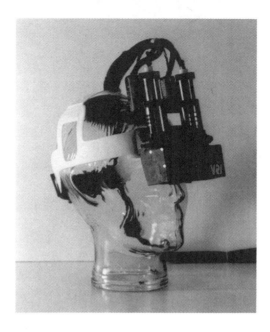

Figure A14   Virtual Reality, Inc. Stereoscopic Minimally Invasive Surgery Vision System 322.

Table A14   Virtual Reality, Inc. Stereoscopic Minimally Invasive Surgery Vision System 322.

Field of view	30° by 30°
Resolution	2 arcminutes
Ocularity	binocular
Focus	fixed
Exit pupil	non-pupil forming optics
Luminance	50 ft-L
See-through	optional
Display type	monochrome CRTs
Weight	"under 2 lb"
Approximate cost	$35 000 (Feb. 94)

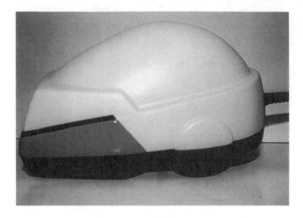

Figure A15   Virtual Reality, Inc. Entertainment Personal Immersive Display Model P2.

Table A15   Virtual Reality, Inc. Entertainment Personal Immersive Display Model P2.

Field of view	58° diagonal
Resolution	11.6 horz. × 8.7 vert. arcminutes*
Ocularity	binocular
Focus	fixed
Exit pupil	non-pupil-forming optics
Luminance	9–10 ft-L
See-through	no
Display type	color liquid-crystal
Weight	"approximately 2 lb"
Approximate cost	$8990 (Feb. 94)

*Note: calculated by authors from data provided by manufacturer.

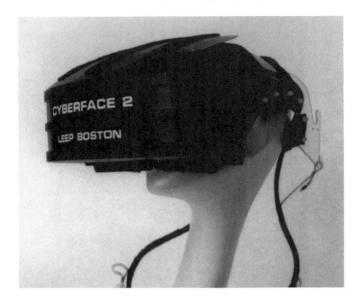

Figure A16 LEEP™ Systems Inc. Cyberface 2™ HMD.

Table A16 LEEP™ Systems Inc. Cyberface 2™ HMD.

Field of view	138/110°
Resolution	21.3 horz. × 43.9 vert. arcminutes (color groups)
Ocularity	binocular
Focus	fixed (beyond infinity to reduce "pixelation")
Exit pupil	non-pupil-forming optics
Luminance	35 ft-L typical
See-through	no
Display type	two liquid-crystal color displays
Weight	2.8 lb + 2 lb counterpoise*
Approximate cost	$8100 (Feb. 1994)

*Note: the basic head-mounted unit is 2.8 lb but an additional counterweight is attached to the back of the head-mounted unit and hangs on the chest of the wearer improving the center of gravity of the system without adding to the rotational inertial mass worn on the head. Total head-supported weight is estimated to be about 4 lb.

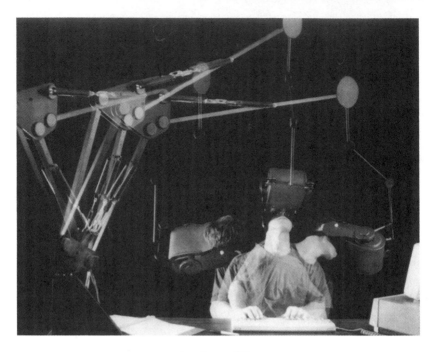

Figure A17 LEEP Systems Inc. Cyberface 3™ Model RS virtual reality interface system.

Table A17 LEEP Systems Inc. Cyberface 3™ Model RS virtual reality interface system.

Field of view	70 to 80°
Resolution	7.1 arcminutes horz. × 21.8 arcmin vert.
Ocularity	binocular (same image to both eyes)
Focus	2 m fixed (convergence at same distance)
Exit pupil	non-pupil-forming optics
Luminance	35 ft-L typical
See-through	no
Display type	backlighted active matrix TFT color liquid-crystal display
Weight	externally supported, head steered system (minimal head supported weight of a few ounces)
Approximate cost	$14 660

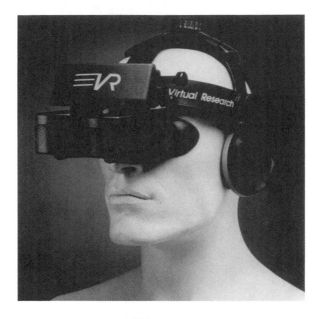

Figure A18 Virtual Research Eyegen3™.

Table A18 Virtual Research Eyegen3™.

Field of view	40° diagonal (3:4 aspect ratio)
Resolution	9.6 horz. × 3.7 vert. arcminutes (calculated)*
Ocularity	binocular
Focus	infinity to 25 cm user adjustable
Exit pupil	non-pupil forming optics
Luminance	data not available
See-through	no
Display type	CRT and mechanical color wheel
Weight	1.75 lb
Approximate cost	$7900 (Feb. 94)

*Note: calculated by authors from data provided by manufacturer.

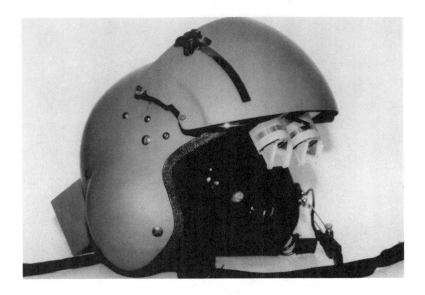

Figure A19   Vista Controls Corp. See-Thru-Armor™ helmet.

Table A19   Vista Controls Corp. See-Thru-Armor™ helmet.

Field of view	approximately 35°
Resolution	approximately 3.5 arcminutes
Ocularity	binocular
Focus	infinity (fixed)
Exit pupil	12 mm
Luminance	data not available
See-through	yes (or adjustable to "see-below")
Display type	two color active matrix liquid-crystal displays
Weight	approximately 5 lb
Approximate cost	$20 000

Figure A20   Optics 1 Incorporated PT-01.

Table A20   Optics 1 Incorporated PT-01.

Field of view	27.5° diagonal
Resolution	<3.2 arcminutes (color triads)
Ocularity	binocular
Focus	yes (ten feet to infinity)
Exit pupil	non-pupil-forming
Luminance	data not available
See-through	no (it is "see under" adjustable)
Display type	two active matrix liquid-crystal displays
Weight	under 14 ounces
Approximate cost	$1695 (stereo version $2395) (Feb. 1994)

7

Eye Tracking in Advanced Interface Design

ROBERT J. K. JACOB

The problem of human–computer interaction can be viewed as two powerful information processors (human and computer) attempting to communicate with each other via a narrow-bandwidth, highly constrained interface (Tufte, 1989). To address it, we seek faster, more natural, and more convenient means for users and computers to exchange information. The user's side is constrained by the nature of human communication organs and abilities; the computer's is constrained only by input/output devices and interaction techniques that we can invent. Current technology has been stronger in the computer-to-user direction than the user-to-computer, hence today's user–computer dialogues are rather one-sided, with the bandwidth from the computer to the user far greater than that from user to computer. Using eye movements as a user-to-computer communication medium can help redress this imbalance. This chapter describes the relevant characteristics of the human eye, eye-tracking technology, how to design interaction techniques that incorporate eye movements into the user–computer dialogue in a convenient and natural way, and the relationship between eye-movement interfaces and virtual environments.

Eye movements and virtual environments

As with other areas of research and design in human–computer interaction, it is helpful to build on the equipment and skills humans have acquired through evolution and experience and search for ways to apply them to communicating with a computer. Direct manipulation interfaces have enjoyed great success largely because they draw on analogies to existing human skills (pointing, grabbing, moving objects in space), rather than trained behaviors. Similarly, we try to make use of natural eye movements in designing interaction techniques for the eye. Because eye movements are so different from conventional computer inputs, our overall approach in designing interaction techniques is, wherever possible, to obtain information from a user's natural eye movements while viewing the screen, rather than requiring the user to make specific trained eye movements to actuate the system. This requires careful attention to issues of human design, as will any successful work in virtual environments. The goal is for human–computer interaction to start with studies of the characteristics of human communication channels and skills and then develop devices, interaction techniques, and interfaces that communicate effectively to and from those channels. We thus begin with a study of the characteristics of natural eye movements and then attempt to recognize appropriate patterns in the raw data obtainable from the eye tracker, turn them into tokens with higher-level meaning, and design interaction techniques for them around the known characteristics of eye movements.

This approach to eye movement interfaces meshes particularly well with the field of virtual environments. The essence of virtual environment and other advanced interface approaches is to exploit the user's pre-existing abilities and expectations. Navigating through a conventional computer system requires a set of learned, unnatural commands, such as keywords to be typed in, or function keys to be pressed. Navigating through a virtual environment exploits the user's existing "navigational commands," such as positioning his or her head and eyes, turning his or her body, or walking towards something of interest. By exploiting skills that the user already possesses, advanced interfaces hold out the promise of reducing the cognitive burden of interacting with a computer by making such interactions more like interacting with the rest of the world. The result is to increase the user-to-computer bandwidth of the interface and to make it more natural. An approach to eye movement interaction that relies upon natural eye movements as a source of user input extends this philosophy. Here, too, the goal is to exploit more of the user's pre-existing abilities to perform interactions with the computer.

Moreover, eye movements and virtual environments both exemplify a new, non-command style of interaction. Some of the qualities that distinguish such interfaces from more conventional types of interaction are shared by other newly emerging styles of human–computer interaction that can collectively be characterized as "non-command-based." In a non-command-based dialogue, the user does not issue specific commands; instead, the computer passively observes the user and provides appropriate responses to, for example, movement of his or her eyes, head, or hands. Non-command-based interfaces will also have a significant impact on the design of future user interface software, because of their emphasis on continuous, parallel input streams and real-time timing constraints, in contrast to conventional single-thread dialogues based on discrete tokens.

BACKGROUND

Physiology and psychology of eye movements

If acuity were distributed uniformly across the visual field, it would be far more difficult to extract meaningful information from a person's eye movement. Instead, receptors are distributed across the retina of the eye in a highly nonuniform way. The *fovea*, located near the center of the retina, is densely covered with receptors, and provides much higher acuity vision than the surrounding areas. The fovea covers approximately one degree field of view, that is, a one-degree angle with its vertex at the eye, extending outwards into space. Outside the fovea, acuity ranges from 15 to 50 per cent of that of the fovea. This peripheral vision is generally inadequate to see an object clearly; for example, to read a word of text generally requires that it be viewed foveally. It follows, conveniently for eye-tracking purposes, that in order to see an object clearly, one must move the eyeball to make that object appear directly on the fovea. A person's eye position as measured by an eye tracker thus gives a positive indication of what he or she is viewing clearly at the moment. Though the density of foveal receptors is not uniform, it is sufficiently high over its approximately one degree area that one can obtain a clear view of an object anywhere in that area. It follows, inconveniently for eye-tracking purposes, that it is not possible to tell where within that approximately one-degree circle the person is looking. In fact, a person is able to pay attention to smaller area than the entire fovea and move this attention around within the fovea without making any eye movements. Thus, no matter how accurately an eye tracker can measure the eyeball position, we can infer the user's attention only to within the one-degree width of the fovea. Further, the relationship between what the person is viewing and what he or she is mentally processing is less straightforward, and, in particular, there can be brief time lags between the two. The eyeball is held in place by three pairs of opposing muscles, which provide motion in an up–down direction, left–right direction, and rotation around an axis from the fovea to the pupil. Interestingly, these six muscles provide little or no proprioceptive feedback to the brain; feedback comes in the form of changes to the image on the retina caused by the eye movements themselves.

The eye does not generally move smoothly over the visual field. Instead, it makes a series of sudden jumps, called *saccades*, along with other specialized movements (Haber and Hershenson, 1973; Young and Sheena, 1975). The saccade is used to orient the eyeball to cause the desired portion of the visual scene fall upon the fovea. It is a sudden, rapid motion with high acceleration and deceleration rates. It is ballistic, that is, once a saccade begins, it is not possible to change its destination or path. A saccade can cover from 1 to 40 degrees of visual angle, but most typically covers 15 to 20 degrees; it typically takes 30–120 ms. The visual system is greatly suppressed (though not entirely shut off) during the saccade. Since the saccade is ballistic, its destination must be selected before movement begins; since the destination typically lies outside the fovea, it must be selected by lower acuity peripheral vision. If an object that might attract a saccade suddenly appears in peripheral vision, there is a 100–300 ms delay before the saccade occurs. There is also a 100–200 ms minimum refractory period after one saccade before it is possible to make another one.

More typically, a saccade is followed by a *fixation*, a period of relative stability during which an object can be viewed. Even during a fixation, the eye does not remain completely still, but engages in several types of small motion, generally within a one-degree radius. It drifts slowly, then is corrected by a tiny saccade-like jump (a microsaccade), which corrects the effect of the drift. In addition, it exhibits a high-frequency tremor, much like the noise in an imperfect servomechanism attempting to hold a fixed position. Fixations typically last between 200 and 600 ms, after which another saccade will occur.

Smooth motion of the eye occurs only in response to a moving object in the visual field. This smooth pursuit motion follows the moving object and is much slower than a saccade. Despite the introspective sensation that the eye is moving smoothly, this motion does not occur when viewing a static scene (or computer screen); it requires a moving stimulus.

Another, more specialized eye movement is called *nystagmus*. It occurs in response to motion of the head (particularly spinning) or viewing a moving, repetitive pattern. It is a sawtooth-like pattern of smooth motion that follows an object across the visual field, followed by a rapid motion in the opposite direction to select another object to follow, as the first one moves too far to keep in view. The motions described thus far are generally made by both eyes in tandem; the eyes also move differentially, making *vergence* movements to converge on an object. They point slightly towards each other when viewing a near object and more parallel for a distant object. Finally, *torsional rotation* occurs about an axis extending from the fovea to the pupil and is thus not detectable by a conventional eye tracker. It seems to depend on neck angle and other factors.

Despite introspective sensation to the contrary, one's eye is rarely stationary. It moves frequently as it fixates different portions of the visual field; even during a fixation it makes small motions; and it seldom remains in one fixation for long. In fact, if the effect of eye movements is negated by creating a fixed image on the retina (as the eye moves, the image moves with it) the image will appear to fade from view after a few seconds (Pritchard, 1961). Normal eye movements prevent such fading from occurring outside the laboratory. Visual perception of even a static scene appears to require the artificial changes we induce by moving our eyes about the scene. The case of a user sitting in front of a desk-top computer display is generally similar to viewing a static scene. We should expect to see steady (but somewhat jittery) fixations, connected by sudden, rapid saccades. We should not expect stationary periods longer than approximately 600 ms. We should not expect smooth motions unless a moving object appears in the display; and we are unlikely to observe nystagmus, vergence, or torsional rotation. For example, the history of 30 seconds of eye movements exhibited by a user working at a computer is shown in Figure 7-1. It contrasts sharply with a typical history of 30 seconds of mouse movements for most users.

Previous work

There is a large and interesting body of research using eye tracking, but the majority of the work has concentrated on using eye-movement data to provide a window on the operation of cognitive processes within the brain or of the eye-movement control mechanism itself (Monty and Senders, 1976; Just and Carpenter, 1980). Research of this type involves retrospective analysis of a subject's eye movements; the eye movements have no effect during the

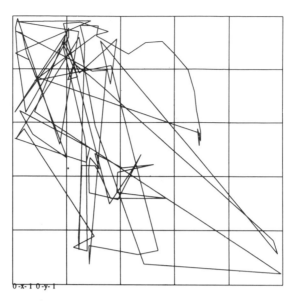

Figure 7-1 A trace of a computer user's eye movements over approximately 30 seconds, while performing normal work (i.e., no eye-operated interfaces) using a windowed display. Jitter within each fixation has been removed from this plot. The display during this time was a Sun window system, with a mail-reading window occupying the left half of the screen, message headers at the top left of the screen, and bodies at the bottom left, and a shell window covering the bottom right quarter of the screen.

experiment itself. Our interest, in contrast, is in using eye movements to affect the user–computer dialogue in real time. There is a much smaller body of research and practice for this situation, much of it concentrated on helping disabled users, such as quadriplegics, who can move their eyes much more effectively than they could operate any other computer input device (Levine, 1981, 1984; Hutchinson *et al.*, 1989). Because their ability to operate other devices is limited or nonexistent, the eye-movement interface need perform only minimally well to provide a significant benefit to such users. Another similar situation occurs for a user whose hands are occupied, such as an airplane pilot. However, these cases hold the eye movement interface to a fairly low standard of performance, since the user has no competing alternative input media. An interface that would normally be rejected as too slow, awkward, or unnatural might still be effective in these cases. We seek instead to use eye tracking to provide an effective input method for a user whose hand might be resting on a mouse, who is fully able and available to operate the mouse, but who will find the eye-movement, based interface better, that is, faster, more convenient, or more natural.

There is a much smaller body of previous research in this area of eye movements, beginning with that of Richard Bolt, who has demonstrated innovative uses of eye movements in user–computer dialogues (Bolt, 1981, 1982; Starker and Bolt, 1990). Floyd Glenn (Glenn *et al.*, 1986) demonstrated the use of eye movements for several tracking tasks involving moving targets. Ware and Mikaelian (1987) reported an experiment in which simple target selection and cursor positioning operations were performed approximately twice as fast with an eye tracker than with a mouse.

Perhaps the work most pertinent to ours is that of Starker and Bolt, which uses natural, real-time eye movements to affect the outcome of a user–computer dialogue. Their system "Analyzes the user's patterns of eye movements and fixations in real-time to make inferences about what item or collection of items shown holds most relative interest for the user. Material thus identified is zoomed-in for a closer look and described in more detail via synthesized speech." Their system displays a planet from the book, *The Little Prince* (Saint-Exupéry). In it, if the user glances around the scene in a general way, a general description of the planet is provided. If, however, the user looks at a pair of staircases, shifting glances between them, the system infers that the user is interested in staircases as a group rather than one specific one, and it provides an appropriate commentary. If the user glances principally at one staircase, then the commentary would describe that one specifically. "The generality or specificity of the system's narrative is a function of the scope and focus of the user's attention, whether wide and covering a group of items . . . or focused in upon some single thing, as inferred from the user's pattern of eye fixations." (Starker and Bolt, 1990).

Another area where eye movements have been used in real-time interfaces is to create the illusion of a larger and higher resolution image than can actually be rendered. This has been demonstrated for flight simulator displays (Tong and Fisher, 1984), and discussed for head-mounted displays. With this approach, the portion of the display that is currently being viewed is depicted with high resolution, while the larger surrounding area (visible only in peripheral vision) is depicted in lower resolution. If the eye tracker is good enough (and/or the coverage of the high-resolution inset is large enough), the user cannot detect the difference between this arrangement and the large, high-resolution display it emulates. Here, however, the eye movements are used essentially to simulate a better display device; the user's eye movements do not alter the basic user–computer dialogue, as we wish to do.

TECHNICAL DESCRIPTION

Eye-tracking technologies

A variety of technologies has been applied to the problem of eye tracking. Some are more suited to laboratory experiments or medical diagnosis than user–computer dialogues. Further details on this and the other eye-tracking methods discussed here can be found in the article by Young and Sheena (1975).

One of the least expensive and simplest eye-tracking technologies is recording from skin electrodes, like those used for making ECG or EEG measurements. Because the retina is so electrically active compared with the rest of the eyeball, there is a measurable potential difference between it and the cornea. Electrodes are placed on the skin around the eye socket, and can measure changes in the orientation of this potential difference. However, this method is more useful for measuring relative eye movements (which require only AC skin electrode measurements) than absolute position (which requires more difficult DC measurements). It can cover a wider range of movement than other tracking technologies, but gives poor accuracy (particularly in absolute position). This method is principally useful for diagnosing neurological problems revealed in the nystagmus eye movements.

The most accurate, but least user-friendly, technology uses a physical attachment to the front of the eye. A non-slipping contact lens is ground to fit precisely over the corneal bulge, and then slight suction is applied (mechanically or chemically) to hold the lens in place. Once the contact lens is attached, the eye-tracking problem reduces to tracking something affixed to the lens, and a variety of means can be used. The lens may have a small mechanical lever, a magnetic coil, or a mirror, all of which can be tracked reliably. This method is obviously practical only for laboratory studies, as it is very awkward, uncomfortable, and interferes with blinking. It also covers a limited range of eye movements. However, it provides accurate data about the nature of human eye movements, which can be used to design effective interaction techniques and to make corrections to the data obtained from more practical, but less accurate, tracking technologies.

Most practical eye-tracking methods are based on a non-contacting camera that observes the eyeball plus image-processing techniques to interpret the picture. The position of the eyeball can be identified by tracking one of its visible features. For example, the boundary between the *sclera* (white portion of the front of the eye) and *iris* (colored portion) is easy to find, but only a portion of it usually remains visible at one time. The outline of the pupil against the iris is a good choice if implemented properly. The eye is usually illuminated by barely visible infrared light, so as not to be disturbing. Under infrared illumination, blue eyes appear dark and may make the black pupil difficult to identify. Shadows, dark eyelashes, and eyebrows may also interfere with identification of the black pupil. This can be alleviated with sophisticated image processing and pattern recognition techniques or, more simply, by illuminating the eye with a light that is coaxial with the camera. Under such illumination, the pupil appears as a bright disk, usually much brighter than surrounding features, regardless of eye color. For retrospective analysis, these approaches can be applied to movies or video tapes of the eye image. For real-time analysis, the same approach is applied to a live video image of the eye.

As described, this approach measures the position of the front of the eyeball in space. For human–computer dialogues, we wish to measure *visual line of gaze*, a line radiating forward in space from the eye and indicating what the user is looking at. To illustrate the difference, suppose the eye tracker detected a small lateral motion of the pupil. It could mean either that the user's head moved in space (and his or her eye is still looking at nearly the same point) or that the eye rotated with respect to the head (causing a large change in where the eye is looking). One solution is to hold the head absolutely stationary, to be sure that any movement detected represents movement of the eye, rather than the head moving in space. This approach is used in laboratory experiments, but it requires a bite board, rather than a chin-rest, for good accuracy.

The more practical approach is to use simultaneous tracking of two features of the eye that move differentially with respect to one another as the line of gaze changes. This allows head movements (the two features move together) to be distinguished from eye movements (the two move with respect to one another). The head no longer need be rigidly fixed; it need only stay within camera range (which is quite small, due to the extreme telephoto lens required). The technique is to shine a collimated beam of infrared light at the front surface of the eyeball, producing a bright glint or corneal reflection, which moves less than the pupil as the eyeball rotates in its socket. The same infrared illumination can provide the corneal reflection and the bright pupil described earlier. The corneal reflection *and* outline of the pupil are then observed by the same video camera; image-processing hardware or software analyzes the image to identify a large, bright circle (pupil) and a still brighter dot (corneal reflection) and compute the center of each. Then absolute visual line of gaze is computed from the relationship between these two points. The temporal resolution of this approach is generally limited to the video frame rate (in particular, it cannot generally capture the dynamics of a saccade). A related method used in the SRI eye tracker (Crane and Steele, 1985) tracks the corneal reflection plus the fourth Purkinje image (reflection from rear of lens of the eye); the latter is dim, so bright illumination of the eye is needed. The reflections are captured by a photocell, which drives a servo-controlled mirror with an analog signal, avoiding the need for discrete sampling. Hence this method is not limited by video frame rate. The technique is accurate, fast, but very delicate to operate; it can also measure accommodation (focus distance).

Current eye-tracking technology is, thus, becoming suitable for ordinary users in settings outside the laboratory. Most of the methods discussed are more suitable for laboratory experiments, but the corneal reflection-plus-pupil outline approach is appropriate for normal computer users, since nothing contacts the subject and the device permits his or her head to remain unclamped. The eye tracker sits several feet away from the subject, and head motion is restricted only to the extent necessary to keep the pupil of the eye within view of the camera. A servomechanism pans and focuses the camera to follow the eye as the subject's head moves. Under ideal conditions, the subject can move within approximately one cubic foot of space without losing contact with the eye tracker. An alternative configuration, less convenient for normal office use, but more useful in virtual environments, is to mount a miniature version of the camera and light source directly on the user's head. That approach is described further in the next section.

This type of equipment is manufactured commercially in both the head-mounted and remote configurations; in our laboratory at the Naval Research Laboratory (NRL), we use an Applied Science Laboratories (Waltham, MA) Model 4250R pupil-plus-corneal reflection eye tracker (Merchant *et al.*, 1974; Young and Sheena, 1975). Figure 7-2 shows the components of this type of eye

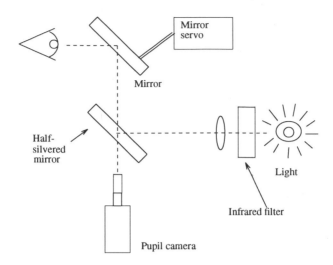

Figure 7-2 Illustration of components of a corneal reflection-plus-pupil eye tracker. The pupil camera and illuminator operate along the same optical axis, via a half-silvered mirror. The servo-controlled mirror is used to compensate for the user's head motions.

tracker. In our laboratory, the user sits at a conventional desk, with a 19 inch Sun computer display, mouse, and keyboard, in a standard office chair. The eye-tracker camera/illuminator sits on the desk next to the monitor. Other than the illuminator box with its dim red glow, the overall setting is thus much like that for an ordinary office computer user. In addition, the room lights are dimmed to keep the user's pupil from becoming too small. The eye tracker transmits the x and y coordinates for the user's visual line of gaze every 1/60 second, on a serial port, to a Sun computer. The Sun performs all further processing, filtering, fixation recognition, and some additional calibration. Software on the Sun parses the raw eye-tracker data stream into tokens that represent events meaningful to the user–computer dialogue. Our user-interface management system, closely modeled after that described by Jacob (1986), multiplexes these tokens with other inputs (such as mouse and keyboard) and processes them to implement the user interfaces under study.

We find that we can generally get an accuracy of two degrees quite easily, and sometimes can achieve one degree (or approximately 0.4 inch or 40 pixels on the screen at a 24 inch viewing distance). The eye tracker should thus be viewed as having a resolution much coarser than that of a mouse or most other pointing devices, perhaps more like a traditional touch screen. An additional problem is that the range over which the eye can be tracked with this equipment is fairly limited. In our configuration, it cannot quite cover the surface of a 19 inch monitor at a 24 inch viewing distance. One further problem is that the eye tracker is designed for use in experiments where there is a "subject" whose eye is tracked and an "experimenter" who monitors and adjusts the equipment. Operation by a single user playing both roles

Figure 7-3   The eye tracker in use in the testbed. The eye tracker camera and light source are located at the lower left of this picture. The camera views the user's eye through a mirror located just below the computer display screen. The eye-tracker electronics are in the rack at the left of the picture, which also contains a monitor that shows the view of the user's pupil as seen by the eye-tracking camera.

simultaneously is somewhat awkward because, as soon as you look at the eye-tracker control panel to make an adjustment, your eye is no longer pointed where it should be for tracking. Figure 7-3 shows the eye tracker in use in our interaction technique testbed.

Improvements in performance and cost of eye-tracking equipment have come rather slowly in recent years. The accuracy of an eye tracker that is useful in a real-time interface is limited by the size of the fovea, since a user generally need not position his or her eye more accurately than the width of the fovea (about one degree) to see an object sharply. Finer accuracy from an eye tracker might be needed for eye movement research, but not for our purpose. The eye's normal jittering further limits the practical accuracy of eye tracking. It is possible to improve accuracy by averaging over a fixation, but not in a real-time interface. The accuracy of the best current eye trackers approaches one-degree useful limit imposed by the diameter of the fovea. However, *stability* and *repeatability* of the measurements leave much to be desired. In a research study it is acceptable if the eye tracker fails very briefly from time to time; it may require that an experimental trial be discarded, but the user need not be aware of the problem. In an interactive interface, though, as soon as it begins to fail, the user can no longer rely on the fact that the computer dialogue is influenced by where his or her eye is pointing and will thus soon be tempted to retreat permanently to whatever back-up input modes are available. While eye trackers have dropped somewhat in price, their performance in this regard has not improved significantly. Performance does not appear to be constrained by fundamental limits, but simply by lack of effort in this area, due to its narrow market (Young and Sheena, 1975).

Most eye-tracking techniques measure line of gaze, but not accommodation or focus, i.e., the specific point along the line of gaze at which the user has focused. For a user sitting in front of a flat display screen, this information is usually obvious. In addition, it is customary to track only one eye, since the two eyes generally point together.

Eye trackers in a virtual environment

As an alternative to the remote camera and illuminator, a much smaller version of the camera and collimated light source can be mounted on the user's head, attached to a headband or helmet. The eye tracker then reports the angle of the user's eye with respect to his or her head. A separate magnetic tracker (such as a Polhemus tracker) measures head orientation, and the two data sources together can be used to determine the line of gaze in physical space. In virtual space, however, the head, eye tracker, and display itself all move together, so the head orientation information is not needed to determine line of gaze. The eye-tracker range is the same as with the remote camera, but allowing head motion greatly expands overall range of the device, allowing the user to look anywhere around him or her, rather than on a single display screen. In addition, the relationship between camera and eye is more nearly constant with the head-mounted eye camera, offering the promise of better stability of eye-tracking measurements. In our laboratory, we use a headband-mounted camera and light source as an alternative to the remote unit; the two produce similar video images of the eye and plug into the same video-processing equipment. For many applications, the head-mounted camera assembly, while not heavy, is much more awkward to use than the remote configuration. However, in a virtual environment display, if the user is already wearing a head-mounted display device, the head-mounted eye tracker adds little extra weight or complexity. The eye tracker camera can obtain its view of the eye through a beam splitter, so it need not obscure any part of the user's field of view. Depending on the display optics, some careful engineering may be required so as not to compromise very close viewing distances required by some wide-angle viewing optics; but this appears to be a soluble problem.

INTERFACE DESIGN ISSUES

Problems in using eye movements in a human–computer dialogue

The other half of the application of eye movement input is to make wise and effective use of eye movements, ideally in a non-command-based style. Eye movements, like other passive, non-command inputs (e.g., gesture, conversational speech) are often unintentional or not conscious, so they must be interpreted carefully to avoid annoying the user with unwanted responses to his actions. In eye movements, we call this the "Midas Touch" problem. The problem with a simple implementation of an eye-tracker interface is that people are not accustomed to operating devices simply by moving their eyes. They expect to be able to look at an item without having the look cause an action to occur. At first it is helpful to be able simply to look at what you want and have it occur without further action; soon, though, it becomes like the Midas Touch. Everywhere you look, another command is activated; you cannot look anywhere without issuing a command. Eye movements are an example of how most of the non-command, passive inputs will require either careful interface design to avoid this problem or some form of "clutch" to engage and disengage the monitoring.

The simplest solution would be to substitute an eye tracker directly for a mouse. This is unworkable because of the way the eye moves as well as because of the instability of existing eye-tracking equipment. Compared to mouse input, eye input has some advantages and disadvantages, which must all be considered in designing eye-movement-based interaction techniques.

First, as Ware and Mikaelian (1987) observed, eye-movement input is faster than other current input media. Before the user operates any mechanical pointing device, he or she usually looks at the destination to which he wishes to move. Thus the eye movement is available as an indication of the user's goal before he or she could actuate any other input device. Second, it is easy to operate. No training or particular coordination is required of normal users for them to be able to cause their eyes to look at an object; and the control-to-display relationship for this device is already established in the brain.

The eye is, of course, much more than a high-speed cursor-positioning tool. Unlike any other input device, an eye tracker also tells where the user's interest is focused. By the very act of pointing with this device, the user changes his or her focus of attention; and every change of focus is available as a pointing command to the computer. A mouse input tells the system simply that the user intentionally picked up the mouse and pointed it at something. An eye tracker input could be interpreted in the same way (the user intentionally pointed his or her eye at something), but it can also be interpreted as an indication of what the user is currently paying attention to, without any explicit input action on his or her part.

This same quality is the prime drawback of the eye as a computer input device. Moving one's eyes is often an almost subconscious act. Unlike a mouse, it is relatively difficult to control eye position consciously and precisely at all times. The eyes continually dart from spot to spot, and it is not desirable for each such move to initiate a computer command. Similarly, unlike a mouse, eye movements are always "on." There is no natural way to indicate when to engage the input device, as there is with grasping or releasing the mouse. Closing the eyes is rejected for obvious reasons—even with eye-tracking as input, the principal function of the eyes in the user–computer dialogue is for communication *to* the user. Using blinks as a signal is unsatisfactory because it detracts from the naturalness possible with an eye-movement-based dialogue by requiring the user to think about when to blink. Also, in comparison to a mouse, eye tracking lacks an analogue of the built-in buttons most mice have. Using blinks or eye closings for this purpose is rejected for the reason mentioned. Finally, the eye-tracking equipment is far less stable and accurate than most manual input devices.

During a single fixation, a user generally thinks he or she is looking steadily at a single object—he is not consciously aware of the small, jittery motions. Therefore, the human–computer dialogue should be constructed so that it, too, ignores those motions, since, ideally, it should correspond to what the user *thinks* he or she is doing, rather than what his eye muscles are actually doing. This requires filtering of the raw eye-position data to eliminate the high-frequency jitter, but at the same time we must not unduly slow response to the high-frequency component of a genuine saccade.

In addition, a user may view a single object with a sequence of several fixations, all in the general area of the object. Since they are distinct fixations, separated by measurable saccades larger than the jitter mentioned above, they would be tracked as individual fixations. Following the same rationale, if the user thinks he or she is looking at a single object, the user interface ought to treat the eye-tracker data as if there were one event, not several. Therefore, if the user makes several fixations near the same screen object, connected by small saccades, the fixations are grouped together into a single "gaze," following the approach of Just and Carpenter (1980). Further dialogue processing is performed in terms of these gazes, rather than fixations, since the former should be more indicative of the user's intentions.

Instability is introduced into the output of the eye tracker whenever it fails to obtain an adequate video image of the eye for one or more frames. This could mean that the user blinked or moved his or her head outside the tracked region; if so, such information could be passed to the user interface. However, it could also mean simply that there was a spurious reflection in the video camera or any of a variety of other momentary artifacts. The two cases may not be distinguishable; hence, it is not clear how the user-interface should respond to brief periods during which the eye tracker reports no position. The user may indeed have looked away, but he or she may also think he is looking right at some target on the screen, and the system is failing to respond.

Another simple interface design issue is whether the system should provide a screen cursor that follows the user's eye position (as is done for mice and other conventional devices). If the eye tracker were perfect, the image of such a cursor would become stationary on the user's retina and thus disappear from perception. In fact, few eye trackers can track small, high-frequency motions rapidly or precisely enough for this to be a problem, but it does illustrate the subtlety of the design issues. Moreover, an eye-following cursor will tend to move around and thus attract the user's attention. Yet it is perhaps the *least* informative aspect of the display (since it tells you where you are already looking). If there is any systematic calibration error, the cursor will be slightly offset from where the user is actually looking, causing the user's eye to be drawn to the cursor, which will further displace the cursor, creating a positive feedback loop. We often observe this phenomenon. Of course, if the calibration and response speed of the eye tracker were perfect, feedback would not be necessary, since a person knows exactly where he or she is looking (unlike the situation with a mouse cursor, which helps one visualize the relationship between mouse positions and points on the screen).

We have divided the problem of processing eye movement data into two stages. First we process the raw data from the eye tracker in order to filter noise, recognize fixations, compensate for local calibration errors and other characteristics and imperfections of the eye-tracking hardware, and generally try to reconstruct the user's more conscious intentions from the available information. This processing stage converts the continuous, somewhat noisy stream of raw eye-position reports into discrete tokens (described below) that more closely approximate the user's intentions in a higher-level user–computer dialogue. In doing so, jitter during fixations is smoothed, fixations are grouped into gazes, and brief eye-tracker artifacts are removed. The second half of the process is to provide generic interaction techniques based on these tokens as inputs. Because eye movements are so different from conventional computer inputs, we achieve best results with a philosophy that tries, as much as possible, to use natural eye movements as an implicit input, rather than to train a user to move the eyes in a particular way to operate the system.

PROCESSING THE RAW EYE-MOVEMENT DATA

Local calibration

The first step in processing the raw data from the eye tracker is to introduce an additional calibration process. The eye-tracker calibration procedure produces a mapping that is applied uniformly to the whole screen. No further calibration or adjustment should be necessary. In practice, we found small calibration errors appear in portions of the screen, rather than systematically across it. We introduce an additional layer of calibration into the chain, outside of the eye-tracker computer, which allows the user to make local modifications to the calibration, based on arbitrary points he or she inputs whenever he or she feels it would be helpful. The procedure is that, if the user feels the eye tracker is not responding accurately in some area of the screen, he or she moves the mouse cursor to that area, looks at the cursor, and clicks a button. That introduces an offset, which warps future eye-tracker reports in the vicinity of the given point, i.e., all reports nearer to that point than to the next-nearest local calibration point. (We found this gave better results than smoothly interpolating the local calibration offsets.) The user can do this at any time and in any position, as needed.

In our early experiments, this had the surprising effect of increasing the apparent response speed for object selection and other interaction techniques. The reason is that, if the calibration is slightly wrong in a local region and the user stares at a single target in that region, the eye tracker will report the eye position somewhere slightly outside the target. If the user continues to stare at

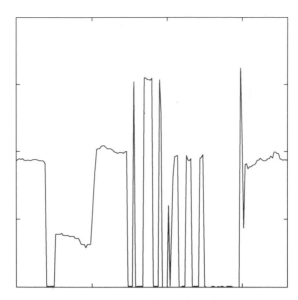

Figure 7-4 Illustration of erratic nature of raw data from the eye tracker. The plot shows one coordinate of eye position vs. time, over a somewhat worse-than-typical three-second period.

it, though, his or her eyes will in fact jitter around to a spot that the eye tracker will report as being on the target. The effect feels as though the system is responding too slowly, but it is a problem of local calibration. The local calibration procedure results in a marked improvement in the apparent responsiveness of the interface as well as an increase in the user's control over the system. Further resistance to calibration errors is provided by an algorithm that accepts fixations outside a selectable object, provided they are fairly close to it and are substantially closer to it than to any other selectable objects.

Fixation recognition

The next step is to analyze the incoming data from the eye tracker and attempt to reconstruct the user's intentional fixations from the raw, jittery, imperfect data received. Such imperfections are caused by both natural and artificial sources: the normal jittery motions of the eye during fixations as well as artifacts introduced when the eye tracker momentarily fails to obtain an adequate video image of the eye.

A view of the type of data obtained from the eye tracker can be seen in Figure 7-4, which plots the x coordinate of the eye position output against time over a relatively jumpy three-second period. (A plot of the y coordinate for the same period would show generally the same areas of smooth vs. jumpy behavior, but different absolute positions.) Zero values on the ordinate represent periods when the eye tracker could not locate the line of gaze, due either to eye-tracker artifacts, such as glare in the video camera, lag in compensating for head motion, or failure of the processing algorithm, or by actual user actions, such as blinks or movements outside the range of the eye tracker. Unfortunately, the two cases are indistinguishable in the eye-tracker output. During the period represented by Figure 7-4, this subject thought he was simply looking around at a few different points on a CRT screen. Buried in these data, thus, are a few relatively long gazes along with some motions to connect the gazes.

Such raw data are quite unusable as input to a human–computer dialogue: while the noise and jumpiness do partly reflect the actual motion of the user's eye muscles, they do not reflect his intentions nor his impression of what his eyes were doing. The difference is attributable not only to the eye-tracker artifacts but to the fact that much of the fine-grained behavior of the eye muscles is not intentional. The problem is to extract from the noisy, jittery, error-filled stream of position reports produced by the eye tracker some "intentional" components of the eye motions, which make sense as tokens in a user–computer dialogue.

One solution would be to use a simple moving average filter to smooth the data. It improves performance during a fixation, but tends to dampen the sudden saccades that move the eye from one fixation to the next. Since one of the principal benefits we hope to obtain from eye motions as input is speed, damping them is counterproductive. Further, the resulting smoothed data do not correctly reflect the user's intentions. The user was not slowly gliding from one fixation to another; he was, in fact, fixating a spot and then jumping ballistically to a new fixation. Instead, we return to the picture of a computer user's eye movements as a collection of jittery fixations connected by essentially instantaneous saccades. We start with an *a priori* model of such saccades and fixations and then attempt to recognize those events in the data stream. We then identify and quickly report the start and approximate position of each recognized fixation. We ignore any reports of eye position during saccades themselves, since they are difficult for the eye tracker to catch and their dynamics are not particularly meaningful to the user–computer dialogue.

Our algorithm is based on that used for analyzing previously recorded files of raw eye-movement data (Lambert *et al.*, 1974; Flagg, 1977) and on the known properties of fixations and saccades. It watches the input data for a sequence of 100 milliseconds during which the standard deviation of the reported eye position remains within approximately 0.5°. As soon as the 100 ms have passed, it reports the start of a fixation and takes the mean of the 100 ms worth of data as the location of that fixation. A better estimate of the location of a fixation could be obtained by averaging over more eye-tracker data, but this would mean a longer delay before the fixation position could be reported to the user-interface software. Our algorithm therefore implies a delay of 100 ms before reporting the start of a fixation. In practice this delay is nearly undetectable to the user. Further eye positions within approximately one degree are assumed to represent continuations of the same fixation (rather than a saccade to a new one). To terminate a fixation, 50 ms of data lying outside one degree of the current fixation must be received. Blinks or artifacts of up to 200 ms may occur during a fixation without terminating it. (These occur when the eye tracker reports a "no position" code.) At first, blinks seemed to

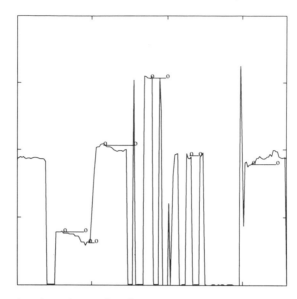

Figure 7-5 Result of applying the fixation recognition algorithm to the data of Figure 7-4. A horizontal line beginning and ending with an *O* marks each fixation at the time and coordinate position it would be reported.

present a problem, since, obviously, we cannot obtain eye-position data during a blink. However (equally obviously—in retrospect), the screen need not respond to the eye during that blink period, since the user cannot see it anyway.

If this algorithm is applied to the noisy data shown in Figure 7-4, we find about six fixations, which more accurately reflects what the user thought he was doing (rather than what his eye muscles plus the eye-tracking equipment actually did). Figure 7-5 shows the same data, with a horizontal line marking each recognized fixation at the time and location it would be reported. Applying the fixation recognition approach to the real-time data coming from the eye tracker yielded a significant improvement in the user-visible behavior of the interface. Filtering the data based on an *a priori* model of eye motion is an important step in transforming the raw eye-tracker output into a user–computer dialogue.

Re-assignment of off-target fixations

Thus far, the processing only translates eye-tracker data into recognized fixations at specific screen locations without reference to what is displayed on the screen. The next processing step uses knowledge of what is actually on the screen, and serves further to compensate for small inaccuracies in the eye-tracker data. It allows a fixation that is near, but not directly on, an eye-selectable screen object to be accepted. Given a list of currently displayed objects and their screen extents, the algorithm will reposition a fixation that lies outside any object, provided it is ''reasonably'' close to one object and "reasonably" distant from all other such objects (i.e., not halfway between two objects, which would lead to unstable behavior). It is important that this procedure is applied only to fixations detected by the recognition algorithm, not to individual raw eye-tracker position reports. The result of this step is to improve performance in areas of the screen at which the eye-tracker calibration is imperfect without increasing false selections in areas where the calibration is good, since fixations in those areas fall directly on their targets and would not activate this processing step.

USER-INTERFACE SOFTWARE

The next step in the process of building a user interface is aided by our user-interface management system (UIMS) (Jacob, 1986), which lends itself to a multi-threaded direct manipulation interaction style typical of an eye-movement-based interface. To use it, the output of the fixation recognition algorithm is turned into a stream of discrete *tokens* suitable for input to the UIMS. Tokens are reported for eye events considered meaningful to the user–computer dialogue, analogous to the way that raw input from a keyboard (shift key went down, letter "a" key went down, etc.) is turned into meaningful events (one ASCII upper case "A" was typed). We report tokens for the start, continuation, and end of each detected fixation. Each such token is tagged with the actual fixation duration to date, so an interaction technique that expects a fixation of a particular length will not be skewed by delays in processing by the UIMS or by the delay inherent in the fixation recognition algorithm. Between fixations, we periodically report a non-fixation token indicating where the eye is, although our current interaction techniques ignore this token in preference to the fixation tokens, which are more filtered. A token is also reported whenever the eye tracker fails to determine eye position for 200 ms and again when it resumes tracking. In addition, tokens are generated whenever a new fixation enters or exits a monitored region, just as is done for the mouse. All tokens, whether generated by eye, mouse, or keyboard, are then multiplexed into a single stream and presented as input to our UIMS.

To implement a user interface with this UIMS, the desired interface is specified as a collection of relatively simple individual dialogues, represented by separate *interaction objects*. The description of all of these interaction objects comprises the user-interface description language (UIDL), which is executed by the UIMS. The interaction objects are connected by an executive that activates and suspends them with retained state, like co-routines. While the overall user-interface may have multiple threads, each individual interaction object has only a single-thread dialogue. A typical object might be a screen button, scroll bar, text field, or eye-selectable graphic object. Since each such object conducts only a single-thread dialogue, with all inputs serialized and with a remembered state whenever the individual dialogue is interrupted by that of another interaction object, the operation of each interaction object is conveniently specified as a simple single-thread state transition diagram that accepts the tokens as input. Each object can accept any combination of eye,

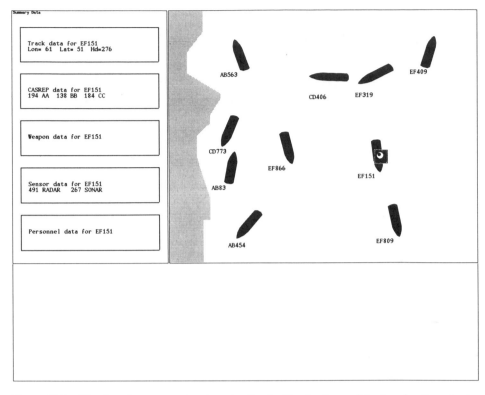

Figure 7-6 Display from eye-tracker testbed, illustrating object selection technique. Whenever the user looks at a ship in the right window, the ship is selected and information about it is displayed in the left window. The square eye icon at the right is used to show where the user's eye was pointing in these illustrations; it does not normally appear on the screen. The actual screen image uses light figures on a dark background to keep the pupil large.

mouse, and keyboard tokens, as specified in its own syntax diagram in the UIDL, and provides a standard method that the executive can call to offer it an input token and traverse its diagram.

The top-level dialogue loop is provided by a standard executive. It operates by assembling the interaction objects and executing each of their state diagrams as a co-routine, assigning input tokens to them and arbitrating among them as they proceed. Whenever the currently active dialogue receives a token it cannot accept, the executive causes it to relinquish control by co-routine call to whatever dialogue can, given its current state, accept it. If none can, the executive discards the token and proceeds.

As an example, each ship in Figure 7-6 responds to a gaze of a certain duration. Each of the ships is implemented as a separate interaction object (but all are of the same class, *Ship*). In addition, each interaction object such as *Ship* also has a lower-level *Gazer* interaction object associated with it to perform the translation of fixations into gazes described above. The Gazer

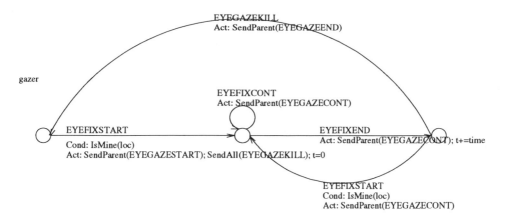

gazer

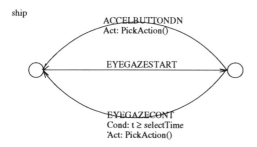

ship

Figure 7-7 Diagrams that specify the syntax of the *Gazer* and *Ship* interaction objects to the user-interface management system.

accepts fixations on its parent object and then combines such consecutive fixations into a single gaze token, which it sends to its parent object (the Ship). Figure 7-7 shows the syntax diagram for Gazer; it accepts the tokens generated by the fixation recognition algorithm (EYEFIXSTART, EYEFIXCONT, and EYEFIXEND), tests whether they lie within its extent or else meet the criteria for off-target fixations described above (implemented in the call to *IsMine*), accumulates them into gazes, and sends gaze tokens (EYEGAZESTART, EYEGAZECONT, and EYEGAZEEND) directly to its parent object. The Ship interaction object syntax then need only accept and respond to the gaze tokens sent by its Gazer. Figure 7-7 also shows the portion of the Ship interaction object syntax diagram concerned with selecting a ship by looking at it for a given dwell time (for clarity the syntax for dragging and other operations described below is not shown in the figure; also not shown are the tokens that the selected ship sends to the other ships to deselect the previously selected ship, if any). When a user operation upon a ship causes a semantic-level consequence (e.g., moving a ship changes the track data), the Ship interaction object calls its parent, an application domain object, to do the work. Although the syntax may seem complicated as described here, it is well matched to the natural saccades and fixations of the eye.

APPLICATIONS OF EYE TRACKING

Interaction techniques

Interaction techniques are specific, yet not bound to a single application. An interaction technique is a way of using a physical input device to perform a generic task in a human–computer dialogue (Foley *et al.*, 1990). It represents an abstraction of some common class of interactive task, for example, choosing one of several objects shown on a display screen. Below, we describe the first eye-movement-based interaction techniques that we have implemented and our observations from using them.

Object selection

Object selection with a mouse is usually done by pointing at the object and then pressing a button to select one object from among several displayed on the screen. The selection might be one of several file icons on a desk-top or, as shown in Figure 7-6, one of several ships on a map. However there is no natural counterpart of the mouse-button press for the eye tracker. We reject using a blink because intentional blinking is not a natural eye movement. We examined two designs—using a button and using dwell time. With the button, the user looks at the desired object then presses a button to indicate that it is to be selected. In Figure 7-6, the user has looked at ship "EF151" and caused it to be selected (for attribute display, described below). With dwell time, the object is selected if the user continues to gaze at it for a sufficiently long time. The two techniques are actually implemented simultaneously, where the button press is optional and can be used to avoid waiting for the dwell time to expire, much as an optional menu accelerator key is used to avoid traversing a menu; this allows the user to make a trade-off between speed and keeping his or her hand free. In practice, however, we found the dwell-time approach alone to be much more convenient, provided the dwell time could be made brief. A long dwell time would be good to ensure that the user does not make inadvertent selection simply by looking around on the display, but it attenuates the speed advantage of using eye movements for input and also reduces the responsiveness of the interface. To allow a reduced dwell time, we make a further distinction: if the result of selecting the wrong object can be undone trivially (that is, selection of a wrong object followed by a selection of the right object causes no adverse effect, the second selection instantaneously overrides the first), then we use a very short dwell time. For example, if selecting an object causes a display of information about that object to appear and the information display can be changed instantaneously, then the effect of selecting wrong objects is immediately undone as long as the user eventually reaches the right one. With a 150–250 ms dwell time, this approach gives excellent results. The lag between eye movement and system response (required to reach the dwell time) is hardly detectable to the user, yet long enough to accumulate sufficient data for our fixation recognition and processing into gazes. The subjective feeling is of a highly responsive system, almost as though the system is executing the user's intentions before he or she expresses them. For situations where selecting an object is more difficult to undo, button confirmation is used rather than a longer dwell time. We found no case where a long dwell time (over $\frac{3}{4}$ second) alone was useful, probably because that is not a natural eye movement (people do not normally fixate one spot for that long) and also it creates the suspicion that the system has crashed.

Continuous attribute display

This object selection interaction technique can be applied effectively to the retrieval of further details or attributes of one of the objects on a display. In Figure 7-6, we provide a separate area of the display for such attributes. The window on the right is a geographic display of ships, while the text window on the left displays attributes of one of the ships, as selected by the user's eye movement. The user can look around the ship window as desired. Whenever the user looks over to the text window, he or she will find the attribute display for the last ship looked at—presumably the one the user is interested in. (The ship remains selected when the user looks away from the ship window to the text window.) However, if the user simply looks at the ship window and never looks at the text area, he or she need not be concerned that his eye movements are causing commands in the text window. Because the text window is double-buffered, changes in its contents are too subtle to be seen by peripheral vision. To notice the change, the user would have to be looking directly at the text window at the time it changed (which, of course, he or she is not—he must be looking at the ship window to effect a change).

Moving an object

If we separate the action of designating an object on the display to be moved from that of moving it, we might use the eye to select the object to be manipulated (moved on a map, in this case) and the mouse to move it. The eye selection is made as described above. Then, the user grabs the mouse, presses a button, drags the mouse in the direction the object is to be moved, and releases the button. There is no visible mouse cursor in this scheme, and the mouse is used as a relative position device—it starts moving from wherever the eye-selected ship was.

As an alternative, the eye might be used to select *and* drag the ship, and a pushbutton to pick it up and put it down. The user selects a ship, then presses a button; while the button is depressed, the ship drags along with the user's eye. (Since the processing described previously is performed on the eye movements, the ship actually jumps to each fixation after about 100 ms and then remains steadily there—despite actual eye jitter—until the next fixation.) When the button is released, the ship is left in its new position.

Before testing, we expected that this second method would be too unpredictable; eye movements would be fine for selecting an object, but picking it up and having it jump around on the screen in response to eye movements would be annoying—a mouse would give more concrete control. Once again, our initial guess was not borne out. While the eye-to-select/mouse-to-drag method worked well, the user was quickly spoiled by the eye-only method. Once you begin to expect the system to know where you are looking, the mouse-to-drag operation seems awkward and slow. After looking at the desired ship and pressing the "pick up" button, the natural thing to do is to look at where you are planning to move the ship. At this point, you feel, "I'm looking right at the destination I want, why do I now have to go get the mouse to drag the ship over here?" With eye movements processed to suppress jitter and respond only to recognized fixations, the motion of the dragging ship is reasonably smooth and predictable and yet appears subjectively instantaneous. It works best when the destination of the move is a recognizable feature on the screen (another ship, or a harbor on a map); when the destination is an arbitrary blank spot, it is more difficult to make your eye look at it, as the eye is always drawn to features.

Eye-controlled scrolling text

The bottom left of Figure 7-8 shows a window of text, which is not large enough to hold all the material to be displayed in it. A row of two upward-pointing arrows is displayed below the last line of the text and above the first line, indicating that there is additional material not shown. If the user looks at the arrows, the text itself starts to scroll. Note, though, that it never scrolls when the user is actually reading the text (rather than looking at the arrows). The assumption is that, as soon as the text starts scrolling, the user's eye will be drawn to the moving display and away from the arrows, which will stop the scrolling. The user can thus read down to end of the window, then, after he or she finishes reading the last line, look slightly below it, at the arrows, in order to retrieve the next part of the text. The arrows are visible above and/or below text display only when there is additional scrollable material in that direction.

Menu commands

Since pop-up menus inherently assume a button, a pull-down menu seemed more appropriate for an eye-movement-based interaction technique. In Figure 7-9, if the user looks at the header of a pull-down menu for a given dwell time (400 ms), the body of the menu will appear on the screen. Next, the user can look at the items shown on the menu. After a brief look at an item (100 ms), it will be highlighted, but its command will not yet be executed. This allows the user time to examine the different items on the menu. If the user looks at one item for a much longer time (1 s), its command will be executed and the menu erased. Alternatively, once the item is highlighted, pressing a button will execute its command immediately and erase the menu. If the user looks outside the menu (for 600 ms), the menu is erased without any command executed. Our initial experience with this interaction technique suggests that the button is more convenient than the long dwell time for executing a menu

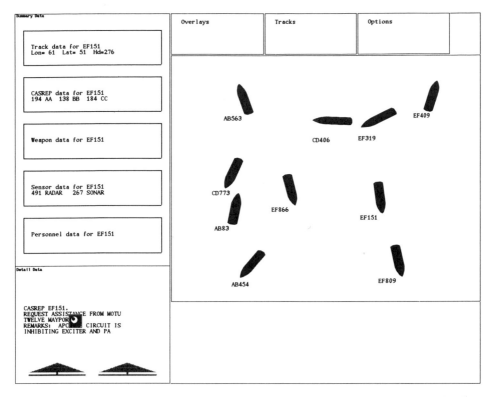

Figure 7-8 Another display from the testbed, showing the scrolling text and other windows.

command. This is because the dwell time necessary before executing a command must be kept quite high, at least noticeably longer than the time required to read an unfamiliar item. This is longer than people normally fixate on one spot, so selecting such an item requires an unnatural sort of "stare." Pulling the menu down and selecting an item to be highlighted are both done very effectively with short dwell times, as with object selection.

A TAXONOMY OF EYE-MOVEMENT-BASED INTERACTION

Direct manipulation and virtual environment interfaces both draw on analogies to existing human skills (pointing, moving objects, and navigating in physical space), rather than trained behaviors. These notions are more difficult to extend to eye-movement-based interaction, since few objects in the real world respond to people's eye movements. The principal exception is, of course, other people: they detect and respond to being looked at directly and, to a lesser and much less precise degree, to what else one may be looking at. We draw two distinctions with respect to eye-movement-based interaction, as shown in Figure 7-10: the nature of the user's eye movements and the nature of

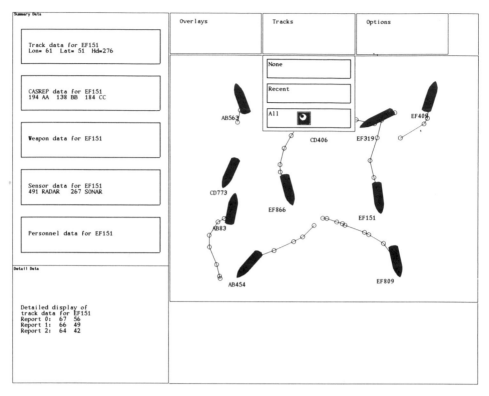

Figure 7-9 Testbed display showing eye-controlled pull-down menu.

the responses. Each of these could be viewed as *natural* (that is, based on a corresponding real-world analogy) or *unnatural* (no real-world counterpart).

With regard to the eye movement axis, within the world created by an eye-movement-based interface, users could move their eyes to scan the scene, just as they would a real-world scene, unaffected by the presence of eye-tracking equipment (*natural* eye movement, on the eye-movement axis of Figure 7-10). The alternative is to instruct users of the eye-movement-based interface to move their eyes in particular ways, not necessarily those they would have employed if left to their own devices, in order to actuate the system (*unnatural* or learned eye movements). On the response axis, objects could respond to a user's eye movements in a natural way, that is, the object responds to the user's looking in the same way real objects do. As noted, there is a limited domain from which to draw such analogies in the real world. The alternative is unnatural response, where objects respond in ways not experienced in the real world.

The possible eye-movement-based interaction techniques resulting from this categorization appear in Figure 7-10. The natural eye-movement/natural response area is a difficult one, because it draws on a limited and subtle domain, principally how people respond to other people's gaze. Starker and Bolt (1990) provide an excellent example of this mode, drawing on the analogy

	Unnatural response	Natural (real-world) response
Unnatural (learned) eye movement	Majority of work, esp. disabled	N/A
Natural eye movement	Jacob (this chapter)	Starker & Bolt, 1990

Figure 7-10 A taxonomy of approaches to eye-movement-based interaction.

of a tour guide or host who estimates the visitor's interests by his or her gazes. In the work described in this chapter, we try to use natural (not trained) eye movements as input, but we provide responses unlike those in the real world. This is a compromise between full analogy to the real world and an entirely artificial interface. We present a display and allow the user to observe it with his or her normal scanning mechanisms, but such scans then induce responses from the computer not normally exhibited by real-world objects. Most previous eye-movement-based systems have used learned ("unnatural") eye movements for operation and thus, of necessity, unnatural responses. Much of that work has been aimed at disabled or hands-busy applications, where the cost of learning the required eye movements ("stare at this icon to activate the device") is repaid by the acquisition of an otherwise impossible new ability. However, we believe that the real benefits of eye-movement interaction for the majority of users will be in its naturalness, fluidity, low cognitive load, and almost unconscious operation; these benefits are attenuated if unnatural, and thus quite conscious, eye movements are required. The remaining category in Figure 7-10, unnatural eye movement/natural response, is of doubtful utility.

NON-COMMAND-BASED USER INTERFACES

Eye-movement-based interaction and virtual environments are two of several areas of current research in human–computer interaction in which a new interface style seems to be emerging. This style represents a change in input from objects for the user to *actuate* by specific commands to passive equipment that simply *senses* parameters of the user's body. Jakob Nielsen describes this property as a *non-command-based* user interface: "This term may be a somewhat negative way of characterizing a new form of interaction, but the unifying concept does seem to be exactly the abandonment of the principle underlying all earlier interaction paradigms: that a dialogue has to be controlled by specific and precise commands issued by the user and processed and replied to by the computer. The new interfaces are often not even dialogues in the traditional meaning of the word, even though they obviously can be analyzed as having some dialogue content at some level, since they do involve the exchange of information between a user and a computer." (Nielsen, 1993.)

Current examples of non-command-based interaction include eye-movement interfaces, virtual environments, some music accompaniment systems, and agents. Previous interaction styles—batch, command line, menu, full-screen, natural language, and even current desk-top or "WIMP" (window-icon-menu-pointer) styles—all await, receive, and respond to explicit commands from the user to the computer. In the non-command style, the computer passively monitors the user and responds as appropriate, rather than waiting for the user to issue specific commands. This distinction can be a subtle one, since any user action, even an involuntary one, could be viewed as a command, particularly from the point of view of the software designer. The key criterion should therefore be whether the user *thinks* he or she is issuing an explicit command. It is of course possible to control one's eye movements, facial expressions, or gestures voluntarily, but that misses the point of a non-command-based interface; rather, it is supposed passively to observe, for example, the user's natural eye movements, and respond based on them. The essence of this style is thus its *non-intentional* quality. Following Rich's taxonomy of adaptive systems (Rich, 1983; Jacob, 1987), we can view this distinction as *explicit* vs. *implicit* commands, thus non-command really means implicit commands.

Eye-movement-based interaction provides an example of several of the characteristics—as well as the problems—of an emerging new user–computer interaction style that combines the non-command attribute with other somewhat correlated characteristics. This style is seen most dramatically in virtual-environment interfaces, but its characteristics are common to a more general class of rich user–computer environments, such as new types of games, musical accompaniment systems, interactive entertainment media, as well as eye-movement-based interfaces. They all share a higher degree of interactivity than previous interfaces—continuous input/output exchanges occurring in parallel, rather than one single-thread dialogue. Most also go a step further from the traditional dialogue towards a more subtle, implicit interchange based on passive monitoring of the user's actions rather than explicit commands. The concepts behind these emerging new interface styles can be better understood by decomposing them into two main attributes (see Figure 7-11).

One of these attributes is command style, the change from explicit to implicit commands, the non-command-based interaction style. As mentioned earlier, non-command can be viewed more precisely as implicit command (in contrast to explicit). An intermediate point can be added along this axis. It still uses explicit commands, but is distinguished by whether interpretation of the user's command is entirely within the user's control or processed in a sufficiently complex way that the user can't easily predict its outcome. This arises in adaptive systems, which interpret a user's commands based on models of his or her state of knowledge and inferred goals and try to correct apparent user errors. The user issues explicit commands, but the precise consequence of each is out of his or her effective control.

The other attribute is interactivity, initially christened non-WIMP (Green and Jacob, 1991), later refined to *highly interactive*. Its fundamental characteristic is a high degree of interactivity between user and computer. We can consider current styles, including direct manipulation, to be essentially turn-taking ("ping-pong style") dialogues with a single input/output stream.

Interactivity	Command style		
	Command-based (Explicit command)	Explicit command with re-interpretation	Non-command (Implicit command)
Half-duplex	Most current interfaces	Command correction (DWIM)	Single-channel music accompaniment, eye-only interfaces
Full-duplex	Air traffic control, command and control		
Highly-interactive	Automobile controls, airplane controls simulators		Next generation: virtual environments, multi-mode eye interfaces

Figure 7-11   A categorization of the components of a new style of user–computer interaction, and examples of some of them.

Even where there are several devices, the input is treated conceptually as a single multiplexed stream, and interaction proceeds in half-duplex, alternating between user and computer. "Highly interactive" interfaces are characterized by continuous interaction between user and computer via several parallel, asynchronous channels or devices. They represent a change from half-duplex to full-duplex (i.e., allowing simultaneous user and computer actions) and from one serialized to several parallel input streams (e.g., meaningful eye input is obtained even while the user is operating a mouse or keyboard). These interfaces attempt to avoid restricting the user's set of valid inputs, no matter what state the application is in. Inputs are also often continuous, in contrast to the discrete, pre-tokenized input obtained from a keyboard and also typically of much higher bandwidth than traditional input devices. This type of input also often arrives in a very raw form, far from that necessary for use in a meaningful dialogue; it must be recognized or otherwise processed before being used in a dialogue. Such interfaces thus require large amounts of input and output bandwidth, which leads to a need for devoting significant hardware resources to processing high bit rates of data as well as to data reduction and recognition algorithms needed to handle such voluminous, but imprecise, inputs.

An intermediate category on this axis can be defined as just "full-duplex," but not "highly interactive." This is a conventional turn-taking dialogue superimposed upon an environment in which other changes occur without user action. Examples include air traffic control, military command and control, and most graphics-based one-player video games. In each, the base dialogue style is half-duplex, but additional changes in the displayed situation may be initiated concurrently with the dialogue, even when it is nominally the user's turn.

The intersection of these two attributes, non-command and highly interactive, characterizes the next generation of user-interface style. In it, commands are received implicitly, and continuous interaction is conducted in parallel over a variety of channels. Though the two attributes are somewhat correlated and often co-occur in new interfaces, considering each in isolation is helpful to provide a more precise understanding of an otherwise fuzzy notion of an emerging new interaction style. For example, practical uses of implicit inputs usually require that the computer monitor the user on a variety of continuous channels simultaneously, hence they are also most often "highly interactive" by this definition.

Within the other categories suggested by Figure 7-11, the *half-duplex/ explicit command* category includes nearly all current interfaces, from command language to direct manipulation (excluding systems like command and control or air traffic control). Despite their differences, they all respond only to explicit commands from a single serialized input stream. The *half-duplex/ implicit command* category is somewhat artificial, the commands are implicit, but they are received over a single channel. Examples include adaptive help or tutoring systems, single-channel musical accompaniment systems, and possibly eye-movement interfaces that use no other input devices. The *highly interactive/explicit command* category is familiar in everyday life, but less often seen in computer interfaces. Automobile or airplane controls are good examples; of course, computer-based simulators of those vehicles provide the same interface. Finally, the *highly interactive/implicit command* category characterizes the next generation of user-interface style. Current examples include virtual environments and multi-mode eye-movement interfaces.

CONCLUSIONS

An eye tracker as an input device is far from "perfect," in the sense that a mouse or keyboard is, and that is caused both by the limitations of current equipment and, more importantly, by the nature of human eye movements. Accuracy obtainable is more similar to a traditional touch screen than a mouse, and the range can barely cover a single CRT display. The equipment, while non-intrusive and non-contacting, is difficult to ignore. Nevertheless, it is perhaps amazing that eye-movement-based interaction can be done at all; when the system is working well, it can give the powerful impression of responding to its user's intentions rather than his or her explicit inputs.

To achieve this, our overall approach in designing interaction techniques is, wherever possible, to obtain information from a user's natural eye movements while viewing the screen rather than requiring the user to make specific eye movements to actuate the system. For example, we tried and rejected long gazes because they are not natural eye movements, preferring to use gazes only as long as natural fixations. We also found it important to search for and recognize fixations in the raw eye tracker data stream and construct our dialogue around these higher-level events.

We saw that designing interaction techniques around a philosophy that emphasizes exploiting natural eye movements meshes well with the virtual environment interaction style, which is also based on natural navigational commands. Eye-movement-based interaction and virtual environment interaction also share the non-command-based property, which will increasingly characterize advanced user–computer interfaces, and, in both areas, working from the natural characteristics of the human users to the interface designs leads to powerful improvements in the naturalness, convenience, and, ultimately, performance obtainable from advanced interface technologies.

Finally, we saw how eye-movement-based interaction and virtual environments are instances of an emerging new style of user–computer interaction. This style is characterized by a change from explicit to implicit commands as well as a change from turn-taking, single-stream dialogues to simultaneous, parallel interactions.

ACKNOWLEDGMENTS

The eye-tracking research described here was conducted while I was a computer scientist at the Naval Research Laboratory in Washington, DC. I want to thank my colleagues at the Naval Research Laboratory, Dan McFarlane, Preston Mullen, Diane Zimmerman, and particularly Linda Sibert, for their help with this research. I also thank an anonymous referee for some very helpful comments and observations on this chapter. This work was sponsored by the US Office of Naval Research.

REFERENCES

Bolt, R. A. (1981) Gaze-orchestrated dynamic windows, *Computer Graphics*, **15**, 109–19

Bolt, R. A. (1982) Eyes at the interface, *Proc. ACM Human Factors in Computer Systems Conf.*, pp. 360–2

Crane, H. D. and Steele, C. M. (1985) Generation-V dual-Purkinje-image eyetracker, *Appl. Opt.*, **24**, 527–37

Flagg, B. N. (1977) Children and television: effects of stimulus repetition on eye activity, *Thesis, Doctor of Education degree*, Graduate School of Education, Harvard University

Foley, J. D., van Dam, A., Feiner, S. K., and Hughes, J. F. (1990) *Computer Graphics: Principles and Practice*, Reading, MA: Addison-Wesley

Glenn, F. A. *et al.* (1986) Eye-voice-controlled interface, *Proc. 30th Annual Meeting of the Human Factors Society*, Santa Monica, CA, pp. 322–6

Green, M. and Jacob, R. J. K. (1991) Software architectures and metaphors for non-WIMP user interfaces, *Computer Graphics*, **25**, 229–35

Haber, R. N. and Hershenson, M. (1973) *The Psychology of Visual Perception*, New York: Holt, Rinehart and Winston

Hutchinson, T. E., White, K. P., Martin, W. N., Reichert, K. C., and Frey, L. A. (1989) Human-computer interaction using eye-gaze input, *IEEE Trans. Systems, Man, Cybernet.*, **19**, 1527–34

Jacob, R. J. K. (1986) A specification language for direct manipulation user interfaces, *ACM Transactions on Graphics*, **5**, 283–317 (Special issue on user interface software)

Jacob, R. J. K. (1987) Human-computer interaction, in S. C. Shapiro (Ed.), *Encyclopedia of Artificial Intelligence*, New York: Wiley, pp. 383–8

Just, M. A. and Carpenter, P. A. (1980) A theory of reading: from eye fixations to comprehension, *Psychol. Rev.*, **87**, 329–54

Lambert, R. H., Monty, R. A., and Hall, R. J. (1974) High-speed data processing and unobtrusive monitoring of eye movements, *Behavior Res. Meth. Instrum.*, **6**, 525–30

Levine, J. L. (1981) *An Eye-Controlled Computer (Research Report RC-8857)*, Yorktown Heights, NY: IBM Thomas J. Watson Research Center

Levine, J. L. (1984) Performance of an eyetracker for office use, *Comput. Biol. Med.*, **14**, 77–89

Merchant, J., Morrissette, R., and Porterfield, J. L. (1974) Remote measurement of eye direction allowing subject motion over one cubic foot of space, *IEEE Trans. Biomed. Eng.*, **BME-21**, 309–17

Monty, R. A. and Senders, J. W. (1976) *Eye Movements and Psychological Processes*, Hillsdale, NJ: Lawrence Erlbaum

Nielsen, J. (1993) Noncommand User Interfaces, *Commun. ACM*, **36**, 83–99

Pritchard, R. M. (1961) Stabilized images on the retina, *Sci. Am.*, **204**, 72–8

Rich, E. (1983) Users are individuals: individualizing user models, *Int. J. Man-Machine Studies*, **18**, 199–214

Starker, I. and Bolt, R. A. (1990) A gaze-responsive self-disclosing display, *Proc. ACM CHI'90 Human Factors in Computing Systems Conf.*, New York: Addison-Wesley/ACM Press, pp. 3–9

Tong, H. M. and Fisher, R. A. (1984) *Progress Report on an Eye-Slaved Area-of-Interest Visual Display (Report No. AFHRL-TR-84-36), (Proc. of IMAGE III Conf.)*, Air Force Human Resources Laboratory, Brooks Air Force Base, TX

Tufte, E. R. (1989) *Visual Design of the User Interface*, Armonk, NY: IBM Corporation

Ware, C. and Mikaelian, H. T. (1987) An evaluation of an eye tracker as a device for computer input, *Proc. ACM CHI+GI'87 Human Factors in Computing Systems Conf.*, pp. 183–8

Young, L. R. and Sheena, D. (1975) Survey of eye movement recording methods, *Behavior Res. Meth. Instrum.*, **7**, 397–429

AUDITORY DISPLAYS

8

The Design of Multidimensional Sound Interfaces

MICHAEL COHEN AND ELIZABETH M. WENZEL

INTRODUCTION

I/O generations and dimensions

Early computer terminals allowed only textual I/O. Because the user read and wrote vectors of character strings, this mode of I/O (character-based user interface, or "CUI") could be thought of as one-dimensional, 1D. As terminal technology improved, users could manipulate graphical objects (via a graphical user interface, or "GUI") in 2D. Although the I/O was no longer unidimensional, it was still limited to the planar dimensionality of a CRT or tablet. Now there exist 3D spatial pointers and 3D graphics devices; this latest phase of I/O devices (Blattner, 1992; Blattner and Dannenberg, 1992; Robinett, 1992) approaches the way that people deal with "the real world." 3D audio (in which the sound has a spatial attribute, originating, virtually or actually, from an arbitrary point with respect to the listener) and more exotic spatial I/O modalities are under development.

The evolution of I/O devices can be roughly grouped into generations that also correspond to the number of dimensions. Representative instances of each technology are shown in Table 8-1. This chapter focuses on the italicized entries in the third-generation aural sector.

Exploring the audio design space

Audio alarms and signals of various types have been with us since long before there were computers, but even though music and visual arts are considered sibling muses, a disparity exists between the exploitation of sound and graphics in interfaces. (Most people think that it would be easier to be hearing- than sight-impaired, even though the incidence of disability-related cultural isolation is higher among the deaf than the blind.) For whatever reasons, the development of user interfaces has historically been focused more on visual modes than aural.

This imbalance is especially striking in view of the increasing availability of

Table 8-1 Generations and dimensions of I/O devices.

Generation/ dimension	Mode	Input	Output
First/1D	textual	keyboard	teletype monaural sound
Second/2D	planar	trackball, joystick mouse touchpad light pen	graphical displays stereo sound
	aural	speech recognition head-tracking	speech synthesis MIDI *spatial sound filtears*
Third/3D	haptic	3D joystick, spaceball DataGlove mouse, bird, bat wand handwriting recognition	tactile feedback: vibrating fingertips force-feedback devices Braille devices, tactor arrays
	olfactory	??	smell emitters
	gustatory	??	?
	visual	head- and eye-tracking	projection systems stereoscopes: head-mounted displays holograms vibrating mirrors

sound in current technology platforms. Sound is frequently included and utilized to the limits of its availability or affordability in personal computers. However, computer-aided exploitation of audio bandwidth is only beginning to rival that of graphics. General sound capability is slowly being woven into the fabric of applications. Indeed, some of these programs are inherently dependent on sound—voicemail, or voice annotation to electronic mail, teleconferencing, audio archiving—while other applications use sound to complement their underlying functionality. Table 8-2 (extended from Deatherage (1972, p. 124), and Sanders and McCormick (1987, p. 148)) lists some circumstances in which auditory displays are desirable.

Because of the cognitive overload that results from overburdening other systems (perhaps especially the visual), the importance of exploiting sound as a full citizen of the interface, developing its potential as a vital communication channel, motivates the exploration of both analogues to other modes of expression and also the evolution of models unique to audio. Computer interfaces present special needs and opportunities for audio communication.

This chapter reviews the evolving state of the art of non-speech audio

Table 8-2 Motivation for using sound as a display mode.

- when the origin of the message is itself a sound (voice, music)
- when other systems are overburdened (simultaneous presentation)
- when the message is simple and short (status reports)
- when the message will not be referred to later (time)
- when the message deals with events in time ("Your background process is finished.")
- when warnings are sent, or when the message prompts for immediate action ("Your printer is out of paper.")
- when continuously changing information of some type is presented (location, metric, or countdown)
- when speech channels are fully employed
- when a verbal response is required (compatibility of media)
- when illumination or disability limits use of vision (an alarm clock)
- when the receiver moves from one place to another (employing sound as a ubiquitous i/o channel)

interfaces, driving both spatial and non-spatial attributes. While we discuss both issues, our emphasis is on neither the backend, the particular hardware needed to manipulate sound, nor the frontend, the particular computer conventions used to specify the control. Rather, the chapter is primarily concerned with their integration—crafting effective matches between projected user desires and emerging technological capabilities.

CHARACTERIZATION AND CONTROL OF ACOUSTIC OBJECTS

Part of listening to a mixture of conversation or music is being able to appreciate the overall blend while also being able to hear the individual voices or instruments separately. This synthesis/decomposition duality is the opposite effect of masking: instead of sounds hiding each other, they are complementary and individually perceivable. For instance, musical instruments of contrasting color are used against each other. Localization effects contribute to this anti-masking by helping the listener distinguish separate sources, be they instruments in an ensemble or voices in the cacophony of a cocktail party (Blauert, 1983, p. 257).

Audio imaging is the creation of sonic illusions by manipulation of stereo channels. For instance, when classical music is recorded, the music from different instruments comes from distinctly different directions. The violins are on the listener's left; the cellos and double basses are on the right; the violas face the listener; and the percussion, woodwind, and brass are to the rear of the orchestra.

In a stereo system, the sound really comes from only the left and right transducers, whether headphones or loudspeakers. Typical audio systems project only a one-dimensional arrangement of the real or mixed sources. In traditional sound reproduction, the apparent direction from which a sound emanates is typically controlled by shifting the balance of the unmodified sound source between the left and right channels. However, this technique yields images that are diffuse, and located only between the speakers.

Table 8-3   Dimensions of sound.

- harmonic content
  - —pitch and register: tone, melody, harmony
  - —waveshape (sawtooth, square, triangle, . . .)
  - —timbre, filtears, vibrato, and equalization
- dynamics
  - —intensity/volume/loudness
  - —envelope: attack, decay, sustain, release (volume shape)
- timing
  - —duration
  - —tempo
  - —repetition rate
  - —duty cycle
  - —rhythm and cadence
  - —syncopation
- spatial location
  - —direction: azimuth, elevation
  - —distance/range
- ambience: presence, resonance, reverberance, spaciousness
- representationalism: literal, everyday ("auditory icons") ↔ abstract ("earcons")

Spatial sound involves technology that allows sound sources to have not only a left–right attribute (as in a conventional stereo mix), but up–down and back–forth qualities as well. It is related to, but goes beyond, systems like quadraphonics and surround sound.[1] Augmenting a sound system with spatial attributes opens new dimensions for audio, making spatial sound a potentially rich analogue of 3D graphics.

Clearly sound has many other qualities besides spatial attributes which contribute to its perceptual and cognitive organization. The various widely discussed (Pollack and Ficks, 1954; Baecker and Buxton, 1987, p. 396; Bly, 1987, p. 420; Mansur, 1987, p. 422) dimensions of sound generally include the attributes shown in Table 8-3. Just as with spatial dimensions, such dimensions can be utilized in an information display context to encourage the perceptual segregation and systematic organization of virtual sources within the interface. Following from Gibson's (1979) ecological approach to perception, the audible world can be conceived of as a collection of acoustic "objects." In addition to spatial location, various acoustic features—such as temporal onsets and offsets, timbre, pitch, intensity, and rhythm—can specify the identities of the objects and convey meaning about discrete events or ongoing actions in the world and their relationships to one another. One can systematically manipulate these features, effectively creating an auditory symbology which operates on a continuum from "literal" everyday sounds, such as the rattling of bottles being processed in a bottling plant (Gaver *et al.*, 1991) to a completely abstract mapping of statistical data into sound parameters (Smith *et al.*, 1990). Principles for design and synthesis can also be gleaned from the fields of music (Blattner *et al.*, 1989), psychoacoustics (Patterson, 1982), user interface design (Blattner and Dannenberg, 1992), and higher-level cognitive studies of the acoustical determinants of perceptual organization (Buxton *et al.*, 1989; Bregman, 1990).

Another obvious aspect of "everyday listening" (Gaver, 1986) is the fact that we live and listen in a three-dimensional world. Thus, a critical advantage of the binaural auditory system is that it allows us to monitor and identify sources of information from all possible locations, not just the direction of gaze. In fact, a good rule of thumb for knowing when to provide acoustic cues is to recall how we naturally use audition to gain information and explore the environment; that is, "the function of the ears is to point the eyes." The auditory system can provide a more coarsely tuned mechanism to direct the attention of our more finely tuned visual analyses, as suggested by the effective linkage between direction of gaze (eye and head movements) and localization accuracy (Perrott *et al.*, 1990; Strybel *et al.*, 1992). In fact, Perrott and his colleagues (Perrott *et al.*, 1991) have recently reported that aurally guided visual search for a target in a cluttered visual display is superior to unaided visual search, even for objects in the central visual field. This omnidirectional characteristic of acoustic signals will be especially useful in inherently spatial tasks, particularly when visual cues are limited and workload is high; for example, in air traffic control displays for the tower or cockpit (Begault and Wenzel, 1992).

Given multiple audio channels, a display[2] system needs a way of perceptually segmenting or distinguishing them from each other. A simple method is by just making the channels of interest louder than their siblings. Spatial sound enhances stream segregation by allowing auditory localization, invoking the "cocktail party effect." The cocktail party effect refers to a phenomenon described in the literature (Cherry, 1953; Arons, 1992) on binaural hearing in which sound source intelligibility is shown to improve when listening dichotically (with two ears), compared to monotically (with one ear). Thus, at a party with many simultaneous conversations, a mingler can still follow any particular exchange by filtering according to

- position
- speaker voice
- subject matter.

Similarly, someone listening to a song distinguishes the streams (voices, instruments, parts) by

- position
- tone/timbre
- melodic line and rhythm.

Spatial dimensions of sound

The goal of spatial sound synthesis is to project audio media into space by manipulating sound sources so that they assume virtual positions, mapping the source channel into three-dimensional space (the perceptual envelope around the sink[3]). These virtual positions enable auditory localization, a listener's psychological separation in space of the channels, via space-domain multiplexing. The simulation techniques being developed to achieve this goal depend critically on our understanding of the perceptual or psychoacoustical cues used by human listeners when localizing sounds in the real world.

Much of our understanding of human sound localization is based on the classic "duplex theory" (Lord Rayleigh, 1907) which emphasizes the role of two primary cues to location, interaural differences in time of arrival and interaural differences in intensity. The original proposal was that interaural intensity differences (IIDs) resulting from head-shadowing determine localization at high frequencies,while interaural time differences (ITDs) were thought to be important only for low frequencies (because of phase ambiguities occurring at frequencies greater than about 1500 Hz). Binaural research over the last few decades, however, points to serious limitations with this approach. For example, it has become clear that ITDs in high-frequency sounds are used if the signals have relatively slow envelope modulations. The duplex theory also cannot account for the ability of subjects to localize sounds along the median plane where interaural cues are minimal (e.g., see Blauert, 1983). Further, when subjects listen to sounds over headphones, they are usually perceived as being inside the head even though interaural temporal and intensity differences appropriate to an external source location are present (Plenge, 1974). Many studies now suggest that these deficiencies of the duplex theory reflect the important contribution to localization of the direction-dependent filtering which occurs when incoming sound waves interact with the outer ears, or pinnae. As sound propagates from a source (e.g., a loudspeaker) to a listener's ears, reflection and refraction effects tend to alter the sound in subtle ways, and the effect is dependent upon frequency. Such frequency-dependent effects, or filtering, also vary greatly with the direction of the sound source, and it is clear that listeners use such effects to discriminate one location from another. Experiments have shown that spectral shaping by the pinnae is highly direction-dependent (Shaw, 1974), that the absence of pinna cues degrades localization accuracy (Roffler and Butler, 1968; Gardner and Gardner, 1973), and that pinna cues are important for externalization or the "outside-the-head" sensation (Plenge, 1974; Durlach et al., 1992).

Such data suggest that perceptually veridical localization over headphones may be possible if this spectral shaping by the pinnae as well as the interaural difference cues can be adequately reproduced. There may be many cumulative effects on the sound as it makes its way to the ear drum, but all of these effects can be coalesced into a single filtering operation, much like the effects of an equalizer in a stereo system. The exact nature of this filter can be measured by a simple experiment in which an impulse (a single, very short sound pulse or click) is produced by a loudspeaker at a particular location. The acoustic shaping by the two ears is then measured by recording the outputs of small probe microphones placed inside an individual's (or an artificial head's; e.g., the KEMAR (Burkhardt and Sachs, 1975) or Neumann heads) ear canals (Figure 8-1). If the measurement of the two ears occurs simultaneously, the responses, when taken together as a pair of filters, include estimates of the interaural differences as well. Thus, this technique allows one to measure all of the relevant spatial cues together for a given source location, a given listener, and in a given room or environment.

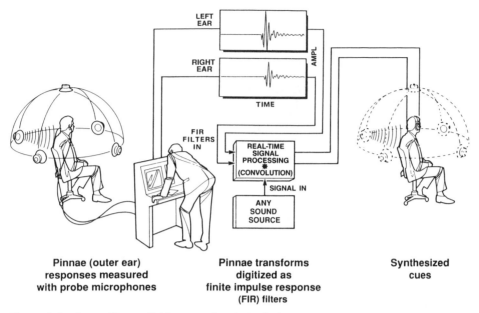

Figure 8-1   3D auditory display: synthesis technique.

Filters constructed from these ear-dependent characteristics are examples of finite impulse response (FIR; also known as tapped delay line) filters and are often referred to as **head-related transfer functions** (HRTFs). Here, HRTF-filtering in the frequency domain manifests as a point-by-point multiplication operation, while FIR-filtering in the time domain occurs via a somewhat more complex operation known as convolution. By filtering an arbitrary sound with these HRTF-based "earprints", it is possible to impose spatial characteristics on the signal such that it apparently emanates from the originally measured location. Of course, the localizability of a sound will also depend on other factors such as its original spectral content; narrowband (pure) tones are generally hard to localize, while broadband, impulsive sounds are the easiest to locate. Filtering with HRTF-based filters cannot increase the bandwidth of the original signal; it merely transforms frequency components that are already present.

A closely related issue to spectral content in the localizability of sound sources is their degree of familiarity. A variety of research indicates that (monaural) features such as peaks and valleys in the spectrum of a sound change systematically with location and appear to be the primary cues for elevation (Roffler and Butler, 1968; Blauert, 1969/1970; Butler and Helwig, 1983; Butler, 1987). Logically, in order for localization to be accurate, spatial cues other than the interaural cues—e.g., cues related to spectral shaping by the pinnae—must be interpreted in light of the original spectrum of the sound source. In effect, the listener must "know" *a priori* what the spectrum of a sound is in order to determine whether a particular feature was "shaped" by the effects of his/her ear structures or was simply present in the source spectrum. In the absence of other disambiguating information, many different spectra could be confused for the same location, and indeed this is often the case (Blauert, 1969/1970; Butler and Helwig, 1983), suggesting that listeners' *a priori* knowledge of source spectra is imperfect. Thus the perception of elevation and relative distance, which both depend heavily on the detection of spectral differences, tend to be superior for familiar signals like speech (Coleman, 1963; Blauert, 1983, p. 104; Begault and Wenzel, 1993). Similarly, spectral familiarity can be established through training (Batteau, 1967).

It should be noted that the spatial cues provided by HRTFs, especially those derived from simple anechoic (free-field, "dry," or echoless) environments, are not the only cues likely to be necessary to achieve veridical localization in a virtual display. Anechoic simulation is merely a first step, allowing a systematic study of the perceptual consequences of synthesizing spatial cues by using a less complex, and therefore more tractable, stimulus. For example, two kinds of error are usually observed in perceptual studies of localization when subjects are asked to judge the position of a stationary sound source in the free-field. One is a relatively small error in resolution ranging from about 1 to 20°, depending upon the experimental paradigm used to estimate localization acuity. In general these paradigms fall into three categories: methods of adjustment (Sandel *et al.*, 1955) which require the subjects to adjust the position of one source to match that of another; discrimination experiments such as those reported by Mills (1958, 1972) which ask subjects to detect whether two successive sounds have changed position; and absolute judgment paradigms which simply ask the subjects to identify the source location by methods such as verbal report or pointing (Stevens and Newman, 1936; Oldfield and Parker, 1984a, 1984b, 1986; Wightman and Kistler, 1989a, 1989b; Makous and Middlebrooks, 1990; Wenzel *et al.*, 1993). Discrimination experiments tend to be constrained primarily by peripheral sensory limitations and measure a just-noticeable difference (JND) or the sensitivity of the subject to various localization cues. Which localization cues are most relevant to a particular JND measurement will depend on the stimulus conditions. For example, discrimination errors are smallest for stimuli in the horizontal plane where the interaural cues are presumably the most important, with a slight auditory "fovea" in that acuity is best directly in front (about 1 to 5°) and worsens for locations out to the side (about 5 to 10°). Absolute judgment paradigms, on the other hand, may be more affected by factors like memory limitations and context effects, and thus are probably more closely related to the conditions that one generally experiences when localizing sounds in a virtual display (simply deciding "where is it?"). Error measures under these circumstances can be considerably larger (about 10 to 20° or more), especially for sources in the rear. There also seems to be a general tendency for errors in elevation to be somewhat larger than for azimuth, although this may depend upon the region of space relative to the listener that is being probed. Of course, error estimates will also be dependent in fairly complex ways upon the bandwidth, duration, spatial span, etc. of the stimuli being localized. For example, the classic study by Stevens and Newman (1936) showed that error magnitudes are dependent on the stimulus frequency, with the greatest errors occurring around 3000 Hz where the interaural phase and level cues are both weakest. For a more complete discussion of the many factors affecting localization acuity and sensitivity measures, see the recent review by Middlebrooks and Green (1991).

Another class of error observed in nearly all localization studies is the occurrence of front↔back reversals. These are judgments which indicate that a source in the front (rear) hemisphere was perceived by the listener as if it were in the rear (front) hemisphere. Reversal confusions in elevation, with up locations heard as down, and vice versa, have also been observed (Wenzel *et al.*, 1991, 1993). Although the reasons for such reversals are not completely understood, they are probably due in large part to the static nature of the stimulus and the ambiguities resulting from the so-called "cone of confusion" (Mills, 1972). Assuming a stationary, spherical model of the head and symmetrically located ear canals (without pinnae), a given interaural time or intensity difference will correlate ambiguously with the direction of a sound source, a conical shell describing the locus of all possible sources. Obviously, the true situation is more complicated; the head is not really a simple sphere with two symmetric holes. However, to a first approximation, the model does seem to predict the pattern of interaural cues actually measured for static sources (Kuhn, 1977; Middlebrooks *et al.*, 1989; Middlebrooks and Green, 1990). While the rigid sphere model is not the whole story, the observed ITD and IID data indicate that the interaural characteristics of the stimulus are inherently ambiguous. In the absence of other cues, both front↔back and up↔down reversals (in fact, confusions between any two points along a particular cone) would appear to be quite likely.

Several cues are thought to help in disambiguating the cones of confusion. One is the complex spectral shaping provided by the HRTFs as a function of location that was described above. For example, presumably because of the orientation and shell-like structure of the pinnae, high frequencies tend to be more attenuated for sources in the rear than for sources in the front (e.g., see Blauert (1983, pp. 107–16)). For stationary sounds, such cues would essentially be the only clue to disambiguating source location. With dynamic stimuli, however, the situation improves considerably. For example, some studies have shown that allowing or inducing head motion improves localization ability by substantially reducing the rate of reversals (Burger, 1958; Thurlow and Runge, 1967; Fisher and Freedman, 1968). With head motion, the listener can potentially disambiguate front/back locations by tracking changes in the magnitude of the interaural cues over time; for a given lateral head movement, ITDs and IIDs for sources in the front will change in the opposite direction compared to sources in the rear (Wallach, 1940).

Another type of localization error is known as in-head localization (IHL). That is, sources sometimes fail to externalize, particularly when the signals are presented over headphones, although IHL has also been observed for real sources (Toole, 1969; Plenge, 1974). The tendency to localize sound sources inside the head is increased if the signals are unfamiliar (Coleman, 1963; Gardner, 1968) or derived from an anechoic environment (Plenge, 1974). Thus, the use of familiar signals combined with cues that provide a sense of environmental context, such as the ratio of direct to reflected energy and other characteristics specific to enclosed spaces, may help to enhance the externalization of images (Coleman, 1963; Gardner, 1968; Laws, 1973; Plenge, 1974; Mershon and King, 1975; Mershon and Bowers, 1979). For example, Begault (1992) recently investigated the effects of synthetic reverberation on the perceived externalization of static, virtual sound sources. He found that, compared to anechoic stimuli, adding reverberant cues nearly eliminated IHL but tended to decrease localization accuracy while having no systematic effect on front↔back confusions. There is also some suggestion that head motion may also be a factor in externalization (Wenzel, 1992, p. 87).

Whether distance, the third dimension in a virtual acoustic display, can be reliably controlled beyond mere externalization is more problematic. It appears that humans are rather poor at judging the absolute distance of sound sources, and relatively little is known about the parameters which determine distance perception (Coleman, 1963; Laws, 1973; Mershon and King, 1975; Mershon and Bowers, 1979; Speigle and Loomis, 1993). Distance judgments depend at least partially on the relative intensities of sound sources, but the relationship is not a straightforward correspondence to the physical roll-off of intensity with distance; i.e., the inverse-square law, which implies a 6 dB decrease in intensity with each doubling of distance. For example, Begault (1991), has reported that a 9 dB increase in intensity is required to produce a halving of the apparent distance of a sound source. Also, as noted above, distance perception also depends heavily on factors like stimulus familiarity.

The addition of environmental effects can complicate the perception of location in other ways. Von Békésy (1960) reports that the spatial image of a sound source grows larger and increasingly diffuse with increasing distance in a reverberant environment, a phenomenon which may tend to interfere with the ability to judge the direction of the source. This problem may be mitigated by the phenomenon known as precedence (Wallach et al., 1949). In precedence, or the "rule of the first wavefront," the perceived location of a sound tends to be dominated by the direction of incidence of the original source even though later reflections could conceivably be interpreted as additional sources in different locations. The impact of the precedence effect is reduced by factors which strengthen the role of the succeeding wavefronts. For example, large enclosed spaces with highly reflective surfaces can result in reflections that are both intense enough and delayed enough (i.e., echoes) to act as "new" sound sources which can confuse the apparent direction of the original source.

However, just as we come to learn the characteristics of a particular room or concert hall, the localization of virtual sounds may improve if the listener is allowed to become familiar with sources as they interact in a particular artificial acoustic world. For example, perhaps simulation of an asymmetric room would tend to aid the listener in distinguishing front from rear locations by strengthening timbral differences between front and rear sources. By taking advantage of a head-tracker in realtime systems, the loop between the auditory, visual, vestibular, and kinesthetic systems can be closed, and we can study the effects of dynamic interaction with relatively complex, but known, acoustic environments. The specific parameters used in such models must be investigated carefully if localization accuracy is to remain intact. It may be possible to discover an optimal trade-off between environmental parameters which enhance externalization and distance perception while minimizing the impact of the resulting expansion of the spatial image which can interfere with the ability to judge the direction of the source.

The above discussion of the perception of localized sound sources is meant primarily to give a sense of the potential complexities involved in any attempt to synthesize both accurate and realistic spatial cues in a virtual acoustic display. See Middlebrooks and Green (1991), Moller (1992), and Wenzel (1992) for somewhat more detailed overviews of localization cues and their synthesis. For an extensive discussion of spatial sound in general, the reader is referred to the in-depth review by Blauert (1983).

Implementing spatial sound

Perhaps the most direct approach to simulating spatial sound distributes sources by physically locating loudspeakers in the place where each source is located, relative to the listener. These loudspeakers could be statically placed, or perhaps moved around by mechanical means. However, such an implementation is cumbersome and certainly not portable. Other approaches use analytic mathematical models of the pinna and other body structures (Genuit, 1986) in order to directly calculate acoustic responses or, alternatively, provide a simplified model of the essential features of previously measured responses of the ear (Kistler and Wightman, 1991). A third approach to accurate realtime spatialization, which is generally emphasized here, concentrates on digital signal processing (DSP) techniques for synthesizing spatial cues from direct measurements of head-related transfer functions (HRTFs).

By measuring, simulating, or modeling the important cues to localization represented in the HRTFs (usually with DSP), many scientists are developing ways of generating and controlling this multidimensional sound imagery (Chowning, 1970, 1977; Martel, 1986; Wenzel et al., 1988a, 1988b; Martens, 1989; Scott, 1989; Sorkin et al., 1989; Fisher, 1990; Kendall et al., 1990; Loomis et al., 1990; Wenzel et al., 1990; Begault and Wenzel, 1992; Wenzel, 1992; Wenzel et al., 1993). The goal of such a sound spatializer is to create the impression that the sound is coming from different sources and different places, just like one would hear "in person." Such a device assigns each source a virtual position with respect to the sink, or listener, and simulates the corresponding auditory positional cues. A display based on this technology exploits the human ability quickly and subconsciously to localize sound sources.

The most frequently used approach to spatial sound generation employs a hardware- or software-based convolution engine that convolves a monaural input signal with pairs of (FIR) digital audio filters to produce output signals for presentation over stereo loudspeakers or headphones. As discussed above, binaural localization cues may be captured by HRTFs, measured for the head and pinna (outer ear) of human or artificial heads in an anechoic environment. For each spherical direction, a left–right pair of these transfer functions is measured, transformed to the time domain, and then stored as FIR filter coefficients (Kendall and Martens, 1984; Gehring, 1987; McKinley and Ericson, 1988; Richter and Persterer, 1989; Wenzel, 1992).

The anechoic implementation of spatial sound described above is often called 'dry'; it includes no notion of a virtual room, and hence no echoes. Conversely, spatial reverberation is a 'wet' technique for simulating the acoustic information used by people listening to sounds in natural environments. A spatial reverberation system creates an artificial ambient acoustic environment by simulating echoes consistent with the placement of both the source and the sink (listener) within a virtual room.

There are two classes of generated echoes: early reflections, which are discretely generated (delayed), and late-field reverberation, which are continuous and statistically averaged. The early reflections are the particular echoes generated by the source, and the late-field reverberation is the non-specific ambience of the listening environment. The early reflections off the floor, walls, and ceiling, provide indirect sound to the listener which can have important perceptual consequences. For example, von Békésy (1960), Mershon and King (1975), Chowning (1977), Mershon and Bowers (1979), Kendall and Martens (1984), and others have demonstrated that the ratio of direct to indirect sound can influence the perceived distance of sound sources.

In practice, room modeling is often limited to rectangular prismatic rooms. This symmetry allows an algorithm such as direct ray-tracing to be used to efficiently determine the propagation delay and direction of individual reflections, which are then spatialized, as if they were separate sources. Each separately spatialized audio source, incident or reflected, requires processing by a separate pair of binaural transfer functions.[4] Late-field reverberation reflects the ambience of the virtual auditorium or listening room. Reverberant implementations of spatial sound, as discussed or instantiated by Kendall and Martens (1984), Kendall et al. (1986a, 1986b), and Martens (1987), employ a recursive, or infinite impulse response (IIR) section to yield dense global reverberation effects. A filter that combines early reflections with late-field reverberation is sometimes called TDR, for tapped-delay-plus-recirculation. The simulation thus models cues to perceived sound direction, sound distance, and room characteristics. This combination of high-order recursive and non-recursive filters enables a spatial reverberation system to implement descriptions of such characteristics as room dimensions and wall absorption, as well as time-varying source and listener positions. Thus, given a monophonic sound source and a specification of source and sink position and motion in a model room, the spatial reverberator approximates the sound field arriving at the model listener's ear drums. In general, however, most of the realtime systems currently available do not implement the full complement of room response characteristics outlined above. Such room modeling requires enormous computational resources and is only beginning to be developed in truly interactive, realtime displays.

Crystal River Engineering Convolvotron

The Crystal River Convolvotron^{TM} is a convolution engine (Wenzel et al., 1988b) that spatializes sound by filtering audio channels with transfer functions that simulate positional effects (see Wenzel (1992)). Other recent devices include the Alphatron and Acoustetron II which are based on lower-cost DSP chips and reduced-complexity algorithms and the Snapshot system which allows one to quickly measure individualized HRTFs in any environment. Specifically, HRTFs in the form of FIRs, are measured using techniques adapted from Mehrgardt and Mellert (1977). Although similar in principle to the impulse response method described earlier, the measurement is actually made with trains of pseudo-random noisebursts to improve the signal-to-noise ratio of the responses. Small probe microphones are placed near each eardrum of a human listener who is seated in an anechoic chamber (Wightman and Kistler, 1989a). Wide-band test stimuli are presented from one of 144 equidistant locations in the free-field (non-reverberant) environment; a different pair of impulse responses is measured for each location in the spherical array at intervals of 15° in azimuth and 18° in elevation (elevation range: −36 to +54°). HRTFs are estimated by deconvolving (mathematically dividing out) the effects of the loudspeakers, test stimulus, and microphone responses from the recordings made with the probe microphones (Wightman and Kistler, 1989a). The advantage of this technique is that it preserves the complex pattern of interaural differences over the entire spectrum of the stimulus, capturing the effects of filtering by the pinnae, head, shoulders, and torso. In order to synthesize localized sounds, a map of "location filters" is constructed from all 144 pairs of FIR filters by first transforming them to the frequency domain, removing the spectral effects of the headphones to be used during playback using Fourier techniques, and then transforming back to the time domain. An overview of the perceptual viability of the basic synthesis technique can be found in Wenzel (1992).

In the Convolvotron, designed by Scott Foster of Crystal River Engineering (Foster, 1990), the map of corrected FIR filters is downloaded from a host computer (IBM-compatible PC) to the dual-port memory of a realtime digital signal processor (Figure 8-2). This set of two printed-circuit boards converts one or more monaural analog inputs to digital signals at a rate of 50 kHz with 16-bit resolution. Each data stream is then convolved with filter coefficients (128 to 512 coefficients/ear; 24-bit integer arithmetic) determined by the coordinates of the desired target locations and the position of the listener's head, "placing" each input signal in the perceptual 3-space of the listener. The resulting data streams are mixed, converted to left and right analog signals, and presented over headphones. The current configuration allows up to four independent and simultaneous anechoic sources with an aggregate computational speed of more than 300 million multiply-accumulate instructions per second (MIPS). This processing speed is also sufficient for interactively simulating a single source plus six first-order reflections (28 sources and reflections in the Acoustetron™, a four-Convolvotron system in a single host computer) with variable surface absorption characteristics in relatively small reverberant environments with head-tracking (Foster et al., 1991; Shinomiya et al., 1993). The hardware design can also be scaled upward to accommodate additional sources and longer filter lengths required for simulating larger enclosures. The Beachtron, a less costly version of the system for the PC, is

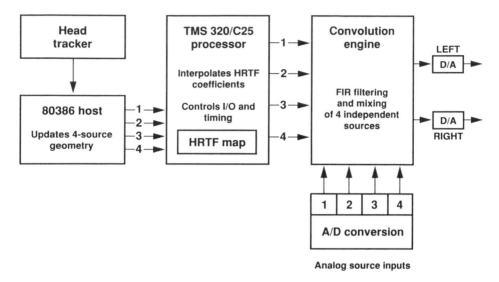

Figure 8-2   The Convolvotron: high-speed realtime digital signal processor.

capable of spatializing two audio input channels (comparable to Focal Point, described later). Currently, this system is anechoic and uses minimum-phase approximations of HRTFs (Kistler and Wightman, 1991; Wightman *et al.*, 1992), which allow a considerable reduction in filter size with minimal perceptual disruption (75 coefficients/ear, 16-bit conversion, 44.1 kHz sampling rate). The Beachtron also includes an onboard Proteus/1xR synthesizer and MIDI (**m**usical **i**nstrument **d**igital **i**nterface) control.

Motion trajectories and static locations at greater resolution than the empirical measurements are simulated by selecting the four measured positions nearest to the desired target location and interpolating with linear weighting functions (Wenzel and Foster, 1993). The interpolation algorithm effectively computes a new coefficient at the sampling interval (about every 20 μs) so that changes in position are free from artifacts like clicks or switching noises. When integrated with a magnetic head-tracking system (like Polhemus (1987)), the listener's head position can be monitored in realtime so that the sources are stabilized in fixed locations or in motion trajectories relative to the user. Again, such head-coupling helps enhance the simulation, since head movements are important for localization (Wallach, 1940; Thurlow and Runge, 1967). This degree of interactivity, especially coupled with smooth motion interpolation and simulation of simple reverberant environments, is apparently unique to the Convolvotron system. In addition, all source code is provided to facilitate the Convolvotron's use as a research tool.

As with any system required to compute data "on-the-fly," the term "realtime" is a relative one. The Convolvotron, including the host computer, has a computational delay of about 30–40 ms, depending upon such factors as the number of simultaneous sources, the duration of the HRTFs used as filters, and the complexity of the source geometry. An additional latency of at least

50 ms is introduced by the head-tracker.[5] This accumulation of computational delays has important implications for how well the system can simulate realistic moving sources or realistic head motion. At the maximum delay, the Convolvotron updates to a new location about every 90 ms (including a 50 ms delay from a low-cost headtracker). This directional update interval, in turn, corresponds to an angular resolution of about 32° when the relative source–listener speed is $360° \, s^{-1}$, 16° at $180° \, s^{-1}$, and so on. Such delays may or may not result in a perceptible lag, depending upon how sensitive humans are to changes in angular displacement (the minimum audible movement angle) for a given source velocity. Recent work on the perception of auditory motion by Perrott and others using real sound sources (moving loudspeakers) suggests that these computational latencies are acceptable for moderate velocities. For example, for source speeds ranging from 8 to $360° \, s^{-1}$, minimum audible movement angles ranged from about 4 to 21°, respectively, for a 500 Hz tone-burst (Perrott, 1982; Perrott and Tucker, 1988). Thus, slower relative velocities are well within capabilities of the Convolvotron, while speeds approaching $360° \, s^{-1}$ may begin to result in perceptible delays, especially when multiple sources or larger filters (e.g., simulations of reverberant rooms) are being generated.

Gehring Research Focal Point

Focal Point[TM] (Gehring, 1987, 1990) comprises two different binaural localization technologies, Focal Point Types 1 and 2. In most Focal Point products the audio is 44.1 kHz sampling rate with 16-bit CD quality. Focal Point Type 1 is the original Focal Point technology, utilizing time-domain convolution with HRTF-based impulse responses for anechoic simulation. It performs binaural convolution in realtime on any audio signal and is portable to most DSP and RISC (reduced instruction set computer) environments; Motorola DSP-based versions for the PC and Macintosh platforms are widely used. Several sets of HRTFS have been demonstrated over the years Focal Point has been available. (One set was measured by the Computer Music Group at Northwestern University using a KEMAR mannequin (Burkhardt and Sachs, 1975).) The current Focal Point HRTFs provide neutral timbre, suitable for music, entertainment, and VR applications.

Typically, Focal Point Type 1 software is downloaded into the DSP upon startup and then updated only when a source is moved; audio processing continues without host CPU interaction, except to reposition a source (by setting three integers). Updating the transfer function in the DSP has a latency of about 3–6 ms, which compares favorably with known visual displays. This update rate, which can be in excess of 300 Hz, is suitable for rapid source motion with respect to the listener.

The Mac and PC versions of Focal Point Type 1 are encapsulated; transfer function synthesis is performed within Focal Point, rather than by the host CPU. This means the entire host resource is available for other applications, such as soundfile playback through Focal Point, direct-to-disk recording concurrently with Focal Point binaural processing, or 3D graphics. The PC version is available as a consumer product.

Focal Point Type 2 (patent pending) is a Focal Point implementation in which sounds are preprocessed offline, creating interleaved soundfiles which can then be positioned in 3D in realtime upon playback. Compared to realtime convolution systems such as Focal Point Type 1, Type 2 is very economical; DSP and other high-speed processing are not required. Although sounds must be preprocessed in advance, Type 2 positioning is very fast, since no convolution pipeline delay is involved and positioning latency is measured in microseconds. Such a process also multiplies the storage requirements of the original sound sample, since a new, spatialized, sample is generated (offline) for each possible position. Type 2 can be used on almost any platform or soundcard with stereo audio capability.

Focal Point Types 1 and 2 can also be MIDI-controlled, allowing notes and sounds to be interactively positioned during musical performance using the many MIDI-based software and hardware products. Focal Point development packages typically include source code and sample C projects for several applications, including headtracking, external control via an RS-232 link, and simultaneous soundfile playback.

AKG CAP (Creative Audio Processor) 340M

A kind of binaural mixing console, CAP (Creative Audio Processor) 340M, has been developed by AKG in Austria (AKG, 1991), based partially on work by Blauert (1984). The system is aimed at applications like audio recording, acoustic design, and psychoacoustic research (Richter and Persterer, 1989). This system is rather large, involving an entire rack of digital signal processors and related hardware, with up to 32 channels that can be independently spatialized in azimuth and elevation along with variable specification of room response characteristics. The sampling rate of the system is 50 kHz with 16-bit floating point conversion (16-bit mantissa plus 3-bit exponent). FIR filters of 100 coefficients per ear are convolved in the time domain with an aggregate computational speed of 340 MFLOPS (millions of floating-point operations per second) on 32-bit floating point arithmetic. The CAP 340M's room simulation algorithm appears to include the ability to impose realtime directional (HRTF) characteristics on the reflected images as well as the direct path, as is the case in the Convolvotron. It also allows simulation of late reverberation using IIR filters. A collection of HRTFs is offered, derived from measurements taken in the ear canals of both artificial heads and individual subjects. A more recent system, the Binaural Audio Processor (BAP 1000), simulates an ideal control room for headphone reproduction using realtime convolution with up to four binaural (HRTF-based) filters (two direct paths plus two mirror-image reflections). The user also has the option of having his/her individual transforms programmed onto a PROM card (Persterer, 1991). Interestingly, AKG's literature mentions that best results are achieved with individualized transforms. So far, the system has not been integrated with interactive head-tracking, so data regarding its motional capabilities are currently not available.

Similar projects in Europe are based on the most recent efforts of Blauert, Poesselt, Lehnert and their colleagues at the Ruhr University at Bochum,

Germany (Boerger *et al.*, 1977; Lehnert and Blauert, 1989; Poesselt *et al.*, 1986). The group at Bochum has been working on a prototype DSP system, again a kind of binaural mixing console, whose proposed features include realtime convolution of HRTFs for up to four sources, interpolation between transforms to simulate motion, and room modeling. The group has also devoted substantial effort to measuring HRTFs for both individual subjects and artificial heads (e.g., the Neumann head), as well as developing computer simulations of transforms.

Head Acoustics

Another researcher in Germany, Klaus Genuit, has founded HEAD Acoustics to develop spatial audio systems. Genuit and his colleagues have also produced a realtime, eight-channel binaural mixing console using anechoic simulations as well as a new version of an artificial head (Gierlich and Genuit, 1989; Genuit *et al.*, 1992). The eight binaural channels can also be adapted to simulate simple room characteristics using a direct path plus up to seven first-order reflections. Genuit's work is particularly notable for his development of a structurally based model of the acoustic effects of the pinnae (e.g., Genuit, 1986). That is, rather than using measured HRTFs, Genuit has developed a parameterized, mathematical description (based on Kirchhoff's diffraction integrals) of the acoustic effects of the pinnae, ear canal resonances, torso, shoulder, and head. The effects of the structures have been simplified; for example, the outer ears are modeled as three cylinders of different diameters and length. The parameterization of the model adds some flexibility to this technique and Genuit states that the calculated transforms are within the variability of directly measured HRTFs, although no data on the perceptual viability of the model is mentioned. Also, since data can be calculated directly, the use of such a parameterized model may obviate the need to be concerned with the required spatial density of measured HRTFs or the nature of the interpolation between measurements needed to achieve smooth motion.

Roland Sound Space (RSS) processor

Roland has developed a system known as the Roland Sound Space (RSS) processing system which attempts to provide realtime spatialization capabilities for both headphone and stereo loudspeaker presentation (Chan, 1991). The basic RSS system allows independent placement of up to four sources using time domain convolution (24-bit arithmetic) with FIR filters based on anechoic measurements of HRTFs for an individual human. Details regarding the length of the filters, the spatial density of the HRTF measurements, and methods of interpolation are not given. The sampling rate is switchable between 44.1 and 48 kHz with four 18-bit A/D converters and eight (four stereo pairs) 20-bit D/A converters. Spatial placement is controlled by MIDI input or by two rotary dials per channel which independently control azimuth and elevation.

Since the RSS is aimed primarily at loudspeaker presentation, it incorporates a technique known as transaural processing, or crosstalk cancellation between the stereo speakers. This additional filtering process is required to compensate for the fact that, in effect, speaker presentation causes the sound to be processed by HRTFs "twice": once by the digital HRTF filters used to manipulate the spatial illusion, and once by the listener's own ears. The transaural technique "divides out" or equalizes the effects of the speaker crosstalk, so that the transfer functions for the frontal direction become flat at the listener's ear canals. This technique seems to allow an adequate spatial impression to be achieved. As Chan (1991) and many others have noted for such speaker presentation systems, localization accuracy suffers as soon as the listener deviates from a listening region near a locus of points equidistant from the two speakers (the "sweet spot"). A sense of increased auditory "spaciousness" (relative to normal stereo techniques) remains relatively intact, however, even for listening positions off the bisector. Chan (1991) also notes that elevation was very difficult to discern with the RSS system. The RSS system can also be used for realtime control of spatial sound over headphones in a similar manner to the systems described above by disabling the transaural processing.

Mixels

The realtime systems described above provide a wide range of simulation capabilities which could be employed as the backend of an interface for a spatial auditory display. Thus, the specific attributes of a particular software control interface may or may not be instantiated, depending on which system is used to generate the spatial audio effects. For example, the simplest and least expensive systems available, such as a single-channel version of the Focal Point or Beachtron systems, will allow only the simplest of anechoic simulations for one or two image sources. Conversely, the large and no doubt expensive array of equipment represented by the CAP 340M could potentially provide a much richer instantiation of a virtual acoustic display.

It is also important to note, however, that the perceptual viability of most of the systems described above (except for the Convolvotron) has not been demonstrated beyond the manufacturers' rather general claims about performance. If such a system is intended for research or other applications that require accurate localization, it is important that the user have access to details about the nature of the simulation techniques and algorithms used in the device. If, on the other hand, simple spatial effects or impression are the primary goal, then a more "black-box" type of approach may be sufficient. Alternatively, a researcher may need or wish to independently test the perceptual validity of a particular device. Such testing will probably require at least some degree of access to the internal controls or software of the spatialization system.

Rather than delve more deeply into particular spatial audio systems, which will no doubt develop as rapidly in the future as the rest of computing technology, the remainder of this chapter concentrates on the nature of the control interfaces that will need to be developed to take full advantage of these new capabilities.

The assumption is that many individually spatialized audio channels will become available so that sound can be modeled in a granular fashion to create a "circumambience." The number of channels corresponds to the degree of spatial polyphony, simultaneously spatialized sound sources. By way of analogy to pixels and voxels, we sometimes call these atomic sounds "mixels," acronymic for sound **mix**ing **el**ements, since they form the raster across which a soundscape is projected, defining the granularity of control.

Non-spatial dimensions and auditory symbology

Auditory icons (Gaver, 1986) are acoustic representations of naturally occurring events that caricature the action being represented. For instance, in the Macintosh SonicFinder (Gaver, 1989), a metallic thunk represents a file being tossed into the trashcan upon deletion, and a liquid gurgling signifies a file being copied. "Earcons" (Sumikawa *et al.*, 1986; Blattner *et al.*, 1989; Blattner and Greenberg, 1989) are elaborated auditory symbols which compose motifs into artificial non-speech language, phrases distinguished by rhythmic and tonal patterns. Earcons may be combined (by juxtaposing these motifs), transformed (by varying the timbre, register, and dynamics), or inherited (abstracting a property). Infosound (Sonnenwald *et al.*, 1990) allows the combination of stored musical sequences and sound effects to be associated with application events, like Prokofiev's use of musical themes in *Peter and the Wolf*.

Auditory icons and earcons are classes along a continuum of display styles, from literal event or data representation to dynamic, symbolic representation, which may be more or less abstract. "Filtears" (Cohen, 1989, 1993b; Cohen and Ludwig, 1991a, 1991b), which depend on the distinction between sources and sinks, are one way of spanning this spectrum.

Sound is malleable under an infinite range of manipulation. Voice and music in particular can be gracefully distorted without loss of intelligibility or euphony. Even though audio channels can be perceptually segmented by virtual location, it is also important to have other attribute cues independent of direction and distance. Filtears are a class of such cues, audio filters implemented as separate attribute cues, superimposing information on sound signals by perceptually multiplexing the audio bandwidth.

Imagine a user telenegotiating with several parties at once, including trusted advisors. Besides whatever spatial array of the various conferees, the user might want to give the advisors' voices a *sotto voce* attribute, perhaps by making their voices sound like whispers, imparting a suggestion of a private utterance, thereby tagging their voices as confidants. If some of the parties (perhaps including some of the advisors) are from outside the user's organization, their voices might be given an *outside* attribute, perhaps by inhibiting any "indoors-suggesting" reverberation, so that their voices seem to come from outside the building. These two separate dimensions of control could be used, separately or together (as in an "off-stage" whisper), to sonically label the voice channels, organizing them mnemonically. (Neither of these examples has actually been implemented yet. The filtears that have been deployed are detailed on page 321.)

Filtears are potentially useful for user interfaces because, unlike an audio zoom feature that simply makes the chosen speaker louder, the extended attributes introduced by spatial sound and filtears are separate from conventional dimensions of control, and they can be adjusted independently. Filtears can be thought of as sonic typography: placing sound in space can be likened to putting written information on a page, with audio emphasis equivalent to *italic*izing or em**bold**ening. Filtears embellish audio channels; they depend on the distinction between source and sink, and warp the channels in some way that is different from parameterizing an original signal.

It is important to note that, while filtears are intended to be perceptually orthogonal to other cues, such independence is difficult to achieve. Sound attributes interact in complex and often unpredictable ways, and such interactions must be taken into account when designing auditory symbologies and implementing them with filtear-type controllers/transformers.

RESEARCH APPLICATIONS

Virtual acoustic displays featuring spatial sound can be thought of as enabling two performance advantages:

Situational awareness   Omnidirectional monitoring via direct representation of spatial information reinforces or replaces information in other modalities, enhancing one's sense of presence or realism.

Multiple channel segregation   By levering off "natural noise cancellation" of the previously described cocktail party effect, spatial sound systems improve intelligibility, discrimination, and selective attention among audio sources in a background of noise, voices, or other distractions. Such enhanced stream segregation allows the separation of multiple sounds into distinct "objects."

Various application fields that exploit these enhanced capabilities are described below.

Sonification

Sonification can be thought of as auditory visualization, and has been explored by scientists (Bly, 1982; Mezrich *et al.*, 1984; Scaletti and Craig, 1991; Blattner and Dannenberg, 1992, ch. 6) as a tool for analysis, for example, presenting multivariate data as auditory patterns. Because visual and auditory channels can be independent of each other, data can be mapped differently to each mode of perception, and auditory mappings can be employed to discover relationships that are hidden in the visual display. This involves some sort of mapping of the analyzed data to attributes like those outlined in Table 8-3. Various researchers (Kendall and Freed, 1988; Kendall, 1990, 1991; Wenzel *et al.*, 1990; Wenzel, 1994) suggest using spatial sound as a component of sonification, and researchers have designed tools for presenting data as an integrated visual and auditory display, whose stereophonic display correlates the sound with position on the monitor. Exvis (Smith *et al.*, 1990) interprets a scatterplot as a texture, a dense distribution of data, and then translates that texture into sound.

Auditory displays for visually disabled users

There is also increasing interest in providing auditory displays for visually disabled users (Vanderheiden, 1989; Loomis *et al.*, 1993). Some researchers, including Lunney *et al.* (1983), Mansur (1984), Mansur *et al.* (1985), have experimented with mapping *x–y* graphs to sound, to convey their information to blind users. An "auditory screen" (Edwards, 1987, 1988) uses a window, icon, menu, pointing device (WIMP) interface to associate musical sound and synthesized speech with tiled screen areas. SeeHear (Nielsen *et al.*, 1988) mapped visual signals from optically scanned objects into localized auditory signals. The Sonic Navigator (Setton, 1990) localizes synthesized speech to the location of the window being read.

Teleconferencing

If a voice can be likened to a long arm, with which one can reach across a room or down a flight of stairs to effectively tap someone on the shoulder, then the telephone lengthens that arm even further, stretching one's presence across continents, oceans, and beyond. Many scientists are exploring computer-controlled teleconferencing systems (Shimada and Suzuki, 1987; Cohen and Koizumi, 1991c, 1992c; Masaki *et al.*, 1991; Miyoshi and Koizumi, 1991; Shimada and Yamasaki, 1991; Tanigawa *et al.*, 1991; Koizumi *et al.*, 1992). Major thrusts have protocols for invoking a rendezvous (Kraemer and King, 1986), suitable architectures for deploying such systems (Sarin and Greif, 1985; Lantz, 1986; Ludwig, 1989; Koizumi, 1991; Takemura *et al.*, 1992), and graphical control (Stefik *et al.*, 1986, 1987; Addeo *et al.*, 1988; Sonnenwald *et al.*, 1990; Kobayashi and Siio, 1993).

Music

Musical applications (Moore, 1983; Kendall and Martens, 1984; Boulez and Gerzso, 1988; Bernardini and Otto, 1989; Cohen and Koizumi, 1991a, 1993a; Lezcano, 1993) feature bouncing and dancing sound. Many spatializers have MIDI interfaces, allowing integration into musical systems. A listener can wander among a marching band or an embracing chord; a composer could program choreography for sonic dancers.

Virtual reality and architectural acoustics

VR systems are computer-generated interactive environments utilizing (typically head-mounted display) 3D graphic scenes and soundscapes, featuring a manual control (Foley, 1987). They are characterized by an intimate link between display and control, in which the user inhabits the system. Various VR researchers, including Fisher *et al.* (1986, 1988); Wenzel *et al.* (1990), have incorporated stereophonic output into their head-mounted display. Direct representation of room geometry and absorption/reflection properties allows sonification of architectural acoustics for acoustical CAD/CAM (Astheimer, 1993; Shinomiya *et al.*, 1993).

Telerobotics and augmented audio reality

"Augmented reality" (Caudell and Mizell, 1992; Feiner *et al.*, 1993a, 1993b; Wellner *et al.*, 1993) is used to describe hybrid presentations that overlay computer-generated imagery on top of real scenes. Augmented audio reality extends this notion to include sonic effects, overlaying computer-generated sounds on top of more directly acquired audio signals. Telepresence delegates a robot slave to act on behalf of the human master. Controlled from afar by a pilot wearing effectors corresponding to robot's sensors, the puppet, a surrogate with feedback, could venture into hazardous environments (fires, toxic waste, nuclear power plants, etc.). By juxtaposing and mixing 'sampled' and 'synthetic' transmissions, scientists are exploring the relationship between telepresence and VR audio presentations: telepresence manifests as the actual configuration of sources in a sound field, as perceived by a dummy-head, say; VR as the perception yielded by HRTF filtering of virtual sources with respect to virtual sinks (Cohen *et al.*, 1993).

Team communication. If several telerobots are working together, their pilots will likely want to communicate with each other. Instead of equipping each robot with a speaker, and letting each operator speak through the respective robot mouth, it is better to 'short-circuit' the communications path, transmitting a pilot's utterance to the other pilots directly, directionalizing to preserve the spatial consistency of the telepresence (Aoki *et al.*, 1992; Cohen *et al.*, 1992).

Sonic cursor. In telemonitoring, one wants to identify the location of a sound object. Using an augmented audio reality system, one could switch between a telemonitored binaural (dummy-head transmitted) and rendered source (synthesized by binaural DSP) to identify the location.

Synesthetic alarm. Synesthesia is the act of experiencing one sense modality as another, and can be used to further blur the distinction between actual and artificial worlds. A telerobot equipped to enter hazardous areas might have infrared or radiation meters. These meters could be thresholded, rendering the danger points as auditory alarms, easily superimposed on the auditory soundscape captured by the robot's ears.

INTERFACE CONTROL VIA AUDIO WINDOWS

"Audio windows" is an auditory-object manager, one potentially powerful implementation of a user interface (frontend) to an audio imaging system. Here, the generalized control model of a window is (by analogy to graphical windows, as in a desktop metaphor) an organizational vehicle in the interface, and has nothing to do with room acoustics. Researchers (Ludwig and Pincever, 1989; Ludwig *et al.*, 1990; Cohen and Ludwig, 1991a, 1991b; Cohen and Koizumi, 1991b, 1992a; Fujino *et al.*, 1991; Koizumi and Cohen, 1993) have been studying applications and implementation techniques of audio windows for use in providing multimedia communications. The general idea is to permit multiple simultaneous audio sources, such as in a teleconference, to coexist in a modifiable display without clutter or user stress. The distribution of sounds in space is intended to realize some of the same kinds of benefits achieved by distribution of visual objects in graphical user interfaces.

A powerful audio imaging user interface would allow the positions of the audio channels to be arbitrarily set and adjusted, so that the virtual positions of the sinks and sources may be constantly changing as they move around each other and within a virtual room. By using an audio window system as a binaural directional mixing console, a multidimensional pan pot,[6] users can set parameters reflecting these positions. Members of a teleconference altering these parameters may experience the sensation of wandering around a conference room, among the teleconferees. Music lovers at a live or recorded concert could actively focus on a particular channel by sonically hovering over the shoulder of a musician in a virtual concert hall. Minglers at a virtual cocktail party might freely circulate. Sound presented in this dynamically spatial fashion is as different from conventional mixes as sculpture is from painting.

Spatial sound applications can be classified according to source (speaker) and sink (listener) mobility. The simplest spatial sound systems allow neither the sources nor the sinks to move. This kind of configuration is still useful for separating channels and, in fact, offers a good checkpoint to spatial sound applications under development; i.e. the several participants in a conference call would project distinct sound images to each other, consistent with their relative virtual (if static) locations. With such a presentation, a user could more easily focus attention on a single speaker or instrument, especially with an audio spotlight (described later).

A simple demonstration of this functionality on a conventional system features three users, each with two telephones, calling each other cyclically (Figure 8-3). Each user's holding the calling and called handsets to different ears demonstrates one application of *stereotelephonics* (Cohen, 1987), the use of stereo effects in telephones.

A system in which the sources are stationary, but the listeners move about (like visitors at a museum) would be useful for displaying orientation, the same way offshore ships get cues from signaling lighthouses, and approaching airplanes use beacons sent from a control tower. The sources might always come from the North, serving as an audio compass, or they might always "point" down, acting like a sonic horizon (Gehring, 1988).

If the sources may move around a static listener, it is as if the user were attending a theatre performance or movie. Air traffic controllers looking out of the control tower perceive the circling airplanes this way, as do seated patrons at a restaurant with strolling violinists. Applications of this class might include an *audio cursor* (Cohen and Ludwig, 1991a; Cohen, 1993b; Cohen et al., 1993), a pointer into 3-space to attract the static user's attention (described later).

Giving both sources and sinks full mobility enables a general spatial data management system in which users can browse through a dataworld of movable

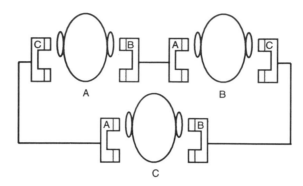

Figure 8-3   Stereotelephonics and 3-way cyclic conferencing.

objects. Teleconferencing applications are perhaps the most obvious example, but more fanciful modes of dance or social intercourse, say, are easily imagined.

INTERFACE DESIGN ISSUES: CASE STUDIES

The issues introduced above are illustrated by three case studies of actual audio-imaging systems, described in the following sections: two employ an egocentric metaphor combined with gestural control, the third is exocentric and controlled graphically.

VEOS is a complete VR system, featuring an immersive frontend, via a head-mounted display and wand, driving both stereographic and stereophonic devices. VEOS/FERN, Mercury, and the Sound Renderer and the Audio Browser (described below) were all developed at HITL, the Human Interface Technology Laboratory at the University of Washington.

Handy Sound also has a gestural frontend. It implements an egocentric perspective (in which users arrange spatial sound sources around themselves), and features a purely manual interface (requiring no keyboard or mouse) driving (via direct manipulation through posture and gesture interpretation) a purely auditory backend (requiring no CRT or visual display); it can be used by blind people as well as by sighted.

MAW is implemented as an exocentric GUI in which users can arrange both themselves and spatial sound objects in configurable rooms. MAW extends conventional WIMP idioms to audio windows. Its features include draggably rotating icons and a hierarchical synthesis/decomposition tool, allowing the spatial configuration of audio channels to reflect their logical organization.

VEOS and Mercury (written with Brian Karr)

VEOS (acronymic for virtual environment operating system) is a platform-independent distributed processing package which combines many separate computers into a networked virtual multiprocessor. This extensible system handles message passing, pattern matching and program control. Combined with FERN (fractal entity relativity node), the system provides distributed database and process management, giving virtual world developers location transparency in the distributed system. FERN is fundamentally a resource administrator for distributed simulation.

Mercury is a self-contained module that interfaces to the virtual environment database, handling both behavior sensing and rendering. The Mercury interface decouples the participant interface from the database, allowing performance to approach the limit of the rendering and position tracking hardware. Similarly, this removes the responsibility for display tasks from the database, allowing both the database (VEOS/FERN) and the renderers to operate at the fastest possible speed.

Mercury maintains an internal representation of the most recent state of the database. The participant experiences this internal representation and is able to move about and interact with entities within it at greater frame rates. Therefore, even though the state of entities in the database may change relatively slowly, the participant can smoothly navigate and interact with objects in the environment. Also, since the renderers are closely coupled with the behavior sensors and the instantaneous state of the external database, aural and visual images are closely registered. Finally, Mercury and its renderers are implemented in a modular fashion, which allows them to be used with almost any VR system. Systems that render new frames only after an entire event loop can benefit most from this approach. Mercury can also be used as an interface to other kinds of software, such as CAD modelers (see Figure 8-4).

Sound Renderer implementation

The Sound Renderer is a software package that provides an interface between a VR system and peripheral audio equipment. Such equipment currently includes:

- spatialization hardware such as the Convolvotron
- sound generation devices such as samplers or synthesizers
- effects processors such as reverberation units.

The current implementation allows for the control of four simultaneous, independent audio sources for each participant using serial communications. The Convolvotron (described on page 302) and geometry software on its host computer are controlled using a serial protocol. Additionally, the Sound Renderer uses the MIDI protocol for control of common audio devices. Some uses for this are:

- triggering raw audio into the spatialization hardware
- manipulating the pitch of the raw audio before convolution to simulate Doppler shift
- controlling effects processors to simulate ambience effects such as reverberation.

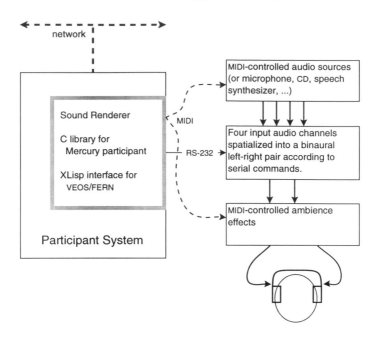

Figure 8-4   Sound Renderer (VEOS/Mercury).

The sound sources currently used include an audio sampler (hosted in a computer), speech-generation hardware, and microphones. The sampler is configured so that the pitch of all sound sources can be independently manipulated, allowing differently spatialized sources to have separate Doppler shifts. The use of MIDI also easily accommodates other audio spatializers which accept MIDI control data.

The Sound Renderer is not itself an application. Rather it is a programming interface which allows world builders to add sound to their environments at a high level of abstraction. This style configuration is typical of many implementations; the world building abstraction and participant model are otherwise novel up to this point.

Mercury interface. To resolve latency and registration issues, the Sound Renderer was tailored to interface at the C-code level, as in the Mercury Participant System. In this case, a Participant System is a self-contained entity that manages participant behavior (position sensors, etc.) and displays in conjunction with a local database containing the current state of a virtual environment as computed by a distributed system. This allows the participant to smoothly interact with a slowly updating database. The Sound Renderer is provided as a C object library which is linked into Mercury. Because both the visual and audio renderers are running in conjunction with the position sensors on the same computer platform, rather than on two separate machines in the distributed system, network delays are eliminated between them, allowing a closer coupling between visual and audio events.

Veos/fern interface. For VR systems such as VEOS/FERN, in which environments are coded in Lisp for distributed platforms, the Sound Renderer has been developed with an XLisp interface. All of the functions of the Sound Renderer are available as an object library which is linked into VEOS at appropriate nodes (i.e., machines from which a Sound Renderer may access serial ports). In the sound renderer, reverberation is simulated with MIDI-controlled processors after spatialization. The reverberant signal is mixed with the spatialized signal as would naturally occur in an enclosed space.

The Audio Browser

The Audio Browser is a hierarchical sound file navigation and audition tool (Whitehead, 1994). Its intent is to speed up the laborious process of selecting appropriate audio segments from vast archives of sound files, and to help sound designers and foley artists familiarize themselves with new audio sample libraries. Sound is naturally time-linear; we cannot scan sound as we would scan a page of text or images. Informal textual descriptions of sound often do not describe the content accurately. Conversely, we can process many audio streams simultaneously, while we cannot interpret many image streams at once. The Audio Browser takes advantage of the fact that we can naturally monitor many audio streams and selectively focus our attention on any particular one, especially if the sources are spatially separated. Audible transitions from node to node in the database are used to give the listener a feeling that they are "moving" through a tree of nodes.

Inclusive implementation. The Audio Browser makes use of the Sound Renderer and Mercury software systems described above. The sound file samples are prearranged, similar sounds collected into single nodes, and nodes arranged into a quad-tree hierarchy. At each node one can hear representative, looped samples from the four children nodes in each of four front quadrants and the sample from the parent node behind, as shown in Figure 8-5. In the inclusive implementation, a graphical representation of the tree is also displayed and the currently auditioned samples are highlighted with a color change.

The listener navigates through the sound file hierarchy by choosing the sound representing the node they wish to follow. The selection is accomplished by flying toward the desired sample, at which point it becomes the parent node behind the listener, as its four child samples begin playing in front. The listener can go back up the tree by flying in reverse. This process is continued until the listener has found the node closest to the desired sound. At this point, the possibly numerous files in the node may be auditioned individually. A more advanced implementation would arrange all files in a node in such a way that they could be inclusively auditioned as well.

Handy Sound

Handy Sound (Cohen, 1989, 1990, 1993b; Cohen and Ludwig, 1991a, 1991b) explores gestural control of an audio window system. The system is of the

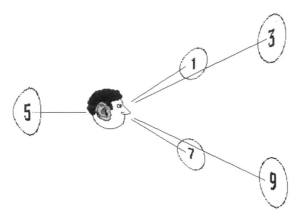

Figure 8-5   Inclusive Audio Browser.

"moving sources/stationary sink" type and uses an egocentric perspective. It thus allows a single user to arrange sources around him/herself with purely manual manipulation (requiring no keyboard or mouse). Handy Sound is motivated (literally and figuratively) by gestures, i.e., spatial motions that convey information. Gestural recognition via a DataGlove is used as input to a spatial sound system, and virtual sound sources manipulated in a 3D presentation. Figure 8-6 illustrates the architecture of the system. Generally in the schematic, digital control data goes down the left, and analog audio signals go up the right.

The user interface of the prototype uses a DataGlove (VPL, 1987) which is coupled with a Polhemus 3Space Isotrak (Polhemus, 1987). The system senses the position and orientation of the wearer's hand, the posture[8] of the user's fingers, and the orientation of the user's head. Such tracking is useful for "soundscape stabilization," the invariance of the perceived location of the sources under reorientation of the user.

3D tracking products like the coupled Polhemus employ a physically stationary standing wave generator (electromagnetic or ultrasonic) and one or more movable sensors. The resulting systems provide 6 parameters in realtime (the $x/y/z$ of the sensor's physical location and roll/pitch/yaw of the sensor's orientation). Finger posture is calculated by measuring flex-induced leakage in fiber optics laid across the finger joints. With a device like a DataGlove, a user can point and gesticulate using a 3D workspace envelope. In Handy Sound, the DataGlove postures and positions are strobed by a Sun workstation, and integrated into gestures which are used to drive the output.

Sound sources (for simulation) are provided by four samplers (Akai, 1989b), synchronized by a MIDI daisy chain, and cued by a MIDI synthesizer. A digital patch matrix (Akai, 1989a), driven via an RPC-invoked (remote procedure call) server, is used to switch in the filtears. The *spotlight*, *muffle*, and *highlight filtears* described below are implemented by an aural exciter (Aphex, 1989) and a low-pass filter (Urei, 1980). Since the number of channels

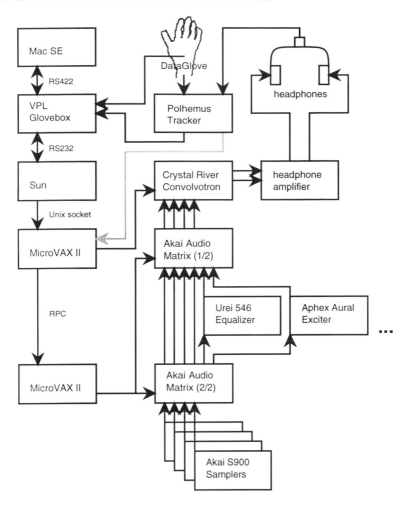

Figure 8-6 Architecture (Handy Sound). Reproduced with permission of the publisher, Academic Press, London; from *Computer Supported Cooperative Work and Groupware*, 1991 (Ed. Saul Greenberg).

in the prototype is fixed, only one channel at a time can be driven through the spotlight or the muffle filtears, and the effects are mutually exclusive (i.e., grabbing an indicated source disables the spotlight as the muffle is enabled), the physical matrix is effectively folded into two logical matrices. The frontend of the system, then, becomes a scheduler, literally handling the dynamic reallocation of the filtear resources.

The backend of the prototype is an enhanced spatial sound system based on the Crystal River Convolvotron. The control (DataGlove box) and presentation (Convolvotron) processes communicate via (internet) **u**ser (unreliable) **d**atagram **p**rotocol (UDP) Unix sockets across an Ethernet.[7] The distributed architecture was designed to modularly separate the client (gestural recognition data model) from the server (spatializer and filtear). By using the DataGlove to drive the Convolvotron, virtual sound sources are manipulated in a full 3D auditory display.

Manipulating source position in Handy Sound

By using a posture characterizer to recognize intuitive hand signs along with full-motion arm interpretation, users can gesturally indicate, select, highlight, and relocate sound sources, mapping the reachable work envelope around the user into the much larger perceptual space. Pointing at a source indicates it, as a prelude for selection by grasping. Grasping and releasing are delimiting postures, which respectively enable and disable repositioning. Repositioning is a gesture defined by grasping accompanied by movement.

The Cartesian coordinates of the DataGlove are mapped into spherical coordinates to give the user an egocentric perspective, as shown in equation (1). To avoid complications imposed by room geometry, the sound sources are constrained to move spherically: azimuth is adjusted horizontally circularly (as opposed to rectilinearly), elevation is adjusted vertically circularly, and distance is adjusted radially with respect to the user. Azimuth (1a) and elevation (1b) track the user's hand, and distance (1c) (which maps inversely cubically[9] to gain in Handy Sound's dry spatialization) is adjusted proportionally to the radial distance difference between the onset and completion of the relocation, measured from the head to the hand.[10]

$$\text{azimuth} = \tan^{-1}\left(\frac{\text{hand}_y - \text{head}_y}{\text{hand}_x - \text{head}_x}\right) - \pi/2 \tag{1a}$$

$$\text{elevation} = \tan^{-1}\left(\frac{\text{hand}_z - \text{head}_z}{\sqrt{(\text{hand}_x - \text{head}_x)^2 + (\text{hand}_y - \text{head}_y)^2}}\right) \tag{1b}$$

$$\text{distance} \mathrel{*}= \frac{|\overline{\text{hand}(t_2)} - \overline{\text{head}(t_2)}|}{|\overline{\text{hand}(t_1)} - \overline{\text{head}(t_1)}|} \tag{1c}$$

The position of the source is tracked continuously during repositioning. Audio panning and volume control are subsumed by spatial location. For example, if the user indicates an object, grabs, and tugs on it, the object will approach. Figure 8-7 illustrates pulling a distant source halfway closer: enamored of a source (represented by concentric rings, whose shading will be explained later) and desiring more intimate proximity, a user repositions it by grasping the proximal projection of its channel, dragging it to a new location, and releasing it.

When the object is released, the azimuth and elevation of the user's hand directly determine the new azimuth and elevation of the object. That is, the azimuthal and elevational control and presentation spaces are the same. Therefore their C/R (control/response) ratio $\equiv 1$. For the distance, however, a

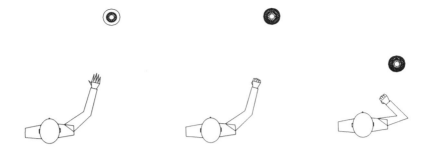

Figure 8-7   Glove at fist site (Handy Sound).

variable radial c/R ratio is employed, in order to gracefully map the near-field work envelope into the entire perceptual space, finessing issues of scale. In effect, the reachable work envelope is magnified to span the auditory space, giving the user a projected telepresence from physical into perceptual space. The closer an object is to the user, the finer the proximal/distal adjustment (and the higher the radial c/R ratio).

Manipulating source quality in Handy Sound

A back-channel is a secondary feedback stream, used to confirm state in control systems. Filtears, which may reflect state information, but do not require a separate display stream, can be used as sonic *piggyback-channels*, since they are carried by the original source signal. These are audio equivalents of changing cursors, state indicators superimposed on a main channel. Implemented on top of a spatial sound system, sonic piggyback-channels have positional attributes as well as filtear qualities; since repositioning and filtearing are (intended to be) orthogonal, an object may be simultaneously moved and filteared.

Since Handy Sound's main display is purely auditory, modality compatibility motivated the use of sonic piggyback-channels. Rather than create independent sound effects and musical motifs to indicate states, Handy Sound employs filtears for selective transformation of source channels.

The gestural commands (and their feedback filtears) recognized and obeyed by Handy Sound are illustrated by the finite state automaton in Figure 8-8, and recapitulated in Figure 8-9, which extends the relocation scenario described earlier (Figure 8-7). Handy Sound implements three types of (sonic piggyback-channel) filtears, described below:

Spotlight. Once audio channels are distributed in space, a telepointer or user-controlled pointer within that space becomes useful. In visual domains, eyegaze selects the focus of attention; there is no direct analogue in audio domains since audition is more omnidirectional than vision. It is easier to detect where someone is looking ("gaze indirection") than to detect what they're listening to. A method of focusing or directing auditory attention is

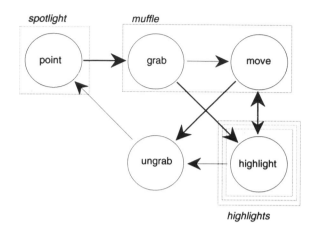

Figure 8-8   State transition and *filtears* (Handy Sound).

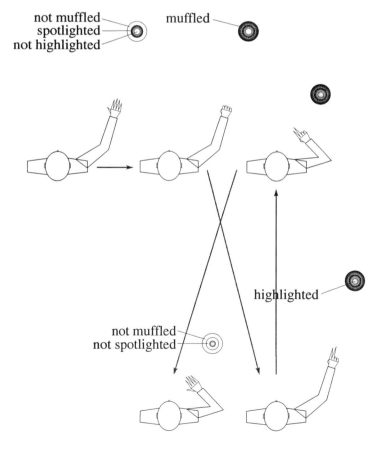

Figure 8-9   Gestured state transitions (Handy Sound).

needed to extend the paradigms of graphical indication into audio conferencing.

One could simply instantiate another independent sound source, an *audio cursor*, to superimpose on the selected sources—for instance, a steady or pulsed tone—but this has the disadvantage of further cluttering the auditory space, especially if multiple cursor positions are allowed. In any case, this feature is available intrinsically: user-movable sources can be used as audio cursors "for free" (except for the loss of a channel). User-programmable sources could be the basis of the horizon or compass applications mentioned earlier. Like a mythical Siren, sound endowed with the ability to move about can also entice users to follow it. Such a "come-hither" beacon might be used to draw attention to a particular place or workstation window in the office.

Handy Sound explicitly implements a perhaps better solution, an audio spotlight, that emphasizes one or more channels (Ludwig and Pincever, 1989; Cohen and Ludwig, 1991a, 1991b; Begault and Wenzel, 1992). This emphasis might comprise any combination of the suite of effects used by audio exciters and aural enhancers: equalization, pitch shifting, amplitude-dependent harmonic emphasis, and frequency-dependent phase shift. The emphasis augments the source channel's acoustic conspicuousness (variously called brightness, clarity, or presence), making it easier to hear and distinguish, without necessarily making it substantially louder. This emphasis can be likened to sonic italicization, an audio shimmering that draws attention to the emboldened source(s) without overpowering the others. However, a spotlight, unlike a cursor, can only emphasize an active channel, and therefore is less useful as a general pointing device.

The spotlight is used to confirm selection of one or more channels—as a prelude to invoking some action (like amplification, muting, or repositioning), or as an end unto itself, since the emphasis makes the selected objects more prominent. The idea is to create a JND, an acoustic enhancement that is noticeable but ignorable, unambiguous but unintrusive.

In practice, as the hand is swept around the room, pointing at the localized sources, confirmation of direction is achieved by having the indicated source emphasized with a spotlight. An audio spotlight is a way of specifying a subset of the channel mix for special consideration—a way of focusing auditorily, bringing a chosen channel out of background cacophony, and selecting it as the object of a subsequent operation.

Muffle. A muffle filtear is used to suggest the grasping of a source. Grabbing a channel, as a prelude to moving or highlighting, muffles its sound, imitating the effect of a hand closed around it. This aural confirmation of a gesture fulfills the user interface principle of conceptual compatibility. The muffling effect is accomplished with a lowpass filter, as a covering hand tends to attenuate the high-frequency components of a sound source. The filtear must be subtle to avoid loss of intelligibility in the selected channel.

Highlights. Highlights are a way of emphasizing audio channels, of endowing them with a perceptual prominence, of promoting and demoting them along a hierarchy of conspicuousness. MAW's highlighting gesture comprises grasping accompanied by a hierarchical specification, represented by extended fingers. Highlights are like an ordered ladder of spotlight-like effects that can be associated with channels. Since they are linked to pointing direction, spotlights cannot be locked on a source, but highlights, which are closely related, may be. Unlike spotlights or muffles, highlights persist beyond the pointing or grasping. They are used to impose a perceptual hierarchical organization on an ensemble of channels. Spotlighting is meant as an immediate feedback feature, guiding selection of a source in a manner analogous to emboldening of the window title bar for graphical interfaces. Highlights are meant as longer-term mnemonic aids, perhaps comparable to choice of font for textural graphical windows.

In a gestural interface like Handy Sound, pointing and grasping are natural postures for indicating and securing. The exact style of extending digits to indicate promotion/demotion in a perceptual hierarchy is culturally sensitive, but the idea of counting on the fingers and thumb is global, and the particular configurations are easily programmed or learned.

Manipulating sound volume in Handy Sound

In order to maintain the purity of the simplified gestural interface, the only way to adjust gain in Handy Sound is to bring a source closer. (Alternatively, additional postures could have been defined to raise or lower the volume of a selected source.) Volume is controlled by closeness/distance effects; gain is set inversely proportional to the virtual distance from the source. While the user might simply adjust the volume of the headphone mixer, the only way to make everyone louder via the gestural interface is by pulling everyone closer individually. The only way to turn a sound off is to push it away until it vanishes, thus making it difficult to retrieve.

Summary

Handy Sound demonstrates the general possibilities of gesture recognition and spatial sound in a multichannel conferencing system. The technology employed, however, is better suited for a concept demonstration than for day-to-day use. The number of spatialized sources is limited to four, with no easy way to scale up. The hardware is complicated, expensive, and unwieldy: the glove itself does not interfere with many other tasks (including writing and typing), but the cables are cumbersome. Further, ambient electromagnetic noise, reflected by metal surfaces in a typical laboratory environment, make reliable operation of the Polhemus tracker difficult beyond a short range, and measurement of orientation (which direction the hand, as opposed to the arm, is pointing) impractical.

The response of the system is somewhat restricted by the speed of the processors and the high bandwidth requirements, forcing the user to be deliberate in manipulating sound objects. The system is tuned using a choke, a parameter specifying how many postural events to coalesce before transmission. Averaging, debouncing, and hysteresis (to clean up noisy data) must be adjusted to match the environment.

There are two sets of data which should be individually calibrated for each user: the ear maps, modeling the HRTFs of the user, and the posture characteristics, calibrating the various hand positions. In practice, without individually tailored HRTFs, the ear maps are not always perceptually precise (Wenzel et al., 1991, 1993; Aoki et al., 1994). Further, active control of (especially multiple) sources is difficult with only an auditory display, even with spotlights, making a visual display useful for confirmation of source placement.

MAW

MAW (Cohen, 1990, 1993a, 1993b; Cohen and Koizumi, 1992c) represents a "moving sources/moving sink: exocentric perspective" style system which allows sources and sinks to be arranged in a horizontal plane. Developed as an interactive teleconferencing frontend, MAW was retrofitted with a batch mode, making it also suitable for automatic, single-user invocation. Its architecture, shown in Figure 8-10, is appropriate for both synchronous and asynchronous applications.

The spatialization backend is provided by any combination of MAW's native Focal Point™ (Gehring, 1990) and external convolution engines, including the Stork and Digital Audio Processor SIM**2 (acronymic for sound **im**age **sim**ulator), in-house DSP modules. The ellipses below the convolution engines in the schematic indicates that any number of these external convolution engines may be deployed, daisy-chained together on a GPIB (**general-purpose interface bus**, or IEEE 488) driven off an SCSI interface (IOtech, 1991). MAW uses configuration files, dynamic maps of virtual spatial sound spaces, to calculate the gain control and HRTF selection for this scalable heterogeneous backend, assigning logical channels to physical devices via a preferences (control) panel. The outputs of all spatialization filters are combined into a stereo pair presented to the user.

The graphical representation of MAW's virtual room is a plan view. This perspective flattening was implemented partly because of its suitability for visual display on a workstation monitor. Figure 8-11 shows a typical view of such an overhead representation (along with the border, buttons, and scrollers that make it a window) as part of a snapshot of a typical session. MAW adopts the simplification that all spatial sound objects are at once 2D sources and sinks. Spatial sound objects have not only rectangular coordinates, but also angular and focal attributes (described later). Visual icons for sources and sinks indicate their orientation by pointing in the direction that the object is facing. Since all the participants are represented by separate icons, a user can adjust another's virtual position as easily as his/her own.

Manipulating source and sink positions in MAW

For the icons used in Figure 8-11, the pictures are clipped to the interior of the circle, so the face of the respective user is like the face of a clock, the single hand pointed in the direction the user is "facing" in its admittedly mixed (frontal/aerial) metaphor. Each of the icons is assigned a unique channel number, used to key the spatializing backend.

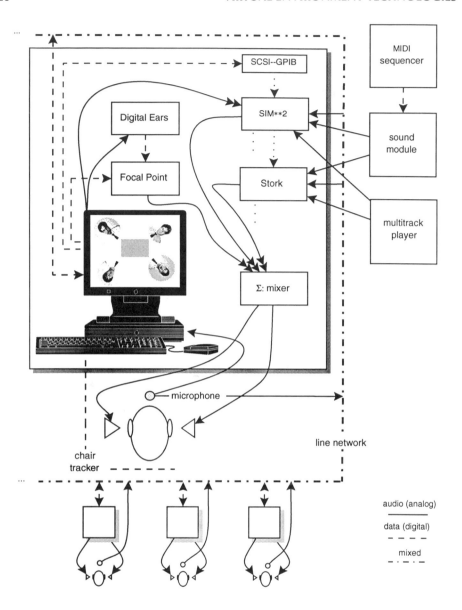

Figure 8-10 System schematic (MAW).

An alternative iconic representation uses top-down pictures of people's heads, as in Figure 8-12. Such a view has the advantage of making the bird's-eye metaphor consistent, but suffers from making the users more difficult to recognize. Another iconic representation uses the first-described "head-and-shoulders" pictures, but replaces the radial azimuth-indicating arm with image rotation, as in Figure 8-10. These various representations may be concatenated, and selected "on the fly," allowing users to change the iconic views according to whim.

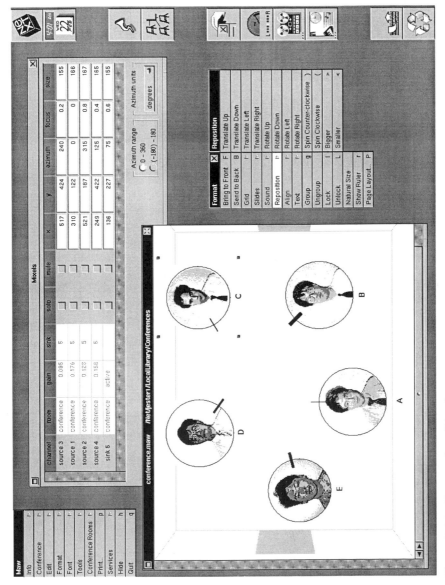

Figure 8-11 Screen shot (MAW).

327

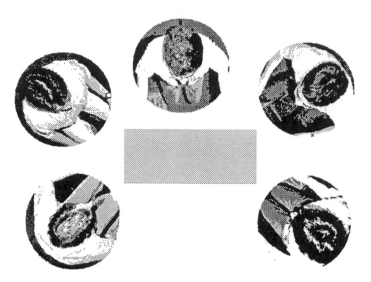

Figure 8-12   Top-down icons (MAW).

As in Handy Sound, the notion of a changing cursor to indicate mode is employed by MAW. In Handy Sound, this feedback role is assumed by filtears, which reflect that an audio source is being indicated, relocated, accented, etc. In MAW, the use of a hand to indicate repositioning is elaborated to distinguish an open hand, suggesting rectilinear translation, from a hand with a pointed pivot finger, suggesting rotation thereabout.

MAW extends WIMP interface conventions to manage spatial sound objects with a variety of interaction styles. Draggably rotating icons, which represent non-omnidirectional sources and sinks, are controlled not only by direct manipulation, but also by arrow keys, chorded with Alternate-, Shift- and Control-keys; menu items and Command-keys; and numeric panels, all employing the object–command (noun–verb) syntax. Various commands move the icons relative to themselves, each other, and the virtual room.

MAW has a chair tracker (Cohen and Koizumi, 1992b), crafted with a Polhemus 3Space Isotrak (Polhemus, 1987), which automatically offsets the azimuth of a particular sink from a (perhaps moving) datum, established via explicit iconic manipulation. The chair tracker blurs the distinction between egocentric and exocentric systems by integrating the egocentric display with ego- and exocentric control, as well as providing the dynamic cues discussed on pages 299, 304, and 318.

As illustrated by Figure 8-13, the virtual position of the sink, reflected by the (graphically exocentric) orientation of its associated graphical icon, pivots ($\mp\delta$) in response to (kinesthetically egocentric) sensor data around the datum/baseline (θ) established by WIMP (exocentric) iconic manipulation. Symmetrically, the system can be thought of as a user of MAW arbitrarily adjusting a (static or moving) orientation established by the chair tracker. Users may exploit both modes interleaved or simultaneously, adjusting or

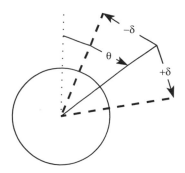

Figure 8-13 Chair tracker geometry (Maw):
exocentric θ, egocentric δ.

amplifying their physical position virtually, like setting flaps and trim tabs on an airplane. The wimp-based operations of Maw can set absolute positions; the chair tracker's reporting of absolute positions has been disabled to allow graphical adjustment. With only wimp-based rotational initialization, the system behaves as a simple tracker, consistent with proprioceptive sensations. Both Maw's wimp-based functions and the chair tracker send positional updates to a multicasting conferencing server, so that everyone in a conference or concert may observe the respective sink spinning (to face a source, for instance, enabling "gaze awareness" (Ishii and Kobayashi, 1992)).

Organizing acoustic objects in Maw

Maw features a cluster utility. Clusters are hierarchically collapsed groups (Schaffer *et al.*, 1993) of spatial sound objects. By bundling multiple channels together, a composite timbre is obtained. Clusters have two main purposes:

Conservation of spatializer resources. Postulating a switching matrix on either side of the spatial sound processor, along with dynamic allocation of spatializer channels, a cluster feature organizes separate input streams that share a single spatializing channel. One application might involve zooming effects. Distant sources would not be displayed; but as it approaches, a cluster would appear as a single point; only to disassociate and distribute spatially as it gets closer. This focus allows navigation in arbitrarily large space, assuming a limited density of point sources. Alternatively, with limited spatializing resources, a user might choose to group a subset of the (less important or less pleasant) channels together, stacking them in a corner or closet.

Logical organization of hierarchical structure. For example, in the context of a concert, individually recording (or mic-ing or synthesizing) the separate instruments, presenting each of the channels to Maw, and mixing them at audition time, rather than in "post-production," allow the instruments to be rearranged by the listener. With the appropriate interface, one could grab onto an orchestral cluster, for instance (shown as part of the concert in Table 8-4), shake it to separate the different instruments, grab one of those instruments and move it across the room. This successive differentiation could go right through concert → orchestra → section → instrument and

Table 8-4   Concert decomposition.

```
concert
  chorus
    soprano
    alto
    tenor
    bass
  orchestra
    strings
      basses
      cellos
      violas
      violins
        G-string
        D-string
        A-string
        E-string
          attack
          decay
            even harmonics
            odd harmonics



    brass
      horns
      trumpets
      trombones
      tuba
    woodwinds
      bassoons
      clarinets
      flutes
      oboes
    percussion
      bass drum
      cymbals
      snare drum
      triangle
      tubular bells
      wood block
      xylophone
      timpani
    other
      harp
      piano
```

actually break down the instrument itself. This super decomposition aspect of the cluster feature could allow, for example, the user to listen to spatially separate strings of a violin.

Unclustering can be likened to viewing the sources through a generalized fish-eye lens (Furnas, 1986; Sarkar and Brown, 1994), which spatially warps the perception of the localized sources to enlarge an area of focus and shrink everything else. That is, when the user indicates a direction of special interest, the sources in that direction effectively approach the user and recede from each other in perspective. While the other objects do not get pushed into the background, the idea is the same: to effect an external rearrangement of sources that complements an internal reordering.

Manipulating sound volume in Maw

In exocentric systems like Maw, it is possible to positionally adjust perceived gain in two different ways: sidle a sink up to a speaker or group of sources, or move the sources nearer to a sink. As in Handy Sound, there is no "volume knob" in Maw; the notion of volume adjustment has been folded into the spatial metaphor.

Maw also provides a more direct way of adjusting gain. The user can resize a selected object by dragging one of the resize handles (knobs) on its bounding rectangle (as in the top right icon of Figure 8-11). The size of a source corresponds to individual gain (amplification); the size of a sink corresponds to general gain (sensitivity). For the sake of parsimony, iconic size (along one linear[11] dimension) is used as a determinant of both metaphorical ear and mouth size. Gain is proportional to the size of the source's mouth (amplification) and the sink's ear (sensitivity), so enlarging an icon makes its owner both louder and more acute. Thus, to make a *single* channel louder or softer, a user simply resizes the respective icon, but to make *everyone* louder or softer, the user need only resize his/her own icon. Gain is also inversely proportional to the distance between the sink and source, so another way to change perceived volume is to have the source and sink approach or recede from each other. A modified frequency-independent cardioidal pattern is used to model the sound field radiation of non-omnidirectional sources. The chosen relationship specifies an azimuth-dependent beaming of the speaker, an idealized directional pattern, with exaggeratable distance effects. Therefore, the overall amplitude of a source $\rightarrow$ sink transmission is independent of the sink's transfer function, and can be specified (Cohen and Koizumi, 1991b, 1992c, 1993b) as a function of focus and mutual position and orientation. Focus represents the dispersion, or beaming, of the sound. For a focus of zero, the radiation pattern is omnidirectional. A focus of greater than zero enables a cardioidal pattern, as if the source were using a megaphone. The icon shown in the top left of Figure 8-14 has focus = 0.1, and a corresponding radiation pattern (sound field density, in which lighter areas indicate greater intensity) in the top right is almost omnidirectional. In contrast, the icon in the bottom left has focus = 0.9 (as indicated by its thicker arm), and its radiation pattern in the bottom right is almost perfectly quiet in the shadow behind the head.

Some systems support multiple visual windows, each featuring a different perspective on a scene. In flight simulators, for example, these might be used to display (egocentric) views out cockpit windows, and/or views from a completely different location—high above the airplane, for example, looking down (exocentrically): a virtual "out-of-body" experience. Since audition is (biasedly) omnidirectional, perhaps audio windows can be thought of as implicitly providing this multiperspective capability, audio sources being inherently superimposed. Maw also features a "schizophrenic" mode, allowing

focus = 0.1

focus = 0.9

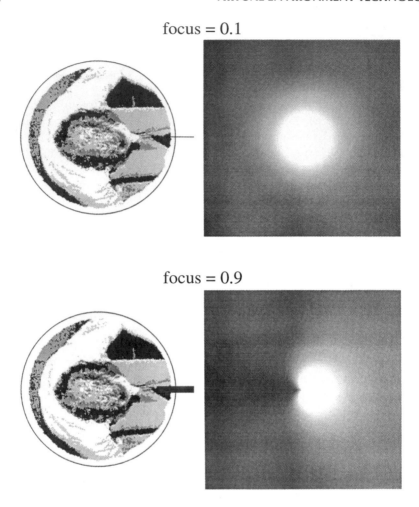

Figure 8-14 Icons and radiation patterns (MAW).

multiple sinks in the same or different conference rooms, explicitly overlaying multiple audio displays.

A simple teleconferencing configuration typically consists of several icons, representing the distributed users, moving around a shared conference space. Each icon represents a source, the voice of the associated user, as well as a sink, that user's ears. However, MAW allows users to have multiple sinks designated (through a preferences panel), effectively increasing their attendance in the conference, enhancing the *quantity* (and not the quality) of presence. Such a feature might be used to pay close attention to multiple sources, even if those sources are not repositionable; just as in ordinary settings, social conventions might inhibit dragging someone else around a shared space. One could pay close attention to multiple instruments in a concert without rearranging the ensemble. One could leave a pair of ears in one conference, while sending another pair to a side caucus, even if the side caucus happens to be in the same room. Such distilled ubiquity, the ability to be anywhere, is better than being everywhere, since it is selective.

The apparent paradoxes of one's being in multiple places simultaneously are resolved by partitioning the sources across the sinks. If the sinks are distributed in separate conference rooms, each source is localized only with respect to the sink in the same room. If multiple sinks share a single conference room, an "autofocus" mode is employed by anticipating level difference localization, the tendency to perceive multiple identical sources in different locations as a single fused source. (This is related to the precedence effect, mentioned on page 300.) Rather than adding or averaging the contribution of each source to the multiple sinks, MAW localizes each source only with respect to the best (loudest, as a function of distance and mutual gain, including focus and orientation effects) sink.

Figure 8-15 illustrates this behavior for a conference (top row) with two sinks, represented by top-down icons, and two different sources, represented by a square and a triangle. In the absence of room acoustics, multiple sinks perceiving a single source is equivalent, via "reciprocity" or symmetry, to a single sink perceiving multiple identical sources. Therefore the exampled scene can be decomposed source-wise into two additive scenes (second row), each single sink combining the parent sinks' perceptions of the respective sources. These configurations reduce (third row), via the "autofocus" level difference anticipation, to the respective sinks and only the loudest source. The loudest source is typically the closest, since the respective pairs of sources are identical, the chorus of phantom sources being a manifestation of the multiple sinks. Finally (bottom row), the additive scenes are recombined, yielding the overall simplified percept.

Summary

Unlike Handy Sound, but like VEOS, MAW is designed to be expandable to a large number of channels, and features two techniques for spatializing multiple channels. One is the ability to locally drive multiple alternate external spatializers, assigning logical channels to heterogeneous physical devices. Further, an arbitrary number of workstations may execute a single conference as a 'distributed whiteboard', each using its own spatializer(s). The outputs of each workstation can then be mixed to form multiple, spatial audio channels.

MAW is intended to interpolate between conventional telephony and VR, but cannot be said to do more than suggest actual acoustic environments. For instance, simulating distance cues is a difficult and not-yet-solved problem which goes beyond MAW's simple gain changes. Besides people's natural inability to estimate distance with precision and MAW's distortion of distance effects, an inverse relation does not perfectly capture real effects (Laws, 1973; Blauert, 1983; Begault, 1991; Wenzel, 1992; Speigle and Loomis, 1993; Begault, 1994). MAW's modeling of source directionality is also not veridical: the selection of a cardioid is somewhat arbitrary, and a flat (frequency-independent) attenuation of gain is not the best model of a rotating source, which should change timbre as well as loudness. It would be more accurate to

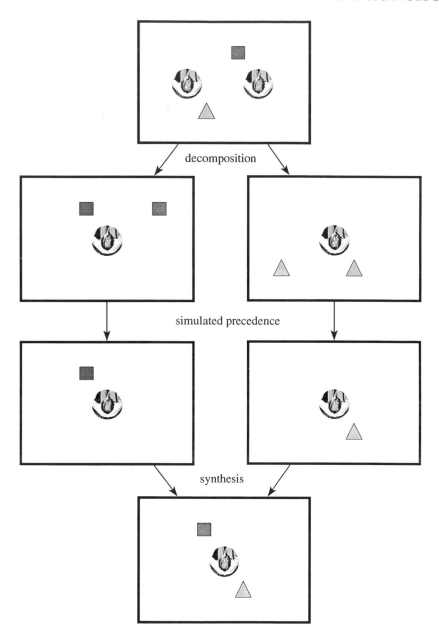

Figure 8-15 Schizophrenic mode with autofocus (MAW).

have a second set of transfer functions that capture these shadow effects, and convolve the digitized source thrice: once for source rotation, and twice (left and right ears) for sink revolution. MAW further over-simplifies reality by neglecting occlusion, the obstruction of a source's sound by other objects in the virtual room; Doppler shifts, the pitch bending exhibited by moving sources;

indirect early reflections (discrete echoes), the ratio of whose energy to that of direct sounds is another cue for estimating distance; and late reverberation, statistically averaged room ambience, which enhances externalization and auditory "spaciousness." The absence of some of these cues is sometimes associated with perceptual errors like front ↔ back reversals (Foster *et al.*, 1991), as mentioned earlier.

CONCLUSIONS

As sound technology matures, and more and more audio and multimedia messages and sessions are sent and logged, the testimony of sound may come to rival that of the written word. Audio windows and other multidimensional sound interfaces organize and control virtual acoustic environments. New media spend their early years recapitulating the modes of older media (McLuhan and Fiore, 1967); the research described by this chapter hopes to abbreviate this phase for audio interfaces by accelerating their conceptual development. Recurrent themes in the design of multidimensional sound systems include perspective, multiuser capability, C/R mapping and feedback (control state) mechanisms, dimensionality, and integration with other modalities.

Both egocentric and exocentric displays are effective paradigms for virtual audio systems. Egocentric displays like VEOS and Handy Sound are most compatible with inclusion-style VR systems: In such an inside-out display, gestural interpretation control is parsimonious, a natural extension of our normal mode of rearranging the world. An exocentric paradigm like MAW's blurs the self/other distinction by iconifying all users with similar tokens. A mouse- and monitor-driven GUI allows manipulation of all the system entities; the metaphorical universe is projected onto an external and egalitarian medium. This is especially important when the user may have multiple existence (as in MAW's schizophrenic mode).

Groupware applications require a permission system to avoid mutex (**mut**ual **ex**clusion) violation on shared entities. Because of its egocentric nature, Handy Sound features individual data models; no notion of synchronized models is imposed. Handy Sound (which was never deployed in a multiuser environment) decouples the control commands from conferencing users, decreeing a null permission system. With such a data model, unconstrained by a physical analog (i.e., the virtual layout may be inconsistent among the users), two users could sit mutually on each other's laps. VEOS allows multiple participants to share a distributed universe, the database cached through Mercury. MAW's exocentric paradigm is more subtle: it requires an abstraction, and depends on social conventions to establish its implicit permission system.

The ability to rearrange objects is important for mnemonic spatial data organization, since a user is most likely to know where something is if he/she put it there. VEOS, Handy Sound and MAW share several features, including the use of a direct manipulation object–command (noun–verb) syntax, continuous feedback and dynamic tracking.

Potential dimensions for a virtual audio system include not only spatial dimensions, but also qualities of orientation, focus, gain, and other features controllable by filtear mechanisms such as those outlined in Table 8-3. Further, in order to support an individually configurable teleconferencing system, a large[12] number of audio channels must be channeled through audio-imaging processors. Other applications, including voicemail, hypermedia, and music, require an arbitrarily large number of separately spatialized sonic channels. For all of these, and any task involving terminal audio management, spatial data organization, or scientific sonification, a grouping mechanism is useful, both as a way of imposing a logical hierarchy on many sources, and in conjunction with an audio switching matrix, as a way of conserving channels. The Audio Browser in VEOS and clusters in MAW provide a way of selectively collapsing dimensions.

Auditory localization, especially distance perception, is difficult. But visual and acoustic displays complement each other; a glance at a map can disambiguate auditory cues (McGurk and McDonald, 1976; Warren et al., 1981). Audio windowing systems can be likened to sonic (analytic) cubism: they present several audio perspectives (on an assembled conference or concert) simultaneously. Multidimensional sound interfaces organize acoustic space, and the interpretation of gestures and the reinterpretation of WIMP conventions seem natural frontends to such systems. Such systems should be designed to exploit innate localization abilities, perception of both spatial and non-spatial attributes, and intuitive notions of how to select and manipulate objects distributed in space. When sound has a physical manifestation, it can become an icon for anything imaginable.

NOTES

1. Surround Sound 360 and THX are two commercial examples of theatrical audio systems, as Circle Vision 360 and Omnimax are examples of analogous visual systems.

2. Throughout this chapter, "display" is used in a general sense to denote presentation or output in any medium.

3. Since the word "speaker" is overloaded, meaning both "loudspeaker" and "talker," "source" is used to mean both, denoting any logical sound emitter. Similarly and symmetrically, "sink" is used to describe a logical sound receiver, a virtual listener.

4. Often, this implies a hardware implementation which devotes a separate (mono → stereo) DSP channel to each image source. Alternatively, as in the Convolvotron (described on page 302), an aggregate binaural impulse response composed of the superposition of the direct and reflected images can be computed on-the-fly for the instantaneous configuration of the source and sink in the environment and then rendered in realtime.

5. An estimate of 50 ms for the effective latency of the head-tracker is probably conservative. It also does not reflect the potentially much more problematic issue of positional "jitter" in current tracking systems (Meyer et al., 1993). For the Convolvotron, and probably all the realtime spatial sound systems described here, latencies through the total system are dominated by the limitations of commercially available

tracking systems. Such latencies and positional jitter are not as critical for the human auditory system, which is less sensitive to changes in angular displacement, as for the human visual system.

6. A **pan**oramic **pot**entiometer controls the placement of a channel in a conventional stereo mix.

7. Ethernet is a trademark of Xerox.

8. This chapter uses the convention of calling (the DataGlove's) recognized static positions "postures," reserving the term "gestures" for the sequential composition of multiple postures.

9. Gain usually falls off as the inverse of the distance, but Handy Sound deliberately exaggerates distance effects.

10. The "$*=$" notation means that each new distance value is determined by the product of the old distance and the gesturally determined scaling factor.

11. The linear dimension that actually determines the gain is (arbitrarily) the width, but since icons are almost always resized while holding the aspect ratio fixed (to avoid graphical distortion), height (or diagonal, or circumference, etc.) would have worked equally well.

12. Since, in a full-duplex conference, every user must spatialize every other user's voice, the total number of mixels, or channels to spatialize simultaneously, grows quadratically, or as $O(|\text{users}|^2)$.

REFERENCES

Addeo, E. J., Dayao, A. B., Gelman, A. D., and Massa, V. F. (1988) An experimental multi-media bridging system, in R. B. Allen (Ed.), *Proc. Conf. on Office Information Systems*, Palo Alto, CA, pp. 236–42

Akai (1989a) *DP3200 Audio Digital Matrix Patch Bay*, Akai Digital P.O. Box 2344, Forth Worth, TX 76113

Akai (1989b) *S900 MIDI Digital Sampler Operator's Manual*, Akai Professional, P.O. Box 2344, Forth Worth, TX 76113

AKG (1991) CAP 340M Creative Audio Processor, AKG Akustischer und Kino-Geräte GmbH; A-1150 Vienna, Austria

Aoki, S., Cohen, M., and Koizumi, N. (1994) Design and control of shared conferencing environments for audio telecommunication, *Presence: Teleoperators and Virtual Environments*, 2(2)

Aoki, S., Koizumi, N., Kusumi, Y., and Sugiyama, K. (1992) Virtual conferencing environment using HRTFs of listeners (in Japanese), in *Proc. IEICE Spring Conf.*, Noda, Chiba, Japan

Aphex (1989) *Aural Exciter Type C Model 103A Operating Guide*, Aphex Systems Ltd., 13340 Saticoy St., North Hollywood, CA 91605

Arons, B. (1992) A review of the cocktail party effect, *J. Am. Voice I/O Soc.*, **12**, 35–50

Astheimer, P. (1993) What you see is what you hear—acoustics applied in virtual worlds, in *VR93: Proc. IEEE Symp. on Research Frontiers in Virtual Reality (in conjunction with IEEE Visualization)*, San Jose, CA, pp. 100–107

Baecker, R. M. and Buxton, W. A. (1987) *The Audio Channel*, Cambridge, MA: Morgan Kaufmann (ISBN 0-934613-24-9) ch. 9

Batteau, D. W. (1967) The role of the pinna in human localization, *Proc. R. Soc.*, B **168**, 158–80

Begault, D. R. (1991) Preferred sound intensity increase for sensation of half distance, *Perceptual and Motor Skills*, **72**, 1019–29

Begault, D. R. (1992) Perceptual effects of synthetic reverberation on three-dimensional audio systems, *J. Audio Eng. Soc.*, **40**, 895–904

Begault, D. R. and Wenzel, E. M. (1992) Techniques and applications for binaural sound manipulation in man-machine interfaces, *Int. J. Aviation Psychol.*, **2**(1), 1–22

Begault, D. R. and Wenzel, E. M. (1993) Headphone localization of speech, *Human Factors*, **35**(2), 361–76

Begault, D. R. (1994) *3-D Sound for Virtual Reality and Multimedia*, Boston: Academic Press (ISBN 0-12-084735-3)

Békésy, G. v. (1960) *Experiments in Hearing*, New York: McGraw-Hill

Bernardini, N. and Otto, P. (1989) Trails: an interactive system for sound location, *ICMC: Proc. Int. Comp. Music Conf.*, Computer Music Association, pp. 29–33

Blattner, M. M. (1992) Messages, Models, and Media, *Multimedia Rev.*, **3**(3), 15–21

Blattner, M. M. and Dannenberg, R. B. (Eds) (1992) *Multimedia Interface Design*, ACM Press, Addison-Wesley (ISBN 0-201-54981-6)

Blattner, M. M. and Greenberg, R. M. (1989) Communicating and learning through non-speech audio, in A. D. N. Edwards (Ed.), *Multi-media Interface Design in Education*, Berlin: Springer

Blattner, M. M., Sumikawa, D. A., and Greenberg, R. M. (1989) Earcons and icons: their structure and common design principles, *Human–Computer Interact.*, **4**(1), 11–44

Blauert, J. (1969/1970) Sound localization in the medial plane, *Acustica*, **22**, 205–13

Blauert, J. (1983) *Spatial Hearing: The Psychophysics of Human Sound Localization*, Cambridge, MA: MIT Press (ISBN 0-262-02190-0)

Blauert, J. (1984) Psychoakustik des binauralen horens [the psychophysics of binaural hearing], in *Proc. DAGA*, Darmstadt, Germany (invited plenary paper)

Bly, S. A. (1982) Presenting information in sound, in *CHI: Proc. ACM Conf. on Computer-Human Interaction*, New York: ACM, pp. 371–5

Bly, S. A. (1987) Communicating with sound, in R. M. Baecker and W. A. S. Buxton (Eds), *Readings in Human-Computer Interaction: A Multidisciplinary Approach*, Cambridge, MA: Morgan Kaufmann, (ISBN 0-934613-24-9) ch. 9

Boerger, G., Laws, P., and Blauert, J. (1977) Stereophonic headphone reproduction with variation of various transfer factors by means of rotational head movements, *Acustica*, **39**, 22–6

Boulez, P. and Gerzso, A. (1988) Computers in music, *Sci. Am.*, **258**(4), 44–50

Bregman, A. S. (1990) *Auditory Scene Analysis*, Cambridge, MA: MIT Press (ISBN 0-262-02297-4)

Bricken, M. (1991) Virtual worlds: no interface to design, in M. Benedikt (Ed.) *Cyberspace: First Steps*, Cambridge, MA: MIT Press

Bricken, W. (1992) Virtual reality: directions of growth, in *Proc. Imagina*, Monte Carlo, pp. I27–I40

Burger, J. F. (1958) Front-back discrimination of the hearing system, *Acustica*, **8**, 301–2

Burkhardt, M. D. and Sachs, R. M. (1975) Anthropomorphic manikin for acoustic research, *J. Acoust. Soc. Am.*, **58**, 214–22

Butler, R. A. (1987) An analysis of the monaural displacement of sound in space, *Percept. Psychophys.*, **41**, 1–7

Butler, R. A. and Helwig, C. C. (1983) The spatial attributes of stimulus frequency in the median sagittal plane and their role in sound localization, *Am. J. Otolaryngol.*, **4**, 165–73

Buxton, W., Gaver, W., and Bly, S. (1989) The use of non-speech audio at the interface (tutorial), ACM/SIGCHI Tutorial No. 10, *ACM Conf. on Human Factors in Computing Systems*, New York

Caudell, T. P. and Mizell, D. W. (1992) Augmented reality: an application of head-up display technology to manual manufacturing processes, in *Proc. Hawaii Int. Conf. on Systems Sciences*, New York: IEEE.

Chan, C. J. (1991) Sound localization and spatial enhancement realization of the roland sound space processor, unpublished handout from a presentation at Cyberarts, Pasadena, CA

Cherry, E. C. (1953) Some experiments on the recognition of speech, with one and with two ears, *J. Acoust. Soc. Am.*, **25**(5), 975–9

Chowning, J. M. (1970) The simulation of moving sound sources, in *Proc. 38th Conv. of the Audio Eng. Soc.*, Audio Engineering Society (Preprint 726 (M-3))

Chowning, J. M. (1977) The simulation of moving sound sources, *Computer Music J.*, **1**(3), 48–52

Cohen, M. (1987) Stereotelephonics, *Internal Memorandum*, IM-000-21460-87-04, Bell Communications Research

Cohen, M. (1989) Multidimensional audio window management, *Technical Memorandum*, TM-NPL-015362, Bell Communications Research

Cohen, M. (1990) Multidimensional audio windows: extending user interfaces through the use of spatial auditory information, *PhD thesis*, Northwestern University

Cohen, M. (1993a) Integrating graphical and audio windows, *Presence: Teleoperators and Virtual Environments*, **1**(4), 468–81

Cohen, M. (1993b) Throwing, pitching, and catching sound: audio windowing models and modes, *IJMMS, J. Person-Computer Interact.*, **39**(2), 269–304

Cohen, M., Aoki, S., and Koizumi, N. (1993) Augmented audio reality: telepresence/VR hybrid acoustic environments, in *Ro-Man: Proc. 2 IEEE International Workshop on Robot and Human Communication*, Tokyo (ISBN 0-7803-1407-7), pp. 361–4

Cohen, M. and Koizumi, N. (1991a) Audio window, in *Den Gaku*, Tokyo Contemporary Music Festival, Music for Computer

Cohen, M. and Koizumi, N. (1991b) Audio windows for binaural telecommunication, in *Proc. Joint Meeting of Human Communication Committee and Speech Technical Committee*, Tokyo: Institute of Electronics, Information and Communication Engineers, Vol. 91, No. 242, SP91-51, HC91-23, CS91-79, pp. 21–8

Cohen, M. and Koizumi, N. (1991c) Audio windows for sound field telecommunication, in *Proc. Seventh Symp. on Human Interface*, Kyoto: Society of Instrument and Control Engineers, pp. 703–9

Cohen, M. and Koizumi, N. (1992a) Audio windows: user interfaces for manipulating virtual acoustic environments, in *Proc. Acoustical Society of Japan Spring Meeting*, Tokyo (special session on *Virtual Reality*, 2-5-12), pp. 479–80

Cohen, M. and Koizumi, N. (1992b) Iconic control for audio windows, in *Proc. Eighth Symp. on Human Interface*, Kawasaki, Japan: Society of Instrument and Control Engineers, pp. 333–40

Cohen, M. and Koizumi, N. (1992c) Exocentric Control of Audio Imaging in Binaural Telecommunication, *IEICE Trans. on Fundamentals of Electronics, Communications and Computer Sciences* (special section on *Fundamental of Next Generation Human Interface*), E75-A(2):164–170. 0916-8508

Cohen, M. and Koizumi, N. (1993a) Audio windows for virtual concerts, in *JMACS: Proc. Japan Music and Computer Science Society Meeting*, Tokyo, No. 47, pp. 27–32

Cohen, M. and Koizumi, N. (1993b) Virtual gain for audio windows, in *VR93: Proc. IEEE Symp. on Research Frontiers in Virtual Reality* (in conjunction with IEEE Visualization), San Jose, CA, pp. 85–91

Cohen, M., Koizumi, N., and Aoki, S. (1992) Design and control of shared conferencing environments for audio telecommunication, in *ISMCR: Proc. Int. Symp. on Measurement and Control in Robotics*, Tsukuba Science City, Japan: Society of Instrument and Control Engineers, pp. 405–12

Cohen, M. and Ludwig, L. F. (1991a) Multidimensional audio window management, *IJMMS, J. Person-Computer Interact.*, **34**(3), 319–36 (special issue on *Computer Supported Cooperative Work and Groupware*)

Cohen, M. and Ludwig, L. F. (1991b) Multidimensional audio window management, in S. Greenberg (Ed.), *Computer Supported Cooperative Work and Groupware*, London: Academic (ISBN 0-12-299220-2), pp. 193–210

Coleman, P. D. (1963) An analysis of cues to auditory depth perception in free space, *Psychol. Bull.*, **60**, 302–15

Deatherage, B. H. (1972) Auditory and other sensory forms of information presentation, in H. P. V. Cott and R. G. Kinkade (Eds), *Human Engineering Guide to Equipment Design*, Washington, DC: US Government Printing Office

Durlach, N. I., Rigpulos, A., Pang, X. D., Woods, W. S., Kulkarni, A., Colburn, H. S., and Wenzel, E. M. (1992) On the externalization of auditory images, *Presence: Teleoperators and Virtual Environments*, **1**(2), 251–7

Edwards, A. D. N. (1987) Modeling blind users' interactions with an auditory computer interface, *Report 25*, Centre for Information Technology in Education, The Open University, Milton Keynes, UK

Edwards, A. D. N. (1988) The design of auditory interfaces for visually disabled users, in *CHI: Proc. ACM Conf. on Computer-Human Interaction*, pp. 83–8

Feiner, S., MacIntyre, B., Haupt, M., and Solomon, E. (1993a) Windows on the world: 2D Windows for 3D augmented reality, in *Proc. UIST'93 (ACM Symp. on User Interface Software and Technology)*, Atlanta, GA

Feiner, S., MacIntyre, B., and Seligmann, D. (1993a) Knowledge-based augmented reality, *Commun. ACM*, **36**(7), 52–62

Fisher, H. and Freedman, S. J. (1968) The role of the pinna in auditory localization, *J. Audiol. Res.*, **8**, 15–26

Fisher, S. (1990) Virtual environments, personal simulation and telepresence, *Multidimensional Media*, pp. 229–36

Fisher, S. S., McGreevy, M., Humpries, J., and Robinett, W. (1986) Virtual environment display system, *ACM Workshop on 3D Interactive Graphics*, pp. 77–87

Fisher, S. S., Wenzel, E. M., Coler, C., and McGreevy, M. W. (1988) Virtual interface environment workstations, in *Proc. Human Factors Soc. 32nd Meeting*, Santa Monica, pp. 91–5

Foley, J. D. (1987) Interfaces for advanced computing, *Sci. Am.*, **257**(4), 126–35

Foster, S. (1990) *Convolvotron*™, Crystal River Engineering, 12350 Wards Ferry Rd, Groveland, CA 95321, (209) 962-6382

Foster, S. H., Wenzel, E. M., and Taylor, R. M. (1991) Real-time synthesis of complex acoustic environments (summary), in *Proc. (IEEE) ASSP Workshop on Applications of Signal Processing to Audio & Acoustics*, New Paltz, NY

Fujino, Y., Kanemaki, N., and Shimamura, K. (1991) An audio window system (in Japanese), in *Proc. IEICE Spring Meeting*, D-255

Furnas, G. W. (1986) Generalized fisheye views, in *CHI: Proc. ACM Conf. on Computer-Human Interaction*, Boston, pp. 16–23

Gardner, M. B. (1968) Proximity image effect in sound localization, *J. Acoust. Soc. Am.*, **43**, 163

Gardner, M. B. and Gardner, R. S. (1973) Problem of localization in the median plane: effect of pinnae cavity occlusion, *J. Acoust. Soc. Am.*, **53**, 400–8

Gaver, W. W. (1986) Auditory icons: using sound in computer interfaces, *Human-Computer Interact.*, **2**(2), 167–77

Gaver, W. W. (1989) The SonicFinder: an interface that uses auditory icons, *Human-Computer Interact.*, **4**(1), 67–94

Gaver, W. W., Smith, R. B., and O'Shea, T. (1991) Effective sounds in complex systems: the ARKola simulation, in *CHI: Proc. ACM Conf. on Computer-Human Interaction*, pp. 85–90

Gehring, B. (1987) *Auditory Localizer Model AL-201 Product Description*, Gehring Research Corporation, 189 Madison Avenue, Toronto, Ontario M5R 2S6, Canada

Gehring, B. (1988) *US Patent 4774515: Attitude Indicator*, 189 Madison Avenue, Toronto, Ontario M5R 2S6, Canada

Gehring, B. (1990) *Focal Point™ 3-D Sound User's Manual*, Gehring Research Corporation, 1402 Pine Avenue, #127; Niagara Falls, NY 14301, (716)285-3930 or (416)963-9188

Genuit, K. (1986) A description of the human outer ear transfer function by elements of communication theory, in *Proc. 12th Int. Congress on Acoustics*, Toronto, Paper B6-8

Genuit, K., Gierlich, H. W., and Künzli, U. (1992) Improved possibilities of binaural recording and playback techniques, in *Proc. 92nd Audio Engineering Society Conv.*, Vienna, Austria, 3PS1.06

Gibson, J. J. (1979) The ecological approach to visual perception, Boston: Houghton Mifflin

Gierlich, H. W. and Genuit, K. (1989) Processing artificial-head recordings, *J. Audio Eng. Soc.*, **37**, 34–9

Handel, S. (1989) *An Introduction to the Perception of Auditory Events*, MIT Press (ISBN 0-262-08179-2)

IOtech (1991) *SCSI488/N Bus Controller*, IOtech, Inc., 25971 Cannon Rd; Cleveland, OH 44146

Ishii, H. and Kobayashi, M. (1992) Clearboard: a seamless medium for shared drawing and conversation with eye contact, in *Proc. CHI'92*, New York, pp. 525–32

Kendall, G. S. (1990) Visualization by ear: Auditory imagery for scientific visualization and virtual reality, in A. Wolman and M. Cohen (Eds), *Proc. Dream Machines for Computer Music*, School of Music, Northwestern University, pp. 41–6

Kendall, G. S. (1991) Visualization by ear: auditory imagery for scientific visualization and virtual reality, *Computer Music J.*, **15**(4), 70–3

Kendall, G. S. and Freed, D. J. (1988) Scientific visualization by ear, *Technical Report*, Evanston, IL: Northwestsern Computer Music, Northwestern University

Kendall, G. S. and Martens, W. L. (1984) Simulating the cues of spatial hearing in natural environments, in *ICMC: Proc. Int. Comp. Music Conf.*, Paris, Computer Music Association, pp. 111–26

Kendall, G. S., Martens, W. L., Freed, D. J., Ludwig, M. D., and Karstens, R. W. (1986a) Image model reverberation from recirculating delays, in *Proc. 81st Audio Engineering Society Conv.*, New York

Kendall, G. S., Martens, W. L. Freed, D. J., Ludwig, M. D., and Karstens, R. W. (1986b) Spatial processing software at northwestern computer music, in *ICMC: Proc. Int. Comp. Music Conf.*, Computer Music Association, pp. 285–92

Kendall, G. S., Martens, W. L., and Wilde, M. D. (1990) A spatial sound processor for loudspeaker and headphone reproduction, in *Proc. Audio Engineering Society 8th Int. Conf.* (ISBN 0-937803-15-4)

Kistler, D. J. and Wightman, F. L. (1991) A model of head-related transfer functions based on principal components analysis and minimum-phase reconstruction, *J. Acoust. Soc. Am.*, **91**, 1637–47

Kobayashi, M. and Siio, I. (1993) Virtual conference room: a metaphor for multi-user real-time conferencing systems, in *Ro-Man: Proc. 2nd IEEE Int. Workshop on Robot and Human Communication*, Tokyo, pp. 430–5

Koizumi, N. (1991) A review of control technology for sound field synthesis (in Japanese), *J. Inst. Telev. Eng. Japan*, **45**(4), 474–9

Koizumi, N. and Cohen, M. (1993) Audio windows: graphical user interfaces for manipulating virtual acoustic environments (in Japanese), in *Proc. 18th Meeting, Society of Computer-Aided Instruction*, Tokyo

Koizumi, N., Cohen, M., and Aoki, S. (1992) Design of virtual conferencing environments in audio telecommunication, in *Proc. 92nd Audio Engineering Society Conv.*, Vienna, Austria (4CA1.04, preprint 3304)

Kraemer, K. L. and King, J. L. (1986) Computer-based systems for cooperative work and group decisionmaking: status of use and problems in development, *Technical Report*, Irvine, CA: University of California

Krueger, M. W. (1991) *Artificial Reality II*, Reading, MA: Addison-Wesley (ISBN 0-201-52260-8)

Kuhn, G. F. (1977) Model for the interaural time differences in the azimuthal plane, *J. Acoust. Soc. Am.*, **62**, 157–67

Lantz, K. A. (1986) An experiment in integrated multimedia conferencing, *Technical Report*, Stanford, CA: Department of Computer Science, Stanford University

Laws, P. (1973) Entfernungshören und das Problem der Im-Kopf-Lokalisiertheit von Hörereignissen (Auditory distance perception and the problem of 'in-head' localization of sound images), *Acustica*, **29**, 243–59

Lehnert, H. and Blauert, J. (1989) A concept for binaural room simulation (summary), in *Proc. (IEEE) ASSP Workshop on Applications of Signal Processing to Audio and Acoustics*, New Paltz, NY

Lezcano, F. L. (1993) A four channel dynamic sound location system, in *JMACS: Proc. Japan Music and Computer Science Society Meeting*, Tokyo, No. 47, pp. 23–6

Loomis, J. M., Hebert, C., and Cicinelli, J. G. (1990) Active localization of virtual sounds, *J. Acoust. Soc. Am.*, **88**(4), 1757–63

Loomis, J., Hebert, C., and Cicinelli, J. G. (1993) Personal guidance system for the visually impaired using GPS, GIS, and VR technologies, in *Proc. 1st Int. Conf. on Virtual Reality and Persons with Disabilities*, San Francisco, CA

Lord Rayleigh (Strutt, J. W.) (1907) On our perception of sound direction, *Phil. Mag.*, **13**, 214–32

Ludwig, L. F. (1989) Real-time multi-media teleconferencing: integrating new technology, *Technical Report*, Red Bank, NJ: Bell Communications Research, Integrated Media Architecture Laborator

Ludwig, L. F. and Pincever, N. C. (1989) Audio windowing and methods for its realization, *Technical Memorandum* TM-NPL-015361, Red Bank, NJ: Bell Communications Research

Ludwig, L. F., Pincever, N. C., and Cohen, M. (1990) Extending the notion of a window system to audio, *(IEEE) Computer* (special issue on *Voice in Computing*), **23**(8), 66–72

Lunney, D., Morrison, R. C., Cetera, M. M., and Hartness, R. V. (1983) A microcomputer-based laboratory aid for visually impaired students, *IEEE Micro*, **3**(4)

Makous, J. C. and Middlebrooks, J. C. (1990) Two-dimensional sound localization by human listeners, *J. Acoust. Soc. Am.*, **87**, 2188–200

Mansur, D. L. (1984) Graphs in sound: a numerical data analysis method for the blind, *Report UCRL-53548*, Lawrence Livermore National Laboratory

Mansur, D. L. (1987) Communicating with sound, in R. M. Baecker and W. A. S. Buxton (Eds), *Readings in Human-Computer Interaction: A Multidisciplinary Approach*, Cambridge, MA: Morgan Kaufmann (ISBN 0-934613-24-9) ch. 9

Mansur, D. L., Blattner, M. M., and Joy, K. I. (1985) Sound-graphs: a numerical data analysis method for the blind, in *Proc. 18th Hawaii Int. Conf. on System Sciences*

Martel, A. (1986) The SS-1 sound spatializer: a real-time MIDI spatialization processor, in *ICMC: Proc. Int. Comp. Music Conf.*, Computer Music Association, pp. 305–7

Martens, W. (1989) Spatial image formation in binocular vision and binaural hearing, in *Proc. 3D Media Technology Conf.*, Montréal, Québec

Martens, W. L. (1987) Principal components analysis and resynthesis of spectral cues to perceived direction, in *ICMC: Proc. Int. Comp. Music Conf.*, San Francisco, Computer Music Association

Masaki, S., Kanemaki, N., Tanigawa, H., Ichihara, H., and Shimamura, K. (1991) Personal multimedia-multipoint teleconference system for broadband ISDN, in *Proc. IFIP TC6/WG6.4 Third Int. Conf. on High Speed Networking*, Amsterdam: Elsevier, pp. 215–30

McGurk, H. and McDonald, J. (1976) Hearing lips and seeing voices, *Nature*, **264**, 746–8

McKinley, R. L. and Ericson, M. A. (1988) Digital synthesis of binaural auditory localization azimuth cues using headphones, *J. Acoust. Soc. Am.*, **83**, S18

McLuhan, H. M. and Fiore, Q. (1967) *The Medium is the Message*, Random House

Mehrgardt, S. and Mellert, V. (1977) Transformation characteristics of the external human ear, *J. Acoust. Soc. Am.*, **61**, 1567–76

Mershon, D. H. and Bowers, J. N. (1979) Absolute and relative cues for the auditory perception of egocentric distance, *Perception*, **8**, 311–22

Mershon, D. H. and King, L. E. (1975) Intensity and reverberation as factors in the auditory perception of egocentric distance, *Percept Psychophys.*, **18**, 409–15

Meyer, K., Applewhite, H. L., and Biocca, F. A. (1993) A survey of position trackers, *Presence: Teleoperators and Virtual Environments*, **1**(2), 173–200

Mezrich, J. J., Frysinger, S., and Slivjanovski, R. (1984) Dynamic representation of multivariate time series data, *J. Am. Stat. Assoc.*, **79**(385), 34–40

Middlebrooks, J. C. and Green, D. M. (1990) Directional dependence of interaural envelope delays, *J. Acoust. Soc. Am.*, **87**, 2149–62

Middlebrooks, J. C. and Green, D. M. (1991) Sound localization by human listeners, *Ann. Rev. Psychol.*, **42**, 135–59

Middlebrooks, J. C., Makous, J. C., and Green, D. M. (1989) Directional sensitivity of sound-pressure levels in the human ear canal, *J. Acoust. Soc. Am.*, **86**, 89–108

Mills, W. (1972) Auditory localization, in J. V. Tobias (Ed.), *Foundations of Modern Auditory Theory, Vol. II*, New York: Academic, pp. 301–45

Mills, W. (1958) On the minimum audible angle, *J. Acoust. Soc. Am.*, **30**, 237–46

Miyoshi, M. and Koizumi, N. (1991) New transaural system for teleconferencing service, in *Proc. Int. Symp. on Active Control of Sound and Vibration*, Tokyo, pp. 217–22

Moller, H. (1992) Fundamentals of binaural technology, *Appl. Acoust.*, **36**, 171–218

Moore, F. R. (1983) A general model for spatial processing of sounds, *Computer Music J.*, **7**(3), 6–15

Nielsen, L., Mahowald, M., and Mead, C. (1988) SeeHear, *Technical Report*, California Institute of Technology

Oldfield, S. R. and Parker, S. P. A. (1984a) Acuity of sound localisation: a topography of auditory space I. Normal hearing conditions, *Perception*, **13**, 601–17

Oldfield, S. R. and Parker, S. P. A. (1984b) Acuity of sound localisation: a topography of auditory space II. Pinna cues absent, *Perception*, **13**, 601–17

Oldfield, S. R. and Parker, S. P. A. (1986) Acuity of sound localisation: a topography of auditory space III. Monaural hearing conditions, *Perception*, **15**, 67–81

Patterson, R. R. (1982) Guidelines for auditory warning systems on civil aircraft, *Paper No. 82017*, Civil Aviation Authority, London

Perrott, D. R. (1982) Studies in the perception of auditory motion, in R. Gatehouse (Ed.), *Localization of Sound: Theory and Applications*, Groton, CN: Amphora, pp. 169–93

Perrott, D. R., Saberi, K., Brown, K., and Strybel, T. Z. (1990) Auditory psychomotor coordination and visual search performance, *Percept. Psychophys.*, **48**, 214–26

Perrott, D. R., Sadralodabai, T., Saberi, K., and Strybel, T. Z. (1991) Aurally aided visual search in the central visual field: effects of visual load and visual enhancement of the target, *Human Factors*, **33**, 389–400

Perrott, D. R. and Tucker, J. (1988) Minimum audible movement angle as a function of signal frequency and the velocity of the source, *J. Acoust. Soc. Am.*, **83**, 1522–7

Persterer, A. (1991) Binaural simulation of an 'ideal control room' for headphone reproduction, in *90th Convention of the AES*, Paris, (Preprint 3062 (k-4))

Plenge, G. (1974) On the difference between localization and lateralization, *J. Acoust. Soc. Am.*, **56**, 944–51

Poesselt, C., Schroeter, J., Opitz, M., Divenyi, P., and Blauert, J. (1986) Generation of binaural signals for research and home entertainment (paper b1-6), in *Proc. 12th Int. Congress on Acoustics*, Toronto

Polhemus (1987) *3SPACE ISOTRAK™ User's Manual*, Polhemus Navigation Science Division, McDonnell Douglas Electronic Company

Pollack, I. and Ficks, L. (1954) Information of elementary multidimensional auditory displays, *J. Acoust. Soc. Am.*, **26**(2), 155–8

Reichter, F. and Persterer, A. (1989) Design and applications of a creative audio processor, in *Proc. 86th Conv. of the Audio Engineering Society*, Hamburg, (Preprint 2782 (U-4))

Robinett, W. (1992) Synthetic experience: a proposed taxonomy, *Presence: Teleoperators and Virtual Environments*, **1**(2), 229–47

Roffler, S. K. and Butler, R. A. (1968) Factors that influence the localization of sound in the vertical plane, *J. Acoust. Soc. Am.*, **43**, 1255–9

Sandel, T. T., Teas, D. C., Feddersen, W. E., and Jeffress, L. A. (1955) Localization of sound from single and paired sources, *J. Acoust. Soc. Am.*, **27**, 842–52

Sanders, M. S. and McCormick, E. J. (1987) *Human Factors in Engineering and Design*, New York: McGraw-Hill, 6th edn (ISBN 0-07-044903-1)

Sarin, S. and Greif, I. (1985) Computer-based real-time conferencing systems, *(IEEE) Computer*, **18**(10), 33–45

Sarkar, M. and Brown, M. (1994) Graphical fisheye views, *Commun. ACM*, **37**(12), 73–84

Scaletti, C. and Craig, A. B. (1991) Using sound to extract meaning from complex data, in E. J. Farrell (Ed.), *Extracting Meaning from Complex Data: Processing, Display, Interaction II, Proc. SPIE*, vol. 1459

Schaffer, D., Zuo, Z., Bartram, L., Dill, J., Dubs, S., Greenberg, S., and Roseman, D. (1993) An experiment comparing variable zoom to standard methods, in *Proc. Graphics Interface*, Toronto: Morgan-Kaufmann

Scott, D. (1989) A processor for locating stationary and moving sound sources in a simulated acoustical environment, in *ICMC: Proc. Int. Comp. Music Conf.*, Computer Music Association, 277–80

Setton, M. (1990) Sonic Navigator™, *Project Report*, Berkeley Systems, Inc.

Shaw, E. A. G. (1974) The external ear, in *Handbook of Sensory Physiology, vol. V/1, Auditory System*, New York: Springer, pp. 455–90

Shimada, S. and Suzuki, J. (1987) A new talker location recognition through sound image localization control in multipoint teleconference system, *IEICE Trans. on Fundamentals of Electronics, Communications and Computer Sciences*, J70-B(9), pp. 491–7

Shimada, S. and Yamasaki, Y. (1991) Evolution of digital signal processing in communication networks (in Japanese), *J. Acoust. Soc. Japan*, 47(7), 491–7

Shinomiya, Y., Sawada, K., and Nomura, J. (1993) Development for real-time acoustic simulation in virtual realities (in Japanese), *J. Acoust. Soc. Japan*, 49(7), 515–21

Smith, S., Bergeron, R. D., and Grinstein, G. G. (1990) Stereophonic and surface sound generation for exploratory data analysis, in J. C. Chew and J. Whiteside (Eds), *CHI: Proc. ACM Conf. on Computer-Human Interaction*, Seattle, WA, New York: Addison-Wesley, pp. 125–32

Sonnenwald, D. H., Gopinath, B., Haberman, G. O., Keese III, W. M., and Myers, J. S. (1990) Infosound: an audio aid to program comprehension, in *Proc. Hawaii Int. Conf. on System Sciences*, Honolulu, HI

Sorkin, R. D., Wightman, F. L., Kistler, D. J., and Elvers, G. C. (1989) An exploratory study of the use of movement-correlated cues in an auditory head-up display, *Human Factors*, 31(2), 161–6

Speigle, J. M. and Loomis, J. M. (1993) Auditory distance perception by translating observers, in *VR93: Proc. IEEE Symp. on Research Frontiers in Virtual Reality (in conjunction with IEEE Visualization)*, San Jose, CA, pp. 92–9

Stefik, M., Bobrow, D., Lanning, S., Tatar, D., and Foster, G. (1986) WYSIWIS revised: Early experiences with multi-user interfaces, in *Conf. on Computer-Supported Cooperative Work*, Austin, TX, pp. 276–90

Stefik, M., Foster, G., Bobrow, D. G., Kahn, K., Lanning, S., and Suchman, L. (1987) Beyond the chalkboard: computer support for collaboration and problem solving in meetings, *Commun. ACM*, 30(1), 32–47

Stevens, S. S. and Newman, E. B. (1936) The localization of actual sources of sound, *Am. J. Psychol.*, 48, 297–306

Strybel, T. Z., Manlingas, C. L., and Perrott, D. R. (1992) Minimum audible movement angle as a function of azimuth and elevation of the source, *Human Factors*, 34(3), 267–75

Sumikawa, D. A., Blattner, M. M., Joy, K. I., and Greenberg, R. M. (1986) Guidelines for the syntactic design of audio cues in computer interfaces, in *Proc. Nineteenth Annual Hawaii Int. Conf. on System Sciences*, Honolulu, HI

Takemura, H., Kitamura, Y., Ohya, J., and Kishino, F. (1992) Distributed processing architecture for virtual space teleconferencing, in S. Tachi (Ed.), *Proc. Second Int. Conf. Artificial Reality and Tele-Existence*, Tokyo, pp. 27–32

Tanigawa, H., Arikawa, T., Masaki, S., and Shimamura, K. (1991) Personal multimedia-multipoint teleconference system, in *Proc. IEEE InfoCom'91*, pp. 1127–34

Thurlow, W. R. and Runge, P. S. (1967) Effects of induced heard movements on localization of direction of sounds, *J. Acoust. Soc. Am.*, 42, 480–8

Toole, F. E. (1969) In-head localization of acoustic images, *J. Acoust. Soc. Am.*, 48, 943–9

Urei (1980) *Dual Parametric Equalizer Model 546 Operating Instructions*, Urei (United Recording Electronics Industries), 8460 San Fernando Rd, Sun Valley, CA 91352

Vanderheiden, G. C. (1989) Nonvisual alternative display techniques for output from graphics-based computers, *J. Visual Impairment Blindness*, 383–90

VPL (1987) *DataGlove Model 2 Operating Manual*, VPL (Visual Programming Language) Research, Inc., 656 Bair Island Rd, Suite 304, Redwood City, CA 94063

Wallach, H. (1940) The role of head movements and vestibular and visual cues in sound localization, *J. Exp. Psychol.*, **27**, 339–68

Wallach, H., Newman, E. B., and Rosenzweig, M. R. (1949) The precedence effect in sound localization, *Am. J. Psychol.*, **57**, 315–36

Warren, D. H., Welch, R. B., and McCarthy, T. J. (1981) The role of visual-auditory "compellingness" in the ventriloquiwm effect: implications for transitivity among the spatial senses, *Percept. Psychophys.*, **30**(6), 557–64

Wellner, P., Mackay, W., and Gold, R. (1993) *Commun. ACM*, **36**(7)

Wenzel, E. M. (1992) Localization in virtual acoustic displays, *Presence: Teleoperators and Virtual Environments*, **1**(1), 80–107

Wenzel, E. M. (1994) Spatial sound and sonification, in G. Kramer (Ed.), *Proc. First Int. Conf. on Auditory Display*, Santa Fe, NM (ISBN 0-201-62603-9), pp. 127–50

Wenzel, E. M., Arruda, M., Kistler, D. J., and Wightman, F. L. (1993) Localization using nonindividualized head-related transfer functions, *J. Acoust. Soc. Am.*, **94**(1), 111–23

Wenzel, E. M. and Foster, S. H. (1993) Perceptual consequences of interpolating head-related transfer functions during spatial synthesis, in *Proc. (IEEE) ASSP Workshop on Applications of Signal Processing to Audio and Acoustics*, New Paltz, NY

Wenzel, E. M., Stone, P. K., Fisher, S. S., and Foster, S. H. (1990) A system for three-dimensional acoustic "visualization" in a virtual environment workstation, in *Proc. First IEEE Conf. on Visualization*, San Francisco, pp. 329–37

Wenzel, E. M., Wightman, F. L., and Foster, S. H. (1988a) Development of a three-dimensional auditory display system, in *CHI: Proc. ACM Conf. on Computer-Human Interaction*, Washington, DC

Wenzel, E. M., Wightman, F. L., and Foster, S. H. (1988b) A virtual display system for conveying three-dimensional acoustic information, in *Human Factors Society 32nd Annual Meeting*, Santa Monica, CA, pp. 86–90

Wenzel, E. M., Wightman, F. L., and Kistler, D. J. (1991) Localization of non-individualized virtual acoustic display cues, in S. P. Robertson, *et al.*, *CHI: Proc. ACM Conf. on Computer-Human Interaction*, New Orleans, LA, New York: Addison-Wesley (ISBN 0-201-51278-5)

Whitehead, J. F. (1994) The Audio Browser: An audio database navigation tool in a virtual environment, in *Proc. Int. Computer Music Conf.*, Århus, Denmark, pp. 280–3

Wightman, F. L. and Kistler, D. J. (1989a) Headphone simulation of free-field listening I: stimulus synthesis, *J. Acoust. Soc. Am.*, **85**, 858–67

Wightman, F. L. and Kistler, D. J. (1989b) Headphone simulation of free-field listening II: psychophysical validation, *J. Acoust. Soc. Am.*, **85**, 868–78

Wightman, F. L., Kistler, D. J., and Arruda, M. (1992) Perceptual consequences of engineering compromises in synthesis of virtual auditory objects, *J. Acoust. Soc. Am.*, **92**, 2332

HAPTIC DISPLAYS

9

Tactile Displays

KURT A. KACZMAREK AND PAUL BACH-Y-RITA

The average adult has approximately $2\,\mathrm{m}^2$ of skin (Gibson, 1968), about 90% hairy, and remainder smooth or glabrous. Although the glabrous areas are more sensitive than the hairy, both types are highly innervated with sensory receptors and nerves (Sinclair, 1981). Tactile displays have utilized both glabrous and hairy skin, the type selected being relative to the sensory display needs of the various investigators.

There are several advantages for selecting the skin as the sensory surface to receive information. (1) It is accessible, extensive in area, richly innervated, and capable of precise discrimination. Further, when the skin of the forehead or trunk is used, the tactile display system does not interfere materially with motor or other sensory functions. (2) The skin shows a number of functional similarities to the retina of the eye in its capacity to mediate information. Large parts of the body surface are relatively flat, and the receptor surfaces of the skin, like the retina, are capable of mediating displays in two spatial dimensions as well as having the potential for temporal integration (summation over time). Thus, there is generally no need for complex topological transformation or for temporal coding of pictorial information for direct presentation onto the accessible areas of the skin, although temporal display factors have been explored with the goal of transmitting spatial information across the skin more quickly than is possible with present systems (Kaczmarek et al., 1984; Bach-y-Rita and Hughes, 1985; Kaczmarek et al., 1985; Loomis and Lederman, 1986). Spatial patterns learned visually can be identified tactually, and vice versa (Epstein et al., 1989; Hughes et al., 1990). (3) Certain types of sensory inhibition, including the Mach band phenomenon and other examples of lateral inhibition originally demonstrated for vision, are equally demonstrable in the skin (Békésy, 1967). (4) Finally, there is evidence that the skin normally functions as an exteroceptor at least in a limited sense: Katz noted that to some extent both vibration and temperature changes can be felt at a distance (Krueger, 1970). For example, a blind person can "feel" the approach of a warm cylinder at three times the distance required by the sighted individual (Krueger, 1970).

Tactile displays in virtual and remote environments

While force feedback is becoming increasingly common in human kinesthetic (force and position) interfaces, tactile (spatial pattern) display has lagged behind. This is somewhat surprising, given our ubiquitous use of touch in everyday life. Tactile cues refine and moderate every manual activity, from grasping a fork to buttoning an overcoat. Lack of adequate display technology has likely restricted tactile access in advanced interfaces, but several companies now manufacture tactile displays for multiple body locations (see list at end of this chapter). Spatial tactile sensors now exist with resolutions better than 1 mm, so tactile information is available. Sensory substitution studies detailed in this chapter demonstrate that tactile feedback need not even be presented to the hands; other body loci should be equally functional, because the brain can learn to project the displayed information onto the remote or virtual environment (VE). We therefore propose that the following applications could benefit significantly from the addition of tactile feedback.

Exploratory tasks with uncertain outcomes are the domain of humans. Planetary and geologic exploration require as much information as possible for appropriate decision making; faithful telepresence will enhance such activities (Held and Durlach, 1992). Tactile feedback is necessary for physical telepresence.

Some environments make visual feedback less useful. High radiation could prevent proper operation of cameras; a muddy sea floor could prevent light transmission (Monkman, 1992). Tactile information, however, would remain intact under these conditions. In the real world, may tasks can be performed with tactile and kinesthetic feedback alone.

Some operations are inherently tactile in nature. Exploring a surface for irregularities and resiliency or elasticity give important clues to its composition and finish in the absence of detailed mechanical and chemical analysis. Virtual surgery, proposed for training medical personnel, would need to reflect the subtle textures of real tissue that differentiate physiological structures.

Tactile feedback can serve as a surrogate for force feedback, greatly reducing hand controller complexity and power consumption. Fingertip force could be conveyed by a large tactor covering the entire fingertip, or by simultaneous activation of many small tactors, which could also be modulated with spatial, tactile patterns.

Finally, entertainment will likely provide a sizable market for VE technology. The availability of "feelies" will be an irresistible attention-getter, for it will help complete the sense of total immersion, or presence, in the virtual world.

Sensory substitution as a model

While the use of tactile displays in virtual and remote worlds is relatively new, much research has demonstrated the utility of tactile displays to partially compensate for human sensory deficits. Sensory substitution systems provide their users with environmental information through a human sensory channel (eye, ear, or skin) different from that normally used. Technological prosthetic devices, first developed for individuals lacking hearing or sight, permit the formation of virtual auditory or visual environments via the sense of touch. Though limited in commercial success, these devices have demonstrated that the skin can receive substantial amounts of information, and will serve as a baseline for our discussions of tactile displays.

Scope

In this chapter, we will summarize the technology developed by many investigators for presenting information to the skin's tactile sense by electrical and mechanical stimulation, examining psychophysiological and technological limitations of present tactile displays, and proposing topics for future research to overcome some of these limitations.

To begin, we will first discuss present and potential future applications of tactile displays, including tactile vision substitution (TVS), tactile auditory substitution, and remote tactile sensing or feedback. This section will emphasize the actual displays and means of processing information for display. We will then review the mechanisms of normal touch perception, including both the physiology and the information-processing ability of the tactile sense and their relevance to display of tactile information. Next, we will discuss the technology for producing tactile sensations by (1) static (or slowly varying) mechanical skin deformation, (2) vibratory (vibrotactile) stimulation, and (3) electrical stimulation of the tactile sense using both surface and subdermal electrodes; typically called electrotactile (or electrocutaneous) stimulation. We will discuss practical operational and engineering considerations for tactile displays, such as comfort, safety, power consumption, and psychological issues. Finally, after briefly reviewing some important considerations for performance and training, we will conclude with a list of manufacturers of tactile displays.

TACTILE DISPLAY DEVICES AND APPLICATIONS

This section provides some examples of the types of tactile display used experimentally and commercially. Because there is substantial functional interchangeability, static mechanical displays, electrotactile (stimulation of touch by surface electrodes), and vibrotactile (vibrating) displays will be treated together. For a broader overview of available devices and applications, we refer the reader to reviews on systems for visual substitution (Bach-y-Rita, 1972; Collins and Bach-y-Rita, 1973; Collins, 1985; Tyler 1990), auditory substitution (Kirman, 1973; Richardson and Frost, 1977; Kirman, 1982; Reed et al., 1982; Sherrick, 1984; Szeto and Christensen, 1988), and other applications (Collins and Madey, 1974; Szeto and Saunders, 1982; Saunders, 1983; Phillips, 1988; Riso, 1988; Szeto and Riso, 1990; Shimoga, 1993; Barfield et al., in press). Electrotactile display technology and applications are extensively reviewed by Szeto and Saunders (1982), Riso et al. (1989), Szeto and Riso

(1990), and Kaczmarek *et al.* (1991). Loomis and Lederman (1986) discuss the perceptual bases for tactile displays, along with a brief review of devices.

Low-technology tactile display

In order to provide a conceptual baseline for discussing technological tactile displays, we will first present three examples of sensory substitution systems that are frequently used as communication methods by blind, deaf, and deaf–blind persons (Kaczmarek, in press). The longevity and success of these mechanically simple methods suggest that their study might provide useful information to the designer of more complex systems (Reed *et al.*, 1990).

Braille

A widely used sensory substitution method is Braille. Using very little instrumentation, the necessary sensory information from the lost sensory domain (vision) is presented in an appropriate format for another, intact, sensory system (touch). In Braille, alphanumeric characters are changed into raised dots; a code based on a rectangular 6-dot matrix (two columns of three dots each, separated by 2.3 mm) was developed to enable blind persons to read with the fingertips.[1] The critical factor is that (with sufficient training) this approach allows the blind person to achieve the same conceptual analysis and mental imagery from reading with the fingertips as the sighted person achieves by reading print. An average Braille reading rate for experienced users is 125 words min^{-1}; 200 words min^{-1} is possible (Library of Congress, 1987).

Sign language

Letters, words, and phrases expressed as hand and body positions and motions can be received visually by the deaf (fingerspelling or American Sign Language) or tactually (in the hand—fingerspelling only) by the deaf–blind. No instrumentation is required. In a comparative study of fingerspelling received visually and tactually (Reed *et al.*, 1990), experienced users interpreted continuous everyday speech in both reception modalities with greater than 80% correct keyword identification at speeds up to 6 letters s^{-1} ≈ 2 syllables s^{-1} (the maximal rate for manual letter production). Production of signs appears to be the limiting factor, at least for visual recognition; 70% correct performance was obtained at 4 syllables s^{-1} presented by high-speed videotape playback. (Tactual performance cannot yet be tested at this speed.) For comparison, a normal speech rate is 4–5 syllables s^{-1}; American Sign Language conveys overall concepts at approximately the same rate as speech.

Tadoma

While sign language requires training by both sender and receiver, in Tadoma the sender speaks normally. The receiver places his/her hands on the face and neck of the sender to monitor lip and jaw movements, airflow at the lips, and vibration on the neck (Reed *et al.*, 1992). Experienced users achieve 80% keyword recognition of everyday speech at a rate of 3 syllables s^{-1} (Leotta *et al.*, 1988). Using no instrumentation, this is the highest speech communication rate recorded for any tactile-only communication system (Reed *et al.*, 1992). Higher rates are possible with reduced comprehension. The richness, quantity, and variety of tactile information available through Tadoma may be responsible for its success. A synthetic Tadoma display (computer-controlled mechanical face), with upper and lower lip and jaw movements, mouth airflow, and laryngeal vibration, approaches the performance of natural Tadoma (Henderson, 1989; Leotta *et al.*, 1988; Tan *et al.*, 1989).

Tactile feedback from tactile sensors

Performing detailed manual tasks is difficult for people with advanced cases of Hansen's disease (leprosy). They lack the sense of touch in the fingers and thus unknowingly injure their hands by grasping objects too tightly. Collins and Madey (1974) developed a tactile feedback system in which strain gages mounted in a special glove measured the force (10 g to 5 kg) on each fingerpad. Each of the 5 sensors controlled the electrotactile stimulation intensity of one forehead electrode (Figure 9-1). Subjects without sensation in the hands were able to distinguish smooth from rough surfaces, soft from hard objects, and by scanning were able to detect edges and corners, in spite of the low resolution of the display. It is likely that the large amount of perceived information from such a low-resolution display comes from (1) spatial information integrated with kinesthetic information received by manually scanning complex objects (haptic exploration) with the few sensors; in effect, forming a "perceptual organ" (Bach-y-Rita, 1972), and (2) receiving texture information from surfaces by the minute, time-dependent frictional vibrations recorded by the sensors (Johansson and Westling, 1987). Kinesthetic information is not necessary to discriminate textures (Loomis and Lederman, 1986).

Informal experiments in our own laboratory similar to those of Collins and Madey suggest that electrotactile stimulation at frequencies of several hundred Hz may be necessary to convey fine-texture information. Rapid sensory adaptation is presently a severe problem for electrotactile stimulation at these high frequencies (Kaczmarek, 1991).

Astronauts in space face a similar lack of sensation (Bach-y-Rita *et al.*, 1987). The gloves of their protective suits reduce touch sensation because they are thick and pressurized. Their hands tire rapidly because they tend to overgrasp objects that could slip out of their grasp. NASA has looked at mainly passive means in which to increase the tactile feedback to the astronaut including movable pins, enhanced fingerpad tactile pads, glove–hand adhesion, and removable fingertips to expose a less bulky, less protected finger. One way to make space activity safer for astronauts is to use remotely controlled robots to perform extravehicular activity (EVA) (Cleland and Winfield, 1985). However, current remote manipulators lack tactile feedback (although some do have force feedback), so it is difficult for the operator to perceive if an object has been properly grasped. In one NASA study (Hannaford and Wood, 1992), the addition of force feedback to a teleoperator reduced the total time to complete three test tasks from 92 s to 63 s. A barehanded time of only 14 s suggests that tactile feedback could further improve performance. (The test

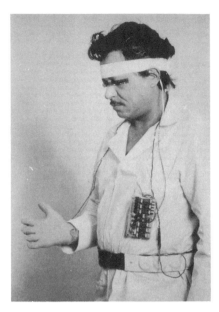

Figure 9-1 This tactile prosthesis by Collins and Madey (1974) measured the pressure at the tips of insensate fingers; the strain gage sensors were mounted to a special glove. The pressure information controlled the stimulation intensity of forehead electrodes by modulating phase width.

tasks were exchange of two blocks, insert nine pegs in holes, and mate and unmate three electrical connectors.)

At the University of Wisconsin, we have investigated tactile feedback systems for space gloves and space telerobots (Bach-y-Rita *et al.*, 1987), and people with insensate feet and hands (common complications of diabetes) (Maalej and Webster, 1988; Wertsch *et al.*, 1988). Pressure sensors on the glove surface, end effector (gripper), shoe insole, and fingers, respectively, control the electrotactile stimulation perceived intensity, e.g. on the abdomen.

Tactile auditory substitution

Based on the early work of Békésy (1955), who discovered that the human ear performs a frequency analysis of incoming sounds at frequency-selective regions in the cochlea, Saunders *et al.* (1981) developed an auditory prosthesis which adjusts the perceived intensity of 16 electrodes, each corresponding to the sound intensity in a given passband in the audio spectrum. This (formerly) commercially available device, the Tacticon™, provided enough "auditory" feedback to improve the speech clarity of deaf children, and to improve auditory discrimination and comprehension in some older patients (Szeto and Riso, 1990). Blamey and Clark (1985) and Boothroyd and Hnath-Chisolm (1988) describe similar eight-channel electrotactile devices based on this "vocoder" principle. Brooks and Frost (1986) and Brooks *et al.* (1986) describe a similar 16-channel vibrotactile device. Unitech Research Inc. (1990) sells a

32-channel electrotactile vocoder; see also Sevrain *et al.* (1990). Preliminary clinical trials showed that the Audiotact™ prosthesis aided in discrimination of phonemes by lipreading, but was not of benefit in subject repetition of connected text (Hughes, 1989; Rakowski *et al.*, 1989). A number of the earlier vocoder-type devices are reviewed by Reed *et al.* (1982), who found few underlying conclusions for the development of a high-performance system; dimensionality (1D vs. 2D display), skin locus (finger vs. abdomen), stimulation mode (electrotactile vs. vibrotactile) had no observable consistent effects on performance. Vocoder users cannot yet perform as well as Tadoma users.

Tactile vision substitution (TVS)

Spatial displays

A two-dimensional matrix of stimulators can display spatial information to the skin similarly to the way the eye presents spatial information to its retina. The television-type camera in a TVS system receives a "visual" image and presents it to the user's skin with vibrotactile or electrotactile stimulators. Each stimulator's intensity (pulse width or amplitude) is controlled by the light intensity at a single camera receptive pixel. Following the initial report (Bach-y-Rita *et al.*, 1969) of successful laboratory use of a vision substitution device, Collins (1970), White (1970), White *et al.* (1970), Bach-y-Rita (1972), Collins and Bach-y-Rita (1973), Craig (1973), Collins and Madey (1974), and others used TVS systems extensively in the early 1970s to study the skin's ability to interpret "visual" information (Figure 9-2). They found that subjects could immediately recognize vertical, horizontal, and diagonal lines. Experienced users could identify common objects and people's faces (Bach-y-Rita, 1972), and perform tasks such as electronic assembly under a microscope (Bach-y-Rita, 1974). Extensive anecdotal comments by one experienced TVS subject are quoted by Bach-y-Rita (1982). With sufficient practice, the "visual" images tactually displayed to the abdomen or back were perceptually projected into the space in front of the camera. This is an example of a general perceptual phenomenon called distal attribution, in which an event is perceived as occurring at a location other than the physical stimulation site (Loomis, 1992b).

A 384-point electrotactile TVS system in development by Unitech Research, Inc. (Madison, WI) offers reliable, painfree abdominal stimulation and stepped electronic zoom capabilities. The authors have found the electrical stimulation of the prototype Videotact™ to be more comfortable than previous electrotactile displays that they have tried. Subjects have navigated in a simple, high-contrast hallway. Planned experiments will determine if electronic and optical zoom systems yield equivalent performance; the second author's early experience suggests that a fast, continuous zoom is useful for complex object recognition (Bach-y-Rita, 1972).

Unfortunately, due partly to limited spatial resolution, tactile masking effects (a strong stimulus obscuring a nearby weaker one), and narrow dynamic

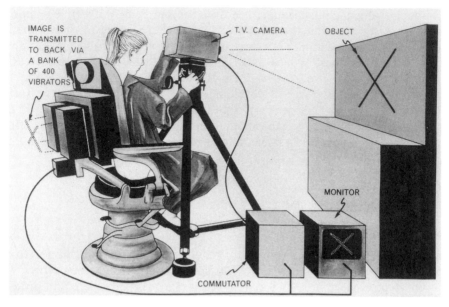

Figure 9-2 This early tactile vision substitution system displayed vibratory patterns on the skin that spatially corresponded to the image recorded by the electronic camera. Experienced subjects were able to recognize common objects and even people's faces (Bach-y-Rita, 1972), although recognition times were as long as one minute for complex scenes.

range, TVS systems are not useful for acquiring information from "cluttered" visual environments such as normal hallways or outdoors and are therefore not presently useful as navigation aids for the blind. Recognition of complex patterns requires manual scanning by the user, slowing the recognition process. We will later discuss information preprocessing steps that may enhance performance.

Tactile reading

Similarly, Linvill and Bliss (1966), Bliss (1969), and Bliss *et al.* (1970) developed the commercially available Optacon (Optical to Tactile Converter by TeleSensory, Mountain View, CA). It converts the outline of printed letters recorded by a small, hand-held camera to vibrotactile letter outlines on the user's fingerpad. The user sweeps the camera across a line of ordinary printed text, with the outline of each letter being converted to an enlarged 6-column $\times$ 24-row vibrating (230 Hz) spatially corresponding (not Braille) pattern on the user's fingerpad (the Optacon II has a 5 $\times$ 20 display). Exceptional blind users can read ordinary printed text at up to 90 words per minute with the Optacon (Hill, 1973); 28 words min^{-1} is more typical (Hislop, 1983). The Optacon^{TM} is the most successful technological sensory substitution device to date, with worldwide sales over 15 000 units, and is the only one to achieve commercial success.

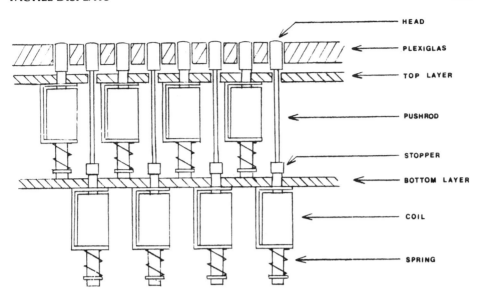

Labels pointing to the figure from top to bottom:
HEAD
PLEXIGLAS
TOP LAYER
PUSHROD
STOPPER
BOTTOM LAYER
COIL
SPRING

Figure 9-3 This static (nonvibrating) mechanical haptic display by Frisken-Gibson *et al.* (1987) used miniature solenoids to produce a relief (height) display of computer graphics.

Interactive haptic displays

Haptic (scanned by fingerpad exploration) display of graphics to blind computer users can potentially reduce information-transfer limitations associated with fixed (attached to the skin) displays (Bach-y-Rita, 1990).[2] The resolution of the tactile sense should also be effectively increased as is evident by the amount of spatial information that can be gathered by exploring an object with a single fingerpad. In an ongoing project, the authors further hypothesize that the ability of the user to use all fingers will provide a tactile analog of peripheral vision, further enhancing performance.

Static tactile displays

Figure 9-3 schematically shows one example of a static tactile display (Frisken, 1987; Frisken-Gibson *et al.*, 1987). This 64-solenoid, four-level display presented graphical information from an IBM PC. While functional, friction was a problem with this complex mechanical device with sliding parts; therefore, no detailed pattern recognition studies were attempted. Power consumption for each solenoid in the fully raised position is 0.5 W, precluding battery operation.

Power consumption is dramatically reduced by using a latching mechanism for each pin/tactor. A prototype updateable Braille cell by Braille Displays, Cambridge, MA, uses one prime mover for all pins, coupled with an individual piezoelectric latch for each of the six pins in each Braille cell. Power consumption for a four-line, 40-cell-per-line display is approx. 20 W, or only 21 mW per pin, if the display is updated once per second.

We are aware of one static mechanical tactile display designed for stationary use on the fingerpad (Johnson, 1990). A prototype device is manufactured by Tini Alloy Co., Inc., San Leandro, CA. Each pin tactor of the 5×6 array requires 0.24 A current to heat a 0.076 mm diameter, 15 mm length Ti–Ni shape-memory alloy wire. Contraction of this wire by 3% moves the tactile tip of a spring cantilever 0.5 mm with a force of 20 g. Actuation time is 0.1 s for 90% of deflection; (passive) recovery time is 1.6 s for 80% return. A 10 Hz actuation–recovery cycle rate seems possible; 4 Hz has been achieved in a similar 0.04 cm^3-volume rotary actuator with active deflection and recovery (Gabriel *et al.*, 1988).

Virtual tactile tablet

Recently, an innovative approach has created a prototype multisensory non-visual interface to graphics-based computers (Boyd *et al.*, 1990). This approach addresses the issue of presenting a "full page" or large pictorial image to the somatosensory system by mounting a fingerpad vibrotactile stimulation array to a mobile/manipulable mouse, allowing haptic exploration of the entire visual/graphic space with a small display. The tactile display device of this system is Virtual Tactile Tablet (or Tactile Puck/Mouse), which consists of a standard absolute-position graphics entry tablet and a specially configured mouse. A 5×20 array of pin vibrotactors (from the Optacon II) is mounted directly above the intersection of the horizontal and vertical segments of the T-shaped mouse to provide a 1-to-1 correspondence of actual to perceived cursor movement. When the screen cursor crosses a line or image segment as the user moves the mouse across the "page" of the tactile tablet, s/he perceives not only the specific construction of the image element projected but also the spatial structure and orientation of that element relative to the overall image through continued haptic "scanning" of the entire image space. This orientation information is important to allow the user to perceive the "big picture," even if it is acquired by scanning. A similar, earlier approach called inTOUCH separated the display (vibrotactile Optacon II) from the display control mouse, thus requiring two hands for operation (Boyd *et al.*, 1990).

Functionally tactile force display

Recent work (Minsky *et al.*, 1990; Minsky, 1995) shows that "tactile" percepts can be communicated through force reflection alone, i.e., without a "spatial" tactile display, if the bandwidth is sufficiently wide (DC to 100–1000 Hz). Bandwidth changes in the 500–1000 Hz range can be perceived.[3] A system called "Sandpaper" (Figure 9-4) consists of a high-performance, force-reflective, two degree-of-freedom (DOF) joystick coupled to a computer model of various virtual materials and surfaces, such as sandpaper, bar gratings, elastic bumps, and spring–mass–damper systems (e.g., weight on a rubber band in molasses). The system user manipulates a cursor on the computer screen and "drags" it across virtual surfaces and material systems with the joystick, receiving force feedback related to the system depicted on the screen (which can be covered up in software to avoid visual cues).

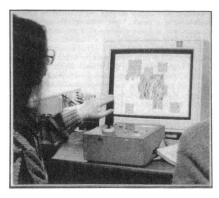

Figure 9-4 A wide-bandwidth, force-reflecting joystick allows a user to probe computer models of variously textured surfaces. The user of the Sandpaper system (Minsky *et al.*, 1990) receives "tactile" information, as if an actual rigid stick were dragged across a real surface.

One of the authors of the present chapter has had personal experience with this system, and perceived sensations that were indeed "textured" and "tactile." While this might appear to be another example of spatiotemporal haptic integration, the perception of roughness does not in general depend on kinesthetic information; roughness estimates are identical for surfaces that are (1) manually scanned, or (2) dragged under a stationary fingerpad (Loomis and Lederman, 1986). The high quality of percepts elicited by this system tends to blur the traditional distinction between kinesthetic (force and position) and tactile (spatial) feedback from remote and virtual environments.

Massie and Salisbury (1994) describe a similar, commercially-available, device with six DOF (three active, three passive).

Other experimental tactile displays

Many other experimental tactile displays have been constructed for experimental use, including an 8×8 vibrating display that is conformable to deep skin contours (Cholewiak and Sherrick, 1981), a 15×15 vibrating array for stimulating the fingers and hand (Kirman, 1974), and a 12×8 vibrotactile forehead display called the Electrophthalm (Starkiewicz *et al.*, 1971). Of particular note is the steerable water jet that can display tactile figures either with cursive tracing or in a raster-scanned format (Collins and Madey, 1974; Collins, 1985). Two-dimensional patterns are traced by a pressurized water stream that is aimed at the skin; a thin, flexible rubber membrane contains the drain water for recirculation.

HUMAN TACTUAL PERCEPTION

Geldard (1960) and Sherrick (1973) lamented that as a communication channel, the tactile sense is often considered inferior to sight and hearing. However, the tactile system possesses some of the same attributes as both of the "primary" senses (Bach-y-Rita, 1972). With over 10 000 parallel channels (receptors) (Collins and Saunders, 1970), the tactile system is capable of processing a great deal of information *if it is properly presented*. This section will therefore summarize the primary mechanisms of human tactual perception.

Humans receive and combine two types of perceptual information when touching and manipulating objects. *Kinesthetic* information describes the relative positions and movements of body parts as well as muscular effort. Muscle and skin receptors and an internal representation of voluntary muscular effort (efference copy) are primarily responsible for kinesthesis; joint receptors serve primarily as protective limit switches (Rabischong, 1981). *Tactile* information describes spatial pressure patterns on the skin given a fixed body position. Everyday touch perception combines tactile and kinesthetic information; this combination is called *haptic perception*. Loomis (1981b) and Loomis and Lederman (1986) provide excellent reviews of these perceptual mechanisms; we will provide primarily those details that pertain directly to the display of tactile information, with or without accompanying kinesthetic information.

Sensory physiology of the skin for normal touch

Skin anatomy

Besides specific fibers for pain sensation, human skin contains six types of cutaneous receptors that have been identified and characterized (Geddes, 1972; Geldard, 1972; Sinclair, 1981; Schmidt, 1986). Note that some receptors are found only in hairy or only in glabrous (hairless) skin. Table 9-1 lists several characteristics of the afferent neural mechanoreceptor systems corresponding to these receptors,[4] following the nomenclature of Schmidt (1986) for hairy skin and Vallbo and Johansson (1984) for glabrous skin; a more detailed presentation can be found in Szeto and Riso (1990). Some of the system characteristics in Table 9-1 are from primate studies (Darian-Smith and Oke, 1980; Freeman and Johnson, 1982; Talbot *et al.*, 1968) where human data are not available.

Neural response of tactile systems to a step change in skin displacement

Phillips and Johnson (1985) and Vallbo and Johansson (1984) provide excellent reviews of the responses of the known system types. Cutaneous mechanoreceptor systems can be roughly classified by the speed of their adaptation to a step change in applied pressure to the skin. An afferent nerve fiber system's response is measured by the change in the firing rate of action potentials; an action potential is always an all-or-none event. Table 9-1 describes the step displacement response of the four traditional systems in glabrous skin: (1) fast adapting, broad receptive field (FA II); (2) fast adpating, small receptive field (FA I); (3) slowly adapting, large-field (SA II); and (4) slowly adapting, small-field (SA I).[5]

Although traditionally included in the above group, the SA II group might not in fact mediate tactile information at all (Bach-y-Rita, 1989). Their large receptive fields have high stimulation thresholds and respond to remote, directional shearing forces in the skin (Johansson, 1978b; Vallbo and Johans-

Table 9-1 Cutaneous tactile receptor systems. SA = Slow adapting; FA = Fast adapting to step mechanical deformation of skin. I = Small, distinct receptive field; II = Large, diffuse field. G = Glabrous skin; H = Hairy skin. Data are from the literature: Talbot *et al.* (1968), Craig (1973), Scharf *et al.* (1973), Johansson (1978a), Johansson and Vallbo (1979), Darian-Smith and Oke (1980), Johansson *et al.* (1980), Sinclair (1981), Vallbo (1981), Freeman and Johnson (1982), Torebjork *et al.* (1984b), Phillips and Johnson (1985), Schmidt (1986), Westling (1986), Bolanowski, *et al.* (1988).

Probable receptor	Class (step indentation response)	Receptive field (mm^2) (median)	Skin type	Frequency range (Hz—most sensitive)	Threshold skin deform μm on hand (median)	Probable sensory corelate	Receptors cm^{-2} on fingertip (palm)	Square-wave grating (mm)
Pacinian corpuscle	FA II (RA II, QA II, PC)	10–1000 (101)	G, H	40–800 (200–300)	3–20 (9.2)	vibration tickle	21 (9)	—
Meissner's corpuscle	FA I (RA I, QA I, RA)	1–100 (12.6)	G	2–200 (20–40)	4–500 (13.8)	touch tickle motion vibration flutter tap	140 (25)	1.5
Hair follicle receptor	FA (RA, QA)	?	H	?	?	touch vibration	—	—
Ruffini ending	SA II	10–500 (59)	G, H	7	40–1500 (331)	none? (see text)	9 (15)	—
Merkel's cells	SA I	2–100 (11.0)	G	0.4–100 (7)	7–600 (56.5)	edge (?) pressure	70 (8)	0.5
Tactile disks	SA	3–50	H	?	?	?	—	—

son, 1984), and elicit no sensation when stimulated in isolation (Torebjork *et al.*, 1984b). SA II units might therefore contribute proprioceptive (position and force) feedback to the motor control of the hand (Knibestol, 1975; Knibestol and Vallbo, 1980; Rabischong, 1981; Tubiana, 1981; Dellon, 1981; Johansson and Vallbo, 1983). It is interesting, however, that Bolanowski *et al.* (1988) identified four *psychophysical* channels for touch perception.

Functional roles of mechanoreceptors

In an excellent review article, Johnson and Hsiao (1992) present the following hypothesis for the functions of the three tactile mechanoreceptor systems in glabrous skin, based on the available psychophysical and neurophysiological data.

> The SA I system is the primary spatial system and is responsible for tactual form and roughness perception when the fingers contact a surface directly and for the perception of external events through the distribution of forces across the skin surface. The FA II system is responsible for the perception of external events that are manifested through transmitted high-frequency vibrations. The FA I system has a lower spatial acuity than the SA I system but a higher sensitivity to local vibration and is responsible for the detection and representation of localized movement between skin and a surface as well as for surface form and texture when surface variation is too small to engage the SA I system.

Perception of nonvibrating stimuli

The sensation produced by mechanical stimulation of the skin is determined by both mechanoreceptor properties and central neural mechanisms (Vallbo and Johansson, 1984). Weinstein (1968) determined the detectable static force applied by a fine wire to most body locations. For men, the lips were the most sensitive, needing 9 dynes for sensation, the fingertips and belly 62 dynes, and the sole of the foot 343 dynes.[6] The thresholds for women on these four locations were 5, 25, 7, and 79 dynes. The fingerpad threshold corresponds to a skin indentation of about 10 μm.

Spatial resolution

This section discusses the basis for tactile spatial resolution; later sections will detail resolution concepts for specific display types.

Two-point limen

Several experimental methods attempt to measure the spatial resolution of the tactile sense. Table 9-2 summarizes the simultaneous two-point discrimination threshold (TPDT) for static, vibrotactile, and electrotactile stimuli on several body locations. The TPDT (the oldest and simplest measure of tactile spatial acuity) is usually defined as the minimal distance at which two simultaneous stimuli are distinguishable from a single stimulus. The numbers in Table 9-2 should be used only as a rough guide to the TPDT; comparisons of absolute numbers between static, vibratory, and electrotactile stimuli may be inaccurate due to the differing methodologies of different investigators. The TPDT is smaller if the stimuli are presented sequentially rather than simultaneously.

Table 9-2 Static simultaneous two-point discrimination threshold (mm).

Body location	Static touch (a)	Vibrotactile	Electrotactile (d)
Fingertip	3	2 (b)	<7 (*)
Palm	10	?	8
Forehead	17	?	?
Abdomen	36	?	10
Forearm	38	?	9
Back	39	11–18 (c)	5 (e)–10
Thigh	43	?	10
Upper arm	44	?	9
Calf	46	?	9

*Note: 7 mm was the smallest distance that could be measured in the first study. Data are from the literature: (a) Weinstein (1968); (b) Bliss (1973); (c) Bach-y-Rita (1972); (d) Solomonow *et al.* (1977); (e) Collins and Madey (1974).

For many years the TPDT was considered to be a limiting factor in the development of tactile displays. For example, the very high two-point limen of the skin of the back might be expected to pose an insuperable barrier to development of a high-resolution sensory substitution system using multifocal stimulation of this skin area. However, the acuity of the senses of touch and pressure exceeds that measured by static TPDT studies. Static determinations, with the "touch compass," do not reveal the actual capabilities of these tactile senses (Davis, 1968). Indeed, as with many other psychophysical determinations, the static two-point limen is not a rigid numerical value; it can be grossly improved by practice, and deteriorates with fatigue or distraction (Boring, 1942). Further, significantly greater resolution can be demonstrated by presentation of patterns rather than individual points. For example, Vierck and Jones (1969) have shown that if relative size judgments are determined, the acuity of a skin area is greater by a factor of ten than that shown in two-point limen studies.[7] In the latter case, integration over several adjoining receptors may allow for the increased resolution. Although still routinely used clinically, the relationship between the static TPDT and functional sensibility has been questioned; Dellon (1981) recommends a moving two-point test.

A functional model of spatiotemporal sensitivity

Bliss (1969) emphasized that the end performance (e.g., pattern recognition ability) is the ultimate measure of a display's effectiveness. Loomis (1981a) and Loomis and Lederman (1986) propose a mathematical model that describes tactile discriminability as a low-pass spatiotemporal filter; tactile presentations with details much smaller or faster than the filter cut-off will be perceptually "blurred," to borrow their analogy to the visual system. Using linear systems theory,

$$r(x, y, t) = \int_{-\infty}^{\infty} \int_{-\infty}^{\infty} \int_{-\infty}^{\infty} s(x', y', t') f(x - x', y - y', t - t') \, dx' \, dy' \, dt' \qquad (1)$$

approximates tactile discriminability where $r(x,y,t)$ is the response to a tactile stimulus $s(x,y,t)$ convolved with the impulse response function $f(x,y,t)$. While the stimulus and response variables may be variously defined and measured, x and y are orthogonal length dimensions and t is time. The spatial part of the impulse response (point spread) function is approximated by the Gaussian distribution function $f(x,y) = \exp[-\pi(x^2 + y^2)c^2]$. A set of experiments that compared blurred visual with fingerpad tactile determination of the orientation (vertical or horizontal) of a two-bar pattern determined that the scaling factor for the fingerpad is $c = 0.163$ mm^{-1}, corresponding to a 5.8 mm half-amplitude width (Loomis and Lederman, 1986). In the spatial frequency domain, this resolution is 0.77 cycle cm^{-1} for a half-amplitude response. Loomis (1990) proposes that this spatial bandwidth, along with several lesser-order factors such as amplitude compression, predicts the discriminability of a given set of characters identified by touch without time constraints.

Based on the spatial model only (equation 1), Figure 9-5 illustrates the

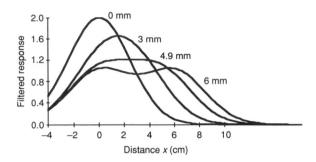

Figure 9-5 Perceptual two-point response on the fingerpad predicted by the spatial filter model proposed by Loomis and Lederman (1986). One point is at zero distance; the second point is at positive distance x of 0, 3, 4.9, and 6 mm, respectively, for the four plots. Individual response peaks from the two points are discernible only when points are separated by more than 4.9 mm. Subjects, however, can discern two points separated by only 3 mm (see text).

predicted combination point spread function for two equal-force points along the x-axis of the fingerpad, separated by distances $a = 0, 3, 4.9,$ and 6 mm:

$$f(x) = \exp[-\pi x^2 c^2] + \exp[-\pi (x - a)^2 c^2] \qquad (2)$$

The filtered (perceptual) representation of this pair of points does not show separate peaks until the separation exceeds 4.9 mm (the exact value is $\sqrt{2}/c\sqrt{\pi}$). If the model applies, the subject should not be able to perceive a dip between the peaks created by two distinct points at the reported TPDT of 3 mm of the fingerpad (Weinstein, 1968). S/he is probably not using an intensive cue to discriminate one point from two because the application force in two-point studies is usually not controlled. The mechanism used for discriminating two points separated by less than 4.9 mm is presently unclear.

Other observations

Notwithstanding the spatial filter described above, the skin can identify a frictionless position shift of a stimulus 10 times smaller than the TPDT (Loomis and Collins, 1978), indicating that the skin's spatial resolution is much better for certain tasks than the TPDT suggests (Loomis, 1981b). Clearly, "spatial resolution" is not a uniquely defined quantity, but depends on the particular type of stimulus and task to be performed (Dellon, 1981); temporal and intensive cues also provide spatial information at the perceptual level (Johnson and Phillips, 1984).

A further illustration of the complexity of spatial processing is the phenomenon of "funnelling," which is the perception of several spatially separated tactile stimuli as one stimulus in between the actual stimulation points (Békésy, 1960, 1967). This could potentially restrict the simultaneous display of multiple tactile objects. The neural mechanisms to account for funnelling are higher than the peripheral afferent nerves (Gardner and Spencer, 1972).

What information is important?

We introduce this section with a simple yet representative human information-processing task. Suppose a person is shown ten pictures of people and is asked to simply identify whether each picture is of a man or a woman. Unless considerable effort is expended to choose ambiguous pictures, this task could probably be accomplished in about 10 s. According to the classical definition of information rate

$$\text{rate (bits s}^{-1}) = (\text{decisions s}^{-1}) \times \log_2 (\text{number of choices in decision}) \quad (3)$$

the information rate of the subject's response is $(1 \text{ decision s}^{-1}) \times \log_2(2 \text{ choices}) = 1 \text{ bit s}^{-1}$. Yet the pictures contain far more pixel "information" than 1 bit each. Indeed, such a pattern recognition task would be formidable for a personal computer (which can perform approximately 10^7 operations s^{-1}).

This admittedly trivial example illustrates the difficulty of defining a useful information-transfer rate for *any* of the human senses, including the tactile sense. The key issue is deciding what information *is* important. Then, formal information theory can be applied meaningfully to predict the usefulness of specific sensory feedback codes.

Clearly, "information" is not a uniquely defined quantity in a system. Biological systems, in particular, exhibit a great deal of divergence (one stimulus may activate hundreds of sensors) and convergence (a single CNS decision may be made on the basis of thousands of neural inputs). While a vibratory stimulus of up to 200 Hz results in synchronized firing of afferent nerve fibers (Lindblom, 1970), showing that the tactile sensing units are capable of great physiological information flow, we perceive only a smooth vibration. A loose description would be that the higher neural centers treat this data stream as highly redundant or trivial. Indeed, J. J. Gibson's definition of information implies some behavioral significance to the information carried in a stimulus (Epstein, 1985). An alternative interpretation is that the volume of neural information from the simple vibrating stimulus is placed into one "chunk" with the redundant, useless information being discarded (Miller, 1956). Information theory would state that the information in the afferent fibers has a low variance; it is somewhat predictable with a constant vibratory stimulus.

Estimates of tactile information flow

The approximate maximal rates of information flow at the receptor level (based on the number of receptors and their afferent nerve fibers) for the eye, skin, and ear are 10^7, 10^6, and 10^5 bits s^{-1}, respectively (Schmidt, 1986). After some perceptual processing and filtering, the massive information stream is reduced to 2–56 bits s^{-1}, the rate at which humans process vibrotactile and electrotactile information at the perceptual level (Table 9-3). Although there are large differences in methodology, we may loosely compare these rates with those quoted by Schmidt (1986) for understanding spoken speech (40 bits s^{-1}) and reading (30 bits s^{-1}).

From equation (3), the number of discernible levels of stimulation (just

Table 9-3 Estimates of perceptual information flow from tactile stimuli.

Source of data	Method	Number of channels	Information rate (bits s^{-1})
Schmidt (1986)	?	?	5
Rollman (1973)	reaction time	1	5
Kokjer (1987)	fusion freq. of vibratory bursts	1	2–56
Kokjer (1987)	Optacon reading	144	5–10
White and Cheatham (1959)	counting stimuli	1	12

noticeable differences or JNDs) is one determinant of information flow. Table 9-4 summarizes these studies; the number of JNDs (choices) has been estimated at from 6 to 59 levels for electrotactile stimulation and 15 levels for vibrotactile stimulation (Geldard, 1960, 1968). The wide electrotactile variations are due in part to the different waveform quantities being manipulated to change the "level." In particular, it is possible that increasing the current by small steps at a slow rate will yield a large number of steps because at each step, some of the perceptual level increase will be lost due to adaptation. Table 9-4 reflects this effect with the number of JNDs for current being higher than the number of JNDs for frequency.

Note that the number of JNDs is not the same as the number of absolute levels that can be reliably classified. For example, only four or five levels of vibrotactile stimulation duration (Geldard, 1960, 1968) and six levels of electrotactile stimulation frequency (Riso *et al.*, 1989) can be reliably classified.[8]

The JND itself is only a measure of channel sensitivity. Table 9-5 summarizes the JND reported for static pressure, electrotactile, and vibrotactile stimulation. The JND is expressed as a percentage because it is approximately proportional to stimulus level or frequency[9]; also see Riso *et al.* (1989); Szeto and Riso (1990).

Table 9-4 Number of discernible levels of stimulation for electrotactile and vibrotactile (VT) stimuli, i.e., number of JNDs. Sub is subdermal stimulation.

Source of data	Location	Variable	Number of levels
Saunders and Collins (1971)	abdomen	current	59
Aiello and Valenza (1984)	abdomen	current	32
Solomonow and Conaway (1983)	palm	frequency	13
Tachi *et al.* (1982)	arm	energy	8–16
Tachi *et al.* (1982)	arm	frequency	6–8
Riso *et al.* (1989)	arm	frequency	11
Riso *et al.* (1989)	arm-Sub	frequency	16
Geldard (1960)	? (VT)	amplitude	15

Table 9-5 Just-noticeable differences of electrotactile, vibrotactile (VT), and mechanical pressure (Mech) stimulation on the skin. Note that frequency JND for vibration is higher if the *subjective* intensity is held constant as a function of frequency (Sherrick and Cholewiak, 1986), rather than with the *physical* amplitude held constant (Keidel, 1973), because the subjective magnitude varies with frequency.

Source of data	Location	Variable	JND %
Collins and Madey (1974)	abdomen	width	>6
Neuman (1987)	arm	current	9–29
	arm (Sub)	current	8–42
Pfeiffer (1968)	?	current	2–6
	?	frequency	>2
Riso et al. (1982)	arm	frequency	15–30
	arm (Sub)	frequency	10–25
Saunders (1973)	abdomen	current	3.5
	abdomen	pulses/burst	10
Solomonow and Conaway (1983)	palm	frequency	19–24
Szeto et al. (1979a)	arm	frequency	16–38
	arm	width	37–46
Szeto and Saunders (1982)	several	width	8–10
	several	current	8–10
Sherrick and Cholewiak (1986)	arm (VT)	frequency	20–25
Keidel (1973)	? (VT)	frequency	5–10
Stevens (1975)	? (Mech)	pressure	20

Spatial and temporal information-processing limitations

The rather rigid limits imposed by the inaccuracy of our absolute judgments can be expanded by the use of both simultaneous and successive discriminations. There are several ways by which the limits of the channel capacity for absolute judgments can be exceeded: (1) we can make relative, rather than absolute, judgments; (2) we can increase the number of dimensions of the stimulus (which can extend the span from 6 to about 150); and (3) we can arrange the task so as to permit one to make a (temporal) sequence of absolute judgments, thereby invoking memory, ". . . as the handmaiden of discrimination" (Miller, 1956).

The absolute judgment and the span of memory are quite different kinds of limitations that are imposed on our ability to process information. Absolute judgment is limited by the amount of information (bits), whereas immediate memory is limited by the number of "items" or "chunks." The number of bits of information is constant for absolute judgment, and the number of chunks of information is constant for immediate memory. The span of immediate memory seems to be almost independent of the number of bits per chunk (Miller, 1956).

Therefore, one must be somewhat cautious in interpreting statements as to channel capacities for information transmission. As Wall (1968) pointed out, such statements usually assume that one is transmitting instantaneous events, but this is not normally the case. The central nervous system takes time to examine incoming signals. What may be an instantaneous event is actually analyzed over a span of time which may be up to seconds in length (Wall, 1968). Indeed, responses of single brainstem cells have been recorded four seconds after each delivery of a single natural somesthetic stimulus (Bach-y-Rita, 1964). While convenient for controlled experiments, the usual technique of asking a subject to immediately respond to a stimulus or group of stimuli may prevent achievement of optimal performance.

There are limits, however, to the cognitive integration of tactile information. Loomis et al. (1991) compared recognition of (1) tactile raised line drawings of common objects for single-fingerpad exploration with (2) a subject-controllable visual window display of a fingerpad-sized area of the same figures. Tactile and visual recognition were identical. However, if the effective field of view was doubled to two adjacent fingers tactually and visually, visual performance (speed and accuracy) improved markedly; tactile performance did not. This suggests the existence of a fundamental limitation in CNS integration of tactile field of view compared with vision. Some of this limitation might be circumvented by the use of a user-controllable electronic zoom feature on a tactile display (Tyler et al., 1992). Manipulating a zoom control, however, takes time and requires manual control by the subject.

For real-time spatiotemporal tasks, such as navigation by a blind person using a tactile vision system, the flood of information so useful to detailed object recognition may need to be reduced so that the salient features are not obscured by a meaningless blur of detail. For example, TVS users could navigate around common indoor obstacles such as tables and chairs, but were unable to cope with a complex outdoor environment. Schemes have been proposed to automatically identify and classify approaching objects sensed by electronic cameras and ultrasonic sonar, verbally identify objects for the traveler, and present only essential spatial orientation cues (e.g., relative position, direction, and range) through a tactile display (Collins and Deering, 1984; Tachi et al., 1982, 1985; Collins, 1985). It seems important, however, not to transform essentially spatial information into a finite set of coded maximally discriminable sensations (White et al., 1970). An analogy from visual perception might be useful here. Imagine trying to create a mental image of the following pattern described in words: "There are four points. Point B is 1 cm above point A, and point C is 1 cm right of point A. Point D is 1 cm above and 1 cm right of point A. Lines connect points A and B, B and D, D and C, and C and A." Although all of the necessary information is unambiguously present, it takes a few moments to realize that this is a square.

In spite of the slowness of a subject to produce a physical response to a tactile stimulus (200 ms) (Rollman, 1973), the perceived stimulation can vary significantly with small variations in the timing of successive stimulations. For example, a subject can detect a 10 ms break in a vibratory stimulus (Howell, 1960); this is shorter than for the visual system (30 ms) but longer than for the auditory system (3 ms). Furthermore, Békésy (1957) and Gescheider (1970) note that if two square-wave mechanical tactile stimulators spaced about 5 cm apart or even on different fingertips are simultaneously pulsed for 1 ms, a single sensation will be felt midway between the stimulators. However, if the pulses are staggered by as little as 0.2 ms, the perceived position of this "phantom" stimulus moves toward the earlier stimulus. An even larger shift in apparent position occurs when the amplitudes of the two stimuli are unequal, with the sensation appearing closer to the stronger stimulus (Gibson, 1968; Alles, 1970; Gescheider, 1970; Mann and Reimers, 1970). Finally, Verrillo (1965) showed that the threshold for vibrotactile stimulation drops as the stimulus time increases to one second, i.e., the tactile sense exhibits temporal summation over one second.

These observations suggest that different types of temporal processing with "time constants" ranging over at least 0.2 ms to greater than 1 min occur in the human somatosensory system. Therefore, the precise effects of such real system characteristics as time delay, time skew between elements, and phase shift are difficult to predict and may need to be determined empirically for a specific system; future research may elucidate some of these mechanisms. It is clear that a tactile percept depends not only upon integration of several cutaneous mechanoreceptor systems that are simultaneously stimulated (Bolanowski et al., 1988), but from a complex spatiotemporal integration of all available information (Geldard, 1985). If a tactile display is used concurrently with other information displays (e.g., visual and/or auditory), the information received from all displays must be consistent to avoid confusion, particularly if the end goal is a feeling of telepresence at an alternate or computer-generated virtual workspace (Held and Durlach, 1992; Loomis, 1992a). By consistent, we mean not that the same information be presented, but only that no conflict exist; the information from the combined displays should convey a unique representation of the workspace.

Spatiotemporal (haptic) information integration

In addition to the cutaneous mechanisms described to this point, the central nervous system uses spatiotemporal information derived from kinesthesis, i.e., the conscious awareness of and movement of the skin surface with respect to the surface being explored. In fact, our everyday use of the "sense of touch" depends on the subconscious integration of time-dependent cutaneous and kinesthetic information (Loomis and Lederman, 1986).

The importance of haptic exploration is confirmed by everyday experience with the tactile sense.[10] For example, an effective strategy for detecting fine surface imperfections or for discriminating surface textures is to run the fingertips, fingernails, or some sharp object over the surface. This maneuver transforms spatial surface features into a dynamic stimulus whose intensity, spectral composition, and temporal structure are related to the surface geometry. From limited parallel spatial information (due to the single contact point), a person can deduce not only the diffuse surface texture, but the relative positions of distinct surface features such as bumps or ridges. When the whole hand is used for exploration, a tactile analog of vision is invoked; while one or two central fingers provide detailed (foveal) information, the cutaneous and kinesthetic (positional) information from the outer fingers provides "peripheral" spatial orientation—the "big picture." Interestingly, this form of

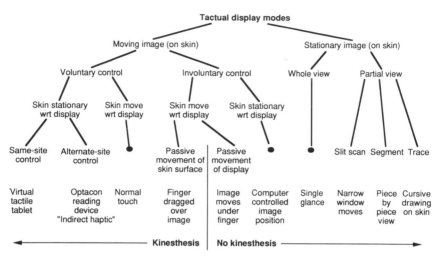

Figure 9-6 The tactual (tactile + kinesthetic) acquisition of information is defined by several criteria. Level I separates moving from stationary images. "Moving" means that a given image feature does not stay in the same skin location; this can be caused by an image moving on the physical display or by the physical display moving with respect to (w.r.t.) the skin. Stationary images may be displayed all at once or in time sequence. Level 2 separates voluntary from involuntary control of a moving image; voluntary control results in "efference copy" information to the brain. Level 3 separates the case where the skin moves w.r.t. the display from the case where the image on the display moves while skin–display alignment is preserved. In either case, the image on the skin moves. Level 4 separates miscellaneous details such as the source of voluntary control, what moves with respect to what, and how a stationary image might be partially presented. The bottom row in the tree provides an example display type or an alternate description for each display mode, only some of which provide kinesthetic information to the brain.

haptic integration is not limited to conscious movements of the stimulated region of skin. The tactile information received by one skin patch can be controlled by movements of distant limbs (e.g., opposite hand) without any degradation in accuracy of tactile pattern recognition (Wiker *et al.*, 1991).

Classification of haptic perception

Figure 9-6 delineates several of the possible modes of tactual information acquisition through a tactile display. (We have deliberately omitted purely kinesthetic perception, such as information received from a teleoperator with force feedback). These modes vary by (1) whether the presented information is spatially fixed or moving with respect to (w.r.t.) the skin, (2) whether the control over moving information is voluntary or involuntary, (3) whether the spatial movement of information is due to the skin moving with respect to the display or due to "windowing" of the displayed information, (4a) whether skin-display movement is due to display movement or due to skin movement, (4b) whether subject-controlled "windowed" information is controlled by movement of the skin site at which the information is displayed, or by an alternate site, and (4c) whether stationary images are displayed in their entirety or in sections. Further classifications, not illustrated because they are so general so as not to alter the classification structure, are (5) stimulation mechanism: static mechanical, electrotactile, or vibrotactile, and (6) spatially corresponding vs. not spatially corresponding display. Further divisions are possible, including such variables as stimulation frequencies, modulation parameters, body site, subject preparedness, etc., although they do not contribute materially to the categorization made here. Note that the kinesthetic information is absent (right side of Figure 9-6) in the stationary modes, as well as in the involuntary modes where the skin is held stationary to the display or the display moves w.r.t. to the stationary skin.

We further propose that Figure 9-6, with the extensions in items (5) and (6) above, form a classification system for tactile displays, building on the model described by Loomis (1991), Loomis and Lederman (1984, 1986) with the hope of further reducing the confusion caused by terms such as "active touch" and "passive touch." For example, the mode of display for the Optacon visual substitution device could be described succinctly as moving, voluntary, skin stationary w.r.t. display, alternate-site control, vibrotactile, spatially corresponding. This mode has been called "indirect haptic" (Tyler *et al.*, 1992). Normal touch would be described as moving, voluntary, skin move w.r.t. display, same site control, static mechanical, spatially corresponding. It is not necessary, though not incorrect, to specify "same site" because this follows automatically from "skin move w.r.t. display."

Experimental findings

Loomis (1991) and Loomis and Lederman (1984) emphasized the need to specify all of the relevant display variables, especially the separate considerations of (1) the presence or absence of kinesthetic information and (2) the voluntary or involuntary nature of spatially moving the pattern, when comparing tactile presentation modes, to avoid confounded results due to "hidden" or interacting variables. With this in mind, the following conclusions can be drawn from the literature. (All of the following studies use presentations that are spatially corresponding and moving unless noted; the Optacon is voluntary, alternate-site control, vibrotactile; raised letters and braille are static mechanical, skin moving w.r.t. display.)

(1) For stationary raised or vibrotactile letters on the fingerpad, palm, back, or abdomen, a sequential partial view (e.g., slit-scan or segment) affords better performance than a whole view only if the letters are small enough that the spatial resolving capability of the particular skin site is challenged (Loomis, 1981b; Loomis and Lederman, 1986). (2) Voluntary control affords no better performance than involuntary control for (a) recognition of letters on the Optacon display (vibrotactile, alternate-site control) (Loomis and Lederman, 1984), or (b) for raised letters or Braille (Loomis and Lederman, 1984; Vega-Bermudez *et al.*, 1991). (3) Vibrotactile presentation of fingerpad-sized simple graphic patterns on an Optacon display is perceived equally well for same-site or alternate-site control (Loomis and Lederman, 1986; Wiker *et al.*,

1991). (4) Whole hand (fingerpads and palm) vibrotactile perception of simple graphic patterns is performed equally well whether the skin moves w.r.t. display or with skin stationary and alternate-site control (Tyler *et al.*, 1992). Subjects preferred using the dominant hand for the alternate-site control (non-dominant hand stationary on display), and also for skin moves w.r.t. display (one hand provides all information). (5) Short letter or graphic presentations reduce the difference between whole-view and sequential performance; absolute performance of all modes also decreases (Loomis and Lederman, 1986).

(6) Recognition of "cookie cutter" shapes (2.5 cm mean diameter) on the palm appears to be better under the normal touch condition than with a stationary, whole view; the case where the shape is passively moved in the hand (moving, involuntary, skin move w.r.t. display, display move) has intermediate performance (Cronin, 1977; Heller, 1980; Heller and Myers, 1983; Loomis and Lederman, 1986). Kinesthesis appears to be important here; movement may also be important.

(7) With larger (approx. 15 cm square) raised patterns, Magee and Kennedy (1980) found that normal touch (fingerpad exploration) was inferior to moving, involuntary, skin move w.r.t. display, skin move acquisition (i.e., subject's hand was externally traced over drawing). This was true even if the cutaneous information was removed by tracing a flat surface. All of the information came from kinesthesis; active control did not help. (8) For geometric patterns and letters presented to the back by a vibrotactile display, a cursively traced presentation (stationary image, traced) results in better recognition than experimenter-panned (moving, involuntary, skin stationary w.r.t. display) presentation of whole figures. (9) For voluntary, skin stationary w.r.t display, electrotactile presentation of simple patterns on the abdomen, a moving, voluntary, alternate-site-control acquisition method is not better than a whole-view stationary display (Tyler *et al.*, 1992). However, when combined with a subject-controlled electronic zoom feature, the "active" acquisition mode is clearly superior, whereas zoom alone does not help. The reason for this interaction, not tested by other groups, is at present unclear.

Conclusions

The results (1)–(4) above suggest that for simple pattern discrimination with drawing sizes of fingerpad size, the display mode may be largely inconsequential, so long as the spatial acuity of the tactile sense is not taxed. With figures that do tax the spatial acuity (very fine spatial details), sequential modes deliver the patterns with lower-spatial-frequency content, circumventing the poor spatial resolution of the tactile sense (Loomis and Lederman, 1986). Studies (6)–(7) suggest that kinesthesis is important for certain figures, but it may be supplied involuntarily (passively). Study (8) showed that if the image is to be presented without subject control, a traced mode is superior; the subject receives only the essential information for pattern recognition. Taken together, studies (7) and (8) highly recommend a traced presentation, even if involuntary. Cursive tracing has been recommended elsewhere (Collins, 1985; Collins and Madey, 1974). Study (9), however, is provocative; it supports the body of anecdotal evidence from the early tactile vision experiments (including study (8) above) that active subject control of tactile pattern position and zoom are very important in more complex tactile–visual environments (White, 1970; White *et al.*, 1970; Beauchamp *et al.*, 1971; Bach-y-Rita, 1972). In the latter, however, the importance of movement, and especially actively controlled movement, may not lie so much in improved pattern perception, but in higher-level cognition such as recovery of three-dimensional spatial information and distal attribution (perceptually relating the reconstructed image to a location away from the tactile display—see below). This is an area ripe for further research; even pattern-recognition testing may not adequately characterize tactile display schemes. It might even be possible that pattern recognition is a poor basis for complex spatiotemporal perception, much as "sensations" have been dismissed as the sole basis for "perception" (White *et al.*, 1970). We might note, however, that many potential applications of tactile displays are essentially basic pattern-recognition tasks.

Distal attribution and telepresence

When a surface is probed with a stick, the surface texture is normally localized at the junction between the probe and the stick, not where the stick is grasped by the hand. Similarly, with the tactile vision substitution system described earlier, experienced subjects perceived the imaged objects in the space in front of the video camera (Bach-y-Rita, 1972), not at the site of the tactile display (abdomen or back). Finally, a teleoperator system with high-performance force reflection can give its human operator the experience of being "in touch with" the remote workpiece. These are three examples of distal attribution, the same perceptual mechanism that causes normal human vision to perceive viewed objects as appearing "out there," rather than at the retina (or the brain!). If sufficient visual, auditory, and tactual (kinesthetic and/or tactile) feedback is provided from a remotely sensed or computer-simulated (virtual) environment to a human observer, s/he may experience "being present in" that environment; this generalization of distal attribution is called *presence* or *telepresence*.

While useful measurements of distal attribution and telepresence are only beginning to be defined, some of the perceptual bases are understood; see the excellent reviews by Held and Durlach (1992) and Loomis (1992a, 1992b) that form the basis for this discussion. Our normal senses of vision, hearing, and even touch externalize stimuli. In everyday living, we perceive a virtual world that normally agrees so closely with the physical world that the difference is imperceptible. The important ingredient for distal attribution to occur appears to be the formation of a perceptual model of received sensory information (afference) as a function of motor control over the sensed environment (efference). Therefore, for remote and virtual environments, one requirement for distal attribution or telepresence is an accurate transmission of sensed or simulated information that changes appropriately with the subject's hand, head, and overall body movements. Degradation of sensory feedback by time delays, inadequate spatial resolution, or conflicting information from different modalities (e.g., vision vs. kinesthesis) not only reduces the sense of otherworldliness, but will contribute to confusion and increase error in task performance (Tyler, 1986).

Ramifications for tactile display design

Clearly, a tactile display system must accommodate the unique sensory characteristics of the skin, particularly if cross-modality (visual-to-tactile or auditory-to-tactile) sensory substitution is attempted. For example, an electro-tactile auditory prosthesis cannot simply use the microphone signal to directly control electrode current because the skin has insufficient high-frequency response. The auditory information must be sufficiently processed to match the properties of the tactile sense, while preserving the fundamental speech–acoustic features of the original acoustic signal.

Dynamic range

The dynamic range (ratio of maximal to minimal signal level) of a given sensor usually does not match the dynamic range of a given tactile display. For example, in a TVS system the range of light input to a camera is much higher than the typically 6–20 dB range of electrotactile stimulation. Some form of amplitude compression or scaling may be desired. For a tactile feedback system, one natural approach might be to implement a transfer function from the pressure sensor to the tactile display so that the perceived stimulation magnitude closely matches the perceived magnitude of the same pressure stimulus on normal skin (Milchus and Van Doren, 1990; Neuman, 1990a; Neuman, 1990b), although such matching is not strictly necessary (Neuman, 1990d).

Spatial resolution

The limited spatial resolution of the skin prohibits whole-frame presentation of very complex graphical patterns. Certain display modes, such as tracing (for line figures) and slit-scan presentation, preserve the original spatial information while reducing its spatial frequency content by sequential presentation (Loomis and Lederman, 1986). Edge enhancement and its special case of outlining are more sophisticated preprocessing steps that may discard some information while improving pattern recognition (Bach-y-Rita, 1972) — by reducing the high spatial frequency content and/or by eliminating "unimportant" informa-tion that may mask the salient features (Collins, 1985). A zoom feature allows smaller spatial features to be resolved; adding to zoom the ability to manually scan an image can greatly improve pattern recognition, at least under some conditions (Tyler et al., 1992).

Information measures

Based on the above absolute-level identification conclusion of Miller (1956), is it useful to optimize tactile display parameters to maximize the number of absolute-level identifications? Perhaps the parameter choice need only guaran-tee some (as yet unspecified) minimum number of levels n. Furthermore, whether the information channel to the tactile display may be quantized to n

levels without loss of end-application system performance remains an open question. Indeed, White *et al.* (1970) suggest that coding for maximal "discrimability" only increases the cognitive load, although we recognize that they were speaking of abstract coding, not a simple limitation in the number of gray levels of a given tactor. Another open question is the relationship between the JND of a display stimulus and the end-application system performance. As we have shown, the tactile sense, like the visual system, is far more capable than these abstract performance measures would suggest. Once a comfortable and controllable display is achieved, the system designer should quickly proceed to optimizing it on user-oriented tasks (Tyler, 1992).

Differential tactile excitation

An electrotactile display stimulates afferent fiber types in different proportions than normal touch. Minimal control is presently available over which fiber types (and hence perceived sensations) are stimulated (Szeto and Riso, 1990). Such differential excitation may be necessary to produce more effective tactile displays (Bolanowski *et al.*, 1988; Vallbo, 1981).

A similar situation exists with a vibrotactile display, where a constant (DC) level is presented as a sinusoidal stimulus. Stimulation frequency, as well as amplitude, can be modulated to provide useful information. Finally, "roughness" information can be presented by appropriate choice of electrotactile stimulation waveforms (Neuman, 1990c, 1991a, 1991b; Van Doren, 1993).

Display modality

Patterson and Katz (1992) provide a substantial history of grip force feedback from myoelectric prosthetic hands. They then present data to support a hypothesis that force feedback is best presented by a force or pressure display, rather than a vibratory one (e.g., vibrotactile), because it is more "natural" or "fitting"; it is certainly more psychologically satisfying, at least initially. This seemingly conflicts with results of tactile vision experiments, which showed that the information transfer was somewhat modality-independent; subjects trained on a vibrotactile display quickly adapted an electrotactile display (Bach-y-Rita, 1972), although electrotactile sensations are somewhat vibratory. A stronger conflict exists, however; after the initial tactile vision training was complete, subjects became quite unaware of the physical stimulus and concentrated on perceptions in the "visual" space in front of the camera. Perhaps this distal attribution needs to occur before the issue of "naturalness" is shelved in the subject's mind. Alternatively, the spatial tasks inherent in the tactile vision studies (as opposed to pressure-discrimination tasks) did not allow the subject to be aware of and confused by competing intensive modalities (pressure vs. vibratory magnitude). This area warrants further research.

TACTILE DISPLAY PRINCIPLES

This section will explain the three primary mechanisms used in tactile displays for exciting the afferent mechanoreceptor system: (1) static mechanical tactile stimulation, (2) vibrotactile stimulation, and (3) electrotactile stimulation. The theory and practice of electrotactile stimulation will be treated in depth because they do not necessarily follow directly from knowledge of conventional tactile perception. We will not discuss some of the more exotic methods such as magnetic (Reilly, 1989; Roth and Basser, 1990; Grandiori and Ravazzani, 1991; Durand et al., 1992), thermal (C/M Research, 1992), ultrasound (Andreeva et al., 1991), and chemical stimulation which may hold future promise.

Static tactile display

Due to high power consumption and the rapid adaptation of the tactile sense to static stimuli, static mechanical "normal touch" displays are infrequently used to display changing tactile information.[11] However, for certain applications such as tactile feedback, a static tactile display may in fact be the golden standard to emulate, i.e., the display deforms the skin exactly as the sensor array is deformed by the grasped object. There is some evidence that a static mechanical display is superior to (modulated pulsatile) vibrotactile or electrotactile displays. Embossed letters are recognized tactually with the fingerpad with 50% accuracy if their height is 4–6 mm; similar accuracy on the Optacon vibrotactile display (230 Hz) requires 12–20 mm height (Loomis and Lederman, 1986; Johnson and Hsiao, 1992).[12]

Vibrotactile display principles

Psychophysics

Extensive studies have shown that the perception of vibrating stimuli depends primarily on skin location, tactor size, gap between tactor and non-moving surround, and vibration amplitude and frequency (Békésy, 1959; Gescheider and Wright, 1968, 1969; Hahn, 1966, 1968, 1973; Berglund and Berglund, 1970; Verrillo, 1985). Geldard (1972) summarizes the sensation threshold for vibrotactile stimulation with a 1 cm^2 vibrator at most body locations. The fingertips are more sensitive than most body locations by at least one order of magnitude. The abdomen, in particular, is 60 times less sensitive than the fingertips to 200 Hz vibration.

In a comprehensive review paper, Verrillo (1985) discusses the mechanisms influencing the sensation threshold of the (glabrous) palm to vibrating stimuli. The vibratory sensation threshold is 5 μm peak amplitude from 25 to 650 Hz for stimulation areas less than 0.05 cm^2. For larger areas, the threshold is frequency dependent,[13] achieving best sensitivity (0.16 μm—one-fifth wavelength of visible light) at 250 Hz with a stimulation area of 5 cm^2.

Temporal summation occurs only for large stimulators at higher frequencies; only the FA II (PC) receptors summate over time. The vibrotactile threshold to a 250 Hz, 2.9 cm^2 stimulus falls by 12 dB as stimulus time increases from 10 ms to 1 s, whereas no threshold shift appears for a 0.02 cm^2 stimulator (Verrillo, 1965). Because the FA II receptors themselves do not show temporal summation in electrophysiological recordings (Talbot *et al.*, 1968), higher neural mechanisms must be responsible for the perceived summation.

Finally, the threshold amplitude for vibrotactile stimulation increases after a strong conditioning stimulus. Gescheider and Verrillo (1978) found that a 10 min stimulus 6 dB over threshold raises the sensation threshold amplitude by 2 dB, while a 40 dB stimulus raises the threshold by 20 dB. This adaptation occurs at least for frequencies from 10 to 250 Hz. Hahn (1968, 1973) reports that a 7 to 25 min conditioning vibrotactile stimulus results in full adaptation, i.e., the sensation threshold does not further increase at longer conditioning stimuli durations. Full recovery from adaptation occurs in approximately 2 min. Furthermore, a conditioning stimulus has more influence on the sensation threshold than on the suprathreshold perceived intensity.

Spatial resolution vs. frequency

If we are restricted to using a vibratory display, it is tempting to select a frequency that will activate the low-temporal-frequency FA I and SA I systems (most sensitive frequencies 10–40 Hz and 5–10 Hz, respectively), with their restricted receptive fields, to achieve a display that responds to fine details. Higher frequencies may be preferable, however. Bliss (1969) and Rogers (1970) showed that subjects identify tactile letters on an 8-column × 12-row pulsatile airjet display most accurately at higher frequencies (160 Hz best in 24–160 Hz range), in spite of the spatially diffuse receptive fields of the FA II (PC).[14]

Practical display requirements

Vibrotactile displays driven with sinusoidal waveforms of 60–250 Hz, at amplitudes at least 10 dB over threshold are recommended. A maximal comfortable displacement of 0.5 mm has been reported for a 1-mm-diameter contactor (Collins, 1970). Non-sinusoidal waveshapes can reduce power consumption at the expense of higher-frequency components which can create excessive acoustical noise (Nunziata *et al.*, 1989). The tactor size is not critical at these frequencies, but a nonvibrating surround around each tactor will help to localize the sensation by preventing traveling waves on the skin.

Electrotactile display principles

Scientific investigation of the sensations produced by controlled, localized electrical stimulation of the skin dates back more than one century (Tschiriew and Watteville, 1879). External stimulation of most cutaneous afferent nerve fibers gives rise to tactile (touch) sensations. The present discussion will describe electrical stimulation of small, distinct patches of skin with surface and subdermal (totally implanted and percutaneous) electrodes. We specifically exclude methods that stimulate nerve bundles to produce diffuse tactile sensations or to block pain (TENS); our focus is on producing distinct, localized sensations that can be controlled to deliver information.[15]

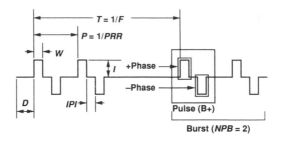

Figure 9-7 Electrotactile waveform variables for balanced-biphasic pulses: delay D, phase width W, interphase interval IPI, current I, time between bursts T, frequency of burst repetition F, period of pulse repetition P, pulse repetition rate PRR, number of pulses/burst NBP.

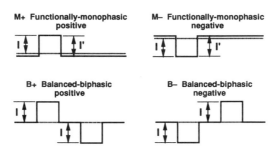

Figure 9-8 Electrotactile pulse types. All four types achieve physiological stimulation while delivering zero net-DC current to the skin, to reduce skin irritation (see text for details).

Waveforms

A great variety of stimulation waveforms can produce distinct, comfortable electrotactile percepts. Since the electrical characteristics of the electrode–skin interface are variable, waveform current (or less commonly, charge or power) is usually controlled rather than voltage. Figure 9-7 shows a reasonably generic current stimulation waveform with balanced-biphasic pulses delivered in repeating bursts; Figure 9-8 shows four different pulse types.[16] Balanced-biphasic pulses have equal positive and negative phases to achieve physiological stimulation with zero net DC current. Similar waveshapes are used for charge-control methods, although they are not necessarily rectangular as shown. The net (average) DC current through the electrode should be close to zero (but see later discussion) to reduce electrochemical skin reactions. Functionally monophasic pulses may also be used if the baseline is shifted to produce zero net DC current. On most skin loci, positive pulses require more stimulation current than negative ones,[17] which are close to balanced-biphasic (Girvin *et al.*, 1982). All of the waveform timing parameters in Figures 9-7 and 9-8 influence the electrotactile sensation.

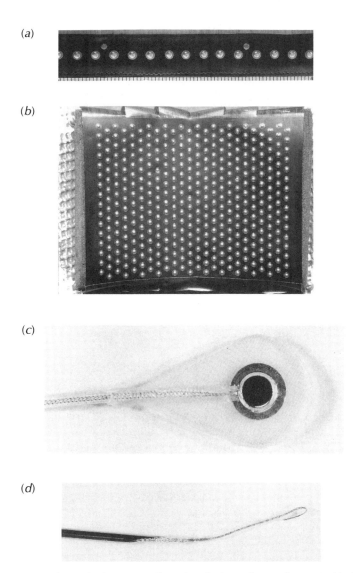

Figure 9-9 Examples of electrotactile stimulation electrodes. (a) Abdominal belt electrode from the Tacticon™ 1600 auditory prosthesis (Tacticon Corp., Concord, CA). The sixteen 5.5 mm-diameter gold-plated electrodes are surrounded by a large common, conductive rubber dispersive electrode (ground plane). Sweat is the electrolyte; water may be used to premoisten. (b) Abdominal electrode array from the prototype Videotact™ visual prosthesis (Unitech Research, Inc., Madison, WI). The 384 titanium electrodes are 2 mm in diameter and are surrounded by a conductive Kapton® ground plane. Electrode gel is liberally applied on the skin before mounting this array. (c) Completely implantable disk electrode. This 3 mm-diameter subdermal platinum–iridium disk, originally designed for skeletal muscle stimulation, is sutured to the underside of the skin, facing outward. (d) Percutaneous wire electrode. This 316L stainless steel wire electrode is inserted 3 cm just under the skin; the active uninsulated area is approximately 1 cm long. (c) and (d) were kindly provided by R. Riso and are described by Riso *et al.* (1989).

Electrodes

Because current flow through the skin is ionic, a transducer (electrode) is needed to convert electron flow in the lead wire to ionic flow. To reduce skin irritation and possible damage, the electrode should not introduce non-native ions into the skin. The electrode must also not react chemically so as to produce an insulating layer between the electrode and the skin. Many electrotactile display systems use titanium electrodes because they are essentially non-reactive, of reasonable cost, and easy to machine; other metals used are gold, platinum, platinum–iridium, silver, and stainless steel. Greatbatch (1981) and Mortimer (1981) review the electrochemistry of implantable metal electrodes; the same general principles apply to skin electrodes.

Figure 9-9 shows several types of electrotactile stimulation electrodes. Many surface electrodes are surrounded by a large-area coaxial, conductive ring (return path) to concentrate stimulation at one skin site, although the return path may be more remote at the risk of stimulating undesired areas. Normally the active electrode area is much smaller than the return electrode so that the higher current density under the active electrode localizes the sensations there.

Stimulation mechanism

Most investigators believe than an electric current passing through the skin directly stimulates afferent nerve fibers (Rollman, 1973; Butikofer and Lawrence, 1978; Szeto and Riso, 1990; Szeto and Saunders, 1982), although Pfeiffer (1968) suggests that small electrodes (1 mm^2) stimulate receptors directly. Some investigators (Blamey and Clark, 1985, 1987) intentionally chose electrode locations to stimulate entire nerve bundles. The sensation resulting from nerve-bundle stimulation is not necessarily confined to a small skin region, and may therefore be less useful for conveying structured spatial information. Stimulation of a hair follicle with a needle electrode produces sensations of vibration or sharp pain depending on the insertion depth (Scharf et al., 1973).

Several mathematical models have recently appeared which predict the stimulation of afferent nerve fibers in response to an external electric field such as that produced by an electrode (Larkin and Reilly, 1984; Reilly and Bauer, 1987; Rattay, 1988, 1989; Veltink et al., 1988, 1989; Reilly, 1989; Altman and Plonsey, 1990; Solomonow, 1991). Of these models, only Larkin and Reilly (1984), Rattay (1988), and Altman and Plonsey (1990) deal with skin surface stimulation electrodes. Rattay (1988) does not consider capacitance; this is a static model. Larkin and Reilly (1984) use an arc discharge (point) stimulation.

Percutaneous stimulation

Fine wire electrodes inserted into the skin also give rise to tactile sensations. Several investigators (Anani et al., 1977; Riso et al., 1982, 1983; 1989; Szeto and Riso, 1990) propose (invasive) percutaneous wire electrodes and entirely implanted subdermal disk electrodes as an alternative to surface electrodes. Among the advantages claimed are a lower JND for pulse rate (frequency), high consistency over time of the sensations evoked, mechanical stability of the electrode interface, and elimination of the need to mount and remove skin electrodes. Special waveforms are required to prevent electrode corrosion (Szeto and Riso, 1990).

Current distribution under surface electrodes

The distribution of the current density J under an electrotactile stimulation electrode is not well understood. For a homogeneous volume conductor, J increases markedly at the electrode edge (Rubenstein et al., 1987; Wiley and Webster, 1982a, 1982b). The conductive path through the skin, however, is not uniform at the microscopic level for any electrode type. Several investigators have shown that current flows through small regions of low resistance— probably sweat ducts, or possibly also sebaceous glands or minute epithelial breaks. The density of low-resistance spots has been reported by Grimnes (1984) as 3–6 spots mm^{-2} on the forearm; Yamamoto et al. (1988) reported 2–3 spots mm^{-2} on the forearm; Saunders (1973) reported 1 spot mm^{-2} on the abdomen. Reilly (1992) quotes an average sweat duct density of 1.6 ducts mm^{-2} on the forearm and 3.7 ducts mm^{-2} on the palm. Panescu et al. (1993) showed that the palm has three times as many conductive pathways as the forearm.

Under large (>100 mm^2) metal electrodes on *dry* skin, one of the skin's conductive paths will occasionally drop suddenly in resistance, shunting much of the electrode current through that pathway (Gibson, 1968; Saunders, 1983). The resulting high current density causes a sudden sharp sting and a red spot on the skin. The sting is most likely to occur with negatively pulsed electrodes. Grimnes (1983b) proposes that a mechanism called electro-osmosis draws water through pores toward a negative electrode. Within about 1 s this considerably increases a pore's conductance and thereby might cause a positive feedback runaway condition in the pore as it rapidly becomes hydrated. Panescu et al. (1992a, 1992b, 1993) alternately propose a combination electrical–thermal model that predicts a runaway condition in some conductive pathways; a particular pathway may initially heat more than the others, dropping its resistance, and assuming an ever-increasing share of the total current. Lin (1984) found that coating 12 mm^2 metal electrodes with a conductive adhesive eliminates the sharp stings. The resistance of the adhesive may serve to equalize the current in several pathways, even if one has lower resistance than the others (Monzon, 1986), or the adhesive may absorb excess water from the pore (Grimnes, 1988), or the flexible adhesive may ensure adequate mechanical and therefore electrical contact between electrode and skin. The exact mechanism is unclear.

If the electrodes are small and well hydrated, sudden stings do not occur. Commercially available electrotactile electrode arrays have used electrode sizes of 24 mm^2 with water and sweat as an electrolyte (Saunders, 1983, 1986) and 3 mm^2 with conductive gel (Sevrain et al., 1990), which increases the effective active area by current spreading. Szeto and Riso (1990) recommend 7–15 mm^2 electrodes for the best-quality sensations.

Subjective description of sensation

Subjects describe electrotactile sensations from surface electrodes qualitatively as tingle, itch, vibration, buzz, touch, pressure, pinch, and sharp and burning pain, depending on the stimulating voltage, current, and waveform, and the electrode size, material, and contact force, and the skin location, thickness, and hydration (Gibson, 1968; Pfeiffer, 1968; Collins and Saunders, 1970; Melen and Meindl, 1971; Mason and Mackay, 1976; Saunders, 1977; Tashiro and Higashiyama, 1981; Szeto and Saunders, 1982; Kaczmarek, 1991). The technique of single-afferent-fiber stimulation with microelectrodes is revealing the sensation qualities associated with activation of the different fiber types (Torebjork et al., 1984b; Vallbo, 1981).[18]

Bishop (1943) found that electrically stimulating the skin in very small areas with spark discharges caused two distinct sensations depending on the location: prick and touch, with the prick locations being more numerous. Moving the stimulus location by as little as 0.1 mm changed the sensation. Therefore, on most skin loci, electrodes of about 1 mm^2 area give a prickly, uncomfortable sensation which becomes painful at levels just above threshold (Saunders, 1983). Larger electrodes result in a more comfortable stimulation described as touch or vibration, probably because: (1) both touch and pain (prick) fibers are stimulated, and the touch sensation can partially mask the pain (Butikofer and Lawrence, 1978), and/or (2) the larger-diameter touch fibers are stimulated at lower current densities than the pain fibers (Veltink et al., 1988). However, even 1 mm position shifts of larger electrodes can change the subjective sensation as well as the sensation and pain thresholds. Because of the great variations in experimental methods and the vagueness of sensation descriptions, it is difficult to predict which stimulation waveforms, body locations, etc. give rise to which types of sensations, much less determine the underlying neural mechanisms. Nevertheless, some investigators have proposed mechanisms (Hallin and Torebjork, 1973; Rollman, 1973; Mason and Mackay, 1976; Butikofer and Lawrence, 1978, 1979).

Stimulation of surface electrodes with current pulses

Figure 9-10 shows the voltage of a 24 mm^2 well-hydrated active electrode on the abdomen relative to a large coaxial (encircling) ground electrode when stimulated with 1 mA, 400 μs duration constant current pulses at a rate of 10 pulses s^{-1} (Kaczmarek and Webster, 1989). Our studies with these well-hydrated electrodes show that the resistive electrical characteristic is quite repeatable (at least for different abdominal locations on one subject). Figure 9-11 shows a model of the electrode–skin interface which explains this waveform. The electrochemical half-cell potential is insignificant considering the high voltages used for stimulation. Consider now only the steady-state electrode voltage V_m near the end of the current pulse. Figure 9-12 shows that this voltage increases nonlinearly with stimulation current; Figure 9-13 shows the same data plotted as static resistance ($R = V_m/I$) vs. current.

The resistive part of the impedance of the electrode–skin interface (R_p in Figure 9-11) drops sharply with increased current (Gibson, 1968; Boxtel, 1977;

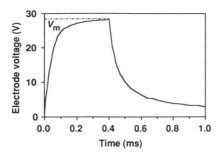

Figure 9-10 Electrode voltage (between 5.5 mm-diameter active electrode and large dispersive electrode) in response to the positive phase of a 1 mA, 400 μs balanced-biphasic current pulse.The negative phase is off the time scale and has the same shape. V_m is the asymptotic maximal voltage, which increases nonlinearly with stimulation current.

Kaczmarek and Webster, 1989; Kaczmarek, 1991; Panescu *et al.*, 1992b). The change in R is localized in the stratum corneum (Boxtel, 1977). Because of this change, electrodes are usually stimulated with constant current rather than constant voltage. One disadvantage of constant current stimulation is that if an electrode makes poor skin contact because of dryness or mechanical noncon-formity, the reduced effective area results in a higher current density and a much stronger, sharper sensation. Saunders (1973) suggests that a constant-power output circuit might be more suitable for electrodes prone to poor contact.

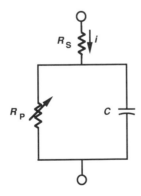

Figure 9-11 An approximate working model that explains the electrical characteristics of the electrode–skin interface consists of a fixed series resistance R_s, a fixed capacitance C, and a parallel resistance R_p that decreases invalue with increasing current. For a 5.5 mm-diameter gold-plated active electrode surrounded by a large (very low resistance) return electrode, approximate parameter values are 600 Ω for R_s, 2 nF for C, and 1–23 kΩ for R_p as stimulation current decreases from 25 to 1 mA. For these values, the electrode–skin interface is well hydrated with sweat.

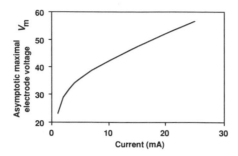

Figure 9-12 The asymptotic maximal electrode voltage for the electrode described in Figure 9-11 increases nonlinearly with increasing stimulation current.

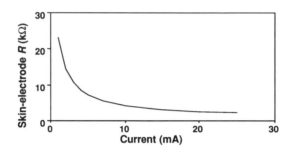

Figure 9-13 The electrode–skin resistance for the electrode described in Figure 9-11 decreases with stimulation current.

Unitech Research, Inc. (Madison, WI) has extensively tested a charge-dump method that delivers comfortable stimulation on the abdomen (Sevrain *et al.*, 1990; Tyler *et al.*, in revision). Stimulation intensity is controlled by the stored charge in a capacitor, which is then discharged into the skin without need for active closed-loop, high-voltage control circuitry. Figure 9-14 shows how the charge dump works; the different + and − voltages serve to reduce pH changes at the electrode–skin interface (Sevrain *et al.*, 1990). The negative phase voltage can vary from 15 to 40 V to set the stimulation intensity. With the 3 mm^2 electrodes (with large coaxial conductive return) well covered with conductive gel, pain is almost impossible to elicit. Interestingly, this scheme approximates voltage control (with a charge limit), because for 80 μs phase widths (the device's upper limit), the capacitors only release approximately one-eighth of their charge into the skin.

Thresholds of sensation and pain

The traditional measure of dynamic range of an electrotactile stimulator is the ratio (threshold of pain):(threshold of sensation) or I_P/I_S. The I_P/I_S ratio reported by various investigators varies from under 2 (6 dB) to about 10 (20 dB) at best (Kaczmarek *et al.*, 1991). This range is limited compared to

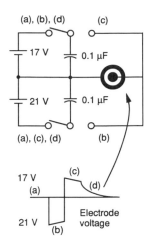

Figure 9-14 Videotact™ charge dump output circuit (see text). The switches are actually field-effect transistors. (a) The capacitors charge while the electrode is disconnected. (b) The lower capacitor discharges into the electrode for a fixed period of time; the phase width. (c) The lower capacitor disconnects and the upper capacitor discharges into the electrode for the same phase width. (d) The electrode is disconnected and both capacitors recharge; the electrode voltage decays due to skin, electrode, and electrode gel characteristics only. The stimulation intensity is determined primarily by the voltage sources and the number of pulses in a burst (one shown); phase width has a lesser effect.

other senses; the ear has a dynamic range of 120 dB and the eye 70 dB. If we assume a maximal comfortable vibratory stimulus amplitude of 0.5 mm for a 0.78 mm^2 stimulator (Collins, 1970), the vibrotactile range of the skin is about 40 dB.

At least four factors account for the variation in the quoted I_P/I_S values. (1) There is no uniform definition of "pain"; it could be defined as mild discomfort to intolerable. (2) The psychological condition and training modify the threshold of pain; experienced subjects tolerate at least twice the stimulation levels of naive subjects (Saunders, 1973). (3) At least for thermally induced pain, noxious stimuli may raise or lower the pain threshold (Torebjork *et al.*, 1984a). (4) The I_P/I_S ratio is a function of electrode size, material, and placement, as well as of the parameters of the stimulation waveform; all of the relevant factors are rarely reported. Finally, the sensation and pain thresholds can change significantly with small (1 mm) changes in electrode position.

Magnitude-based dynamic range

Although the I_P/I_S ratio has been extensively reported in the literature, we believe that it may be misleading. I_P, I_S, and I_P/I_S are *electrical* measures that give little information about the *percept* produced by stimulation. Choosing a waveform that maximizes I_P/I_S does not guarantee a usefully strong or comfortable sensation (Kaczmarek *et al.*, 1992a, 1992b). We propose that a better measure of the dynamic range of a tactile display is the perceived

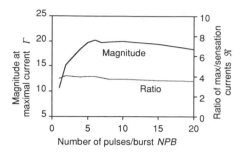

Figure 9-15 The maximal magnitude (at the predetermined maximal current without discomfort) is maximized with 6 pulses per burst. In the range 1–20 pulses per burst, the ratio of maximal current to sensation threshold does not vary much. Frequency of burst repetition was 15 Hz, pulse repetition rate within a burst was 350 Hz, and phase width was 150 μs.

magnitude at the maximal current without discomfort $\psi(I_M)$; note that $I_P \approx 1.3$ I_M. Figure 9-15 shows both dynamic range indices as a function of the number of pulses per burst. For the plot of maximal magnitudes $\psi(I_M)$, the stimulation current is set at the predetermined maximal level without discomfort for that particular value of number of pulses per burst; the magnitude shown is therefore the strongest stimulation that is considered to be of adequate quality. While I_M/I_S varies little, $\psi(I_M)$ is maximized at 6 pulses per burst; indeed this waveform is qualitatively more comfortable than one with only one pulse per burst.

Mechanism of sensation and pain thresholds, and stimulation comfort

Figure 9-16 shows that the required sensation threshold current increases with decreasing phase width, suggesting that the threshold of sensation is determined by the pulse charge (current × duration). Alternately, a first-order system with a time constant of 100–500 μs might describe this relationship (Sherrick and Cholewiak, 1986). Geddes and Baker (1989) and Mouchawar *et al.* (1989) review several competing mathematical descriptions of this strength–duration relationship. Because of the limited electrotactile temporal integration of the skin and the reduction of I_P/I_S with longer durations, current pulses with duration less than 0.5 ms are the most appropriate. For pulse durations longer than 500 μs, the pain threshold drops more quickly than the sensation threshold (Gibson, 1968), indicating that different integration mechanisms may determine the sensation and pain thresholds.

The electrotactile sensation and pain thresholds vary with body location. For a gelled 8.4 mm² coaxial stainless steel electrode pulsed for 100 μs, the sensation threshold varies from 2 mA on most trunk sites to about 7 mA on the palmar and plantar surfaces (Solomonow and Preziosi, 1982).

The I_P/I_S ratio (and probably the magnitude-based dynamic range as well)

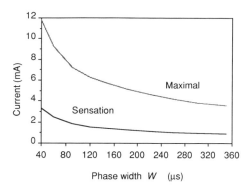

Figure 9-16 Sensation threshold current and maximal current without discomfort vs. phase width.

increases with electrode size as long as sudden stings do not occur. Saunders (1973, 1983) and Szeto and Riso (1990) report that 7–15 mm^2 is the optimal area of metal electrodes on the (hairy) abdomen; this is a compromise between larger electrodes (higher I_P/I_S) and smaller electrodes (less possibility of sudden stings). Gibson (1968) specified 175 to 700 mm^2 area for hairy skin and 50 mm^2 for glabrous skin. However, Gibson used longer pulses (500 vs. 10 μs) and may have used conductive gel (possibly equalizing current flow in the current pathways) under electrodes while Saunders did not.

Finally, spatial integration may be the best way to improve the magnitude-based dynamic range of a multi-electrode display. The 384-point Videotact^{TM} abdominal array described earlier produces a comfortable, strong tactile sensation when many small (3 mm^2) closely spaced electrodes are stimulated, although the perceived intensity of a single electrode is quite weak.

Skin condition

This has a profound influence on I_P/I_S and on the magnitude-based dynamic range and comfort of stimulation; dry skin has a high impedance and a prickly sensation (likely due to nonuniform current distribution). Effective skin preparation ranges from applying electrodes 20 min prior to stimulation to allow sweat to build up (Mason and Mackay, 1976), to premoistening the skin with water (Szeto and Saunders, 1982) or saline (Saunders, 1973) before applying the electrodes. Once stimulation starts, sweat production increases and provides sufficient moisture. While commercial conductive electrode gels provide a low skin resistance, they can short-circuit adjacent electrodes in a closely spaced array and increase the required current levels. Furthermore, the gel can dry out and require reapplication after several hours of operation. At least one display manufacturer does recommend gel (Sevrain et al., 1990; Tyler, 1992). Excessive body oil (an insulator) may be removed with a saline–detergent–alcohol solution (Collins and Madey, 1974).

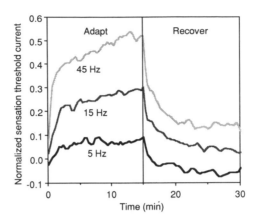

Figure 9-17 The electrotactile sensation threshold rises with time (sensory adaptation). The rate and amount of adaptation increase with frequency of burst repetition. The waveform was balanced-biphasic positive (B+), phase width 150 μs, six pulses per burst at a pulse repetition rate of 350 Hz. Zero normalized current represents the pre-adapted sensation threshold; a normalized current of one represents the pre-adapted maximal current without discomfort.

Sensory adaptation

The subjective intensity of a continuous train of pulses decreases with time due to adaptation.[19] The adaptation rate varies with frequency; while little adaptation occurs at 10 Hz, the sensation produced by a 1000 Hz pulse train decreases within seconds (Szeto and Saunders, 1982). As with vibrotactile stimulation, electrotactile adaptation has more effect at the sensation threshold than at suprathreshold levels. Bursts of stimulation (Figure 9-7) reportedly reduce the adaptation (Collins and Saunders, 1970).

A detailed study of electrotactile adaptation (Kaczmarek, 1991) found that the electrotactile sensation threshold elevation due to adaptation increased substantially with burst repetition rate F (Figure 9-17). The threshold elevation after 15 min was approximately 0.43 times the difference between the adapting current (0.7) and the initial threshold when the 15 Hz adapting stimulus was presented for 10 s out of each 20 s interval. Waveforms with 6 pulses per burst adapted twice as much as waveforms with either 1 or 2 pulses per burst.

Subjective magnitude of electrotactile stimulation

The subjective intensity (magnitude) of a train of pulses is increased by raising the pulse current, phase width, or, to a lesser extent, pulse rate (or burst rate if gated into bursts). If the pulses are gated into bursts, increasing the number of pulses per burst also increases the intensity (Sachs *et al.*, 1980; Milchus and Van Doren, 1990; Neuman, 1990a, 1990b). Several investigators (Rollman, 1973; Cross *et al.*, 1975; Sachs *et al.*, 1980) have attempted to fit electrotactile data to Stevens' power law (Stevens, 1962): $\psi = (\phi - \phi_0)^n$, where ψ is the subjective magnitude, ϕ_0 is the sensation threshold,[20] and ϕ is the stimulus level (in this case, current). While the exponent n varied from 0.7 to 3.5 in various studies, only Rollman's data were taken from a localized cutaneous sensation (electrode away from nerve bundles). For this case n increased from 2.3 to 3.0 (with ϕ_0 set to 0) as the number of pulses in a burst increased from 1 to 30. The value n (rate of subjective magnitude growth) is high compared to other sensory modalities such as pressure on the palm of the hand ($n = 1.5$), vibration ($n = 0.95$), and loudness of a 1 kHz tone ($n = 0.3$) (Stevens, 1962). This result indicates that the stimulation current must be carefully controlled to avoid unpleasantly strong sensations. Finally, McCallum and Goldberg (1975) suggested that a power relationship may not even be the most appropriate. In a later study using equal-size pairs of 50 mm^2 forearm electrodes, Higashiyama and Rollman (1991) found that for a different power function, $\psi = (\phi/\phi_0{}^n)$, n varied from 1.6 to 2.1.

Both phase width (Collins and Saunders, 1970) and frequency modulation (Blamey and Clark, 1985) have also been used for electrotactile displays. Saunders (1973) describes an intensity-modulation technique using pulse bursts ($PRR = 10$ kHz) in which the number of pulses in each burst varies from 0 to 40. Szeto (1985) found that subjects perceive a constant stimulation intensity (but varying "quality") if phase width and frequency (Figure 9-7 with one pulse per burst) are varied according to the relationship

$$\log W = 2.82 - 0.412 \ (\log F) \tag{4}$$

where W is the phase width in microseconds and F is the frequency in Hz. In contrast, Menia and Van Doren (in press) reported that perceived intensity was independent of stimulation frequency, and that perceived "pitch" was independent of stimulation current. They discuss how a slightly different experimental method (silent gaps between stimuli), or a different waveform (10 pulses per burst, 1 kHz pulse repetition rate), might be responsible for this apparent discrepancy.

Pain

Painful sensations are a major disadvantage of electrotactile stimulation, although comfortable stimulation is normally assured if several design recommendations are adhered to. The three most common types of pain or discomfort are: (1) prickly sensations at all stimulation levels, (2) sudden stings at low-to-moderate stimulation levels, and (3) burning sensations at high stimulation levels (Mason and Mackay, 1976). At least on hairy skin, prickly sensations and sudden stings are best avoided by using electrodes of approximately 10 mm^2 area and allowing sweat to build up (Saunders, 1983) or by using conductive electrode gel. Partial loss of electrode contact reduces the effective electrode area and may therefore lead to prickly, painful sensations. Limiting the maximal voltage to 50–70 V under poor-contact conditions can help to prevent sharp sensations (Szeto and Riso, 1990); the charge-dump circuit in Figure 9-14 uses this principle. Burning sensations usually represent the upper limit of electrotactile stimulation intensity. Note that we distinguish a burning sensation from true thermal damage to the skin.

PRACTICAL CONSIDERATIONS

Psychological issues

Historically, the greatest barriers to widespread use of complex "complete replacement" sensory aids for the blind and deaf, and perhaps for other tactile display applications as well, have not been primarily technological (Bach-y-Rita, 1979, 1982). Humans are resistant to switching information channels and will cling to an old channel as long as it is marginally useful. Even congenitally blind persons who later recover physiological use of the eyes through surgery do not necessarily "see"; the cognitive processes for interpreting and associating the visual sensations with prior experience do not yet exist (Bach-y-Rita, 1972). Cosmetic, convenience, and social issues also influence usefulness.

For example, although a blind person's long cane has significant spatial-sensing limitations, it is inexpensive and always works; it does not require adjustments, battery recharging, or repair (unless it simply breaks). The second author, however, remains convinced that the inherent capacity of the brain to modify function (brain plasticity) both as a response to injury or sensory loss, and as a response to functional demand, offers a strong basis for expecting sophisticated sensory augmentation systems to be successful. He noted more than 25 years ago (Bach-y-Rita, 1967) that ". . the ability of the brain to extract the data and recreate subjectively the image captured by the artificial receptor would depend on the adaptability, or plasticity, of the brain. There is ample evidence . . . that the brain is capable of adapting to a variety of extreme conditions. That a successful . . . system is not presently in use may not be due to limited functional capabilities of the brain; it may be due to the fact that an artificial receptor system has not yet been constructed to challenge the adaptive capacities of the human brain."

Some of the same principles may influence the acceptance of tactile displays in virtual environments, rather than strict replacement or substitution applications. It is presently unclear how much advantage may be gained by adding tactile feedback mechanisms to existing visual, auditory, and kinesthetic information channels in automobiles, aircraft, teleoperators, and "virtual worlds"; user acceptance may be a separate issue altogether. Hard data are needed here.

Safety

Burns

Electrodes and vibrators can both generate sufficient heat to cause painful sensations of heat as well as burns. LaMotte (1978), in a review of thermally induced pain, reports that for a 3 s application of radiant heat to a 7.5 mm-diameter ($44 \, mm^2$) patch of glabrous skin on the hand, the average threshold temperatures for perception of warmth and pain without tissue damage are 40 and 47°C, respectively. Three minutes of exposure at 49°C are required to cause a minor burn. In terms of radiant energy, the pain and burn thresholds are $0.92\,\mathrm{W\,cm^{-2}}$ and $2.0\,\mathrm{W\,cm^{-2}}$, respectively, for 3 s exposures (Geldard, 1972). However, Taige (1986) found that $113\,\mathrm{mm^2}$-area vibrotactile transducers are uncomfortably warm at continuous average power levels exceeding only 62 mW ($55\,\mathrm{mW\,cm^{-2}}$). This lower power is likely due to the fact that the bulky transducers (and mounting hardware) are in physical contact with the skin, trapping heat, in contrast with the radiant heat studies.

Burns under electrodes are potentially of at least three types. First, electrochemical burns due to a net flow of ions are prevented by ensuring that the net DC current flow at an electrode is close to zero—but see later comments on skin irritation. Next, large thermal burns are not likely to occur at the frequencies of interest in tactile display systems ($<1\,\mathrm{kHz}$) unless the stimulation level is driven well into the pain region. For example, from data in Kaczmarek et al. (1992a), a $24\,\mathrm{mm^2}$ electrode requires approximately 10 mA for 150 μs pulses, 6 pulses per burst at a 15 Hz burst rate to cause pain. If we assume the maximal voltage to be 50 V (Kaczmarek and Webster, 1989), the average power at the electrode is 13.5 mW, or $56\,\mathrm{mW\,cm^{-2}}$ power density, well below the burn level.

Finally, tiny black marks (0.25 mm diameter) are visible on the skin under magnification after sudden stings from an electrode. Mason and Mackay (1976) propose that the marks are burns caused by high power density in a single conductive pathway. However, their calculations assume that the dynamics of the electrode voltage and current are measurable during a sting with a stripchart recorder and that most of the current flows through one pathway.

Electrotactile skin irritation

Szeto and Riso (1990) and Szeto and Saunders (1982) present comments on skin irritation as well as report on a 10 h/day, two-week trial in which five subjects wore stimulators driving silver coaxial electrodes on the upper arm. They found that while a balanced-biphasic waveform caused the least long-term skin irritation, a functionally monophasic waveform caused less transient skin reddening. They concluded that either waveform is suitable. However, Szeto and Saunders (1982) recommend biphasic pulse pairs to prevent the net electrochemical reactions that occur even with capacitively coupled (no net DC flow) monophasic pulses. Riso et al. (1989) report that long-term use of percutaneous electrodes rarely cause skin infection; they recommend daily cleaning with alcohol.

It has been recently determined that the best stimulation waveform to reduce skin irritation (or subdermal electrode corrosion) is an asymmetric biphasic shape (Scheiner et al., 1990; Sevrain et al., 1990; Riso et al., 1991). This is because the zero net-DC charge associated with the balanced-biphasic waveform does not guarantee the absence of electrochemical reactions at the electrode–tissue interface, although it is a reasonable approximation.

Electric shock

By standard design principles, to prevent the possibility of cardiac fibrillation, subject-connected electrical instrumentation should be designed so that the maximal current flow across the user's torso is under 0.1 mA at any time (Olsen, 1992), even if there is a circuit fault or if a body part contacts another metal object, grounded or otherwise. However, these guidelines were written primarily for monitoring equipment. Electrotactile stimulation uses currents up to 50 mA, but at short phase widths (10 μs). The product of current and phase width, or charge, is the important criterion for electrical safety. With a maximal voltage of 1 kV, ventricular fibrillation requires at least 50 μC charge (Reilly, 1992); we recommend that the stimulator be designed to deliver less than 50 μC (pulsatile charge) and less than 1 mA DC current with any foreseeable failure. These criteria are readily achieved with redundant parallel *RC* networks in series with the active electrodes, or by the use of "charge dump" output circuitry (Figure 9-14). Kaczmarek *et al.* (1991) provide further details and a usable design. Reilly (1992) provides a detailed summary of electrical safety principles.

Comfort

Electrotactile

The maximal level of comfortable electrotactile stimulation varies between individuals and even varies within one individual. The user will ideally have a simple means of adjusting the stimulation level and quickly turning it off if necessary. As discussed earlier, stimulus quality is best with consistent electrode contact, a waveform chosen for a high magnitude-based dynamic range, and the use of spatial integration over several electrodes to achieve strong sensations.

Vibrotactile

This is comfortable with amplitudes up to 0.5 mm for a 1 mm diameter (0.79 mm^2) stimulator (Collins, 1970) unless the heat generated at the stimulator is greater than 62 mW cm^{-2} (Taige, 1986).

General

The mechanical comfort of any tactile display is heavily influenced by the method used to hold the display to the skin. A compromise must often be made between performance and comfort. For example, the sensation produced by electrotactile stimulation is most comfortable when the electrode–skin interface is wet with perspiration or electrode gel, and with the electrodes held firmly against the skin.

Repeatability and spatial uniformity

Because of the high variations in thresholds of electrotactile sensation and pain between subjects, a fixed relationship between the desired information (e.g., force) and the stimulation parameter (e.g., current) is not practical or desirable. The system user must be free to adjust the stimulation intensity and dynamic range as desired. Tursky and O'Connell (1972) showed that for a single subject, suprathreshold levels are more repeatable than the sensation threshold.

With the exception of the approximate fingerpad sensitivity maps by Melen and Meindl (1971), we are not aware of any published studies for electrotactile or vibrotactile stimulation which report the amount of variation of sensation or pain thresholds over an array of stimulators on one body surface. Our studies indicate that electrotactile sensation thresholds for stimuli delivered with a $24\,mm^2$ gold-plated electrode vary 3:1 over the lower abdominal surface (64 locations tested, mean current 1.62 mA, $\sigma = 0.43$ for 100 μs balanced-biphasic pulses, 100 Hz), with no observable spatial patterns. In contrast, Tyler (1992) has noticed that many subjects are less sensitive at the center of the abdomen than at the sides, with occasional insensitive patches elsewhere on the abdomen.

Power consumption

Low system power consumption is desirable in portable tactile display systems. This section comments on the power consumed by example tactile displays.

Electrotactile

A $24\,mm^2$-area electrode driven at the maximal current without discomfort, averaged over seven subjects, consumes between 1.2 and 4.9 mW with balanced-biphasic pulses, phase width 150 μs, frequency 15 Hz, pulse repetition rate 350 Hz, number of pulses per burst varying from 1 to 6 (Kaczmarek et al., 1992a). Notice that more power is required with the 6-pulses-per-burst waveform, even though the current is smaller: 5.2 mA vs. 7.0 mA at 1 pulse per burst. The 6-pulse-per-burst waveform has a higher magnitude-based dynamic range (Kaczmarek et al., 1992a). In a practical electrotactile display, only a fraction of the stimulators may be active at a given time, leading to an average power dissipation as low as 1 μW per pixel (Collins and Saunders, 1970). Subdermal stimulation requires only 10–22 μW (Riso et al., 1989) because of the lower voltage; the high resistance of the epidermis is absent.

Vibrotactile

Kovach (1985) used the mechanical properties of the skin to estimate the mechanical power dissipated in abdominal skin for a 250 Hz, $12.6\,mm^2$ vibrotactile stimulator. The threshold power is 0.4 mW, with an "adequate" continuous stimulation level 8 dB higher requiring 2.5 mW, close to Collins' (1970) estimate of 10 mW for a $0.79\,mm^2$-area stimulator; also see Sherrick (1984). The electrical power consumption of the actual $12.6\,mm^2$ vibrator (Star Micronics QMB-105 audio transducer) is considerably higher (138 mW for sine waves at threshold) due to conversion inefficiency and coupling losses. The resulting energy-conversion efficiency of 0.29% is too low for practical use of this transducer; highly specialized transducers with higher efficiencies (0.5–15%) have been developed for research work (Sherrick, 1984). Finally, as with electrotactile stimulation, only a small percentage of the stimulators will be active at any given time, reducing considerably the average power consumption.

Static mechanical tactile

These arrays, using electromechanical solenoids or the shape-memory alloy system described earlier, typically require at least 1 W per pixel to produce forces well above threshold, making them impractical for limited-power applications. They also suffer from severe adaptation to constant stimuli lasting longer than 1 s, although this may not be a limitation for dynamic applications. With slowly varying stimuli, latching mechanisms can reduce power consumption while increasing mechanical complexity.

PERFORMANCE EVALUATION

Developing an optimal tactile information display requires some objective method to evaluate the performance of the display. Preferably, numerical performance criteria need to be established regarding issues such as information transfer and practicality. Each of the performance criteria can then be optimized by varying the parameters of the display (waveforms, modulation, coding, etc.). A possible list of performance criteria for display development is:

(1) Minimal power consumption
(2) Maximal stimulation comfort
(3) Minimal post-stimulation skin irritation
(4) Minimal sensory adaptation
(5) Maximal information transfer measured by:
   (a) minimal JND of the modulation parameters current, width, frequency, and number of pulses per burst
   (b) minimal error in identifying the absolute stimulation level of a randomly stimulated electrode
   (c) minimal error in manually tracking a randomly varying target stimulus
(6) Maximal dynamic range:
   (a) maximal comfortable level/sensory threshold
   (b) maximal range of perceived intensities
(7) Minimal variation of sensory threshold and maximal comfort level with the precise electrode location on a given skin region
(8) Fastest or most accurate spatial pattern recognition

However, performance criteria should be chosen carefully with the final system application in mind. Do the chosen evaluation method criteria mimic (at least in theory) the final task? For example, if the final application is a tactile feedback system from a telerobotic gripper to convey texture and slip information as well as grip force to the human operator, are small changes in the JND (system gain) really meaningful? In light of the conclusion by Miller (1956) that the absolute identification of stimuli levels is a high-level process largely independent of the sensory modality, it may be meaningful to optimize a cutaneous display for the greatest number of discriminable levels only if the end task requires absolute judgments. Furthermore, such absolute judgments might be better provided by a warning-signal approach where some appropriate circuit or microprocessor algorithm makes the judgments. Tracking methodologies (Triggs *et al.*, 1973; Szeto and Lyman, 1977; Szeto *et al.*, 1979b; Jansson, 1983; Riso and Ignagni, 1985; Szeto and Chung, 1986) may be among the most useful evaluation tools because they are dynamic and thus approximate a whole class of real-time tasks; they can incorporate both spatial and temporal information. Where practical, final task measures (such as workpiece assembly time with a teleoperator) are preferable to more abstract, traditional, criteria. Finally, with multiple performance measures for a system there will likely be no unique set of optimal parameters (Kaczmarek *et al.*, 1991); engineering judgment will determine which performance measures are most important.

TRAINING

In order to effectively use information from a tactile display, particularly if it is used as part of a sensory augmentation system, the brain must mobilize a number of mechanisms that can collectively be included in the definition of brain plasticity (Bach-y-Rita, 1967, 1972, 1989). These require time and practice to mobilize. The acquisition of telepresence and distal attribution with either visual prostheses or teleoperators is not immediate (Epstein *et al.*, 1986); training is required to form the requisite mental model of afference (perceived patterns on display) as a function of efference (voluntary control) (Held and Durlach, 1992; Loomis, 1992a). Since tactile feedback has not been commonplace in virtual and remote environment applications, we will present examples from illustrative visual substitution studies.

For example, subjects using tactile vision substitution devices learn to treat the information arriving at the skin in its proper context. Thus, at one moment the information arriving at the skin has been gathered by the TVS camera, but at another it relates to the usual cutaneous information (pressure, tickle, wetness, etc.). The subject is not confused; when s/he scratches his/her back under the matrix s/he does not "see" anything. Even during task performance with the sensory system, the subject can perceive purely tactile sensations when s/he is asked to concentrate on these sensations.

The learning process may be similar to that which takes place in children with normal sensory and motor systems, or in adults learning a foreign language or Morse code, or in deaf persons learning sign language. As learning progresses, more and more of the information extraction processes become automatic and unconscious, and the "chunking" phenomena discussed by Miller (1956) may allow the number of bits per chunk to increase. For example, a blind subject looking at a tactile display of objects must initially consciously perceive each of the relative factors such as the perspective of the table, the precise contour of each object, and the size and orientation of each object, and the relative position of parts of each object to others nearby. With experience, information regarding several of these factors is simultaneously gathered and evaluated. Thus, concepts of "chunking" appear to apply to the development of increased information transfer through a sensory substitution system.

Users of the Optacon can immediately recognize vertical, horizontal, and diagonal lines presented to the display. Forty to fifty hours of training enable tactile reading rates of 10–20 words min^{-1} (Bliss *et al.*, 1970; Craig, 1977); further training typically raises the rate to about 28 words min^{-1} (Hislop, 1983). Users' self-reports suggest that 30–60 words min^{-1} are common after 1–2 years of experience (Craig, 1977). For the exceptional reading rate of 90 words min^{-1}, over 100 h of experience are required. One exception is notable; Craig (1977) found two extraordinary subjects who could read 70–100 words min^{-1} after only a few hours of Optacon experience. (They both had 17–30 h prior training on discrimination and recognition tasks, but still far outperformed other subjects.)

Most users of the early tactile vision system could recognize familiar objects after approximately 20 h of training, even when the objects were partially covered or changed in orientation (Bach-y-Rita, 1971). Distal attribution with the TVS system typically developed during the first 2–5 hours of training (Collins and Bach-y-Rita, 1973).

The benefit of tactile pattern recognition training transcends any particular set of patterns. Subjects trained on one pattern set perform better on a completely different set, indicating development of more general tactile-information-processing skills (Epstein *et al.*, 1989; White *et al.*, 1970).

CONCLUSION

As demonstrated in this chapter, the information-acquisition and -processing capabilities of the tactile sense rival those of the visual and auditory systems. In addition to accepting informational constructs from the usual communicative senses, human touch mediates control of the neuromuscular system, which is itself crippled in the absence of tactual feedback. Virtual and remote environment presentations will therefore be complete only in the presence of both kinesthetic *and* tactile feedback. A first generation of usable technological tactile displays exists today and can be incorporated into present systems, once some methods for rendering useful tactile information are developed.

Future research is needed to (1) determine the information requirements (range, resolution, etc.) for tactile feedback systems, (2) determine what gains in performance and level of realism can be gained by the use of tactile feedback, (3) develop algorithms to deliver appropriate information to the display, and finally, (4) redefine today's tactile displays to meet the needs of future tactile feedback systems.

COMPANIES THAT MANUFACTURE TACTILE DISPLAYS

Some of the following information was quoted from Salisbury and Srinivasan (1992) with permission of the second author of that report.

Begej Corp., 5 Claret Ash Rd., Little, CO 80127, 303-932-2186 sells fingertip (37-tactor) and tool-mounted (128-tactor) tactile arrays.

EXOS, Inc., 2A Gill St., Woburn, MA 01801, 617-229-2075 sells a fingertip vibrotactile stimulator called Touch Master.

Braille Displays, 186 Massachusetts Ave., Cambridge, MA, 02139, 617-491-8912, sells prototype static tactile modules with four Braille cells each that can be stacked horizontally to display four lines of Braille text, with 40 characters per line.

TeleSensory, N. Bernardo Ave., Mountain View, CA, 415-960-0920, sells the Optacon II reading device for the blind, featuring a 100-point vibrotactile fingerpad display.

TiNi Alloy Co., 1144 65th St., Unit A, Oakland, CA 94608, 415-658-3172 sells 9-tactor shape-memory-alloy static mechanical tactile arrays.

Unitech Research Inc., 702 N. Blackhawk Dr., Madison, WI, 53705, 608-238-5244 sells the Audiotact 32-channel abdominal electrotactile auditory substitution prosthesis and is completing development of the Videotact 768-tactor abdominal electrotactile stimulation system.

GLOSSARY

A *balanced-biphasic* current pulse for electrotactile stimulation has a positive and a negative current phase of equal duration and magnitude for an approximately zero net-DC current.

A *coaxial* (also called *concentric* or *annular*) electrode consists of an active center electrode insulated from a larger annular surrounding dispersive electrode for the return current path.

Distal attribution is the phenomenon whereby events are normally perceived as occurring external to our sense organs.

Efference copy, in the context of this chapter, is information about commanded muscular effort that is available to higher neural centers.

Electrotactile (also called *electrocutaneous*) stimulation evokes tactile (touch) sensations within the skin at the location of the electrode by passing a pulsatile, localized electric current through the skin. Information is delivered by varying the amplitude, frequency, etc., of the stimulation waveform.

A *functionally monophasic* current pulse for electrotactile stimulation has a single positive or negative current phase. To minimize skin irritation, a train of such pulses has an approximately zero net-DC current.

A *haptic display* presents to a user's skin spatial information that is under motor control of the user. Control of information display acquisition may occur by (1) directly scanning the display with a receptive skin surface, e.g., fingertips, or (2) by indirect means, e.g., using hand motions to control the presentation of information delivered to abdominal skin.

Haptic perception (tactual perception) combines tactile and kinesthetic information; this is "normal touch" (Loomis and Lederman, 1986).

The *just-noticeable difference* (JND) is the smallest change is a physical stimulus, such as frequency or amplitude of vibration, that can be reliably detected by a subject.

Kinesthetic perception is information about the relative positions of and forces on body parts, possibly including efference copy.

Masking is a sensory/perceptual phenomenon in which a weak stimulus can be obscured by a (temporally or spatially) nearby intense stimulus.

Percutaneous electrodes for electrotactile stimulation are subdermally placed and pass through the skin to an external connection.

Sensory substitution is the use of one human sense to receive information normally received by another sense, i.e., auditory or by visual information received through the skin.

Spatial integration occurs when a tactile receptor or neuron (or its central nervous system connection) sums a stimulus over some area of the skin.

Static tactile stimulation is a slow local mechanical deformation of the skin that varies the deformation amplitude directly rather than the amplitude of a fixed frequency of vibration. This is "normal touch" for grasping objects, etc.

Subdermal electrodes for electrotactile stimulation are implanted just under the skin.

Tactile perception is information about spatial pressure patterns on the skin with a fixed kinesthetic position.

Telepresence (or *presence*) consists primarily of visual, auditory, thermal, kinesthetic, and/or tactile feedback to a person from a remote (or virtual) environment, giving the person the experience of "being in" the remote location (Loomis, 1992b).

Temporal integration occurs when a tactile receptor or neuron (or its central nervous system connection) sums a stimulus over time.

Texture is a combination of surface roughness, hardness, elasticity, and viscosity.

Vibrotactile stimulation evokes tactile sensations using mechanical vibration of the skin, typically at frequencies of 10–500 Hz. Information is delivered by varying the amplitude, frequency, etc. of the vibration.

A *virtual environment* is a real-time interactive computer model that attempts to display visual, auditory, and tactual information to a human user as if s/he were present at the simulated location. An airplane cockpit simulator is one example.

ACKNOWLEDGMENTS

The authors appreciate the assistance and ideas provided by Dr Jack Loomis, University of California at Santa Barbara; Dr Mandayam Srinivasan, Massachusetts Institute of

Technology, and Mitchell Tyler and Dr John Webster, University of Wisconsin at Madison. The National Eye Institute grant R01-EY10019 provided partial support for both authors. The first author acknowledges the financial support of his wife Nancy while preparing the first draft of the manuscript.

NOTES

1. An extended 8-dot system is also available, but not yet popular.

2. Loomis *et al.* (1991) showed that by using two adjacent fingerpads, subjects could not identify raised line drawings any more accurately or quickly than with one fingerpad. The hope is that in a less-restrictive mode, e.g., with the fingers free to move with respect to each other or even lift off of the display, each user will develop a unique scanning strategy, discarding spurious tactile information by choice of fingerpad position, and reducing the perceptual confusion caused by masking effects on a fixed display.

3. Unpublished experiments at the University of Wisconsin have shown that an electrotactile abdominal display at similarly high frequencies can convey very fine spatial details when controlled by a fingerpad pressure sensor on the user's hand—heavily gloved to reduce natural sensation.

4. We will not maintain the strict separation of "receptors" from their corresponding afferent nerve fibers as is found in the neurophysiological literature; we note, however, that the two descriptions are not entirely interchangeable.

5. Note that in the literature, FA II is also called PC (Pacinian corpuscle), and FA is also called RA (rapidly adapting) or QA (quickly adapting). Finally, FA (without a I or II designation) sometimes refers specifically to FA I receptors, and sometimes it refers to both FA I and FA II.

6. Many investigators report these forces in mass units: $1 \, mg = 0.981$ dynes at standard gravity.

7. Similarly, in the visual system, while the maximal visual (grating) acuity is approximately 0.5 minute of arc (Shlaer, 1937), vernier acuity is only two seconds of arc (Stigmar, 1970).

8. This is not likely a limitation of the tactile sense, however. Miller (1956) found that subjects classifying pitch and loudness of tones, counting dots presented on a screen, identifying locations of tactile stimuli, recall of spoken words and numbers, and similar tasks could typically "process" from five to nine discrete pieces of information . . . which averages to his "magical" number seven.

9. Weber's Law (Werner, 1974) states that the just noticeable difference for many psychophysical metrics (e.g., pressure, vibratory and auditory frequency and amplitude, brightness) is proportional to the physical magnitude.

10. We might also note in comparison that the human visual system performs unconscious, but measurable, scanning motions with the eye muscles to prevent image fading due to sensory adaptation; these motions are essential for normal vision (Beauchamp *et al.*, 1971).

11. However, some commercial displays exist; see list at the end of this chapter.

12. This is probably due to cutaneous mechanoreceptor recruitment. The 230 Hz Optacon display excites only FA I and FA II receptor systems; normal touch excites also the SA I system, which has the finest spatial resolution.

13. Verrillo (1985) explains this characteristic with the "duplex model," which states

that at least two functional types of receptors (Pacinian and non-Pacinian) are present. The Pacinian (FA II) system integrates stimuli spatially and therefore is responsible for the threshold curve at stimulator areas larger than $0.05 \, \text{cm}^2$, while the non-Pacinian system does not, and accounts for the response to small-area stimulators. Further psychophysical studies by Gescheider *et al.* (1985) and Bolanowski *et al.* (1988) suggest that three and four, respectively, receptor populations mediate touch in glabrous skin.

14. This improvement at high frequencies, however, may be a sampling rate effect. At the tested presentation rates of 12 and 30 words min^{-1} (5 letters per word average), a given pixel traverses the eight display columns at a rate of 8 or 20 columns s^{-1}, respectively. Therefore, only a few stimulation cycles for each pixel position are possible at the lower frequencies. As for the spatial resolution, even if the FA II are recruited, the fine spatial information is still provided by the smaller-field FA I receptors (Johnson and Hsiao, 1992; Phillips and Johnson, 1985).

15. We will also exclude mechanical sensations such as those that occur when a dry patch of skin moves over the electrode surface during ~50 Hz stimulation, producing a weak vibrating sensation that may be felt at currents as low as 1 μA (Mallinckrodt *et al.*, 1953). Grimnes (1983a) calls this sensation electrovibration and shows that it is due to electrostatically generated mechanical deformation of the skin, not electrical stimulation of neurons, as occurs in conventional electrotactile stimulation. Strong and Troxel (1970) describe a manually scanned haptic fingerpad display based on this principle. Ongoing research in our laboratory is attempting to increase the low-intensity percepts produced by this method.

16. The literature contains inconsistent waveform terminology. Frequently, M+ and M− waveforms as shown in Figure 9-8 (with zero net DC current and nonzero baseline) are called "biphasic" because they have positive and negative parts. B+ and B− are sometimes called "biphasic with equal positive and negative parts." A zero-baseline monophasic waveform (with a net DC current) is never used for electrotactile stimulation due to rapid skin irritation resulting from electrochemical reactions at the electrode–skin interface (Saunders, 1983). Therefore, we use the terms "functionally monophasic" for M+ and M− and "balanced-biphasic" for B+ and B− to avoid ambiguity. Finally, the two phases of a balanced-biphasic waveform pulse (Figure 9-7) are often called pulses (with the result that interphase intervalis called "interpulse interval"). Introducing the term "phase" avoids the above ambiguity, and uniquely specifies the interpulse and interphase timing relationships.

17. Our recent experiments show that on the fingertip, as opposed to other locations such as the abdomen and forearm, M− pulses produce a weak, diffuse sensation, while M+ pulses feel much like the balanced-biphasics (Kaczmarek *et al.*, 1994).

18. In microelectrode single-fiber stimulation studies, FA II system stimulation gives rise to sensations of deep, diffuse vibration or tickling (20–50 Hz); FA I to tapping (1 Hz), flutter (10 Hz), or vibration (50 Hz); SA I to pressure (>10 Hz). Sensations of sharp and dull (burning) pain are respectively elicited by stimulation of Aδ and C nociceptor afferents (which terminate in free nerve endings).

19. Sensory adaptation can be measured by at least two different methods: (1) decrease in the perceived intensity of a constant stimulus, and (2) elevation of the sensation threshold at a skin site previously conditioned by an intense adapting stimulus.

20. ϕ_0 is sometimes set arbitrarily to zero. We do not think this is advisable for electrotactile stimulation, because the sensation threshold current is a substantial fraction of any perceivable and non-painful current level, and is therefore not negligible.

REFERENCES

Aiello, G. L. and Valenza, M. A. (1984) Psychophysical response to electrocutaneous stimulation, *IEEE Trans. Biomed. Eng.*, **BME-31**, 558–60

Alles, D. S. (1970) Information transmission by phantom sensations, *IEEE Trans. Man-Machine Systems,* **MMS-11**, 85–91

Altman, K. W. and Plonsey, R. (1990) Point source nerve bundle stimulation: effects of fiber diameter and depth on stimulated excitation, *IEEE Trans. Biomed. Eng.*, **BME-37** 688–98

Anani, A. B., Ikelda, K. and Korner, L. M. (1977) Human ability to discriminate various parameters in afferent electrical nerve stimulation with particular reference to prostheses sensory feedback, *Med. Biol. Eng. Comput.*, **15** 363–72

Andreeva, I. G., Vartanyan, I. A. and Tsirul'nikov, E. M. (1991) Summational properties of the somatosensory systems during tactile sensations elicited by electric current and focused ultrasound, *J. Evolutionary Biochem. Physiol.* (transl. from Russian by Consultants Bureau of New York), **27**, 65–8

Bach-y-Rita, P. (1964) Convergent and long latency unit responses in the reticular formation of the cat, *Exp. Neurol.* **9**, 327–44

Bach-y-Rita, P. (1967) Sensory plasticity, *Acta Neurol. Scand.*, **43**, 417–26

Bach-y-Rita, P. (1971) A tactile vision substitution system based on sensory plasticity, in T. D. Sterling *et al.* (Eds), *Visual Prosthesis: The Interdisciplinary Dialogue*, New York: Academic, pp 281–90

Bach-y-Rita, P. (1972) *Brain Mechanisms in Sensory Substitution*, New York: Academic

Bach-y-Rita, P. (1974) Visual information through the skin—A tactile vision substitution system, *Trans. Am. Acad. Ophthalmol. Otolaryngol.*, **78**, OP-729–OP-739

Bach-y-Rita, P. (1979) The practicality of sensory aids, *Int. Rehab. Med.*, **1**, 87–9

Bach-y-Rita, P. (1982). Sensory substitution in rehabilitation, in L. Illus and M. Sedgwick (Eds), *Rehabilitation of the Neurological Patient*, Oxford: Blackwell Scientific Publications, pp. 361–83

Bach-y-Rita, P. (1989) Physiological considerations in sensory enhancement and substitution. *Europa Medicophys.*, **25**, 107–27

Bach-y-Rita, P. (1990) Three dimensional spatial graphics for blind computer users, in K. Fellbaum (Ed.), *Access to Visual Computer Information by Blind Persons: State of the Art and Proposals for Projects*, Berlin: Technical University of Berlin, Institute of Telecommunications, pp. 81–5

Bach-y-Rita, P., Collins, C. C., Saunders, F. A., White, B. and Scadden, L. (1969) Vision substitution by tactile image projection, *Nature*, **221**, 963–4

Bach-y-Rita, P. and Hughes, B. (1985) Tactile vision substitution: some instrumentation and perceptual considerations, in D. H. Warren and E. R. Strelow (Eds) *Electronic Spatial Sensing for the Blind*, Dordrecht: Martinus Nijhoff, pp. 171–86

Bach-y-Rita, P., Webster, J. G., Tompkins, W. J. and Crabb, T. (1987) Sensory substitution for space gloves and for space robots, in *Proc. Workshop on Space Telerobotics, Jet Propulsion Laboratory*, Publ. 87–13, pp. 51–7

Barfield, W., Hendrix, C., Bjorneseth, O., Kaczmarek, K. A., and Lotens, W. (1995), Comparison of human sensory capabilities with technical specifications of virtual environment equipment, *Presence: Teleoperators and Virtual Environments* (in press)

Beauchamp, K. L., Matheson, D. W. and Scadden, L. A. (1971) Effect of stimulus-change method on tactile-image recognition, *Percept. Motor Skills*, **33**, 1067–70

Békésy, G. v. (1955) Human skin perception of traveling waves similar to those of the cochlea, *J. Acoust. Soc. Am.*, **27**, 830–41

Békésy, G. v. (1957) Sensations on the skin similar to directional hearing, beats, and harmonics of the ear, *J. Acoust. Soc. Am.*, **29**, 489–501

Békésy, G. v. (1959) Synchronism of neural discharges and their demultiplication in pitch perception on the skin and in hearing, *J. Acoust. Soc. Am.*, **31**, 338–49

Békésy, G. v. (1960) *Experiments in Hearing*, New York: McGraw-Hill

Békésy, G. v. (1967), *Sensory Inhibition.*, Princeton, NJ: Princeton University Press

Berglund, U. and Berglund, B. (1970) Adaptation and recovery in vibrotactile perception, *Percept. Motor Skills*, **30**, 843–53

Bishop, G. H. (1943) Responses to electrical stimulation of single sensory units of skin, *J. Neurophysiol.*, **6**, 361–82

Blamey, P. J. and Clark, G. M. (1985) A wearable multiple-electrode electrotactile speech processor for the profoundly deaf, *J. Acoust. Soc. Am.*, **77**, 1619–21

Blamey, P. J. and Clark, G. M. (1987) Psychophysical studies relevant to the design of a digital electrotactile speech processor, *J. Acoust. Soc. Am.*, **82**, 116–25

Bliss, J. C. (1969) A relatively high-resolution reading aid for the blind, *IEEE Trans. Man-Machine Systems*, **MMS-10**, 1–9

Bliss, J. C. (1973) Summary of three Optacon-related cutaneous experiments, in *Proc. Conf. Cutan. Commun. Sys. Dev.*, pp. 84–94

Bliss, J. C., Katcher, M. H., Rogers, C. H., and Shepard, R. P. (1970) Optical-to-tactile image conversion for the blind, *IEEE Trans. Man-Machine Systems*, **MMS-11**, 58–65

Bolanowski, S. J., Gescheider, G. A., Verrillo, R. T., and Checkosky, C. M. (1988) Four channels mediate the mechanical aspects of touch, *J. Acoust. Soc. Am.*, **84**, 1680–94

Boothroyd, A. and Hnath-Chisolm, T. (1988) Spatial, tactile presentation of voice fundamental frequency as a supplement to lipreading: results of extended training with a single subject, *J. Rehab. Res. Dev.*, **25**, 51–6

Boring, E. G. (1942) *Sensation and Perception in the History of Experimental Psychology*, New York: Appleton

Boxtel, A. v. (1977) Skin resistance during square-wave electrical pulses of 1 to 10 mA, *Med. Biol. Eng. Comput.* **15** 679–87

Boyd, L. H., Boyd, W. L., and Vanderheiden, G. C. (1990) *The Graphical User Interface Crisis: Danger and Opportunity*, University of Wisconsin-Madison: Trace R&D Center

Brooks, P. L. and Frost, B. J. (1986) The development and evaluation of a tactile vocoder for the profoundly deaf, *Can. J. Pub. Health*, **77**, 108–13

Brooks, P. L., Frost, B. J., Mason, J. L., and Gibson, D. M. (1986) Continuing evaluation of the Queen's University tactile vocoder I: Identification of open set words, *J. Rehab. Res. Dev.*, **23**, 119–28

Butikofer, R. and Lawrence, P. D. (1978) Electrocutaneous nerve stimulation—I: model and experiment, *IEEE Trans. Biomed. Eng.*, **BME-25**, 526–31

Butikofer, R. and Lawrence, P. D. (1979) Electrocutaneous nerve stimulation—II: stimulus waveform selection, *IEEE Trans. Biomed. Eng.*, **BME-26**, 69–75

Cholewiak, R. W. and Sherrick, C. E. (1981) A computer-controlled matrix system for presentation to the skin of complex spatiotemporal patterns, *Behav. Res. Method Instrum.*, **13**, 667–73

Cleland, J. G. and Winfield, D. L. (1985) *NASA Workshop Proceedings: Extravehicular Activity Gloves*, Research Triangle Institute

C/M Research (1992) *Displaced Temperature Sensing System X/10 Product Brochure*, Houston, TX

Collins, C. C. (1970) Tactile television—mechanical and electrical image projection, *IEEE Trans. Man-Machine Systems*, **MMS-11**, 65–71

Collins, C. C. (1985) On mobility aids for the blind, in D. H. Warren and E. R. Strelow (Eds), *Electronic Spatial Sensing for the Blind*, Dordrecht: Martinus Nijhoff, pp. 35–64

Collins, C. C. and Bach-y-Rita, P. (1973) Transmission of pictorial information through the skin, *Adv. Biol. Med. Phys.*, **14**, 285–315

Collins, C. C. and Deering, M. F. (1984) A microcomputer based blind mobility aid, in *Proc. IEEE Frontiers Eng. Comput. Health Care*, pp. 52–6

Collins, C. C. and Madey, J. M. J. (1974) Tactile sensory replacement, in *Proc. San Diego Biomed. Symp.*, pp. 15–26

Collins, C. C. and Saunders, F. A. (1970) Pictorial display by direct electrical stimulation of the skin, *J. Biomed. Systems*, **1**, 3–16

Craig, J. C. (1973) Pictorial and abstract cutaneous displays, in *Proc. Conf. Cutan. Commun. System. Dev.*, pp. 78–83

Craig, J. C. (1977) Vibrotactile pattern perception: extraordinary observers, *Science*, **196**, 450–2

Cronin, V. (1977) Active and passive touch at four age levels, *Dev. Psychol.*, **13**, 253–6

Cross, D.V., Tursky, B. and Lodge, M. (1975) The role of regression and range effects in determination of the power function for electric shock, *Percept. Psychophys.*, **18**, 9–14

Darian-Smith, I. and Oke, L. E. (1980) Peripheral neural representation of the spatial frequency of a grating moving across the monkey's finger pad, *J. Physiol.*, **309**, 117–33

Davis, H. (1968) Epilogue: a chairman's comments on the neural organization of sensory systems, in D. R. Kenshalo (Ed.), *The Skin Senses*, Springfield, IL: Charles C. Thomas, pp. 589–92

Dellon, A. L. (1981) *Evaluation of Sensibility and Re-Education of Sensation in the Hand*, Baltimore, MD: Williams and Wilkins

Durand, D., Ferguson, A. S., and Dulbasti, T. (1992) Effect of surface boundary on neuronal magnetic stimulation, *IEEE Trans. Biomed. Eng.*, **39**, 58–64

Epstein, W. (1985) Amodal information and transmodal perception, in D. H. Warren and E. R. Strelow (Eds) *Electronic Spatial Sensing for the Blind*, Dordrecht: Martinus Nijhoff, pp. 421–30

Epstein, W., Hughes, B., and Schneider, S. (1986) Is there anything out there?: a study of distal attribution in response to vibrotactile stimulation, *Perception*, **15**, 275–84

Epstein, W., Hughes, B., Schneider, S. L., and Bach-y-Rita, B. (1989) Perceptual learning of spatiotemporal events: evidence from an unfamiliar modality, *J. Exp. Psychol.*, **15**, 28–44

Freeman, A. W. and Johnson, K. O. (1982) A model accounting for effects of vibratory amplitude on responses of cutaneous mechanoreceptors in macaque monkey, *J. Physiol.*, **323**, 43–64

Frisken, S. F. (1987) A 64-solenoid, 4-level haptic display for the blind, *M.S. Thesis*, Electrical Engineering, University of Wisconsin-Madison

Frisken-Gibson, S. F., Bach-y-Rita, P., Tompkins, W. J., and Webster, J. G. (1987) A 64-solenoid, four-level fingertip search display for the blind, *IEEE Trans. Biomed. Eng.*, **BME-34**, 963–5

Gabriel, K. J., Trimmer, W. S. N., and Walker, J. A. (1988) A micro rotary actuator using shape memory alloys, *Sensors and Actuators*, **15**, 95–102

Gardner, E. P. and Spencer, W. A. (1972) Sensory funneling. I. Psychophysical observations of human subjects and responses of cutaneous mechanoreceptive afferents in the cat to patterned skin stimuli, *J. Neurophysiol.*, **35**, 925–53

Geddes, L. A. (1972) *Electrodes and the Measurement of Bioelectric Events*, New York: Wiley

Geddes, L. A. and Baker, L. E. (1989) *Principles of Applied Biomedical Instrumentation*, 3rd edn, New York: Wiley

Geldard, F. A. (1960) Some neglected possibilities of communication, *Science*, **131**, 1583–8

Geldard, F. A. (1968) Body English, *Psychol. Today*, **2**, 43–7

Geldard, F. A. (1972) *The Human Senses*, New York: Wiley

Geldard, F. A. (1985) The mutability of time and space on the skin, *J. Acoust. Soc. Am.*, **77**, 233–7

Gescheider, G. A. (1970) Some comparisons between touch and hearing, *IEEE Trans. Man-Machine Systems*, **MMS-11**, 28–35

Gescheider, G. A., Sklar, B. F., Van Doren, C. L., and Verrillo, R. T. (1985) Vibrotactile forward masking: psychophysical evidence for a triplex theory of cutaneous mechanoreception, *J. Acoust. Soc. Am.*, **78**, 534–43

Gescheider, G. A. and Verrillo, R. T. (1978) Vibrotactile frequency characteristics as determined by adaptation and masking procedures, in D. R. Kenshalo (Ed.), *Sensory Functions of the Skin of Humans*, New York: Plenum, pp. 183–203

Gescheider, G. A. and Wright, J. H. (1968) Effects of sensory adaptation on the form of the psychophysical magnitude function for cutaneous vibration, *J. Exp. Psychol.*, **77**, 308–13

Gescheider, G. A. and Wright, J. H. (1969) Effects of vibrotactile adaptation on the perception of stimuli of varied intensity, *J. Exp. Psychol.*, **81**, 449–53

Gibson, R. H. (1968) Electrical stimulation of pain and touch, in D. R. Kenshalo (Ed.), *The Skin Senses*, Springfield, IL: Charles C. Thomas, pp. 223–60

Girvin, J. P., Marks, L. E., Antunes, J. L., Quest, D. O., O'Keefe, M. D., Ning, P., and Dobelle, W. H. (1982) Electrocutaneous stimulation I. The effects of stimulus parameters on absolute threshold, *Percept. Psychophys.*, **32**, 524–8

Grandiori, F. and Ravazzani, P. (1991) Magnetic stimulation of the motor cortex — theoretical considerations, *IEEE Trans. Biomed. Eng.*, **38**, 180–91

Greatbatch, W. (1981) Metal electrodes in bioengineering, *CRC Crit. Rev. Biomed. Eng.*, **5**, 1–36

Grimnes, S. (1983a) Electrovibration, cutaneous sensation of microampere current, *Acta. Physiol. Scand.* **118**, 19–25

Grimnes, S. (1983b) Skin impedance and electro-osmosis in the human epidermis, *Med. Biol. Eng. Comput.*, **21**, 739–49

Grimnes, S. (1984) Pathways of ionic flow through human skin in vivo, *Acta. Derm. Venerol. (Stockh)*, **64**, 93–8

Grimnes, S. (1988) Personal communication

Hahn, J. F. (1966) Vibrotactile adaptation and recovery measured by two methods *J. Exp. Psychol.*, **71**, 655–8

Hahn, J. F. (1968) Tactile adaptation, in D. R. Kenshalo (Ed.), *The Skin Senses*, Springfield, IL: Charles C. Thomas, pp. 322–6

Hahn, J. F. (1973) Vibratory adaptation, in *Proc. Conf. Cutan. Commun. System Dev.*, pp. 6–8

Hallin, R. G. and Torebjork, H. E. (1973) Electrically induced A and C fiber responses in intact human skin nerves, *Exp. Brain Res.*, **16**, 309–20

Hannaford, B. and Wood, L. (1992) Evaluation of performance of a telerobot, *NASA Tech Briefs*, **16**(2), Item #62

Held, R. M. and Durlach, N. I. (1992) Telepresence: *Presence: Teleoperators and Virtual Environments*, **1**, 109–12

Heller, M. A. (1980) Reproduction of tactually perceived forms, *Percept. Motor Skills*, **50**, 943–6

Heller, M. A. and Myers, D. S. (1983) Active and passive tactual recognition of form, *J. Gen. Physiol.*, **108**, 943–6

Henderson, D. R. (1989) Tactile speech reception: development and evaluation of an improved synthetic Tadoma system, *MS Thesis*, Massachusetts Institute of Technology

Higashiyama, A. and Rollman, G. B. (1991) Perceived locus and intensity of electrocutaneous stimulation, *IEEE Trans. Biomed. Eng.*, **38**, 679–86

Hill, J. W. (1973) Limited field of view in reading lettershapes with the fingers, in *Proc. Conf. Cutan. Commun. System Dev.*, pp. 95–105

Hislop, D. W. (1983) Characteristics of reading rate and manual scanning patterns of blind Optacon readers, *Human Factors*, **25**, 379–89

Howell, W. C. (1960) On the potential of tactual displays: an interpretation of recent findings, in *Symposium on Cutaneous Sensitivity, U.S. Army Med. Res. Lab. Rep. No. 424*, pp. 103–13

Hughes, B., Epstein, W., Schneider, S., and Dudock, A. (1990) An asymmetry in transmodal perceptual learning, *Percept. Psychophys.*, **48**, 143–50

Hughes, B. G. (1989) *A new electrotactile system for the hearing impaired*, National Science Foundation Final Project Report, ISI-8860727, July 18, Sevrain-Tech, Inc.

Jansson, G. (1983) Tactile guidance of movement, *Int. J. Neurosci.*, **19**, 37–46

Johansson, R. S. (1978a) Tactile afferent units with small and well demarcated receptive fields in the glabrous skin area of the human hand, in D. R. Kenshalo (Ed.), *Sensory Functions of the Skin of Humans*, New York: Plenum, pp. 129–45

Johansson, R. S. (1978b) Tactile sensibility in the human hand: Receptive field characteristics of mechanoreceptive units in the glabrous skin area, *J. Physiol.*, **281**, 101–23

Johansson, R. S. and Vallbo, A. B. (1979) Detection of tactile stimuli. Thresholds of afferent units related to psychophysical thresholds in the human hand, *J. Physiol.*, **297**, 405–22

Johansson, R. S. and Vallbo, A. B. (1983) Tactile sensory coding in the glabrous skin of the human hand, *Trends in Neurosci.*, **6**, 27–32

Johansson, R. S., Vallbo, A. B., and Westling, G. (1980) Thresholds of mechanosensitive afferents in the human hand as measured with von Frey hairs, *Brain Res.*, **184**, 343–51

Johansson, R. S. and Westling, G. (1987) Signals in tactile afferents from the fingers eliciting adaptive motor responses during precision grip, *Exp. Brain Res.*, **66**, 141–54

Johnson, A. D. (1990) *Shape-Memory Alloy Tactical Feedback Actuator (AAMRL-TR-90-039)* (available through NTIS), August, Tini Alloy Co., Inc., Oakland, CA, under sponsorship of Harry G. Armstrong Aerospace Medical Research Laboratory, Wright-Patterson AFB, OH

Johnson, K. O. and Hsiao, S. S. (1992) Neural mechanisms of tactual form and texture perception, in W. M. Cowan *et al.* (Eds), *Annual Review of Neuroscience, vol. 15*, Palo Alto, CA: Annual Reviews, pp. 227–50

Johnson, K. O. and Phillips, J. R. (1984) Spatial and nonspatial neural mechanisms underlying tactile spatial discrimination, in C. v. Euler *et al.* (Eds), *Somatosensory mechanisms*, London: Macmillan, pp. 237–48

Kaczmarek, K., Bach-y-Rita, P., Tompkins, W. J., and Webster, J. G. (1985) A tactile vision-substitution systsem for the blind: computer-controlled partial image sequencing, *IEEE Trans. Biomed. Eng.*, **BME-32**, 602–8

Kaczmarek, K. A. (in press) Sensory augmentation and substitution, *CRC Handbook of Biomedical Engineering*, Boca Raton, FL: CRC Press

Kaczmarek, K. A. (1991) Optimal Electrotactile Stimulation Waveforms for Human Information Display, *Ph.D. Thesis*, Dept. Electrical and Computer Engineering, University of Wisconsin-Madison

Kaczmarek, K. A., Bach-y-Rita, P., Tompkins, W. J., and Webster, J. G. (1984) A time-division multiplexed tactile vision substitution system, in *Proc. Symp. Biosensors (IEEE)*, pp. 101–6

Kaczmarek, K. A., Kramer, K. M., Webster, J. G., and Radwin, R. G. (1991) A 16-channel 8-parameter waveform electrotactile stimulation system, *IEEE Trans. Biomed. Eng.*, **BME-38**, 933–43

Kaczmarek, K. A. and Webster, J. G. (1989) Voltage-current characteristics of the electrotactile skin–electrode interface, in *Proc. Ann. Int. Conf. IEEE Eng. Med. Biol. Soc.*, pp. 1526–7

Kaczmarek, K. A., Webster, J. G., Bach-y-Rita, P., and Tompkins, W. J. (1991) Electrotactile and vibrotactile displays for sensory substitution systems, *IEEE Trans. Biomed. Eng.*, **38**, 1–16

Kaczmarek, K. A., Webster, J. G., and Radwin, R.G . (1992a) Maximal dynamic range electrotactile stimulation waveforms, *IEEE Trans. Biomed. Eng.*, **9** 701–15

Kaczmarek, K. A., Webster, J. G., and Radwin, R. G. (1992b) Maximal dynamic range electrotactile stimulation waveforms, in *1992 SID Int. Symp. Digest of Tech. Papers*, pp. 667–70

Kaczmarek, K. A., Tyler, M. E., and Bach-y-Rita, P. (1994) Electrotactile haptic display on the fingertips: preliminary results, *Proc. 16th Ann. Int. Conf. IEEE Eng. Med. Biol. Soc.*, pp. 940–1

Keidel, W. F. (1973) The cochlear model in skin stimulation, in *Proc. Conf. Cutan. Commun. System Dev.*, pp. 27–32

Kirman, J. H. (1973) Tactile communication of speech: a review and analysis, *Psychol. Bull.*, **80**, 54–74

Kirman, J. H. (1974) Tactile perception of computer-derived formant patterns from voiced speech, *J. Acoust. Soc. Am.*, **55**, 163–9

Kirman, J. H. (1982) Current developments in tactile communication of speech, in W. Schiff and E. Foulke (Eds), *Tactual Perception: A Sourcebook*, Cambridge: Cambridge University Press

Knibestol, M. (1975) Stimulus response functions of slowly adapting mechanoreceptors in the human glabrous skin area, *J. Physiol.*, **245**, 63–80

Knibestol, M. and Vallbo, A. B. (1980). Intensity of sensation related to activity of slowly adapting mechanoreceptive units in the human hand, *J. Physiol.*, **300**, 251–67

Kokjer, K. J. (1987) The information capacity of the human fingertip, *IEEE Trans. System Man. Cybern.*, **SMC-17**, 100–2

Kovach, M. W. (1985) Design considerations for the construction of a vibrotactile array, *M.S. Thesis*, Biomed. Eng., Ohio State University, Columbus; OH

Krueger, L. E. (1970) David Katz's Der Aufbau der Tastwelt (the world of touch): a synopsis, *Percept. Psychophys.*, **7**, 337–41

LaMotte, R. H. (1978) Intensive and temporal determinants of thermal pain, in D. R. Kenshalo (Ed.), *Sensory Function of the Skin of Humans*, New York: Plenum, pp. 327–58

Larkin, W. D. and Reilly, J. P. (1984) Strength/duration relationships for electrocutaneous sensitivity: Stimulation by capacitive discharges, *Percept. Psychophys.*, **36**, 68–78

Leotta, D. F., Rabinowitz, W. M., Reed, C. M., and Durlach, N. I. (1988) Preliminary results of speech-reception tests obtained with the synthetic Tadoma system, *J. Rehab. Res. Dev.*, **25**, 45–52

Library of Congress (1987) *About Braille*, May, National Library Service for the Blind and Physically Handicapped

Lin, C. (1984) Electrodes for sensory substitution, *M.S. Thesis*, Electrical Engineering, Univ. of Wisconsin-Madison

Lindblom, U. (1970) The afferent discharge elicited by vibrotactile stimulation, *IEEE Trans. Man-Machine Systems*, **MMS-11**, 2–5

Linvill, J. G. and Bliss, J. C. (1966) A direct translation reading aid for the blind, *Proc. IEEE*, **54**, 40–51

Loomis, J. M. (1981a) On the tangibility of letters and braille, *Percept. Psychophys.*, **29**, 37–46

Loomis, J. M. (1981b) Tactile pattern perception, *Perception*, **10**, 5–27

Loomis, J. M. (1990) A model of character recognition and legibility, *J. Exp. Psychol.: Human Percept. Perf.*, **16**, 106–20

Loomis, J. M. (1991) *Factors Limiting the Tactile Perception of Form: Final Report*, Grant NS-15129 from National Institute of Neurological and Communicative Disorders and Stroke; grant DC-00143 from National Institute of Deafness and other Communication Disorders, March, Dept. of Psychology, University of CA, Santa Barbara

Loomis, J. M. (1992a) Distal attribution and presence, *Presence: Teleoperators and Virtual Environments*, **1**, 113–9

Loomis, J. M. (1992b) Presence and distal attribution: phenomenology, determinants, and assessment, in *Proc. SPIE Conf. on Human Vision, Visual Proc., Digital Disp.*

Loomis, J. M. and Collins, C. C. (1978) Sensitivity to shifts of a point stimulus: an instance of tactile hyperacuity, *Percept. Psychophys.*, **24**, 487–92

Loomis, J. M., Klatzky, R. L., and Lederman, S. J. (1991) Similarity of tactual and visual picture recognition with limited field of view, *Perception*, **20**, 167–77

Loomis, J. M. and Lederman, S. H. (1984) What utility is there is distinguishing between active and passive touch? Paper presented at the *Ann. Meeting of the Psychonomic Society*

Loomis, J. M. and Lederman, S. J. (1986) Tactual perception, in K. R. Boff *et al.*, *Handbook of Perception and Human Performance: vol II, Cognitive Processes and Performance* New York: Wiley, pp. 31.1–31.41

Maalej, N. and Webster, J. G. (1988) A miniature electrooptical force transducer, *IEEE Trans. Biomed. Eng.*, **BME-35**, 93–8

Magee, L. E. and Kennedy, J. M. (1980) Exploring pictures tactually, *Nature*, **283**, 287–8

Mallinckrodt, E., Hughes, A. L., and Sleator Jr, W. (1953) Perception by the skin of electrically induced vibrations, *Science*, **118**, 277–8

Mann, R. W. and Reimers, S. D. (1970) Kinesthetic sensing for the EMG controlled "Boston Arm", *IEEE Trans. Man-Machine Systems*, **MMS-11**, 110–5

Mason, J. L. and Mackay, N. A. M. (1976) Pain sensations associated with electrocutaneous stimulation, *IEEE Trans. Biomed. Eng.*, **BME-23**, 405–9

Massie, T. M. and Salisbury, J. K. (1994) The PHANToM haptic interface: A device for probing virtual objects, in *Proc. ASME Winter Ann. Meet.*, vol. 1, pp. 295–302

McCallum, P. and Goldberg, H. (1975) Magnitude scales for electrocutaneous stimulation, *Percept. Psychophys.*, **17**, 75–8

Melen, R. D. and Meindl, J. D. (1971) Electrocutaneous stimulation in a reading aid for the blind, *IEEE Trans. Biomed. Eng.*, **BME-18**, 1–3

Menia, L. L. and Van Doren, C. L. (in press). Independence of pitch and loudness of an electrocutaneous stimulus for sensory feedback, *IEEE Trans. Rehab. Eng.*

Milchus, K. L. and Van Doren, C. L. (1990) Psychophysical parameterization of synthetic grasp force feedback, in *Proc. Ann. Int. Conf. IEEE Eng. Med. Biol. Soc.*, pp. 2275–6

Miller, G. A. (1956) The magical number seven, plus or minus two: some limits on our capacity for processing information, *Psychol. Rev.*, **63**, 81–97

Minsky, M. (1995) Computational haptics *Ph.D. Thesis* (in press), Massachusetts Institute of Technology, Media Arts and Sciences

Minsky, M., Ouh-young, M., Steele, O., Brooks, F. P. J., and Behensky, M. (1990) Feeling and seeing; issues in force display, in *Proc. 1990 Symp. on Interactive 3D Graphics*, pp. 235–43, 270

Monkman, G. J. (1992) An electrorheological tactile display, *Presence: Teleoperators and Virtual Environments*, **1**, 219–28

Monzon, J. E. (1986) Noninvasive cardiac pacing electrodes, *M.S. Thesis*, Dept. of Electr. and Comput. Eng., University of WI-Madison

Mortimer, J. T. (1981) Motor Prostheses, in V. B. Brooks (Ed.), *Handbook of Physiology, section I, The Nervous System*, Bethesda, MD: American Physiological Society, pp. 155–87

Mouchawar, G. A., Geddes, L. A., Bourland, J. D., and Pearch, J. A. (1989) Ability of the Lapicque and Blair strength-duration curves to fit experimentally obtained data from the dog heart, *IEEE Trans. Biomed. Eng.*, **BME-36**, 971–4

Neuman, M. R. (1987) *Artificial Sensory Transducers: Quarterly Progress Report, 2*, Feb. 11, Applied Neural Control Laboratory, Electronics Design Center, and Department of Obstetrics and Gynecology, Case Western Reserve University, Cleveland, OH

Neuman, M. R. (1990a) *Prosthetic Sensory Transducers: Quarterly Progress Report, 2*, April 15, Applied Neural Control Laboratory, Electronics Design Center, and Department of Obstetrics and Gynecology, Case Western Reserve University, Cleveland, OH

Neuman, M. R. (1990b) *Prosthetic Sensory Transducers: Quarterly Progress Report, 1*, Jan. 1, Applied Neural Control Laboratory, Electronics Design Center, and Department of Obstetrics and Gynecology, Case Western Reserve University, Cleveland, OH

Neuman, M. R. (1990c) *Prosthetic Sensory Transducers: Quarterly Progress Report, 5*, Jan. 15, Applied Neural Control Laboratory, Electronics Design Center, and Department of Obstetrics and Gynecology, Case Western Reserve University, Cleveland, OH

Neuman, M. R. (1990d) *Prosthetic Sensory Transducers: Quarterly Progress Report, 4*, Oct. 15, Applied Neural Control Laboratory, Electronics Design Center, and Department of Obstetrics and Gynecology, Case Western Reserve University, Cleveland, OH

Neuman, M. R. (1991a) *Prosthetic Sensory Transducers: Quarterly Progress Report, 8*, August 11, Applied Neural Control Laboratory, Electronics Design Center, and Department of Obstetrics and Gynecology, Case Western Reserve University, Cleveland, OH

Neuman, M. R. (1991b) *Prosthetic Sensory Transducers: Quarterly Progress Report, 7*,

May 10, Applied Neural Control Laboratory, Electronics Design Center, and Department of Obstetrics and Gynecology, Case Western Reserve University, Cleveland, OH

Nunziata, E., Perez, C., Jarmul, E., Lipetz, L. E., and Weed, H. R. (1989) Effect of tactile stimulation pulse characteristics on sensation threshold and power consumption, *Ann. Biomed. Eng.*, **17**, 423–35

Olsen, W. H. (1992) Electrical safety, in J. G. Webster (Ed.), *Medical Instrumentation: Application and Design*, 2nd edn, Boston: Houghton Mifflin, pp. 751–92

Panescu, D., Cohen, K. P., Webster, J. G., and Stratbucker, R. A. (1993) The mosaic electrical characteristics of the skin, *IEEE Trans. Biomed. Eng.*, **BME-40**, 434–9

Panescu, D., Webster, J. G., and Stratbucker, R.,A. (1992a) A nonlinear finite element model of the electrode–electrolyte–skin system, *IEEE Trans. Biomed. Eng.*, **41**, 681–7

Panescu, D., Webster, J. G., and Stratbucker, R. A. (1992b) A nonlinear electrical–thermal model of the skin, *IEEE Trans. Biomed. Eng.*, **41**, 672–80

Patterson, P. E. and Katz, J. A. (1992) Design and evaluation of a sensory feedback system that provides grasping pressure in a myoelectric hand, *J. Rehab. Res. Dev.*, **29**, 1–8

Pfeiffer, E. A. (1968) Electrical stimulation of sensory nerves with skin electrodes for research, diagnosis, communication and behavioral conditioning: a survey, *Med. Biol. Eng.*, **6**, 637–51

Phillips, C. A. (1988) Sensory feedback control of upper- and lower-extremity motor prostheses, *CRC Crit. Rev. Biomed. Eng.*, **16**, 105–40

Phillips, J. R. and Johnson, K. O. (1985) Neural mechanisms of scanned and stationary touch, *J. Acoust. Soc. Am.*, **17**, 220–4

Rabischong, P. (1981) Physiology of sensation, in R. Tubiana (Ed.), *The Hand* Philadelphia: Saunders, pp 441–67

Rakowski, K., Brenner, C., and Weisenberger, J. M. (1989) Evaluation of a 32-channel electrotactile vocoder (abstract), *J. Acoust. Soc. Am.*, **86**, suppl. 1 S83

Rattay, F. (1988) Modeling the excitation of fibers under surface electrodes, *IEEE Trans. Biomed. Eng.*, **BME-35**, 199–202

Rattay, F. (1989) Analysis of models for extracellular fiber stimulation, *IEEE Trans. Biomed. Eng.*, **BME-36**, 676–82

Reed, C. M., Delhorne, L. A., Durlach, N. I., and Fischer, S. D. (1990) A study of the tactual and visual reception of fingerspelling, *J. Speech Hearing Res.*, **33**, 786–97

Reed, C. M., Durlach, N. I., and Bradia, L. D. (1982) Research on tactile communication of speech: a review, *AHSA Monographs*, **20**, 1–23

Reed, C. M., Rabinowitz, W. M., Durlach, N. I., Delhorne, L. A., Bradia, L. D., Pemberton, J. C., Mulcahey, B. D., and Washington, D. L. (1992) Analytic study of the Tadoma method: improving performance through the use of supplementary tactile displays, *J. Speech Hearing Res.*, **35**, 450–65

Reilly, J. P. (1989) Peripheral nerve stimulation by induced electric currents: exposure to time-varying magnetic fields, *Med. Biol. Eng. Comput.*, **27**, 101–10

Reilly, J. P. (1992) *Electrical Stimulation and Electropathology*, Cambridge: Cambridge University Press

Reilly, J. P. and Bauer, R. H. (1987) Application of a neuroelectric model to electrocutaneous sensory sensitivity: parameter variation study, *IEEE Trans. Biomed. Eng.*, **BME-34**, 752–4

Richardson, B. L. and Frost, B. H. (1977) Sensory substitution and the design of an artificial ear, *J. Psychol.*, **96**, 258–85

Riso, R. R. (1988) Sensory augmentation for enhanced control of FNS systems, in A.

Mital (Ed.), *Ergonomics in Rehabilitation*, New York: Taylor and Francis, pp. 253–271

Riso, R. R. and Ignagni, A. R. (1985) Electrocutaneous sensory augmentation affords more precise shoulder position command for control of FNS orthoses, in *Proc. RESNA 8th Ann. Conf.*, pp. 228–30

Riso, R. R., Ignagni, A. R., and Keith, M. W. (1989) Electrocutaneous sensations elicited using subdermally located electrodes, *Automedica*, **11**, 25–42

Riso, R. R., Ignagni, A. R., and Keith, M. W. (1991) Cognitive feedback for use with FES upper extremity neuroprostheses, *IEEE Trans. Biomed. Eng.*, **BME-38**, 29–38

Riso, R. R., Keith, M. W., Gates, K. R., and Ignagni, A. R. (1983) Subdermal stimulation for electrocutaneous communication, in *Proc. Sixth Ann. Conf. Rehab. Eng.*, pp. 321–3

Riso, R. R., Szeto, A. Y. J., and Keith, M. W. (1982) Comparison of subdermal versus surface electrocutaneous stimulation, in *Proc. IEEE Frontiers of Engineering in Health Care Conf.*, pp. 343–7

Rogers, C. H. (1970) Choice of stimulator frequency for tactile arrays, *IEEE Trans. Man-Machine Systems*, **MMS-11**, 5–11

Rollman, G. B. (1973) Electrocutaneous stimulation, in *Proc. Conf. Cutan. Commun. System Dev.*, pp. 38–51

Roth, B. J. and Basser, P. J. (1990) A model of the stimulation of a nerve fiber by electromagnetic induction, *IEEE Trans. Biomed. Eng.*, **BME-37**, 588–97

Rubenstein, J. T., Spelman, F. A., Soma, M., and Suesserman, M. F. (1987) Current density profiles of surface mounted and recessed electrodes for neural prostheses, *IEEE Trans. Biomed. Eng.*, **BME-34**, 864–75

Sachs, R. M., Miller, J. D., and Grant, K. W. (1980) Perceived magnitude of multiple electrocutaneous pulses, *Percept. Psychophys.*, **28**, 255–62

Salisbury, J. K. and Srinivasan, M. A. (1992) *Virtual Environment Technology for Training*, BBN #7661, March, The Virtual Environment and Teleoperator Research Consortium at the Massachusetts Institute of Technology

Saunders, F. A. (1973) Electrocutaneous displays, in *Proc. Conf. Cutan. Commun. System Dev.*, pp. 20–6

Saunders, F. A. (1977) Recommended procedures for electrocutaneous displays, in F. T. Hambrecht and J. B. Reswick (Eds), *Functional Electrical Stimulation: Applications in Neural Prostheses*, New York: Marcel Dekker, pp. 303–9

Saunders, F. A. (1983) Information transmission across the skin: high-resolution tactile sensory aids for the deaf and the blind, *Int. J. Neurosci.*, **19**, 21–8

Saunders, F. A. (1986) *Tacticon 1600 Electrotactile Sensory Aid for the Deaf: User's Guide*, Concord, CA: Tacticon Corporation

Saunders, F. A. and Collins, C. C. (1971) Electrical stimulation of the sense of touch, *J. Biomed. Systems*, **2**, 27–37

Saunders, F. A., Hill, W. A., and Franklin, B. (1981) A wearable tactile sensory aid for profoundly deaf children, *J. Med. Systems*, **5**, 265–70

Scharf, B., Hyvarinen, J., Poranen, A., and Merzenich, M. M. (1973) Electrical stimulation of human hair follicles via microelectrodes, *Percept. Psychophys.*, **14**, 273–6

Scheiner, A., Mortimer, J. T., and Roessmann, U. (1990) Imbalanced biphasic electrical stimulation: muscle tissue damage, in *Proc. Ann. Int. Conf. IEEE Eng. Med. Biol. Soc.*, pp. 1486–7

Schmidt, R. F. (1986) Somatovisceral sensibility, in R. F. Schmidt (Ed.), *Fundamentals of Sensory Physiology*, New York: Springer, pp. 30–67

Sevrain, C. J., Schramm, H. R., Schmidt, D. G., Hooper, P. S., and Thomas, M. P. (1990) Electro-tactile stimulator, *U.S. Patent #4,926,879*

Sherrick, C. E. (1973) Current prospects for cutaneous communication, in *Proc. Conf. Cutan. Commun. Systems Dev.*, pp. 106–9

Sherrick, C. E. (1984) Basic and applied research on tactile aids for deaf people: progress and prospects, *J. Acoust. Soc. Am.*, **75**, 1325–42

Sherrick, C. E. and Cholewiak, R. W. (1986) Cutaneous sensitivity, in K. R. Boff *et al.* (Eds), *Handbook of Perception and Human Performance*, New York: Wiley, pp. 12.1–12.58

Shimoga, K. B. (1993) A survey of perceptual feedback issues in dextrous telemanipulation: Part II. Finger touch feedback, *IEEE Annu. Virtual Reality Int. Symp.*, Seattle, WA, 271–9

Shlaer, S. (1937) The relation between visual acuity and illumination, *J. Gen. Physiol.*, **21**, 165–88

Sinclair, D. (1981) *Mechanisms of Cutaneous Sensation*, New York: Oxford University Press

Solomonow, M. (1991) Comments on 'Point source nerve bundle stimulation: Effects of fiber diameter and depth on stimulated excitation' and Authors' reply, *IEEE Trans. Biomed. Eng*, **BME-38**, 390

Solomonow, M. and Conaway, C. (1983) Plasticity in electrotactile frequency discrimination, in *Proc. IEEE Frontiers Eng. Comput. Health Care Conf.*, pp. 570–4

Solomonow, M., Lyman, J., and Freedy, A. (1977) Electrotactile two-point discrimination as a function of frequency, body site, laterality, and stimulation codes, *Ann. Biomed. Eng.*, **5**, 47–60

Solomonow, M. and Preziosi, M. (1982) Electrotactile sensation and pain thresholds and ranges as a function of body site, laterality and sex, in *Proc. IEEE Frontiers Eng. Health Care Conf.*, pp. 329–31

Starkiewicz, W., Kurprianowicz, W., and Petruczenko, F. (1971) 60-channel elektroftalm with CdSO4 photoresistors and forehead tactile elements, in T. D. Sterling *et al.* (Eds), *Visual Prosthesis: The Interdisciplinary Dialogue*, New York: Academic Press, pp. 295–9

Stevens, S. S. (1962) The psychophysics of sensory function, in W. Rosenblith (Ed.) *Sensory Communication*, Cambridge: MIT Press, pp. 1–33

Stevens, S. S. (1975) *Psychophysics*, New York: Wiley

Stigmar, G. (1970) Observation on vernier and stereo acuity with special reference to their relationship, *Acta Opthalmol.*, **48**, 979–98

Strong, R. M. and Troxel, D. E. (1970) An electrotactile display, *IEEE Trans. Man-Machine Systems*, **MMS-11**, 72–9

Szeto, A. Y. J. (1985) Relationship between pulse rate and pulse width for a constant-intensity level of electrocutaneous stimulation, *Ann. Biomed. Eng.*, **13**, 373–83

Szeto, A. Y. J. and Christensen, K. M. (1988) Technological devices for deaf-blind children: needs and potential impact, *IEEE Eng. Med. Biol. Mag.*, **7**, 25–9

Szeto, A. Y. J. and Chung, Y. (1986) Effects of training on human tracking of electrocutaneous signals, *Ann. Biomed. Eng.*, **14**, 369–81

Szeto, A. Y. J. and Lyman, J. (1977) Comparison of codes for sensory feedback using electrocutaneous tracking, *Ann. Biomed. Eng.*, **5**, 367–83

Szeto, A. Y. J., Lyman, J., and Prior, R. E. (1979a) Electrocutaneous pulse rate and pulse width psychometric functions for sensory communications, *Human Factors*, **21**, 241–9

Szeto, A. Y. J., Prior, R. E., and Lyman, J. (1979b) Electrocutaneous tracking: a methodology for evaluating sensory feedback codes, *IEEE Trans. Biomed. Eng.*, **BME-26**, 47–9

Szeto, A. Y. J. and Riso, R. R. (1990) Sensory feedback using electrical stimulation of the tactile sense, in R. V. Smith and J. H. Leslie Jr (Eds), *Rehabilitation Engineering*, Boca Raton, FL: CRC Press, pp. 29–78

Szeto, A. Y. J. and Saunders, F. A. (1982) Electrocutaneous stimulation for sensory communication in rehabilitation engineering, *IEEE Trans. Biomed. Eng.*, **BME-29**, 300–8

Tachi, S., Tanie, K., Komoriya, K., and Abe, M. (1982) Electrocutaneous communication in seeing-eye robot (MELDOG), in *Proc. IEEE Frontiers of Eng. in Health Care Conf.*, pp. 356–61

Tachi, S., Tanie, K., Komoriya, K., and Abe, M. (1985) Electrocutaneous communication in a guide dog robot (MELDOG), *IEEE Trans. Biomed. Eng.*, **BME-32**, 461

Taige, P. (1986) A power minimizing stimulus for electromechanical vibrators used in a portable tactile vision substitution system, *M.S. Thesis*, Bio-Medical Engineering, Ohio State University

Talbot, W. H., Darian-Smith, I., Kornhuber, H. H., and Mountcastle, V. B. (1968) The sense of flutter-vibration: comparison of the human capacity with response patterns of mechanoreceptive afferents from the monkey hand, *J. Neurophys.*, **31**, 301–34

Tan, H. Z., Rabinowitz, W. M., and Durlach, N. I. (1989) Analysis of a synthetic Tadoma system as a multidimensional tactile display, *J. Acoust. Soc. Am.*, **86**, 981–8

Tashiro, T. and Higashiyama, A. (1981) The perceptual properties of electrocutaneous stimulation: sensory quality, subjective intensity, and intensity–duration relation, *Percept. Psychophys.*, **30**, 579–86

Torebjork, H. E., LaMotte, R. H., and Robinson, C. J. (1984a) Peripheral neural correlates of magnitude of cutaneous pain and hyperalgesia: simultaneous recordings in humans of sensory judgements of pain and evoked responses in nociceptors with C-fibers, *J. Neurophysiol.*, **51**, 325–39

Torebjork, H. E., Schady, W., and Ochoa, J. (1984b) Sensory correlates of somatic afferent fibre activation, *Human Neurobiol.*, **3**, 15–20

Triggs, T. J., Levison, W. H., and Sanneman, R. (1973) Some experience with flight-related electrocutaneous and vibrotactile displays, in *Proc. Conf. Cutan. Commun. System Dev.*, pp. 57–64

Tschiriew, S. and Watteville, A. d. (1879) On the electrical excitability of the skin, *Brain: J. Neurol.*, **2**, 163–80

Tubiana, R. (1981) Architecture and functions of the hand, in R. Tubiana (Ed.), *The Hand*, Philadelphia: Saunders, pp. 19–93

Tursky, B. and O'Connell, D. (1972) Reliability and interjudgement predictability of subjective judgements of electrocutaneous stimulation, *Psychophysiol.*, **9**, 290–5

Tyler, M. (1992) Personal communication

Tyler, M., Hooper, P., Wysocki, D., and Bach-y-Rita, P. (in revision) A dynamic multielectrode electrotactile display: the effects of peak voltage, pulse phase width, number of pulses, and geometric area on the perception of haptic threshold, *IEEE J. Rehab. Eng.*

Tyler, M., Hooper, P., Wysocki, D. and Bach-y-Rita, P. (1992) *Haptic Display of Computer Graphics for the Blind*, Grant no. 7-R43-EY08166-02, March 13, National Eye Institute

Tyler, M. E. (1986) A quantitative analysis of human performance in manual tracking movements, *M.S. Thesis*, University of California-Berkeley

Tyler, M. E. (1990) Tactile devices and perception, in *Handbook on State-of-the-Art Technology: Proc. of the Sixth Int. Conf. on Computer Aids for the Visually Impaired*

Unitech Research Inc. (1990) *Audiotact Product Brochure*, Unitech Research Inc., Madison, WI

Vallbo, A. B. (1981) Sensations evoked from the glabrous skin of the human hand by electrical stimulation of unitary mechanosensitive afferents, *Brain Res.*, **215**, 359–63

Vallbo, A. B. and Johansson, R. S. (1984) Properties of cutaneous mechanoreceptors in the human hand related to touch sensation, *Human Neurobiol.*, **3**, 3–14

Van Doren, C. L. and Menia, L. L. (1993) Representing the surface texture of grooved plates using single-channel, electrocutaneous stimulation, in R. T. Verrillo (Ed.), *Sensory Research: Multimodal Perspectives*, Hillsdale, NJ: Lawrence Erlbaum, pp. 177–97

Vega-Bermudez, F., Johnson, K. O., and Hsiao, S. S. (1991) Human tactile pattern recognition: active versus passive touch, velocity effects, and patterns of confusion, *J. Neurophysiol.*, **65**, 531–46

Veltink, P. H., Alste, J. A. v., and Boom, H. B. K. (1988) Influences of stimulation conditions on recruitment of myelinated nerve fibers: a model study, *IEEE Trans. Biomed. Eng.*, **BME-35**, 917–24

Veltink, P. H., Veen, B. K. v., Struijk, J. J., Holsheimer, J., and Boom, H. B. K. (1989) A modeling study of nerve fascicle stimulation, *IEEE Trans. Biomed. Eng.*, **BME-36**, 683–92

Verrillo, R. T. (1965) Temporal summation in vibrotactile sensitivity, *J. Acoust. Soc. Am.*, **37**, 843–6

Verrillo, R. T. (1985) Psychophysics of vibrotactile stimulation, *J. Acoust. Soc. Am.*, **77**, 225–32

Vierck, C. J. and Jones, M. B. (1969) Size discrimination on the skin, *Science*, **163**, 488–9

Wall, P. D. (1968) Comment, in D. R. Kenshalo (Ed.), *The Skin Senses*, Springfield, IL: Charles C. Thomas, p. 550

Weinstein, S. (1968) Intensive and extensive aspects of tactile sensitivity as a function of body part, sex and laterality, in D. R. Kenshalo (Ed.), *The Skin Senses*, Springfield, IL: Charles C. Thomas, pp. 195–218

Werner, G. (1974) The study of sensation in physiology: psychophysical and neurological correlations, in V. B. Mountcastle (Ed.), *Medical Physiology*, St. Louis: Mosby, pp. 551–74

Wertsch, J. J., Bach-y-Rita, P., Price, M. B., Harris, J., and Loftsgaarden, J. (1988) Development of a sensory substitution system for the insensate foot, *J. Rehab. Res. Dev.*, **25**, 269–70

Westling, G. K. (1986) Sensori-motor mechanisms during precision grip in man, *Ph. D. Thesis*, Umea University, Sweden

White, B. W. (1970) Perceptual findings with the vision-substitution system, *IEEE Trans. Man-Machine systems*, **MMS-11**, 54–8

White, B. W., Saunders, F. A., Scadden, L., Bach-y-Rita, P., and Collins, C. C. (1970) Seeing with the skin, *Percept. Psychophys.*, **7**, 23–7

White, C. T. and Cheatham, P. G. (1959) Temporal numerosity: IV. A comparison of the major senses, *J. Exp. Psychol.*, **58**, 441–4

Wiker, S. F., Vandereheiden, G., Lee, S., and Arndt, S. (1991) Development of tactile
    mice for blind access to computers: importance of stimulation locus, object size,
    and vibrotactile display resolution, in *Proc. Human Factors Soc. 35th Ann.
    Meeting*, pp. 708–12
Wiley, J. D. and Webster, J. G. (1982a) Analysis and control of the current distribution
    under circular dispersive electrodes, *IEEE Trans. Biomed. Eng.*, **BME-29**, 381–5
Wiley, J. D. and Webster, J. G. (1982b) Distributed equivalent-circuit models for
    circular dispersive electrodes, *IEEE Trans. Biomed. Eng.*, **BME-29**, 385–9
Yamamoto, T., Yamamoto, Y., Yasuhara, K., Yamaguchi, Y., Yasumo, W., and
    Yoshida, A. (1988) Measurement of low-resistance points on the skin by dry
    roller electrodes, *IEEE Trans. Biomed. Eng.*, **35**, 203–9

10

Kinesthetic Displays for Remote and Virtual Environments

BLAKE HANNAFORD AND STEVEN VENEMA

Humans perceive their surrounding environment through five sensory channels, popularly labeled "sight," "sound," "taste," "smell," and "touch." All of these modalities are fused together in our brains into an apparently seamless perception of our world. While we typically place the most importance on our visual sense, it is our sense of touch which provides us with much of the information necessary to modify and manipulate the world around us. This sense can be divided into two categories: the kinesthetic sense, through which we sense movement or force in muscles and joints; and the tactile sense, through which we sense shapes and textures. This chapter will focus on the use of kinesthetic sense in realistic teleoperation and virtual environment simulations.

HISTORY

Artificial kinesthetic feedback techniques were first developed in the field of teleoperation—robot manipulators remotely controlled by human operators. In teleoperation, the perceptions from a physically remote environment must be conveyed to the human operator in a realistic manner. This differs from virtual reality in which the perceptions from a *simulated* environment are conveyed to the user. Thus, teleoperation and virtual environments communities share many of the same user interface issues but in teleoperation the need for detailed world modeling is less central.

The earliest remote manipulation systems were operated by direct mechanical linkages and the operator viewed the workspace directly through windows (see Figure 10-1) (Goertz, 1964). Perhaps because of their relative simplicity and high performance, little was learned about sensory requirements for remote manipulation from these early devices. When remote manipulation was developed for long distances and mobile platforms, electronic links became mandatory. The earliest attempts drove the remote manipulator with a position signal only and no information was returned to the operator about contact

Figure 10-1 Early teleoperator system with mechanical kinesthetic force feedback for handling toxic materials.

force. In the original mechanical designs, force information was intrinsically available because the linkages (actually metal tape and pulley transmissions) were relatively stiff, low-mass, connections between the operator and the environment. With the shift to electronic links, the loss of kinesthetic information was immediately apparent to the operators. The first artificial kinesthetic displays arose to provide improved functionality for remote manipulators.

Since the early remote manipulators, teleoperation has grown into a large field of research and development. Many of the issues in kinesthetic teleoperation interfaces (e.g., mechanism design, control system design and stability, performance evaluation, human factors) have direct applications to kinesthetic interactions with virtual environments. However, issues specific to kinesthetic simulation have only recently begun to be addressed. Thus, much of the information presented in this chapter is drawn from the field of teleoperation.

Characteristics of the kinesthetic channel

There are two different roles for kinesthetic sensations. The first is body position sense. This is available at all times internally and is implicitly consistent with most virtual environments. Although it is possible to modify this internal kinesthesia (see below), in most teleoperation and virtual environments we wish to leave the user's perception of body position and movement unmodified. The other major role of kinesthesia is sensing and controlling contact between the body and the external environment. Although tactile sensations obviously play a significant role in sensing and control of contact force, there are major exceptions when a tool is used or where heavy gloves are worn (as in space). In these situations, kinesthesia plays a dominant role. The kinesthetic sensations related to contact with the environment must be reproduced with high fidelity in realistic teleoperation and virtual environment systems.

There is a fundamental difference between kinesthetic information and that of other modalities such as visual and auditory displays. The visual and auditory channels are one-way, information-only flows. Vision involves collection and analysis of reflected photons generated by existing light sources. Hearing involves the collection and analysis of sound waves from the environment but does not generate significant sounds. Although head movements play a key role in 3D aural and visual perception, they do not involve energetic interaction in the physical variables being sensed. In both cases, energy flows in one direction from the environment to the human and thus the visual or aural environment can be (1) recorded or synthesized, and (2) replicated (displayed) by an information system. In contrast, the kinesthetic sensations fundamentally involve a bidirectional flow of energy between the human and environment. The relevant form of energy here is mechanical energy whose rate of change (power) is determined instantaneously by the product of the contact force and the velocity of the contact point. This means that kinesthetic sensations cannot be reproduced by an information system alone. A further consequence of this key distinction is that it is usually not meaningful to consider the ability to display a simulated environment separately from the ability to modify the simulated environment.

With kinesthetic interaction it is usually the case that to sense the environment *is* to modify the environment. This is true because in general, energy can flow from the user to the environment through the kinesthetic channel. Of course one can imagine an environment for which this is untrue. For example a room made of concrete should remain unmodified in spite of human kinesthetic interaction. In this case, a substantial impedance mismatch exists between the human and the environment, and so almost no energy flows. Since no energy flows, the environment is unmodified. Thus, unlike any other modality, the behavior of the kinesthetic channel is determined in equal parts by the user and the environment (real or simulated).

Physics: position/force simultaneity

The technical problem for virtual environments and teleoperators then is how to reproduce the bidirectional properties of mechanical energy flow. The term "force feedback," which is often used in this context suggests that one approach is to sense velocity (for many purposes velocity and position can be used interchangeably as long as mathematical bookkeeping is in order) and "apply" the appropriate force to the operator. In fact, this is a popular method of simulating kinesthetic interaction, but is not the only one. For example, we can do the opposite: sense force, and apply velocity feedback to create the same mechanical energy flow.

The usual implementation constraint is that with technological actuators, one of the two variables must be sensed and left alone while the other is controlled. This is a fundamental physical restriction if an energetic system is to be interfaced to information-only systems. When treated as sensed and actuated variables, force and velocity can be considered information. When applied to an energetic interaction they cannot be separated because they represent the physical flow of energy.

What information needs to be conveyed to reproduce the kinesthetic sensation of contact? This is a complex question because of the many possible modes of contact between objects and the existence of multiple contact points for example at the fingertips and palmar surfaces. However, just as a useful visual display can sometimes be obtained with a low-resolution monoscopic, monochrome device, a useful kinesthetic display need not reproduce the full sensation of contact at all surfaces of the hand. First, consider the modeling of a point contact such as that between the tip of a tool held in the hand and an external environment. At the point of contact, three directional components of force are sufficient to reproduce the contact. However, since the hand is a short distance away from the contact point, torques will be developed around these three axes in the hand. Thus, complete information about the contact at the user's hand requires six numbers at each instant of time: the force in three directions, and the torques about these three axes.

Simulation

Even in the simplest case, which is limited to a single degree of freedom, there is a progression of levels of realism which can be attempted in a system designed for kinesthetic display (Figure 10-2). The first is to simulate a dynamical system (i.e., linear second-order) which is permanently attached to the user's hand at the kinesthetic display. The kinesthetic display thus appears to have a certain mass (different from its real mass), damping, and spring-like behavior relative to some equilibrium point. The control system necessary to achieve this effect is the well-known "impedance control" (Hogan, 1985a, 1985b, 1985c). However, for the purposes of simulating the kinesthetic aspect of contact with "virtual worlds," this is usually inadequate because we must allow the operator to selectively come into contact with discrete simulated objects which are localized in space. The second-order model driving the

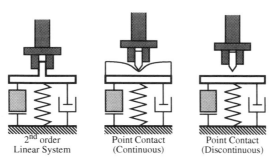

Figure 10-2 Levels of realism in kinesthetic displays.

impedance controller is global in that it applies to all values of position. In the next level of realism, simulation of discrete objects, we require different models for each object which are local to a region of space. We can conceptually divide these object models into two classes according to the hardness of their surfaces. Objects with soft surfaces will cause force to increase gradually as contact is made while those with hard surfaces will cause discontinuous force trajectories. This distinction can be made quantitative with reference to the capability of the display to generate rapidly changing forces. Assuming that "hard" objects will populate virtual environments, the rapidity with which a display can calculate and apply forces to the human hand determines the level of realism. All of the above have considered the simple case of point contact. Future systems of increasing realism will have to contend with generalized types of contact such as line contact, surface contact, etc. (Funda and Paul, 1990), and eventually to the complexities of contact with the multi-fingered hand.

What bandwidth is required to reproduce the kinesthetic sensation of contact? This is also a complex question because the frequency content of contact information depends upon the human operator as well as the contacted object. Unfortunately, contact between hard objects generates rapidly changing forces and thus very high (audio) frequencies. Although the human hand is covered with compliant material, we often hold tools made of hard material, and can sense the forces of contact between them and other hard objects. Convincing reproduction of either remote or simulated hard contact will be technologically extremely difficult for the foreseeable future due to the high mechanical bandwidths required.

Physiology

In humans, the kinesthetic channel is mediated by specific physiological pathways, organs, and brain centers. Muscles, specialized kinesthetic sensors, and reflexes all interact to determine our kinesthetic interactions.

Muscle cannot be viewed as either a "pure" force generator nor a source of velocities (Hannaford and Winters, 1990). Its complex dynamics mean that force and velocity, while not independent, are constrained to an abstract surface in the dimensions of force, velocity, and length. This makes analytical modeling of the kinesthetic channel very difficult although some progress has been made in numerical simulation (Hannaford and Fiorini, 1988; Hannaford and Anderson, 1988).

Muscle spindles are specialized muscle fibers within skeletal muscle which transduce stretch of muscle and the rate of stretch. Various spindle endings have greater or lesser position sensitivity vs. velocity sensitivity, and all have substantial nonlinear response. Much evidence indicates that these are a primary sensor for our sensation of body position (Goodwin et al., 1972). For a detailed but accessible review, see (Clark and Horch 1986), for detailed analytical models, see Agarwal and Gottlieb, 1982; Hasan and Stuart (1988).

The muscle spindle turns out to be very sensitive to vibration applied to the tendon (Matthews and Watson, 1981). Spindle firing in response to applied vibration can give rise to strong subjective sensations of body movement. Several experiments indicate that vibration-induced movement illusions are not mediated by skin receptors (Goodwin et al., 1972; Matthews and Watson, 1981; Matthews, 1984). Therefore, the potential exists for creating kinesthetic displays by generating artificial kinesthetic sensation through tendon vibration. Golgi tendon organs encode muscle force, but their role in kinesthesia and movement control remains controversial (Matthews, 1972). One additional measure of muscle force available for kinesthesia is the so-called "efferent copy," the registration of the level of muscle effort commanded by the central nervous system.

Body reference frame/object extent

Beyond the detailed mechanisms of kinesthetic interaction, there are additional significant differences between kinesthesia and other modalities. First, visual sensations appear to exist in a space which is external to the observer. Mechanisms such as the optokinetic and vestibular-ocular reflexes help to compensate for variables such as head movements which would destroy this illusion, but most impressively, visual images do not appear to move when the eye moves in space (for example, due to voluntary saccadic eye movements) in spite of large displacements on the retina (see Howard (1982). This property is absent from the kinesthetic sense in that kinesthetic sensations are always perceived with respect to specific limbs of the body—a body reference frame as opposed to a world reference frame. In some cases, the kinesthetic perceptions may be externalized, for example, to the end of a tool held in the hand (see Chapter 9 on "Tactile Displays").

Another remarkable characteristic of the visual system is its spatially global representation. When we view a complex scene, our eye movements generate a scan-path (Noton and Stark, 1971) during which our retinas image a sequence of detailed spots on the scene. Our foveal vision only extends about one half a degree, yet our subjective perception is of a wide field at high resolution. Kinesthetic contact sensations, however, are spatially localized to specific objects. Even a small movement away from contact with a surface, for example, instantly eliminates the sensation of contact. If kinesthesia were like the visual system, we would have an active perception of contact with an object even after we have let it go.

KINESTHETIC DISPLAYS

As described in the earlier section on physics: position/force simultaneity, the fundamental task in reproducing kinesthetic sensation is reproducing the bidirectional exchange of mechanical energy. This section will examine the various methods that can be used to create a kinesthetic display.

Contact modeling

The primary technology for kinesthetic displays are active joysticks connected to sensors and actuators. Network theory (Chua *et al.*, 1987; Paynter, 1961) allows us to model the interaction between the operator and the simulated or remote environment. Specifically, the bond-graph method (Chua *et al.*, 1987) allows us to model the energy exchange between the kinesthetic display and operator in terms of the generalized quantities "effort" and "flow." This notation, applicable to both electrical and mechanical energy transmission, is very useful when modeling control systems where both forms of energy transmission are present simultaneously.

The generalized variables have physical dimensions which depend on the type of system being modeled (see Table 10-1). In the case of a kinesthetic display, the mechanical variables are most convenient. Using the mechanical variables, the physical interaction can be schematically described as in Figure 10-3 where f represents a force, v represents a velocity and $z(v)$ represents a generalized mechanical impedance (mass, static and viscous friction, etc., as a function of v and its time-derivatives and time integrals). Using Kirchhoff's Law, the loop equation for this system is:

$$f_1 - z_1(v_P) - z_2(v_P) - f_2 = 0 \qquad (1)$$

or

$$f_1 - z_1(v_P) = f_2 + z_2(v_P) = f_P \qquad (2)$$

Equation (2) shows that the contact force is determined equally by the operator and the kinesthetic display. Thus, it is possible to control at most one of the two mechanical system variables, "force" and "velocity." This analysis

Table 10-1 Generalized system variables.

Electrical systems		Generalized system variables	Mechanical systems	
Units	Variables		Variables	Units
$V = \mathrm{NmC}^{-1}$	voltage	effort	force	$F = \mathrm{N}$
$I = \mathrm{Cs}^{-1}$	current	flow	velocity	$V = \mathrm{ms}^{-1}$
$P = \mathrm{Nms}^{-1}$	power	power	power	$P = \mathrm{Nms}^{-1}$
$E = \mathrm{Nm}$	energy	energy	energy	$E = \mathrm{Nm}$

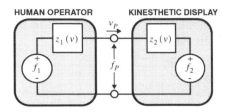

Figure 10-3   One-port model of a kinesthetic display and human operator.

suggests two different types of display: those that control the force being applied to the operator and those that control the velocity of the display. In both cases, the uncontrolled variable is available for the operator to change as a system input.

Force-feedback displays

The most common approach to implementing kinesthetic interaction is to sense the operator's velocity/position, and to apply force at the point where the velocity is sensed. We will assume that this contact point is the operator's hand. Although kinesthetic displays could be developed for other parts of the body, the hand is the primary human kinesthetic port for detailed manipulation tasks; thus the high cost of these devices dictates that initial efforts be applied to the hand.

The amount of force to be applied is determined by the remote or simulated interaction. For example, in a virtual environment simulation, the force is calculated from the response of a simulated object to the displacement observed at the operator interface. In teleoperation, in place of the model, a robot manipulator is moved by the same displacement as the human, and the robot contact force is used as the force-feedback command.

A mechanism capable of implementing this mode of kinesthetic display must have several characteristics:

(1) It must allow uninhibited movement of the operator's hand when no contact is meant to be conveyed.
(2) It must accurately reproduce the forces intended to be applied.
(3) It must be capable of sufficiently large forces so that contact can be simulated/reproduced with rigid objects.
(4) It must have sufficiently high bandwidth so that transients due to making and braking of contact can be reproduced with sufficient fidelity.

Interestingly, these characteristics are the same as the requirements for robot manipulators capable of contact force control. Both parallel and serial mechanisms[1] are in principle capable of meeting the above criteria. To date, the most successful designs have been serial linkages (like most robot arms). Except as noted, serial mechanisms will be considered in the rest of this chapter.

In a force-feedback display mechanism, actuators are selected which are good open-loop generators of force or torque such as DC servo motors. If, in addition, the mechanism connecting the motor to the operator's hand is designed to be highly back drivable (point (1) above, see the section on Dynamics below) then the force applied to the operator's hand will be a well-defined function of the motor inputs (inverse of the Jacobian matrix transpose, see Craig, 1989). Position sensors on the motion axes are sufficient to detect the operator's motion for transmission to the slave manipulator or virtual environment (see Hannaford, 1989 for details of coordinate transformations).

Displacement-feedback displays

The second major approach to kinesthetic display is to sense applied force and to impose a controlled displacement on the display.

The displacement to be applied to the display is determined by the remote or simulated interaction. In a virtual environment simulation, the displacement is calculated by a dynamic world model from the response of the simulated object to the measured operator contact force. In teleoperation, the remote robot manipulator is programmed to apply the same contact force as measured at the human hand, and the resulting displacement is used as the displacement command for the display.

A displacement-feedback mechanism must have the same characteristics as those listed in the previous section. From the point of view of design, however, it is useful to restate the characteristics as follows:

(1) It must be rigid enough to completely block the operator's hand when contact is meant to be conveyed with a rigid object.
(2) It must accurately reproduce the displacements intended to be applied.
(3) It must be sufficiently back drivable so that free motion can be reproduced without excessive drag on the operator.
(4) It must have high bandwidth so that transients can be reproduced with sufficient fidelity.

These characteristics are the same as the requirements for robot manipulators capable of accurate position trajectory following. As with force-feedback displays, both parallel and serial mechanisms are capable of meeting these criteria. In theory, parallel mechanisms are stiffer than serial linkages, and so may be better for this kind of system. A negative is that they generally have smaller work volumes.

In a displacement-feedback mechanism, the actuators must be good generators of displacement, independent of applied forces. Examples include hydraulic actuators, and highly geared DC motors with position feedback control. If, in addition, the mechanism is sufficiently stiff, the displacement applied to the operator's hand will be a well-defined function of the motor displacements (the Jacobian matrix (Craig, 1989)). Force sensors in the joints or at the hand grip can detect the operator's applied forces/torques, and send them to the slave manipulator or virtual environment.

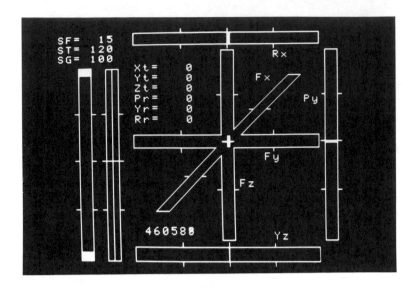

Figure 10-4 JPL force/moment bar-graph display.

Displacement-feedback display mechanisms tend to be more expensive for a given level of performance than force-feedback designs. This is because (1) force/torque sensors are more expensive than position sensors, and (2) true position actuators are not available. In practice, very stiff actuators are used with position-feedback control. Thus, in addition to force sensors, position sensors and a servo control system for position is required. These systems also tend to be heavier due to the required stiff structure.

Cross-modal displays

Cross-modal displays have been used as a substitute for true kinesthetic displays. This type of display keeps the user feedback in the information domain and thereby avoids the difficulties of reproducing or simulating bilateral energy flow. This can be done if one of the variables from the simulated or remote contact is controlled by the operator, and the other is displayed to the operator at a different point or through a different sensory modality. With a cross-modal display, the power at each operator port is zero but information about the simulated or remote interaction is conveyed. An example of such a cross-modal display is a bar graph display of contact force information in teleoperation (see Figure 10-4) (Bejczy and Dotson, 1982; Corker *et al.*, 1985). In this example, all six degrees of freedom of force/torque information are displayed in a pseudo-3D visual arrangement. Although the information is comprehensible to the operator with some effort, it was not shown to improve force control performance (Hannaford, 1987). This is probably due to the extra cognitive burden of transforming and interpreting visual information into the force/torque domain relative to the hand.

Exploratory methods

Kinesthetic display devices are still an immature technology. Much work of an exploratory nature is still being conducted. One concept which will be discussed here are devices employing brakes.

In a recent set of experiments, electrically operated brakes were fitted to a display mechanism and used to simulate contact with rigid objects (Russo *et al.*, 1990). The idea is that being passive mechanisms, brakes could achieve rigidity comparable to hard contact without high servo control gains and the potential for instability.

While the idea of employing passive mechanical elements has merit, the use of brakes has two fundamental limitations. First, although brakes can act almost instantaneously in time, their effect is to constrain velocity to zero. This is different from surface contact in which an inequality constraint is applied to position, but kinetic energy is unchanged or reduced by a certain amount at each contact "bounce." Secondly, the breaks act only in the directions determined by the mechanism axes. Thus, it is impossible for a device based on brakes to simulate contact with a surface which is not aligned with the mechanism axes.

KINESTHETIC DISPLAY DESIGN AND SELECTION ISSUES

While each of the above approaches to implementing kinesthetic display has its own unique advantages and requirements, all kinesthetic displays must satisfy some minimum set of kinematic, dynamic and physiological requirements to ensure adequate physical and human-factors performance. This section focuses on these requirements and some of the trade-offs that must occur when selecting desired capabilities. Examples of quantitative requirements and capabilities for some specific mechanisms are found in Fischer *et al.* (1990) and McAffee and Fiorini (1991).

Kinematics

As already discussed in the section on contact modeling, a kinesthetic display must be capable of exchanging energy with an operator using the mechanical system variables "force" and "velocity." The fact that these variables must coexist simultaneously at the operator/display interface means that the display mechanism must be capable of continuous contact with the operator while the point of the operator/display interface is moving. Additionally, since forces have to be either measured or applied (depending on the type of display), a common "ground" or reference frame must exist between the operator and the display; without this feature, the two would simply drift apart. The most common approach to meeting these requirements is a kinematically articulated mechanism with joints and articulated links configured with one end connected to the "ground" and the other end connected to the operator's hand. Other, more exotic approaches are possible using indirect contact methods of applying forces such as reaction jets or magnetic fields. However, these approaches will not be considered here.

A display's kinematic parameters describe the interrelation between the display's various degrees of freedom (DOFs) or joints. A commonly used convention for these parameters is called the Denavit–Hartenberg (DH) notation (Denavit and Hartenberg, 1955; Craig, 1989). With the coordinate frames that come with the DH notation, the four parameters for each DOF can be represented by a 4×4 homogeneous transform matrix, **T**, between a given DOF and the next DOF in the kinematic chain. Thus the kinematic structure of an n-DOF mechanism can be summarized by a series of n homogeneous transforms. These matrices can then be used to analyze the kinematic performance of the mechanism.

The following subsections examine each of the kinematic considerations for a kinesthetic display mechanism.

Degrees of freedom

Perhaps the most important kinematic parameter is the number of DOFs. Since, by definition, a DOF allows motion along (prismatic motion) or around (revolute motion) a single axis, the number of positions and orientations that a mechanism can achieve is strongly correlated with the number of DOFs. For example, a mechanism with a single prismatic DOF can only achieve motion along a single line in space while a mechanism with two nonparallel prismatic DOFs can achieve motion in a plane. In general, the greater the number of DOFs, the greater the number of directions in which forces and velocities can be controlled/sensed simultaneously. Complete freedom of motion for 3D spatial positioning and 3D orientation requires a minimum of six DOFs for any mechanism.

The complexity and cost of a kinesthetic display mechanism increases with increasing DOF. This is due to the corresponding increase in the number of actuators, sensors, and joints that the mechanism must support. This additional equipment also increases mass, inertia, friction, and backlash which can degrade dynamic performance of the overall mechanism and increase manufacturing costs.

Workspace

While a 6DOF kinesthetic display may be capable of complete freedom of motion for spatial positioning and orientation, mechanical limitations will limit the range of motion along each motion axis of the display. When all DOFs are considered simultaneously the ranges of motion describe the "workspace" of the display. The shape of the workspace for a 2DOF display is easily described by plane geometry; the workspace of a higher-DOF display can be much more difficult to represent mathematically due to its higher dimensionality.

In general, a kinesthetic display should be capable of matching some subset of the workspace of the human arm. The size of this workspace depends on the type of task that is to be done. For example, a high-dexterity task such as mechanical watch assembly requires precision motions in a relatively small workspace directly in front of the operator. In contrast, manipulating large objects requires less precise motions over a much larger workspace.

Singularity analysis

A display mechanism is said to be "singular" when one or more joints is at a motion limit ("workspace boundary" singularities) or when two or more joint axes become parallel ("workspace interior" singularities). While in a singular condition, the mechanism loses one or more of its DOFs (Craig, 1989). The Jacobian matrix relates joint velocities (θ) to Cartesian velocities (V) by

$$V = J(\theta)\,\dot{\theta} \tag{3}$$

The Jacobian matrix becomes singular at the mechanism singularities. This means that J^{-1} is nonexistent and that the relation

$$\dot{\theta} = J^{-1}(\theta)\,V \tag{4}$$

is undefined. Thus, for $V \neq 0$, one or more joint velocities will approach infinity as θ approaches a singularity.

This analysis using the Jacobian matrix also extends to the force domain. The equation,

$$\tau = J^{T}(\theta)\,F \tag{5}$$

relates joint torques (τ) to Cartesian forces (F). If the Jacobian matrix is singular, it has lost full rank and it becomes impossible to apply Cartesian forces/torques in one or more orthogonal directions. Looking at the inverse relation,

$$F = (J^{T})^{-1}(\theta)\,\tau \tag{6}$$

we also see that as θ approaches a singularity the Cartesian forces/torques in one or more directions go to infinity.

From this kinematic analysis we see that the display mechanism should be designed such that no singularities are encountered within the workspace that the operator is expected to use.

Human interface

The kinesthetic display must be suitable for human use and comfort. The display's performance is constrained not only by the kinematic constraints of the mechanism itself, but by those of the human arm that is grasping it. Thus, the display mechanism must be kinematically suited to the human arm so that an operator's desired range of motion can be tracked by the display. The display must also be designed for human comfort. While the work volume of the human arm is very large (Umek and Lenarcic, 1991), humans perform most tasks in a small region directly in front of their bodies. This region is important because it is naturally aligned with visual and other sensory inputs. Fine manipulation activities performed outside this zone can be fatiguing but the larger volume may be required for applications involving exploration of immersive environments.

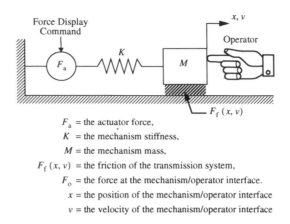

F_a = the actuator force,
K = the mechanism stiffness,
M = the mechanism mass,
$F_f(x, v)$ = the friction of the transmission system,
F_o = the force at the mechanism/operator interface.
x = the position of the mechanism/operator interface
v = the velocity of the mechanism/operator interface

Figure 10-5 Dynamic model of one-dimensional kinesthetic display.

Dynamics

The dynamics of the kinesthetic display mechanism can distort the forces and velocities intended to be displayed to the operator. Faithful reproduction of hard contact, for example, requires high bandwidth (quick) response (Uebel *et al.*, 1991). Therefore, the fidelity of a force-feedback display system is inherently limited by the display mechanism itself. To better understand these limitations we consider a highly simplified one-dimensional model of a force-feedback display consisting of an actuator and transmission (Figure 10-5). This type of display outputs a contact force while allowing the operator to control velocity (see the earlier section on force-feedback displays). The ideal display would allow the perfect transmission of commanded force ($F_o = F_a$) while accurately measuring the display's velocity ($v_m = v$). However, the summing forces on the mass show that the force applied to the operator is related to the actuator force by:

$$F_o = F_a - F_f(x, v) - M\dot{v} \qquad (7)$$

Thus, the force available to the operator is reduced by terms accounting for the friction and inertia of the display mechanism. In this simplified model, the stiffness, K, does not effect force transmission.

The following subsections discuss some of the effects of each of the parameters in the above model. In this discussion we consider the effects of these parameters on the transfer of force from display to operator and the transmission of velocity from the operator to the display.

Mass

We can see from equation (7) that the mass of the display interferes with the transmission of actuator forces to the operator by opposing changes in display velocity. This opposing force is proportional to the display's acceleration. Unfortunately, during collisions, we can expect high accelerations. Thus minimization of display mass is an important design issue.

If the display mechanism becomes multidimensional, the dynamics become more complex. In particular, unless the device is of a dynamically decoupled design such as a Cartesian mechanism, Coriolis and centripetal terms dependent on velocity will further "absorb" actuator force when velocity is significantly different from zero such as at the beginning of an impact.

The display must also be capable of supporting its own weight in a gravity field. If this were not true, then the operator would have to support the weight of the display—an undesired force having nothing to do with the task. As the display configuration changes while moving through the work volume, either active compensation (via computer-controlled offsets to actuator forces) or passive counterbalancing techniques must be used. In the latter case, the mass of the counterbalances adds significantly to the inertial problems. In the former case, the actuators must be capable of generating additional torque to offset the gravity load.

In the case of a displacement display, the mass will interfere with the transmission of force from the operator to the display. This results in the same negative effects as in the case of the force feedback display.

Friction

Equation (7) shows that friction also absorbs some of the actuator output force. Friction is often modeled as the sum of three components: static friction, which is the "break-away" force required to allow two parts in mutual contact to begin relative motion, Coulomb friction, which is a constant force which resists motion, independent of the magnitude of velocity, and viscous friction, which is a force proportional to the relative velocity of the mutual contact surfaces. However, it is important to note that friction is actually a much more complex phenomenon than this model suggests. Even with this simplified model, only viscous friction can be modeled in a linear system; the other two are nonlinear functions of velocity.

Friction occurs where mutual contact surfaces are in relative motion; it is present in bearings as well as geared and cabled transmissions (Townsend and Salisbury, 1987) and many actuators. Some electric motors also exhibit a friction-like behavior called torque ripple where the force output is a function of actuator position.

Since $F_f(x, v)$ is likely to have significant magnitude near zero velocity, friction becomes especially important when the display's velocity is near zero such as during contact with rigid objects. Therefore, minimizing the static and Coulomb friction in the kinesthetic display is also an important design consideration.

Stiffness

The stiffness of a display describes how the mechanism deforms under static or dynamic loads. While stiffness in the simple model of Figure 10-5 does not absorb dynamic actuator force like mass and friction, it does allow the two ends of the display to have different velocities. Since many systems measure velocity by monitoring the velocity of the actuator, the stiffness of the display limits the accuracy of the velocity measurement as it flexes under loads. When an operator attempts to control the velocity (and position) of a display with non-infinite stiffness, distortions can occur as the mechanism flexes in an oscillatory manner (Minsky et al., 1990).

Energy conversion

An "ideal" technological actuator acts as a variable force or velocity source for the display in which the output variable is a linear function of its input signal. However, real actuators have various linear and nonlinear properties which cause them to deviate from their "ideal" behavior. Actuators also have output limits due to physical constraints (e.g., resistive heating in motors and overpressure in hydraulic pistons); attempting to exceed these limitations can cause degradation of actuator performance or even catastrophic failure.

The dynamics of the actuators therefore cannot be neglected if truly high-fidelity kinesthetic display is to be achieved.

Kinesthetic display examples

There are a large number of existing kinesthetic display designs. Many of these designs are now marketed commercially through spin-off companies. Shimoga (1993) has surveyed force displays and other master devices for controlling multi-fingered hands in dexterous telemanipulation. Shimoga's paper contains extensive tabular summaries of the capabilities of these devices. Although these tables are often necessarily incomplete they often contain useful pointers to workers in the field. Table 10-2 contains summarized information on the force-feedback devices reviewed in Shimoga's paper (1993).

The following sections discuss one example of each type of kinesthetic display.

Salisbury/JPL force-feedback display

One of the most highly developed force-feedback displays is the Salisbury/JPL display (McAffee and Ohm, 1988) (see Figure 10-6). This six-axis device allows the user's hand to move anywhere and to any orientation within a roughly 2 ft^3 (0.06 m^3) work volume. Each axis of motion is motorized with DC servo

Table 10-2 Characteristics of force displays (Shimoga, 1993).

Name of device	Force sensing	Force feedback			Portability	Source reference
		Actuator	Resolution	Max. force		
Oomichi Device	●	electric	?	?	good	Oomchi et al., 1987
Utah	●	hydraulic	analog	?	good	Jacobson et al., 1989
Iwata	×	electric	?	3.3 N	good	Iwata, 1990
Jau/JPL	●	electric	?	?	good	Jau, 1990
Portable Master	●	pneumatic	0.005 N	22 N	very good	Burdea, 1991
New Master	●	pneumatic	0.005 N	22 N	very good	Burdea et al., 1992

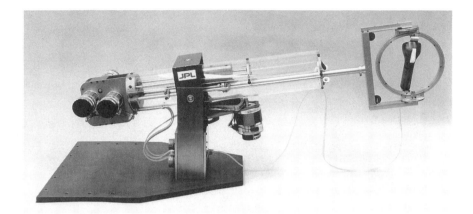

Figure 10-6   Salisbury/JPL force-feedback display.

motors connected via precision cable drives. The motors are located at the opposite end of the cylindrical body of the device to assist in balancing the device. The cable drive transmission is the key technology which enables high performance in all of the above measures.

An important design feature of the Salisbury display is the location of the singular point of its wrist mechanism: the last three axes are arranged so that their singular configuration corresponds to full flexion of the operator's wrist. In this configuration, the operator's own skeletal structure is also singular so that the display mechanism singularity does not reduce the useful range of motion.

Utah displacement display

A recently developed example using the displacement-feedback method is the anthropomorphic master/slave arm/hand built by the University of Utah (see Figure 10-7) (Jacobsen *et al.*, 1991). This high-bandwidth teleoperator system uses proprietary hydraulic actuators to implement a displacement-feedback display worn as an exoskeleton. The system senses force applied by the human operator to the joints of the display mechanism, and controls the device to achieve a displacement based on that of a kinematically identical slave arm. The system uses metal-foil strain gages to sense the user's applied force. In the important case of free motion, the actuators must remove the effective forces due to the exoskeletal device by regulating the force readings to zero.

IMPLEMENTATION ISSUES

Current implementations

Kinesthetic displays have been studied in detail over the last few decades. However, it has only recently become computationally tractable to consider the implementation of kinesthetic display of simulated environments. Only a few

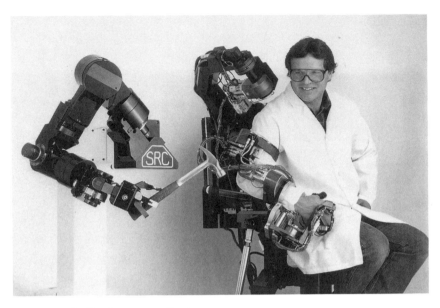

Figure 10-7 Utah displacement display.

applications with this type of capability have been explored to date. One exciting application is in the field of biochemistry. Here, a kinesthetic display allows manipulation of various molecules to study how they best "fit" together. Ouh-young *et al.* (1988) have used this technique to study how particular molecules can bind to particular receptor sites on a protein or nucleic acid molecule. Molecules with desirable binding properties may be useful in the design of new drugs.

Another application is in the field of microteleoperation where a kinesthetic display is used to navigate along a surface being scanned by a scanning-tunneling microscope (STM) (Hollis *et al.*, 1990; Robinett *et al.*, 1992). The STM measures the current flow through a voltage-biased tip; this current varies as a function of the tip's distance from the sample surface. In this application, the tip distance is servoed to maintain a constant current as the probe moves along the sample. The changing distance is then fed back to a kinesthetic display to give the operator a kinesthetic sensation of moving along the sample surface.

This type of application illustrates an important domain of application for kinesthetic simulation: instead of interfacing with a strictly simulated environment, simulated kinesthetic feedback can be added to a real-time physical application that is not inherently kinesthetic in nature. This additional kinesthetic sense may enhance the overall human interface to the application.

Future research challenges

The field of kinesthetic displays is relatively new; the potential applications to the simulation of virtual environments have only begun to be realized. While much can be borrowed from the field of telerobotics, there remain many open research issues which must be resolved before high-fidelity kinesthetic simulation is possible.

The "hard-contact" problem

As shown in Figure 10-3, the interface between the human operator and the kinesthetic display can be modeled as an energy port. The electromechanical components of the display, combined in series with the neuromuscular components of the human operator's arm, form a highly complex, nonlinear physical system. The interconnection of various masses, stiffnesses, and frictions produce a system which is susceptible to instabilities when included in a closed-loop position or force control architecture. Instabilities are most prevalent during simulated contact with high-stiffness ("hard") surfaces. This is due to the near-discontinuous change in the operating characteristics of the system between the no-contact and "hard" contact conditions. Hannaford and Anderson (1988) studied this issue for force-reflecting teleoperators. Minsky *et al.* (1990) have begun to explore these issues for simplified display mechanisms using linear models. However, much research remains to be done in this area.

Real-time dynamic modeling

When simulating virtual environments without a kinesthetic display, there is no requirement that objects in the environment must follow any particular physical law. However, since kinesthetic simulation requires an exchange of energy between the operator and objects in the environment, more emphasis must be placed on the modeling of these physically energetic processes. Recent research in visual graphics simulations has developed new techniques for the physical modeling of energetic interactions between simulated objects (Barzel and Barr, 1988). These modeling techniques need to be extended to include the kinesthetic interaction with a force display.

Mechanism design

A large number of force display mechanisms have been designed for specific applications in different research laboratories. While literature abounds on these specific designs (for examples, see the *Proceedings of IEEE Robotics and Automation Conference* for the last several years), only a few publications (Brooks and Bejczy, 1985; Fischer *et al.*, 1990; Brooks, 1990; McAffee and Fiorini, 1991) have begun to address the need for a general methodology for designing or selecting a force display for a given set of applications.

CONCLUSIONS

Humans rely on all of our five sensory channels when manipulating the world around us. Virtual environment implementations have traditionally focused on the visual aspects of the simulation and, to a lesser degree, the aural channel. The addition of a kinesthetic display to a virtual environment adds a whole new dimension of realism to the simulation and opens the door to several useful applications in the areas of mechanical design, environmental design, and machine-operator training. While much research remains to be done in the area of kinesthetic display mechanisms and kinesthetic display simulations, the current state of the art allows at least rudimentary forms of these displays to be added to existing virtual environment implementations.

NOTE

1 A serial mechanism is one in which the actuators are connected to the load in series, i.e., in a "kinematic chain." In a parallel mechanism, all actuators connect to the load directly.

REFERENCES

Agarwal, G. C. and Gottlieb, G. L. (1982) Mathematical modeling and simulation of the postural control loop: part I, *CRC Crit. Rev. Bioeng.*, **8**, 93–134

Barzel, R. and Barr, A. H. (1988) A modeling system based on dynamic constraints, *Proc. IEEE SIGGRAPH Conf.*, August, Atlanta, GA

Bejczy, A. K. and Dotson, R. S. (1982) A force torque sensing and display system for large robot arms, *Proc. of IEEE Southeastcon 82*, April, Destin, FL

Brooks, T. L. (1990) Telerobot response requirements, *STX Systems Corporation, Technical Report* STX/ROB/90-03

Brooks, T. L. and Bejczy, A. K. (1985) Hand controllers for teleoperation: a state-of-the-art technology survey and evaluation, *JPL Publication 85-11*, NASA Jet Propulsion Laboratory

Burdea, G. C. (1991) Portable dextrous feedback master for robot telemanipulation, *US Patent* no. 5,004,391

Burdea, G. C., Zhuang, J., Roskos, E., Silver, D., and Langrana, N. (1992) A portable dextrous master with force feedback, *Presence*, **1**, 29–44

Chua, L. O., Desoer, C. A., and Kuh, E. S. (1987) *Linear and Non-linear Circuits*, New York: McGraw-Hill

Clark, F. J. and Horch, K. W. (1986) Kinesthesia, in *Handbook of Perception and Human Performance*, Boff *et al.* (Eds), New York: Wiley-Interscience

Corker, K., Bejczy, A. K., and Rappaport, B. (1985) Force/torque display for space teleoperation control experiments and evaluation, *Proc. of the 21st Annual Conf. on Manual Control*, June, Columbus, OH

Craig, J. (1989) *Introduction to Robotics: Mechanics and Control*, 2nd edn, New York: Addison-Wesley

Denavit, J. and Hartenberg, R. S. (1955) A kinematic notation for lower-pair mechanism based on matrices, *J. Appl. Mech.*

Fischer, P., Daniel, R., and Siva, K. V. (1990) Specification and design of input devices for teleoperation, *Proc. of IEEE Robotics and Automation Conf.*, May, Cincinnati, OH

Funda, J. and Paul, R. P. (1990) Teleprogramming: overcoming communication delays in remote manipulation, *Proc. Int. Conf. on Systems, Man, and Cybernetics*, November, pp. 873–5

Goertz, R. C. (1964) Manipulator systems development at ANL, *Proc. of the 12th Conf. on Remote Systems Technology*, November, ANS, pp. 117–36

Goodwin, G. M., McCloskey, D. I., and Matthews, P. B. C. (1972) The contribution of muscle afferents to kinesthesia shown by vibration induced illusions of movement and the effects of paralysing joint afferents, *Brain*, **95**, 705–48

Hannaford, B. (1987) Task level testing of the JPL-OMV smart end effector, *Proc. of the JPL-NASA Workshop on Space Telerobotics, vol. 2* (JPL Publication 87-13), July, Pasadena, CA, pp. 371–80

Hannaford, B. (1989) A design framework for teleoperators with kinesthetic feedback, *IEEE Trans. Robot. Autom.*, **5**, 426–34

Hannaford, B. and Anderson, R. (1988) Experimental and simulation studies of hard contact in force reflecting teleoperation, *Proc. IEEE Conf. on Robotics and Automation*, April, pp. 584–9

Hannaford, B. and Fiorini, P. (1988) A detailed model of bilateral (position/force) teleoperation, *Proc. Int. Conf. on Systems, Man, and Cybernetics*, August, Beijing, pp. 117–21

Hannaford, B. and Winters, J. M. (1990) Actuator properties and movement control: biological and technological models, in *Multiple Muscle Systems*, J.M. Winters (Ed.), Berlin: Springer

Hasan, Z. and Stuart, D. G. (1988) Animal solutions to problems of movement control: the role of proprioceptors, *Am. Rev. Neurosci.*, **11**, 199–223

Hogan, N. (1985a) Impedance control: an approach to manipulation: part I—theory, *J. Dyn. Systems, Meas. Contr.*, **107**, 1–7

Hogan, N. (1985b) Part II: impedance control: an approach to manipulation: implementation, *J. Dyn. Systems, Meas. Contr.*, **107**, 8–16

Hogan, N. (1985c) Part III: impedance control: an approach to manipulation: applications, *J. Dyn. Systems, Meas. Contr.*, **107**, 17–24

Hollis, R. L., Salcudean, S., and Abraham, D. W. (1990) Toward a tele-nanorobotic manipulation system with atomic scale force feedback and motion resolution, *Proc. IEEE Micro Electro Mechanical Systems Conf.*, February, Napa Valley, CA, pp. 115–19

Howard, I. P. (1982) Human visual orientation, Chichester: Wiley

Iwata, H. (1990) Artifical reality with force-feedback: development of a desktop virtual space with compact master manipulator, *ACM Computer Graphics*, **24**, 165–70

Jacobsen, S. C., Iverson, E. K, Davis, C. C, Potter, D. M., and McLain, T. W. (1989) Design of a multiple degree of freedom force reflective hand master/slave with a high mobility wrist, *Third Topical Meeting on Robotics and Remote Systems*, March

Jacobsen, S. C., Smith, F. M., Backman, D. K., and Iversen, E. K. (1991) High performance, high dexterity, force reflective teleoperator II, *Proc. ANS Topical Meeting on Robotics and Remote Systems*, February, Albuquerque, NM

Jau, B. M. (1990) Anthropomorphic form fingered robot hand and its glove controller, *Proc. IEEE Conf. on Engineering in Medicine and Biology, vol. 12*, November, Philidelphia, PA, pp. 1940–41

Matthews, P. B. C. (1972) Mammalian Muscle Receptors and their Central Actions, London: Edward Arnold

Matthews, P. B. C. (1984) Evidence from the use of vibration that the human long-latency stretch reflex depends upon the spindle secondary afferents, *J. Physiol.*, **348**, 383–415

Matthews, P. B. C. and Watson, J. D. G. (1981) Action of vibration on the response of cat muscle spindle Ia afferents to low frequency sinusoidal stretching, *J. Physiol.*, **317**, 419–46

McAffee, D. A. and Fiorini, P. (1991) Hand controller design requirements and performance issues in telerobotics, *Proc. of 5th ICAR Conf.*, June, Pisa

McAffee, D. A. and Ohm, T. (1988) Teleoperator subsystem/telerobot demonstrator: force reflecting hand controller equipment manual, *NASA JPL Document*, no. D-5172

McGrath, G. J. and Matthews, P. B. C. (1973) Evidence from the use of vibration during procaine nerve block to the tonic stretch reflex of the decerebrate cat, *J. Physiol.*, **235**, 371–408

Minsky, M. *et al.* (1990) Feeling and seeing: issues in force display, *Proc. 1990 Symp. on Interactive 3D Graphics*, Snowbird, UT

Noton, D. and Stark, L. (1971) Scanpaths in saccadic eye movements while viewing and recognizing patterns, *Vision Res.*, **11**, 929–42

Oomchi, T., Miyatake, T., Mekawa, A., and Hayashi, T. (1987) Mechanics and multiple sensory bilateral control of a finger manipulator, in R. Bolles and B. Roth (Eds), *Proc. Int. Symp. on Robotics Research*, Cambridge, MA: MIT Press, pp. 145–53

Ouh-young, M. *et al.* (1988) Using a manipulator for force display in molecular docking, *Proc. IEEE Robotics and Automation, vol. 3*, Philadelphia

Paynter, H. M. (1961) *Analysis and design of engineering systems*, Cambridge, MA: MIT Press

Robinett, W. *et al.* (1992) The nanomanipulator project: an atomic scale teleoperator, *1992 SIGGRAPH Course Notes on Implementation of Immersive Virtual Worlds*

Russo, M., Tadros, A., Flowers, W., and Zelter, D. (1990) Implementation of a three degree of freedom motor/brake hybrid force output device for virtual environment control tasks, *Human Machine Interfaces for Teleoperators and Virtual Environments Conf.*, March, Santa Barbara, CA (NASA Conference Publication 10071)

Shimoga, K. B. (1993) Survey of perceptual feedback issues in dexterous telemanipulation: part I. finger force feedback, *Proc. IEEE VRAIS-93*, September, Seattle, pp. 263–70

Townsend, W. and Salisbury, K. (1987) Effect of Coulomb friction and sticktion on robot force control, *Proc. of IEEE Conf. on Robotics and Automation*

Uebel, M., Ali, M. S., and Minis, I. (1991) The effect of bandwidth on telerobot system performance, *NASA Technical Paper 3152*

Umek, A. and Lenarcic, J. (1991) Recent results in evaluation of human arm workspace, *Proc. 5th ICAR*, June

11

Input Devices and Interaction Techniques for Advanced Computing

I. SCOTT MacKENZIE

One enduring trait of computing systems is the presence of the human operator. At the human–computer interface, the nature of computing has witnessed dramatic transformations—from feeding punched cards into a reader to manipulating 3D virtual objects with an input glove. The technology at our fingertips today transcends by orders of magnitude that in the behemoth calculators of the 1940s. Yet technology must co-exist with the human interface of the day. Not surprisingly, themes on keeping pace with advances in technology in the human–computer interface and, hopefully, getting ahead, underlie many chapters in this book. The present chapter is no exception. Input devices and interaction techniques are the human operator's baton. They set, constrain, and elicit a spectrum of actions and responses, and in a large way inject a personality on the entire human–machine system. In this chapter, we will present and explore the major issues in "input," focusing on devices, their properties and parameters, and the possibilities for exploiting devices in advanced human–computer interfaces.

To place input devices in perspective, we illustrate a classical human-factors interpretation of the human–machine interface (e.g., Chapanis, 1965, p. 20). Figure 11-1 simplifies the human and machine to three components each. The internal states of each interact in a closed-loop system through controls and displays (the machine interface) and motor-sensory behaviour (the human interface). The terms "input" and "output" are, by convention, with respect to the machine; so input devices are inputs to the machine controlled or manipulated by human "outputs." Traditionally human outputs are our limbs—the hands, arms, legs, feet, or head—but speech and eye motions can also act as human output. Some other human output channels are breath and electrical body signals (important for disabled users).

Interaction takes place at the interface (dashed line in Figure 11-1) through an output channel—displays stimulating human senses—and the input channel. In the present chapter, we are primarily interested in controls, or input devices; but, by necessity, the other components in Figure 11-1 will to some extent participate in our discussion.

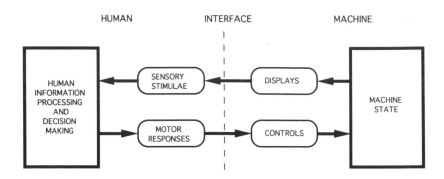

Figure 11-1 The human–machine interface. Input devices are the controls humans manipulate to change the machine state.

Two broad themes in this chapter are *interaction* and *technology*. A familiar message is that interaction is the key to pushing the frontier and that technology should evolve and bend to serve interaction, rather than interaction conforming to technology. This is a contestable viewpoint. Advances in technology are often independent of the consequences or possibilities for human–computer interaction or other applied disciplines. Basic research fields such as materials science or semiconductor physics push the boundaries of science, addressing fundamental questions and spawning "low-level deliverables" (e.g., semiconductor devices that are smaller, faster, denser, more efficient, etc.). Through engineering and design, deliverables eventually filter up into commercial products (cf. technology). As human-factors researchers or human–machine system designers, we should fully expect to mold interaction scenarios within a given resource base—today's technology. Although technological constraints tend to vanish simply by waiting for new advances, interaction problems persist since their solution requires multidisciplinary research and design efforts that are often ill-defined and qualitative. This is where the greatest challenges lie.

In advanced virtual environments, goals are to empower the user, to instrument all or part of the body, and to force the machine to yield to natural dialogues for interaction. In the following paragraphs we will describe the state-of-the-art and identify trends in input devices and interaction techniques. There is a substantial existing resource base upon which to proceed (the time is right!); however, as we shall see, many of the more utopian visions will remain just that until the technology delivers more.

TECHNOLOGY

In this section, we focus on technological characteristics of present and future input devices. While specific devices are cited, the intent is not to list and categorize the repertoire of devices. Previous surveys have adequately summarized tablets, touch screens, joysticks, trackballs, mice, and so on (e.g., Greenstein and Arnault, 1987; Sherr, 1988). Eye tracking as an input technology is discussed in Chapter 7, and will not be included here. Technological considerations presented herein include the physical characteristics of input devices (with examples from real devices), properties that define and distinguish devices, models for summarizing or predicting performance, and parameters that can be measured and controlled to optimize interaction. We begin with the physical characteristics of the transducers embedded within input devices.

Transducers

The most simplistic, technology-centered view of input and output devices is at the electro-mechanical level of the transducer. Transducers are energy converters. For input devices the conversion is usually from kinetic energy (motion) or potential energy (pressure) to electric energy (voltage or current). By far the most common input transducer is the switch. The hardware supporting mouse buttons and alphanumeric keys is the most obvious example. Motion applied to the switch opens or closes a contact and alters the voltage or current sensed by an electronic circuit. Many "high-level" devices are an aggregate of switches. The x–y pointing capability of mice and trackballs, for example, is often implemented by photoelectric switches. A beam of light is interrupted by perforations in a rotating wheel driven by the mouse ball or trackball. Light pulses stimulate phototransistors that complete the conversion of kinetic energy to electric energy (see Figure 11-2).

Joysticks are commonly available in two flavors. Displacement or isotonic joysticks move about a pivot with motion in two or more axes. The 544-G974 from Measurement Systems, Inc., for example, is a three-axis displacement joystick sensing x and y pivotal motion as well as twist (see Figure 11-3(a)). Deflection is $\pm 15°$ about the x and y axes and $\pm 10°$ of twist.

Force sensing or isometric joysticks employ resistive strain gauges which undergo a slight deformation when loaded. An applied force generates compression or tension in a wire element bonded to a load column. The wire element undergoes compression or tension which changes its resistance. This effects a change in voltage or current in the interface electronics. An example is the 426-G811, also from Measurements Systems, Inc. (see Figure 11-3(b)). This four-axis joystick senses x, y, and z force, and torque about the twist axis. Up to 10 lb of force is sensed in the x and y axes, and 20 lb in the z axis. Torque up to 32 in-lb is sensed in the twist axis. Deflection is slight at 0.65 inches for the x and y axes, 0.25 inches for the z axis, and $9°$ for the twist axis.

Although most input devices are manually actuated, we should acknowledge the microphone as an important input device. Converting acoustic energy to electric energy, microphones are the transducers that permit us to talk to our computer. Speech input will be mentioned briefly later in connection with multimodal input; however specific problems in speech input and recognition are beyond the scope of this chapter.

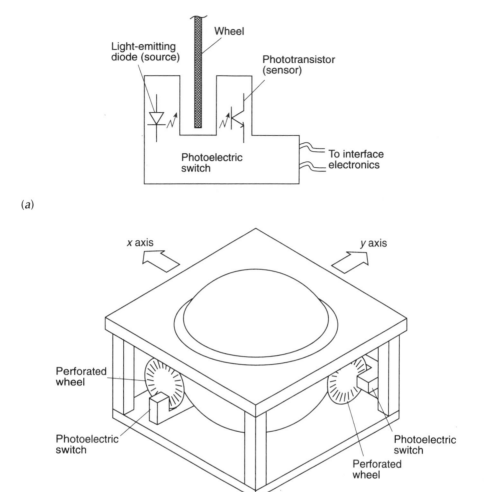

Figure 11-2 A photoelectric switch as an input transducer. (*a*) A light-emitting diode provides a source of light and stimulates a phototransistor sensor, switching it on and off. The light beam is interrupted by a rotating perforated wheel. (*b*) Two photoelectric switches sense *x* and *y* motion of a rolling trackball.

Gloves, 3D trackers, and body suits

The technology underlying many successful input devices, such as the mouse or QWERTY keyboard, is mature and stable. Of greater interest to this book's audience is the requisite technology of future input devices. Body suits and input gloves represent two input technologies holding tremendous promise in bringing technology to interaction. Juggling or conducting an orchestra are human activities with the potential of entering the world of human–machine dialogues; yet, significant inroads—on purely technological grounds—must be

(a)

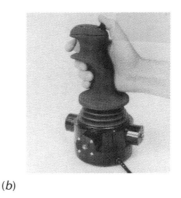
(b)

Figure 11-3 (a) A three-axis displacement joystick senses tilt about the base and twist about the vertical axis. (b) A four-axis isometric joystick senses force in the x, y, and z axes, and torque in the twist axis.

achieved first. Applications such as these do not exist at present, except in a primitive form in research laboratories. A challenge for researchers is to get the technology into the mainstream as an entertainment medium or a means of performing routine tasks in the workplace.

Devices such as gloves and body suits are really a complement of transducers working in unison to deliver fidelity in the interface. Most gloves combine a single 3D tracker and multiple joint sensors. The *DataGlove* by VPL Research, Inc. is a thin Lycra glove with a magnetically coupled 3D tracker mounted on it (see Figure 11-4). Bending in the two proximal joints is measured by the attenuation of a light signal in each of two fiber optic strands sewn along the fingers and thumb. Position and orientation measurements are accurate to 0.13 inches RMS and 0.85° RMS at 15 inches. Data are transferred

Figure 11-4 The VPL *DataGlove*. Two optical strands are sewn along each finger to sense bend in two joints. A single strand sewn on the thumb senses single-joint motion.

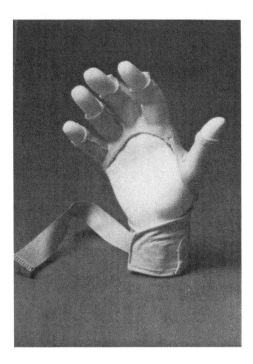

Figure 11-5   The Virtex *CyberGlove* includes 22 resistive-bend sensors. Three bend and one abduction sensor are used for each finger and thumb. Thumb and pinkie cross-over and wrist rotation are also sensed.

over RS232 or RS422 links at rates up to 38.4 kilobaud. Sampling rate is 30 Hz or 60 Hz. The DataGlove, first introduced at CHI '87 by Zimmerman *et al.* (1987),[1] was the first input glove to gain widespread use in the research community (although earlier devices date from about 1976; see Krueger, 1991, ch. 4). Options are available for abduction sensing (on the thumb, index, and middle fingers) and force feedback.

The DataGlove has been criticized because of its nonlinear mapping between joint movement and the intensity of the reflected light (Green *et al.*, 1992). As well, the lack of abduction sensing (on the standard model) limits the number of hand positions that can be detected, for example, in gesture recognition tasks (Weimer and Ganapathy, 1989; Fels and Hinton, 1990; Takahashi and Kishino, 1991).

The *CyberGlove* by Virtual Technologies includes 22 resistive-strip sensors for finger bend and abduction, and thumb and pinkie rotation. The mapping is linear with 8 bits of resolution per sensor (see Figure 11-5). A force-feedback option is available. The strip sensors are a more natural transducer for sensing bend and abduction than the optical fibres in the VPL DataGlove. Their presence is less apparent, more comfortable, and easily extends to applications beyond the hand. Complete body instrumentation is possible through custom

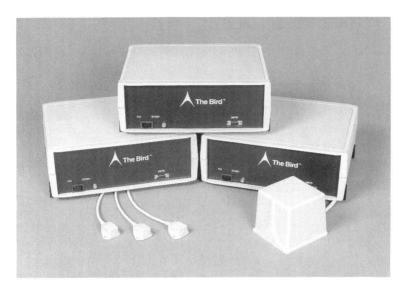

Figure 11-6 The Ascension *Bird* 3D electromagnetic tracker includes a sensor (bottom center), a source (right), and interface electronics.

sewn suits covering the torso or limbs. The strip sensors can be added in the suit's material at any anatomical position where bend is to be sensed.

An inexpensive input glove is the *Power Glove* by Mattel, designed as an input device for the Nintendo Entertainment System (video game). It was used in a low-end system known as *Virtual Reality on Five Dollars a Day* (Pausch, 1991). *x*, *y*, and *z* location, and wrist rotation, are determined using ultrasonic receivers (two on the glove) and transmitters (three, wall-mounted). Bend in the thumb and first three fingers is detected to 2 bits of resolution via strain gages. Seventeen buttons on the forearm padding provide various select functions.

There are several 3D trackers in current use, including the Polhemus *Isotrack* (e.g., Ware and Baxter, 1989), the Ascension Technology Corp. *Bird* (see Figure 11-6) and the Logitech *2D/6D Mouse* (e.g., Deering, 1992; Feiner *et al.*, 1992). A transmitter or source mounted in the vicinity of the user generates an electromagnetic or ultrasonic field that is picked up by a sensor mounted on the glove (or torso, head, etc.). A cable from the sensor to the interface electronics completes the loop permitting six-degree-of-freedom localization of hand position and orientation. The six degrees of freedom are the spatial coordinates with respect to the *x*, *y*, and *z* axes, and the angular orientations around each axis, known as pitch, roll, and yaw. The cable is sometimes called a "tether" since it confines body motion near the interface electronics. A problem with the widely used Polhemus device is that nearby metallic objects interfere with the source/sensor signal. This has inspired some alternate technologies such as optical tracking using infrared transmitters and receivers (Wang *et al.*, 1990) or ceiling-mounted video cameras (Fukumoto *et al.*, 1992).

Device properties

Input devices possess numerous properties and parameters which can enhance or limit performance. For this discussion, "properties" are the qualities which distinguish among devices and determine how a device is used and what it can do. They place a device within a "design space"—a framework for comparison and analysis.

Device properties cannot be adjusted or optimized (unlike device parameters; see below). For example, cursor positioning is relative using some devices (e.g., touch tablets), but absolute with others. There is no middle ground. In relative positioning, motion (or force) applied to the device influences the motion of the cursor relative to its current position. In absolute positioning, the cursor position on the display maps to specific, absolute spatial coordinates on the device. This property distinguishes devices and determines the sorts of action that may be easier on one device but harder on another.

"Clutching" is an interaction property inherent in tablets, mice, and other devices using relative positioning. Clutching is the process of disengaging, adjusting, and re-engaging the input device to extend its field of control. This is necessary when the tracking symbol, whether a cursor on a planar CRT or a virtual hand in 3-space, cannot move because the controlling device has reached a limit in its physical space. The most obvious example is lifting and repositioning a mouse when it reaches the edge of the mouse-pad; however, many input devices for virtual environments require constant clutching to allow the user to attain new vantages in a potentially huge task space. In such situations, clutching is implemented through a supplemental switch or through gestural techniques such as grasping. Characteristics such as this affect performance, but quantitative distinctions are difficult to measure because they are highly task dependent.

Device models

A model is a simplified description of a system to assist in understanding the system or in describing or predicting its behavior through calculations. The "system" in this sense is the set of input devices. Models can be broadly categorized as descriptive or predictive. Several ambitious descriptive models of input devices have been developed. One of the earliest was Buxton's (1983) taxonomy which attempted to merge the range of human gestures with the articulation requirements of devices. In Figure 11-7, devices are placed in a matrix with the primary rows and columns (solid lines) identifying what is sensed (position, motion, or pressure) and the number of dimensions sensed (1, 2, or 3). For example, potentiometers are 1D (left column) but a mouse is 2D (center column); trackballs are motion sensing (center row) but isometric joysticks are pressure sensing (bottom row). Secondary rows and columns (dashed lines) delimit devices manipulated using different motor skills (sub-columns) and devices operated by direct touch vs. a mechanical intermediary (sub-rows). For example, potentiometers may be rotary or sliding (left

		Number of Dimensions						
		1		2			3	
Property Sensed	Position	Rotary Pot	Sliding Pot	Tablet & Puck	Tablet & Stylus	Light Pen	Floating Joystick	3D Joystick	M
				Touch Tablet		Touch Screen			T
	Motion	Continuous Rotary Pot	Treadmill	Mouse			Trackball	3D Trackball	M
			Ferinstat				X/Y Pad		T
	Pressure	Torque Sensor					Isometric Joystick		T

Figure 11-7   Buxton's (1983) taxonomy places input devices in a matrix by the property sensed (rows), number of dimensions sensed (columns), requisite motor skills (sub-columns), and interaction directness (sub-rows; from Buxton, 1983).

sub-columns); screen input may be direct through touch or indirect through a light pen (top sub-rows).

Foley *et al.* (1984) provided a two-tiered breakdown of graphics tasks and listed devices suited to each. Six main tasks were identified: *select*, *position*, *orient*, *path*, *quantify*, and *text entry*. Within each category a complement of sub-tasks was identified and appropriate device mappings offered. For example, two of the position sub-tasks were "direct location" and "indirect location." The touch panel was cited for the direct location task and the tablet, mouse, joystick, trackball, and cursor control keys were cited for the indirect location task. Foley *et al.*'s (1984) taxonomy is useful because it maps input devices to input tasks; however, it does not provide a sense of the device properties that generated the mappings. The strength of Buxton's (1983) taxonomy is its focus on these properties.

Researchers at Xerox PARC extended the work of Buxton (1983) and Foley *et al.* (1984) into a comprehensive "design space" where devices are points in a parametric design space (Card *et al.*, 1990, 1991; Mackinlay, *et al.*, 1991). Their model captures, for example, the possibility of devices combining position and selection capabilities with an integrated button. (Selection is a discrete property outside the purview of Buxton's taxonomy.)

The models above are descriptive. They are useful for understanding devices and suggesting powerful device–task mappings; but they are not in themselves capable of predicting and comparing alternative design scenarios. Their potential as engineering (viz., design) tools is limited.

	Science		Development Technique (engineering)
	Descriptive	Predictive	
Human Characteristics	Norman 4-stages Norman slips (Perceptual Models) (Cognitive Psychology) Egan et al user abilities	Routine cognitive skill GOMS, NGOMSL, CCT Unified cognitive models MHP, Soar, ACT* ETIT Fitts' Law	KL-Model PUMS Fitts' Law
Machine	Input device taxonomies Buxton et al; Foley et al; Mackinlay et al.	State-transition (CSP, CCS, ESTEREL), Squeak, PIE, Alexander PAC, PPS Grammar Models BNF, CLG, TAG, ETAG, DTAG Fitts' Law	Fitts' Law

Figure 11-8 Models for human and machine characteristics of importance to human–computer interaction (from Marchionini and Sibert, 1991).

The point above surfaced in a workshop on human–computer interaction (HCI) sponsored by the US National Science Foundation (Marchionini and Sibert, 1991). The participants were leading researchers in human–computer interaction. Among other things, they identified models that are important for the future of HCI. These were organized in a matrix identifying scientific vs. engineering models as relevant to human vs. machine characteristics. In Figure 11-8, the device models discussed above are found at the intersection of machine characteristics and descriptive scientific models. Interesting in the figure is the relative paucity of models cited as useful engineering tools, at both the human and machine level (right column). Three engineering models were cited: the Keystroke-Level (KL) model of Card *et al.* (1980); the Programmable User Model (PUM) of Young *et al.* (1989); and Fitts' law (Fitts, 1954; see MacKenzie, 1992). These models are all predictive. They allow performance comparisons to be drawn before or during the design process. The idea is that interface scenarios can be explored *a priori* with performance comparisons drawn to aid in choosing the appropriate implementation. A challenge for HCI researchers, therefore, is to bring basic research results to the applied realm of engineering and design—to get the theory into the tools. Newell and Card (1985) elaborate further on this point.

Device parameters

A parameter is any characteristic of a device or its interface which can be tuned or measured along a continuum of values. Input parameters are the sorts of features controlled or determined one way or another by designers or by system characteristics. Output parameters are the dependent variables or performance measures commonly studied in research by, for example, manipulating "device" or an input parameter as an experimental factor. Presumably a setting exists for each input parameter that yields optimal performance on the range of output parameters.

Some parameters, such as mass, resolution, or friction, are "in the device" or its electronics, and can be designed in, but cannot be tuned thereafter. Others exist in the interface software or system software. Examples are sampling rate or the control–display (C–D) relationship. Still others exist through a complex weave of transducer characteristics, interface electronics, communications channels, and software. Lag or feedback delay is one such example.

Although some parameters can be adjusted to improve performance, others are simply constraints. Resolution, sampling rate, and lag are parameters with known "optimal" settings. Resolution and sampling rate should be as high as possible, lag as low as possible. Obviously, these parameters are constrained or fixed at some reasonable level during system design. Although typical users are quite unconcerned about these, for certain applications or when operating within a real-time environment, limitations begin to take hold.

Resolution

Resolution is the spatial resolving power of the device/interface subsystem. It is usually quoted as the smallest incremental change in device position that can be detected (e.g., 0.5 cm or 1°); however, alone the specification can be misleading. This is illustrated in Figure 11-9, showing device position (input) vs. the position reported (output) over a spatial interval of 10 arbitrary units. The ideal case is shown in (*a*): The resolution is 1 unit and it is reported in precise, equal steps over the range of device movement. In (*b*) nonlinearity is introduced. Resolution in the middle of the field of movement is very good ($\approx$0.25 units output @ 5 units input), but it is poor at the extremes ($\approx$1.5 units output @ 1 unit input). Another important trait is *monotonicity*. Positive changes in device position should always yield positive changes in the output; however, this is often not the case as illustrated in (*c*). Other non-ideal characteristics (not shown) are *offset*, which results if the step function shown in (*a*) is shifted up or down; and *gain*, which results if the slope of the step function differs from unity. In the interface electronics, temperature sensitivity is the main culprit compromising performance. It must be remembered that the number of steps is usually quite large (e.g., thousands) and resolution specifications must be met for each degree of freedom. Very small changes in voltage or current must be sensed in the interface electronics on multiple input channels. If the transducers are magnetically coupled, then interference or noise may be the main cause of poor resolution, nonlinearity, etc.

Touch screens, tablets, and other devices using finger or stylus input have apparent resolution problems since it is difficult to resolve finger or stylus position to the same precision as the output display (a single pixel). In fact the resolving power of the input device often exceeds that of the output device; however the input/output mapping is limited by the contact footprint of the input device (e.g., the width of the fingertip).

3D trackers have resolution better than 1 inch and 1 degree; but this varies with the proximity of the sensor to the source and other factors. Resolution

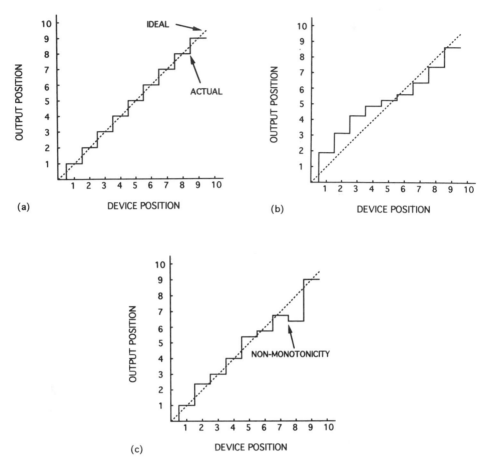

Figure 11-9 Resolution. (a) The ideal case for 1 unit of resolution over 10 units of movement. In (b) nonlinearity is introduced showing degraded resolution at the extremes of movement rather than in the center. (c) Non-monotonicity occurs when the output fails to increase uniformly with the input.

often sounds impressive in specification sheets; but when application demands increase, such as widening the field of use or combining two or three trackers, limitations become apparent. The specification sheets of 3D trackers are surprisingly sparse in their performance details. Is the resolution cited a worst-case value over the specified field of use, or is it "typical"? How will resolution degrade if two or more trackers are used? What is the effect of a large metal object five meters distant? These questions persist.

Resolution will constrain a variety of applications for 3D virtual worlds. The motions of a dancer are difficult to capture with any justice because of the large expanse of movements required. Sensing the common action of tying one's shoelaces would be a formidable task for a pair of input gloves controlling virtual hands in a simulated environment. Resolution is one constraint in this case because the movements are extremely intricate.

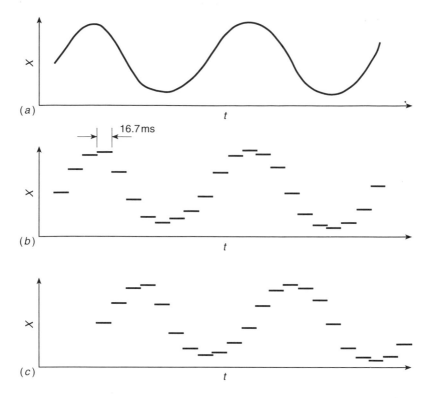

Figure 11-10   Sampling rate and lag. Sinusoidal back-and-forth motion of a mouse at 6 Hz is shown in (*a*). At 60 Hz sampling, the cursor appears as in (*b*). With three samples of lag, cursor motion is delayed as in (*c*).

Sampling rate

Sampling rate is the number of measurements per unit time (e.g., samples per second) in which the position of the input device is recorded. It is the input analog of the refresh rate for updating the output display. The rate of sampling begins to constrain performance when input or output motion is quick. Typical rates are from 10 to 100 samples per second. This is fine for many applications, but may be inadequate for real-time 3D environments which must sense and respond to the natural, sometimes rapid, motions of humans. Acts such as tying one's shoelaces or juggling involve a series of quick, intricate, coordinated hand motions that would require, among other things, a high sampling rate. In the more common application of capturing temporal cues in gestures for a sign language, sampling rate has been cited as a constraint (Fels and Hinton, 1990; Takahashi and Kishino, 1991).

Sampling rate is illustrated in Figure 11-10 parts (*a*) and (*b*). A mouse can be wiggled back-and-forth easily at rates up to about 6 Hz. Figure 11-10(*a*) shows this as a sinusoid with the back-and-forth motion of the hand on the vertical axis and time on the horizontal axis. If the mouse position is sampled at 60 Hz (every 16.7 ms) with immediate updates of the screen, there will be about 10 updates of the cursor for each back-and-forth motion of the mouse. Cursor motion will appear as in Figure 11-10(*b*). The loss of fidelity is obvious.

A high sampling rate is essential in 3D virtual worlds because of spatial dynamics. In the mouse example above, the back-and-forth motion of the hand and cursor will not exceed about 10 cm. If the controlling device is a 3D tracker attached to the head, similar back-and-forth motion (a few cm at the nose) will translate into very large movements in the visual space in very small time intervals. Smooth viewing motion necessitates a high sampling rate with immediate display refreshes.

Lag

Lag is the phenomenon of not having immediate updates of the display in response to input actions. High sampling and refresh rates are wasted if the re-drawn viewpoint does not reflect the immediately preceding sample, or if the sample does not capture the immediate habit of the user. One reason this may occur is the drawing time for the scene. If the image is complex (e.g., thousands of texture-mapped polygons with 24-bit colour), then drawing time may take two or three (or more) sampling periods. Green and Shaw (1990) describe a client-server model which lessens this effect.

If updates are delayed by, say, three samples, then the cursor motion for our earlier example is degraded further as shown in Figure 11-10(*c*). Lag can cause a variety of non-ideal behaviors, even motion sickness (Deyo and Ingebretson, 1989; Laurel, 1991; Krueger, 1991, p. 128; Hettinger and Riccio, 1993). All current 3D trackers have significant lag, in the range of 30 ms to 250 ms (depending on how and where measurements are made). Furthermore, the source of the lag is not always obvious and is difficult to measure. The sampling rate for input devices and the update rate for output devices are major contributors; but lag is increased further due to "software overhead"—a loose expression for a variety of system-related factors. Communication modes, network configurations, number crunching, and application software all contribute.

Significant lags occur in most teleoperation systems, whether a remote microscope for medical diagnosis (Carr *et al.*, 1992) or a space-guided vehicle (Ferrell and Sheridan, 1967). Evidently, lags more than about 1 s force the operator into a move-and-wait strategy in completing tasks. Since lag is on the order of a few hundred milliseconds in virtual environments, its effect on user performance is less apparent.

In one of the few empirical studies (Liang *et al.*, 1991) measured the lag on a Polhemus Isotrak. They found lags between 85 ms and 180 ms depending on the sampling rate (60 Hz vs. 20 Hz) and communications mode (networked, polled, continuous output, direct, and client-server). Although the software was highly optimized to avoid other sources of lag, their results are strictly best-case since an "application" was not present. Substantial additional lag can be expected in any 3D virtual environment because of the graphic rendering required after each sample. Liang *et al.* (1991) proposed a Kalman predictive filtering algorithm to compensate for lag by anticipating head motion. Apparently predictive filtering can obviate lags up to a few hundred milli-

	Lag (ms)				Performance Degradation
Measure	8.3	25	75	225	at Lag = 225 ms[a]
Movement Time (ms)	911	934	1059	1493	63.9%
Error Rate (%)	3.6	3.6	4.9	11.3	214%
Bandwidth (bits/s)	4.3	4.1	3.5	2.3	46.5%

[a]relative to lag = 8.3 ms

Figure 11-11 Motor-sensory performance in the presence of lag. The dependent variables movement time, error rate, and bandwidth are all degraded as lag is introduced. Performance degrades dramatically at 225 ms of lag (from MacKenzie and Ware, 1993).

seconds; however, beyond this, the overshoot resulting from long-term prediction is more objectionable than the lag (Deering, 1992).

In another experiment to measure the human performance cost, lag was introduced as an experimental variable in a routine target selection task given to eight subjects in repeated trials (MacKenzie and Ware, 1993). Using a 60 Hz sampling and refresh rate, the minimum lag was, on average, half the sampling period or 8.3 ms. This was the "zero lag" condition. Additional lag settings were 25, 75, and 225 ms. Movement time, error rate, and motor-sensory bandwidth were the dependent variables. Under the zero lag condition (8.3 ms), the mean movement time was 911 ms, the error rate was 3.6%, and the bandwidth was 4.3 bits s^{-1}. As evident in Figure 11-11, lag degraded performance on all three dependent variables. At 225 ms lag (compared to 8.3 ms lag), movement times increased by 63.9% (to 1493 ms), error rates increased by 214% (to 11.3%), and bandwidth dropped by 46.5% (to 2.3 bits s^{-1}). Obviously, these figures represent serious performance decrements.

The communication link between the device electronics and the host computer may prove a bottleneck and contribute to lag as the number of sensors and their resolution increases. The CyberGlove by Virtual Technologies provides greater resolution of finger position than many gloves by including more sensors—up to 22 per glove. However, correspondingly more data are required. At the maximum data rate of 38.4 kilobaud, it takes about 5 ms just to relay the data to the host. Alone this is trivial, however, a trade-off is evident between the desire to resolve intricate hand formations and the requisite volume of "immediate" data. If we speculate on future interaction scenarios with full body suits delivering the nuances of complex motions—a common vision in VR—then it is apparent that lag will increase simply due to serial bias in the communications link. Since technological improvements can be expected on all fronts, lag may become less significant in future systems.

Optimality and control-display gain

Unlike resolution, sampling rate, and lag, some parameters are "tunable" along a continuum. Presumably, a setting exists which leads to optimal human performance. This is an elusive claim, however, because no clear definition of "optimal" exists. How does one measure optimality? Quantitative measures such as task completion time or error rate are commonly used, but are narrow

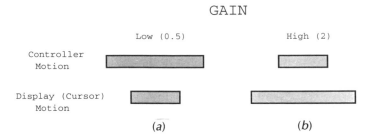

Figure 11-12 Contol–display (C–D) gain. (*a*) Under low gain a large controller movement is required for moderate cursor movement. (*b*) Under high gain a slight controller movement yields significant cursor movement.

and do not capture important qualitative aspects of the interface. Ease of learning, skill retention, fatigue, effort, stress, etc., are important qualities of an optimal interface, but are difficult to measure. This idea has been studied extensively in an area of human factors known as *human engineering* (e.g., Chapanis, 1965; Wickens, 1987). As a brief example, if a relative positioning system is employed, the nuisance of clutching may go unnoticed in an experiment that only required a narrow field of motion. If frequent clutching results in a subsequent application of the same technology, then frustration or stress levels may yield highly *non-optimal* behavior which eluded measurement in the research setting.

Even though task completion time and error rate are easily measured in empirical tests, they are problematic. Getting tasks done quickly with few errors is obviously optimal, but the speed-accuracy trade-off makes the simultaneous optimizing of these two output variables difficult. This is illustrated by considering control–display (C–D) gain. C–D gain expresses the relationship between the motion or force in a controller (e.g., a mouse) to the effected motion in a displayed object (e.g., a cursor). Low and high gain settings are illustrated in Figure 11-12.

Although a common criticism of research claiming to measure human performance on input devices is that C–D gain was not (properly) optimized, close examination reveals that the problem is tricky. Varying C–D gain evokes a trade-off between gross positioning time (getting to the vicinity of a target) and fine positioning time (the final acquisition). This effect, first pointed out by Jenkins and Connor (1949), is illustrated in Figure 11-13.

Presumably, the optimal setting is at the intersection of the two curves in Figure 11-13, since the total time is minimized (Chapanis and Kinkade, 1972). However, minimizing total target acquisition time is further confounded by a non-optimal (viz., higher) error rate. This was illustrated in an experiment which varied C–D gain while measuring the speed and accuracy of target acquisitions (MacKenzie and Riddersma, 1994). Twelve subjects performed repeated trials of a routine target acquisition task while C–D gain was varied through LOW, MEDIUM, and HIGH settings. As expected, the total target acquisition time was lowest at the MEDIUM setting (see Figure 11-14(*a*)).

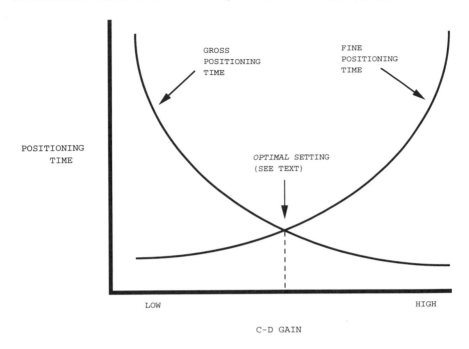

Figure 11-13 Low and high gains evoke a trade-off between gross positioning time and fine positioning time. Total positioning time is minimized at the intersection of the two.

However, the error rate was highest at the MEDIUM setting (Figure 11-14(*b*)). So, the claim that an optimal C–D gain setting exists is weak at best. Other factors, such as display size (independent of C–D gain setting), also bring into question the optimality of this common input device parameter (Arnault and Greenstein, 1990).

The linear, or first-order, C–D gain shown in Figure 11-12 maps controller displacement to cursor (display) displacement. In practice, the C–D gain function is often nonlinear or second order, mapping controller velocity to some function of cursor velocity. Examples include the Apple Macintosh mouse and Xerox Fastmouse. Figure 11-15 illustrates a variety of first-order (dashed lines) and second-order (solid lines) C–D gains.

The second-order gains are of the form,

$$V_d = kV_c^2$$

where V_d is the display (cursor) velocity and V_c is the controller velocity. Note that the second-order function crosses several first-order points as the controller velocity increases. A variation of this, which is easier to implement in software, uses discrete thresholds to increment k as the controller velocity increases. This relationship is

$$V_d = kV_c$$

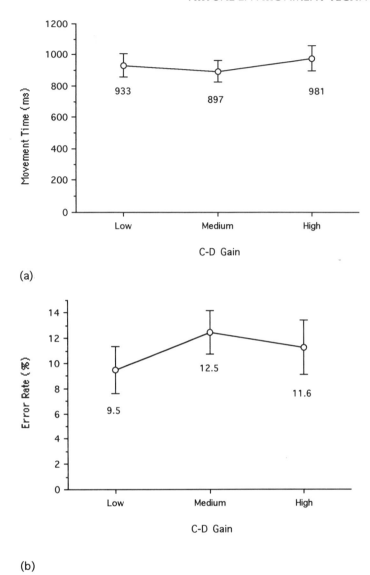

Figure 11-14 C–D gain and the speed-accuracy trade-off. Positioning time is lowest under MEDIUM gain, but error rates are highest (from MacKenzie and Riddersma, 1994).

where k increases by steps as V_c crosses pre-determined thresholds. Second-order C–D gains have been explored as a means to boost user performance (Jackson, 1982; Rogers, 1970); however, there is no evidence that performance is improved beyond the subjective preference of users. Jellinek and Card (1990) found no performance improvement using several second-order C–D gain relationships with a mouse, and suggested the only benefit is the smaller desk-top footprint afforded by a second-order C–D gain.

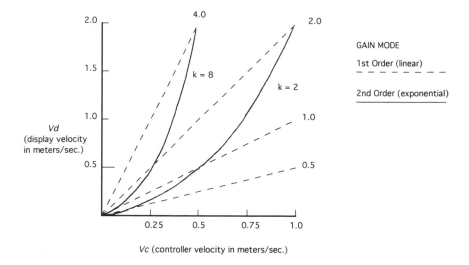

Figure 11-15 Linear vs. exponential mappings for C–D gain. Under exponential mapping, cursor velocity increases nonlinearly by k times the square of the controller velocity.

INTERACTION

Today's software products invariably boast "user friendly" interfaces. This rather empty phrase would lead us to believe that human interface problems are of historical interest only. Not true. The problem of "interaction" persists. The 2D CAD tools of yesterday were precursors of today's 3D tools supporting an enhanced palette of commands and operations to control the workspace. The flat world of CRTs has stretched to its limit, and now 3D output (in numerous forms) is the challenge.

Input/output mappings

On the input side, challenges go beyond migrating from 2D devices (e.g., a mouse) to 3D devices (e.g., a glove). Paradigms for interaction must evolve to meet and surpass the available functionality. It is apparent that *movement* is of increasing importance in the design of human–computer interfaces. Static considerations in the design of interfaces, such as command languages and menu layouts, give way to the dynamics of an interface—the human is a performer acting in concert with system resources.

One theme for 3D is developing interactions for mapping 2D devices into a 3D space. The mouse (for pointing), mouse buttons (for selecting or choosing), and keyboards (for specifying or valuating) are extensively used to capture and control 3D objects. Such interaction was demonstrated, for example, by Bier (1990) in manipulating polyhedrons using a technique called "snap dragging"; by Chen *et al.* (1988) in a three-axis rotation task using three simulated slider controls; by Houde (1992) for grasping and moving furniture in a 3D room; by

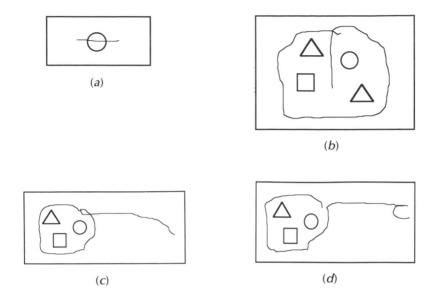

Figure 11-16 Gestures for graphic editing. (a) Delete an object by stroking through it. (b) Delete a group of objects by circling and finishing the stroke within the circle. (c) Move a group by circling and releasing outside the circle. (d) Copy by terminating with a "c" (from Kurtenbach and Buxton, 1991).

Mackinlay *et al.* (1990) to specify the direction and extent of real-time navigation in 3-space; and by Phillips and Badler (1988) to manipulate limb positions and joint displacements of 3D animated human figures. These pseudo-3D interfaces do not employ gloves or other inherently 3D input technology, so the available devices—the mouse and keyboard—were exploited.

Perceptual structure

Notwithstanding the success, low cost, and ease of implementation of the interaction styles noted above, a lingering problem is that an interaction technique must be learned. The interaction is not intuitive and, in general, there is no metaphoric link to everyday tasks. Such contrived mappings are criticized on theoretical grounds because they violate inherent structures of human perceptual processing for the input and output spaces (Jacob and Sibert, 1992). Besides force-fitting 2D devices into 3-space, there is the coincident problem of the different senses engaged by the devices vs. those stimulated by the task. Stated another way, input/output mappings of force-to-force, position-to-position, etc., are always superior to mappings such as force-to-position or force-to-motion.

Consider the joysticks mentioned earlier. The three-degree-of-freedom displacement joystick (Figure 11-3(*a*)) senses pivotal motion about a base, and twist about the *y* or vertical axis. A strong match to perceptual structures results when the task (output space) directly matches the properties sensed (input space). For example, a task demanding pivotal positioning of an object about a point combined with y-axis rotation would be ideal for this joystick: The input/output mapping is position-to-position. The four-degree-of-freedom isometric joystick in Figure 11-3(b) could perform the same task but with less fidelity, because of the force-to-position mapping.

There is some empirical support for the comparisons suggested above. Jagacinski and colleagues (1978, 1980) tested a displacement joystick in 2D target acquisition tasks. Position-to-position and position-to-velocity mappings were compared. Motor-sensory bandwidth was approximately 13 bits s^{-1} for the position-to-position system compared to only 5 bits s^{-1} for the position-to-velocity system. Kantowitz and Elvers (1988) used an isometric joystick in a 2D target acquisition task using both a force-to-position mapping (position control) and a force-to-motion mapping (velocity control). Since the application of force commonly evokes motion, a force-to-motion mapping seems closer to human perceptual processing than a force-to-position mapping. Indeed, performance was significantly better for the force-to-motion mapping compared to force-to-position mapping.

Additionally, motions or forces may be linear or rotary, suggesting that, within either the force or motion domain, linear-to-linear or rotary-to-rotary mappings will be stronger than mixed mappings. Thus, the use of a linear slider to control object rotation in the study by Chen et $al.$ (1988) cited earlier is a weak mapping.

Jacob and Sibert (1992) focused on the "separability" of the degrees of freedom afforded by devices and required by tasks. The claim is that "non-separable" degrees of freedom in a device, such as x, y, and z positioning in a 3D tracker, are a good match for a complex task with similar, non-separable degrees of freedom. Conversely, a device with "separable" degrees of freedom, such as the three-degree-of-freedom joystick in Figure 11-3(a), will work well on complex tasks with multi-, yet separable, degrees of freedom. Any complex task with relatively independent sub-tasks, such as simultaneously changing the position and colour of an object, qualifies as separable.

Gestures

By far the most common interaction paradigm heralding a new age of human–machine interaction is that of *gesture*. There is nothing fancy or esoteric here—no definition required. Gestures are actions humans do all the time, and the intent is that intuitive gestures should map into cyberspace without sending users to menus, manuals, or help screens. Simple actions such as writing, scribbling, annotating, pointing, nodding, etc. are gestures that speak volumes for persons engaged in the act of communicating. The many forms of sign language (formal or otherwise), or even subtle aspects of sitting, walking or driving a bicycle contain gestures.

What is articulated less emphatically is that human–computer interfaces that exploit gestures are likely to spawn new paradigms of interaction, and in so doing redefine intuition. This is not a criticism. Today's intuition is the result of evolution and conscious design decisions in the past (e.g., pull-down menus). One of the most exciting aspects of interface design is imagining and experimenting with potential human–computer dialogues with gestural input.

Gestures are high-level. They map directly to "user intent" without forcing the user to learn and remember operational details of commands and options. They "chunk" together primitive actions into single directives. One application for gestural input is to recognize powerful yet simple commands (viz., strokes) for manipulating text, such as those proofreaders adopt when copy-editing a manuscript. Can editing an electronic document be as direct? Numerous prototype systems have answered a resounding "yes" (e.g., Goldberg and Goodisman, 1991; Wolf and Morrel-Samuels, 1987). The gesture of circling an object to select it is simple to implement on a mouse- or stylus-based system and can yield fast and accurate performance, particularly when multiple objects are selected (Buxton, 1986; Jackson and Roske-Hofstrand, 1989).

In an editor for 2D graphical objects, Kurtenbach and Buxton (1991) demonstrated a variety of gestures that simplify selecting, deleting, moving, or copying individual objects or groups of objects. As evident in Figure 11-16, the gestures are simple, intuitive, and easy to implement for a mouse or stylus. Recognition, as with speech input, remains a challenge. The open circle in Figure 11-16(d), for example, is easily recognized by humans as a slip, but may be misinterpreted by the recognizer. Other problems include defining and constraining the scope of commands and implementing an undo operation (Hardock, 1991).

For the artist, gestural input can facilitate creative interaction. Buxton (1986) demonstrated a simple set of gestures for transcribing musical notation. As evident in Figure 11-17, the most common musical notes (shown across the top) map intuitively to simple strokes of a stylus (shown below each note).

Many touch technologies, such as the stylus or touch screen, sense pressure to 1 bit of resolution—enough to implement the "select" operation. This is insufficient to capture the richness of an artist's brush stokes, however. In a stylus-based simulation of charcoal sketching (Bleser et al., 1988), pressure was sensed to 5 bits of resolution and x and y tilt to 7 bits. This permitted sketching with lines having thickness controlled by the applied pressure, and texture controlled by tilt. The results were quite impressive.

The applications above are all 2D. Some of the most exciting new

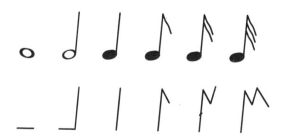

Figure 11-17 Gestures for transcribing musical notation. The most common notes (top) are easily mapped to simple gestures (bottom; from Buxton, 1986).

paradigms are those for direct, gestural interaction using an input glove in 3D virtual worlds. In fact, gesture recognition may be the easiest interaction task to cast with a glove. Pointing, delimiting a region of space, or rapid flicks of the wrist or arm are innate properties of hand and arm motion. Comparing gloves with mice and keyboards, the problems seem reversed. Selecting, specifying, choosing, etc. are easy with mice and keyboards, but defy the glove. This problem has been noted by Krueger (1991), who calls input gloves, *gesture technology*. Sweeping motions with the hand, as though performing an action, are natural for gloves; selecting or initiating action is hard.

Typically, a glove is the input device, and a 3D graphical hand, or virtual hand, acts as a cursor. For example, Sturman *et al.* (1989) used a DataGlove to pick up and move 3D objects. When the virtual hand viewed on the CRT crossed a threshold region near an object, grasping with the hand locked the object to the graphical hand. The object moved with the graphical hand until the grasping posture was relaxed. An alternate technique is to use the index finger to point and thumb rotation to select (Weimer and Ganapathy, 1989).

Tactile and force feedback

That input gloves are inherently a gesture technology follows from a feedback void. Imagine the task of reaching behind a piece of virtual equipment to turn it on. Without the sense of force or touch, this task is formidable: the virtual hand passes through the equipment without any sense of the presence of the chassis or on/off switch.

It is naive to dig deep into "input" without recognizing the interdependency with output. The visual channel, as (computer) output, is primary; but the tactile and force senses are also important. This is implicit in the earlier reference to "force-to-force" as one example of an appropriate perceptual structure for input/output mapping. A few examples of force and tactile feedback pertaining to the design of interface devices follow. For detailed discussions of the mechanisms and human perception of tactile stimulation, see Chapter 9.

A simple use of tactile feedback is shape encoding of manual controls, such as those standardized in aircraft controls for landing flaps, landing gear, the throttle, etc. (Chapanis, 1965). Shape encoding is particularly important if the operator's eyes cannot leave a primary focus point or when operators must work in the dark.

Not surprisingly, systems with tactile feedback, called *tactile displays*, have been developed as a sensory replacement channel for handicapped users. The most celebrated product is the Octacon, developed by Bliss and colleagues (Bliss *et al.*, 1970). This tactile reading aid, which is still in use, consists of 144 piezoelectric bimorph pins in a 24×6 matrix. A single finger is positioned on the array (an output device) while the opposite hand maneuvers an optical pickup (an input device) across printed text. The input/output coupling is direct; that is, the tactile display delivers a one-for-one spatial reproduction of the printed characters. Reading speeds vary, but rates over 70 words min^{-1} after 20 hr of practice have been reported (Sorkin, 1987).

Figure 11-18 Tactile and force feedback. Tactile feedback is provided by a solenoid-driven pin in the mouse button. Force feedback (friction) is provided by a magnetic field between an electromagnet inside the housing (not shown) and an iron mouse pad (from Akamatsu and Sato, 1992).

A tactile display with over 7000 individually movable pins was reported by Weber (1990). Unlike the Octacon, both hands actively explore the display. With the addition of magnetic induction sensors worn on each index finger, user's actions are monitored. A complete, multi-modal, direct manipulation interface was developed supporting a repertoire of finger gestures. This amounts to a graphical user-interface without a mouse or CRT—true "touch-and-feel" interaction.

In another 2D application called *Sandpaper*, Minski *et al.* (1990) added mechanical actuators to a joystick and programmed them to behave as virtual springs. When the cursor was positioned over different grades of virtual sandpaper, the springs pulled the user's hand towards low regions and away from high regions. In an empirical test without visual feedback, users could reliably order different grades of sandpaper by granularity.

Akamatsu and Sato (1992) modified a mouse, inserting a solenoid-driven pin under the button for tactile feedback and an electromagnet near the base for force feedback (see Figure 11-18). Tactile stimulus to the fingertip was provided by pulsing the solenoid as the cursor crossed the outline of screen objects. Force feedback to the hand was provided by passing current through the electromagnet to increase friction between the mouse and an iron mouse pad. Friction was high while the cursor was over dark regions of the screen (e.g., icons) and was low while over light regions (background). In an experiment using a target acquisition task, movement time and accuracy were improved with the addition of tactile and force feedback compared to the vision-only condition (Akamatsu *et al.*, in press). A similar system was described by Haakma (1992) using a trackball with corrective force feedback to "guide" the user towards preferred cursor positions. One potential benefit in adding force and tactile feedback is that the processing demands of the visual channel are diminished, freeing up capacity for other purposes.

Some of the most exciting work explores tactile feedback in 3D interfaces. Zimmerman *et al.* (1987) modified the DataGlove by mounting piezoceramic benders under each finger. When the virtual fingertips touched the surface of a virtual object, contact was cued by a "tingling" feeling created by transmitting a 20–40 Hz sine wave through the piezoceramic transducers. This is a potential solution to the blind touch problem cited above; however, providing appropriate feedback when a virtual hand contacts a virtual hard surface is extremely difficult. Brooks *et al.* (1990) confronted the same problem:

> Even in a linear analog system, there is no force applied until the probe has overshot [and] penetrated the virtual surface. The system has inertia and velocity. Unless it is critically damped, there will be an unstable chatter instead of a solid virtual barrier. (p. 183)

They added a brake—a variable damping system—and were able to provide reasonable but slightly "mushy" feedback for hard-surface collision.

It is interesting to speculate on the force equivalent of C–D gain. Indeed, such a mapping is essential if, for example, input controls with force feedback are implemented to remotely position heavy objects. The force sensed by the human operator cannot match that acting on the remote manipulator, however. Issues such as the appropriate mapping (e.g., linear vs. logarithmic), thresholds for sensing very light objects, and learning times need further exploration.

Custom hand-operated input devices (not gloves) with force feedback are also described by Bejczy (1980), Iwata (1990), and Zhai (1993).

Multi-modal input

The automobile is a perfect example of multi-modal interaction. Our hands, arms, feet, and legs contribute in parallel to the safe guidance of this vehicle. (A formidable challenge would be the design of a single-limb system for the same task.) With eyes, ears, and touch, we monitor the environment and our car's progress, and respond accordingly. In human-to-human communication, multi-modal interaction is the norm, as speech, gesture, and gaze merge in seamless streams of two-way intercourse. Equally rich modes of interaction have, to a limited extent, proven themselves in human–computer interaction.

Multi-modal interaction has exciting roots in entertainment. The movie industry made several leaps into 3D, usually by providing the audience with inexpensive glasses that filter the screen image and present separate views to each eye. Andy Warhol's *Frankenstein* is the most memorable example. "Smellorama" made a brief appearance in the B-movie *Polyester*, starring Devine. At critical points, a flashing number on the screen directed viewers to their scratch-and-sniff card to enjoy the full aromatic drama of the scene. A prototype arcade game from the 1960s called *Sensorama* exploited several channels of input and output. Players sat on a "motorcycle" and toured New York city in a multi-sensory environment. Binaural 3D sounds and viewing optics immersed the rider in a visual and auditory experience. The seat and handlebars vibrated with the terrain and driver's lean, and a chemical bank behind a fan added wind and smell at appropriate spots in the tour (see Krueger, 1991).

Back in the office, multi-modal input to computing systems occurs when more than one input channel participates simultaneously in coordinating a complex task. The input channels are typically the hands, feet, head, eyes, or voice. Two-handed input is the most obvious starting-point. Experimental psychologists have shown that the brain can produce simultaneously optimal solutions to two-handed coordinated tasks, even when the tasks assigned to each hand are in a different physical space and of different difficulties (Kelso *et al.*, 1979). For human input to computing systems, Buxton and Myers (1986) offer empirical support in an experiment using a positioning/scaling task. Fourteen subjects manipulated a graphics puck with their right hand to move a square to a destination, and manipulated a slider with their left hand to re-size the square. Without prompting, subjects overwhelmingly adopted a multi-modal strategy. Averaged over all subjects, 41% of the time was spent in parallel activity.

Mouse input with word processors permits limited two-handed interaction. Selecting, deleting, moving, etc., are performed by point–click or point–drag operations with the mouse while the opposite hand prepares in parallel for the ensuing **DELETE**, **COPY**, or **PASTE** keystrokes. However, when corrections require new text, multi-modal input breaks down: the hand releases the mouse, adopts a two-handed touch-typing posture, and keys the new text. Approximately 360 ms is lost each way in "homing" between the mouse and keyboard (Card *et al.*, 1978).

One novel approach to reduce homing time, is to replace the mouse with a small isometric joystick embedded in the keyboard. Rutledge and Selker (1990) built such a keyboard with a "Pointing Stick" inserted between the G and H keys and a select button below the space bar (Figure 11-19). They conducted a simple experiment with six subjects selecting circular targets of random size and location using either the mouse or Pointing Stick. The task began and ended with a keystroke. Three measurements were taken: homing time to the pointing device, point–select time, and homing time to the keyboard. As shown in Figure 11-20, performance was 22% faster overall with the Pointing Stick. Homing times for the Pointing Stick were less than for the mouse, particularly for the return trip to the keyboard (90 ms vs. 720 ms). Although the mouse was faster on the point–select portions of the task, the subjects were expert mouse users; so, further performance advantages can be expected as skill develops with the Pointing Stick. We should acknowledge, however, that the mouse uses position-to-position mapping and the Pointing Stick, force-to-velocity mapping. There may be inherent advantages for the mouse that will hold through all skill levels.[2]

Another technique for two-handed input in text-editing tasks is to free-up one hand for point–select tasks and type with the other. This is possible using a one-handed technique known as Half-QWERTY (Matias *et al.*, 1993; see Figure 11-21). Intended for touch typists, the Half-QWERTY concept uses half a standard keyboard in conjunction with a "flip" operation implemented on the space bar through software. Using only the left (or right) hand, typists proceed as usual except the right-hand characters are entered by pressing and holding the space bar while pressing the mirror-image key with the left hand. The right hand is free to use the mouse or other input device. The claim is that learning

Figure 11-19 The Pointing Stick. An isometric joystick is embedded between the G and H keys and a select button is below the space bar.

time for the Half-QWERTY keyboard is substantially reduced with touch typists because of skill transfer. In an experiment with ten touch typists, an average one-handed typing speed of 35 words min^{-1} was achieved after 10 hr of practice. Each subject attained a one-handed typing speed between 43% and 76% of their two-hand typing speed. Prolonged testing with a limited subject pool indicates that speeds up to 88% of two-handed typing speeds may be attained with one hand. Besides applications for disabled users and portable computers, the Half-QWERTY keyboard allows the full point–select capabilities of the mouse in parallel with text editing and entry.

| Measurement | Task Completion Time (ms)[a] | | Pointing Stick Advantange |
	Mouse	Pointing Stick	
Homing Time to Pointing Device	640 (110)	390 (80)	39%
Point-Select Time	760 (190)	1180 (350)	-55%
Homing Time to Keyboard	720 (120)	90 (130)	875%
Total	2120 (260)	1660 (390)	22%

[a] standard deviation shown in parentheses

Figure 11-20 Task completion times for the mouse and Pointing Stick. The Pointing Stick has a 22% advantage overall (from Rutledge and Selker, 1990).

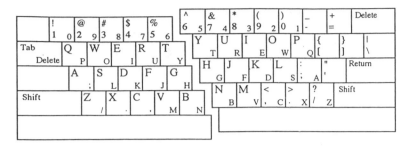

Figure 11-21 The Half-QWERTY keyboard. Subjects type with either the left hand or right hand. The keys reflect in a mirror image from one side to the other. Using the left hand, a "y" is entered by pressing and holding the space bar while pressing "t" (from Matias *et al.*, 1993).

Speech is a powerful channel for multi-modal input. The ability to combine speech input with pointing is particularly important with 3D input, since selecting is kinesthetically difficult. The potential for speech input has been shown in numerous successful implementations. In an experiment using speech and gesture input, Hauptmann (1989) asked 36 subjects to perform rotation, translation, and scaling tasks using hand gestures and/or speech commands of their own choosing. Subjects were told a computer was interpreting their verbal commands and gestures through video cameras and a microphone; however, an expert user in an adjoining room acted as an intermediary and entered low-level commands to realize the moves. Not only did a natural tendency to adopt a multi-modal strategy appear, the strategies across subjects were surprisingly uniform. As noted, "there are no expert users for gesture communications. It is a channel that is equally accessible to all computer users." (p. 244.)

Early work in multi-modal input was done at the MIT Media Lab. In Bolt's (1980) *Put-that-there* demo, an object displayed on a large projection screen was selected by pointing at it and saying "put that." The system responded with "where." A new location was pointed to, and replying "there" completed the move. Recent extensions to this exploit the latest 3D technology, including input gloves and eye trackers (Bolt and Herranz, 1992; Thorisson *et al.*, 1992). A 3D object is selected by spoken words, by pointing with the hand, or simply by looking at it. Scaling, rotating, twisting, relative positioning, etc., are all implemented using two hands, speech, and eye gaze. Speech specifies what to do and when to do it; hand positions, motions, or eye gaze specify objects, spatial coordinates, relative displacements, or rotations for the moves. This is illustrated schematically in Figure 11-22.

CHALLENGES

In the previous pages, we have presented numerous input devices, their characteristics, and key issues for the design of interaction dialogues for high-performance computing machines. Yet, the goals seem as distant as ever.

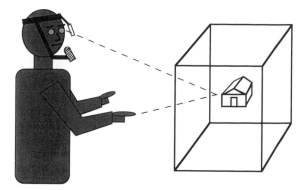

Figure 11-22 Multi-modal interaction. Speech, eye gaze, and pointing combine to control a virtual world.

There are so many new, powerful, and untapped scenarios in which to apply the latest technology, that with every problem solved a half-dozen others emerge. If it were not for this, however, the field would be bland and routine. The excitement of new possibilities, of making technology do what was once impossible, of devising interactions to redefine intuition, is why so many dedicated researchers and designers enter and persist in this field.

There are numerous challenges ahead. So-called adaptive or intelligent systems promise to embed a familiar edict for interface designers: "know thy user." These systems will know and understand us, and mold to our strengths, weaknesses, and preferences. They will know when we are having a good day and when a little prompting is due.

An idea behind 3D virtual worlds is to instrument all or part of the user's body, to permit natural multi-modal 3D interaction. This necessitates a large number of degrees of freedom for positioning and orientation with large volumes of data at high sampling rates. Interference between sensors, transducers, and the environment will add noise to the data. The task of embedding intelligence in the interface may be superseded by the more basic recognition of postures and gestures: what is the user doing?

Virtual worlds are the pervasive theme of this book; however, many issues in input and interaction are outstanding. The promises will be met only when "deliverables" appear and enter the mainstream worlds of work and entertainment. The constraints of resolution, sampling and refresh rates, and lag will probably be met on purely technological grounds. Appropriate interaction—tactile and force feedback, gestures, multi-modal input/output, etc.—will be harder to achieve and integrate due primarily to the demands of diverse users and unique and complex applications.

Telerobotics (or remote manipulation) is an area where input devices and interaction techniques are key players. The strong interest in telerobotics is a central focus of *Presence: Teleoperators and Virtual Environments*, a new journal dedicated to remote and virtual environments (see also Sheridan, 1992). Unlike virtual reality, telerobotics works in a physical world where objects are too dangerous, too complex, or too distant for direct human contact. Yet, the objects are real. Since many of the interface issues are common between such virtual and physical environments (e.g., perceptual mappings, force feedback), research and design efforts will be complementary. Matching device affordances with high-fidelity interaction dialogues remains a challenge for future research and design efforts.

NOTES

1. CHI '87 was the 1987 conference of the ACM's Special Interest Group on Computer–Human Interaction (SIGCHI).

2. The Pointing Stick has recently surfaced in IBM's ThinkPad notebook computer. It is marketed as the TrackPoint II.

REFERENCES

Akamatsu, M., MacKenzie, I. S., and Hasbroucq, T. (in press) A comparison of tactile, auditory, and visual feedback in a pointing task using a mouse-type device, *Ergonomics*

Akamatsu, M. and Sato, S. (1992) Mouse-type interface device with tactile and force display: multi-modal integrative mouse, *Proc. of the 2nd Int. Conf. on Artificial Reality and Tele-Existence (ICAT '92)*, Tokyo, Japan, pp. 178–82

Arnault, L. Y. and Greenstein, J. S. (1990) Is display/control gain a useful metric for optimizing an interface? *Human Factors*, **32**, 651–63

Bejczy, A. K. (1980) Sensors, controls, and man-machine interface for advanced teleoperation, *Science*, **208**, 1327–35

Bier, E. A. (1990) Snap-dragging in three dimensions, *Computer Graphics*, **24**, 193–204

Bleser, T. W., Sibert, J. L., and McGee, J. P. (1988) Charcoal sketching: returning control to the artist, *ACM Trans. Graphics*, **7**, 76–81

Bliss, J. C., Katcher, M. H., Rogers, C. H., and Sheppard, R. P. (1970) Optical-to-tactile image conversion for the blind, *IEEE Trans. Man-Machine Systems*, **MMS-11**, 58–65

Bolt, R. (1980) Put-that-there: voice and gesture at the graphics interface, *Computer Graphics*, **14**, 262–70

Bolt, R. A. and Herranz, E. (1992) Two-handed gesture in multi-modal natural dialog, *Proc. of the ACM SIGGRAPH and SIGCHI Symp. on User Interface Software and Technology*, New York: ACM, pp. 7–14

Brooks, Jr., F. P., Ouh-Young, M., Batter, J. J., and Kilpatrick, P. J. (1990) Project GROPE: haptic displays for scientific visualization, *Computer Graphics*, **24**, 177–85

Buxton, W. (1983) Lexical and pragmatic considerations of input structures, *Computer Graphics*, **17**, 31–7

Buxton, W. (1986) Chunking and phrasing and the design of human-computer dialogues, in H.-J. Kugler (Ed.), *Proc. of the IFIP 10th World Computer Conf.—Information Processing '86*, Amsterdam: Elsevier Science, pp. 475–80

Buxton, W. and Myers, B. A. (1986) A study in two-handed input, *Proc. of the CHI '86 Conference on Human Factors in Computing Systems*, New York: ACM, pp. 321–6

Card, S. K., English, W. K., and Burr, B. J. (1978) Evaluation of mouse, rate-controlled isometric joystick, step keys, and text keys for text selection on a CRT, *Ergonomics*, **21**, 601–13

Card, S. K., Mackinlay, J. D., and Robertson, G. G. (1990) The design space of input devices, *Proc. of the CHI '90 Conf. on Human Factors in Computing Systems*, New York: ACM, pp. 117–24

Card, S. K., Mackinlay, J. D., and Robertson, G. G. (1991) A morphological analysis of the design space of input devices, *ACM Trans. Office Inform. Systems*, **9**, 99–122

Card, S. K., Moran, T. P., and Newell, A. (1980) The keystroke-level model for user performance time with interactive systems, *Commun. ACM*, **23**, 396–410

Carr, D., Hasegawa, H., Lemmon, D., and Plaisant, C. (1992) The effects of time delays on a telepathology user interface, *Technical Report No. CS-TR-2874*, College Park, MD: University of Maryland, Computer Science Department

Chapanis, A. (1965) *Man-Machine Engineering*, Belmont, CA: Wadsworth

Chapanis, A. and Kinkade, R. G. (1972) Design of controls, in H. P. Van Cott and R. G. Kinkade (Eds), *Human Engineering Guide to Equipment Design*, Washington, DC: US Government Printing Office, pp. 345–79

Chen, M., Mountford, S. J., and Sellen, A. (1988) A study in interactive 3-D rotation using 2-D control devices, *Computer Graphics*, **22**, 121–9

Deering, M. (1992) High resolution virtual reality, *Computer Graphics*, **26**, 195–202

Deyo, R. and Ingebretson, D. (1989) Implementing and interacting with real-time microworlds, *Course Notes 29 for SIGGRAPH '89*, New York: ACM

Feiner, S., MacIntyre, B., and Seligmann, D. (1992) Annotating the real world with knowledge-based graphics on a see-through head-mounted display, *Proc. of Graphics Interface '92*, Toronto: Canadian Information Processing Society, pp. 78–85

Fels, S. S. and Hinton, G. E. (1990) Building adaptive interfaces with neural networks: the glove-talk pilot study, *Proc. of INTERACT '90*, Amsterdam: Elsevier Science, pp. 683–8

Ferrell, W. R. and Sheridan, T. B. (1967) Supervisory control of remote manipulation, *IEEE Spectrum*, **4**, 81–8

Fitts, P. M. (1954) The information capacity of the human motor system in controlling the amplitude of movement, *J. Exp. Psychol.*, **47**, 381–91

Foley, J. D., Wallace, V. L., and Chan, P. (1984) The human factors of computer graphics interaction techniques, *IEEE Computer Graphics Appl.*, **4**, 13–48

Fukumoto, M., Mase, K., and Suenaga, Y. (1992) Finger-pointer: a glove free interface, *Poster Presented at the CHI '92 Conf. on Human Factors in Computing Systems*, Monterey, CA

Goldberg, D. and Goodisman, A. (1991) Stylus user interfaces for manipulating text, *Proc. of the ACM SIGGRAPH and SIGCHI Symp. on User Interface Software and Technology*, New York: ACM, pp. 127–35

Green, M. and Shaw, C. (1990) The DataPaper: living in the virtual world, *Proceedings of Graphics Interface '90*, Toronto: Canadian Information Processing Society, pp. 123–30

Green, M., Shaw, C., and Pausch, R. (1992) Virtual reality and highly interactive three dimensional user interfaces, *CHI '92 Tutorial Notes*, New York: ACM

Greenstein, J. S. and Arnault, L. Y. (1987) Human factors aspects of manual computer input devices, in G. Salvendy (Ed.), *Handbook of Human Factors*, New York: Wiley, pp. 1450–89

Haakma, R. (1992) Contextual motor feedback in cursor control, *Poster presented at the CHI '92 Conf. on Human Factors in Computing Systems*, Monterey, CA

Hardock, G. (1991) Design issues for line-driven text editing/annotation systems, *Proc. of Graphics Interface '91*, Toronto: Canadian Information Processing Society, pp. 77–84

Hauptmann, A. G. (1989) Speech and gestures for graphic image manipulation, *Proc. of the CHI '89 Conference on Human Factors in Computing Systems*, New York: ACM, pp. 241–5

Hettinger, L. J. and Riccio, G. E. (1993) Visually induced motion sickness in virtual environments, *Presence*, **1**, 306–10

Houde, S. (1992) Iterative design of an interface for easy 3-D direct manipulation, *Proc. of the CHI '92 Conference on Human Factors in Computing Systems*, New York: ACM, pp. 135–42

Iwata, H. (1990) Artificial reality with force-feedback: development of desktop virtual space with compact master manipulator, *Computer Graphics*, **24**, 165–70

Jackson, A. (1982) Some problems in the specification of rolling ball operating characteristics, *Int. Conf. on Man/Machine Systems*, Middlesex, UK: Thomas/Weintroub, pp. 103–6

Jackson, J. C. and Roske-Hofstrand, R. J. (1989) Circling: a method of mouse-based selection without button presses, *Proc. of the CHI '89 Conf. on Human Factors in Computing Systems*, New York: ACM, pp. 161–6

Jacob, R. J. K. and Sibert, L. E. (1992) The perceptual structure of multidimensional input device selection, *Proc. of the CHI '92 Conf. on Human Factors in Computing Systems*, New York: ACM, pp. 211–18

Jagacinski, R. J., Hartzell, E. J., Ward, S., and Bishop, K. (1978) Fitts' law as a function of system dynamics and target uncertainty, *J. Motor Behavior*, **10**, 123–31

Jagacinski, R. J., Repperger, D. W., Moran, M. S., Ward, S. L., and Glass, B. (1980) Fitts' law and the microstructure of rapid discrete movements, *J. Exp. Psychol.: Human Percept. Perform.*, **6**, 309–20

Jellinek, H. D. and Card, S. K. (1990) Powermice and user performance, *Proc. of the CHI '90 Conf. on Human Factors in Computing Systems*, New York: ACM, pp. 213–20

Jenkins, W. L. and Connor, M. B. (1949) Some design factors in making settings on a linear scale, *J. Appl. Psychol.*, **33**, 395–409

Kantowitz, B. H. and Elvers, G. C. (1988) Fitts' law with an isometric controller: effects of order of control and control-display gain, *J. Motor Behavior*, **20**, 53–66

Kelso, J. A. S., Southard, D. L., and Goodman, D. (1979) On the coordination of two-handed movements, *J. Exp. Psychol.: Human Percept. Perform.*, **5**, 229–38

Krueger, M. W. (1991) *Artificial Reality II*, Reading, MA: Addison-Wesley

Kurtenbach, G. and Buxton, B. (1991) GEdit: A testbed for editing by contiguous gestures, *SIGCHI Bull.*, **23**, 22–6

Laurel, B. (1991) *Computers as Theatre*, Reading, MA: Addison-Wesley

Liang, J., Shaw, C., and Green, M. (1991) On temporal-spatial realism in the virtual reality environment, *Proc. of the ACM SIGGRAPH and SIGCHI Symp. on User Interface Software and Technology*, New York: ACM, pp. 19–25

MacKenzie, I. S. (1992) Fitts' law as a research and design tool in human-computer interaction, *Human-Computer Interact.*, **7**, 91–139

MacKenzie, I. S. and Riddersma, S. (1994) CRT vs. LCD: Empirical evidence for human performance differences. *Behavior and Information Technol.*, **13**, 328–37

MacKenzie, I. S. and Ware, C. (1993) Lag as a determinant of human performance on interactive systems, *Proc. of the INTERCHI'93 Conf. on Human Factors in Computing Systems*, New York: ACM, pp. 488–93

Mackinlay, J. D., Card, S. K., and Robertson, G. G. (1990) Rapid controlled movement through a virtual 3D workspace, *Computer Graphics*, **24**, 171–6

Mackinlay, J. D., Card, S. K., and Robertson, G. G. (1991) A semantic analysis of the design space of input devices, *Human-Computer Interact.*, **5**, 145–90

Marchionini, G. and Sibert, J. (1991) An agenda for human-computer interaction: science and engineering serving human needs, *SIGCHI Bull.*, **23**, 17–32

Matias, E., MacKenzie, I. S., and Buxton, W. (1993) Half-QWERTY: a one-handed keyboard facilitating skill transfer from QWERTY, *Proc. of the INTERCHI'93 Conf. on Human Factors in Computing Systems*, New York: ACM, pp. 88–94

Minski, M., Ouh-Young, M., Steele, O., Brooks, Jr, F. P., and Behensky, M. (1990) Feeling and seeing: issues in force display, *Computer Graphics*, **24**, 235–70

Newell, A. and Card, S. K. (1985) The prospects for psychological science in human-computer interaction, *Human-Computer Interact.*, **1**, 209–42

Pausch, R. (1991) Virtual reality of five dollars a day, *Proc. of the CHI '91 Conf. on Human Factors in Computing Systems*, New York: ACM, pp. 265–70

Phillips, C. B. and Badler, N. I. (1988) Jack: a toolkit for manipulating articulated figures, *Proc. of the ACM SIGGRAPH Symp. on User Interface Software and Technology*, New York: ACM, pp. 221–9

Rogers, J. G. (1970) Discrete tracking performance with limited velocity resolution, *Human Factors*, **12**, 331–9

Rutledge, J. D. and Selker, T. (1990) Force-to-motion functions for pointing, *Proc. of IFIP INTERACT'90: Human-Computer Interaction*, Amsterdam: Elsevier, pp. 701–6

Sheridan, T. B. (1992) *Telerobotics, Automation, and Human Supervisory Control*, Cambridge, MA: MIT Press

Sherr, S. (Ed.) (1988) *Input Devices*, San Diego, CA: Academic

Sorkin, R. D. (1987) Design of auditory and tactile displays, in G. Salvendy (Ed.), *Handbook of Human Factors*, New York: Wiley, pp. 549–76

Sturman, D. J., Zeltzer, D., and Pieper, S. (1989) Hands-on interaction with virtual environments, *Proc. of the ACM SIGGRAPH Symp. on User Interface Software and Technology*, New York: ACM, pp. 19–24

Takahashi, T. and Kishino, F. (1991) Hand gesture coding based on experiments using a hand gesture interface device, *SIGCHI Bull.*, **23**, 67–73

Thorisson, K. R., Koons, D. B., and Bolt, R. A. (1992) Multi-modal natural dialogue, *Proc. of the CHI '92 Conf. on Human Factors in Computing Systems*, New York: ACM, pp. 653–4

Wang, J.-F., Chi, V., and Fuchs, H. (1990) A real-time optical 3D tracker for head-mounted display systems, *Computer Graphics*, **24**, 205–15

Ware, C. and Baxter, C. (1989) Bat brushes: on the uses of six position and orientation parameters in a paint program, *Proc. of the CHI '89 Conf. on Human Factors in Computing Systems*, New York: ACM, pp. 155–60

Weber, G. (1990) FINGER: a language for gesture recognition, *Proc. of INTERACT '90*, Amsterdam: Elsevier Science, pp. 689–94

Weimer, D. and Ganapathy, S. K. (1989) A synthetic visual environment with hand gesturing and voice input, *Proc. of the CHI '89 Conf. on Human Factors in Computing Systems*, New York: ACM, pp. 235–40

Wickens, C. D. (1987) *Engineering Psychology and Human Performance*, New York: Harper Collins

Wolf, C. G. and Morrel-Samuels, P. (1987) The use of hand-gestures for text-editing, *Int. J. Man-Machine Studies*, **27**, 91–102

Young, R. M., Green, T. G. R., and Simon, T. (1989) Programmable user models for predictive evaluation of interface design, *Proc. of the CHI '89 Conf. on Human Factors in Computing Systems*, New York: ACM, pp. 15–19

Zhai, S. (1993) Investigation of feel for 6DOF inputs: isometric and elastic rate control for manipulation in 3D environments, *Proc. of the Human Factors and Ergonomics Society 37th Annual Meeting—1993*, Santa Monica: Human Factor Society, pp. 323–7

Zimmerman, T. G., Lanier, J., Blanchard, C., Bryson, S., and Harvill, Y. (1987) A hand gesture interface device, *Proc. of the CHI+GI '87 Conf. on Human Factors in Computing Systems*, New York: ACM, pp. 189–92

III

INTEGRATION OF TECHNOLOGY

Presence and Performance Within Virtual Environments

WOODROW BARFIELD, DAVID ZELTZER,
THOMAS SHERIDAN, AND MEL SLATER

Recent developments in display technology, specifically head-mounted displays slaved to the user's head position, techniques to spatialize sound, and computer-generated tactile and kinesthetic feedback allow humans to experience impressive visual, auditory, and tactile simulations of virtual environments. However, while technological advancements in the equipment to produce virtual environments have been quite impressive, what is currently lacking is a conceptual and analytical framework in which to guide research in this developing area. What is also lacking is a set of metrics which can be used to measure performance within virtual environments and to quantify the level of presence experienced by participants of virtual worlds. Given the importance of achieving presence in virtual environments, it is interesting to note that we currently have no theory of presence, let alone a theory of *virtual presence* (feeling like you are present in the environment generated by the computer) or *telepresence* (feeling like you are actually "there" at the remote site of operation). This in spite of the fact that students of literature, the graphic arts, the theater arts, film, and TV have long been concerned with the observer's sense of presence. In fact, one might ask, what do the new technological interfaces in the virtual environment domain add, and how do they affect this sense, beyond the ways in which our imaginations (mental models) have been stimulated by authors and artists for centuries?

Not only is it necessary to develop a theory of presence for virtual environments, it is also necessary to develop a basic research program to investigate the relationship between presence and performance using virtual environments. To develop a basic research program focusing on presence, several important questions need to be addressed. The first question to pose is, how do we measure the level of presence experienced by an operator within a virtual environment? We need to develop an operational, reliable, useful, and robust measure of presence in order to evaluate various techniques used to produce virtual environments. Second, we need to determine when, and under what conditions, presence can be a benefit or a detriment to performance. For example, in controlling actual vehicles or telerobots, where we absolutely depend on feedback, we have inadequate knowledge of how the operator's sense of presence contributes either to ultimate performance—apart from providing necessary feedback for control. Is what really matters the bits of information, coded with sufficiently high resolution in stimulus magnitude in time and space, and displayed to the appropriate sensory modality? And is the sense of "presence" simply a concomitant benign phenomenon, or even a distraction? Or is the quality of "presence" the critical psychological indicator of physical stimulus sufficiency? Similar questions are appropriate for training and learning. Knowledge of results is known to be essential. A sense of participation and involvement is known to help a great deal. When simulation and virtual environments are employed, what is contributed by the sense of presence *per se*? When simulation and virtual environments are used in conjunction with actual vehicles or dynamic systems in the field, providing embedded or *in situ* training/planning capability, we do not have design/ operating principles for how best to use the virtual and actual capabilities together.

There are many additional questions which need to be answered before virtual environment technologies are fully integrated into our interfaces. For example, there is the question of the effect of prolonged exposure to virtual environments on the human's ability to re-adapt to the real world, especially when the stabilization of the virtual environment is poor. Will extended experience in "cyberspace" affect the participant's ability to perform basic tasks such as spatial orientation upon re-entering the real world? Finally, there are a series of questions which need to be answered concerning just what factors produce presence within virtual environments. For example, what are the characteristics of the medium (e.g., field of view, resolution, frame update rate) and message (world construct) which produce the sense of presence? A display with a large field of view will produce more optical flow in the periphery and thus may be more beneficial in contributing to the sense of presence than displays with lesser fields of view. However, systems with lesser fields of view may present a higher resolution in the fovea. Thus, it is important to know which of these factors are more important for presence and which factors lead to better performance when using virtual environment technology for a given task. These are difficult questions because we expect that factors such as field of view and update rate will show both main effects and interactions. For example, a fast update rate may be more essential to achieving a sense of presence in high-fidelity environments than in low, due to differential suspension of belief. However, for given tasks the combination of a large field of view with a slow update rate may result in the same level of performance as with a fast update rate and lesser field of view. The potentially non-additive nature of the factors used to produce virtual environments necessitates a rigorous research program to study presence.

The purpose of this chapter is to discuss the concept of presence in the context of virtual environments focusing briefly on the technology used to produce virtual environments and by focusing on conditions which may produce a sense of presence within virtual environments. Furthermore, this chapter proposes several measurable physical variables that may determine presence including virtual presence and telepresence. We also discuss several aspects of human performance that might be (differentially) affected by these forms of presence. In essence, the concept of presence represents the underlying theme or conceptual framework for the work being done in the field of virtual environments. Thus, each of the following chapters comprising this book contributes to this theme either by discussing the technology used to produce computer-simulated auditory, visual, tactile, and kinesthetic virtual environments or by discussing the human factors and psychological issues associated with the design and use of virtual worlds.

PRESENCE IN THE WORLD

To discuss presence in the context of virtual environments, it is first necessary to discuss the concept of presence in the non-virtual or real world. "Presence" generally refers to the sense of being present in time or space at a particular location (Webster's II Dictionary, 1984). Thus, presence is a cognitive state which occurs when the brain processes and makes sense of the myriad of stimulus information impinging upon the human's sensory systems. We propose that the concept of presence, that is, the sense of "being there," or of a person or thing "being here" (Wells, 1992), serves as the underlying conceptual framework for virtual environments.

As noted, presence of an environment occurs when the human senses information from the world. Using information derived from the senses, higher cognitive centers in the brain process visual, tactile, kinesthetic, olfactory, proprioceptive, and auditory information to form an impression of the world. An important point to emphasize is that it is necessary for attentional resources to be directed to stimulus information before the sense of presence can occur. We will return to this important idea in a later section. Finally, the sense of presence is not confined to complex spatial or auditory displays. It could be argued that presence can occur as a result of reading a captivating book, viewing a movie or play, or by simply daydreaming of another time or place. However, it is important to carefully differentiate between concepts that may result in similar observable effects, but which are not the same. For example, the movie-goer who visibly flinches at a particularly shocking scene, or who cries during an emotional scene, may well feel very involved in the story, and identify with the main characters, but have no sense at all of "being there" that is associated with presence.

It is important to note that the sense of presence one experiences in the real world is derived primarily by a subset of sensory information impinging upon the human's sensory systems. Consider a real-world example, the act of viewing a movie at the local theater. Even though the person viewing the movie receives visual, auditory, tactile, kinesthetic, proprioceptive, and olfactory sensory information, information from the visual and auditory modalities dominate this experience. In fact, the tactile and kinesthetic information received from the position of the observer's body on the theater chair does not contribute to the "presence" or involvement which results from viewing and listening to the movie. It is even possible that these cues may compete for the participant's attentional resources and thus serve to lower the level of presence for the "movie experience." The fact that presence for an environment can occur when the observer attends to only a subset of the sensory information impinging upon the senses, has significance for producing presence in virtual environments. We believe that it is possible to invoke a high level of presence in virtual environments without having to stimulate every sensory system of the human. In fact, many current virtual environment systems successfully invoke presence by stimulating only the visual and auditory modalities, and for teleoperator applications, tactile and kinesthetic feedback provides strong cues for presence.

Finally, it is interesting to note that there are two types of presence that a person can experience without computer stimulation of the senses: (1) the sense of presence that the observer has of the actual environment he/she is in, and (2) the sense of presence the observer has of a different environment (in time or space), for example, daydreaming of the beach on a tropical island.

THE BASIC COMPONENTS OF A VIRTUAL ENVIRONMENT SYSTEM

A virtual environment is a computer-simulated world consisting of software representations of real (or imagined) agents, objects and processes; and a human–computer interface for displaying and interacting with these models. A typical virtual environment system consists of three basic components: (1) computer hardware and software to model and render images; (2) a logical interface that specifies what parameters of the virtual environment and its models can be changed, and when; and (3) a physical interface consisting of one or more visual, haptic or auditory displays for presenting the virtual environment to the human participant using, for example, stereoscopic images, spatialized sound, or computer-generated tactile feedback; and a set of sensing devices to monitor the human's actions, e.g., a Space Ball or a Power Glove with a Polhemus position-sensing device. Figure 12-1 shows a virtual environment participant interacting with a virtual object using a 6-degree-of-freedom (6 DOF) input device; the stereo image(s) is projected onto a 6 ft by 8 ft rear-lit screen.

The new and driving technologies which have impacted the development of virtual environments are high-density video, high-resolution and fast computer-graphics, head-coupled display, instrumented "data gloves" and "body suits," and high-bandwidth, multi-degree-of-freedom force-feedback and cutaneous stimulation devices. Virtual environment devices are now being integrated into actual control stations in the field, so that the operator can use such virtual "what-would-happen-if" exercises for *in situ* planning and embedded training. However, research and development in virtual environment modeling and interface technology is certainly not new. The very first electronic digital computing engines were used to compute physically based models of fluid flow

Figure 12-1 Example of a user interacting with a virtual object. A large screen projection system is used to display the virtual images. (Picture courtesy of the Sensory Engineering Laboratory (SEL), University of Washington.)

and ballistic trajectories (Harvard Computation Laboratory, 1985). And since that time, researchers have been studying ways of expanding the human–machine interface to enable more "natural" communication and interaction with computer systems and computational models. For example, MIT graduate Ivan Sutherland in 1968 demonstrated the use of a head-mounted display for computer-generated images (Vickers, 1982). In the 1960s, Michael Noll at Bell Labs developed what he called "a three-dimensional machine communication tactile device" which allowed a user to feel a simulated object (Noll, 1972). What is new to the scene is the advent of graphics workstations capable of rendering reasonable visual approximations of familiar objects in near-real time, coupled with commercially available whole-hand input devices, such as the DataGlove, as well as head-mounted displays that provide a wide field of view slaved to the user's head motions (Fisher *et al.*, 1986; Blanchard *et al.*, 1990.

BASIC DEFINITIONS AND TERMS

In this section, definitions proposed by Sheridan (1992b) focusing on the basic concepts and terms associated with the virtual environment domain are presented in order to acquaint the reader with the concepts associated with presence and to provide a framework for other chapters. Currently, there are many terms being introduced in the literature relating to virtual environments the meanings of which may not be clear to readers or may never have been well defined. The reader should note that the following concepts are from a wide range of fields, including computer science, robotics, and human factors. This emphasizes the interdisciplinary nature of the work being done to design and evaluate virtual environments. The discussion of terminology that follows will not be comprehensive nor, for those terms offered, provide the last word, as developments in this field are occurring rapidly.

There are many new technologies emerging that are likely to have a large impact on both the experience of *virtual environments* (e.g., a computer-simulated vehicle or system by which user, trainee, or planner can try out alternative actions and get realistic feedback) and *teleoperation* (human remote control of vehicles, manipulators and other systems using video, audio, kinesthetic and tactile feedback from the remote site). In either case, given a sufficiently high-fidelity display, a mental attitude of willing acceptance, and a modicum of motor "participation," the human operator can experience a sense of "telepresence" (sense of being physically present with real object(s) at the remote teleoperator site) or "virtual presence" (sense of being physically present with visual, auditory, or force displays generated by a computer). Figure 12-2 illustrates these terms and their interrelations. A more general definition of presence for virtual environments has been given by Slater and Usoh (1993). We will present this definition now, in order to initiate the discussion, although the remainder of this chapter will say more about how presence should be conceptualized, measured, and defined. Slater and Usoh refer to *presence* as the extent to which human participants in a virtual environment allow themselves to be convinced while experiencing the effects of a computer-synthesized virtual environment that they are somewhere other than where they physically are—that "somewhere" being determined by the image, sounds, and physical sensations provided by the computer-synthesized virtual environment to their senses.

Teleoperator

Tele means at a distance and *operator* means that which operates. To *operate* can mean to transform the physical environment by an energy exchange, or it can mean to transform information from one configuration to another. These components might suggest that a teleoperator is any entity that transforms energy or information at a distance, which is still an insufficient definition, for it could mean anything that transforms energy or information at a distance from anything else. However, in common usage, the *operator* part of teleoperator has come to mean machine, not human and the *tele* part has come to mean at a distance from and controlled by a human operator. Hence the accepted definition: *A teleoperator is a machine that operates on its environment and is controlled by a human at a distance.* A simple stick or hand tool is a teleoperator. So is a much more complex robotic device in outer space or on the ocean bottom that is remotely controlled by a human. So is a remotely controlled motor-operated pump or valve or other device that does not manipulate in the usual sense. A teleoperator need not be anthropomorphic (exhibit human form), and it can be either a telesensor (e.g., a remotely panned and tilted video camera) or a telemanipulator or a combination. In either case it must include a remotely controlled actuator.

When the term teleoperator is used in relation to humans, and distant environments, there could be an ambiguity—whether the teleoperator is a

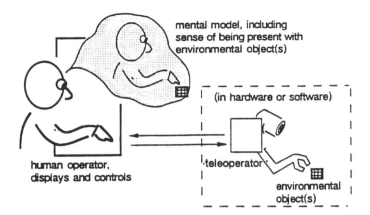

Figure 12-2 In telepresence, displays and operator actions result in a mental model that includes the sense of being present with actual environmental object(s). In virtual presence, software substitutes for actual teleoperator and environmental objects. (From Sheridan, 1992a. Presence: *Teleoperators and Virtual Environments*, Volume 1(1), MIT Press.)

human doing the operating on the distant environment or is a machine operating on its immediate environment at a distance from the human. The accepted meaning within the teleoperator engineering and human-factors community, is the latter. The teleoperator is the machine that actually does the operation of sensing and/or modifying its environment. It is controlled from a distance by a human operator, often using special displays and controls to communicate to the teleoperator.

We can speak of a *teleoperator* (or *teleoperation*) *system* (which includes the teleoperator, as well as the human operator's displays and controls and the communication system) much as we would speak of a television system (which sees at a distance) or a telephone system (which speaks at a distance). Any of these systems can be understood to include the human operator, or not. One simply has to be specific about bounding the reference system. Incidentally, if the term teleoperator were used to refer only to a human we would need a different term for the machine actually doing the operation on its own environment. No other generic term has currency, so there should be no ambiguity. Hence, to repeat: A teleoperator is a machine that operates on its environment and is controlled by a human at a distance.

Manually controlled teleoperator. This is a subclass of teleoperator in which all movements are guided continuously by the human operator. Sometimes the word "direct" has been used instead of "manual" here, but "direct" combined with "tele" seems a contradiction.

Master–slave teleoperator. This is a subclass of direct- or manual-controlled teleoperator in which the human positions the master, which provides a reference signal to a servo-mechanism to position the slave in conformance to the master. Master–slave can also refer to master-force to slave-force conformance. In the teleoperation sense, a master–slave teleoperator system has two subsystems: (1) the *master device*, which typically is a multi-degree-of-freedom, more-or-less anthropomorphic (having a serial-kinematic form like a human arm) mechanical device, positioned directly by a human operator; and (2) a *slave device*, which typically is isomorphic to (having the same form as) the master. The latter is often equipped with an end effector (a hand for grasping, or a specialized tool to perform some specialized task). Either or both forces or displacements at the slave end may be scaled up or down relative to those at the master end (with energy added or subtracted to achieve proper control) and still be kinematically equivalent. If not kinematically equivalent, there must be coordinate transformations to make the slave end effector follow the master.

Rate-controlled teleoperator. This is a direct-controlled teleoperator in which the position of the human operator's control device specifies the velocity of the teleoperator's movement.

Robot

Unlike the other terms under discussion, this term has been available for some years in most dictionaries. Derived from the Slavic word for *work*, it is usually attributed to Karel Capek's Play R.U.R. for *Rossum's Universal Robots*. A robot is a machine that *performs functions ordinarily ascribed to human beings, or operates with what appears to be almost human intelligence* (adapted from Webster's Third International Dictionary). The Robot Institute of America has defined a robot as a *reprogrammable multifunctional manipulator designed to move material, parts, tools, or specialized devices through variable programmed motions for the performance of a variety of tasks*. A strict technical definition suitable for the purpose of this chapter requires that the robot's actions be determined by a computer, based at least in part on artificial exteroception (sensing of its external environment) and in part on an internal program. In this sense robot implies autonomous control, at least with respect to some state variables and/or for short periods of time.

Telerobot. This term came into fashion within the space teleoperation community in the 1970s. In the generic sense a *telerobot is a robot controlled at a distance by a human operator.* Such a definition does not contradict the strict definition of robot provided its autonomy is understood to be partial. Thus *a telerobot is a subclass of teleoperator that, once instructed by a human, may perform limited sensing or manipulation tasks autonomously.* In essence, a telerobot is the subclass of teleoperator complementary to the direct-manual teleoperator, i.e., the two classes are mutually exclusive and, so far as we know, collectively exhaustive.

Supervisory control

The term can refer to human supervisors of other humans in a social organization, or to hardware or software that supervises other hardware or software, as, for example, a computer's operating system supervises other software components. The term "supervisory control" is most often applied to human supervisors of telerobots, where supervising means *instructing by (1) specifying subgoals, constraints, criteria, or procedures to a computer*, and (2) *receiving back a variety of information about a telerobot's state or performance, often in summary form*. From such information the supervisor monitors whether the telerobot is achieving the task, whether it has completed the task, or whether it has failed. If either of the latter conditions is the case, the supervisor intervenes to reprogram or control manually. The supervisor is also responsible for planning new commands and learning from past observations. Supervisory control does not require physical remoteness, though some degree of functional remoteness is inherent. In the strict sense, supervisory control requires that the machine being supervised has some degree of intelligence and is able to perform automatically once programmed (i.e., is a telerobot in the general sense, which also includes semiautomatic systems such as aircraft and manufacturing plants). In a less strict sense, commanding any complex machine in high-level language and monitoring any complex system using synoptic (summarizing) displays of complex state relations has sometimes been called supervisory control, even though the control loop closure may be continuous through the human operator.

Telepresence

Sheridan (1992b) takes the term to mean that the human operator receives sufficient information about the teleoperator and the task environment, displayed in a sufficiently natural way, that the operator feels physically present at the remote site. This can be a matter of degree. Normally, an operator, on reflection, knows where he or she really is, but yet can suppress disbelief to enhance the effect. The illusion of telepresence can be compelling if the proper technology is used. A restrictive and specialized definition of telepresence used in space teleoperator development requires that the teleoperator's dexterity match that of the bare-handed human operator. In a loose sense, telepresence may be achieved through artistry without high technology, for example, by clever storytelling. In this sense it is synonymous with virtual presence (see below), but it seems best to retain telepresence to refer to the sense of presence in actual environments (including prerecording and later reproduction of display of an actual environment). The projection of the participant's cognitive and perceptual abilities to the remote site can also be referred to as telepresence. Finally, the manual manipulation of events at a remote site is defined as *teleoperator control*.

Virtual presence, virtual environment, virtual reality, artificial reality

A *virtual environment* is an interactive, multisensory, three-dimensional, computer-synthesized environment. *Virtual presence* refers to the human's level of presence or inclusion within a virtual environment. In a recent article, Sheridan (1992b) defined virtual presence as the sense of being physically present with visual, auditory, or force displays generated by computer. We extend this definition to include cognitive presence in a virtual environment as well. The terms "virtual presence", "virtual environment", "virtual reality", "artificial reality" are experienced by a person when sensory information generated only by and within a computer and associated display technology compels a feeling of being present in an environment other than the one the person is actually in. Thus, Sheridan (1992b) takes these terms to be essentially synonyms, though one might argue that virtual presence is an experience and the others are what is experienced. In some ideal sense, and presumably with sufficiently good technology, a person would not be able to distinguish between actual presence, telepresence, and virtual presence. Note that we regard the terms *virtual reality* and *artificial reality* to be linguistically self-contradictory and therefore more troubling than the terms *virtual presence* and *virtual environment*.

Tele-anything-else

Many other tele-words have been used in recent years. Some of them are intended as "more pure" substitutes, suchas *tele-chirics* (the latter, of Greek etymology, for telemanipulation). Some other terms, such as *teleprioprioception*, *telekinesthesis*, or *teletouch*, simply modify conventional terms to mean the corresponding events are done at an acceptable distance from the human operator.

COMPONENTS OF THE "VIRTUAL ENVIRONMENT" EXPERIENCE

Several authors have discussed factors which describe the virtual environment experience and thus relate to the sense of presence, including Lavroff (1992), Robinett (1992), Wells (1992) and Zeltzer (1992). In this section we will focus in detail on Zeltzer's (1992) taxonomy of Virtual Environment systems, which is based on three main components, *autonomy* (computational models and processes), *interaction* (logical interface), and *presence* (physical interface). The resulting "AIP-cube" provides a useful qualitative tool for thinking about the kinds of models and interfaces one ought to provide for various virtual environment applications. Moreover, such a taxonomy can help us to describe, categorize, compare and contrast virtual environment systems; and also help us to identify application areas and avenues of research to pursue.

In contrast, rather than attempting to define the constituent components of a virtual environment system, Wells and Lavroff have each tried to characterize the factors associated with the virtual environment experience. According to Wells, this experience is *immersive*, *interactive* and *intuitive*. *Immersive* means that the participant is completely surrounded by the computer simulation. *Interactive* means that the participant's actions affect the simulation, and conversely, the simulation can affect the participant. Finally, *intuitive* means that the participant communicates with the simulation using actions that are familiar and natural, which is one property of what Zeltzer and others have called *task-level* interaction. Lavroff argues that the virtual environment experience is immersive, in agreement with Wells. *Manipulation* is a further characteristic, in that the participant can affect objects in the simulation, and will, in turn, receive sensory cues from the objects, again, in agreement with

Wells' *interactive aspect*. Finally, Lavroff suggests that the participant can *navigate* through a virtual environment. In our view, each of these qualities can be realized in a properly constructed virtual environment system. It is also important to note that not all of these qualities may be required for a particular application.

Robinett proposed a detailed taxonomy that attempts to categorize the varieties of virtual environment and teleoperator systems. This analysis is based on the spatial and temporal relationships among the human participant, the human–computer interface, and the simulation software or teleoperator system. In addition, he characterizes systems in terms of the displays, actuators and sensors that are used. In our view, Robinett's taxonomy is in many ways complementary to Zeltzer's (presented below). Indeed, in Robinett's taxonomy, the dimensions labeled *display type*, *sensor type*, *action measurement type* and *actuator type* reflect a principled attempt to begin to describe and quantify multi-modal interfaces to virtual environment and teleoperator systems, which are represented along a single axis only—the "presence" axis—in Zeltzer's work.

ZELTZER'S AIP CUBE

Autonomy

We can speculate that the sense of presence within a virtual environment might be greater if the computer-synthesized objects in the virtual environment exhibit some level of autonomy. Objects in the real world exhibit a range of autonomy, e.g., except for complying with the laws of physics, a rock exhibits no autonomous behavior. On the other hand, animals, humans and robots maintain more or less rich repertoires of behaviors. In the same way, simulated objects and actors in a virtual environment ought to be capable of a range of more or less autonomous behaviors. At one extreme, a computational model in computer graphics may be a passive, geometric data structure with no associated procedures. We may apply the usual affine transformations (Foley, *et al.*, 1990) to these models and then render them. At the other extreme are virtual actors capable of reactive planning, and, ultimately, more powerful knowledge-based behaviors. Between these extremes, we can augment models of objects and agents in various ways, for example, with procedures that account for the mechanical properties of rigid and non-rigid objects, yielding what has come to be known as physically based models. Autonomy, then, is a qualitative measure of the ability of a computational model to act and react to simulated events and stimuli, ranging from 0 for the passive geometric model to 1 for the most sophisticated, physically based virtual agent.

Interaction

In this context *interaction* refers to the software architecture of the human–machine interface of the virtual environment system. In its most basic form, we need to specify the degree of access to model and system parameters at run-time. What are the system and model "control knobs"? When and how during the simulation can the human participant modify system and model parameters? The range is from 0 for "batch" processing in which no interaction at run-time is possible, to 1 for comprehensive, real-time access to all model parameters. Most current graphics systems are indeed highly interactive, such that real-time manipulation of rigid objects is often controlled by joysticks, knobs or a mouse. In other application domains, such as computational fluid dynamics, interaction remains quite limited due to the computational cost of updating the model at each time step.

Note that autonomy implies levels of abstraction, which are crucial to the representation of behaviors. And, as has been discussed in detail elsewhere, interaction paradigms vary as one accesses model parameters at different levels of abstraction (Zeltzer, 1991). Moreover, merely providing direct access to many parameters is not necessarily productive, since it is easy to overwhelm a user with the sheer number of parameters that must be attended to in order to accomplish a given task. This has been referred to as the *degrees-of-freedom problem* (Turvey *et al.*, 1982). This means that in a complex work domain such as a virtual environment with many actors and processes, the input operations must be properly organized so as to functionally reduce the number of degrees of freedom that must be directly controlled—irrespective of the input modality, whether through the keyboard, conventional graphical input devices, or through hand-motion measurement devices such as the DataGlove. The latter, while increasing the sense of presence, does not necessarily reduce the complexity of the control task; that really depends on understanding the functional relationships among input parameters (Vicente and Rasmussen, 1990), and implementing the proper abstraction classes, which is what is represented by the autonomy–interaction plane.

Presence

We are immersed in a very high bandwidth stream of sensory input, organized by our perceiving systems, and out of this "bath" of sensation emerges our sense of being in and of the world. This feeling is also engendered by our ability to affect the world through touch, gesture, voice, etc. The *presence axis* provides a rough, lumped measure of the number and fidelity of available sensory input and output channels. Rather than measuring the subjective feeling of being present, the intention is to measure the bits of information displayed to the appropriate sensory modality, as well as the bandwidth and resolution, etc., of the various sensing devices used to monitor the actions of the human participants. Later in this chapter, we will discuss techniques for describing and measuring these quantities.

A discussion of presence is quite meaningless without specifying the application domain and the task requirements. For example, consider the head-mounted display and the null stimulus, which we can think of as a structureless, diffuse, evenly illuminated visual field, the so-called *Ganzfeld* (Cornsweet, 1970; Grind, 1986). What visual cues should be provided to the head-mounted display wearer, beyond this null stimulus, so that he or she feels "present" in some environment? Clearly, the visual field must provide some structured imagery lest the wearer feel immersed in a featureless void. Gibson suggests that the experience of perceiving some volume of space requires at least the presentation of texture gradients that can be interpreted as a surface (Mace, 1977). Alternatively, fixed reference points (Howard, 1986, 1991) or a uniformly moving visual field can also give rise to a perception of space (Hochberg, 1986), but is stereo viewing required to feel present? Should a collimated display be provided? What level of photorealism is appropriate? To answer these and other questions, we need to specify present *where* and for what *purpose*.

In terms of visual requirements for virtual environments, Ellis (1991) at NASA/Ames introduced the concept of *virtualization* to refer to the visual cues necessary to create a virtual environment (see Chapter 2). Virtualization is defined by Ellis as *"the process by which a human viewer interprets a patterned sensory impression to be an extended object in an environment other than that in which it physically exists."* As an example, consider a three-dimensional computer-generated image perceived as floating in front of the display screen, produced by a stereoscopic display system. According to Ellis there are three aspects of virtualization which when combined create the illusion that one is experiencing a virtual world or a virtual object within that world: these include the concepts of virtual space, virtual image, and virtual environment. The virtual space effect relies on pictorial depth cues to create the impression of a three-dimensional object projected onto a two-dimensional display surface. These depth cues include texture gradients, perspective, shading, and occlusion. According to Ellis, the second form of virtualization refers to the perception of the virtual image. Three-dimensional virtual images are perceived by the addition of accommodation, vergence, and stereoscopic disparity cues (accommodation and vergence are in conflict with stereoscopic displays). Finally, according to Ellis, virtual environments are produced when observer-slaved motion parallax, depth of focus variation, and a wide field of view display without a prominent frame are used to present images.

In practice, implementation of virtual environments is guided by what has been called *selective fidelity* (Johnston, 1987). It is not possible to simulate the physical world in all its detail and complexity, so for a given task we need to identify carefully the sensory cues that must be provided for a human to accomplish the task, and match as closely as possible the human perceptual and motor performance required for the task. Determining the operational parameters inevitably involves many trade-offs among cost, performance, and efficiency. For visual cues, such parameters include throughput of geometric primitives, visual update rate, and display resolution, all of which are critical numbers for any computer image generator. Unfortunately, in many of these areas, current technology falls far short.

Just as the conventional logical input devices (e.g., locator and valuator) allow us to separate functionality from the operational detail of physical input devices (Foley *et al.*, 1990), we distinguish between *interaction* (i.e., the degree to which model parameters can be accessed at run-time) and the means of

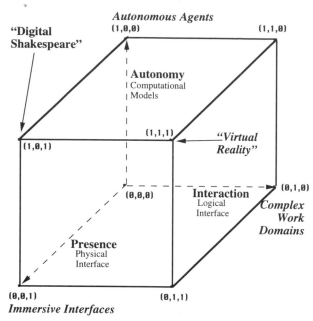

Figure 12-3 The AIP cube. (From Zeltzer, 1992. Presence: *Teleoperators and Virtual Environments*, Volume 1(1), MIT Press.)

accessing those parameters. Therefore, an analysis of the kinds of input devices provided belongs also to the measure of presence: are the input devices designed to monitor our movements and speech, or are they constructed to measure the motions we impart to special kinematically constrained assemblies such as buttons (vertical motion), dials (rotary motion) and the mouse (2D translations)? Put another way, a widely accepted working hypothesis states that using our familiar sensorimotor skills to manipulate virtual objects directly by means of whole-hand input devices like the VPL DataGlove, contributes to our sense of presence much more than writing programs, twisting knobs or pushing a mouse to accomplish the same task. Thus the presence dimension provides a measure of the degree to which input and output channels of the machine and the human participant(s) are matched.

The three axes, autonomy, interaction, and presence, define a coordinate system we can use as a qualitative measure of virtual environment systems. Let us examine the positive octant formed by the three axes (see Figure 12-3).

At the origin $(0, 0, 0)$ we have essentially the situation as it obtained in the early 1960s—models with no autonomy, and systems with no interaction and no presence (i.e., batch processing of simple graphical models, with the results portrayed on a pen plotter or perhaps output to a film recorder).

In contrast, the corner $(1, 1, 1)$ is our "grail": fully autonomous agents and objects which act and react according to the state of the simulation, and which are equally responsive to the actions of the human participant(s). In addition, sensory stimulation provided to the participant(s) in the virtual environment is indistinguishable from what would be expected in a physical setting. That is to say, this node represents a hypothetical future system in which one could feel a cool breeze on the back of one's neck, or experience what it is like to pull 9 Gs in a high-performance jet aircraft. Is such a system achievable? Probably not without some form of direct stimulation of nervous tissue, about which we will not speculate. Is such a system desirable? Certainly not for all applications. For example, if one were teleoperating a real or virtual robot performing what for a human would be a physically demanding task, one would quickly be overcome with fatigue if all the forces experienced by the robot were reflected back to the human participant. Moreover, if the robot were in some hostile environment say, a nuclear reactor on fire, or a battlefield one certainly would want to restrict the presence cues!

The point $(0, 1, 0)$ represents a system where all model parameters are subject to user control at run-time. Conventional commercial animation systems approach such a point, providing dozens if not hundreds of parameters that can be directly modified by the user, generally through the use of conventional input devices, e.g., tablet and mouse. For the most part, users of such systems must operate on passive two- and three-dimensional geometrical abstractions which forces them to construct synthetic events in all their detail. The sheer number of details that must be specified can be overwhelming, which makes the control task very difficult, and also requires users to be quite expert with respect to design and animation techniques.

Currently available virtual environment systems begin to approach the point $(0, 1, 1)$, since, in general, there is a non-trivial amount of interaction with object models in the system and an interesting (and often compelling) level of presence is implemented through the use of a binocular head-mounted display with wide, head-slaved field of view and glove-like whole-hand input devices (Sturman, 1992). For example, in the "RB2" system previously offered by VPL, participants could interact with a graphic simulation of a robot manipulator, by "grabbing" the end-effector with the DataGlove and moving the arm, i.e., updating the position and orientation of the robot gripper (Blanchard et al., 1990). Autonomy is low, however, since the computational models in these systems are for the most part rather passive geometric data structures with few attached procedures.

Continuing around the base of the cube, the point $(0, 0, 1)$ represents a non-interactive system with sophisticated sensory stimulation devices, which is based on passive, geometric models that are neither autonomous nor modifiable in real time. For example, a precomputed conventional animation sequence viewed with head-mounted display and haptic feedback would approach this corner of the AIP-cube. The "Star Tours" attraction at Disneyland is another example of such a system.

The point $(1, 0, 1)$ represents an interesting combination in which autonomy is high, i.e., the simulation contains virtual actors and physically based models, and where presence is high, but there is little or no interaction with characters. Zeltzer argues that such a system could be, and likely will be, quite successful commercially. Imagine being able to put on a head-mounted display and stroll among virtual actors performing, say, a play by Shakespeare. High autonomy means that the virtual actors could respond to, say, natural language scripts describing the performance, a topic of much recent research (Ridsdale et al.,

1986; Badler and Webber, 1991; Zeltzer, 1993) and which would go far toward making such "virtual theater" pieces economical to produce. One would be able to view the action from various viewpoints, and perhaps even rewind or fast-forward the piece. However, the virtual actors would be entirely oblivious to the viewer's virtual presence.

The corner $(1, 0, 0)$ represents a graphic simulation with physically based agents and virtual actors, viewed on a conventional display device with no interaction. Portions of the animation Grinning Evil Death, for example, are prototypical of such a piece (McKenna et al., 1990).

Finally, the corner $(1, 1, 0)$ represents something close to the "bolio" virtual environment system which was implemented at MIT (Zeltzer et al., 1989). The bolio system supported a number of autonomous models, and also provided comprehensive and varied access to model parameters. However, the level of presence in that virtual environment system was not high, since "natural" input was limited to kinematic, whole-hand input, and the MIT researchers at the time did not use a head-mounted display.

The AIP-cube with its three axes autonomy, interaction and presence provides a conceptual tool for organizing our understanding of current virtual environment technology. In this scheme, for example, "virtual reality" is an appropriate label for the unattainable node in which the value of all three components is unity. It is not clear how to rigorously quantify these components, however, and much work remains, for example in understanding how to measure selective fidelity.

In the autonomy domain, work on physically based modeling of rigid and non-rigid bodies continues in many laboratories, including work on anthropo-metric (Lee et al., 1990) and physically based jointed figure motion (Wilhelms et al., 1988; McKenna and Zeltzer, 1990), and reactive planners (Zeltzer and Johnson, 1991). In terms of interaction, the problem is to understand how to organize and functionally abstract complex control spaces to make them more amenable to safe and effective human operation. In terms of presence, we need to improve our understanding of human perception for several reasons. First, a better understanding of human sensory mechanisms will make it possible for us to design and implement effective devices for enhancing presence, e.g., haptic feedback. Other perceptual phenomena, such as binaural hearing, may be stimulated artificially, but at great computational expense (Wenzel and Foster, 1990), so that algorithm and hardware development is necessary to realize economical, real-time devices. Second, there are presence cues that are simply not practical to synthesize, and we therefore need to know how to suggest sensations or substitute other kinds of cues when possible or appropriate. For example, applying the linear and angular accelerations experienced by the pilot of a high-performance jet aircraft is simply not possible to achieve in a ground-based flight simulator (Rolfe and Staples, 1986). However, a sufficient understanding of the sensory processes involved makes it possible to provide a variety of cues which sum to a fairly convincing experience of being in a moving cockpit.

Finally, it is important to develop a taxonomy of tasks in terms of sensory input: for a given task, what sensory cues are necessary, and which cues are dispensable but improve performance? Are there sensory cues which do not affect performance *per se*, but which enhance the aesthetics of the operations or the work place? Are there sensory cues that interfere with performance and which should be avoided?

AUGMENTED REALITY

In addition to the use of a head-mounted display to present an immersive computer-generated virtual world to the virtual environment participant, a number of researchers are currently developing systems which combine the real world (typically live video) with the virtual world (i.e., computer graphics) (Feiner, 1993; Lion *et al.*, 1993) (see Chapter 14). The relationship between these systems and presence is quite interesting as they allow a variety of real-world and virtual-world combinations to be developed. Such systems will be especially useful for training applications and should invoke a high sense of presence for tasks such as maintenance and repair.

As a rationale for overlay systems consider the following: the trend in virtual environment design has been to laboriously model scenes with many polygons and eventually present computer-generated stereoscopic imagery of these scenes through opaque head-mounted displays. Unfortunately, few contemporary workstations have sufficient power to render the number of polygons necessary to create a complex scene at 30 frames a second. However, note that the "real world" offers a wealth of varying environments, realism, and detail, and by capturing the complexity and richness of the real world using video, it is then not necessary for a programmer to model the captured environment using computer graphics.

There is precedence for such an approach as virtual interface pioneers such as Myron Krueger (Krueger, 1991), have already integrated real-world imagery into their works by means of monoscopic video. Other researchers have also explored overlay techniques. For example, Bajura *et al.* (1992), at the University of North Carolina performed a similar composite, but with monocular video imagery, as did Deering (1992) in his 1992 Siggraph Video. In an empirical study, Milgram *et al.* (1991) composited stereo computer-generated imagery with stereo video, and studied subjects' ability to make absolute size and distance judgments about real objects using a virtual pointer, which could be scaled and translated through the overlay space. Performance with stereoscopic virtual pointers was similar to that of real pointers.

However, unlike standard monoscopic video imagery, the real world conveys a compelling sense of depth. An overlay system developed at the Laboratory for Interactive Computer Graphics and Human Factors at the University of Washington recognizes this dimensionality, as their system imports the real world into the computational environment by means of stereoscopic live motion video. They use this live motion video to enhance the virtual environment by compositing the stereo video underneath the computer-generated stereo imagery, and displaying the combined imagery on a large field-of-view (6 ft by 8 ft) back-lit screen. The real-world imagery forms the

Figure 12-4 Photograph representing augmented reality using a see-through head-mounted display. (Picture courtesy of Professor Michitaka Hirose, Department of Mechanical Engineering, University of Tokyo, Japan.)

Table 12-1 Taxonomy of combined stereoscopic overlaid imagery.

Foreground imagery	Background imagery	Description	Applications
CGI*	CGI	multiple synthetic realities	virtual worlds
CGI	video	virtual overlay	HUD, training
Video	CGI	video overlay	multimedia
Video	video	multiple video realities	telepresence, image processing

*CGI = computer-generated imagery.

majority of the virtual environment (Figure 12-4). The computer-generated imagery (CGI) is used as an enhancement to the scene. Stereo video provides a compelling sense of presence for viewers. Table 12-1 presents a taxonomy of overlay systems with suggested applications.

TECHNIQUES TO MEASURE PRESENCE AND PERFORMANCE WITHIN VIRTUAL ENVIRONMENTS

There is an obvious need for measures of virtual presence and telepresence that are operational (repeatable by anyone using proper procedures), reliable (will produce the same result at a later date), useful (can be applied), and robust. A measure of presence will aid software designers in evaluating virtual worlds and will aid human-factors engineers in designing studies which relate presence within virtual environments to performance. However, the literature

does not even offer us a useful measure of "presence," though Ne
324 in Sheridan *et al.*, 1987), Held and Durlach *(1992)*, and o.
stressed the need for an objective measure. Partially this is due to the
in measuring presence, and that only recently have advances in
environment technology motivated the need for such a measure.

The difficulty associated with measuring virtual presence or telepresen
that presence is a mental manifestation, much like the concepts "mer.
workload" and "mental model." Since presence is a mental manifestation, it
not so amenable to objective-physiological definition and measurement.
Therefore, as with mental workload and mental models, indirect measures such
as subjective reports and performance measures may form the basis for
measuring presence. As a way to approach the problem of measuring presence,
we will look closely at techniques from psychology and human factors and
indicate which techniques are good candidates for presence.

Principal determinants of presence

Sheridan (1992a) proposed that there are at least three principal determinants
of the sense of presence. The first principal determinant represents the extent
of sensory information, i.e., the bits of information concerning a salient
variable transmitted to appropriate sensors of the observer. The second
principal determinant of presence is the control of relation of sensors to
environment, e.g., the ability of the observer to modify his viewpoint for visual
parallax or visual field, or to reposition his head to modify binaural hearing, or
the ability to perform a haptic search. The third determinant of presence is the
ability to modify the physical environment, e.g., the extent of motor control to
actually change objects in the environment or their relation to one another.
These determinants may be represented as three orthogonal axes (see Figure
12-5) since the three can be varied independently in an experiment. Perceived
extent of sensory information is sometimes regarded as the only salient factor.
Sometimes the other two are lumped together as "user interaction" (Zeltzer,
1992). Figure 12-5 shows "perfect presence" as the maximum of all three,
though it is far from clear by what function "presence" is determined by
combinations of the three. It surely is not a simple vector sum.

Lines of constant information communicated are suggested in the figure to
indicate that the extent of sensory information is a much greater consumer of
information (bits) than are the two control components, "control of sensors"
and "ability to modify environment." We are not suggesting that the three
principal determinants of presence operate alone, in fact we expect them to be
task dependent. It seems that there are two major properties of tasks that
affect behavior, both subjective and objective. These Sheridan (1992a) calls
task difficulty and *degree of automation*. Task difficulty may be defined in terms
of entropy measures, such as Fitts' *index of difficulty* (Fitts, 1954). Degree of
automation means the extent to which the control of the task (the ability to
modify the environment) is automatic as opposed to being manual. There is a
scale from manual to automatic, where intermediate levels of automation are
normally called supervisory control.

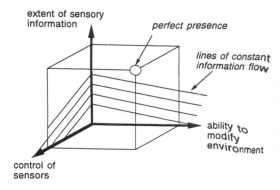

Figure 12-5 Principal determinants of sense of presence for a given task. (From Sheridan, 1992a. Presence: *Teleoperators and Virtual Environments*, Volume 1(1), MIT Press.)

Given the three independent determinants of presence we see the larger research challenge to be the determination of the dependent variables: (1) *sense of presence*, as measured by *subjective rating* and *objective measures*, (2) objective *training efficiency*, and (3) ultimate *task performance*. This mapping is illustrated (Sheridan, 1992a) in Figure 12-6. Tasks in which presence, learning, and performance interrelate take many forms in time and space and stimulus intensity (e.g., brightness, loudness, force). Sometimes the dynamic aspects of sensing and control are the most important. Sometimes it is the relation of stimuli in space.

Before one can suggest specific techniques to measure presence it is useful to approach this problem by formulating block-like diagrams representing the basic processes or stimuli which may determine or influence presence. Figure 12-7 provides a simple organizational framework for exploring the concept of

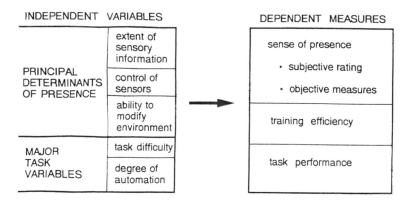

Figure 12-6 Experimental determination of presence, learning, efficiency, and performance. (From Sheridan, 1992a. Presence: *Teleoperators and Virtual Environments*, Volume 1(1), MIT Press.)

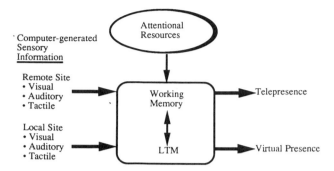

Figure 12-7 Virtual presence or telepresence occurs when attentional resources are allocated to stimulus events which are generated by a computer or associated technology. (From Barfield and Weghorst, 1993.)

presence in virtual environments (Barfield and Weghorst, 1993). The figure indicates the importance of attentional resources for virtual presence and telepresence. This simplistic model shows that incoming sensory information is processed at several levels within the human's information-processing system. When attentional resources are allocated to computer-generated sensory information, such as visual information provided by a head-mounted display, tactile information provided by tactors, or auditory information provided by head-related transfer functions, presence for that stimulus event(s) occurs.

Multidimensional aspects of presence

When discussing measurement techniques, it is important to note that presence is a multidimensional construct, i.e., the level of presence that an operator experiences in a virtual environment will be related to a number of variables which, when combined, will add to the sensation of presence. These will include hardware, software, subject, and task variables. To emphasize the multidimensional nature of presence consider the following points. Surely, presence will be related to the fidelity of the computer input to each of the human senses as well as the field of view provided by the visual display. For example, a high-resolution color display with a wide field of view should be more effective than a low-resolution monochrome screen with a small field of view in inducing presence. In addition, the update rate, the speed of the simulation, will surely influence the level of presence experienced by the virtual environment participant. For example, given a virtual world of many polygons, without sufficient computing resources, the scene will not move smoothly in response to the viewer's head movements. Such a system will greatly impair the operator's ability to use motion parallax as a depth cue and to discriminate self-movement from object movement (Piantanida *et al.*, 1993). Of course, we would expect presence to be low in such a system. However, as the update rate increases to an acceptable level (we need to determine this value), the sense of presence should correspondingly increase.

The frame rate is yet another variable which we propose will have a major influence on presence. The frame rate, which is controlled by hardware, represents the number of images the eyes see each second (Piantanida *et al.*, 1993). Preliminary evidence (Airey *et al.*, 1990) suggests that six frames per second is sufficient to produce the "virtual reality" illusion, while at least 20 frames per second is necessary for interactivity to appear to "increase rapidly." Finally, the reader should note that there is an important relationship between the frame rate and the update rate which has relevance for presence. If a system has a frame rate of 60 Hz, but an update rate of only 4 Hz, then the system will present 15 consecutive images of the same scene before the next 15 images of the same scene are presented. We postulate that a slow update rate will surely result in less presence.

Another issue which has relevance for presence is the capability of virtual environment equipment to present stimuli which match the capabilities and limits of the human's sensory systems. As an example, consider the visual field of view provided by a head-mounted display. Current commercial head-mounted displays provide a field of view in the range between 80° to 120° horizontally and 60° to 80° vertically. In comparison, the maximum field of view for humans given achromatic targets is approximately 60° of visual angle above and below the center and more than 100° to both sides. Since current systems provide smaller fields of view than we are accustomed to in the real world, what effect will these lesser fields of view have on the sense of presence in virtual environments and on performance? In fact, a large field of view may not be necessary for all tasks, especially if the task requires excessive amounts of attentional resources. However, we do not know if this holds for presence.

The resolution of the display will also have a strong influence on the level of presence experienced by the virtual environment participant. In terms of display resolution, the capabilities of current head-mounted displays lag far behind the capability of the human's visual system to resolve detail. For example, the commercially available EyePhone presents to each eye an array of 360 by 240 pixels in a field of view that measures approximately 80° horizontally and 60° vertically. Thus, each pixel subtends about 13 minutes of arc at the retina. This is roughly equivalent to having 20/200 visual acuity on the Snellen eye chart. Compare these values to the foveal visual acuity of the human, which is approximately 30 seconds of arc and 20/20 on the Snellen chart. However, display resolution is an area where technological advancements are occurring rapidly. More recent systems provide 1280×1024 pixel resolution and when used to view an image at a distance of 57 cm, produce a pixel subtense of 1.5 minutes of arc, resulting in an improved visual acuity of 20/30.

In addition to issues relating to the characteristics (e.g., resolution, update rate, etc.) of individual display technologies, we also need to carefully evaluate the many trade-offs involved in creating virtual worlds. For example, with head-mounted displays, there is a trade-off between resolution and field of view for a fixed number of pixels. Resolution is less with a large field of view, conversely, resolution is higher with a smaller field of view. A low-resolution display will reduce the viewer's ability to resolve detail and orientation of objects in the virtual environment as well as the observer's ability to resolve an object's velocity, especially those objects far away (Piantanida *et el.*, 1993). In contrast, performance for the above tasks will improve with higher resolution. However, if higher resolution is achieved at the expense of field of view, performance for tasks requiring information in the periphery will suffer. The optimum solution, of course, is high spatial resolution (4K by 4K pixels of 1 minute of arc subtended angle) and a wide field of view (at least 140° horizontally and 80° vertically) (Weghorst, 1991). However, it is not possible to produce these specifications given current technology.

Another hardware-oriented issue for presence is to determine whether presence is enhanced using a head-mounted display, or if presence for a given task will be sufficient using a stereoscopic (i.e., non-immersive) display. In fact, it is possible that not all applications will require immersive interfaces. For example, researchers at MIT have implemented a virtual environment for planning plastic surgery procedures on the human face which uses a conventional workstation CRT and a mouse-and-window interface (Pieper *et al.*, 1992). This design decision is supported by the physicians who have evaluated the system (Pieper, 1991). In contrast, virtual environment or teleoperator systems which must support manipulation or command-and-control tasks, would benefit from stereo, head-tracked, wide-field-of-view displays (Kim *et al.*, 1988; Hirose *et al.*, 1990; Zeltzer and Drucker, 1992). Specifically when a head-mounted display should be used, and for which tasks, is another important basic research question which needs to be answered.

Psychophysical and subjective measures

Subjective and psychophysical techniques provide procedures which can be used to unobtrusively assess the level of presence experienced by the operator within a virtual environment. There are two main benefits of subjective techniques: (1) they do not disrupt performance and, (2) they are relatively easy to administer. However, the validity of these techniques must be clearly demonstrated for the particular virtual environment application.

As mentioned previously, presence is a multidimensional construct. However, typical rating scales are unidimensional, i.e., they arc designed to measure one aspect of a phenomenon, say time load with the construct of mental workload. Subjective measures though need not be unidimensional. If the dimensions (factors) comprising presence are carefully qualified, subjects should be able to give reliably different responses for the different factors which will comprise presence. This has certainly been true of mental workload, and multifactor rating procedures (Sheridan and Simpson, 1979) now form the basis of mental workload applications. Multiple dimensions can also be inferred from unidimensional ratings of "psychological distance" between stimuli (Sheridan, *et al.*, 1972). A common multidimensional assessment technique for mental workload developed by NASA is shown in Table 12-2. The NASA TLX scale (Hart and Staveland, 1988) assesses work load on each of five seven-point scales and has a formal prescription for how the multiple scales may be combined to form a single measure of work load.

Table 12-2 NASA TLX scale; rating scale (from Hart and Staveland, 1988).

Title	Endpoints	Descriptions
Mental demand	low/high	How much mental and perceptual activity was required (e.g., thinking, deciding, calculating, remembering, looking, searching, etc.)? Was the task easy or demanding, simple or complex, exacting or forgiving?
Physical demand	low/high	How much physical activity was required (e.g., pushing, pulling, turning, controlling, activating, etc.)? Was the task easy or demanding, slow or brisk, slack or strenuous, restful or laborious?
temporal demand	low/high	How much time pressure did you feel due to the rate or pace at which the tasks or task elements occurred? Was the pace slow and leisurely or rapid and frantic?
Performance	perfect/failure	How successful do you think you were in accomplishing the goals of the task set by the experimenter (or yourself)? How satisfied were you with your performance in accomplishing these goals?
Effort	low/high	How hard did you have to work (mentally and physically) to accomplish your level of performance?

In Figure 12-8 we present a few sample questions to measure presence. The reader should note that a questionnaire designed to measure presence should be organized around several categories. For example, questions related to input devices, the visual display, the auditory display, tactile and kinesthetic feedback, etc., would make up such a questionnaire. Further, important issues such as the design of the questions and how they are anchored, need to be determined by pilot studies.

In order to test the relationship between subject and equipment variables in terms of presence, a series of factorial studies needs to be performed. The basic idea is to design a factorial study such as that shown in Figure 12-9, and use the responses to the above questions (or other response variables such as task performance) to serve as the dependent variable(s) to measure presence and performance. In this simplistic study, main effects for display resolution and type of display could be computed as well as the two-way interaction between display resolution and type of display.

Psychophysical measures

The next section discusses the use of psychophysical techniques to measure presence. The discussion focuses on only a few standard techniques. More complete reviews of psychophysical techniques can be found in Kling and Riggs (1971). Generally, psychophysical techniques are used to relate the physical magnitude of a stimulus with the observer's subjective rating of the stimulus magnitude. For example, a typical psychophysical study might involve asking a subject how loud a noise was and then comparing this response to a standard

----

To what extent did you experience a sense of being "really there" inside the virtual environment?

A little   A lot
1   2   3   4   5   6   7

How realistic was your interaction with the virtual objects?

A little   A lot
1   2   3   4   5   6   7

Did the objects in the computer-generated world look real?

A little   A lot
1   2   3   4   5   6   7

Was the "force feedback" provided by the hand controller realistic?

A little   A lot
1   2   3   4   5   6   7

Figure 12-8 Example of questions which could be used to subjectively measure presence within virtual environments.

physical measure of sound intensity. With the psychophysical experiment the subject is instructed in advance to make a certain type of judgment regarding the stimulus and the mathematical relationship between the stimulus and the response is obtained.

Psychophysics is interested in four types of classic problems (Snodgrass, 1975), each of which relates to presence and performance within virtual environments. The first problem is to determine whether the stimulus is there; this is a problem of detection which involves sensory thresholds. The second classic psychophysical problem is to determine what the stimulus is; this is a problem of recognition. The third psychophysical problem is to determine whether a particular stimulus is different from another stimulus; this is a

Display Resolution

                  640 x 480 (NTSC)   1280 x 1024
          Monoscopic

Type of
Display   Stereoscopic

Figure 12-9 Hypothetical 2×2 factorial experiment for the study of virtual presence as a function of display type and resolution.

problem of discrimination. Finally, the fourth problem is to determine how different a particular stimulus is from another; this is a question of scaling. As noted, each of these classic psychophysical problems has direct relevance for measuring presence and performance within virtual environments.

It is particularly important to determine how the operator's level of presence within a virtual environment varies as a function of the techniques used to produce the virtual environment. For example, does an operator "feel" more presence within a virtual environment with a lag time of say 5 ms or a lag time of 100 ms? Or, to phrase this a different way: "What is the incremental increase in presence which occurs when a system presents a lag time of 5 ms compared to a lag time of 100 ms?" A very straightforward psychophysical relationship is represented by $R = f(S)$, where R is a response, typically in the form of a verbal report ("My level of presence is 5," using a 1–7 scale), and S is a particular physical stimulus of a defined value or magnitude (say 1024×1280 pixel resolution). The response need not always be a verbal report, for example with spatialized sound the subject may be instructed to manually adjust one tone to match another in pitch.

There are two basic sets of methodologies involving psychophysical techniques. The first set of measurement techniques is relevant when the task is to determine the threshold of a stimulus. Consider the task of detecting whether a virtual object is present at a particular location within the virtual environment. As we move closer to the object's location in the virtual environment, at some distance to the object the size of the object will be such, i.e., have sufficient pixel resolution, that the operator will just be able to detect it. This is an example of an absolute threshold. However, if the task is to determine whether two virtual objects are different in texture from one another, this is an example of a difference threshold. That is, whether we can detect if they are different depends on our difference threshold for texture. It is important to recognize that detection of stimuli, including those in virtual environments, is a statistical rather than an all-or-none phenomenon. If a stimulus is presented randomly during half the trials at some fixed intensity near threshold, on some proportion p of trials the observer will correctly detect the stimulus, on $1 - p$ trials the observer will not detect the stimulus. In many studies, the stimulus intensity at which $p = 0.75$ is taken as the absolute threshold (random guessing yields 0.5).

The method of limits is a classic technique used to derive the threshold value for a stimulus. With this technique, the observers are asked whether they perceived the stimulus or not for each stimulus presentation. In terms of virtual environments, the method of limits may provide useful techniques to investigate whether the threshold for spatialized sound changes as a function of the earprint used to listen to the sound. There are three variations of this technique. In the ascending method of limits, the stimulus is set far enough below the absolute threshold so that it is never detected, then it is increased in small steps until the subject reports detecting the stimulus. In the descending method of limits, the general procedure is the same except that the stimulus is set to a value above the threshold and then decreased until the subject reports that he/she no longer detects it. Finally, with the staircase method, the subject is presented with a repeated stimulus which automatically decreases in intensity when it is detected, followed by the next trial; or the next stimulus is increased in intensity if it is not detected for a given trial.

In a typical discrimination experiment two stimuli in temporally or spatially discrete positions are presented, and the subject's task is to say whether the second stimulus is greater than, less than, or equal to the first or standard stimulus. Such techniques may be particularly useful for studies in the visualization of statistical data. The two quantities of interest are the point of subjective equality, the value at which the variable is perceived to be equal to the standard, and the value of just noticeable difference (JND) between the standard and the variable. The JND can be defined as that difference which is correctly identified 50 per cent of the time (guessing yields 33% in this case).

All psychophysics involves scaling, the assignment of numbers to stimuli according to a nominal, ordinal, interval, or a ratio scale of measurement. With nominal scaling, numbers or other symbols are used to categorize objects as different with respect to the measured response, but say nothing about how they are ordered, how far apart they are from each other, or how big they are. In ordinal scaling the stimuli can be ordered with respect to some property. For example, the fidelity of three virtual worlds rendered with three different shading algorithms (e.g., Lambertian, Phong, Blinn) can be ordered first, second, or third. However, with this technique nothing can be said about how much more "realistic" one virtual world is compared to another. With interval scaling, the assigned numbers reflect differences between stimuli, as well as order. Finally, with ratio scaling, the assigned numbers reflect both differences and ratios between stimuli.

Nominal scaling involves recognition. A subject is presented one of n stimuli and asked what he/she recognizes it to be. The subject must form an internal model of the standard stimulus then compare successive stimuli with the model. The stimuli in recognition experiments may vary along a single dimension, such as intensity, or simultaneously along several. A question of major interest is the number of different stimuli that can be correctly identified as a function of the number of dimensions along which they vary and their relative spacing along those dimensions. A consistent finding is that for unidimensional stimuli, the number that can be identified is of the order of seven. Such findings have direct relevance for the design of auditory, visual, and tactile virtual objects.

Ordinal scaling involves rank ordering of stimuli with respect to some attribute. Suppose the subject is to rank order how easy it is to rotate a virtual object given several 6 DOF input devices. He can be given subsets of k stimuli from the set of n and asked to rank within that subset, giving the rank of 1 to the input device that is easiest to use, and the rank of k to the one that is hardest to use. When $k = 2$, the method is called paired comparisons, when $k = n$ all the comparisons are made at once. When $k < n$ the ranking of a particular input device is the frequency in which it is chosen over all other input devices.

In category scaling, subjects are given some number of categories prior to the study and instructed to assign stimuli, one at a time, to one of the n

categories (so far this is nominal scaling). Subjects are instructed to make the subjective widths or intervals of categories equal. These instructions imply that responses are on an interval rather than an ordinal scale. Typically, the number of categories is odd and the subject is presented with the extremes of the stimulus range at the beginning of the study to anchor his judgments.

One ratio scaling method is magnitude estimation where the subject is presented with a standard stimulus to which the experimenter assigns a number. To subsequent stimuli of different intensities the subject is asked to assign numbers such that the ratio between the assigned number and the standard reflects the ratio between the sensation produced by the variable and the sensation produced by the standard. For example, if the standard is given the number 10, he is told to assign 20 to the stimulus twice as great with respect to the variable, and 5 to the stimulus with half the magnitude of the standard. One application of the magnitude estimation technique for the design of virtual environments may involve a comparison of real vs. computer-generated textures. In such a study, using magnitude estimation, the real texture(s) would be assigned an arbitrary value, say 10, and the subject would be asked to compare virtual images of different textures based on the standard.

Physiological measures

Ultimately, it will be important to have objective measures for presence since objective measures can often be obtained more conveniently than subjective ones. Further, some people, for example, physical scientists and engineers, tend to feel more comfortable with objective measures. The basic idea behind physiological measures for presence is that just as humans experience changes in physiological parameters in response to novel or unusual stimuli in the real world, given sufficiently realistic stimuli in a virtual environment, the human should experience similar physiological changes. According to Sanders and McCormick (1993) physiological indices can be classified by the major biological systems of the body: cardiovascular, e.g., heart rate or blood pressure; respiratory, e.g., respiration rate for oxygen; nervous, e.g., electric brain potentials or muscle activity; sensory, e.g., visual acuity, blink rate, or hearing acuity; and blood chemistry, e.g., catecholamines.

There are a number of physiological measures that might be used to investigate presence. Two of these measures will be briefly reviewed here. It has been shown that the diameter of the pupil correlates with the resource demands for a large number of diverse cognitive tasks (Kahneman et al., 1967; Wickens, 1992). As reported in Wickens (1992) these include short-term memory load, reaction time, and logical problem solving. For example, pupillary responses (dilation) during mental tasks differ as a function of mental workload, with both the amplitude and the duration of the response being dependent on workload (Beatty, 1982). However, these responses are only on the order of tenths of a millimeter, thus making measurement difficult. As a measure of presence, it may be relevant to determine if pupillary response (dilation) also occurs in response to virtual objects.

The evoked potential is a series of voltage oscillations or components that are recorded from the surface of the scalp to indicate the brain's electrical response to environmental events (Wickens, 1992). The wave form of the evoked potential recorded from the scalp, the evoked brain potential (EP), is a physiological technique to measure mental workload. As a stimulus is processed, a prominent late-positive or P300 component in the wave form of the evoked potential of the scalp is generated. Just as the P300 wave is used to assess mental workload, it may be of interest to determine if this measure also has relevance for presence.

Performance measures

As with physiological reactions, behavioral responses to exclusively virtual events may provide a measure of the degree of presence experienced within an environment. The notion here is that presence in a virtual environment necessitates a sense that the participant no longer inhabits the physical space but now occupies the computer-generated virtual environment as "place" (Barfield and Weghorst, 1993). Of particular interest are responses to virtual events that directly contradict the appropriate response to a concurrent natural world event. An example scenario suitable to this approach would be "mixed" natural and virtual environments in which "perceptual capture" across environments affects performance on simple tasks. Degree of presence should be predictive of the predominant direction of capture. This will be due to the suspension of disbelief, meaning that the operator in a virtual environment must imagine that the world portrayed is real, without being jarred out of this belief by the world's behavior (Bates, 1992). For example, a low-resolution display with a small field of view will interfere with the extent to which a display system is transparent to the operator more so than a high-resolution display with a wide field of view (Held and Durlach, 1992), in essence interfering with the operator's suspension of disbelief. One type of measure that has face validity is response to unexpected and perhaps threatening stimuli (Held and Durlach, 1992). If a virtual object is suddenly seen (and/or heard binaurally) to be on a collision course with one's head, does the subject blink, or duck? If the subject is controlling a virtual automobile displayed to be heading for a crash, or a virtual aircraft showing signs of stalling, does the operator take immediate appropriate action? If a subject is controlling a virtual baseball bat, does the subject take immediate actions if the ball is thrown towards his head? Another type of measure might be a socially conditioned response to virtual social encounters: unpremeditated reaching out to grasp something being handed over, or to shake hands or cheer, or an utterance of "Hello," "I beg your pardon," or "Gesundheit," as appropriate.

There is also the question of the effect of prolonged exposure to virtual environments on the human's ability to re-adapt to the real world, especially when the stabilization of the virtual environment is poor. Are participants disoriented after a given length of exposure to virtual environments? One possible method to test the effect of prolonged exposure to virtual environments is to administer a battery of cognitive and psychomotor tests to the subjects after they "come out" of a virtual world. The independent variable(s) could be the length of exposure to a virtual environment, display characteristics, etc. The following represent the type of dependent variables that could be used to access disorientation: (1) rotary pursuit tasks, measured using eye–hand coordination, (2) body balance, measured using an infrared stability platform, and (3) visual acuity, perception of motion, motion prediction, and spatial relations, all measured using psychometric tests.

EMPIRICAL STUDIES OF PRESENCE

There have been some attempts to study presence empirically, mainly using subjective measures of the type discussed in the previous section. Slater and Usoh (1993) have used the technique of case-control experimental studies to isolate various contributory factors to presence in a systematic way. In a case-control study, subjects are randomly assigned to different groups. The groups all undergo an experiment carried out under identical conditions, except that there is a systematic variation of a control (or independent) variable across the groups. Here, some measure of "presence" is the response (or dependent) variable, and the purpose is to see if there are differences between the measured response for the groups. If there are such differences, and they are statistically significant, then—other things being equal—it can be inferred that the independent variable accounts for the variation in the response—tentatively, the independent variable can be used to explain the response, and hence may be regarded as a causative factor.

The application context of the work of Slater and Usoh has been architectural walkthrough, where it was particularly important to establish that an immersive virtual environment system could deliver a sense of presence in virtual buildings to participants such as architects and their clients. Slater and Usoh have distinguished between external and internal factors contributing to presence, and the relationship between presence, the virtual body and the proprioceptive system. We discuss each of these in turn, beginning with the subjective measures that they have used throughout their studies. This is followed by a discussion of supporting evidence from other studies, and a conclusion concerning the relationship between presence and enjoyment.

Subjective measures

Three aspects contributing to the sense of presence were considered by Slater and Usoh. First, the most obvious aspect of this state of consciousness is the sense of "being there" in the environment portrayed by the virtual reality system. Second, a high sense of presence in the virtual environment should lead to the participant experiencing objects and processes in the virtual world as (temporarily) more "real" than those aspects of the real world in which the virtual environment experience is actually embedded (i.e., the physical area of the virtual environment laboratory). Should this happen, the participant is likely to momentarily "forget" about the external physical world, and treat the virtual world as real. Third, having experienced a virtual environment, how

Table 12-3   Three questions relating to the sense of presence.

1. Being there	2. The presenting reality	3. Seeing/visiting
Please rate your sense of being there in the computer-generated world . . .	To what extent were there times during the experience when the computer-generated world became the "reality" for you, and you almost forgot about the "real world" outside?	When you think back about your experience, do you think of the computer-generated world more as something that you saw, or more as somewhere that you visited?
In the computer-generated world I had a sense of "being there" . . .	*There were times during the experience when the computer-generated world became more real or present for me compared to the "real world" . . .*	*The computer-generated world seems to me to be more like . . .*
1. not at all	1. at no time	1. something that I saw
.	.	.
.	.	.
.	.	.
7. very much	7. almost all of the time	7. somewhere that I visited

does the participant remember it—is it more like a place that was visited, or is it more like images that were seen? (This can be used, perhaps, to distinguish the kind of "presence" or involvement due to watching an engrossing film, compared to presence in an immersive environment.)

Based on these ideas a questionnaire was constructed that employs a seven-point ordinal scale (Slater and Usoh, 1993) as shown in Table 12-3. The results of these three questions can be used separately, and also combined into one overall scale, for example, by taking the median of the three answers given by the respondent as the combined measure. The problem with an ordinal scale is that it is statistically unsound to use the results in, for example, a multiple-regression analysis as the dependent variable—only an interval or ratio scale is suitable for this purpose. A conservative way to combine the three scores, to allay the statistical objection, is to only take answers above a certain minimum (for example, a score of at least 6) as indicating a "positive" result, and then count the number of such positive results. The combined score would now be a genuine count (from 0 to 3), and the resulting variable could be used in a logistic (or binary) regression analysis. This was the technique adopted by Slater and Usoh.

External and internal factors

Earlier, we discussed the principal determinants of presence. We refine this here by considering distinct classes of such determinants that we refer to as "external" and "internal" (Slater and Usoh, 1994a). *External* factors are all those resulting from the virtual environment system itself—that is the hardware components, peripherals, software and models used to generate the experience. For example, the extent of sensory information is such an external factor—it is wholly determined by the hardware and software of the virtual environment system. In particular, the size of the field of view, whether or not there is the capability for binaural auditory output, the type of graphics illumination model used, the frame and update rates, are all products of the hardware and software systems. However, the individual participant does not simply absorb the sensory data offered by the virtual environment display, but (unconsciously) filters these through the characteristics of his or her particular sensory, perceptual and cognitive systems: the specific characteristics of sight, hearing, mental models, and beliefs of that individual person. Just as in everyday reality, different people can experience identical events in quite a different manner from one another. These are the *internal* determinants, ranging from structural aspects, such as whether the person has the physical capability for binocular vision, to psychological aspects, such as the typical mental patterns associated with how they process sensory data.

A particularly strong relationship was found between subjective scores on presence and a very simple model relating to internal processing of sensory information. This "neuro-linguistic programming" model (for example, Dilts *et al.*, 1979) holds that people tend to rely differentially on visual (V), auditory (A), and kinesthetic (K) sensory data to construct their models of reality, and to have a preference for one of these representation systems. For example, the extent of sound in the environment might be essential for one person to function effectively, to "make sense" of the world, and yet nearly irrelevant for another. Should this be the case, a visually rich but auditorially poor virtual environment is likely to induce a higher sense of presence for those who are visually dominant compared to those who are more auditorially dominant. Slater and Usoh attempted to test this hypothesis in two different experiments. In the first (1994a) they used essays written by subjects after their virtual environment experience, and counted the numbers of visual, auditory and kinesthetic references and predicates per sentence, in order construct scores possibly relating this measure to presence. A multiple regression analysis relating the ordinal scale 1 of Table 12-3 to these V, A, and K variables found a very high and significant correlation, and in particular that, other things being equal, the higher the V score the higher the presence, and the higher the A score the lower the presence (K will be discussed later). This was to be expected since the virtual environment system provided almost exclusively visual information, with only a small amount of sound.

A problem with this first experiment was that an assessment of sensory preference was obtained from essays written after the virtual environment experience of the experimental subjects. A second and more rigorous study (1994b) used a questionnaire to obtain indicators of sensory preference several days before the actual virtual environment experience. Here the combined measure of presence was used (counting the number of 6 or 7 scores across the three questions of Table 12-3), and a logistic regression analysis once again revealed a strong correlation with the V, A, and K scores.

Such analysis could be important for the development of virtual environments, since it allows the possibility of tailoring environments to the needs of particular groups of users. For example, a profession likely to have strong visual preference (maybe architecture) might not require much auditory input in order to obtain a sufficient sense of presence for their tasks. On the other hand, the model could be used to explain failures of systems to deliver presence: for example, where a great deal of attention had been paid by system designers to generating a very high degree of visual realism for a group of users for whom the V stream of data is not particularly useful without strong auditory correlates.

The virtual body

The representation of the human in the virtual environment may be of critical importance. Held and Durlach (1992) argue, in the context of teleoperator systems, that important requirements for enhancing telepresence are that:

(1) the operator can view effector movements—for example, move his/her hands and see them move;
(2) there is a high correlation between movements of the operator sensed directly and the actions of the slave robot;
(3) there is an identification between the operator's own body with that of the slave robot;
(4) there is a similarity in visual appearance between the operator and slave robot.

If we apply these ideas in the context of immersive virtual environments, a representation of the human body and its activity inside the virtual environments is required, and we call this the "virtual body" (VB). The VB is slaved to movements of the participant's real body, in so far as these can be inferred from the tracking devices employed. Badler *et al.* (1993) have discussed the technical problems associated with the mapping from human movements to the VB.

In the first experiment discussed by Slater and Usoh above (1994a), the subjects were divided into two groups, an experimental group which had a full-body representation, and a control group where the VB representation was simply a 3D arrow with position and orientation slaved to (right) hand movements. There were 17 subjects in this study, eight in the control group and nine in the experimental group. The full VB representation responded to movements and orientation of the hand-held 3D mouse (this was used to determine virtual arm and hand movements and orientation), and the HMD tracker was also used to determine whole-body orientation. This independent variable (whether or not the subject had a full VB representation) proved to be statistically significant in the regression model discussed above, and enhanced the reported sense of presence. Moreover there was an important relationship between this and the participants' "kinesthetic" representation system. A preference for this system would be indicated by frequent references by the subjects in their essays to "feelings" and to movements of the body or limbs. It was found that, other things being equal, for those in the experimental group the higher the degree of kinesthetic preference the higher the presence score, whereas for those in the control group, the higher the degree of kinesthetic preference, the lower the sense of presence. These results do tie in with points (1)–(4) above: those subjects with a high kinesthetic preference perhaps need a VB with behavior that correlates highly with their own sensed movements, and one with which they can identify.

The question of "identification" is crucial—it may be important to have a VB, but if participants reject it then this may be worse, with respect to presence, than not having one at all. For example, a minority of subjects who notice that their virtual left arm cannot be moved by moving their real left arm (since there is no tracking information) have one of two observable and extreme reactions: they become dissociated from the arm, or even from the whole VB, making comments similar to those reported by Oliver Sacks (1985) when patients have lost their sense of proprioception; or alternatively, they carry out behaviors to enforce a match between their proprioceptive feedback and the visual information—that is, matching their real left arm with the virtual left arm. The second (1994b) experiment by Slater and Usoh included a sub-study to explicitly examine this phenomenon: the virtual left arm was programmed to mirror the behavior of the virtual right arm (which was slaved to the tracking device). Four out of the 24 subjects matched their real left arms to the behavior of the virtual ones. The only difference between these subjects and the remainder was that they had a significantly higher average score on the K representation system (more than double).

The importance of participants associating with their VBs was highlighted in a study on navigation (Slater *et al.*, 1994c). Here, two different methods were used for moving at ground level through the virtual environment, in the context of architectural walkthrough. The control group utilized the hand-held pointing device and pressed a button to move in the direction that their virtual right hand was pointing. The experimental group used a method where they could "walk in place," and a pattern recognizer analyzing the stream of data from the HMD distinguished between such walking in place behavior from any other kind of behavior. When it determined that the walking in place behavior was occurring, it would move the subject forward in the direction of gaze. (Both groups were able to take a few real steps, with the limitation imposed only by the effective tracker range.) The point about the experimental group, is that their bodily sensations of "walking" would be more closely matched to the visual information indicating vection, than would have been the case with those in the "point and button press" control group. The same measure of presence was used as discussed above, and all subjects were asked about their degree of association with the VB (a response on an ordinal seven-point scale). The statistical analysis revealed that for those in the experimental group, the higher the association with the VB the higher the sense of presence, whereas there was no such relation for those in the control group.

The VB used in these experiments was a crude polygonal representation of a real human body. How closely, if at all, does the VB representation have to match that of a real body? Point (4) above suggests that there should be a close relationship, at least in the teleoperator context. There is some evidence to support this, although from quite a different virtual environment paradigm—a "second person" or "out of the body" system. A survey was carried out by

Carrie Heeter (1992) of 160 people who used the BattleTech Center in Chicago. In this system, called Enter 3-D Second Person VR, a video camera is pointed at the participants who see themselves in a stereo 3D scene with which they are able to interact. They accomplish this by moving their real bodies, and the chroma keyed video signal overlays their body on the 3D scenes, thus showing a faithful reproduction of their real appearance in a virtual world. When their video representation touches a computer-generated object, this may react—for example, in an undersea simulation an octopus could be grabbed and carried around. Heeter reports that "Of those who tried the demos, 71% considered the 'being on the screen' to be their real self, rating their screen self either more real than the 'being the camera pointed at' (29%) or as real as the 'being the camera pointed at' (42%). Only 26% felt that the being the camera pointed at was their only real self." Here there is a clear identification with the virtual body, even though it is not located at the same physical place as the real body that is the center of the sensory experience. Interestingly, some of the subjects were shown the full video representation of themselves, and others were shown only its shadow silhouette. They were all asked to rate their enjoyment on an 11-point (0 to 10) scale, with 10 being "very enjoyable." Those who saw the silhouette as self-representation rated the experience as 5.8 on the average, whereas those who saw the full video representation had an average rating of 8.0.

However, this is only really scant evidence of the need for a VB representation that looks like the real body. A more rigorous experiment requires several control groups, where other representations are used that, while functionally consistent and learnable, do not look like the human body. Perhaps it is equally possible and enjoyable for people to adopt the appearance of a tiger, provided that the mapping from real movements to virtual movements is quickly learned and transparent. Indeed, Heeter quotes Jaron Lanier as expressing surprise at the "ease with which people adapted to inhabiting non-human shapes, such as lobsters, in virtual worlds."

Continuity of environment

We have seen that presence may be enhanced by a suitable VB representation that locates the participant in the virtual environment. If there is identification with the VB, and the VB is portrayed to the senses as being in the virtual environment, then the participant is likely to generate a (suspension of dis-) belief that he or she is in that environment. However, a further condition must be that the environment itself is capable of being considered as a place—that is, it is relatively constant and continuous through time. Evidence for this has come from an interesting and unusual study borrowing a technique often used by anthropologists and sociologists studying a community—ethnography. This requires detailed observation, insofar as possible without prejudgments, of the target community in action. "The principal goal of ethnographic reporting is to share what was observed . . . the description of one culture with another, in this case, that of field geologists with virtual presence engineers and scientists . . ." (McGreevy, 1992). McGreevy of NASA Ames Research Center carried out such a study of two field geologists working in a Mars-like terrain, in the Mojave Desert in Southern California.

McGreevy found that the "continuity of continuous existence is the glue that binds the will, via locomotion and manipulation, to predictable translation and rotation relative to objects within a relatively predictable environment." That is, the geologists were able to use their bodies in a familiar and predictable way in relationship to the environment, and the environment itself was stable and continuous through time, so that constant and repeatable relationships could be established between behavior and results. To maintain a sense of presence in a virtual environment, a similar continuity and stability must be established—it would be impossible to maintain presence in a location which changed in a manner that could not be learned and predicted—in other words, the environment must be "place like." This is similar to the idea of Barfield and Weghorst (1993) who write that ". . . presence in a virtual environment necessitates a belief that the participant no longer inhabits the physical space but now occupies the computer generated virtual environment as a 'place'." It also connects with question 3 of Table 12-3 above.

Enjoyment

As was pointed out at the start of this chapter, at the moment we do not know how presence may contribute to task performance—other than in the sense of the fairly obvious, such as the need for continuous feedback. Can an architect really "know" what it will be like to be in a building only by looking at external screen images of it, even with high-resolution and accurate lighting models? Almost certainly presence is necessary for those applications that do require participants to be surrounded by the environment, rather than looking at it from the outside. An interesting secondary connection between presence and task performance, however, has emerged from an experiment reported in Barfield and Weghorst (1993). Weghorst found that presence may be positively correlated with a subjective reporting of "enjoyment." If this is the case, since enjoyment is likely to be associated with efficiency of task performance, it would be evidence for a positive association between presence and task performance.

In this study 86 subjects undertook two immersive interactive fly-throughs of complex environments, and full data was subsequently available from 70 subjects. Presence was measured subjectively on ten-point scales with three questions that proved to be highly correlated: The sense of being there, the sense of inclusion in the virtual world, and the sense of presence in the virtual world. Factors found to be significantly correlated with at least one of these are shown in Table 12-4.

From an analysis of the inter-correlations amongst the variables, Weghorst concluded that all three indicators of presence were predictive of "overall enjoyment," and that this in itself could be an important reason for enhancement of the sense of presence. This was further supported in a second study of 69 children involved in building a virtual world, where it was found that responses to "Did you feel you were part of the virtual world?" were

Table 12-4 Factors affecting presence within an immersive virtual environment.

Positive correlations	Negative correlations
Ability to get around	
Display color quality	image clarity
Ease of navigation	
Orientation within the virtual world	being lost
Comfort with computers	
Display comfort	
Introspection	
Overall enjoyment	
Engaging	

From Weghorst, HITL, University of Washington.

significantly and positively correlated with "How much did you enjoy designing and building a virtual world?"

Enjoyment is not only a worthy cause in itself, but may be economically as well as psychologically beneficial. Further research would be needed to verify the positive association between enjoyment and presence, and indeed the direction of causality.

SUMMARY

This chapter focused on describing and defining virtual presence and telepresence in the context of virtual environments. As discussed throughout the chapter, relatively little empirical work has been done to determine how presence should be conceptualized, manipulated, and measured. This chapter (and book) is a first step in that direction. It is hoped that the material contained in this chapter will motivate additional thinking on this topic and, in addition, lead to empirical work on determining what factors produce presence within virtual environments, and when presence is a benefit or possibly a detriment to performance.

ACKNOWLEDGMENTS

This work was supported in part by NHK (Japan Broadcasting Corp.), National Science Foundation Grants (DMC-8857851, CDA-8806866, IRI-8712772, DARPA/Rome Laboratories), the Office of Naval Research, equipment grants from Apple Computer, Silicon Graphics and Hewlett-Packard, and a software donation from Alias Research Corporation. M. Slater's contribution is supported in part by the London Parallel Applications Centre, the UK Department of Trade and Industry, and Science and Engineering

Research Council. We thank Dav Lion and Craig Rosenberg for their contributions to the "augmented reality" section.

REFERENCES

Airey, J. M., Ruhlf, J. H., and Brooks, F. P. (1990) Towards image realism with interactive update rates in complex virtual building environments, *Proc. 1990 Symp. in Interactive 3D Graphics*, March 25–28, Snowbird, UT; also (1990) *Computer Graphics*, **24**, 41–50

Badler, N., Hollick, M. J., and Granieri, J. P. (1993) Real-time control of a virtual human using minimal sensors, *Presence: Teleoperators and Virtual Environments*, **2-1**, 86

Badler, N. I. and Webber, B. L. (1991) Animation from instructions, in N. Badler *et al.* (Eds), *Making Them Move: Mechanics, Control and Animation of Articulated Figures*, San Mateo, CA: Morgan Kaufmann, pp. 51–93

Bajura, M., Fuchs, H., and Ohbuchi, R. (1992) Merging virtual objects with the real world, *Computer Graphics*, **26**, 203–10

Barfield, W. and Weghorst, S. (1993) The sense of presence within virtual environments: a conceptual framework, in G. Salvendy and M. Smith (Eds), *Human Computer Interaction: Software and Hardware Interfaces*, Amsterdam: Elsevier, pp. 699–704

Bates, J. (1992) Virtual reality, art, and entertainment, *Presence: Teleoperators and Virtual Environments*, **1**, 133–8

Beatty, J. (1982) Task-evoked pupillary response, processing load, and the structure of processing resources, *Psychol. Bull.*, **91**, 276–92

Blanchard, C., Burgess, S., Harvill, Y., Lanier, J., Lasko, A., Oberman, M., and Teitel, M. (1990) Reality built for two: a virtual reality tool, *Proc. 1990 Symp. in Interactive 3D Graphics*, March 25–28, Snowbird, UT, also (1990) *Computer Graphics*, **24**, 35–6

Cornsweet, T. N. (1970) *Visual Perception*, San Diego: Harcourt Brace Jovanovich

Deering, M. (1992) High Resolution Virtual Reality, *Computer Graphics*, **26**, 195–202

Dilts, R., Grinder, J., Bandler, R., DeLozier, J., and Cameran-Bandler, L. (1979) *Neuro-Linguistic Programming I*, Meta Publications

Ellis, S. R. (1991) Nature and origins of virtual environments: a bibliographical essay, *Computing Systems Eng.*, **2**, 321–47

Feiner, S. (1993) Virtual worlds research at Columbia University, *Virtual Reality Systems*, **2**, 63–6

Fisher, S. S., McGreevy, M., Humphries, J., and Robinett, W. (1986) Virtual environment display system, in *Proc. 1986 ACM Workshop on Interactive Graphics*, October 23–24, pp. 77–87

Fitts, P. M. (1954) The information capacity of the human motor system in controlling the amplitude of movement, *J. Exp. Psychol.*, **47**, 381–91

Foley, J. D., VanDam, A., Feiner, S. K., and Hughes, J. F. (1990) *Computer Graphics: Principles and Practice*, Reading, MA: Addison-Wesley

Grind, W. A. (1986) Vision and the graphical simulation of spatial structure, *Proc. 1986 ACM Workshop on Interactive Graphics*, October 23–24, pp. 197–235

Hart, S. G. and Staveland, L. E. (1988) Development of NASA-TLS: results of empirical and theoretical workload, in P. A. Hancock and N. Meshkayi (Eds), *Human Mental Workload*, Amsterdam: North-Holland

Harvard Computation Laboratory (1985) *Proc. of a Symp. on Large-Scale Calculating Machinery*, January, Cambridge, MA: MIT Press

Heeter, C. (1992) Being there: the subjective experience of presence, *Presence: Teleoperators and Virtual Environments*, **1**, 262–71

Held, R. M. and Durlach, N. I. (1992) Telepresence, *Presence: Teleoperators and Virtual Environments*, **1**, 109–12

Hirose, M., Myoi, T., Liu, A., and Stark, L. (1990) Object manipulation in virtual environment, *6th Symp. on Human Interface*, October 24–26, Tokyo, pp. 571–6

Hochberg, J. (1986) Representation of motion and space in video and cinematic displays, in K. Boff *et al.* (Eds), *Handbook of Perception and Human Performance, vol. 1*, New York: Wiley, pp. 22-1–22-64

Howard, I. P. (1986) The perception of posture, self motion, and the visual vertical, in K. Boff *et al.* (Eds), *Handbook of Perception and Human Performance, vol. 1*, New York: Wiley, pp. 18-1–18-62

Howard, I. P. (1991) Spatial vision within egocentric and exocentric frames of reference, in S. R. Ellis (Ed.), *Pictorial Communication in Real and Virtual Environments*, London: Taylor and Francis, pp. 338–58

Johnston, R. S. (1987) The SIMNET visual system, in *Proc. Ninth ITEC Conf.*, November 30–December 2, Washington, DC, pp. 264–73

Kahneman, D., Beatty, J., and Pollock, I. (1967) Perceptual deficits during a mental task, *Science*, **157**, 218–19

Kim, W. S., Liu, A., Matsunaga, K., and Start, L. (1988) A helmet mounted display for telerobotics, in *Proc. IEEE COMPCON*, San Francisco, CA

Kling, J. W. and Riggs, L. A. (1971) *Experimental Psychology*, 3rd edn, New York: Holt, Rinehart and Winston

Krueger, M. W. (1991) *Artificial Reality II*, Reading, MA: Addison-Wesley

Lavroff, N. (1992) *Virtual Reality Playhouse*, Waite Group Press

Lee, P., Wei, S., Zhao, J., and Badler, N. (1990) Strength guided motion, *Computer Graphics*, **24**, 253–62

Lion, D., Rosenberg, C., and Barfield, W. (1993) Overlaying three-dimensional computer graphics with stereoscopic live motion video: applications for virtual environments, *Proc. of the Society for Information Displays*, pp. 483–6

Mace, W. M. (1977) James J. Gibson's strategy for perceiving: ask not what's inside your head, but what your head's inside of, in R. Shaw and J. Bransford (Eds), *Perceiving, Acting, and Knowing: Toward an Ecological Psychology*, Hillsdale, NJ: Lawrence Erlbaum Associates, pp. 43–65

McGreevy, M. W. (1992) The presence of field geologists in Mars-like terrain, *Presence: Teleoperators and Virtual Environments*, **1**, 375–403

McKenna, M., Atherton, D., and Sabiston, B. (1990) *Grinning Evil Death*, Computer Animation, MIT Media Lab

McKenna, M. D. and Zeltzer, D. (1990) Dynamic simulation of autonomous legged locomotion, in *Proc. ACM SIGGRAPH 90*, August 6–10, Dallas, TX, pp. 29–38

Milgram, P., Drascis, D., and Grodski, D. (1991) Enhancement of 3-D video displays by means of superimposed stereo-graphics, *Proceedings of the Human Factors Society 35th Annual Meeting*, pp. 1457–61

Noll, A. M. (1972) Man-machine tactile communication, *SID Journal*, July/August

Piantanida, T., Boman, D. K., and Gille, J. (1993) Human perceptual issues and virtual reality, *Virtual Reality*, **1**, 43–52

Pieper, S. (1991) CAPS: computer-aided plastic surgery, *Ph.D. Thesis*, Massachusetts Institute of Technology

Pieper, S., Rosen, J., and Zeltzer, D. (1992) Interactive graphics for plastic surgery: a task-level analysis and implementation, in *Proc. 1992 Symposium on Interactive 3D Graphics*, March 29–April 1, Cambridge, MA: ACM Press, pp. 127–34

Ridsdale, G., Hewitt, S., and Calvert, T. (1986) The interactive specification of human animation, in *Proc. Graphics Interface 86*, Toronto, Ont., pp. 121–30

Robinett, W. (1992) Synthetic experience: a proposed taxonomy, *Presence: Teleoperators and Virtual Environments*, **1**, 229–47

Rolfe, J. M. and Staples, K. J. (Eds) (1986) *Flight Simulation*, Cambridge, UK: Cambridge University Press

Sacks, O. (1985) *The Man Who Mistook His Wife for a Hat*, Picador

Sanders, M. S. and McCormick, E. J. (1993) *Human Factors in Engineering and Design*, 7th edn, New York: McGraw-Hill

Sheridan, T. B. (1992a) Musings on telepresence and virtual presence, *Presence: Teleoperators and Virtual Environments*, **1**, 120–5

Sheridan, T. B. (1992b) Defining our terms, *Presence: Teleoperators and Virtual Environments*, **1**, 272–4

Sheridan, T. B., Kruser, D. S., and Deutsch, S. (Eds) (1987) Human factors in automated and robotic space systems, *Proc. of a Symp.*, Washington, DC: National Research Council, p. 324

Sheridan, T. B., Romney, A. K., and Nerlove, S. B. (1972) *Multidimensional Scaling: Volume I, Theory*, New York: Seminar Press

Sheridan, T. B. and Simpson, R. W. (1979) Towards the definition and measurement of mental workload of transport pilots, flight transportation, *Man-Machine Systems Laboratory Technical Report*, DOT-OS-70055, Cambridge, MA: MIT Press

Slater, M. and Usoh, M. (1993) Presence in immersive virtual environments, *IEEE Virtual Reality Int. Symp.*, pp. 90–6

Slater, M. and Usoh, M. (1994a) Representation systems, perceptual position and presence in virtual environments, *Presence: Teleoperators and Virtual Environments*, **2.3**, 221–34

Slater, M., Usoh, M., and Steed, A. (1994b) Depth of presence in virtual environments, *Presence: Teleoperators and Virtual Environments*, **3.2**, 130–44

Slater, M., Usoh, M., and Steed, A. (1994c) Steps and ladders in virtual reality software and technology, *Proc. of the VRST '94 Conference, Sponsors ACM/SIGCHI and ISS*, Singapore, G. Singh, S. K. Feiner, and D. Thalmann (Eds), World Scientific, pp. 45–54

Snodgrass, J. G. (1975) Psychophysics, in B. Scharf (Ed.), *Experimental Sensory Psychology*, Scott, Foresman Co.

Sturman, D. J. (1992) *Whole-hand input, Ph.D. Thesis*, Massachusetts Institute of Technology

Turvey, M. T., Fitch, H. L., and Tuller, B. (1982) The problems of degrees of freedom and context-conditioned variability, in J. A. S. Kelso (Ed.), *Human Motor Behavior*, Hillsdale, NJ: Lawrence Erlbaum Associates, pp. 239–52

Vicente, K. J. and Rasmussen, J. (1990) Mediating direct perception in complex work domains, *Ecol. Psychol.*, **2**, 207–49

Vickers, D. L. (1982) Head-mounted display terminal, in J. B. K. Booth (Ed.), *Tutorial: Computer Graphics*, 2nd edn, IEEE Computer Society, pp. 164–71

Webster's II Dictionary (1984) Riverside Publishing Co.

Weghorst, S. (1991) Inclusive biomedical visualization, *Human Interface Technology Technical Report*, no. HITL-R-91-2

Wells, M. J. (1992) Virtual reality: technology, experience, assumptions, *Human Factors Soc. Bull.*, **35**, 1–3

Wenzel, E. M. and Foster, S. H. (1990) Realtime digital synthesis of virtual acoustic environments, in *Proc. 1990 Symp. in Interactive 3D Graphics*, March 25–28, Snowbird, UT, pp. 139–40

Wickens, C. (1992) *Engineering Psychology and Human Performance*, 2nd edn, Harper Collins

Wilhelms, J., Moore, M., and Skinner, R. (1988) Dynamic animation: interaction and control, *The Visual Computer*, **4**, 283–95

Zeltzer, D. (1991) Task level graphical simulation: abstraction, representation and control, in N. Badler *et al.* (Ed.,) *Making Them Move: Mechanics, Control and Animation of Articulated Figures*, San Mateo, CA: Morgan Kaufmann, pp. 3–33

Zeltzer, D. (1992) Autonomy, interaction, and presence, *Presence: Teleoperators and Virtual Environments*, **1**, 127–32

Zeltzer, D. (1993) Virtual actors and virtual environments: defining, modeling and reasoning about motor skills, in L. McDonald and J. Vince (Eds), *Interacting with Virtual Environments*, New York: Wiley

Zeltzer, D. and Drucker, S. (1992) A virtual environment system for mission planning, in *Proc. 1992 IMAGE VI Conf.*, July 14–17, Phoenix, AZ, pp. 125–34

Zeltzer, D. and Johnson, M. (1991) Motor planning: specifying and controlling the behavior of autonomous animated agents, *J. Visualization Computer Anim.*, **2**, 74–80

Zeltzer, D., Pieper, S., and Sturman, D. (1989) An integrated graphical simulation platform, in *Proc. Graphics Interface 89*, June 19–23, pp. 266–74

13

Cognitive Issues in Virtual Reality

CHRISTOPHER D. WICKENS AND POLLY BAKER

Virtual reality involves the creation of multisensory experience of an environment (its space and events) through artificial, electronic means; but that environment incorporates a sufficient number of features of the non-artificial world that it is experienced as "reality." The cognitive issues of virtual reality are those that are involved in *knowing* and understanding about the virtual environment (cognitive: to perceive and to know). The knowledge we are concerned with in this chapter is both short term (Where am I in the environment? What do I see? Where do I go and how do I get there?), and long term (What can and do I learn about the environment as I see and explore it?).

FEATURES OF VIRTUAL REALITY

Given the recent interest in virtual reality as a concept (Rheingold, 1991; Wexelblat, 1993; Durlach and Mavor, 1994), it is important to consider that virtual reality is not, in fact, a unified thing, but can be broken down into a set of five features, any one of which can be present or absent to create a greater sense of reality. These features consist of the following five points.

1. Three-dimensional (perspective and/or stereoscopic) viewing vs. two-dimensional planar viewing. (Sedgwick, 1986; Wickens *et al.*, 1989). Thus, the geography student who views a 3D representation of the environment has a more realistic view than one who views a 2D contour map.

2. Dynamic vs. static display. A video or movie is more real than a series of static images of the same material.

3. Closed-loop (interactive or learner-centered) vs. open-loop interaction. A more realistic *closed-loop* mode is one in which the learner has control over what aspect of the learning "world" is viewed or visited. That is, the learner is an active navigator as well as an observer.

4. Inside-out (ego-referenced) vs. outside-in (world-referenced) frame-of-reference. The more realistic inside-out frame-of-reference is one in which the image of the world on the display is viewed from the perspective of the point of ego-reference of the user (that point which is being manipulated by the control). This is often characterized as the property of "immersion." Thus, the explorer of a virtual undersea environment will view that world from a perspective akin to that of a camera placed on the explorer's head; rather than, for example, a fixed camera pointing north, or one mounted behind the user, following the user's track, but not his or her momentary orientation. For conventional navigational displays, the ego-referenced vs. world-referenced contrast has an analog with fixed north-up vs. rotating track-up electronic maps (Baty *et al.*, 1974; Harwood and Wickens, 1991; Aretz, 1991; Wickens *et al.*, 1994). It is important to note that the frame of reference can be varied independently for orientation and location.

5. Multimodal interaction. Virtual environments employ a variety of techniques for user input, including speech recognition and gestures, either sensed through a "DataGlove" (Zimmerman *et al.*, 1987) or captured by camera. The user experiences the virtual environment through enhanced forms of feedback. These can include the proprioceptive or kinesthetic feedback from body motion, tactile feedback when encountering virtual objects of varying surface textures (Minsky *et al.*, 1990), force feedback felt from a joystick or other hand grip (Brooks *et al.*, 1990), and the auditory feedback produced by sophisticated techniques of 3D localized sound (Begault and Wenzel, 1992). Compared with keyboards and mice, the rich interaction possible in virtual environments is closer to the way in which we interact with the physical world.

These five elements, summarized in Table 13-1, are not entirely independent of one another. For example, the frame-of-reference feature has a different meaning if the environment is static than if it is dynamic. However, it is also easy to see how each "layer" of realism can be peeled away or added as desired. In this regard, it is also important to realize that each layer brings with it added costs, or added sources of unreliability in equipment maintenance. As a consequence, prior to implementation in operational systems, these costs should be justified in terms of their performance or education benefit. Since there has been little cognitive research carried out on "complete" virtual

Table 13-1 Components of virtual reality.

	Less real	More real
Dimensionality	2D	3D
Motion	static	dynamic
Interaction	open loop	closed loop
Frame of reference	outside-in (God's eye)	inside-out (user's eye)
	world-referenced	ego-referenced
Multi-modal interaction	limited	multi-modal

environment systems with all features present, our emphasis in this chapter will be on research that has focused on subsets of the features.

Uses of virtual environment systems

The importance of parsing virtual environment systems into their components is that this provides the designer more flexibility to "tool" or configure a system in a way that is most appropriate for a particular use. If some components are more important than others in a given context, then greater emphasis can be placed on their implementation, while other, less critical ones can be approximated, or abandoned altogether. This will be a particularly valuable exercise if the abandoned component is one that would bring with it high costs.

As with any complex technology, implementing this approach with virtual environments requires an understanding of the task goals of the user and the strengths and weaknesses of the user's perceptual system so that the system may be designed appropriately. In the following, we describe four general categories of tasks for which virtual environment systems have intended to serve, each of which may highlight the importance of certain virtual environment features to a greater or lesser extent.

1. On-line performance. Here we refer to systems where the virtual environment is providing the operator with direct manipulation capabilities in a remote, or non-viewable environment. This may describe the operation of a remote manipulator, such as an undersea robot, space shuttle arm (McKinnon and Kruk, 1991), or hazardous waste handler (Sheridan, 1987, 1992), the control of a remotely piloted vehicle (McGovern, 1991), or the task of navigating through a virtual database to obtain a particular item (Newby, 1992). Three general human performance concerns are relevant in these environments: (1) closed-loop perceptual motor performance should be good (that is, errors should be small, reactions should be fast, and tracking of moving targets should be stable); (2) situation awareness should be high (Sarter and Woods, 1991; Endsley, in press) (that is, the user should have more global knowledge of the location of objects in the environment, relative to his or her location beyond those that are the direct object of manipulation and/or avoidance: situation awareness of the current state of these objects becomes critical if abnormal conditions develop, requiring the user to modify the plan of action); and (3) workload or cognitive effort should be low.

2. Off-line training and rehearsal. Virtual environments have been proposed as a tool for rehearsing critical actions in a benign, forgiving environment, in preparation for target performance in a less forgiving one. This may involve practicing lumbar injection for spinal or epidural anesthesia (Bostrom *et al.*, 1993), maneuvering a space craft (Eyles, 1991; Grunwald and Ellis, 1993), carrying out rehearsal flights prior to a dangerous mission (Bird, 1993; Williams *et al.*, 1994), or practicing emergency procedures in a variety of systems (Baum, 1992). The primary criterion here is the effective transfer of training from practice in the virtual environment to the "true reality" target environment.

3. On-line comprehension. The goal of interacting with a virtual environment may be reaching understanding, comprehension or "insight" regarding the structure of an environment. For example, the scientist interacting with a database may be doing so with the objective of obtaining understanding of the data (McGreevy, 1991)—perceiving relations, constraints and constancies that were not apparent from a more abstract rendering. The chemist or drug developer may be exploring ways that particular molecules can be combined or "docked" (Brooks, 1993), or the radiologist may be trying to understand the topology of a brain tumor. Thus insight and discovery are the goals, and it is ideal (although not mandatory) that these processes take place WHILE the operator is interacting, rather than at a later period of time.

4. Off-line learning and knowledge acquisition. The goal here is the transfer of knowledge, acquired in a virtual environment, to be employed, later in a different more abstract form (Brelsford, 1993). This situation typifies the recent enthusiasm for the role of virtual environment systems in education (Wickens, 1992a).

Clearly the four categories listed above overlap to some extent, and hard and fast boundaries cannot be drawn between them. However, research has informed us that features of virtual reality (Table 13-1) that may benefit some categories may, generally speaking, disrupt performance in others. For example, the feature of closed-loop interaction is not necessarily ideal for on-line performance. Robots and autopilots usually can do a better job of fine coordination and tracking of well-defined visual targets than can human manipulators. However, a substantial database reviewed by Wickens (1992a) reveals that closed-loop interaction is a key feature for understanding, and the long-term knowledge acquisition characterizing categories 2, 3, and 4 above. Correspondingly, the inside-out framework often improves category 1 manipulation (tracking) performance, but may work to the detriment of situation awareness and long-term knowledge acquisition (category 4).

The importance of these task display dependencies may be enhanced by the fact that very different visual systems may be involved in perceptual-motor coordination and navigation, from those involved in the perceptual understanding of spatial location (Bridgeman, 1991; Shebilske, 1991). Equally relevant is the distinction between *ambient* visual systems involved in general orientation, and *focal* visual systems required for object recognition (Liebowitz, 1988). The relative importance of these different kinds of task in a user's application will dictate the importance of display concerns that address properties of the visual system in question.

In the following section, we describe in more detail a series of issues and cognitive phenomena that bear on the effectiveness of virtual environment systems for these different uses. This description can help us understand the specific linkages between different features of virtual environment systems, and the uses for which those systems are intended, as these are mediated by the cognitive capabilities of the user. Our approach to classifying these phenomena is through a more detailed analysis of the cognitive and perceptual-motor tasks that must be performed by the virtual environment user. Understanding these, and the constraints that they impose on the human operator, will help formulate guidelines for the design of effective virtual environment systems.

TASK ANALYSIS

The appropriate implementation of virtual environment systems depends upon a careful analysis both of the demands of the particular task to be performed with the virtual environment technology and of the constraints and limitations of the human user. The primary features of such analysis are described below, in the context of a human operator, who is performing an inherently spatial task (space is, after all, the metaphor of virtual environments). The operator has a very wide sensory bandwidth, a more limited perceptual bandwidth and very constraining limits on both attention (the ability to process several separate channels of input concurrently) and working memory (e.g., remembering where s/he has been, or remembering an arbitrary command string). The operator also brings to the interface a high level of natural perceptual-motor coordination, and a large repertoire of facts and knowledge about how the world operates. In some respects the virtual environment adheres to these properties of the real world. Yet in other respects, such properties can or will be violated by the system. For example, typical visual-vestibular coupling is often missing, the control–display loop may be delayed, travel is constrained neither by inertia nor the rigidity of objects encountered, and the vertical gravitational force is absent. Bearing these features in mind, virtual environments can be characterized by a number of key "tasks" that may need to be performed.

Search

The user often needs to find an object of interest in the virtual environment. Depending upon the environment, this object may be a reference in a database (Newby, 1992), an item in a menu (Jacoby and Ellis, 1992), a fact in a hypertext space (Golovchinsky and Chignell, 1993), a particular data point in a scientific database, or a tumor in the representation of body tissue. Often the object of the search is specified in a format different from and more abstract than its rendering in the virtual environment. Furthermore, the object may not necessarily be visible in that space at the time it is desired. Hence, successful search is facilitated by providing an electronic map of the environment. Brooks reports repeatedly finding it necessary to present two views to the user, one of which is an egocentric view of the scene. The second view, presented on a separate screen or as an inset into the main display, is an exocentric view providing an overall map of the virtual world. This is similar to the topographic maps produced by the US Geological Survey, in which the location of the quadrant is outlined in a small state map in the upper left corner. Brooks observes that users often start out using the overall map view and move to the egocentric view only when they have developed an adequate internal mental map of the virtual world (Brooks, 1988). Similar endorsement for the importance of an overall map comes from Reichlen (1993). Users, wearing a tracked head-mounted display and seated in a swivel chair, turned to see different sections of a map of Boston; they reported the need for being able to "back up" and get a bigger view.

Human factors research reveals that three features of electronic maps are desirable in order for them to support visual search. First, maps should contain a minimal amount of unnecessary clutter (Hofer and Palen, 1993; Mykityshyn and Hansman, 1993; Kuchar and Hansman, 1993). A large amount of research in the visual search literature reveals the retarding effect of clutter (Teichner and Mocharnuk, 1979; Van Der Heijden, 1992), and hence it is appropriate that decluttering options of any map be provided. Still, it is apparent that what is clutter at one moment (or for one user) may be necessary information at (or for) another. If there is any uncertainty about the potential relevance of certain sorts of information, the best solution may be to render the "questionable clutter" in faint,but still visible intensity (background mode), so that awareness of the presence of the information can be maintained even while it does not distract processing of the necessary information.

Second, a flexible frame of reference should be provided (Aretz, 1991; Harwood and Wickens, 1991; McKinnon and Kruk, 1991). Users should be able to orient the map into either a "canonical frame" (with geographical maps, this is "north-up"), or into a "track-up" ego-referenced frame, in which the top of the map corresponds to the momentary direction of view in virtual environment space. This rotating map feature will alleviate the difficulties that map users encounter when traveling in a direction that is opposite from the canonical orientation of the map, a difficulty directly related to the cost of mental rotation (Shepard and Cooper, 1982; Shepard and Hurwitz, 1984; Harwood and Wickens, 1991; Aretz, 1991; Aretz and Wickens, 1992). It will also alleviate problems of translating the "exocentric view" of the world to the egocentric frame-of-reference necessary for control and movement through the space (Ellis *et al.*, 1991). The difference, of course, between the map and the virtual environment view is that the former is expressed at a more "abstract," less "real" level. It will likely be two-dimensional, may have abstracted or symbolic representation of objects and landmarks, and will encompass a wide field of view. Its value, of course, is that the map can depict, at once, the entire domain of the virtual environment, along with more abstract goals, landmarks, and objects, necessary to maintain situation awareness.

Third, it is important to provide an electronic "tie" or link between location and orientation of designated objects (including oneself) in the abstract map coordinates, and in the virtual environment. For example, one's own current location and heading could be specified on the map, while positions and landmarks which the user wishes to designate on the map, can also be highlighted in the virtual world. Correspondingly, because of the importance of orthogonal reference lines in our own natural environment (Howard, 1986;

Franklin and Tversky, 1990; Tversky, 1991), it would appear important that the depiction of corresponding orthogonal reference lines, stabilized in world coordinates (e.g., horizon, vertical), be made continuously visible. The idea of an "electronic link" between different representations of the space is embodied in the important concept of visual momentum (Woods, 1984), a concept that will be elaborated in the section "Three human-factors guidelines in learning" later in this chapter.

Virtual environments populated by more abstract concepts can also be "mapped." Knepp et al. (1982) developed a display concept to support information search through, and retrieval from, a multidimensional database: the display featured a small, but consistently oriented picture of the full database in the form of a cube, and the currently examined item was highlighted. A study by Vicente and Williges (1988), nicely supported the concept of "world maps" in information retrieval from a hierarchically organized database in which users had experienced problems of "cognitive disorientation." Vicente and Williges found that the presence of a map of the file-organization, and of a cursor highlighting the momentary position within the file structure, provided significant benefits to user "orientation."

Navigation

Appropriate implementation of the human factors of navigation assists the virtual environment user to answer four questions: Where am I now? What is my current attitude and orientation? Where do I want to go? How do I travel there?—and then supports the actual navigational travel through the virtual environment space to the desired destination. Answers to the questions of "where am I" and "where do I want to go," are of course supported by the design electronic maps, as discussed in the previous section. The actual mechanism of navigation through the virtual environment presents a number of challenging cognitive and perceptual-motor issues, because most of the physical constraints that normally accompany navigation and locomotion through real space are removed. Where possible, these mechanisms should capitalize as much as possible about how humans normally move through real space (Warren and Wertheim, 1990). Travel in many virtual environment systems takes the form of real-world metaphors, where head-trackers, hand-trackers, treadmills, gloves, and joysticks are used to indicate viewer position and orientation, and where the viewpoint is moved smoothly through the environment. Some systems also provide discrete point-to-point navigation, allowing the user to specify a goal and instantly travel to it, or to "zoom" at very fast speeds, rapidly passing by objects in the environment. Virtual travel should represent a compromise between two features: speed and flexibility on the one hand, and situation awareness on the other.

The advantages of speed and flexibility (i.e., rapid travel to any part of the environment) are apparent, but their costs pertain to the loss of situation awareness that may result. Situation awareness—my understanding of where I am in the overall context—decreases when computer intelligence and automation take over many of the normally human functions in navigation, a concern that has been repeatedly expressed in the aviation community (Wiener, 1989; Billings, 1991; Sarter and Woods, 1994). If a computer instantly takes me to my goal, which I have expressed via abstract commands, I have no way of knowing about the intervening or surrounding "terrain," and I may need that knowledge should unexpected things suddenly happen, or if an important part of my task relates to later recall of that terrain. In contrast, I might well have implicitly acquired this knowledge had I been forced to navigate on my own through the environment to reach the goal.

Of course there are many levels of compromise between fully manual and fully automatic navigation; one could let the user choose course headings and allow the virtual environment system to automatically fly those. One could either control the speed of movement through the environment, or one could allow the computer to control the speed. In the latter case the system might either impose a constant speed or, using a technique that has considerable merit, impose a logarithmically diminishing speed, as the next destination is approached (Flach et al., 1990). Similarly, in point-of-interest movement (Macinlay et al., 1990), the user specifies a target location by picking a point on some object in the virtual environment. The system moves the user viewpoint to a spot that is close to and facing the selected point. The movement is logarithmic, covering the same percentage of current viewer-to- object distance on each frame and rotating to align the view direction. This concept, which illustrates the value of task-dependent design, allows rapid navigation through empty space, but longer exposure to the environment as critical user choice points are approached, and it is important that these choices be well informed by longer perceptual experience.

The effectiveness of a particular navigational metaphor may be a function of the task and of the type of the virtual environment. Ware evaluated three different ways of using a hand-held six-degrees-of-freedom (6DOF) input device ("the bat") in exploration, search, and viewpoint control tasks in three different environments and found significant differences in user preferences and user performance (Ware and Jessome, 1988; Ware and Osborne, 1990). For example, the "flight vehicle" metaphor, in which the bat is used to control translational and rotational velocity, was the most useful in exploring a "maze" environment, but was judged worst for navigating around a "cube" environment. An interesting observation is the effect of the sense of scale. The cube environment, consisting of a single cube, was perceived to be small and it would be unnatural to "fly" in so constrained a space. The preferred strategy for the cube was the "environment-in-hand" metaphor, in which the bat is used to move and rotate the entire environment. In contrast, this metaphor was seen as inappropriate for a "road signs" environment, which was perceived to be very large—something a human could not simply pick up and move around.

If a design is chosen to make available some continuous form of interactive control, via manipulation of a joystick or hand position for example, then two important design issues come to the fore: the influence of visual depiction of surfaces and on perceptual biases of slant and distances, and the stability of the perceptual motor loop. While these issues are related—faulty perception of space may disrupt the control loop—they are not mandatorily coupled since different visual systems are involved in each (Shebilske, 1991). Each will be addressed in turn.

Perceptual biases

The discussions of human space perception as it effects travel and navigation is far broader than can be done service in this chapter (see Howard, 1986; Sedgwick, 1986; Regan *et al.*, 1986; Warren and Wertheim, 1990 for excellent reviews). However, it is important to briefly mention certain key biases that can distort perception of the location and orientation of objects and surfaces in virtual environments. While the navigation in a virtual environment may obviate the physical danger of "collisions" with objects and surfaces, in many environments such events can still be disorienting. Furthermore, in some areas like manipulating a virtual spacecraft or robot off-line, in order to store a trajectory which can later be implemented on the real system, virtual collisions should be minimized because of the possibility that they might be inadvertently stored and then implemented with the real system. Collision avoidance can be supported by the accurate perception of locations and surfaces.

The "ecological" school of psychology has supported a program of research to identify the cues that humans use to judge motion and orientation in the natural world (Gibson, 1979; Warren and Wertheim, 1990). The conclusions from this work, reinforced by work that has examined the causes of pilot illusions in flight (O'Hare and Roscoe, 1990) emphasize the importance of regularly spaced texture, and level surfaces to support the accurate perception of gradients, slant, and optic flow, and the time until a moving object collides with a solid surface (Regan *et al.*, 1986; Wolpert, 1990; Stevens, 1991; Lee and Moray, 1992).

Ellis, McGreevy, and their colleagues at NASA Ames (McGreevy and Ellis, 1986; Ellis *et al.*, 1987, 1989, 1990, 1991) have conducted a programmatic series of studies to evaluate and model the biases in perceived object location that result from different three-dimensional display renderings, how these are influenced by differing viewing parameters, and whether location judgments are made from an egocentric perspective ("where is X relative to me"), or an exocentric one ("where is X relative to Y"). The latter distinction is critical to our understanding of virtual environment issues because it directly maps onto the frame-of-reference feature. In particular, this research has focused on two perceptual biases: (1) the "virtual space effect" which describes the biases in perceived location of objects resulting from a display magnification (wide field of view) or minification (narrow field of view) that is inappropriate given the viewing distance between the eyes and the display surface, and (2) the "2D–3D effect," which describes the perceived "rotation" of vectors towards a plane which is more closely parallel to the viewing plane than is appropriate (see Figure 13-1). That is, an underestimation of the slant of a surface (Perrone, 1982).

This modeling has direct implications for the choice of the frame of reference: the ego-referenced display, typical of virtual environment systems, or the outside-in world-referenced display (see Figure 13-2). While both biases may be manifest in the ego-referenced display, their effects may be enhanced

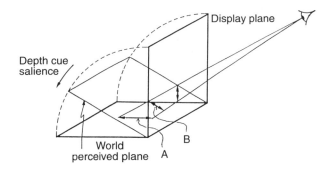

Figure 13-1 The figure illustrates the extent to which the true position of two objects in 3D space, indicated by the two ends of the horizontal vector, (A) will be perceptually "rotated" upwards, (B) when the scene is viewed on a display (i.e., the points are projected onto a vertical surface). The extent of this bias will be magnified if perceptual depth cues are impoverished and reduced if those cues are enhanced (from Wickens *et al.*, 1989).

in the world-referenced display because they may distort both the perception of other objects' locations *and* the perception of one's own location. This difference can explain why three-dimensional displays can provide more effective tools for navigating when they are presented from one's own ego-referenced perspective (Haskell and Wickens, 1993) than from an outside-in world-referenced perspective (Wickens *et al.*, 1994; Prevett and Wickens, 1994).

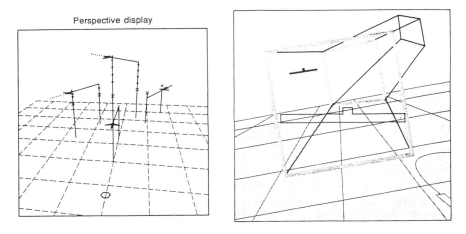

Figure 13-2 Contrasting examples of exocentric (left) and egocentric (right) displays. The exocentric cockpit display of traffic information (Ellis, *et al.*, 1987) depicts the aircraft in which the user sits, in the center of the grid. The egocentric primary flight display (Haskell and Wickens, 1993), depicts a schematic view directly from the eye point of the pilot sitting in the vehicle.

The work of Ellis, McGreevy and their colleagues has also addressed different *display-enhancement* techniques that can alleviate these biases, such as the inclusion of grids and posts (Figure 13-2) to help identify the location of objects in an orthogonal Euclidian coordinate space (Ellis *et al.*, 1987), the use of cubes or other known 3D objects whose parallel surface form is known *a priori* in the perspective scene, the use of stereo to provide a more accurate sense of depth (Ellis *et al.*, 1991), and the use of a compass rose, depicted both in a perspective view and in a 2D map view to facilitate the calibration of angles in the former (Ellis and Hacisalihzade, 1990).

Visual-motor coupling

While virtual environment interfaces may be argued to be "natural" in principle, there are many features that can disrupt or distort the natural coupling of actual reaching and walking, so as to create problems of stability and disorientation, lessons that have been well learned in the flight community (Wickens, 1986; Baron, 1988). Five critical issues relate to *gain, time delay, order, travel-view decoupling*, and *field of view*.

1. Gain. Any given control input by the human user, designed to translate or rotate, can be related to a change in display view (or viewer position and orientation in the virtual environment space) by any arbitrary setting of system gain. Low gains will require a lot of displacement to obtain a given display change, and therefore a lot of effort. High gains, while more efficient, lead to greater chances of instability and overcontrol. Optimal gains involve a trade-off between these factors (Wickens, 1986). The best point on the trade-off function depends upon the nature of the task: fine adjustment of position requires a lower gain than does rapid travel, for example. Also, because of stability concerns, the optimal gain depends very much upon the system time delay which, as we see below, is a very real issue in virtual environment systems.

2. Time delay. High-gain systems, coupled with significant time delays or lags in updating the visual world based upon operator control input, will be quite susceptible to closed-loop instability (Jagacinski, 1977; Wickens, 1986). This becomes a very real concern if complex imagery must be updated by computer graphics to accomplish the control-based changes in viewer position and orientation. Research in flight simulation has shown that display lags as short as 50 ms can significantly impact performance, and lags much longer than that can lead to undesirable control oscillations (Wickens, 1986). In supporting navigation in the virtual environment, it is necessary to parse the user input, determine the new viewpoint, and produce the new imagery. With the rich visual scene display required for many virtual environments, it is easy to see how this could present a problem. Airey *et al.* (1990) found that below six frames per second, users choose to navigate using an overall map view requiring less intensive image updating; only when the frame update rate improved beyond six frames per second, would users navigate in the egocentric scene view.

Different solutions can be adopted to address the problems of time delay. For example, one could maintain gain (or position update rate) at a low enough level, slaved for example to maximum image update rate, so that instability problems are never encountered. The slower update may frustrate the user, but overshoot problems related to instability will not result. Experiments in predictive filtering of the user input stream have had some success in reducing the lag between user movement and display update (Liang et al., 1991). Alternatively, computer-generated imagery can be simplified in order that substantial negative impacts are never encountered (Pausch, 1991), or "adaptive" or "progressive" imagery can be used: drawing simplified views during navigation and progressing to more detailed views when the user has come to rest. This latter technique has been used successfully in architectural walkthroughs (Airey et al., 1990), as well as other applications. When following this course, care should be taken to provide sufficient texture information to achieve a realistic sense of forward motion (Larish and Flach, 1990). Of course, simplified imagery diminishes the sense of visual reality, but from the perspective of user engagement, user "presence" within the environment, and overall system performance, it is well worth the price. Brooks advises always depicting motion realistically, no matter what else suffers (Brooks, 1988). Moreover, data we discuss below suggest that, regarding image quality and complexity, "more is not always better."

3. Control order. Control order refers to the qualitative nature of the change in system state (and therefore display state) that results from a change in position of the control. In the most natural virtual environment the control order is zero. That is, a given change in position (e.g., a given joystick or head rotation angle or a step forward), will lead to a given change in the viewed environment. But for many aspects of virtual environment navigation or manipulation (see below), a *first-order* or rate control dynamics could be implemented such that a fixed change in control position yields a constant *rate of change* or velocity of viewpoint position or angle. The advantage of one order over the other depends very much upon whether the *goals* of the virtual environment task are to produce velocity or position (Notterman and Page, 1962; Wickens, 1986). In navigation, the primary goal is usually to travel and therefore to produce a given movement (velocity). Hence, first-order control (rate control) is typically the order of choice when control is exerted by some hand manipulation. On the other hand, if desired distances of change are small, so final *position* is the most important criterion, then zero-order (position) control gains greater utility. (If navigation is achieved by walking, obviously a zero-order control is the logical candidate.)

4. Travel-view decoupling. An important cognitive issue in virtual environment design is whether to allow the direction of motion to be decoupled from the direction of gaze at the virtual environment world. While this makes a certain amount of "ecological" sense (we can easily look to the side while we walk forward), the features of such an option in a virtual environment may not be easy to implement (Mercurio and Erickson, 1990). The decoupling of head rotation, body movement, and the experienced visual field that is normally encountered in true reality, is governed by an elaborate, highly instinctive and automatic mechanism within the brain (Wertheim, 1990), one that can be considerably disrupted when navigation or rotation is achieved by artificial electronic means. This disruption will be exacerbated when the delays between control and display update are nontrivial relative to the time between control inputs. The added degrees of freedom created by allowing both kinds of motion concurrently contribute to the complexity of the control problem, unless navigation is actually achieved by walking. An alternative solution is to provide a wide field of view, and allow the operator to stop and "hover," before inspecting right and left.

5. *Field of view.* The term "field of view" can have two somewhat confusing meanings. One describes the amount of the virtual environment that is viewable without moving the head. Here, for example, a sufficient degree of minification (a "fisheye" view) can present a full 360° field of view, like a panoramic picture collapsed into 30°. The second which we refer to as the *viewing angle* refers to the width subtended by the viewable display surface, measured in units of visual angle. This angle, of course, is dictated jointly by the width of the display and the viewer's distance from the display. In normally viewing the real world, these two are equivalent and defined by the limiting sensory resolution at extreme levels of peripheral vision. If full virtual environment systems capture all viewing parameters of the real world, the two will be also equivalent. When the two are equivalent, the perceived position of things corresponds to where one would reach to touch them. It is, of course, electronically possible to vary either aspect of the field of view as required. Human characteristics impose four consequences of such variation. (1) Wider fields of view clearly support greater situation awareness of surrounding objects and terrain. (2) As noted above, the down-side of wide fields of view (unless coupled with proportional increase in viewing angle) is that they distort the perceived position of and perceived distance from objects (McGreevy and Ellis, 1986). This may create real hazards for vehicle control, based upon such displays (Roscoe, 1991). (3) Wider viewing angles provide a more compelling sense of forward motion, given the sensitivity of peripheral vision to motion, and the enhanced tracking performance that results when peripheral vision is available (Wickens, 1986). (4) The down-side of this compulsion is that, if forward motion is not accompanied by corresponding vestibular inputs (e.g., from walking), and a mismatch between vestibular and visual perception results, this will invite motion sickness (Andersen and Braunstein, 1985; Oman, 1991).

Manipulation

Many virtual environment systems are designed to support the manipulation of objects. Issues of grasping and tactile feedback in such manipulations are well addressed in Chapter 9 (see also McKinnon and Kruk, 1991). From the standpoint of the current discussion of cognitive factors, several of the same issues are relevant as were of concern in the previous section on navigation. The accurate depiction of location and orientation of surfaces and objects is again critical as discussed above. Once again, issues of display gain and time lag are important as these dictate stability of the control loop. In particular, because manipulation often requires both high spatial and temporal precision, the interaction of gain and time delay on stability becomes even more of a concern. For example, Sturman found that at 6–10 frames per second, their "whole-hand interface" for grasping and manipulating objects was natural and effective, but at 3 frames per second, it was difficult or impossible to use (Sturman *et al.*, 1989).

Another critical parameter is the order of the perceptual motor loop discussed above, whose optimum value must be determined by task/goal analysis. If the goal is to make the manipulator match the velocity of a *moving* target (e.g., in order to capture a tumbling satellite), or to *travel* a long distance, a first-order rate control is preferable. But if the distance is short, and a precise fixed *position* or *location* is the goal in the virtual environment, then a zero-order control is optimal (Wickens, 1986). Switching logic can, of course, be employed to allow the operator to choose between orders as the task demands. It also turns out that the optimum kind of feedback on the manipulator, whether isometric (rigid and force sensitive) or isotonic (free moving and position sensitive) depends on the control order (Buxton, 1990). For a six-degree-of-freedom hand manipulator, used to manipulate the orientation and location of a cursor in virtual space, Zhai and Milgram (1993) found that isometric control is optimal for first-order dynamics, and isotonic control (e.g., a sensor that responds to the position and orientation of the hand) is optimum for zero-order dynamics.

Multimodal interaction styles that often characterize virtual environments can aid in manipulation tasks. For example, some systems use an audible click to signify when the virtual manipulator has successfully connected with a virtual object, and haptic displays, in which force information is fed back to the user through a finger apparatus or hand-grip, have been found to give a two-fold improvement in user performance over purely visual displays. In one study, the force cue was seen to be more helpful in grasping virtual blocks than either stereoscopic viewing or variable viewpoint. In another study, haptic display by itself was found to be better than visual display alone for manipulating an object in a force field. Force cues improved performance in a complex manipulation task involving molecular docking. In this study, chemists who were provided with force cues reported having a better feel of the force field at the active site of the molecule and a better understanding for the docking behavior of the various drugs that were tried (Brooks *et al.*, 1990).

Another important cognitive issue in manipulation is the frame of reference of the display: should the view be that of the eye view in a real world, or a view mounted from the end of the manipulator (McKinnon and Kruk, 1991)? The former frame of reference would appear most desirable since this configuration is both an extension of natural experience (the eye gaze is not slaved to the hand), and conforms to Roscoe's (1968) principle of the moving part. This principle dictates that the moving part of a display, relative to the stable display "frame," should conform to that which moves in the world (or, in this instance, in the user's most typical experience of that world). Alternatively, it may be desirable to provide multiple simultaneous views. In a system to plan radiation treatment, it was found to be advantageous to provide an overall view of the treatment apparatus and orthogonal views of the tumor area, as well as a "beam's-eye" view that sighted down the direction of the radiation beam (Mosher et al., 1986).

Perception and inspection

A goal of many virtual environments is to inspect objects within that environment, in order to gain an understanding of what is there, to select or identify certain patterns, and so forth. These perceptual tasks impose somewhat different demands than do those imposed by the perceptual side of the perceptual motor loop used in travel. Quite different features of reality may be important to support these different task demands. In navigational travel, for example, accurate depiction of spatial relations is important, and it is equally important to retain visual features of the environment that produce a rich experience of spatial extent (Warren and Wertheim, 1990). Correspondingly, the accuracy of motion representation is quite important to support control stability. However, for object inspection and recognition, motion fidelity becomes less critical, while light and shadowing (Barfield et al., 1988) and motion parallax (Prazdny, 1986) may play a relatively greater role than do stereo and texture gradients (Wickens et al., 1989).

Some important data from research on the formatting of instructional material also bear on the degree of realism with which objects to be inspected should be rendered for accurate perception. Here the lesson is that "more is not necessarily better" (Wickens, 1992b). In particular, research findings suggest that stick or schematic figures often surpass photographic images for guiding users through task procedures (Dwyer, 1967; Schmidt and Kysor, 1987; Spencer, 1988). Stick figures preserve shape, and indeed may be used to exaggerate distinctive shapes (and thereby enhance perceptual identification), while dispensing with fine texture information. (Any use of stick figures in virtual environments, however, should always proceed with the awareness that the depth cue of interposition or occlusion—the hiding of a distant figure by a nearer one—is an "all purpose" cue to depth (Wickens et al., 1989). That is, if stick figures are used, then hidden line algorithms should be employed.) Users of computer imagery technology for visualization in medicine and science have valued the role of computer technology to present *less* reality (e.g., decluttering), rather than more, for problem-solving in the rendered environment (Gershon et al., 1993).

Naturally, to reiterate the point made in this section, decisions about the level of visual realism necessary for inspection and recognition must be based upon task analysis of *what* is to be recognized, or discriminated. If texture *is* important (say, for discriminating geological features on a Martian landscape), then obviously it should not be sacrificed, but other properties might well be sacrificed in order to compensate (e.g., speed of image updating). It is important that explicit consideration of these trade-offs and sacrifices be made, based upon the task analysis.

Learning

There are really four different forms of learning that might be fostered in a virtual environment, each influencing the different features listed in Table 13-1 to be either preserved, or sacrificed.

1. Procedural learning. As we have noted in the previous section, greater (e.g., photographic) visual realism will not necessarily be helpful, and may, in fact, be detrimental in enabling operators to learn a set of procedures to be performed in an interactive environment (e.g., fault management training in an aircraft). The closed-loop interactive feature is a clear asset, however, for such learning to proceed.

2. Perceptual motor skill learning. Here the objective is to teach some generic perceptual motor skill; typical examples include flying, training for certain medical procedures or for assembly or repair tasks. For such skills, the need to be an active participant in the control loop appears to be important (Kessel and Wickens, 1982), as does concern for the appropriate dynamics, similar to those of the target task (Lintern and Wickens, 1991). The requirement for enhanced sensory feedback appears to be quite task specific. For example, there is little evidence from flight simulation research that dynamic simulator motion is a characteristic of simulators that leads to better mastery of flying skills (Koonce, 1979; Lintern, 1987; O'Hare and Roscoe, 1990). However, realistic proprioceptive feedback is necessary for skill acquisition in tasks such as spinal injection (Bostrom *et al.*, 1993). High levels of visual realism do not appear to be necessary for the training of skills such as landing an aircraft (Lintern, 1991). However, it may well be that specific aspects of proprioceptive feedback from controls—mimicking the real transfer environment, are important for effective learning to take place (Lintern and Wickens, 1991).

3. Spatial learning and navigational rehearsal. A virtual environment may be used to allow one operator to rehearse a particular, one-time skill, given that the system designer has awareness of the composition of the specific environment. At one level of scale, this might typify the surgeon practicing for a specific surgical operation, which will require understanding of the morphology of a particular brain, and a tumor or abnormality contained therein. At a quite different level of scale, it might typify the helicopter pilot, rehearsing a particularly dangerous rescue mission, who wishes to learn the specific features of the approaching ground terrain and the rescue site. Some research in flight simulation has suggested the features of virtual reality important for such a task. For example, Aretz (1991) concluded that the egocentric (rotating) frame of reference on an electronic map inhibited the pilot's ability to form a "mental map" of the environment (although it did not inhibit the ability to fly the specific maneuver). This mental map could be critical if the pilot were suddenly required to depart from the pre-rehearsed plan. Williams and Wickens (1993) concluded that greater visual realism of the environment in navigational rehearsal flights did not lead to better performance of those flights in a transfer environment; but reinforcing a more general conclusion about learning, they also found that remaining in the active control loop during rehearsal proved to be of great importance for later retention of the rehearsal flight maneuver (see also Foreman et al., 1990). This advantage of being in the active control loop remains, however, only so long as the mental workload of flying remains relatively low. (Williams et al., 1994). Interestingly, however, subjects who studied a two-dimensional map of the route to be flown, achieved just as effective navigation performance on the rehearsal flight as subjects who practiced on the closed-loop flight through the virtual environment. Furthermore, map study provided the subjects with a superior mental map of the environment.

Building an accurate mental map of a physical space presented as a virtual environment is hindered by some types of display equipment. Head-mounted displays, while good at immersing the user in the virtual environment and increasing the user's feeling of "presence" in the virtual environment, provide a limited field of view. Henry and Furness (1993) found that individuals wearing head-mounted displays underestimated the dimensions of a set of rooms in a virtual museum. Individuals who walked through the actual museum made accurate judgments; those who viewed the synthetic museum on a regular computer monitor underestimated, but not as much as those wearing helmets (Henry and Furness, 1993). These results are consistent with earlier work that shows that perception of size and distance diminishes with a decreasing field of view. Environments such as the CAVE (Cruz-Neira et al., 1992) and the Virtual Portal (Deering, 1993) use multiple large screens (10 ft × 10 ft) and rear-projection to create a room-sized environment with a more natural field of view.

A somewhat different form of spatial learning was examined by Wickens et al. (1994), who examined how well subjects understood (learned) the shape of a complex three-dimensional surface, as a function of whether they had previously experienced aspects of that surface with either high (three-dimensional, stereo) or lower (two-dimensional, mono) realism. While the 3D perceptual augmentations assisted subjects in answering questions about the database as they were actually viewing the display, these enhancements provided only limited support for later memory and understanding of the surface shape. Furthermore, the addition of stereo to the three-dimensional perspective view had no added benefit to later understanding.

4. Conceptual learning. When a virtual environment system is designed to support conceptual understanding of a phenomenon, whether for the scientist or the student, two features appear to be of critical importance. First, as in other forms of learning, active closed-loop exploration, rather than passive viewing, seems to be important (Gregory, 1991; Wickens, 1992a). Second, a key feature of any long-term conceptual knowledge is the availability of alternative knowledge representations of the same material. Virtual environments can provide a variety of representations—Brooks observes that each new visualization of a particular molecule produces a different insight (Brooks, 1988). Brelsford (1993) found that teaching physics concepts through virtual environment manipulations to a naive group of both junior high school and college students led to better retention of the physics concepts than teaching the same concepts via lecture. However, to best support a successful learning experience, it is important that a virtual environment exposure to the concepts is experienced *in conjunction with* and *related to*, alternative, more abstract representations. For example, the student, experiencing a physical phenomenon through a virtual environment, should also, at the same time, experience this same phenomenon via its graphical interpretation, its verbal description and its symbolic formula. Providing alternative representation of the same learning phenomenon, however, only satisfies part of the requirements for successful learning. It is also important for the learner to understand how those representations are related to each other, an issue we address below in our discussion of the concept of visual momentum.

THREE HUMAN-FACTORS GUIDELINES IN LEARNING

The previous discussion has focused on the set of characteristics of cognitive processes and tasks that may be used in a virtual environment. We consider now a set of three relevant human-factors principles that have been shown both to help performance and, if carefully applied, should also facilitate learning in such an environment.

Consistency

The general human-factors guidelines for consistency of display representation have been well validated by research. In fact, several studies have shown that it is better to have a pair of tasks (or stimulus-response mappings) that are consistent with each other even though both may have less compatible stimulus-response mappings, than to make one more compatible, but create inconsistency between them (Chernikoff *et al.*, 1960; Duncan, 1979; Andre and Wickens, 1992). Inconsistency of representation creates confusion, high cognitive effort and is a possible source of error if actions carried out in one context have effects on the system that are not consistent with similar actions in a different context. Aircraft designers remain quite concerned about the sorts of inconsistencies between cockpit layouts that can breed errors through negative transfer (Braune, 1989).

Examples of inconsistency that might appear in virtual environment design would include the inconsistency provided by different modes of navigation (e.g., high gain vs. low gain), or frames of reference (e.g., inside-out, outside-in). When such inconsistency between modes is present, it is important that the user be provided with salient reminders of what mode is in effect.

Ironically, one of the guidelines we have cited above for effective use of virtual environments in a learning environment may, at first glance, appear to violate the guideline for consistency. We noted above that an advantage of virtual environment systems is their ability to provide the student learner with a novel ego-centered viewpoint of the material to be learned (e.g., viewing an inside-out exploration of an archeological site, rather than studying a God's-eye map). To be valuable in education, however, the novel perspective must be cognitively linked in the learner's mind, with a more abstract top-down, outside-in (global) perspective, so that the learner may see how the two relate. In the same way, as we argued before, the student of physics should both experience forces directly through experimentation and manipulation, and understand them at a more abstract level via language, equations, and graphs. We argue that the "inconsistency" of representation in these cases (e.g., ego-centered and world-centered) is necessary because it provides a *redundancy* of experience; the potential downside of this inconsistency can be addressed by application of the principle of *visual momentum*. These two human-factors design concepts—redundancy and visual momentum—will now be addressed in turn.

1. Redundancy. A well-validated principle in the human factors of design concerns the advantage of redundancy in presenting information in a variety of forms; whether these are low-intensity signals to be detected (Colquhoun and Baddeley, 1967), patterns to be classified (Garner and Felfoldy, 1970; Carswell and Wickens, 1990), or, in the context most relevant here, instructions to be mastered (Booher, 1975; Stone and Gluck, 1980; Nugent, 1987; see Wickens, 1992b for a summary).

Redundancy here is different from *repetition*, and describes the presentation of identical or related information in alternative formats (e.g., graphs, pictures, speech, print, principles, case studies). It is apparent that such redundancy has at least three potential advantages: (1) it enables the information flow from computers to learners to be less vulnerable to learner shifts in attention (e.g., between auditory and visual channels). (2) For learning, it accomplishes the goal of long-term storage of material by achieving memory traces in different representational formats (graphs vs. words). Basic principles of learning theory have instructed that multiple representations in memory increase resistance to forgetting (Tulving and Thomson, 1973). (3) Again, for learning, redundancy allows different users (learners) to capitalize on the format of information display that is most consistent with their cognitive style (Yallow, 1980).

2. Visual momentum. In previous pages we have outlined the case for the learner to receive alternative viewpoints, perspectives, or format representations of the same underlying data scheme. In a different context we have also noted the importance of the user understanding the spatial configuration of the environment in both a virtual environment and a more abstract map representation, to see how these are related. At the same time, as we have noted, the urge for diversity of representations may be at odds with the desirable feature of maintaining consistency. Fortunately, these two competing goals—diversity and consistency—can be partially reconciled through application of the principle of visual momentum.

The concept of visual momentum represents an engineering design solution proposed to address the issues of becoming cognitively lost as the display user traverses through multiple displays pertaining to different aspects of the same system or database (Woods, 1984; Wise and Debons, 1987). The concept was originally borrowed from film editors, as a technique to provide the movie viewer with an understanding of how successively viewed film cuts relate to each other (Hochberg and Brooks, 1978). When applied to the viewing of successive display frames, either of actual space (e.g., maps), or "conceptual space" (e.g., topologically related components in a process control plant, nodes in a menu or database, or graphical representations of data), the concept of visual momentum may be captured in terms of three basic guidelines.

a. Use consistent representations. This guideline of course reiterates a principle that was set forth above. Unless there is an explicit rationale for changing some aspects of a display representation, aspects should not be changed. However, when it is necessary to show new data, or present a new representation of previously viewed data, the principles of visual momentum dictate that display features should show the relation of the new data to the old. The next two guidelines show how this may be accomplished.

b. Use graceful transitions. When changes in representation will be made over time, abrupt discontinuities may be disorienting to the user. For example, in a virtual environment view, the transition from a small-scale wide angle perspective to a large-scale close-up perspective may be cognitively less disorienting if this change is made by a rapid but continuous "blow-up." In virtual environment systems, the use of discrete, instantaneous navigational mechanisms, rather than continuous ones, would endanger the sense of geographical orientation, because of the loss of visual momentum.

c. Highlight anchors. An anchor may be described as a constant invariant feature of the displayed "world," whose identity and location are always prominently highlighted on successive displays. For example, in aircraft attitude displays that might be viewed successively in various orientations, the direction of the vertical (or the horizon) should always be prominently highlighted (Weintraub and Ensing, 1992). In map displays, which may be reconfigured from inside-out to outside-in, in order to accommodate different task demands, a salient and consistent color code might be used to highlight both the northerly direction and the heading direction (Andre *et al.*, 1991). In Aretz' (1991) study of helicopter navigation, discussed above, anchoring was successfully used to portray the orientation and angle subtended by the forward field of view as a "wedge," depicted on a north-up map. In displays used to examine components of a complex chemical or electrical process, the direction of causal flow (input–output) could be prominently highlighted. In the design of "you are here" maps, visually prominent landmarks in the forward view, highlighted on the map, offer such an anchor (Levine, 1982).

In virtual environments in general, we suggest that abstract representations of the space may be characterized both by key objects that are the target of navigation and by a *canonical axis* (e.g., "north," "up"). Adherence to visual momentum principles would dictate that both the location and orientation of these should be made prominently visible in the ego-referenced virtual environment view, while the current ego location, along with the momentary direction of view (or heading if they are decoupled), may be depicted in the more abstract world-referenced representation.

EFFORT AND WORKLOAD

The concepts of effort and mental workload (Hancock and Meshkati, 1988) are relevant to our discussion of cognitive factors in virtual reality in two respects. First, it is obvious that for virtual environments to be useful to performance, designers must focus on reducing the cognitive effort of users at the interface (Sweller *et al.*, 1990). Well-performing and powerful systems that impose very high cognitive loads upon the users will probably not be heavily employed. Less obvious perhaps is the conclusion that many features intended to enhance reality will, unless they are accurately and precisely implemented, increase, rather than reduce, cognitive workload. For example, hand pointing to indicate direction of travel has been found to be a source of increased effort (Mercurio and Erickson, 1990), and very high levels of visual reality, if imposing lags in updating the visual display following control inputs, may also increase effort (Wickens, 1986). Hence, some withdrawal from high reality may be workload reducing rather than workload enhancing.

Secondly, the first author has argued elsewhere (Wickens, 1992a; Lintern and Wickens, 1991) that it is important to distinguish between the effort directed towards on-line performance (which generally should be minimized by incorporating design features like direct manipulation), and the effort allocated to learning or mastery of task-related information. If certain components of the virtual-world interface do force more effort to be allocated to understanding relationships between the different representations of information presented in the represented data, then those components will be beneficial to learning, even if they may be components of lesser, rather than greater, reality. It is by invoking this concept of learning-related effort that we can account for our findings that the features of the virtual environment interface which sometimes lead to lower levels of performance (and greater levels of effort) may also produce learning and mastery that is as effective or more effective than less effortful features. Merwin and Wickens (1991), for example, found that a two-dimensional graphics interface led to worse performance but just as good retention as did the 3D interface. Wickens *et al.* (1994) found similar results comparing a mono (less real) with a stereo (realism) view of scientific data; and as we noted above Williams and Wickens (1993) found that subjects who were asked to learn about terrain via map study, learned better than those who were passively flown through a highly realistic visual graphics world depicting the terrain. In these examples, those features that extracted a greater toll of effort in understanding and navigating the virtual environment (and perhaps *because* they do so) were found to engender greater long-term learning of the material presented within that space.

CONCLUSIONS

In conclusion, virtual reality is a technology that will likely grow in use and importance. It is therefore essential to realize that all components of a virtual environment system need not be retained (or retained at high levels of fidelity) for the technology to be useful. In fact, full fidelity is at a minimum, very costly; it may degrade system reliability and, in some circumstances, degrade system performance. A cognitive analysis of tasks performed by the virtual environment user, such as that presented here, can serve as a useful basis for understanding the features that might be preserved under different circumstances. Such an analysis can also form the basis for generating the needed research on the importance of these components for different tasks.

ACKNOWLEDGMENTS

We wish to acknowledge the support of a grant from the National Science Foundation (NSF IRI 90-21270) and from NASA Ames Research Center (NASA NAG 2-308) in preparation of this chapter. We also wish to acknowledge the valuable comments and contributions of Mingpo Tham.

REFERENCES

Airey, J. M. *et al.* (1990) Towards image realism with interactive update rates in complex virtual building environments, *Proc. of the 1990 Workshop on Interactive 3D Graphics*, Snowbird, UT, March 25–28, in *Computer Graphics*, **24**, 41–50

Andersen, G. J. and Braunstein, M. L. (1985) Induced self-motion in central vision, *J. Exp. Psychol.: Human Percept. Perform.*, **11**, 122–32

Andre, A. D. and Wickens, C. D. (1992) Compatibility and consistency in display-control systems: implications for aircraft decision aid design, *Human Factors*, **34**, 639–53

Andre, A. D., Wickens, C. D., Moorman, L., and Boschelli, M. M. (1991) Display formatting techniques for improving situation awareness in the aircraft cockpit, *Int. J. Aviation Psychol.*, **1**, 205–18

Aretz, A. J. (1991) The design of electronic map displays, *Human Factors*, **33**, 85–101

Aretz, A. J. and Wickens, C. D. (1992) The mental rotation of map displays, *Human Perform.*, **5**, 303–28

Barfield, W., Sanford, J., and Foley, J. (1988) The mental rotation and perceived realism of computer-generated three-dimensional images, *Int. J. Man-Machine Studies*, **29**, 669–84

Baron, S. (1988) Pilot control, in E. Wiener and D. Nagel (Eds), *Human Factors in Aviation*, San Diego: Academic, pp. 347–85

Baty, D. L., Wempe, T. E., and Huff, E. M. (1974) A study of aircraft map display location and orientation, *IEEE Trans. Systems, Man, Cybernet.*, **SMC-4**, 560–8

Baum, D. R. (1992) Virtual training devices: illusion or reality? *Proc. of the 14th Annual Interservice/Industry Training Systems and Education Conference*, Nov.

Begault, D. R. and Wenzel, E. M. (1992) Techniques and applications for binaural sound manipulation in human-machine interfaces, *Int. J. Aviation Psychol.*, **2**, 23–38

Billings, C. (1991) Toward a human-centered aircraft automation philosophy, *Int. J. Aviation Psychol.*, **1**, 261–70

Bird, J. (1993) Sophisticated computer gets new role: system once used only in fighters helping in Bosnia, *Air Force Times*, October 25, p. 8

Booher, H. R. (1975) Relative comprehensibility of pictorial information and printed words in proceduralized instructions, *Human Factors*, **17**, 266–77

Bostrom, M. *et al.* (1993) Design of an interactive lumbar puncture simulator with tactile feedback, *Proc. of IEEE Virtual Reality Annual Int. Symp. (VRAIS)*, September 18–21, Seattle, WA, pp. 280–6

Braune, R. J. (1989) *The Common/Same Type Rating: Human Factors and Other Issues*, Anaheim, CA: Society of Automotive Engineers

Brelsford, J. W., Jr (1993) Physics education in a virtual environment, *Proc. of the 37th Annual Meeting of the Human Factors and Ergonomics Society*, Santa Monica, CA: Human Factors and Ergonomics Society, pp. 1286–90

Bridgeman, B. (1991) Separate visual representations for perception and for visually guided behavior, in S. R. Ellis *et al.* (Eds), *Pictorial Communication in Virtual and Real Environments*, London: Taylor and Francis, pp. 316–27

Brooks, F. P. (1988) Grasping reality through illusion: Interactive graphics serving science, *Proc. of CHI '88*, May 15–19, Washington, DC, pp. 1–11

Brooks, F. P. (1993) *Keynote address presented at the IEEE Symposium on Visualization*, October 27–29, San Jose, CA

Brooks, F. P. *et al.* (1990) Project GROPE—haptic display for scientific visualization, *Proceedings of SIGGRAPH '90* August 6–10, Dallas, TX, in *Computer Graphics*, **24**, 177–85

Buxton, W. (1990) The pragmatics of haptic input, Tutorial 26 Notes, *CHI '90, ACM Conf. on Human Factors in Computing Systems*, Seattle, WA

Carswell, C. M. and Wickens, C. D. (1990) The perceptual interaction of graphical attributes: configurality, stimulus homogeneity, and object integration, *Percept. Psychophys.*, **47**, 157–68

Chernikoff, R., Duey, J. W., and Taylor, F. V. (1960) Effect of various display-control configurations on tracking with identical and different coordinate dynamics, *J. Exp. Psychol.*, **60**, 318–22

Colquhoun, W. P. and Baddeley, A. D. (1967) Influence of signal probability during pretraining on vigilance decrement, *J. Exp. Psychol.*, **73**, 153–5

Cruz-Neira, C. *et al.* (1992) The CAVE: audio-visual experience automatic virtual environment, *Commun. ACM*, **35**, 65–72

Deering, M. F. (1993) *Explorations of Display Interfaces for Virtual Reality*, pp. 141–7

Duncan, J. (1979) Divided attention: the whole is more than the sum of the parts, *J. Exp. Psychol.: Human Percept. Perform.*, **5**, 216–28

Durlach, N. I. and Mavor, A. S. (Eds) (1994) *Virtual Reality: Scientific and Technical Challenges*, Washington, DC: National Academy Press

Dwyer, F. M. (1967) Adapting visual illustrations for effective learning, *Harvard Educational Rev.*, **37**, 250–63

Ellis, S. R. and Hacisalihzade, S. S. (1990) Symbolic enhancement of perspective displays, *Proc. of the 34th Annual Meeting of the Human Factors Society*, Santa Monica, CA: Human Factors Society, pp. 1465–9

Ellis, S. R., McGreevy, M. W., and Hitchcock, R. J. (1987) Perspective traffic display format and airline pilot traffic avoidance, *Human Factors*, **29**, 371–82

Ellis, S. R., Smith, S., and Hacisalihzade, S. (1989) Visual direction as a metric of visual space, *Proc. of the 33rd Annual Meeting of the Human Factors Society*, Santa Monica CA: Human Factors Society, pp. 1392–5

Ellis, S. R., Tharp, G. K., Grunwald, A. J., and Smith, S. (1991) Exocentric judgments in real environments and stereoscopic displays, *Proc. of the 35th Annual Meeting of the Human Factors Society*, Santa Monica, CA: Human Factors Society, pp. 1442–6

Endsley, M. (in press) Toward a theory of situation awareness, *Human Factor*

Eyles, D. E. (1991). A computer graphics system for visualizing spacecraft in orbit, in S. R. Ellis *et al.* (Eds), *Pictorial Communication in Virtual and Real Environments*, London: Taylor and Francis, pp. 196–206

Flach, J. M., Hagen, B. A., O'Brien, D., and Olson, W. A. (1990) Alternative displays for discrete movement control, *Human Factors*, **32**, 685–96

Foreman, N., Foreman, D., Cummings, A., and Owens, S. (1990) Locomotion, active choice, and spatial memory in children, *J. Gen. Psychol.*, **117**, 215–32

Franklin, N. and Tversky, B. (1990) Searching imagined environments, *J. Exp. Psychol.: Gen.*, **119**, 63–76

Garner, W. R. and Felfoldy, G. L. (1970) Integrality of stimulus dimensions in various types of information processing, *Cognitive Psychology*, **1**, 225–41

Gershon, N. *et al.* (1993) Is visualization really necessary? The role of visualization in science, engineering and medicine, in G. M. Nielson and D. Dergeron (Eds), *Proceedings Visualization 1993*, Los Alomitos, CA: IEEE Computer Society Press, pp. 343–6

Gibson, J. J. (1979) *The Ecological Approach to Visual Perception*, Boston: Houghton Mifflin

Golovchinsky, G. and Chignell, M. (1993) Queries-R-links: Graphical markup for text navigation, *Interchi '93*, pp. 454–60

Gregory, R. L. (1991) Seeing by exploring, in S. R. Ellis *et al.* (Eds), *Pictorial Communication in Virtual and Real Environments*, London: Taylor and Francis, pp. 328–37

Grunwald, A. J. and Ellis, S. R. (1993) Visual display aid for orbital maneuvering: experimental evaluation, *J. Guid. Contr. Dyn.*, **16**, 145–50

Hancock, P. A. and Meshkati, N. (1988) *Human Mental Workload*, Amsterdam: North-Holland

Harwood, K. and Wickens, C. D. (1991) Frames of reference for helicopter electronic maps: the relevance of spatial cognition and componential analysis, *Int. J. Aviation Psychol.*, **1**, 5–23

Haskell, I. D. and Wickens, C. D. (1993) Two- and three-dimensional displays for aviation: a theoretical and empirical comparison, *Int. J. Aviation Psychol.*, **3**, 87–109

Henry, D. and Furness, T. (1993) Spatial perception in virtual environments, *Proc. IEEE Virtual Reality Annual Int. Symp. (VRAIS)*, September 18–21, Seattle, WA, pp. 33–40

Hochberg, J. and Brooks, V. (1978) Film cutting and visual momentum, in J. W. Senders *et al.* (Eds), *Eye Movements and the Higher Psychological Functions*, Hillsdale, NJ: Erlbaum

Hofer, E. F. and Palen, L. A. (1993) Flight deck information managements: an experimental study of functional integration of approach data, *Proc. of the 7th Int. Symp. on Aviation Psychology*, Columbus, OH: Dept. of Aviation, Ohio State University

Howard, I. P. (1986) The perception of posture, self motion, and the visual vertical, in

K. R. Boff *et al.* (Eds), *Handbook of Perception and Human Performance, vol. I: Sensory Processes and Perception, vol. I*, New York: Wiley, pp. 18-1–18-62

Jacoby, R. H. and Ellis, S. R. (1992) Using virtual menus in a virtual environment, *Proc. of the SPIE Technical Conf. 1666*, San Jose, CA

Jagacinski, R. J. (1977) A qualitative look at feedback control theory as a style of describing behavior, *Human Factors*, **19**, 331–47

Kessel, C. J. and Wickens, C. D. (1982) The transfer of failure-detection skills between monitoring and controlling dynamic systems, *Human Factors*, **24**, 49–60

Knepp, L., Barrett, D., and Sheridan, T. B. (1982) Searching for an object in four or higher dimensional space, *Proc. of the 1982 IEEE Int. Conf. on Cybernetics and Society*, Seattle, WA, pp. 636–40

Koonce, J. M. (1979) Predictive validity of flight simulators as a function of simulator motion, *Human Factors*, **21**, 215–23

Kuchar, J. K. and Hansman, R. J., Jr (1993) An exploratory study of plan-view terrain displays for air carrier operations, *Int. J. Aviation Psychol.*, **3**, 39–54

Larish, J. F. and Flach, M. J. (1990) Sources of optical information useful for perception of speed of rectilinear self-motion, *J. Exp. Psychol.: Human Percept. Perform.*, **16**, 295–302

Lee, J. D. and Moray, N. (1992) Trust, control strategies and allocation of function in human-machine systems, *Ergonomics*, **35**, 1243–70

Levine, M. (1982) You-are-here maps: psychological considerations, *Environ. Behavior*, **14**, 221–37

Liang, J. *et al.* (1991) On temporal-spatial realism in the virtual reality environment, *Proceedings of UIST '91*, Hilton Head, SC, November 11–13, pp. 19–25

Liebowitz, H. (1988) The human senses in flight, in E. Wiener and D. Nagel (Eds), *Human Factors in Aviation*, San Diego: Academic, pp. 83–110

Lintern, G. (1987) Flight simulation motion systems revisited, *Human Factors Soc. Bull.*, **30**, 1–3

Lintern, G. (1991) An informational perspective on skill transfer in human-machine systems, *Human Factors*, **33**, 251–66

Lintern, G. and Wickens, C. D. (1991) Issues for acquisition in transfer of timesharing and dual-task skills, in D. Damos (Ed.), *Multiple Task Performance*, London: Taylor and Francis

Macinlay, J. D. *et al.* (1990) Rapid controlled movement through a virtual 3D workspace, *Proc. of SIGGRAPH '90*, August 6–10, Dallas, TX, in *Computer Graphics*, **24**, 171–6

McGovern, D. E. (1991) Experience and results in teleoperation of land vehicles, in S. R. Ellis *et al.* (Eds), *Pictorial Communication in Virtual and Real Environments*, London: Taylor and Francis, pp. 182–95

McGreevy, M. W. (1991) Virtual reality and planetary exploration, *29th AAS Goddard Memorial Symp.*, Washington, DC

McGreevy, M. W. and Ellis, S. R. (1986) The effect of perspective geometry on judged direction in spatial information instruments, *Human Factors*, **28**, 439–56

McKinnon, G. M. and Kruk, R. V. (1991). Multi-axis control in telemanipulation and vehicle guidance, in S. R. Ellis *et al.* (Eds), *Pictorial Communication in Virtual and Real Environments*, London: Taylor and Francis, pp. 247–64

Mercurio, P. J. and Erickson, T. D. (1990) Interactive scientific visualization: an assessment of a virtual reality system, *Proc. of INTERACT*

Merwin, D. H. and Wickens, C. D. (1991) 2D vs. 3D display for multidimensional data visualization: the relationship between task integrality and display proximity,

Proc. of the 35th Annual Meeting of the Human Factors Society, Santa Monica, CA: Human Factors Society

Minsky, M. *et al.* (1990) Feeling and seeing: issues in force display, *Proc. of the 1990 Workshop on Interactive 3D Graphics*, March 25–28, Snowbird, UT, in *Computer Graphics*, **24**, 235–43

Mosher, C. E. J. *et al.* (1986) The virtual simulator, *Proc. of the 1986 Workshop on Interactive 3D Graphics*, October 23–24, Chapel Hill, SC, pp. 37–42

Mykityshyn, M. and Hansman, R. J. (1993) Electronic instrument approach plates: the effect of selective decluttering on flight crew performance, *Proc. of the 7th Int. Symp. on Aviation Psychol.*, Columbus, OH: Dept. of Aviation, Ohio State University

Newby, G. (1992) An investigation of the role of navigation for information retrieval, *Proc. of ASIS*

Notterman, J. M. and Page, D. E. (1962) Evaluation of mathematically equivalent tracking systems, *Percept. Motor Skills*, **15**, 683–716

Nugent, W. A. (1987) A comparative assessment of computer-based media for presenting job task instructions, *Proc. of the 31st Annual Meeting of the Human Factors Society*, Santa Monica, CA: Human Factors Society, pp. 696–700

O'Hare, D. and Roscoe, S. N. (1990) *Flightdeck Performance: The human factor*, Ames, IA: Iowa State University

Oman, C. M. (1991) Sensory conflict in motion sickness: an observer theory approach, in S. R. Ellis *et al.* (Eds), *Pictorial Communication in Virtual and Real Environments*, London: Taylor and Francis, pp. 362–76

Pausch, R. (1991). Virtual reality on five dollars a day, *CHI '91 Proc.*, ACM, pp. 265–9

Perrone, J. A. (1982) Visual slant underestimation: a general model, *Perception*, **11**, 641–54

Prazdny, K. (1986) Three-dimensional structure from long-range apparent motion, *Perception*, **15**, 619–25

Prevett, T. T. and Wickens, C. D. (1994) *Perspective displays and frame of reference: Their interdependence to realize performance advantages over planar displays in a terminal area navigation task*, Technical Report ARL-94-8/NASA-94-3, Savoy, IL: University of Illinois, Institute of Aviation, Aviation Research Laboratory

Regan, D. M., Kaufman, L., and Lincoln, J. (1986) Motion in depth and visual acceleration, in K. R. Boff *et al.* (Eds), *Handbook of Perception and Human Performance, vol. I: Sensory Processes and Perception*, New York: Wiley, pp. 19-1–19-46

Reichlen, B. A. (1993) Sparcchair: a one hundred million pixel display, *Proc. IEEE Virtual Reality Annual Int. Symp. (VRAIS)*, September 18–21, Seattle, WA, pp. 300–7

Rheingold, H. (1991) *Virtual Reality*, New York: Summit Books

Roscoe, S. N. (1968) Airborne displays for flight and navigation, *Human Factors*, **10**, 321–32

Roscoe, S. N. (1991) The eyes prefer real images, in S. R. Ellis and M. Kaiser (Eds), *Pictorial Communication in Virtual and Real Environments*, London: Taylor and Francis, pp. 577–86

Sarter, N. B. and Woods, D. D. (1991) Situation awareness: a critical but ill-defined phenomenon, *Int. J. Aviation Psychol.*, **1**, 45–58

Sarter, N. and Woods, D. (1994). Pilot interaction with cockpit automation II. *Int. J. Aviation Psychol.*, **4**(1), 1–28

Schmidt, J. K. and Kysor, K. P. (1987) Designing airline passenger safety cards, *Proc.*

of the 31st Annual Meeting of the Human Factors Society, Santa Monica, CA: Human Factors Society, pp. 51–5

Sedgwick, H. A. (1986) Space perception, in K. Boff *et al.* (Eds), *Handbook of Perception and Performance, vol. I: Sensory Processes and Perception*, New York: Wiley, pp. 21-1–21-57

Shebilske, W. L. (1991) Visuomotor modularity, ontogeny and training high-performance skills with spatial instruments, in S. R. Ellis *et al.* (Eds), *Pictorial Communication in Virtual and Real Environments*, London: Taylor and Francis, pp. 305–15

Shepard, R. N. and Cooper, L. A. (1982) *Mental Images and their Transformations*, Cambridge, MA: MIT Press

Shepard, R. N. and Hurwitz, S. (1984) Upward direction, mental rotation, and discrimination of left and right turns in maps, *Cognition*, **18**, 161–93, also in S. Pinker (Ed.), *Visual Cognition*, Cambridge, MA: MIT Press, pp. 163–93

Sheridan, T. B. (1987) Supervisory control, in G. Salvendy (Ed.), *Handbook of Human Factors*, New York: Wiley, pp. 1243–68

Sheridan, T. B. (1992) *Telerobotics, Automation, and Human Supervisory Control*, Cambridge, MA: MIT Press

Spencer, K. (1988) *The Psychology of Educational Technology and Instructional Media*, London: Routledge

Stevens, K. A. (1991) The perception of three-dimensionality across continuous surfaces, in S. R. Ellis *et al.* (Eds), *Pictorial Communication in Virtual and Real Environments*, London: Taylor and Francis, pp. 449–59

Stone, D. E. and Gluck, M. D. (1980) How do young adults read directions with and without pictures? *Technical Report*, Ithaca, NY: Cornell University, Department of Education

Sturman, D. J. *et al.* (1989) Hands-on interaction with virtual environments, *Proc. of UIST '89*, November 13–15, Williamsburg, VA, pp. 19–24

Sweller, O., Chandler, P., Tierney, P., and Cooper, M. (1990) Cognitive load as a factor in the structuring of technical material, *J. Exp. Psychol.: Gen.*, **119**, 176–92

Teichner, W. H. and Mocharnuk, J. B. (1979) Visual search for complex targets, *Human Factors*, **21**, 259–76

Tulving, E. and Thomson, D. M. (1973) Encoding specificity and retrieval processes in episodic memory, *Psychol. Rev.*, **80**, 352–73

Tversky, B. (1991) Distortions in memory for visual displays, in S. R. Ellis *et al.* (Eds), *Pictorial Communication in Virtual and Real Environments*, London: Taylor and Francis, pp. 61–75

Van Der Heijden (1992) *Selective Attention in Vision*, London: Routledge

Vicente, K. J. and Williges, R. C. (1988) Accommodating individual differences in searching a hierarchical file system, *Int. J. Man-Machine Studies*, **29**, 647–68

Ware, C. and Jessome, D. R. (1988) Using the bat: a six-dimensional mouse for object placement, *IEEE Computer Graphics Appl.*, **8**, 65–70

Ware, C. and Osborne, S. (1990) Exploration and virtual camera control in virtual three-dimensional environments, *Proc. of the 1990 Workshop on Interactive 3D Graphics*, March 25–28, Snowbird, UT, in *Computer Graphics*, **24**, 175–83

Warren, R and Wertheim, A. H. (Eds) (1990) *Perception and Control of Self-motion*, Hillsdale, NJ: Erlbaum

Weintraub, D. J. and Ensing, M. J. (1992) *The Book of HUD—A Head-up Display State of the Art Report*, CSERIAC SOAR 91-2, Wright-Patterson AFB, OH

Wertheim, A. H. (1990) Visual, vestibular, and oculomotor interactions in the perception of object motion during egomotion, in R. Warren and A. H. Wertheim (Eds), *Perception and Control of Self-motion*, Hillsdale, NJ: Erlbaum, pp. 171–217

Wexelblat (1993) *Virtual Reality: Applications and Explorations*, Orlando, FL: Academic Press

Wickens, C. D. (1986) The effects of control dynamics on performance, in K. Boff *et al.* (Eds), *Handbook of Perception and Performance, vol. II*, New York: Wiley, pp. 39-1–39-60

Wickens, C. D. (1992a) Virtual reality and education, *Proc. of the IEEE Int. Conf. on Systems, Man, and Cybernetics*, vol. 1, New York: IEEE, pp. 842–7

Wickens, C. D. (1992b) *Engineering Psychology and Human Performance*, 2nd edn, New York: Harper Collins

Wickens, C. D., Liang, C. C., Prevett, T., and Olmos, O. (1994) Egocentric and exocentric displays for terminal area navigation, *Proc. of the 38th Annual Meeting of the Human Factors and Ergonomics Society*, Santa Monica, CA: Human Factors Society

Wickens, C. D., Merwin, D. H., and Lin, E. (1994) The human factors implications of graphics enhancements for the visualization of scientific data: dimensional integrality, stereopsis, motion, and mesh, *Human Factors*, **36**, 44–61

Wickens, C. D., Todd, S., and Seidler, K. (1989) Three-dimensional displays: perception, implementation, and applications, *University of Illinois Institute of Aviation Technical Report*, ARL-89-11/CSERIAC-89-1, Savoy, IL: Aviation Research Laboratory; (also CSERIAC SOAR 89-001, AAMRL, Wright-Patterson AFB, OH, December)

Wiener, E. L. (1989) *Human factors of advanced technology ("glass cockpit") transport aircraft*, NASA Contractors Report 177528, Moffett Field, CA: NASA Ames Research Center

Williams, H. P. and Wickens, C. D. (1993) A comparison of methods for promoting geographic knowledge in simulated aircraft navigation, *University of Illinois Institute of Aviation Technical Report*, ARL-93-9/NASA-93-3, Savoy, IL: Aviation Research Laboratory

Williams, H. P., Wickens, C. D., and Hutchinson, S. (1994) Realism and interactivity in navigational training: a comparison of three methods, *Proc. of the 38th Annual Meeting of the Human Factors and Ergonomics Society*, Santa Monica, CA: Human Factors Society

Wise, J. A. and Debons, A. (1987) Principles of film editing and display system design, *Proc. of the 31st Annual Meeting of the Human Factors Society*, Santa Monica, CA: Human Factors Society, pp. 121–4

Wolpert, L. (1990) Field-of-view information for self-motion perception, in R. Warren and A. H. Wertheim (Eds), *Perception and Control of Self-motion*, Hillsdale, NJ: Erlbaum, pp. 101–26

Woods, D. D. (1984) Visual momentum: a concept to improve the cognitive coupling of person and computer, *Int. J. Man-Machine Studies*, **21**, 229–44

Yallow, E. (1980) *Individual differences in learning from verbal and figural materials, Aptitudes Research Project Technical Report No. 13*, Palo Alto, CA: School of Education, Stanford University

Zhai, S. and Milgram, P. (1993) Human performance evaluation of manipulation schemes in virtual environments, *Proc. IEEE Virtual Reality Annual Int. Symp. (VRAIS)*, September, Seattle, WA

Zimmerman, T. *et al.* (1987) A hand gesture interface device, *Proc. of CHI '87 and Graphics Interface*, April 5–7, Toronto, Canada, pp. 189–92

14

Augmented-Reality Displays

WOODROW BARFIELD, CRAIG ROSENBERG,
AND WOUTER A. LOTENS

Recent technological advancements in virtual environment equipment have led to the development of augmented reality displays for applications in medicine, manufacturing, and scientific visualization (Bajura *et al.*, 1992; Janin *et al.*, 1993; Milgram *et al.*, 1991; Lion *et al.*, 1993). However, even with technological advances in virtual environment equipment, the development of augmented reality displays are still in the early stages of development, primarily demonstrating the possibilities, the use, and the technical realization of the concept. The purpose of this chapter is to review the literature on the design and use of augmented reality displays, to suggest applications for this technology, and to suggest new techniques to create these displays. In addition, the chapter also discusses the technological issues associated with creating augmented realities such as image registration, update rate, and the range and sensitivity of position sensors. Furthermore, the chapter discusses human-factors issues and visual requirements that should be considered when creating augmented-reality displays.

Essentially, an augmented-reality display allows a designer to combine part or all of a real-world visual scene, with synthetic imagery. Typically, the real-world visual scene in an augmented-reality display is captured by video or directly viewed. In terms of descriptions of augmented reality found in the literature, Janin *et al.* (1993) used the term "augmented reality" to signify a see-through head-mounted display (HMD) which allowed the user to view his surroundings with the addition of computer graphics overlaid on the real-world scene. Similarly, Robinett (1992) suggested the term "augmented reality" for a real image that was being enhanced with synthetic parts; he called the result a "merged representation". Finally, Fuchs and Neuman (1993) observed that an augmented-reality display combined a simulated environment with direct perception of the world with the capability to interactively manipulate the real or virtual object(s).

Based on the above descriptions, most current augmented-reality displays are designed using see-through HMDs which allow the observer to view the real world directly with the naked eye. However, if video is used to capture the real world, one may use either an opaque HMD or a screen-based system to view the scene (Lion *et al.*, 1993). Thus, in this chapter we use a more general description of an augmented reality display in which the HMD may or may not be a component of the system, and the HMD may or may not be see-through. Finally, while the focus of this chapter is on visually based augmented realities, using the other sensory modalities, e.g., auditory and tactile, other types of "augmented reality" displays are possible. A later section discusses this interesting topic. However, unless otherwise noted, when the term "augmented reality" is used in this chapter, it refers to the combination of video or a real-world scene, with overlaid computer graphics.

ADVANTAGES OF AUGMENTED-REALITY DISPLAYS

Typically, in "virtual reality" a stereoscopic scene is viewed using an opaque HMD providing the viewer with a sense of immersion. With this type of display, the generated world consists entirely of computer graphics. However, for several applications it may be desirable to use as much as possible of the real world in the scene rather than creating a new scene using computer-generated imagery. For example, in medical applications the physician must view the patient to perform surgery, and in telerobotics the operator must view the remote scene in order to perform tasks such as controlling the path of a robot's arm. In addition, for tasks such as maintaining or repairing equipment it is necessary for the repair person to see the actual equipment.

A main motivation for the use of augmented-reality displays relates to the computational resources necessary to generate and update computer-generated scenes. When designing virtual environments, the more complex the scene, the more the computational resources which must be used to render the scene, especially for real-time applications. However, the concept of augmented reality is to enhance the real world with synthetic imagery. Therefore, this approach does not require a scene that consists entirely of computer graphics. Instead, synthetic imagery is used as a supplement to the real-world scene. In addition, for many applications of augmented reality, the synthetic component of the augmented-reality display will not require highly realistic imagery. For example, some applications in augmented reality may require only line graphics or text, typically monochrome, overlaid on top of the real-world scene. This was the case in the augmented-reality system developed by Janin *et al.* (1993), where only 30–40 monochrome lines per frame were needed to augment a real-world scene with wiring-diagram information.

An additional reason why it may be desirable to combine synthetic imagery with real-world scenes is to maintain the high level of detail and realistic shading that one finds in the real world. As noted, to model the complexity of the real world using entirely computer graphics would not only be a very tedious task but would require tremendous computational resources. This is an important point because currently one of the most time-consuming aspects of designing virtual environments is associated with the laborious process of modeling complex scenes. The incorporation of computer-generated objects with the real-world scene will provide the designer with a rich visual scene to start with, one that will not have to be painstakingly modeled and rendered using extensive computational resources.

Another potential benefit associated with the use of augmented-reality displays is related to the problem of simulator sickness. Vertigo, dizziness induced by sensory mismatches within display environments, can be a problem when one uses an HMD to view a virtual world. Metzger (1993) postulated that an augmented-reality display may minimize the effect of vertigo because this type of display system still provides the observer an anchor in reality. For example, if the participant starts to feel uneasy, instead of having to remove the HMD to orient himself, an observer using a see-through HMD can simply look down at his hands or feet to orient himself with the real world. Finally, another reason why the real-world scene may be important to include in a visual display is if the task is to show an annotation to the real world. In this case the real world is obviously needed. An example of this would be a training exercise in which it is desirable to allow the trainee to use a real object in the exercise, but to access overlaid graphics of the scene to perhaps emphasize maintenance or repair steps, or to show the internal structure of an object.

VISUAL DISPLAY SYSTEMS FOR AUGMENTED REALITY

Generally, to create a computer-generated augmented reality, the following equipment is necessary: (1) hardware for displaying visual images; (2) a position and orientation sensing system; (3) hardware for combining the computer graphics and video images into one signal (which may be any TV standard or digital video) and (4) the associated system software (Janin *et al.*, 1993). As mentioned, there are two main ways in which the real-world and computer-generated imagery may be combined to form an augmented scene. The first method involves the direct viewing of the real world with overlaid computer-generated imagery as an enhancement. In this case, the real-world image and the computer-generated image(s) are combined optically. The second method involves combining camera-captured video of the real world with computer-generated imagery viewed using either an opaque HMD, or a screen-based display system. If the augmented reality involves video of the real world, then the electronic merging (see keying in a later section) of the computer graphics and the video images are determined on a pixel by pixel basis, a procedure used by Fuchs and Neuman (1993). In summary, given a see-through HMD, opaque HMD, or a screen-based system for augmented reality, the following two basic types of augmented reality can be created.

- *Opaque HMD or screen-based augmented reality.* These systems can be used to view local or remote video views of real-world scenes, combined with overlaid computer graphics. The viewing of a remote scene is an integral component of telepresence applications.
- *Transparent HMD augmented reality.* This system allows the observer to view the real world directly using half-silvered mirrors with computer-

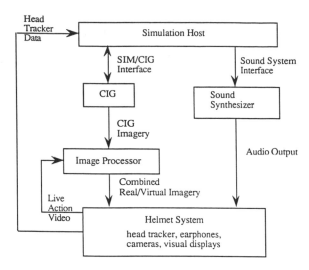

Figure 14-1 System overview of Metzger's augmented reality system. (Copyright 1993 Metzger, LORAL Advanced Distribution Simulation, Inc.)

graphics electronically composited into the image. An advantage of this system is that the real world can be directly viewed and manipulated.

To further describe the basic components of an augmented-reality system we present Metzger's (1993) flow diagram of an opaque HMD with the real world represented by video input (Figure 14-1). A detailed description of a screen-based augmented-reality system developed at the University of Washington is presented in a later section to describe an alternative procedure to create an augmented-reality environment. In Metzger's system, the video image is captured using a single camera mounted on the top of an HMD. This produces a monoscopic (non-stereo) image of the real world. If a stereoscopic real-world image is required for the application, then two cameras can be mounted on the HMD and calibrated to provide the appropriate parallax to create stereoscopic images. In either case, the acquired video signal(s) is electronically combined with the computer-generated scene and transmitted to liquid-crystal display (LCD) or cathode ray rube (CRT) screens mounted inside the HMD. The synthetic image is generated using a computer graphics workstation with sufficient power to model and render the scene that is being displayed. The real-world video is input along with the real-time computer-generated imagery, into a video luminance or chrominance keyer. The result is that the user sees both the video image of the world outside the helmet as well as the computer-generated graphics which are overlaid on top of the video signal.

Table 14-1 provides additional examples of the use of video and computer graphics for the design of visual displays. In the table, CGI refers to computer-generated imagery and video typically refers to an NTSC image (525 lines) of a real environment (remote or local) that is acquired using one or two video cameras mounted on an HMD or perhaps on a robot located at a remote

Table 14-1 Classification of visual imagery for video, virtual, and augmented-reality displays.

Type of visual stimulus	Description	Typical applications
Video only	• analog or digital images of real scene	• television, telepresence, surveillance
CGI only	• virtual environments, computer graphics	• scientific visualization entertainment, 3D CAD, virtual world development
CGI and real-world	• computer graphics overlaid on real scene	• manufacturing, medicine, augmented reality
CGI with video of the real world	• video-captured real-world scene combined with CGI	• training, knowledge enhancement, military applications, augmented reality

site. The first visual stimulus listed in Table 14-1 represents a video image of the real world. This is not a direct example of an augmented-reality display; however, since video imagery can be used as part of an augmented-reality scene it is included in the table. A video image can be captured and presented in an analog or digital format and displayed using either a TV monitor, projection system, or HMD. The primary applications for video include entertainment, education, and telepresence. For telepresence applications, the addition of head-tracking equipment combined with a visual display is necessary. The second listing in the table is concerned with CGI only. Using CGI it is possible to create a virtual environment using a stereo-ready computer graphics monitor, projection system, or HMD. To create an immersive virtual environment, the addition of head-tracking equipment combined with an HMD is necessary.

Of particular interest in Table 14-1 are the two types of augmented-reality displays. The first type of augmented-reality display consists of a computer-generated image(s) overlaid on top of the real world. As noted, this is accomplished using a see-through HMD. A see-through HMD uses one (monoscopic) or two (stereoscopic) half-silvered mirror systems which allow the user to look through the mirror(s) and simultaneously view the real-world scene and the computer-generated imagery (Figure 14-2). Note that whenever a see-through HMD is used to view synthetic imagery, the resolution of the HMD is a limiting factor in the visualization of the augmented scene. For example, some commercial HMDs provide resolutions of 720 by 480 pixels in a 60° field of view, equivalent to 20/100 visual acuity. Thus, when an observer uses a see-through HMD for augmented reality, the observer is quite aware of the limited resolution of the synthetic imagery compared to the real-world scene. The second main type of augmented-reality display listed in Table 14-1 consists of an opaque HMD with combined synthetic and video imagery (Figure 14-3). With this system both graphics and video are presented at approximately the same low resolution.

However, there are some advantages associated with using video for augmented environments; with a video image it is possible to further process the visual information captured by the cameras to enhance or highlight a particular portion of the image. In addition, it is possible to mount the cameras

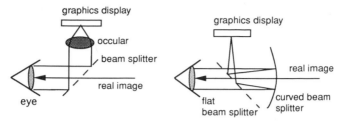

Figure 14-2 Schematic diagrams of see-through HMDs for augmented reality. The display on the left includes an ocular which magnifies the displayed image which is then projected on the retina. The viewer is able to see the real-world directly through the beamsplitter (half-silvered mirror) with overlaid imagery. In the figure on the right, a similar display is shown, the difference being the use of mirror optics to display the graphical image on the retina.

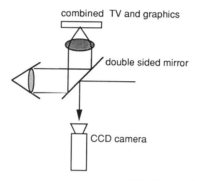

Figure 14-3 This figure shows an opaque HMD display that can be used for augmented-reality applications. With an opaque HMD, the viewer sees the combined image on displays mounted inside the HMD. With this display the real-world imagery is captured with one or two small CCD cameras, typically mounted on the HMD. Note that when using one camera, the nodal point of the camera should be located as close as possible to the position between the two eyes of the viewer. When using two cameras, the nodal point of the cameras should be located as close as possible to the position of the viewer's two eyes.

in an environment that is not local to the viewer. Finally, another benefit associated with the use of video for augmented realities is that it is possible to remove parts of the video scene and place synthetic imagery over the removed part. This, of course, is not possible using real-world imagery. Regardless of the type of display technology used to create an augmented-reality display, the user has to cognitively assimilate the two images. The cognitive issues associated with switching between two overlaid visual images are discussed in a later section.

VIDEO KEYING AND IMAGE REGISTRATION

The following sections discuss some of the basic issues involved in the design of augmented-reality displays. The first issue, video keying, is relevant when an opaque HMD with video input is used to create an augmented-reality scene. The second issue, image registration, is relevant for all types of augmented-reality systems.

Video keying

When an opaque HMD is used as part of an augmented-reality system, video and synthetic images are mixed using a video keyer to form an integrated scene. Video keying is a process that is widely used in television, film production, and computer graphics. As a familiar example of keying, consider the TV broadcast of the weather report. A TV weatherman standing in front of a weather map points to areas of interest on the map. In actuality, the weatherman is standing in front of a blue screen and a video keyer is used to superimpose a computer-generated map over the blue background. Keying is also extensively used in music video clips, combining different video sources or a single video source with computer-generated imagery.

When using a video keyer to design augmented-reality scenes, one signal contains the foreground image while the other signal contains the background image. The keyer combines the two video signals to produce a combined video signal which is then sent to the display device. Furthermore, keying can be done using composite or component video signals. A composite video signal contains information about color, luminance, and synchronization, thus combining three pieces of video information into one signal. With component video, luminance and synchronization are combined, but chroma information is delivered separately. The two types of keyers that are used in either video, film production, or augmented-reality environments, chroma and luminance keyers, are discussed next.

Chroma keying involves specifying a desired foreground key color. Foreground areas containing the key color are then electronically replaced with the background image. Typically, a keyer combines the foreground and background images in a proportion determined by the "key level." This results in the background image being replaced with the foreground image in areas where the background image contains the chroma color (Jack, 1993). A chroma keyer has the ability to replace pixels in the background image when a particular color in the foreground image is used, usually blue or black. If blue is used for keying, blue parts in the foreground image act as holes through which the background image is displayed. If a video image of the real world is chosen as the foreground image, parts of the scene that should show the computer-generated world are rendered blue. The reason why the color blue is typically used for chroma keying is that the shade of blue used, termed chromakey blue, rarely shows up in human skin tones (Metzger, 1993). In contrast, if video of the real world is chosen as the background image, the computer-generated environment will be located in the foreground.

A luminance keyer works in a similar manner to a chroma keyer, however, a luminance keyer combines the background image wherever the luminance (Y-component of the video signal) values are below a certain threshold. Luminance keying involves specifying the desired threshold of the foreground

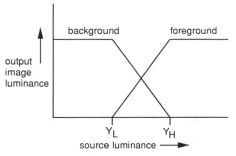

Figure 14-4 Principle of soft keying, using two threshold values for luminance. Below the value of Y_L only the background image is shown, above Y_H only the foreground. In between these values the images are overlaid.

luminance (or brightness) Y_{FG}. Foreground areas containing luminance levels below the keying level are replaced with the background image. This hard-keying implementation may be replaced with soft keying by specifying two threshold values of the foreground video signal: Y_H and $Y_L(Y_L < Y_H)$. Between the two luminances the images are both shown, with brightness changing proportionally with Y_{FG}, as depicted in Figure 14-4.

If the luminance keying is done using RGB sources, Y_{FG} (the intensity of the foreground) may be obtained by the following equation which is used to convert between RGB and NTSC:

$$Y_{FG} = 0.299R' + 0.587G' + 0.114B'$$

Luminance and chroma keyers both accomplish the same function but use of a chroma keyer can result in a sharper key and has greater flexibility, whereas a luminance keyer is typically lower resolution and has less flexibility. Metzger (1993) used a luminance keyer (as part of the NewTek Video Toaster board hosted in an Amiga computer) for his augmented-reality system. He concluded that one should consider the importance of lighting conditions when video keying. Specifically, it is important to make sure that the keyer accommodates the variations in color and lighting that in a natural image may be present at the sections that are to be replaced.

Image registration

In many applications, the visual requirement for a virtual environment is only that the generated scene look consistent to the viewer. For most augmented-reality applications, however, an additional requirement is that the computer-generated images accurately register with the surroundings in the real world (Janin *et al.*, 1993). For example, consider a medical application; when computer-generated images are overlaid onto a patient, a careful registration of the computer-generated imagery with the patient's anatomy is crucial (Bajura *et al.*, 1992; Lorensen *et al.*, 1993). In terms of developing scenes for augmented-reality displays, the problem of image registration, or positioning of the synthetic objects within the scene in relation to the real objects, is both a difficult and important technical problem to solve (Figure 14-5).

Figure 14-5 Example of superimposed images and the problem of registration. The left image shows the registration before calibration, the right image after calibration. (Copyright 1993 Oyama, Tsunemoto, Tachi, and Inoue, Mechanical Engineering Laboratory, Tsukuba Science City, Japan. Presence: *Teleoperators and Virtual Environments*, Volume 2(2), MIT Press.)

Image registration is an important issue regardless of whether one is using a see-through or an opaque HMD to view the augmented-reality environment. For example, for medical tasks, such as performing a fine-needle aspiration biopsy of a breast tumor, a very close registration of the real and computer-generated stimuli is absolutely necessary (Bajura *et al.*, 1992). With applications that require close registration (as most do), accurate depth information has to be retrieved from the real world in order to carry out the calibration of the real and synthetic environments. Without an accurate knowledge of the geometry of the real-world and computer-generated scene, exact registration is not possible.

To properly align video and computer-generated images with respect to each other, several frames of reference must be considered. Janin *et al.* (1993) (using an HMD) and Lorensen *et al.* (1993) (using a screen-based system) have discussed issues of image calibration in the context of different frames of reference for augmented reality. In Lorensen's medical example, two coordinate systems were necessary, a real-world coordinate system and a virtual-world coordinate system. Alignment of the video and computer-generated imagery was done manually. Lorensen pointed out that this procedure worked well when anatomical features of the patient were easily visible.

More detailed information concerning image registration is shown in Figure 14-6 from Janin *et al.* (1993). This figure shows several coordinate systems which must be taken into account in order to accurately register real and synthetic images for a manufacturing application. In general, the position-sensing transmitter is located at a fixed and known position in the real environment and the position-sensing receiver is mounted on an HMD. As shown in Figure 14-6, a point on the top of the work bench is projected onto the virtual screen. Objects in the real world which are located on the work bench are defined by means of a world coordinate system. The virtual screen coordinate system is computed based on the location of the virtual screen with

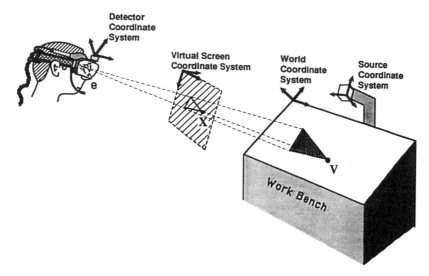

Figure 14-6 Schematic drawing representing four coordinate systems which can be used for image registration. (Copyright 1993 Janin, Mizell, and Caudell, Boeing Computer Services.)

respect to the optics of the physical display. The virtual screen parameters include three rotational and the three translational components that define the location of the virtual screen relative to the world coordinate system. In stereoscopic augmented reality there are two virtual screens (one for each eye) that define the viewport.

In addition, there are two other coordinate systems that must be taken into account, those which relate to the position sensor that detects head position and rotation (receiver), and those which relate to the position transmitter. The position sensor receives a signal from the source (transmitter); this information is used to track head position. Both the transmitter and the receiver, as shown in Figure 14-6, are described in terms of the coordinate system associated with them. The transmitter is a real-world object and is rigidly attached to the world coordinate system. As the user moves his head, the position and orientation of the receiver change with respect to the source. In addition, there are a few parameters that can change across users. These parameters include the interocular distance between the user's eyes (average about 64 mm) as well as the vertical distance from the position sensor (located at the top of the head) to the horizontal plane of the eyes. For accurate registration of images, these two user parameters must be accounted for on an individual basis within the calibration of the system.

According to Janin *et al.* (1993) the most useful accuracy measurement for an augmented-reality system is the error in the projected image relative to the real image. Simple geometry shows that the projected error (E) scales linearly with the positional error (P) and as the sine of the orientation error ψ:

$$E = P + D \sin \psi$$

where D is the distance between the transmitter and receiver.

Using a Polhemus Isotrack position sensor Janin and colleagues were able to achieve about 0.2 inches translational error and 2 degree rotational error, leading to a projection error of about 0.8 inches at 18 inches (they point out that the next generation of position sensors will lead to higher accuracy). A finer calibration can be achieved using the Dual Camera Metrology procedure as described by Janin *et al.*, (1993) and Sid-Ahmed and Boraie (1990). This procedure involves computing several parameters, such as the location of the viewer's eye in virtual screen coordinates, the horizontal and vertical resolution of the virtual screen, and a 4×4 matrix to transform the real-world coordinate system to the virtual-screen coordinate system. Using a calibration image it is possible to compute the positional dismatch between the current virtual location of an object and its desired location by measuring the location and orientation of the position sensor. Using this information, the transformation matrix can be calculated so that the dismatch goes to zero. They reported that this procedure results in a translational accuracy of better than 0.05 inches using 640×480 video cameras and given the field of view of the display used in their study.

In addition, Janin and colleagues present a third technique that can be used to measure the accuracy with which virtual images are registered with real-world images. This method involves the subject aligning a crosshair, viewed through an HMD, with objects of known position and geometry in the real world. Because this crosshair is not head tracked it moves with the user's head, this allows the vector from the position tracker to the real-world object to be measured. The alignment procedure is done from multiple viewing positions and orientations, and, as reported by Janin and colleagues, allows a level of accuracy in terms of projection errors of 0.5 inches, the approximate resolution of the position sensor.

Another design issue for augmented realities is concerned with the optics of the camera lens used to acquire the real-world video image and the optics of the HMD. The focal length of a camera is the distance between the near nodal point of the lens and the focal plane, when the focus of the lens is set to infinity. There are two nodal points in a compound lens system. The front nodal point is where the rays of light entering the lens appear to aim. The rear nodal point is where the rays of light appear to have come from, after passing through the lens. Camera lenses which may be used to design augmented-reality displays may vary in field of view. For example, a typical wide-angle lens has an 80° field of view, a standard lens a 44° field of view and a typical telephoto lens a 23° field of view. The use of a zoom lens that has the capability to change from wide-angle to telephoto views of the scene is desirable for augmented-reality displays as this allows the researcher to match the field of view of the real-world scene to the field of view of the computer-generated scene. In addition, depth of field, described as the distance from the nearest to the furthest parts of a scene which are rendered sharp at a given focusing setting, is another important variable to consider for augmented-reality displays. Depth of field increases as the lens is stepped down (smaller lens aperture), when it is focused for distant objects, or when the lens has a short focal length. In some cases it is desirable to have a large depth of field when using an augmented-reality system in order to maximize the amount of the scene that is in focus.

Edwards *et al.* (1993) from the University of North Carolina at Chapel Hill have discussed the above issues in the context of augmented reality. Their system consisted of the Flight Helmet from Vision Research using LEEP optics and two color LCDs as displays, positioned to provide a 75° horizontal field of view. Video images were acquired using two miniature charge-coupled device (CCD) or digital imaging cameras. A CCD camera is similar to traditional analog cameras; however, after light has passed through the lens of a digital camera it falls on a CCD, a grid of light-sensitive elements that alters its electrical output as a function of the amount of light falling on it. The field of view of the image is a function of the focal length of the lens and also a function of the size of the CCD detector. For an augmented-reality display, the field of view of the camera lens and the field of view of the HMD's optics must match exactly. If not, magnification or minification of the real-world scene will occur and the foreground and the background images will not be accurately registered. They are matched if:

$$y/D = s/f$$

where y is the HMD image size, D its distance from the eye to the screen, s is the size of the CCD sensor array, and f is the focal length of the camera.

Edwards *et al.* (1993) gave an example of calculating the camera's focal length, with LEEP optics as part of the HMD. Given the height of the LCD screens for the Flight Helmet ($y = 595.2$ mm), and their positions with respect to the LEEP optics ($D = 1178.4$ mm), the vertical field of view can be calculated as $\tan^{-1}$ (595.2/1178.4), or 26.8°. In addition, the camera sensor size (s above) can be used to calculate the focal length, f, that should be used for the camera lens.

Other important variables to consider when designing an augmented-reality display include the horizontal disparity (horizontal offset) of the two cameras, and the convergence angle of the two cameras. Some basic information on these variables is provided by Milgram *et al.* (1991) who used video cameras to create a stereo real-world image superimposed with a stereo computer-generated pointer. In their system, the cameras, each with a focal length of 8 mm, were separated by 0.118 m and were set to converge at 0.965 m. Therefore images further than 0.965 m from the camera appeared behind the plane of the monitor (i.e., uncrossed disparity) and those closer than 0.965 m appeared in front of the plane of the monitor (i.e., crossed disparity). Furthermore, if the video of the real world is to appear as if viewed through the user's eyes, the two miniature cameras must act as if they were at the same physical location of the wearer's eyes. Edwards *et al.* (1993) tried several different camera configurations to find the best combination of these factors for augmented-reality displays. They determined that the inter-pupillary nodal distance is an important parameter to consider for applications which require close to medium viewing distances for depth judgments and that "off-axisness" is hard to get used to when objects are close to the viewer. Placing the cameras in front of the wearer's eyes may result in perfectly registered video and computer-generated images, but the images of the outside world seen through the HMD will appear magnified and thus closer than they actually are. In addition, further refinements are possible by adjusting the horizontal tilt and disparity of the display. The horizontal tilt represents the convergence angle of the display and the disparity represents the horizontal distance between the center of the two displays.

SYSTEM DESIGN ISSUES FOR AUGMENTED REALITY DISPLAYS

In addition to the design problems addressed above, there are several other issues of relevance for the design and use of augmented-reality displays. These include the frame rate, update rate, system delays, and the range and sensitivity of the tracking sensors. As noted by Piantanida *et al.* (1993) the frame rate is a hardware-controlled variable determining the number of images presented to the eye per second. Systems that use the NTSC standard present two interlaced fields at 60 Hz, presenting together 30 frames per second. For interlaced video this is a reasonable rate, but for non-interlaced video a frame rate this low can cause annoying flicker, visual fatigue, and reduced sensitivity to motion (Piantanida *et al.*, 1993). Monoscopic augmented-reality displays that show an image to one eye, for example the "modified" Private Eye used by Feiner and colleagues (1993), use an LED display with a 50 Hz refresh rate showing 25 lines with 80 characters per line. Augmented reality displays which show stereo images alternately to the left and right eye typically use a scan rate doubler to transmit 120 frames per second so that each eye has an effective frame rate of 60 Hz (Lion *et al.*, 1993).

Given that augmented reality displays present images of varying levels of complexity (normally at 60 Hz) a more important variable to consider is the update rate. The update rate of the display is the rate at which new (different) images are presented to the viewer. Consider the following example: if a display has a frame rate of 60 Hz, but an update rate of only 3 Hz then the system will present 20 images of the same scene to the viewer before 20 images of the next scene are shown (Piantanida *et al.*, 1993). Thus, given these values only three different images per second will be shown even though the frame rate is 60 Hz. With an update rate this low, if the observer using an augmented-reality display moves his head, the real and computer-generated images will no longer be registered until the next update. What limits the update rate is the relationship between the complexity of the scene and the computational power of the computer system used to generate the scene. This relationship is especially important for computationally intensive applications such as medical imaging. For example, in augmented-reality displays for medicine, X-ray computer tomography (CT) and magnetic resonance imaging (MRI), images are superimposed over the patient's anatomy. Bajura *et al.* (1992) pointed out that the images in the virtual environment are registered to the real world given the update rate limit of the tracking and display system and not with the acquisition-rate limit of the image acquisition system. They also pointed out that lag in image generation and tracking is noticeable in all

HMDs but is dramatically accentuated with see-through HMDs. In this case, the real-world view moves appropriately with head movements but the computer-generated imagery lags behind. This is a critical problem if exact image registration is required. For virtual environments, in many cases it is sufficient to only know the approximate position of the user's head. Small errors are not easily discernible because the visual system tends to override the conflicting signals from his or her vestibular and proprioceptive system. However, in augmented reality, small errors in registration are easily detectable by the visual system.

Several of the problems associated with head tracking were addressed by Sowizral and Barnes (1993) and Azuma (1993). Sowizral and Barnes noted that the theoretical accuracy (accuracy without interfering noise) of a tracker depended on the type of tracker used: with the Polhemus Isotrak an accuracy of 2 degrees of rotation (2 inches at a 5 ft distance) can be obtained, with the Logitech 6 DF tracker 0.2 to 0.3 rotational degrees of accuracy can be obtained. The ultrasound principle of the latter is more suitable than the electromagnetic principle of the former, due to electromagnetic noise in the typical environment. What are the head-tracking requirements for augmented-reality displays? As stated by Azuma, a tracker must be accurate to a small fraction of a degree in orientation and a few millimeters in position. Errors in head orientation (pitch, roll, yaw) affect image registration more so than errors in head position (x, y, z), leading to the more stringent requirements for head-orientation tracking. Azuma stated that positional tracking errors of no more than 1 to 2 mm are maximum for augmented reality.

Piantanida *et al.* (1993) noted that there are two types of system delays which will affect performance in augmented reality: computational and sensor delays. As the complexity of the computer-generated image increases, the computational delay is a major factor determining the update rate of a display. In addition, sensor delay, the time required by the system to determine that the viewer has made a movement that requires updating the display, is an important variable in determining performance in augmented reality. Many HMD-based systems have combined latencies over 100 ms, which become very noticeable.

In addition to basic visual factors (e.g., resolution and field of view) which should be considered in the design of augmented-reality displays, cognitive factors should be considered in the design as well. Users of systems form mental models of the system they interact with and the mental model they form influences their performance. With augmented-reality displays the designer will have to take into account two mental models of the environment, the mental model of the synthetic imagery and of the real image. The design challenge will be to integrate the two stimuli in such a way that a single mental model will be formed of the augmented scene (Figure 14-7). It is then relevant to ask, what aspects of the two stimuli will lead to an integrated mental model? Probably, the more realistic the two stimuli, the more likely the participant will suspend disbelief and view the augmented scene as one singular environment. In addition, the more the two images match in terms of brightness and color, the more the two images will be viewed as one scene. Furthermore, the better the

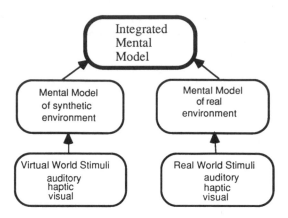

Figure 14-7 The synthetic and real-world stimuli may be combined to form a mental model of the augmented-reality environment.

image registration, the more likely that the scene will form an integrated whole.

Some preliminary information on how well users may form mental models of augmented-reality environments is provided by research on head-up displays (HUDs). Stokes *et al.* (1990) reviewed the literature on HUDs, discussing issues such as HUD symbology, and optical and attentional factors. They noted that an important issue associated with HUDs is the operator's ability to divide attention between the real-world and synthetic imagery. For medical augmented reality, allocating attentional resources as one cognitively switches between the two sources of information may lead to a decrement in performance with serious consequences. Some preliminary evidence from research on HUDs suggests that it may in fact be difficult to switch attention between projected HUD symbology and the real-world scene. For example, pilots have been shown to turn off the HUD during critical phases of a mission. Thus, a relevant question to pose for augmented-reality environments is the extent to which overlaid imagery may interfere with the visualization of the real-world image and performance of a task.

Another important issue to consider when designing displays which include synthetic and real-world imagery is display clutter. Without a careful consideration of how the two types (synthetic and real-world) of information should be combined, display clutter may result and thus interfere with performance. Furthermore, it is obvious that the synthetic imagery should not be allowed to obscure important parts of the real-world scene.

Both of the above issues, display clutter and attentional resources, are relevant for augmented-reality displays. However, the extent of their relevance for augmented reality is a function of the level of image registration required for the task. For some augmented-reality displays, it will be necessary that the synthetic imagery register quite accurately with the real-world environment; for example, in medicine a CT image must be exactly registered with the patient's anatomy. In contrast, some applications may only require that the synthetic image or text appear in the observer's field of view. How each of these tasks uses attentional resources and how display clutter affects performance is an important topic for future research.

THE UNIVERSITY OF WASHINGTON AUGMENTED REALITY SYSTEM

Different technical methods have been used to produce augmented-reality displays. The type of augmented-reality display that is used for a particular application will vary according to task requirements, and whether the display should be see-through, opaque, or screen-based. In addition, perceptual requirements, such as resolution, color, and the inclusion of stereoscopic vision in either the computer-generated or live video modes will influence the selection of the system. Lion *et al.* (1993) developed a screen-based augmented reality display that provides stereoscopy for both virtual and real-world components and uses low-cost components only, apart from the computer and the (not essential) large-screen video projector. This equipment is described here in detail; other systems will be explained more briefly in the next section. It is convenient to describe the system in terms of video capture, computer graphics rendering, and signal integration (Figure 14-8).

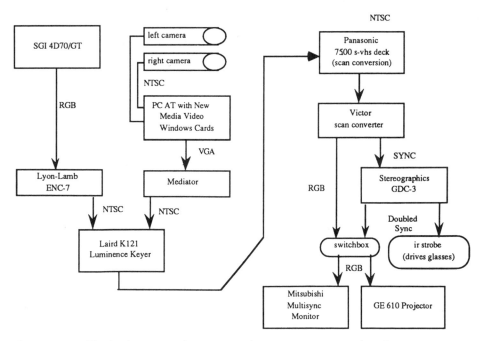

Figure 14-8 Block diagram of Lion *et al.* (1993) augmented-reality stereoscopic system. The images are viewed using either a 6 ft by 8 ft screen back-lit by a General Electric 610 RGB projection system or displayed using a high-resolution 19 inch color monitor.

Figure 14-9 Example of image displayed using a large-screen projection system used for virtual environments and augmented-reality displays. (Picture courtesy of Sensory Engineering Laboratory (SEL), University of Washington.)

The University of Washington system allows researchers to display stereo video combined with stereo computer graphics. With this system the viewer is able to see a stereoscopic view of himself and the environment he is in, projected onto a 6 ft by 8 ft screen (Figure 14-9). In addition, using keying, computer-generated images are overlaid over the stereo video (Figure 14-10). A Stereographics display system was used to present stereo computer graphics. This system is described in detail by Lipton (1991). This system displays left- and right-eye perspective views alternately at twice the normal frame rate (120 Hz) (Figure 14-11). The participant wears shutter glasses that fully occlude the right eye when the left-eye view is being displayed, and occlude the left eye when the right-eye view is displayed. In this manner, the participant perceives a flicker-free stereoscopic pair of images at the normal frame rate (60 Hz), while what is truly being displayed is alternate left- and right-eye views at double the normal frame rate.

Video capture and image rendering

The video capture aspect of the augmented-reality system is composed of two commercially available camcorders. The video images are captured using two New Media Video Windows hosted in an AT computer. The two New Media Video Window boards also combine the two camera signals into one VGA format signal $(2 @ 640 \times 485 \rightarrow 1 @ 640 \times 480)$. The VGA signal is then converted to an S-VHS signal $(1 @ 640 \times 480 \rightarrow 1 @ 640 \times 485)$, by means of a VideoLogic Mediator. Arrangement and alignment of the cameras are of particular importance for image registration. Vertical parallax must be elimin-

Figure 14-10 Example of augmented-reality scene displayed using a 19 inch monitor. (Picture courtesy of Sensory Engineering Laboratory (SEL), University of Washington.)

ated, and appropriate symmetric convergence must be established, based upon the target scene, focal length of the camera lenses, and position of the cameras with respect to the scene. The video cameras are typical consumer-grade Hi 8 video cameras made by Ricoh and mounted on a special mounting bracket that enables the two cameras to be positioned side by side and their convergence angle adjusted. Thus far we have primarily used trial and error to "calibrate" the convergence angle of the video cameras; however, this is a very poor solution if accurate image registration is important.

Figure 14-11 Left-eye and right-eye view of operator shown in Figure 14-9. The images are time multiplexed and presented using a stereo-ready monitor. (Picture courtesy of Sensory Engineering Laboratory (SEL), University of Washington.)

The computer-generated imagery is rendered by a Silicon Graphics Indigo2 Extreme at NTSC resolution (525×485). The computer graphics signal is converted from RGB + Sync component format to an S-VHS signal at the same resolution by a Lion Lamb ENC-7. This is necessary because the chroma key compositing takes place in the S-VHS format.

Signal integration

The two S-VHS signals, foreground computer-generated image and background imported video, are combined by a Laird Telemedia K121 linear keyer ($2 @ 640 \times 485 \rightarrow 1 @ 640 \times 485$). At this stage, the single S-VHS signal is converted into a format compatible with our time-multiplexed display system, which requires a separate synchronization signal. First, a conversion from component Y/C to composite NTSC is done by a Panasonic 7500 S-VHS deck. Second, the signal is converted from composite NTSC to component RGB + Sync by a Victor Scan Converter. Next, synchronization is taken from the Victor and sent to the Stereographics GDC-3 scan rate doubler, to drive the Stereographics active shutter glasses and the display. The display device may be either a large-format General Electric Imager 610 projection system ($6\,\text{ft} \times 8\,\text{ft}$ back-lit screen), or a high-resolution 21 inch Mitsubishi multisync monitor, each at a resolution of 1280×1024 pixels.

The large rear-lit projection screen allows an extremely wide field of view for augmented-reality applications. For example, at a viewing distance of 36 inches, the field of view subtended by the screen is 106° in the horizontal direction. Due to the use of the large screen projection system the horizontal spatial resolution is only 13.6 dpi. For comparison a computer monitor provides very crisp imagery, with spatial resolutions between 75 and 100 dpi. In contrast to the projection system, when using a viewing distance of 18 inches from the computer monitor, the field of view subtends only 47°.

STUDIES ON AUGMENTED REALITY

Several recent studies have been published on the topic of augmented reality. These studies represent a wide range of interesting and important applications. In the following section we summarize several of these papers and, when the information is available in the literature, list the hardware used by a particular research team to create an augmented reality.

Fitzmaurice's (1993) creative contribution to augmented reality was to develop a portable computer display with the ability to associate electronic information with the physical location of objects in the environment. One of his main ideas was that physical objects anchor information to a particular location in 3D space. For example, consider an automobile: the control panel anchors information about the amount of fuel remaining, speed, oil temperature, etc., to the physical location of the control display. The engine anchors information about the carburetor, fuel pump, radiator, etc., to the front end of the car. The idea is that using a hand-held computer with a position tracker,

Figure 14-12 An active map which emits various layers of information is accessed by the palm-top unit. (Copyright 1993 Fitzmaurice, University of Toronto.)

relevant information about objects in the environment can be delivered to the user at the right place and time. In Fitzmaurice's system the palm-top display (a small flat panel display) essentially acts as a window into what he termed an "information space." Because the handheld computer contains a position tracker, it is "aware" of its location and orientation with respect to the physical environment. Thus, when a database related to the location of an object in the physical environment is encountered, the display shows that information (Figure 14-12). The input devices on the display (buttons) can be used to access pull down menus and to select options. Fitzmaurice's experience is that by using the display, the sense of spatial localization of information is as strong as if delivered using a stereo system. The basic hardware for this system consists of a Casio 4 inch LCD color TV, with an Ascension Byrd 6 DOF position tracker. The images are produced by a Silicon Graphics 4D/310 Iris workstation on a 19 inch diagonal monitor and relayed to an LCD TV by a video camera.

Wellner (1993) presents an interesting example of augmented reality which does not require an HMD to view the scene. This system, developed at Xerox and termed the DigitalDesk, places the computer world into the world of the user. With DigitalDesk, using cameras pointing at a display surface, computer-generated visual information is directly projected on the real world. The idea is to make a real-world physical workstation more like a computer. In his system, this is accomplished by augmenting paper using the capabilities of a computer. Specifically, a computer display is projected onto a desk; video cameras pointed down at the desk detect what the user is doing. The system can read documents placed on the desk and can respond to interactions with pens or bare fingers. Thus, since the real world is used in the display, computing power

Figure 14-13   Example of an overlaid image using the Private Eye. (Copyright 1993 Feiner, Blair MacIntyre, and Seligmann, Columbia University.)

can be used for tasks such as pattern recognition of video images of the real world, rather than the rendering of synthetic images. Whenever a paper document is put on the desk, an associated data file is activated and a projector above the desk fills in the virtual parts (numbers, images, text) by means of an overlay on the real object. Wellner (1993) demonstrated this concept with three applications, a calculator, a cut-and-paste editor, and a shared desk. Using the calculator, numbers that are indicated with a finger or a stylus are identified by a rectangle of light. A tap on the desk confirms the choice and reads the number in. Arithmetic operators are read from a projection on another sheet, that also contains an area for presenting the result. In a similar way the cut-and-paste editor allows for replacing and copying drawings or text. The area to be processed is indicated with two corners, in the same way as in drawing programs. The shared desk acts almost like a video overlay of someone else's paper and hands over the real paper. Computing resources are used for the scaling and positioning of papers and for making a distinction between the pointing devices used by the participants. In terms of usability, according to the author, the first user experiences are encouraging. However, there are many technical problems involved in this design, including pattern recognition of objects and hands, limitation in the resolution of the cameras, lighting conditions, and calibration. In addition, Wellner observed that working with the DigitalDesk requires a level of disciplined behavior. One important aspect is to avoid obscuring of the desk by hands and arms, another is that tapping on the desk may inadvertently activate the input process.

Feiner *et al.* (1993) has been a main contributor to the emerging field of augmented reality (Figure 14-13). Feiner and colleagues are especially interested in augmenting the real world with knowledge. Specifically, their

Figure 14-14 Photograph of the virtual dome. (Picture courtesy of Professor Michitaka Hirose, Department of Mechanical Engineering, University of Tokyo, Japan.)

knowledge-based augmented reality system is designed to explain how to perform 3D spatial tasks, such as the repair of equipment. The knowledge-based graphics component of Feiner's augmented-reality system is called the Intent Based Illustration System (IBIS). IBIS is designed to make design decisions such as, choosing viewpoints, avoiding occlusion of objects, choosing rendering style, etc. The system will also adapt to design or system constraints forced upon it by the user or the application. One application of the system is to assist a repair person in maintaining a laser printer. This is accomplished by overlaying the location of the toner cartridge and paper tray on a real laser printer using a see-through monocular HMD.

The system runs on various computers, each serving a specific purpose for the system design. For example, the IBIS runs on an HP 9000 380 TurboSRX graphics workstation and the HMD is based on a Private Eye display, served by an Intel 486-based PC. The tracking processes of head and objects, transduced by Logitech and Ascension sensors, run on different workstations. All system software is written in C and C++.

The system designed by Hirose *et al.* (1993) is not an augmented-reality display as such, since no computer-generated image is used, but the techniques used are interesting for the purpose of this chapter. Images taken from a video camera, by scanning the surroundings, are projected into a virtual dome, using texture mapping computer-graphics techniques. The observer uses an HMD to view the virtual dome providing a sense of immersion within the visually captured environment (Figure 14-14). A particular feature of the system is that the camera updates the projection around the observer's area of view more frequently than elsewhere. The camera is mounted on a support that spins

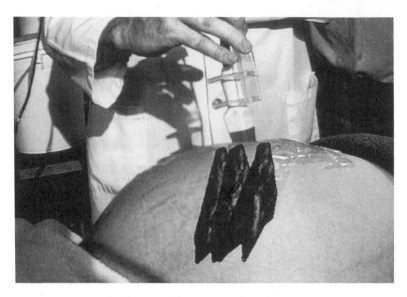

Figure 14-15 Picture of ultrasound image of a fetus superimposed over the mother. (Picture courtesy of the Department of Computer Science, University of North Carolina, Chapel Hill.)

around a pivot. When the camera swings around, objects enter the field of view at one side and leave at the opposite side. Between these events the camera position has moved, resulting in different points of view for the objects. This effect is used to obtain depth information. In front of the camera are two vertical slits, at the borders of the field of view. The angle over which the camera mount has to be turned to see an object in the other slit is measured, using edge detection of the object. Angles are determined each 2 degrees of horizontal rotation and each 4 degrees vertical rotation. This grid is used to construct the left- and right-eye images necessary for stereo viewing. To create an augmented-reality display, it is only necessary to overlay computer-generated imagery on the video view of the world. The hardware for this system consists of a Sony XC-711RR CCD camera, which feeds images to a Silicon Graphics IRIS 4D 210 VGX workstation with a Video frame grabber. The video images are presented to the observer using a VPL HMD.

Milgram *et al.* (1991) performed a study to determine the ability of subjects to estimate distances in a teleoperation setting, using a stereoscopic augmented-reality display. Specifically, Milgram and colleagues measured the accuracy of distance judgments using a virtual pointer overlaid onto a video scene. The connecting line between two indicated points was used as a tape-measure. Subjects viewed a stereoscopic monitor in four different "tape-measure" conditions: a real or virtual pointer, combined with a real or virtual scene. The real scene was created by displaying stereo images, obtained using a pair of video cameras. The results showed that in all conditions there was the same systematic bias (25 seconds of arc) when pointing in front of the target (locations in the spatial scene). Furthermore, the accuracy of distance

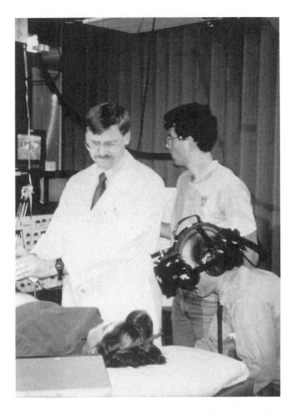

Figure 14-16 Picture of the display technology used to view the image shown in Figure 14-15. (Picture courtesy of the Department of Computer Science, University of North Carolina, Chapel Hill.)

judgments using a virtual pointer was 30 seconds of arc less than with a real pointer, regardless of the type of the target.

Bajura *et al.* (1992) used ultrasound images of a pregnant subject as an application for augmented reality (Figures 14-15 and 14-16). The physician used a handheld scanner to produce ultrasound echographs. A tracker was mounted to the scanner in order to track the position and orientation of the scanner. A second tracker was mounted to the head of an observer, together with a miniature camera. The successive 2D ultrasound images obtained were used to build a 3D database, which was then rendered for two offset eyepoints (to create stereo images). The ultrasound image was thus seen as a 3D image, stable in space. The real-world scene, captured by the camera, was merged with the left synthetic image and the resultant left and right images were presented by means of an opaque HMD.

For tracking the physician's head movements, a Polhemus sensor was used. The scanner data (Irex System III) was digitized with a Matrox MVP/S frame grabber and preprocessed using Sun workstations. The image rendering was performed using a Pixel-Planes 5 parallel processor, taking into account the user's head position. Left- and right-eye NTSC frames were produced, of which the left frame was luminance keyed (Grass Valley Group Model 100) with the camera image (Panasonic GP-KS 102). The presentation was done using a VPL EyePhone. The update rate of the graphics was only 2 Hz.

In Metzger's (1993) augmented-reality system, real and synthetic images were mixed, using chroma keying. Metzger demonstrated the features of his system by showing a synthetic helicopter cresting a real-world hill. The author mentions that an exact match between the real and synthetic world was a major hurdle when designing this system. Indoor scenes seem to be less critical in this respect than outdoor scenes and wireless equipment is regarded as desirable to increase the range of the display. The hardware for the system consisted of a Virtual Research Flight Helmet, with a Toshiba IK-M40A miniature videocamera, and an Ascension Technologies Bird tracker mounted on top of the helmet. The real-world image was shown as a monoscopic image while the synthetic images were generated with a LORAL GT100 image generator, producing RGB output, which was converted to NTSC format. A NewTek Video Toaster keyer was used to combine the two real and synthetic images, producing a broadcast-quality NTSC signal for the Flight Helmet.

Deering (1993) produced shaded virtual objects combined with live video images, using video keying. This was done using a modified camcorder, showing the result to the observer in the viewfinder. A 6 DOF tracking device was mounted to the camera which allowed for stabilization of the virtual object in the image of the real world when the observer moved around with the camera. Essentially, the camera served as a one-eye HMD. While Deering suggested several useful applications for his system, the current system is demonstrated with a single virtual object only. However, in Deering's system, shadows of the virtual objects overlaid on the real world are included. Special attention is paid to the problem of the occlusion of virtual objects when they move behind real objects. To account for occlusion, the Z-buffer contained depth information of virtual objects in the scene. More complex techniques would be required to mix see-through real objects with virtual objects. The limitation in position information accuracy may cause jitter of the virtual objects relative to the image of the real environment. The hardware he used generates NTSC format, with a 640×480 pixel resolution, filling a 40° field of view. The virtual objects are generated with a Sun SPARCstation 2GT. Tracking is performed by Logitech ultrasonic trackers.

As noted above, Lion *et al.* (1993) designed a screen-based augmented-reality system with cost as a major consideration. In their system, both real and synthetic images were projected onto a large screen in stereo. This system is unique insofar as it applies a simple algorithm to occlude the generated image where it should disappear behind the real world. The actual demonstration of the system's capabilities is a computer-generated crown of stars, circling around the person's head. A clipping plane is defined for the synthetic image and is yoked to the position of the head tracker. When the person moves his head the clipping plane moves with him. Using a luminance keyer, synthetic imagery in front of the clipping plane replaces live video, behind the plane it is suppressed. Although many potential applications are listed, the main purpose of the development is to provide a technology for training. The technical details of this study have been explained more extensively above.

MULTIMODALITY AUGMENTED-REALITY DISPLAYS

The above discussion seems to suggest that augmented reality is specifically visual; however, this conclusion is not justified. Although in many cases images are the primary interest in augmented-reality environments, they are not the only one. For example, Feiner *et al.* (1993) emphasized the importance of knowledge to augment the real world. In addition, it is quite clear that auditory and haptic information can be used to augment the real world as well. We propose that the enhancement of the real world with auditory and haptic information will lead to novel interface techniques for human interaction with complex systems. Not only will we be able to see virtual objects merged with real world stimuli, we will also be able to place computer-generated sounds over the real object to enhance its visibility or perhaps to change its meaning. Furthermore, by overlaying computer-generated haptic feedback with real-world objects, we will be able to change the parameters of how an object feels. This may allow the quality of touch to vary as a function of the application and not the material property of the object. However, by overlaying haptic sensations on real-world objects, one will not only experience the virtual sensations from the virtual interface equipment but also the real tactile and kinesthetic sensation from the actual real-world object. Thus, related to the problem of cognitively switching between two different visual stimuli as discussed above, it will be important to determine how best to integrate the two sources of haptic feedback to avoid interference and to enhance the performance of the task for a given application.

Table 14-2 shows a number of single-modality and multi-modality augmented-reality displays and the potential tasks that they can help perform. In the table, visual, auditory and haptic information, and their respective combinations, are considered. The most common methods of presentation of these modalities have been selected, rather than trying to exhaust the possibilities. The olfactory and gustatory senses have been excluded from the table, mainly because the technology to produce the virtual equivalents of these stimuli is lacking.

Several terms used in the table need to be defined. In an *overlaid* augmented-reality scene, the virtual image(s) is combined with the real-world image. An example is a wireframe overlay in which the real-world imagery is not occluded by the virtual world imagery. In a *merged* augmented reality scene, the real-world image is replaced by objects shown in the virtual world, thus real-world objects are occluded by virtual-world objects. Finally, the term "virtual stimuli" is used in Table 14-2 to refer to computer-generated stimuli such as stereoscopic images, spatialized sound, or tactile stimulation. The primary purpose of the information in the table is to stimulate thinking and research on different types of augmented-reality displays.

Table 14-2 Various types of augmented realities as a function of different sensory modalities, and potential tasks that can be performed with various methods of presentation of augmented reality. The virtual stimulus is present in addition to the real stimulus.

Virtual stimulus	Method of presentation	Potential tasks
Visual	*General comments*	*All techniques can be applied in mono as well as in stereovision if the task requires this*
	Opaque HMD with merged real and virtual images	Tasks that require 360° visual surround and high visual fidelity; tasks that involve visual registration with the operator's own body
	See-through HMD with overlaid real and virtual images	Tasks that require 360° visual surround; tasks that require large instantaneous field of view; tasks that require high real-world resolution; particularly suited for local environments
	Merged images on monitor or projection screen	Minimizes instrumentation worn by the user; easy implementation of multiple participants; tasks that require high visual fidelity
Auditory	*General comments*	*Merged augmented reality might be achieved by removing real-world sounds with active noise reduction*
	Free-field loudspeaker	Minimizes instrumentation worn by the user; requires as many speakers as there are sound-source locations; unrestricted hearing of real-world sound; tasks that require accurate localization of sound; does not require individual calibration
	Convolved sound presented via loudspeakers	Minimizes instrumentation worn by the user; suitable for multiple and moving sound sources; only produces high definition of sound source with individualized earprint; unrestricted hearing of real-world sound; suitable for multiple participants (with user location restrictions)
	Convolved sound presented via headphones	For tasks involving multiple participants; allows purposeful reduction of unwanted real-world audio; suitable for tasks that require high definition of sound source localization
Haptic	*General comments*	*For tasks such as telepresence, remote manipulation of objects; tactile devices interfere with perception of real-world tactile information; tactile devices are currently restricted to limited skin surface area*

Table 14-2 — *contd.*

Virtual stimulus	Method of presentation	Potential tasks
	Body-mounted force-exerting devices usually using pneumatics or electromagnetic forces	Tasks that are aided by providing resistive forces that counteract the contraction of muscles; these displays afford the capability of moderate levels of freedom of motion (examples include training users for interacting in low- or high-gravity environments and with force feedback from grasping motions)
	World-mounted force-exerting devices: usually involving hydraulics or electromechanical equipment	Tasks that require scaling forces that are imparted by the user or displayed to the user (example: power steering in an automobile)
	Body-mounted tactile displays	Tasks that involve detection of physical contact such as detection of surface location and surface property characteristics; wide range of applications for the visually or hearing impaired
Visual and auditory	*General comments*	*Many combinations of presentation methods may be made, but not all combinations show good symbiosis; this bimodal augmented reality may be more compelling than any monomodal augmented reality*
	HMD combined with earphones	Tasks that require mobility of the user; tasks that require a high degree of spatial orientation or tasks that involve searching for targets
	Computer monitor or projection system combined with convolved sound presented via two speakers	High-fidelity sound and images; multiple participant tasks; tasks with limited mobility of user; minimal instrumentation worn by the users
Visual and haptic	*General comments*	*These modalities are particularly suited for the investigation and manipulation of non-auditory virtual objects in a real environment*
	Computer monitor or projection system combined with world-mounted force-feedback devices	Manipulation of very heavy objects or very accurate positioning of objects in a real world (objects may be virtual)
	HMD combined with tactile display	Tasks where the user may touch real and virtual objects in a fully inclusive environment; tasks that include exploration of virtual surface characteristics or boundaries
Auditory and haptic	*General comments*	*These modalities reinforce rather than supplement each other and can be used for auditory and haptic warning devices*

Table 14-2—*contd.*

Virtual stimulus	Method of presentation	Potential tasks
	Spatialized sound from multiple speakers combined with tactile display	Reinforcement of collision detection of objects where direct visual control lacks sufficient accuracy; auditory and haptic exploration of virtual environments
Visual, auditory, and haptic	*General comments*	*This represents the most advanced multi-modal augmented reality; and may be applicable for tasks that require a strong feeling of presence*

Selected application areas

Several interesting applications for the use of augmented-reality environments have emerged from the literature. For example, consider the remote manipulation of robots for tele-existence or telemanipulation tasks (Oyama *et al.*, 1993) (Figure 14-17). In this application, synthetic imagery may be superimposed over the real-world scene to enhance the visibility of the remote environment under degraded visibility conditions. As another example, consider the use of augmented reality for recreational activities. Along these lines, Anderson (1993) developed a "virtual batting cage" in which a participant with a real bat was able to practice batting against a virtual pitcher throwing a virtual baseball (Figure 14-18). Several other recreational activities, such as tennis and skiing, will surely benefit from augmented-reality technology as well.

One of the more important applications for augmented reality is the visualization of medical images in the context of the patient's anatomy. Currently, MRI and CT images are viewed independently of the patient's physical body. The use of augmented-reality displays will allow MRI and CT images to be superimposed over the patient's anatomy which may assist in tasks such as the planning of surgical procedures. Researchers from the Department of Computer Science at the University of North Carolina, Chapel Hill, have pioneered the development of medical augmented reality. For example, Fuchs and Neuman (1993) investigated the use of three-dimensional medical images superimposed over the patient's anatomy for non-invasive visualization of internal human anatomy. Specifically, in their application, a physician wearing an HMD viewed a pregnant woman, with an ultrasound scan of the fetus overlaid on the woman's stomach. Walking around the patient allowed the doctor to observe the fetus in 3D perspective and with reference to the mother's body.

Other researchers, such as Lorensen and colleagues (1993), and Gleason and colleagues at the Surgical Planning Laboratory of Brigham and Woman's Hospital and Harvard Medical School, have also investigated the use of augmented-reality environments for medical visualization. Specifically,

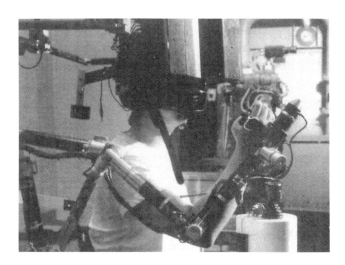

Figure 14-17 Master system used for a telerobotic/augmented reality application. (Copyright 1993 Oyama, Tsunemoto, Tachi, and Inoue, Mechanical Engineering Laboratory, Tsukuba Science City, Japan. Presence: *Teleoperators and Virtual Environments*, Volume 2(2), MIT Press.)

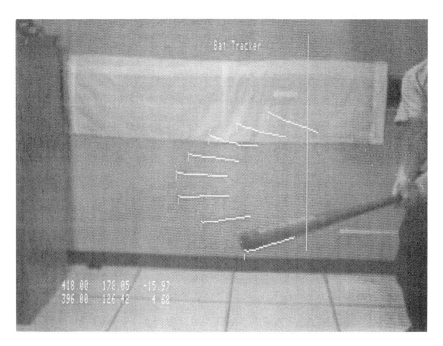

Figure 14-18 Batter swinging a bat as seen through a camera view. (Copyright 1993 Anderson, AT&T Bell Laboratories. Presence: *Teleoperators and Virtual Environments*, Volume 2(1), MIT Press.)

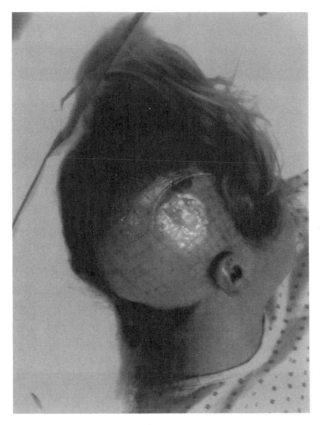

Figure 14-19 Preoperative video registration of a tumor superimposed over the patient's body. (Picture courtesy of Gleason, Kikinis, Lorensen, and Jolesz, Surgical Planning Laboratory of Brigham and Woman's Hospital and Harvard Medical School.)

Gleason *et al.* (1994) used three-dimensional images to assist in preoperative surgical planning and simulation of neurosurgical and craniofacial cases. They built an augmented-reality display which allowed the surgeon to superimpose three-dimensional images with the surgeon's operative perspective. Surgical simulation provides the ability to interact with the reconstructed virtual objects, such as viewing different surgical approaches or displaying only a limited number of anatomic structures or objects. Gleason *et al.* (1994) described the effectiveness of their augmented-reality system for intraoperative neurosurgical procedures in the context of 16 cases. Figure 14-19 shows a striking image of a tumor, registered with a video-image of the head of a young patient. From the same research team, Lorensen *et al.* (1993) presented a case study which involved the removal of a tumor at the top of a patient's brain. Before making any incisions, the surgical team viewed computer models of the underlying anatomy of the patient's brain surface and tumor, mixed with a live video image of the patient. The combined video and computer image was used to help the surgeon plan a path to the diseased tissue. The video of the patient, enhanced by the computer models, showed the extent of the tumor's intrusion beneath the brain's surface.

Another application for augmented-reality environments is telecommuting. Social, economical and environmental motives have urged governments to stimulate telecommuting, but its acceptance is progressing slowly. It is estimated that in the USA four million will be involved in telecommuting by 1995, increasing to 30% of the workforce by 2020. Thus far, companies that have implemented telecommuting are generally positive, but others fear the lack of control over employees and find implementation in the current organization difficult (Olsen, 1989). Telecommuters themselves miss the social environment of the corporate workplace (Chee and Tng, 1990). Augmented reality can remove these obstacles by the creation of augmented workplaces that allow natural access to colleagues, documents, information and meetings. What needs to be developed is an affordable augmented-reality platform, which is versatile enough to serve in different workplaces over a range of applications.

Janin and colleagues at Boeing Computer Services (1993) developed an augmented-reality display designed to support manufacturing processes. With their system, a see-through HMD and a head-tracker were used to place graphical overlays on real production boards and tables, providing technical information such as wiring schemes. Their application required only 30 to 40 simple wireframe images, which were generated at a rate of 20 frames per second. Other design criteria included accurate head-tracking over a large volume of space, low weight and good stability of the HMD, and easy calibration. For acceptance as a work tool, reasonably cheap deployment is another requirement.

Furthermore, augmented-reality displays can aid in training. The general idea is that augmented reality will allow the physical body of the trainee to be visually present in the system by means of a live stereoscopic video system (Lion et al., 1993). For example, consider the problem of teaching pronunciation in a speech pathology setting. The participant in this system is trying to learn a new set of phonemes. The cameras are pointed at him and he watches his image on a display through shutter glasses. Superimposed over the video head is a three-dimensional wire-frame model of his face, spatially located over the real face. A wire frame in this application provides maximum contrast against the real face. A personal model could be generated from the actual face by a CyberWare Scanner in the form of a polygon mesh. Head tracking could be performed by any of the available 6 DOF trackers. The polygonal representation could be manipulated in 3D to form various phonemes, that have to be imitated. Such an application would provide immediate feedback in an individually tailored setting, and would exploit the human's ability to mimic facial gestures. Sports training and rehabilitative medicine applications will follow the same overlay strategy.

As a final application area consider the field of architecture. Architects frequently present designs by overlaying photographic imagery of present sites with synthetic imagery of proposed buildings. In some cases, full animations are produced showing the proposed building in its intended setting. Instead of modeling the site, a video registration could be made from the environment, recording the position and orientation of the camera. Then, the camera position and orientation can be used to drive an animation of the proposed building. The animation could be composited on top of the video footage (Deering, 1992), saving the animator from having to model the entire setting. For an interactive presentation, the participant would be on the site, wearing an overlay HMD, looking at the synthetic building as if it were there. In summary, the above examples represent only a subset of what is possible with augmented-reality environments; we believe that developments will occur rapidly in this field, producing a host of new application areas.

ACKNOWLEDGMENTS

The writing of this chapter was supported by grants from the National Science Foundation (DMC8857851 and CDA8806866) to Woodrow Barfield. In addition, the TNO Institute for Human Factors provided support to Wouter Lotens for the writing of this manuscript. Dav Lion is acknowledged for his contribution to the development of the University of Washington Augmented Reality System.

REFERENCES

Anderson, R. L. (1993) A real experiment in virtual environments: a virtual batting cage, *Presence: Teleoperators and Virtual Environments*, **2**(1), 16–33

Azuma, R. (1993) Tracking requirements for augmented reality, *Commun. ACM*, **36**, 50–1

Bajura, M., Fuchs, H., and Ohbuchi, R. (1992) Merging virtual objects with the real world: seeing ultrasound imagery within the patient, *Computer Graphics*, **26**, 203–10

Chee, S. Y. and Tng, H. (1990) Telecommuting: attitudes of female computer professionals in Singapore, in Kaiser and Opelland (Eds), *Desktop Information Technology*, Amsterdam: North-Holland, pp. 193–207

Deering, M. F. (1992) High resolution virtual reality, *Computer Graphics*, **26**, 195–202

Deering, M. F. (1993) Explorations of display interfaces for Virtual Reality, *Proc. IEEE Virtual Reality Annual Int. Symp.*, Seattle, WA, September 18–22, pp. 141–7

Edwards, E. K., Rolland, J. P., and Keller, K. P. (1993) Video see-through design for merging of real and virtual environments, *Proc. IEEE Virtual Reality Annual Int. Symp.*, September 18–22, Seattle, WA, pp. 223–33

Feiner, S., MacIntyre, B., and Seligmann, D. (1993) Knowledge based augmented reality, *Commun. ACM*, **36**, 53–62

Fitzmaurice, G. W. (1993) Situated information spaces and spatially aware palmtop computers, *Commun. ACM*, **36**, 39–49

Fuchs, H. and Neuman, U. (1993) A vision telepresence for medical consultation and other applications, *Proc. of ISRR-93, Sixth Int. Symp. on Robotics Research*, October, Hidden Valley, PA

Gleason, P. L., Kikinis, R., Black, P. McL., Alexander, E., Stieg, P. E., Wells, W.,

Lorensen, W., Cline, H., Altobelli, D., and Jolesz, F. (1994) Intraoperative image guidance for neurosurgical procedures using video registration, submitted to *Neurosurgery*

Hirose, M., Yokoyama, K., and Sata, S. (1993) Transmission of realistic sensation: development of a virtual dome, *Proc. IEEE Virtual Reality Annual Int. Symp.*, September 18–22, Seattle, WA, pp. 125–31

Jack, K. (1993) *Video Demystified: A Handbook for the Digital Engineer*, CA: HighText

Janin, A. L., Mizell, D. W., and Caudell, T. P. (1993) Calibration of head-mounted displays for augmented reality applications, *Proc. IEEE Virtual Reality Annual Int. Symp.*, September 18–22, Seattle, WA, pp. 246–55

Lion, D., Rosenberg, C., and Barfield, W. (1993) Overlaying three-dimensional computer graphics with stereoscopic life motion video: applications for virtual environments, *Society of Information Display Int. Symp.*, May 18–29, Seattle, WA, pp. 483–6

Lipton, L. (1991) *The CrystalEyes Handbook*, San Rafael, CA: Stereographics Corporation

Lorensen, W., Cline, H., Nafis, C., Kikinis, R., Altobelli, D., and Gleason, L. (1993) Enhancing reality in the operating room, *Proc. Visualization '93*, October 25–29, San Jose, CA, pp. 410–15

Metzger, P. J. (1993) Adding reality to the virtual, *Proc. IEEE Virtual Reality Annual Int. Symp.*, September 18–22, Seattle, WA, pp. 7–13

Milgram, P., Drascis, D., and Grodsky, D. (1991) Enhancement of 3D-video displays by means of superimposed stereo-graphics, *Proc. of the 35th Annual Meeting of the Human Factors Society*, September 2–6, San Francisco, CA, pp. 1457–61

Olsen, M. H. (1989) Work at home for computer professionals: current attitudes and future prospects, *ACM Trans. Inform. Systems*, **7**, 317–38

Oyama, E., Tsumemoto, N., Tachi, S., and Inoue, Y. (1993) Experimental study on remote manipulation using virtual reality, *Presence: Teleoperators and Virtual Environments*, **2**(2), 112–34

Piantanida, T., Boman, D. K., and Gille, J. (1993) Human perceptual issues and virtual reality, *Virtual Reality*, **1**, 43–52

Robinett, W. (1992) Synthetic experience: a proposed taxonomy, *Presence: Teleoperators and Virtual Environments*, **1**, 227–47

Sid-Ahmed, M. A. and Boraie, M. T. (1990) Dual cameras calibration for 3-D machine vision metrology, *IEEE Trans. on Instrumentation and Measurements*, **39**, 512–16

Sowizral, H. A. and Barnes. J. C. (1993) Tracking position and orientation in a large volume, *Proc. IEEE Virtual Reality Annual Int. Symp.*, September 18–22, Seattle, WA, pp. 132–9

Stokes, A., Wickens, C., and Kite, K. (1990) *Display Technology: Human Factors Concepts*, Warrendale, PA: Society of Automotive Engineers, Inc.

Wellner, P. (1993) Digital desk, *Commun. ACM*, **36**, 87–96

Index